ISBN 978-0-265-79231-5
PIBN 10890091

JOURNAL

OF THE

DEPARTMENT OF AGRICULTURE

OF

WESTERN AUSTRALIA.

ISSUED BY DIRECTION OF

THE HONOURABLE THE MINISTER FOR AGRICULTURE.

(VOL. XIV., JULY TO DECEMBER, 1906.)

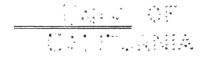

PERTH:
BY AUTHORITY: FRED. WM. SIMPSON, GOVERNMENT PRINTER.

—

1906.

4A).

⌈Registered at the General Post Office for transmission by Post as a Newspaper.⌉

JOURNAL

OF THE

DEPARTMENT OF AGRICULTURE

OF

WESTERN AUSTRALIA.

Editor: THE DIRECTOR OF AGRICULTURE.

PUBLISHED MONTHLY.

Vol. XIV.—Part 1.

JULY, 1906.

PERTH:

BY AUTHORITY: FRED. WM. SIMPSON, GOVERNMENT PRINTER.

1906.

WESTERN AUSTRALIAN GOVERNMENT.

IMMIGRATION.

Nominated Passages.

Persons having friends and relatives in the United Kingdom who are desirous of emigrating to Western Australia may obtain passages at half the ordinary fares by nominating them to the Hon. Colonial Secretary in Perth.

Fares from £6 10s. to £14 10s.

Clerks, artizans, and mechanics will **not** be accepted.

Advanced Passages.

Working men and others resident in the State may obtain an advance of passage money, including railway fares from port of arrival to destination, to bring their wives and families from the Eastern States and New Zealand to this State.

Such advances to be repaid within six or twelve months, according to the amount advanced.

A responsible guarantor must be provided.

Special Concessions are provided for Settlers taking up Land.

Full particulars can be obtained upon application to the Under Secretary, Colonial Secretary's Department, Perth.

By order,

F. D. NORTH,

Under Secretary.

JOURNAL

OF THE

Department of Agriculture

OF

WESTERN AUSTRALIA.

Vol. XIV.	JULY 23, 1906.	Part 1.

EDITOR'S NOTES.

NETTING FOR FARMERS.—The Fisheries Department has on hand about 1,200 yards of fishing netting which has been confiscated. It has been decided to sell the same. Farmers and others who require string netting for any purpose would do well to put themselves into communication with the Under Secretary.

PRIZE FOR PACKING APPLES.—The conditions under which the special pri e offered by the Government for the best packed consignment of apples landed at Bremen have been fulfilled. Messrs. Smith and Johnson, of Mt. Barker estate, being awarded first place. A full report of the shipment appears elsewhere in this issue.

SPRAYING FOR FUNGUS.—It cannot be impressed too often on the attention of fruit-growers that fungus once established cannot be cured, but only prevented from spreading. In order to keep vines and trees free from this disease, preventive measures must be used early. As soon as pruning is over, scrape off all loose bark and spray.

SEED POTATOES.—Applications have been made to the Department for the purchase of seed potatoes. The extent of the experimental trials at Hamel were not sufficient to provide the public with seed potatoes. Those requiring seed are recommended to place their orders early with their merchants. An interesting article on the preparation of seed potatoes for planting is published in this issue.

MOHAIR.—There is evidence of a growing demand for mohair. As an adjunct to our flocks, the angora goat cannot be too highly spoken of. They require less attention, care, and feeding than any other animal on the farm. They can also be put to most valuable use as scrub clearers; so that, taken all round, a farmer is certainly wanting in business acumen if he neglects to establish a flock of angoras.

BROODY HENS.—The question has been raised that if one of the birds competing in the egg-laying contest went broody what would be done? The matter being referred to the poultry expert, Mr. Robertson stated that a a broody hen would never be allowed to remain on the nest of a night, but would be taken out of the pen and put into a coop with broad slats on the bottom to keep the bird from sitting on the ground, and fed sparingly.

FLOCK BOOK FOR AUSTRALIA.—We have received a notification from the central committee of the "Flock-Book for British Breeds of Sheep in Australasia," stating that it is intended to shortly publish Volume III. of this book, and asking that this fact be made known amongst the breeders of British breeds in the State. The book was formerly confined to Victoria only. Any communications addressed to Mr. Patterson, secretary Royal Agricultural Society of Victoria, will receive attention.

SUMMER FODDER.—From experiments made on the Chapman State Farm, it is evident that farmers will make a mistake in waiting until spring before sowing for fodder crops. All crops must be well grown before the advent of the hot summer sun. The grasses that seemed to withstand the heat best were paspalum, Rhodes grass, African Wonder grass and Sheep's Burnet. These can be planted in early spring with a certain amount of assurance that they will continue to grow throughout the summer.

SUGAR FOR CATTLE.—From experiments tried by some of our progressive farmers, it has been demonstrated that sugar given in the food of live stock is a most valuable addition to its feed. Molasses can be used in the place of sugar when preferred. It not only assists to keep the animals in good health, but materially aids fattening. This, in the case of cattle, pigs, and sheep that are being prepared for market, is a matter of great importance. The increase in value is about five times the cost of the sugar given.

BLIGHT-PROOF STOCKS.—A correspondent asks :—When an apple is worked on a blight-proof stock, does that imply that the roots are also blight-proof, seeing that all apple trees sold by nurserymen are worked twice? Yes; the roots are blight-proof as well as the stem. It is important that all parts beneath the surface of the ground should be blight-proof. The object of the double working is to save time. When young trees of Northern Spy or Majetine are obtainable, then it is only necessary to work on the stem above ground.

Fine crop of Rape grown at Katanning.

(*See* letterpress.)

FARM LABOUR.—An advertisement appears in this issue calling the attention of farmers to the fact that experienced farmers and farm labourers are arriving weekly as immigrants from the United Kingdom, and that many of them are anxious to obtain employment on farms in this State. The Government will therefore be glad to receive applications from those who desire to obtain any farm assistance, or who can offer employment. Applications should be made to Mr. James Longmore, Superintendent Government Labour Bureau, Perth.

FINE CROP OF RAPE.—In this issue is published an illustration of a very fine crop of rape, grown by Mr. F. H. Piesse, M.L.A., at Katanning. The land is of a second class quality, light sandy loam (about 9½ inches deep) on clay subsoil. Seed was sown at the rate of four pounds to the acre, fertilised with 50 pounds of superphosphate. The crop grew rapidly and continuously from the first rains. The area is 100 acres, and has been carrying 1,000 ewes and lambs for some weeks. To lamb raisers this should be an object lesson well worth emulating.

SUGAR PRODUCTION.—Particulars of the last sugar crop show that in the central and southern districts of Queensland white labour has supplanted the employment of coloured persons. In that State 50,897 tons were produced by white labour and 101,362 tons by black labour. In New South Wales 18,019 tons were produced by white labour and 1,964 tons by black. The grand totals were:—By white labour, 68,916 tons; by black labour, 103,326 tons; total production of Australia, 172,242 tons. The bounty paid in Queensland was £111,550 and that paid in New South Wales was £36,234; total, £147,784.

CLEARING FERN LANDS.—Complaints are frequently made of the after growth of bracken and ferns on newly-cleared fern lands. A settler stated that he had a lot of trouble for two or three years in trying to rid the ground of young growth from the fern roots left in after clearing. Eventually he used a disc harrow; since then he has not seen a sign of either bracken or fern. Other settlers, questioned, favour running a roller over the ferns so as to break the leaf stalks without tearing them off the parent plant; the sap is then partly used up in feeding that bruised leaf and its tension is not sufficient to start the growth of other vigorous fronds. With a little patience and perseverance the plant dies of exhaustion.

EGG PRESERVATIVE.—On the 15th of June last year, three dozen eggs were received from Messrs. Gardner Bros. that had been treated with a preservative. The eggs were boxed, sealed, and stored in one of the Departmental rooms, and on the 15th June last, just 12 months afterwards, the box was opened and the eggs tested. They were found to be somewhat shrunken in bulk but perfectly fresh, and suitable for cooking purposes. The trial was rather a severe test, as there is never any reason why they should be kept so long. From what could be seen of the test, it is reasonable to suppose that had they only been kept three or four months, that their condition would have been very much better and more like the fresh article.

THE. VALUE OF LIME.—The following letter appears in the Melbourne *Leader*:—"Mr. J. Brock, of Steel Creek, got six bags of slack lime to try it on potatoes. It gave such satisfaction, that last year he took nine bags and used it in 1½ acre of potatoes, putting a small handful on each seed. He has just ordered 20 bags more, as he tells me the crop has given 10 tons per acre. He also put the lime on some maize, putting it in drills and dusting it with lime. This crop grew 10 feet high, and was shown at the Yarra Glen Show. Mr. Brock has given permission to do as you like with this. I am quite satisfied that his statement is correct, as a Mr. Hargraves got 19 bags a little time ago, having seen the result of the lime on Mr. Brock's crops. Mr. Brock worked in the lime quarry here some time ago, so I know him well."

DWARF FRUIT TREES.—It is often a matter of wonder that those whose orchards are so situated as to be exposed to gully or other strong winds do not go in for the dwarf kinds of fruit trees. Some say that the tall trees are best because the limbs are out of the way of horses, and the ground is easier cultivated. Against this is the great loss of fruit (wind-falls), broken limbs, etc., and unsightly leaning trees. Quite 50 to 75 per cent. of fruit is lost every year from the winds, and what is left requires a lot of climbing or long ladders to reach, the trees being materially injured by breaking off fruit spurs and laterals. A dwarf tree will produce as much bloom and sit as heavy a crop as a tall tree in a favourable position; the cost of picking is considerably less, and the lowness of the branches assist to keep the ground and roots cool and protected from the burning rays of the summer sun.

FRUIT TREES FROM SEED.—A correspondent asks, "Will it do to plant seeds such as pear or their pips or peach nuts in the places it is intended to allow the trees to permanently remain, and to graft and bud as they grow in such places, and not rear them in a nursery as is usually done?" There is no doubt that such a thing could be done, and strong and sturdy trees would be the result, but it would be eight or nine years or even more before they would bear, and this is a great consideration. The system could only be recommended for localities that were not suitable to ordinary plant growth. The fact of lifting trees from the nursery bed in order to transplant necessitates the severance of the tap root and pruning of the roots, which greatly stimulates the early bearing of fruit. In any case, the trees must be either grafted or budded in order to have the fruit true to name.

HORSES EATING SAND.—Reports have reached the Department from settlers complaining of horses suffering from sand in the bowels, and asking for a remedy and advice. The matter being referred to the acting Government veterinary surgeon, Mr. Burns states that—"It is a common complaint at the present time of the year, when young grass is coming up, and the roots not being strong enough to prevent horses when feeding from pulling up the whole of the plant, as a consequence a certain amount of sand or dirt that adheres to the roots is taken into the stomach of the animal. For a remedy, the bowels should be kept open with raw linseed oil, and the following mixture given in the feed every night for one week:—

Pulv. iron carbonate	...	...	...	2 drms.
„ gentian	...	...	...	2 drms.
„ common salt ...	...	...	...	2 drms."

CROP ROTATION.—Amongst the advantages to be gained from a rational plan of crop rotation are the following:— Soil fertility is retained and, under certain conditions increased. The plant food of the soil is more economically appropriated. There is not the same necessity for application of manures. Weeds which thrive amongst certain crops are checked, and often exterminated, by resorting to a change from one crop to another of a different order. Plant diseases and insect pests may be checked and often prevented, by a systematic change of crops. Cultivation necessary for the successful culture of one crop may materially benefit a different crop to follow. The locality of live stock is continuously being changed, allowing the pastures to sweeten and the destruction of parasitic disease germs. The farm work is more evenly distributed throughout the year, which brings about continuous employment and a more settled class of agricultural labourers. Risk of failure is minimised by not staking all in one venture. It allows of monetary returns being available at various seasons of the year.

RED SCALE PARASITE:—It is pleasing to know that we have the assurance of our orchard inspectors that the red scale parasite has thoroughly established itself in this State, and can be seen on infested trees in and around Perth, where it is multiplying with great rapidity. This is a chalcid fly that was found in China, and is an internal parasite. An enlarged illustration of this insect will be found on p. 573 of the Handbook of Horticulture and Viticulture published by this Department. A ladybird from Jerusalem has also worked great havoc by feeding on the red scale. Both these friendly insects were introduced in November of last year by Mr. Compére, the Government Entomologist, and were received by Inspector Newman, who is in charge of this work. They were at once placed in breeding jars, and as they bred out were distributed on infected trees, when they were watched and cared for. It is anticipated that there will be sufficient numbers hatched out in the spring to supply most of the demand likely to be made. Those having red scale in their orchards should send in their applications for parasites, which will be booked and insects sent out, so soon as the weather is warm enough to enable collecting to commence.

AUSTRALIAN WHEAT.—Exports of wheat and flour from the Commonwealth since the commencement of the present season, on 16th December last, up till 16th June this year, approximated 23,256,969 bushels of wheat and 913,002 sacks of flour, or a total wheat equivalent of 27,639,377 bushels, of an estimated value of £4,419,000. The following are the figures :—

From—				Wheat. Bushels.		Flour. Sacks.
Victoria	...	...	...	10,082,776	...	373,914
South Australia	...	...	...	9,194,730	...	308,378
New South Wales	...	...	...	3,979,462	..	229,660
Queensland	...	...	...	—		1,050
Total	...	...		23,256,968	...	913,002

The total includes 18,738,803 bushels for Europe, 3,343,158 bushels for South Africa, 857,076 bushels for India and Colombo, 2,418,710 bushels for South America, and the balance—2,281,630 bushels—for other countries. The second experimental shipment of 45,900 bushels of wheat was sent last year from this State, and it is fair to surmise that in a little while we shall take our place with the other States in regard to exporting wheat and flour.

CARROTS FOR FEEDING.—Many years since, when the appearance of the dreaded " disease " threatened the extinction of the potato, the carrot was by competent authorities held to be its legitimate successor. We know more than one flourishing suburban dairyman who makes large use of sliced potatoes for his cows, and analysis has proved the carrot to have a much higher feeding value. Says a well-known English authority : "Carrots form a palatable and nutritious food for almost every species of stock. Mixed with chaff, there are few things that will better support the horse, and colts are brought into excellent condition when fed with them. To the cow they afford a wholesome food, and colour and flavour the butter much more agreeably than turnips. The hog eats them ravenously, and thrives upon them, and if the veterinary surgeon were to state his opinion, it would be that the carrot is one of the most valuable medicines which he has at his command." In the form of a poultice, it will give a healthy appearance to foul ulcers, and it will heal cases of grease where everything else fails. When colts, and young horses, too, are recovering from catarrh or strangles, and it is doubtful what turn the disease will take, there is nothing so likely to recall the appetite and to turn the scale in favour of life. Carrots will sometimes have a similar although not so decided effect in the case of cattle.

PORK-PRODUCING FOODS.—According to an exchange, the Wiltshire (E.) County Council carried out recently some pig-feeding experiments which are of an extremely interesting and instructive nature. The dry feed was soaked over night, at the rate of a peck to five gallons of water, except when milk was used, when it replaced its own volume of water. The potatoes were boiled, and the foods were not given them in a sloppy condition. Appended are the points given to the different feeds :—

(1.) Barley-meal, milk, potatoes, 1,000 points.
(2.) Barley-meal and milk, 903 points.
(3.) Maize-meal and milk, 877 points.
(4.) Maize-meal and bean-meal, 590 points.
(5.) Barley-meal, 519 points.
(6.) Maize-meal and pea-meal, 489 points.
(7.) Maize-meal, 484 points.
(8.) Barley-meal and bran, 409 points.
(9.) Maize-meal and bran, 404 points.

The most suitable meat for bacon production was obtained from barley-meal and bran. Maize alone was found to produce excessive fat.

THE DANYSZ EXPERIMENTS: —After some considerable delay, the Federal Government has decided that permission be given to break the seals that hold Dr. Danysz's microbes, with the proviso that all experiments shall be made in the laboratory only, until such time as the Government is assured that that out-of-doors experiments will be perfectly harmless to human beings or any domestic animal. There seems every probability that the microbe Dr. Danysz has introduced for the extermination of rabbits is already in the States. Dr. J. Ashburton Thompson, President of the Board of Health, Sydney, explained that many microbes found in the New South Wales rabbit are known to exist in rabbits all over the world, and it is therefore most likely that search would reveal something parallel to Dr. Danysz's microbe. Dr. Tidswell has, as a matter of fact, isolated a microbe that caused an epidemic disease amongst rabbits at Yalgogrin, New South Wales, and that microbe is still kept living and active, and might, if necessity arose, be cultivated and made sufficiently virulent for experiments such as those Dr. Danysz proposes to carry out. An epidemic amongst rabbits has just been reported from the Cobar district, New South Wales, and Dr. Danysz may be asked to investigate it, with the object of adopting a local disease for his experiments.

DESTRUCTION OF WEEDS.—Crops generally are looking well in most localities. In some they are more advanced than in others, but in all localitiet weeds are doing well. Thistles, nettles, and other vile and unwelcome intruders top all and show up above both corn and grass. They will keep ahead, too, if allowed. Check them before their propagation. In discussing this question with a farmer the other day, we did not agree. He held they were best cut when fully developed. I contented that it was more advantageous to cut them when quite young. Let me give reasons for my belief. When cut young the plants are full of sap. This runs out and weakens the roots very much. If cut early a second growth will occur, but this is much more weakly than the first, and never attains a matured seed-producing condition again. If these weaker growths are cut in with corn and hay they do not bulk objectionably in the fodder, and they often almost shrink to disappearance in the harvesting. When, however, they are left to grow big, and are on the point of making their seed, more or less of this is sure to fall out, and then of a surety there will be more weeds, more worry, and more expense in time to come in attempting to expel them. Farmers must have noticed that in cutting thistles when in flower they appear to be in no way near being possessed of ripe seed, but when they lie on the surface in the sun for a few days the flower heads have a peculiar way of drying, becoming woolly or fluffy, then they burst, and so tens of thousands of seed are dispersed. This is an occurrence almost sure to happen in late cutting.

FRUIT CONSUMPTION.—It is often remarked that people do not purchase enough fruit, the excuse being given that "it is too dear;" yet, if the truth were known, this is not so in a majority of cases, the real reason being that would-be purchasers are debarred from obtaining the fruit they require. To explain, the retail fruiterers in the large towns have always a good show of really fine and first-class fruits tempting enough for anyone; but when would-be customers enter some shops to buy they are served from the back of the displayed fruit with an inferior article. We have seen people open their packages after purchase and noted the disgust with which the bad and half-rotten goods are brought to view, often to be thrown away. This practice by a certain class of fruit sellers is dishonest and mitigates more against the consumption of fruit than the high prices that sometimes rule. Shopkeepers expose what are supposed to be samples of different fruits ticketed with a price, which the purchaser is prepared to give for the article exhibited. To put an inferior grade into a bag and charge the price quoted for the better article is dishonesty. Good fruit should be sold as such, while second class and inferior should be sold at a less rate. In the packing of berries and small fruits, the same practice is indulged in, the punnets or boxes being topped with firm, large specimens, while the bulk often consist of very inferior fruit indeed. It should always be borne in mind that the first aim of all growers and retailers should be the establishment of a reputation. Pack with honest care, price the best fruit at the sum you are prepared to sell it for, and see that your customers get the best when they are prepared to give you the price asked. Many a man would under the circumstances buy fruit to take home, that at present he refrains from doing, as he does not like to disappoint his little ones by displaying bad and inferior fruit when he leads them to expect something they could eat and enjoy.

How to Feed Chaff.—It is somewhat surprising to find the different ideas that pertain to the making and using of chaff in the different parts of the country. In the term "chaff," as here used, is included all kinds of "chop" or artificial chaff made by cutting up fodder material of all kinds. Every chaff-cutter has change-wheels by which the length of the chop is regulated, and the length desired is various in different districts. Theoretically, long chop is required by cows because they must chew the cud and require a fairly decent length of stuff for this end, but actually in some districts the short or quarter-inch length is preferred. Again most horsemen prefer the short length of chop for their horses, but the writer knows of one district where the half-inch cut is in almost universal use. It would be interesting to know if there is any reason for these differences, for the writer prefers and believes in short stuff for horses, and long—even one inch long —for cows. If the animals do not thrive on nor like these appropriate sizes, then it is because they have been used to the other, and it is only a matter of a short time to get them to take to the right size as far as palatability is required. If, on the other hand, the animals tend to scour or be costive, then it must be due to the nature of the fodder and not to the size to which it is chopped. Natural chaff, that from wheat and oats, is small enough and fine enough, but there is no need to cut straw or hay fodder so fine or short. A great fuss is made by some over the taking out of the dust. Where horses are fed out of nosebags this is probably a necessity, for where nosebags are common there windbroken horses are plentiful, but for cows or other stock it is quite unnecessary—more especially where fed in an open manger, or where the food is wetted. The dust is largely vegetable fibre, which is quite as good food as the clean chop, and where it is formed of grit. it does the animals no more harm than the stones in the crop of a bird Chaff cutting is, of course, a comparatively modern affair, for our grandfathers did not practice it, as it started with our fathers, but it is usually work well bestowed, for we can use up and make palatable much inferior stuff, and make an ordinary quantity go a long way.

THE CULTIVATION OF GRASSES.

By Percy G. Wicken.

In response to a large number of inquiries made by settlers on the subject of grasses, the Department of Agriculture has recently imported a large quantity of seed from England of varieties of grass most likely to give satisfactory results in the drier parts of this State. These grasses include Cocksfoot, Timothy, Tall Fescue, Tall Oat Grass, Wallaby Grass, Rib Grass, Hungarian Forage Grass, White Clover, Burnet, and Chicory. These grasses are most likely to stand the period of dry weather experienced during the summer months. The deeper rooted grasses are enabled to obtain their moisture from the subsoil, and it is thought that they will probably help to shelter those that are not so deeply rooted. A short description and an illustration of each of the above-mentioned grasses is given with these notes. A mixture has been made in the proportion of—

Cocksfoot	8lbs.
Timothy	6lbs.
Tall Fescue	8lbs.
Chicory	4lbs.
Tall Oat Grass	2lbs.
Wallaby Grass	5lbs.
Burnett	2lbs.
Rib Grass	1lb.
White Clover	1lb.
Hungarian Forage Grass	3lbs.

This makes a total of 40lbs., sufficient to sow one acre. About 30 acres of this mixture have been sewn at the State Farm, Narrogin; 25 acres at Hamel; and 2 acres at the State Farm, Chapman. The balance has been distributed to settlers in all parts of the country, both as a mixture and in separate lots; and the results obtained from the different farms should provide valuable data for future guidance in laying down permanent pastures.

In preparing land for grasses, it should be remembered that we are preparing for a crop that is expected to last for some considerable time, and that it is necessary to give the ground a thorough working before planting the seed. It should be ploughed as deeply as possible, then scarified and harrowed until a fine tilth is obtained. It should then be allowed to lie fallow until the weed seeds in the soil have had sufficient time to germinate. When this has taken place, the land should be scarified and harrowed until the weeds are all killed. The fertiliser should then be sown; it may either be sown broadcast or by means of a wheat-drill, using only the fertiliser box. As the crop is likely to last for several years, a lasting manure should be used. Bonedust can be used for this purpose, or, better still, bonedust mixed with a little superphosphate. This should be sown at the rate of 1½ cwt. per acre. When the grass begins to make a good growth, a top dressing of more soluble fertiliser, such as nitrate of soda and sulphate of potash, should be applied.

As soon as the fertiliser has been sown, the land should be harrowed, and the seed may be sown broadcast, either by hand or by one of the machines made for the purpose. A very useful machine is shown in the accompanying illustration.

Seeding Barrow.

It is a hand-barrow, carrying a seed-box 12 feet in width, and is made by Messrs. Hunt & Son, London. It can be adjusted to sow from 1lb. of turnip or rape seed per acre upwards, and will sow all kinds of seed from turnips or clover to peas. Its cost does not exceed £5. It is not hard to push, and one man can sow from 12 to 15 acres per day, and the seed is sown as evenly as possible.

The mistake is often made of planting grass seed too deeply or on too rough ground. The seed is very small and, if covered deeply, the young shoots are unable to force their way to the surface. The best way is to sow the seed on a rolled surface and to cover it by means of a light brush harrow; even if this does not appear to cover all the seed, the majority of it will germinate if sown at a favourable time. In this climate it is best to sow the seed as early in the season as possible, either in April or May, according as to whether the season is late or early. This enables the young plants to get a good root hold before the weather becomes hot. If it is not possible to sow the seed early in the autumn, they should not be sown during the middle of winter, when the ground is wet and cold, but should be kept back until the worst of the wet is over. Our experience tells us that spring-sown grasses, except in some of the southern districts, do not do so well as those sown in the autumn.

Not less than 40lbs. of grass seed should be sown per acre; in fact, many of the American writers recommend 60lbs. of seed. The best results are not obtained where thin growing is practised; the grass should cover the ground and shelter it from the hot sun; the habit of grass is to grow thickly, and it is not advisable to attempt to economise by sowing a small quantity of seed.

Many settlers are unable to sow a large area with grasses, as they have not sufficient land cleared to enable them to grow their wheat crops and to lay down an area with grass, but they may do much to improve the feeding properties of their paddocks by sowing a handful of grass seed in all the stump holes and soft patches in the paddock, while by running a scarifier through any clear places and broadcasting a little seed, the carrying capacity of the land may be increased.

Many mistakes are made, and pastures that would otherwise do well are ruined, by being overstocked and the grass eaten right out to the roots. To obtain the best results from a pasture, it should be divided up into small

PLATE I.—Rough Cocksfoot (*Dactylis glomerata*).

paddocks, and as soon as one paddock is eaten down the stock should be shifted into another, and the first one allowed to recuperate. By this means the pastures will yield much better and last longer than if the stock are kept continuously feeding and running over the whole area.

The way in which the greatest results will, I think, be obtained in this State will be to lay down two pastures, one paddock sown with such grasses as are mentioned in this article, and a second paddock with such grasses as will give the greatest amount of fodder during the hot, dry months, and which I intend to write about in a future article. The paddock containing the summer grasses would be allowed to remain unstocked all the winter and spring months, when the stock would be kept on the English-grass paddock. During the early summer the summer-grass paddock would make a good growth, and when the English-grass paddock was beginning to go off the stock could be removed, if this paddock was not stocked during the drier months it would yield better, and with the first autumn rains would soon be able to carry the stock again, when the summer-grass paddock could be given a rest. No stock should be allowed to graze on a young grass paddock until the plants have been able to obtain a good root hold. Many crops are ruined by allowing the crowns of the plant to be eaten out before the roots are established. It is a good plan to cut the first crop from a grass paddock for hay, and not allow the stock on until it has grown up again. A grass paddock should not be allowed to seed the first season, as this tends to exhaust the plant. If there are not sufficient stock in the paddock to keep it eaten down, a sythe or mowing machine should be run over the paddock when the grass has flowered, so as to cut all the stalks before the seed matures.

Another important matter in planting grasses is to obtain good seed. Grass seed rapidly deteriorates when exposed, and then the percentage of germination is very unsatisfactory. Only good, fresh seed should be purchased, and it is not profitable to purchase inferior seed for the purpose of saving a few pence per pound and have, perhaps, only half the crop come up. The best seed is shipped from Europe, in zinc-lined cases, and these cases should not be opened until the seed is required for sowing. Grass seed should not be carried in stock from one season to another, but fresh supplies should be obtained every season.

For the illustrations and botanical notes accompanying this article we are indebted to Mr. Martin Sutton's work on Permanent and Temporary Pastures. The Best Forage Plants, by Dr. F. G. Stebler and the Settler's Guide:

COCKSFOOT GRASS.

Dactylis Glomerata.

This is sometimes known as Orchard Grass; it is a perennial plant, and grows, under favourable circumstances, to a height of three to four feet. Cocksfoot is a grass that has come under the notice of farmers very considerably of late. Owing to its drought-resisting qualities, it is particularly valuable for sowing in a dry district. It has been tried in numbers of places in this State, and has proved one of the best winter and early summer grasses we have yet obtained. Although it dries up during the long period of dry weather, it rapidly becomes green again with the first showers of rain. In cooler and moister localities, it makes an excellent permanent pasture grass. All kinds of stock are fond of it, and sheep fatten on it. It grows well on high, ridgy land and stands heat well, making it a valuable grass for this climate. It yields a good supply of green feed during the summer, from September to January or February. It should be sown in the autumn, so that it gets a good root hold before the weather becomes hot. It can either be cut and made into hay or ensilage or fed off by stock. It is one of the most suitable grasses to put in a mixture of grass seed for the purpose of forming a permanent pasture. It is one of the hardiest of the perennial grasses. About 40lbs. of seed are required for an acre, if sown by itself. Seed can be purchased from any seedsman in Perth, the cost being about 8d. per lb. The seed should be sown broadcast on a well-prepared surface and lightly harrowed in. This grass should form the base of any mixture laid down for permanent pasture in the drier districts.

DESCRIPTION OF PLATE I.—ROUGH COCKSFOOT (*Dactylis Glomerata*).

Roots fibrous; rootstock perennial. Stems 2 to 3 feet, erect, stout, and smooth. Leaves broad, keeled, and rough; sheath scabrid; ligule long. Panicle secund, spreading below, close and pointed above. Spikelets three-to five-flowered, laterally compressed, and closely clustered at the end of the branches. Empty glumes smaller than flowering glumes, unequal, keeled, and hairy on upper part of the keel, pointed at summit. Flowering glumes with hairy keel, pointed, and ending in a short awn. Palea bifid at summit, and fringed at base. Grows in pastures, woods, orchards, and waste places throughout Europe, North Africa, North India, and Siberia.

ANALYSIS.		Grass in Natural State.		Dried at 212° Fahr.
Water		60·74	...	—
*Soluble albuminoids		·25	...	·62
**Insoluble albuminoids		1·50	...	3·81
Digestible Fibre		11·30	...	28·78
Woody fibre ... .•		16·24	...	41·36
†Soluble mineral matter		2·04	...	5·19
††Insoluble mineral matter		·91	...	2·32
Chlorophyll, soluble carbo-hydrates, etc.		7·02	...	17·92
		100·00	...	100·00
*Containing Nitrogen		·04	...	·10
**Containing Nitrogen		·24	...	·61
	Albuminoid Nitrogen	·28	...	·71
Non-albuminoid Nitrogen		·18	...	·46
	Total Nitrogen	·46	...	1·17
†Containing Silica		·35	...	·89
††Containing Silica		·51	...	1·29

TIMOTHY GRASS.

Phleum Pratense.

This is a very favourite grass in the United States of America; but so far, in this State, it has succeeded much better in moist localities than in the dry districts. At the Hamel State Farm the grass has made splendid growth, and for the southern districts this grass is likely to prove of considerable value. For drier districts the quantity of seed should be reduced.

Timothy is a perennial grass, and will grow, under favourable circumstances, to a height of two to three feet. It thrives best on moist or rich

PLATE XIV.

PHLEUM PRATENSE

PLATE II.—Timothy Grass or Meadow Catstail (*Phleum pratense*).

soils or clayey land. It is of high feeding value, and is said to contain more nourishment when it is ripe and dry than when it is green and in flower. It is largely used for cutting for hay. When grown on dry soils, Timothy forms a bulbous swelling at the base of the stems, from which next year's growth starts. It is only advisable, therefore, to pastue this grass lightly, or, better still, to have it cut by a mowing machine and made into hay or fed to stock in a green state as required. The seed is readily obtainable in the State, and is not expensive. If sown alone, 30lbs. is sufficient for an acre. The seed should be sown broadcast in a well-prepared soil and lightly harrowed in.

In the southern districts Timothy grass can be sown with a better chance of success than in the eastern districts.

DESCRIPTION OF PLATE II.—TIMOTHY GRASS, OR MEADOW CATSTAIL
(Phleum Pratense.)

Rootstock perennial, somewhat creeping. Stems 1 to 3 feet, erect and smooth. Leaves short, flat, and soft; sheath smooth; ligule oblong. Panicle spike-like, cylindrical, elongate, and compact. Spikelets one-flowered, laterally compressed. Empty glumes larger than flowering glumes, equal, each with stiff hairs on the keel and a short scabrid terminal awn. Palea minute and pointed. Flowering glumes much smaller than empty glumes, toothed and awnless. Grows in meadows and pastures throughout Europe, North Africa, Siberia, and Western Asia.

ANALYSIS.

	Grass in Natural State.		Dried at 212° Fahr.
Water	39·99	...	—
*Soluble albuminoids	·25	...	·43
**Insoluble albuminoids	2·19	...	3·63
Digestible fibre	12·74	...	21·23
Woody fibre	31·97	...	53·27
†Soluble mineral matter	3·59	...	5·98
††Insoluble mineral matter	1·26	...	2·09
Chlorophyll, soluble carbo-hydrates, etc.	8·01	...	13·37
	100·00	...	100·00
*Containing Nitrogen	·04	...	·07
**Containing Nitrogen	·35	...	·58
Albuminoid Nitrogen	·39	...	·65
Non-albuminoid Nitrogen	·48	...	·80
Total Nitrogen	·87	...	1·45
†Containing Silica	·27	...	·45
††Containing Silica	·69	...	1·15

TALL FESCUE GRASS.
Festuca Elatior.

There are a large number of Fescues, all of them valuable grasses under different conditions. Nearly all the varieties have been tried at the State farms, and so far the Tall Fescue has proved the most hardy, has flourished well under adverse conditions, kept green, and provided a supply of green feed during the hot weather; and has, in my estimation, proved the most successful for a dry climate of any of the introduced English grasses. This does not apply to W.A. only, but has been the experience in the

Eastern States. Where there is a heavy rainfall in the summer, there are many grasses that may give better results, but during a long period of dry weather such as we experience, Tall Fescue will give as good an account of itself as any of the English grasses.

It is a perennial grass, growing, under favourable circumstances, to a height of from three to four feet. It is a very productive and strong-growing variety, and is eaten by stock both as hay or green feed. It does best on a somewhat heavy soil, but thrives well in sand and under adverse conditions. It is of good feeding value and can either be sown alone or as one of the grasses in a mixture. If sown alone, about 40lbs. of seed per acre are required. The seed is somewhat more expensive than the general run of English grass seed, and will be about 2s. 6d. per lb. in small quantities. If the grass is sown in drills the quantity of seed required may be reduced very considerably. During the last year the seed has been somewhat scarce, and the supply ordered from London has been late in arriving owing to the difficulty in obtaining the seed. A large area will be planted in this State this season and the results will be interesting, as, if it comes up to expectations, an increased area will be sown for next season.

DESCRIPTION OF PLATE III. —TALL FESCUE (*Festuca Elatior—Var. Fertilis*).

Rootstock perennial, somewhat stoloniferous. Stems 3 to 6 feet, erect and smooth. Leaves broad, flat, and scaberulous; sheath smooth; ligule short. Panicle diffuse and nodding. Spikelets many-flowered, half an inch long or more, lanceolate. Empty glumes shorter than flowering glumes, acute and unequal. Flowering glumes broad, rough, and toothed at the apex. Palea acute and ribbed, with hairy nerves. Grows in damp pastures and wet places throughout Europe, North Africa, and North America.

ANALYSIS.

	Grass in Natural State.		Dried at 212° Fahr.
Water	71·25	...	—
Soluble albuminoids	—	...	—
*Insoluble albuminoids	1·31	...	4·50
Digestible fibre	6·80	...	23·65
Woody fibre	14·25	...	49·56
Soluble mineral matter	1·09	...	3·79
†Insoluble mineral matter	·56	...	1·95
Chlorophyll, soluble carbo-hydrates, etc....	4·74	...	16·55
	100·00	...	100·00
*Containing Nitrogen	·21	...	·72
Non-albuminoid Nitrogen	·13	...	·45
Total Nitrogen	·34	...	1·17
†Containing Silica	·31	...	1·08

TALL OAT GRASS.

Avena Elatior.

This grass is said to succeed well on sandy soils. It is a valuable pasture on account of its coming into growth very early in the spring and affording a supply of early feed for the stock; it stands fairly well into the summer and is worth a place in any mixture put down to provide a permanent pasture.

PLATE III.—Tall Fescue (*Festuca elatior—Var. fertilis*).

There is a native grass somewhat similar to the kangaroo grass known as *Anthistiria Avenaca*, or Tall Oat Grass. These grasses are not similar, but having the same name may lead to confusion. It is in cases like this where the Latin name helps us to distinguish between various grasses.

Seed should be sown in the autumn with the first rains; it should be broadcasted on the surface and lightly harrowed in.

If sown by itself, 40lbs. of seed per acre is required; but it is better sown as part of a mixture. Seed can be obtained from any Perth seedsman.

WALLABY GRASS.

Danthonia Semiannularis.

A perennial grass found in nearly all parts of Australia. It varies in height according to the soil and climate. It is a very hardy, deep-rooted grass, and, being indigenous to Australia, should prove better able to adapt itself to the local conditions than grasses which are exotic. This grass is often sown by itself; it grows rapidly and soon provides a good quantity of fodder; it stands the dry weather very well and keeps green well into the hot weather; it stands grazing well and makes an excellent food for stock. The seed ripens early in the summer—November or December—but if cut down before the seed ripens the grass will soon grow again. Tall Wallaby Grass and Dwarf Wallaby Grass are often mentioned, but it is most probable that the grass is the same and only affected by the conditions under which it grows. This grass has been grown at Hamel State Farm and has done exceeding well, while in the Eastern States it has been cultivated in many places with successful results and provides feed for stock nearly all the year round. The seed is of a very fluffy nature and is extremely light; when pressed into bags, it forms a mass like kapock and has to be rubbed apart and either mixed with other seeds, or if sown alone, with sand or dry ashes before being sown. From 30 to 40 pounds would be required to sow an acre. The seed can be obtained in Sydney or New Zealand, and costs about 2s per pound in Sydney. If sown with a mixture, the fluffy nature of the seed will check the mixture from flowing through the drill and provision for sowing the seed faster must be made.

DESCRIPTION OF PLATE IV.—R. BR. WALLABY GRASS (*Danthonia Semiannularis*).

Reference to Plate.—A, spikelet; B, floret, closed, showing the three semiannular rings of hairs on the back of glume; C, floret, open; D, grain, back and front views. All variously magnified.

RIB GRASS.

Plantago Lanceolata.

This is a well-known grass, although not suitable as a pasture by itself, and should form part of any mixture of grasses sown. It is a perennial grass and grows about six inches in height. The leaves are broad and taper towards both ends; they have broad flat ribs, from which the plant takes its name. At the joint of the leaf with the crown of the plant there are tufts of white woolly fibres. It produces its foliage very easily in the spring, and lasts until the weather becomes hot. It is not so readily eaten by stock as the other grasses mentioned, but when mixed with other grasses the sheep will keep it eaten down. If sown by itself, about 30lbs. of seed is required

PLATE IV.—R. Br. Wallaby Grass (*Danthonia semiannularis*).

इ.स.

PLATE V.—Hungarian Forage Grass, or Awnless Brome Grass (*Bromus inermis*).

for an acre, but it is usually sown with other grasses, and about 2lbs. per acre added to the mixture. The seed is very small. It can be obtained from almost any seedsman in Perth and is not expensive.

HUNGARIAN FORAGE GRASS.

Bromus Inermis.

This is a very valuable grass; it is also known as Broome Grass, and is said to be named from the Hungarian plains. These plains are a tract of dry, sterile country, on which this grass did remarkably well. It is now to be found in all parts of the world, and has proved very successful in America and in parts of Australia. It is one of the deep-rooted grasses, the roots, where able to do so, penetrating to a depth of two or three feet into the subsoil; this gives it great drought-resistiug properties and for this property it is worth an extended trial. It is said to thrive well in a sandy soil, and so far the results obtained in this State are most encouraging.

It is a perennial grass and is one of the earliest to start into growth in the spring. It is readily eaten by all kinds of stock, and the analyses shows it is richer in flesh-forming constituents than the well-known Italian Rye Grass. It is a long-lived grass and will stand, under favourable conditions, for years. During the spring and early summer months it affords abundance of succulent fodder, and keeps green, if not grazed too heavily, nearly all the year. In common with most of these grasses, it does not make much growth during the very dry period at the end of the summer. The seed should be sown with the first autumn rains, on well-prepared soil, at the rate of 40lbs. per acre, and lightly harrowed in. The seed can be obtained in Perth in small quantities from any seedsman. Large supplies would have to be ordered from England or America sufficiently early to permit of them arriving in time for sowing in April.

It has grown remarkably well in the South-Western portion of this State.

DESCRIPTION OF PLATE V.—HUNGARIAN FORAGE GRASS (*Bromus inermis*).

Fig. A. Entire plant in flower.

  ,, 1. Spikelet before flowering.

  ,, 2. Lower pale, dorsal surface.

  ,, 3. False fruit, ventral surface (the two lines to the right indicate the maximum and minimum natural size).

  ,, 4. False fruit, dorsal surface.

  ,, 5. False fruit, side-view.

  ,, 6. Caryopsis, ventral surface (the two lines to the right indicate the maximum and minimum natural size).

  ,, 7. Caryopsis, dorsal surface.

  ,, 8. Caryopsis, side-view.

  ,, 9. Transverse section of a lateral shoot (two entire leaf-sheaths and two rolled blades).

  ,, 10. Transverse section of the blade of a culm leaf from the midrib to the margin.

  ,, 11. The ligule.

WHITE CLOVER.

Trifolium repens.

Clovers belong to the leguminous order of plants, and possess the power of obtaining their supplies of nitrogen from the air. All pastures should have a certain proportion of leguminous plants among them, so as to provide a proper ration for stock. White Clover is a hardy perennial plant, and, for the purpose of supplying a leguminous plant, a few pounds should be added to all mixtures of pasture grasses. It is of a creeping habit and of low growth, and intertwines among the grasses, and helps to make a thick mass of herbage. It is very sweet and of high feeding value, and is sought after by the stock.

It will not yield any great supply of fodder if sown by itself, but does better when sown in a mixture.

There are many other kinds of clover which make a heavier growth under favourable circumstances, but none are so hardy as the White Clover. The seed should be sown on a finely-prepared land and lightly harrowed in. If sown by itself, from 15 to 20 lbs. per acre is required, but it is generally sown in the proportion of 2lbs. to 40lbs. of mixed grass seed. The seed can be obtained from any Perth seedsman.

DESCRIPTION OF PLATE VI.—PERENNIAL WHITE CLOVER (*Trifolium Repens Perenne*).

Rootstock perennial. Stems solid, prostrate, creeping, rooting at the nodes. Stipules lanceolate-cuspidate. Leaves on long stalks. Leaflets obtuse or obcordate; margins finely toothed, generally with a white curved band. Peduncles axillary, long, erect, bearing a globose head of flowers. Pedicels deflexed after flowering. Calyx-teeth unequal, subulate, slightly shorter than tube. Corolla persistent, white or pink, turning brown. Pods three- to four-seeded. Native of Europe, North Africa, Asia, India, and North America.

ANALYSIS.

	Clover in Natural State.		Dried at 212° Fahr.
Water	80·59	...	—
*Soluble albuminoids	·36	...	1·88
**Insoluble albuminoids	1·44	...	7·56
Digestible fibre	4·83	...	24·71
Woody fibre	4·73	...	24·36
†Soluble mineral matter	1·59	...	8·20
††Insoluble mineral matter	·81	...	4·21
Chlorophyll, soluble carbo-hydrates, etc.	5·65	...	29·08
	100·00	...	100·00
*Containing Nitrogen	·058	...	·30
**Containing Nitrogen	·23	...	1·21
Albuminoid Nitrogen	·288	...	1·51
Non-albuminoid Nitrogen	·29	...	1·51
Total Nitrogen	·578	...	3·02
†Containing Silica	·13	...	·69
††Containing Silica	·30	...	1·56

PLATE VI.—Perennial White Clover (*Trefolium repens perenne*).

CHICORY.

Cichorium intybus.

This well-known perennial plant is indigenous to Europe and Asia, where it is found growing wild. It is a very deep-rooted plant, and stands the dry weather well. It is a good fodder plant for sheep, and supplies a large amount of green leaves, and for this reason is included in the mixture. During dry seasons sheep will eat the roots in the ground, and do well when there is apparently nothing for them to eat. When used as a fodder, it should not be allowed to seed, as then it rapidly becomes fibrous and loses its feeding properties. Once established, it is somewhat difficult to eradicate, as the roots go deeply into the ground, and when cut by the plough the cut portions of the roots send out fresh roots.

If sown by itself, it is best sown in drills, so that the rows can be cultivated and kept free from weeds. When sown in rows, about 5lbs. of seed is required to sow an acre; if sown broadcast, 10lbs. are required. The seed is somewhat larger than the grass seeds, and may be harrowed in with an ordinary harrow.

Seed can be obtained from most of the Perth seedsmen. Apart from its value as a fodder, the root, which somewhat resembles a parsnip in appearance, is dried and used for the purpose of mixing with coffee. For drying purposes, the roots are cut into strips and allowed to dry in the sun. There is a limited demand for chicory for blending with coffee.

SHEEP'S BURNET.

Poterium sanguisorba.

This is a perennial herb. It grows from one to two feet in height, and possesses a long tap root, which enables it to withstand a long spell of dry weather, and helps it to remain green well into the summer, while during the winter months it grows rapidly. When it is young it makes a good fodder plant, particularly for sheep, but if allowed to get old it becomes woody, and is not so relished by the stock. It will stand a considerable amount of stocking, and can be kept continually eaten down without destroying the plant. It is not often sown by itself, except when it is grown for seed, but makes a valuable addition to a mixture. After a light shower of rain it will very quickly send out green shoots, and provide a little green feed. Seed should be sown in the autumn, if possible, but in moister districts it may be left until the spring. Seed should be harrowed in and lightly covered. When sown by itself, 10lbs. of seed is required if broadcasted, and 5lbs. if drilled; but it is generally sown with a mixture of grasses, 2lbs. to 3lbs. per acre being added to the grass seed. Seed can be obtained from most local seedsmen, and the price is about 1s. 6d. per lb. This plant is noted for its drought-resisting qualities, and its ability to thrive upon a variety of soils, both poor and rich, and also its perennial habit, which enables it to grow year after year from the same roots.

PEA OR GROUND NUT.

(*Arachis hypogea.*)

By G. Chitty Baker.

Not a year goes by that the *Journal* does not advocate the cultivation of the pea or ground-nut, also sometimes called earth-nut and monkey-nut. The demand for this article is ever on the increase, yet no steps seem to be made to catch up to the requirements. It is one of the easiest crops grown, and most productive. Besides the value of the nut proper the foliage makes a splendid fodder at a season when feed is scarce. The roots are also impregnated with a larger proportion of nitrogenous nodules than almost any other plant grown, which considerably enhances the richness of the soil. These nodules are shown in Fig. II. of the illustration accompanying this article.

The plant will grow in any light, friable soil. Sandy soil, however, suits it best, one with a good retentive subsoil, not clay; in fact, it will thrive in soils that are almost useless for any other kind of production. The pods, which contain from one to three kernels apiece, usually two, invariably take their colour from that of the soil, and as the light-coloured nuts are mostly in demand, it follows that light sandy soils are the best to plant in. Another reason where sandy soils have the advantage is in cleaning the nuts, the sand being easily shaken off, leaving a clean, bright nut that always fetches the highest price. So that as the most of our waste lands are allowed to remain dormant by reason of their sandy nature, it is a very strong argument why this useful plant should be extensively cultivated. Pea-nuts may follow almost any crop, except that of the sweet potato, which is very similar in its habits and requirements. Lime is very essential, and should it be intended to grow a crop on ground deficient in lime, it must be applied with no unstinted hand.

In preparing the ground no better advice can be given than that published in the *Queensland Agricultural Journal* when it stated that "The land should be prepared as for potatoes, except that shallower ploughing is needed—say from four to five inches. The object of this shallow ploughing is to secure a firm bed on which the nuts may rest. If the ploughing is too deep, the result is that the roots run down to too great a depth, the nuts take longer to ripen, are harder to harvest, and, unless the soil is very porous or thoroughly well drained, they run the danger of destruction owing to an excess of moisture. When the soil has been reduced to a good tilth, the land should be marked off in rows four feet apart and crossrows be drawn two feet apart. The nuts before planting must be divested of their shells. Two or three seeds are then dropped at the intersections of the rows and covered with from one inch to 1¼ inches of soil—not more. In from 10 days to a fortnight the young plants will be up. Every miss should be replanted at the earliest possible moment. The ground must then be kept thoroughly clean until the vines begin to cover the intervening spaces. Next comes the time for laying by, the vines having extended nearly half-way across the rows. This is done by running a plough lightly once in the middle, between the rows, and drawing the earth up to the rows with the hoe, care being taken not to cover the vines and to disturb their position as little as possible, as the nuts will now be forming. It will be necessary also to guard against making the bed too high. Soon after this the vines will cover the whole ground and choke every other growth.

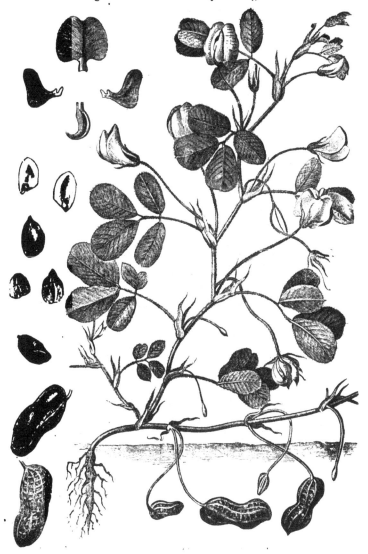

FIG. I.—Pea-nut or Earth-nut (*Arachis hypogea*).

"The yellow pea-shaped flowers are produced in bunches of from five to seven. After flowering, the flower stalk gradually bends down and forces its point with the incipient seed pod into the earth, where it gradually swells and ripens with about two nuts to each pod. When the vines have quite died, off, either naturally or after a frost, harvesting should begin. This work must be done in dry weather. The vines are mown off or cut off with a sickle. These may be used as fodder. The stems are drawn out by hand, the earth is shaken off the nuts, and the bunches laid down near the row. Next day they are laid out under cover on a straw platform, and in a fortnight afterwards the nuts are stripped off. This method, however, is only adopted in countries where labour is cheap. The simplest and cheapest method of harvesting is to run the plough under the roots, turning the nuts uppermost. They are then dealt with as described. At the fortnight's end, the nuts are either separated from the haulms by hand, or, if the crop is large, by means of a machine called Crocker's separator, which separates the nuts into three grades, the heaviest, and consequently, the most unripe nuts being delivered into one compartment and the ripest and lightest into another. This machine will grade from 15,000 to 20,000 nuts in a day.

. " The next business is to thoroughly dry the nuts, for if not well dried they will turn dark, musty, and lose 50 per cent. of their value. A bushel of nuts weighs 22lbs., and the minimum price is 2d. per lb., or £18 per ton for good, ripe, dry, bright-coloured nuts. (In Perth as much as sixpence per pound for ton lots has been offered.) The yield per acre ranges from 40 to 120 bushels per acre; two bushels in the pod will plant one acre. The uses of the pea-nut are numerous, but its chief value as a commercial product is the oil it contains. The yield of oil is set down at from 16 to 50 per cent. It is largely used as an adulterant of olive, sesame, and cocoanut oils, whilst it possesses the enormous advantage over olive oil in being the product of an annual plant instead of requiring many years for the plant which produces it to mature.

" In the East Indies some 150,000 acres are devoted to pea-nut culture. whilst in the United States about 3,000,000 bushels annually are produced. There is a large and ever-increasing demand for oil seeds all over the world, and also in Australia, where there would be no difficulty in disposing of the crop. In Barbados the average yield is 2,000lbs. of nuts per acre, and yields of 4,000lbs. are not uncommon."

TIME TO SOW.

With this crop, the same as any other, good seed is of the first importance. By good seed is meant nuts that are full and been allowed to thoroughly ripen before harvesting. Out of one lot of seed planted three years ago only one per cent. germinated. Last year I sowed them much thicker, and every seed germinated. The seed should be sown early in September or so soon as the ground becomes free from excessive moisture, and warm enough to start the seed in a week's time, and should show through the ground in ten or twelve days from sowing. To sow in cold wet ground only courts failure.

The earlier the sowing the better the harvest. The crop takes from six to seven months to thoroughly mature, and when sown later, the winter rains commence before the plants have done growing, the ground becomes wet and cold, the nuts dirty and muddy, and the crop generally much reduced in value. From experiments tried last year, I would advise that a row or two be sown fairly thick, so that when misses occurred, the space could be filled from these rows. As stated above I sowed thickly last year,

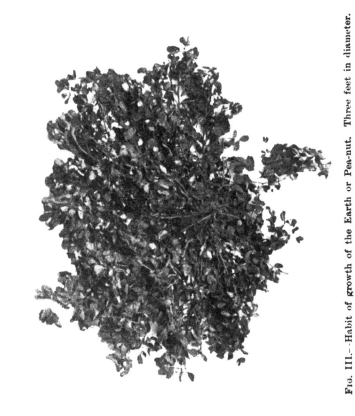

Fig. III.—Habit of growth of the Earth or Pea-nut. Three feet in diameter.

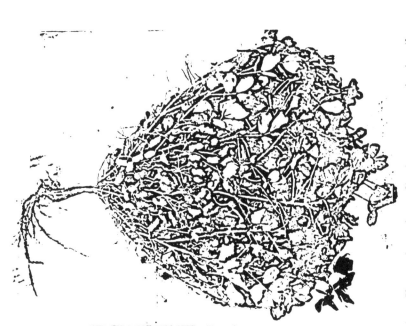

Fig. II.—A plant of the Earth or Pea-nut, showing the nitrogenous nodules on the roots. Grown at South Perth.

and from those that came up I transplanted as many as I could find room for, and watched the result. At first I was somewhat dubious as to their success, owing to the fact that even in young seedlings a very long tap root exists, which in very many cases was broken in lifting. The plants did not make near so much tops, but on digging them up the yield was very much larger from the transplanted plants both in number and size of the nuts, than from those allowed to remain. The only drawback to the general adoption of this system is that it is absolutely necessary to give them a good watering when so transplanted, unless a wet day is selected for the operation, in which case early cultivation must be given in order to loosen the ground that would necessarily be trampled on and hardened when shifting the plants.

FERTILISERS.

As stated above, lime is more essential than anything else, animal and nitrogenous manures should never be used. When grown on ground rich in nitrogen, very heavy tops will be the result, with but a few nuts and most of them empty. Bonedust, superphosphate, and potash are the best. These can be applied in the proportions, by weight, of five, two, and one, at the rate of two cwt. to the acre at the time of sowing the seed. In places where marl can be obtained, no better substance can be used for adding lime to the soil. It is without doubt the specific fertiliser for the pea-nut.

CULTIVATION.

In about two weeks from the time of planting, providing the weather is favourable, the young plants ought to have made sufficient growth to show up all misses, these spaces should be filled up at once. The first cultivation should be made as early as possible, throwing the earth away from the plants into the centre; the second working so soon as the laterals commence to spread, when the soil should be thrown back, taking care not to cover the runners; a third and final cultivating should be made as soon as flowering commences, the main object being to keep the ground well open up to this stage after which they may be allowed to follow their own sweet will, when they will soon spread all over the ground, effectually choking the growth of all weeds. The appearance of a crop of pea-nuts at this stage is most pleasing and, to quote an enthusiast, a thrifty crop of pea-nuts at the time approaching maturity is a most magnificent sight. The vines having met each other in all directions, the whole crop, from a little distance, looks as if the ground were covered with a carpet of velvet-plush. No other crop in existence provides such a sight at a season when most herbage is turning yellow from the heat of the sun and want of moisture.

On the matter of harvesting, this has already been dealt with in an early part of this article. The only other item to touch on is that of saving the seed. Too much attention cannot be given to the selection of the best plants. Dry the whole of the plant out in the open; after all signs of moisture have disappeared, pick the nuts and spread them in a dry place (not warm) where they will be subjected to currents of fresh air; in about three weeks they can be bagged and kept until planting time. The one thing to guard against is mildew; the slightest moisture left in the husks will soon start them moulding, and if packed in heaps the whole lot becomes a rotten, stinking mass.

OPINIONS OF OTHERS.

Mr. Despeissis in his Handbook on Horticulture and Viticulture of Western Australia, speaking of the pea-nut states :--

"These annual leguminous plants thrive to great perfection in Western Australia. In Spain, Algeria, South America, and India they constitute an important industry. The nuts are graded, sacked, and sold in large quantities for eating, while an enormous amount is crushed in mills, where the oil—of which the nut contains over 40 per cent.—is extracted, and the residue compressed and sold for feeding stock.

"The oil, which is largely used for lighting and for soap making, is imported into Australia in large quantities.

"The nuts are first crushed and cold pressed, yielding an almost colourless oil, of pleasant taste and smell, which is used as an adulterant of salad oil. The paste is then sprinkled with water and pressed again, cold, the oil being used mostly for illumination. The third oil is next extracted from the steamed paste, and is in great demand for soap making, while the residual cake constitutes excellent food for stock.

"The climate best suited for the cultivation of earth-nuts is one free from frost for about five months. The soil should be free and light, to permit the easy penetration of the flowering organs, which curve downwards into the ground, where they enlarge and ripen. A gravelly loam with a retentive clay subsoil suits it well. Lime or marl, if not naturally present, must be added either with the fertilisers used or independently; without lime the nuts will not develop properly, a large proportion being empty shells, called 'pops.'"

In the United States every farmer makes it his business to grow enough for his own wants. They are mostly grown between rows of those crops that take from two to three years to mature, the nitrogen collected by the plants greatly benefiting the crops remaining in the ground after the nuts have been harvested. An American farmer thus sums up the advantages of growing earth-nuts:—"They have no insect enemies; you are always sure of the crop; poor, sandy land that will not grow any other crop to pay will give a fine return in earth-nuts; such lands will readily yield from 50 bushels per acre without any additional fertilisers that would not yield a low return of corn. The vines make the finest hay, the nuts always command a ready sale for oil-making; they also make the best of pig-feed, even after the oil is extracted; the residue is made into cakes for cattle, poultry, etc., besides which hundreds of thousands of bushels are annually used for human consumption. Horses will leave lucerne to feed on earth-nut vines; you can get two bushels of earth-nuts ready while you would get less than one bushel of corn. They will fatten hogs quicker than anything else, and keep them healthier. Some people say they are not worth the trouble. Those who have tried them in a proper way know better, for they obtain money all the year round from them. Keep them clean in the early stages of their growth and you will never need to worry about the crop, for that will be there when you start to harvest."

Some useful notes on the cultivation of the earth-nut appeared in the October issue, 1905, on page 293 of vol. xii. of the *Journal*.

LIME DEPOSIT AT PINJARRA.

By T. I. WALLAS.

The Deposits exist on land belonging to Mr. William Patterson. They are contained within a rectangular area of 135 acres, which adjoins the main South-Western Railway line, on the East at a distance of a mile and a half North of Pinjarra Station.

The boundary of the area extends from the South-West junction of Mr. Patterson's boundary fence with the railway, for a distance of 45 chains along the railway Northward, and for a distance of 30 chains Eastward.

The Eastern boundary of the area is within a distance of half-a-mile of the Perth-Bunbury main road. The deposit is, therefore, exceptionally well placed for accessibility, and facility of transport, both by road and rail. A right-of-way for cartage should be available from the South-East boundary fence limit to the Perth-Bunbury main road.

As the land is practically on a level with the railway a truck line could be run from the main line to any part of the deposit, without difficulty and at slight expense.

The deposit extends through the whole area, and exists as a series of outcrops of cow mounds and ridges.

Borings and excavations have been made at several points. In some of the pits excavations have been carried to a depth of eight feet. These show the limestone in unbroken deposit apparently of uniform quality.

The limestone is free from organic admixture, and is easy of excavation.

Samples for analysis were taken from five different points. These have been examined by the Government Analyst's Department, and show the following results:—

	No. 1.	No. 2.	No. 3.	No. 4.	No. 5.
Carbonate of Lime ...	75·69	75·55	66·87	81·54	91·38

Calculated percentage composition of dry sample. These give an average of 78·20 of dry carbonate of lime.

The samples are practically free from magnesia and common salt, and the other constituents per cent., silicia, alumina, and trace of iron, in no way depreciate the value of the limestone. The quality may be classed as good, and capable of profitable use as agricultural manure, building lime, or as material for manufacturing cement.

In a previous report of mine on the deposit at Lime Lake (See *Journal of Agriculture*, March, 1906, page 221), I pointed out the need and value of lime to the agriculture of this State, thus:—

"The soil of the greater part of the agricultural land . . . resulting largely from the breaking down of granitic rock, is seriously lacking in lime. Moreover, the soil of the country generally, served by many centuries' growth of coarse vegetation, sodden and starved by lack of cultivation, and exhausted of many elements of nutrition by dense forest growths, calls for the use of lime—a substance needed for the growth of almost all crops, as a sweetening and drying agent, as a chemical force to release and change the various soil constituents unavailable until so acted upon, and to provide nutrition for the life processes of the essential soil-enriching organisms."

Every practical farmer knows the value of lime to his industry, and in this State the fullest opportunity should be given to agriculturists to acquire, easily and cheaply, this material, which is necessary to them.

Under the methods and conditions which, hitherto, have obtained in agriculture in this State—continuous, exhaustive, single-cropping, which so speedily reduces fertility—more and more lime will be needed on the land which has been brought under crop, and the necessity of the application of scientific knowledge must speedily be recognised and acted upon if the State desires prosperity. The Government of the United States, America—still an infant as time counts in the world—gives an example to all the nations, in the amazing development and prosperity which have followed an early practical recognition of the value of scientific help to agriculture as the prime industry of the country.

The motto of its Agricultural Department is: "Agriculture is the foundation of manufacture and commerce."

Just in proportion to the practical recognition of this fact will the development and welfare any country proceed. This, however, is neither the place, nor the opportunity to preach either the gospel of science or the gospel of lime.

I suggest that the reservation and acquisition of every useful lime deposit within the agricultural areas, as an essential to the country's welfare, should be recognised by every Government of the State.

The surveyors of the Lands Department should be required to examine and report every lime deposit met with in the course of their field work.

GOOMALLING AND COWCOWING AREAS.

By PERCY G. WICKEN.

In accordance with instructions received I left Perth on 27th June for a trip to the Goomalling district. Goomalling was reached on the following day, and on the 29th we made a start to visit a number of farms in the vicinity. We first went in a northerly direction. At five miles out we came to the farm of Mr. M. Cooma, who has an area of 1,100 acres, and although he has only been in residence for two years has 300 acres under crop and 200 acres cleared ready to fallow. Last year Mr. Cooma harvested 16 bushels per acre from the land sown with wheat. Mr. Cooma uses bonedust and superphosphate mixed together as a fertiliser, and finds it gives the best results.

About one mile further on is the farm belonging to Mr. H. Slater, who has about 1,400 acres in his homestead, besides grazing leases. He has 850 acres under crop and 250 ready for fallow. He only started to clear the land about four years ago. The timber on the land consists of salmon gum, gimlet, and jam. Mr. Slater has about 800 sheep and 20 working horses. A nice stone house has been erected on the property. The wheat crop yielded last year 16 bushels per acre, while 100 acres of hay yielded three tons of hay per acre.

At 12 miles from Goomalling we pass the homestead of Mr. M. Slater, who has a nice brick house erected, and a large area of land cleared and under cultivation.

Three miles further on we come to the homestead of Mr. C. Chitty, called Batbatting. Mr. Chitty, who is one of the pioneer settlers of the district, has about 11,000 acres under lease and about 600 acres under crop, and has some of the best wells in the district. The timber consists of jam, salmon gum, and gimlet.

On the following day we visited Mr. W. Eaton, of Margerin, six miles south of Goomalling, and one of the older settlers. Mr. Eaton has about 500 acres under crop, and states that he finds it unnecessary to use fertiliser as he gets such good crops without.

Messrs. Lockyer and Sons have a large area of land adjoining Goomalling, and the railway line runs through their property. They have about 1,100 acres under wheat, and are still busy seeding. They also carry a considerable number of stock.

On Saturday evening I delivered a lantern lecture on agricultural subjects at Goomalling; there was an attendance of about 20.

On Sunday morning we started out for a tour of the Koombekine and Cowcowing districts, under the guidance of Mr. Fraser, the secretary of the Koombekine Progress Association. About one mile from Goomalling we pass the homestead of Mr. Slater, who is the pioneer settler of this district, Mr. Slater and his sons have 20,000 acres of land, and 1,450 acres under crop, four acres under vines, about 3,000 sheep, as well as cattle and horses. In the garden at this place are two large date palm trees, one of which is now bearing fruit.

For some miles we follow the road to Dowerin, to which place a light line of railway is now being built from Goomalling. At Four-Mile Feed, Mr. T. Maloney has 700 acres; this is his first year and he has succeeded in getting 80 acres under crop. The timber consists of jam, York gum, and salmon gum.

At Eight-mile rock, where we leave the Dowerin road for Koombekine, Messrs. Bently Bros. have about 400 acres, and 100 acres under crop.

Two miles along this road, Messrs. Cawell Bros. have about 400 acres of forest country, and 150 acres under crop; on the opposite side of the road Mr. W. Kelly has 1,500 acres of mixed country, and 200 acres under crop.

Four miles further on, Mr. A. Watson has 300 acres of gimlet country, 160 acres cleared and under crop.

Another three miles brings us to Mr. J. Evans's farm. This consists of 1,700 acres of good soil, of which he has 300 acres under crop and 200 acres ready to fallow. Last year, Mr. Evans had 200 acres under crop and obtained a yield of seven bags of wheat to the acre, and some that was cut for hay yielded three tons per acre. Mr. Evans used about 40lbs. of superphosphate to the acre. He has some fine draught horses, also pigs and fowls. Mr. Evans states that two years ago he obtained without fertiliser, 831 bags of wheat from 110 acres of new land.

Mr. Henning has a nice property at Koombekine and another one five miles north, known as Emuming Well. These properties contain about 6,000 acres, of which about 300 acres are cleared and 240 acres under crop. Mr. Henning has a number of sheep and cattle and some very well-bred poultry, ducks, and geese. The run is well supplied with water.

Adjoining Mr. Hennings' Koombekine property, Mr. F. Davis has 260 acres, of which 45 are cleared and under crop.

About a mile south-east of Koombekine, Mr. T. Holmes has about 700 acres, of which 430 are cleared and under crop. Mr. Holmes last year is said to have obtained 1,400 bags of wheat from 250 acres, and the land was not ploughed, only cleared and worked with the cultivator, and no fertiliser was used.

Adjoining Mr. Holmes, Mr. C. Anderson has 1,000 acres of land and about 100 acres under crop. He has also sheep, pigs, and poultry.

Three miles to the south, Mr. T. Evans holds 300 acres, of which about 150 acres are under crop. Mr. Evans has also 475 acres on the bank of the Koombekine Lake, and had last year 75 acres under crop, and obtained four bags to the acre without any fertiliser.

On Monday we proceeded from Koombekine to Ejanding; the distance is about 11 miles. On the way we passed farms held by Mr. R. McCue, who holds about 700 acres and has about 170 acres under crop. Mr. G. Williams, who has only been on his holding for 18 months, has 160 acres cleared and under crop, and has done all the work himself; in addition to which he has got a house, stable, and shed erected.

Messrs. Marshall and Sons have taken up homestead blocks, and have about 50 acres under wheat. About half-way along the road we pass White's Well, where there is a good supply of permanent fresh water, and a proposed townsite, and steps are being taken to obtain an Agricultural Hall.

The Ejanding Area has mostly been taken up by new settlers. Mr. F. Fraser, Secretary of the Koombekine Progress Association, has 1,400 acres of forest country, which includes a fresh water lake, and he has made a start at clearing the timber, and hopes next year to have an area under crop. Mr. G. Farmer has 1,000 acres, and has ringbarked 400 acres. Mr. J. Jones has taken up over 1,000 acres, and some has been ringbarked. Mr. Stuart has 1,000 acres adjoining the rabbit fence on the north side of Ejanding reserve. He has built a house, and done some ringbarking. As this area has only recently been taken up, not many of the selectors have yet commenced operations. Adjoining the rabbit-proof fence 3,000 acres have been reserved for water supply at Ejanding. This area, which contains samples of nearly all the soils to be found in the district, the residents are anxious to have utilised as an experimental farm. The timber consists of salmon gum, gimlet, morrell, York gum, jam, and mallee, and a small area of sand plain. It contains two small lakes of fresh water, a soak at the west end, and a deep well at the east end, and all contain good stock water. A cleared road runs right through the reserve, and it provides easy access to the railway at Dowerin.

From Ejanding to Cowcowing Lake is a distance of 15 miles in an easterly direction, the road passes through the reserve and crosses the rabbit-proof fence at the 44-mile gate from Cunderdin, at the Doodardin Well, where one of the boundary riders of the rabbit-proof fence has his camp. A run down hill through morrell, salmon gum, and jam country brings us to the edge of the lake. The lake at this part consists of a large flat covered with sand fire bush (*Salicornia*), of which there are several varieties and which is said to be good feed for stock. Following on the south shore of the lake for about seven miles we come to Nalcain, the old head-quarters of Messrs. Dempster Bros., who held this part of the country until recently as a pastoral lease. Messrs. Dempster Bros. improved the property by excavating several tanks, which are now available to settlers taking up the land. On approaching Nalcain we come into the salt bush country, and further east there are large areas of saltbush country—there are several kinds of saltbush growing, but the principal one is the Old Man saltbush (*Atriplex nummularia*) ; this is excellent grazing country and stock can be fattened rapidly, provided the land is not overstocked.

Five miles past Nalcain we come to Messrs. Smith and Jones' camp, who have taken up 2,000 acres of the country, and have made a start clearing. They have a small area under crop this season, which they hope to extend by next year. Adjoining them several other settlers have started ringbarking their blocks. Warramuggin, where Mr. McFadyen has secured 5,000 acres, adjoins Messrs. Smith and Jones. Mr. McFadyen last year fattened 750 sheep on this block, and has done a little clearing and fencing, and also grown a little hay.

Four miles further on we come to Buckley's tank, which is a waterhole situated in a large salt bush plain, very similar to the saltbush plains in the Riverina country in New South Wales. On this plain a number of cattle are now being fattened. At this point we cross the plain and reach the north shore of the lake. Here we are again in forest country, consisting of a strong loamy soil, and timbered with morrell, salmon gum, gimlet, and jamwood. As we have now reached the end of settlement in this direction we now retrace our way to Warramuggin, where we camp for the night.

The description of Cowcowing as a lake is somewhat misleading, as the area is mostly a series of plains running into the timber, and covered with sand fire bush and saltbush, and which are not covered with water. Here and there in the plain are large depressions varying in area, which during the winter become filled with water, and when the water dries up are covered with salt deposit. On these areas no vegetation grows.

It is stated by settlers that this forest country on the north shore of the lake is known to extend northwards for a considerable distance, some of the settlers having been 15 miles through it without coming to any change, while to the north-east it is said there is a large area of saltbush plains. These areas are all available for settlement, and if means of communication were provided this land would soon be planted with wheat, and carry a large number of stock. At the furthest part of the journey we were only about 50 miles from Goomalling by road, and if the railway now being extended from Goomalling to Dowerin were continued for another 30 miles it would reach the Cowcowing area, and it is stated that there are fully 500,000 acres of land in the vicinity that would be taken up for wheat-growing. The total distance from Perth, *via* Northam, would only be about 150 miles, and settlers in the district would be very favourably situated as regards marketing their produce. The question of rainfall is one of much interest to settlers, and many varying statements are made, but there are no authentic records. According to the rainfall charts the area is about half-way between the 10 and 15 inch rainfall lines, and comparing the locality with other places we can put it down at from 12 to 14 inches per annum. Mr. McFadyen, at Warramuggin, took out a rain gauge last year, and from May, 1905, to May, 1906, he registered 11·5 inches. If this rainfall can be reckoned on, it is quite sufficient to mature the wheat crop.

On the following day, after walking over a portion of the plains, we returned to Koombekine, driving along a cleared track for the whole of the distance. Most of this country is still open for settlement, and very little improvements have yet been done. The rabbit-proof fence was passed at the 36-mile gate, and between that and Koombekine an area of sand plain was passed through. The following morning we drove from Koombekine to Goomalling along a different road to the one we came out by, and passed the following selections. Mr. J. Cottrell, who has 80 acres under crop. Mr. E. Cottrell has about 200 acres under crop. Mr. J. Anderson at Dowerin has about 400 acres cleared and partly under crop. Mr. Foreman has 80 acres under crop. Mr. F. Brain has 160 acres under crop; Mr. J. Watson 210 acres under crop; Messrs. Link and Phillips 300 acres under crop; and Mr. J. Gangel 260 acres under crop.

All these settlers are busy clearing more land and the area under crop will be greatly increased next year.

During the trip we passed through 9,300 acres of land under wheat, while a much larger area is being cleared ready for future cultivation. This district is making rapid progress and will in the near future add very considerably to the quantity of wheat produced in this State.

STATE FARM, HAMEL.

REPORT ON MAIZE.

By G. F. BERTHOUD.

Red Hogan.—Sown 23rd November, 1905; growth fairly robust; height 9 to 10 feet; stalks do not stand up well, badly laid by the high east winds. Ripe second week in April; planted 4 x 3 feet; one plant per hill; produce one cob per stalk, long and well filled; grain large and bright yellow. Yield, 58 bushels per acre. Late variety; not suitable for this locality.

Gold Cap.—Sown 23rd November, 1905; growth even and healthy; stalks strong, stand up well; height 9 feet; one cob per stalk, which is short, thick-set, and well filled with red grain, tipped bright yellow; planted 4ft. x 3ft.; two plants per hill; ripe middle April. Yield, 68 bushels per acre. Good late variety, which requires a long season and strong moist land.

Brazilian Flour.—Sown 5th December, 1905; growth good; stalks tall and thin; height 9 feet; plants stool out freely; first-class variety for ensilage; ripe late, end of April; two medium-sized cobs per stalk, well filled with smooth, pure white grain; planted 6ft. x 4ft.; two plants per hill. Yield, 51 bushels per acre. Late variety, requiring good soil and warm climate.

Kansas.—Sown 5th December, 1905; growth very strong and even; height 9 feet; one large and well filled cob per stalk; grain large, bright yellow; plant firm; stands up very well; ripe late, end of April; planted 4ft. x 3ft.; two plants per hill. Yield, 81 bushels per acre. Requires good moist land; one of the most productive and best varieties tested here.

Ninety Day Flint.—Sown 11th December, 1905; growth, fair and even; height 8ft.; one to two cobs per stalk; well filled with yellow flinty grain; ripe early, first week in April; planted 4ft. x 3ft.; two plants per hill; fair yield of 48 bushels (average) per acre. Early hardy variety.

Yellow Hogan.—Sown 1st December, 1905; growth, strong; height 9ft.; stalks weak, badly laid by high winds; one cob per stalk, large and well filled with deep bright yellow grain; planted 6ft. x 6ft.; three plants per hill; ripe very late, first week in May. Yield, at the rate of 37 bushels per acre. Late variety, not suitable for this locality.

Old Gold.—Sown 8th December, 1905; growth even; height 8ft.; cobs, one per stalk, of fair size and well filled; grain deep yellow; ripe middle April; planted 4ft. x 3ft.; two plants per hill. Yield good, at the rate of 58 bushels per acre. Second, early, good.

Crossbred No. 1 Red.—Sown 9th December, 1905; growth tall, 9ft; late and slow of growth; requires good soil and long season; ripe end of April; planted 4ft. x 3ft.; two plants per hill; cobs of fair size and well filled; grain of various shades of red. A very distinct and decorative variety; plant stools out well. Yield, at rate of 71 bushels per acre. Fair, late variety.

Old's Reliance.—Sown 9th December, 1905; growth rather slow and weak; height 8ft.; stands up fairly well; cob medium size, one per stalk; grain yellow; ripe middle April; planted 4ft. x 3ft.; two plants per hill. Yield poor, 17 bushels per acre. Second, early.

Austin's Colossal.—Sown 11th December, 1905; growth good, but slow; height 10ft.; one large cob per stalk; grain bright yellow; ripe late, first week in May; planted 4ft. x 3ft.; two plants per hill. Yield good, rate of 65 bushels per acre. Productive, late variety, requiring strong moist land and warm climate to mature properly.

Holt's Strawberry.—Sown 5th December, 1905; growth tall, stands up fairly well; height 10ft.; one large cob per stalk, well filled; grain large, soft, and floury; colour white striped and flashed with bright red and yellow; ripe end of April; planted 6ft. x 4ft.; two plants per hill. This distinct variety requires good soil and long season to mature properly. Yield, rate of 32 bushels per acre.

Reid's Yellow Dent.—Sown 6th December, 1905; healthy, vigorous grower; height 9ft. to 10ft.; plant stools well; cobs large and well filled, one per stalk; grain deep, colour rich yellow; planted 4ft. x 3ft.; two plants per hill; ripe middle April. Yield good, rate of 68 bushels per acre. Fair; main crop variety.

Hickory King.—Sown 6th December, 1905; growth fair, stalks slim; height 8ft., stands up fairly well; plant stools out freely, good for ensilage; cobs one per stalk, rather badly filled; grain white, large, and deep; ripe end of April; planted 4ft. x 3ft.; two plants per hill. Late variety. Yield, rate of 32 bushels.

White Dawn.—Sown 7th December, 1905; growth quick and even; height 8ft., stands up fairly well; one cob per stalk, well filled with pure white grain; ripe middle April; planted 4ft. x 3ft.; 2 plants per hill. Fair; second early variety. Yield, rate of 52 bushels per acre.

REPORT ON CEREALS.

Oats.

Variety.	Date of Sowing.	Yield.	Remarks.
	1905.	bushels.	
Early "Champion," Funk's ...	23rd May	10¼	Growth affected by wet. Very poor
"Big Four," Old's	22nd May	10¼	Badly damaged by wet. Poor variety
"Gray Winter," Woods ...	23rd May	10¼	Very poor. Spoiled by wet
"Alaska," Old's	Do.	9¼	Straw weak. The wet causing the very low yield
"Early Ripe"	22nd May	27¾	Reliable variety for dry district
"Golden Fleece"	Do.	8	Very poor, with weak straw
"White Tartar," Harris ...	Do.	10½	Poor yield. Straw of a coarse nature
"Wisconsin No. 4," Old's ...	23rd May	10¼	Very badly damaged by wet. Poor
"Huskless," Chinese	Do.	6	Very badly damaged by wet
"Burt's Early"	22nd May	31	Good. Useful for dry districts
"Storm King," Garton's ...	2nd May	27	Late variety. Has coarse straw. Was damaged by wet
"Falman White"	4th May	26¾	Fair for grain
"Brown-Garton's Excelsior"	2nd May	21¾	Late variety. Damaged by wet. Poor
"Nassengrunder"	6th May	19½	Heads badly filled. Straw of fair quality
"Dollar"	Do.	14½	Late variety and poor. Badly damaged by wet
"Short White Italian" ...	8th May	15	Poor, with weak straw. Badly damaged by wet
"Giant Dakota," Funk's ...	4th May	24¾	Mid-season variety. Fair for grain
"Black," Garton's Pioneer ...	8th May	20½	Poor. Spoiled by wet

Fertiliser: Complete manure, 3cwt. per acre. Eighteen varieties of oats, averaging 16¾ bushels per acre.

Wheat.

Variety.	Date of Sowing.	Yield.	Remarks.
	1905.	bushels.	
"Galland's Hybrid"	26th May	16½	Ripe, 18th December. Late, strong, and prolific. Stands wet
"Paros"	Do.	8¾	Ripe 15th December. Tall mid-season; damaged by wet.
"Kubanka"	25th May	9¾	Ripe 16th December. Maccaroni; very good for dry places.
"Centennial"	Do.	8¼	Ripe 15th December. Tall mid-season; damaged by rain
"Cumberland"	26th May	12¼	Ripe 5th December. Good, new, early variety; prolific in dry places
"John Brown"	29th May	8¾	Ripe 16th December. Plot badly flooded. Yield light
"Huguenot"	31st May	6¾	Ripe 15th December. Tall growth, very uneven

WHEAT—continued.

Variety.	Date of Sowing.	Yield.	Remarks.
	1905.	bushels.	
"Persian"	16th June	11	Ripe 15th December. Distinct dwarf bearded variety
"Bastard"	Do.	13¾	Ripe 15th December. Russian variety, tall and bearded
"Busca Nera"	25th May	7¼	Ripe 20th December. Tall bearded kind; damaged by wet
"Bobs"	29th May	10¼	Ripe 17th December. Good variety, but poor here owing to floods
"New Era," Garton's	21st June	15	Ripe 20th December. Growth fair. Good straw and grain
"Lucky Talavera"	Do.	19	Ripe 20th December. Good midseason variety. Damaged by wet
"White Lammas"	Do.	15	Ripe 20th December. Good for hay and grain. Plot flooded
"Galland's Hybrid"	24th June	16½	Ripe 23rd December. Prolific late variety. Stands wet better than others
"Plover"	Do.	15	Ripe 16th December. Second early. Good milling grain
"X Bred I/J"	Do.	17	Ripe 8th December. Early, but badly damaged by wet
"Toby's Luck"	23rd June	16¼	Ripe 10th December. Early. Poor and uneven owing to wet
"Red King," Garton's ...	Do.	7½	Ripe 3rd January. Very late variety. Growth slow but fair
"Medeah"	Do.	13	Ripe 15th December. Maccaroni wheat. Damaged by wet
"Tardent's Blue"	Do.	17¾	Ripe 18th December. Main crop. Good for hay and grain
"Alpha"	Do.	22	Ripe 10th December. Good early variety, but patchy owing to wet
"Russian Summer"	Do.	9	Ripe 15th December. Spoiled by wet. Inferior variety
"Atlanti"	22nd June	11¼	Ripe 15th December. Growth tall. Heads heavily bearded
"Bobs"	19th June	20	Ripe 16th December. This plot damaged by wet. Good milling
"White Pearl," Garton's ...	20th June	11	Ripe 7th January. Very late variety. Growth healthy. Fair
"Andros," Greek	29th June	9	Ripe 15th December. Fair growth. Inferior milling variety
"Paine's Defiance"	Do.	14½	Ripe 18th December. Even growth. Bearded. Fairly prolific

These wheats were grown on new land, fallowed in spring, and re-ploughed and cultivated late in autumn. Manure at the rate of 3cwt. complete fertiliser per acre. Seed sown in drills. The growth was seriously damaged by heavy rains and floods late in July and August. Taken as a whole the yields are poor.

MANURE TEST PLOTS.

WHEAT.—Variety : "Alpha."

Fertiliser (kind and quantity per acre).	Date of Sowing.	Yield.	Remarks.
Guano, 3cwt.	1905. 28th June	bushels. 12⅜	Growth, fair; height, 2 to 3 feet; heads, medium size
Nitrate of Soda, 1½cwt. ...	Do.	1⅞	Growth, very poor ; height, to 12 inches
Comp. Manure, 3cwt. ...	Do.	13 1/16	Growth, patchy ; height, 24 to 30 inches ; heads, fair
„ „ N., 3cwt. ...	Do.	13 1/16	Growth, rather more uneven and weak than the last
Ammonia Sulphate, 1½cwt. ...	Do.	2⅘	Growth, poor and weak ; height, 1 to 2 feet
Superphosphate, 3cwt. ...	Do.	11 11/16	Growth, fair ; height, 2 to 3 feet ; heads, small
Bonedust (fine), 3cwt. ...	Do.	17 7/16	Growth, good and fairly even ; height, 3 feet. The best of these plots
No Manure	Do.	1 7/16	Growth, very slow and weak ; height, 9 to 12 inches ; heads, small and thin
Thomas's Phosphate, 3cwt. ...	Do.	11 11/16	Growth, very uneven ; height, 18 to 30 inches ; heads, small
Potash Sulphate, 1½cwt. ...	Do.	⅜	Growth, very poor. The worst plot of the lot
Lime, 10cwt.	Do.	2 7/16	Growth, slow and poor ; height, 12 to 18 inches ; heads, small. Damaged by wet
Blood and Bonedust, 3cwt. ...	Do.	15 1/16	Growth, uneven but fairly good to 3 feet ; heads, fair

NOTE.—Manure test plots were very carefully done on new land fallowed and well-tilled during previous summer, a space of three feet being allowed around and between the different plots. The sowing was later than it should have been. The heavy rains and floods which followed soon after the plants came up seriously damaged all the plots, washing out the more soluble manures, such as the Nitrate and Potash. Bonedust and the slow-acting manures gave the most favourable results.

HOPS.

The plot devoted to this crop was planted 18 months ago with imported sets of the "Oregon" variety. The plants are now fairly strong, clean, and free from insect pests, etc. The vines have made vigorous growth, covering two tall poles per hill. These yielded a fair crop of catkins, which ripened rather unevenly. Some were discoloured and damaged by the high eastern winds which prevail here during the summer months. The hops picked during the week are of good quality, being rich in lupulin and of pleasant aroma. The yield is at the rate of 2,250lbs. green, which would give about 600lbs. of cured hops per acre. The green hops were placed in shallow wood and hessian trays and sun-dried. When pressed I shall forward samples to your office for testing. It is very doubtful if this crop will pay to cultivate here, owing to the high cost of labour for picking, etc.

"BROOM CORN"

.(Variety: "Weber's Improved Evergreen.")

A small plot of this was sown in October. The plants have made tall and very healthy growth. Part of the bushes matured, and were cut during the week. They are of good colour, and to 20 inches in length. I consider that this would be a payable side crop for farmers to grow on suitable land.

A STARLING SCARE.

In the March issue of the *Journal* a report appeared dealing with an alleged discovery of Starlings at Guildford. It seems, after exhaustive inquiries made into the matter, those reporting the presence of these birds were unacquainted with the Starling, and mistook some other bird for them. In a report on the matter Inspector Whittington states:—

"According to instructions I again proceeded to West Guildford to continue investigating the rumour concerning the intruding, and depredations of the Starling, or birds seen by Mr. Giles, on his property and thought to be such. Although there is no possible doubt about the frugivorousness of the birds detected by the above-named gentleman, yet I was unable to find anyone in the district able to give any information or description that would lead me to imagine the birds in question were really Starlings. Mrs. Giles informed me that Mr. Giles was still away on his farm, and that he had not been home since my last visit, but that she had kept eyes open constantly, but had seen nothing of the birds since my inquiries. On inspecting the prints of the Wattle birds and Starling in the *Journal of Agriculture*, she could see no resemblance in either to the birds she and her husband saw eating the grapes, and when I described the build and colour of the Starling, it did not coincide with the impression the other birds had left on her memory. I also called on Mrs. Jourdain again, so that I might show her the prints of the birds in the *Journal* as I had Mr. Giles, but she immediately recognised the Wattle bird at sight from the print, and declared it was not like the birds she had taken for the Starling, but when I turned to the print of the Starling she did not know it in any possible way, and was rather surprised when I informed her it was a picture of the English Starling, and with my description of the colour of the birds she was quite convinced that the birds she had taken for Starlings were not Starlings, but resembled more the Mutton birds of Melbourne. During my conversation with Mrs. Jourdain, she mentioned that Mrs. Addarbrook, of Ansby-road, had also seen strange birds in her garden. So I called on the last-mentioned lady and told her I was investigating the subject, and she at once put a veto on the Starling scare by stating that she was an English woman and knew the Starling well, and she was positive the birds she saw were strangers, but not Starlings. I could find no other person in the place that had seen strange birds of any kind."

SPROUTING SEED POTATOES.

By G. CHITTY BAKER.

The general rule amongst potato growers in this State is to plant seed while the eyes are still dormant. The system of germinating, or starting the growth first, is one that has made great strides in England, and has been the means of developing an immense industry.

In all districts where early potatoes are grown to any extent, the sprouting of the seed is an important feature. The plant grows quicker and tubers are formed much earlier than is the case when seed is planted before first being allowed to sprout. The sprouting is done by placing the tubers on dry shelves or floor, special boxes being used in which they are placed.

The boxes most generally used in England, Jersey, and Ayrshire, are here illustrated. Figure I. shows one with the proper measurements:

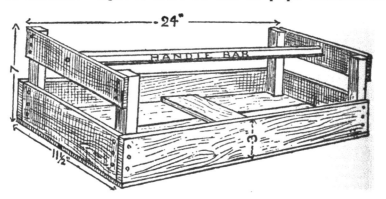

FIG. I.—Box for Sprouting Potatoes.

two feet long, one foot wide, corner pieces seven inches long, with a slab across the ends to strengthen them; as these boxes, when filled, are piled one on top of the other, sometimes 25 to 30 being in one tier, it can be easily understood that the corner pieces, which carry all the weight, must be very strong, and these are made from 3 x 2 pine.

FIG. II.—Another style of box; this is also used
for gathering fruit.

The box shown in Fig. II. is not quite as deep as the former, and is minus the cross-piece or handle-bar. This box is six inches longer and six inches wider, both hands being required to move them, while in the other one hand only is used. Boxes of the pattern of Fig. I. should not cost more than ninepence each, and sixpence for Fig. II. About 30 of the larger boxes are required to hold enough potatoes to plant one acre of ground and nearly twice that number of the smaller one, Fig. I. As these boxes will, with care, last very many years, the first cost is the only one; unless a trifle now and again may be required for repairs. The case described in Fig. II. is also used in the summer for gathering fruit from the orchard. A pile of these is placed at the foot of each tree, and when filled, the cart goes along gathering them up, stacking them one on top of the other, and taking them to the packing-house; by these means, soft and very ripe fruit are easily handled without bruising or injury of any sort. Good, sound, whole tubers of medium size from 1¼-inch to 2 inches in diameter being the best for boxing, the smaller ones proving unsatisfactory, while the only objection to the use of larger ones is the extra cost that is entailed for seed.

Figure III. shows the case filled with tubers well sprouted, ready for planting out.

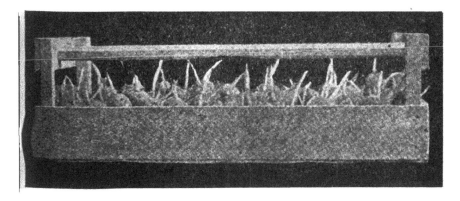

Fig. III.—Box containing potatoes sprouted and ready for planting.

Tubers must never be cut before boxing, but in the case where very large ones are used it is advisable to pinch off all shoots but one that start from the crown of the potato. This will induce all or most of the other eyes to start. The tuber can then be divided at the time of planting, rubbing the cut part in dry wood ashes and planting at once, when little or no harm will result, unless the ground is very wet, when rot must be guarded against. The boxes when filled are stacked one on top of the other. They should be placed in some dry shed or room fairly well lighted; an ideal spot is in the stable or cow-house, boards being placed across the ceiling joists and the boxes on top. They must not be excluded from the light, for if left in the dark, long irregular shoots will be the result, too weakly to be of any value. Shoots when allowed to grow in a pit, heap, or dark places are usually white, brittle, slender in the stem, long-jointed, and easily detached from the tuber. With seed boxed and properly exposed to the light in a well-ventilated place, the shoots will generally be found to be of a bluish-green colour, thick in the stem, short-pointed, very elastic and tough, and firmly attached to the tuber.

Figure IV.—Shovel used for carrying potatoes from boxes to the ground:—

Fig. IV.—Shovel used to carry tubers from
the boxes to the furrows.

As it is not intended to deal with the planting or the cultivating of the potato in this article, it will be sufficient to draw attention to Fig. IV., a device used to transfer the seed from the boxes to the ground. These can be easily made from kerosene tins cut diagonally, each tin making two shovels, a piece of wire for a handle completing the device.

Acknowledgments are due to the Highland and Agricultural Society of Scotland for the blocks used in this article, which are taken from the published report of the transactions of that Society.

HINTS ON CIDER-MAKING.

By M. T. NUNDY.

These few remarks are intended to try and induce farmers in Western Australia to take an interest in the above industry—particularly those who live in districts and whose land is suitable to plant apple trees and grow apples specially for cider-making.

I will describe a small cider mill and the plant necessary, suitable for a farmer or would be sufficient for half a dozen if they joined in the cost of erection. I am not attempting to describe an up-to-date mill, fitted with the latest machinery—the Americans have the best plants—and for some years the best and largest firms at home have been adopting their crushing rollers and presses.

In the first place great care is required in gathering the apples when ripe, to keep them as clean as possible. Care should also be taken not to mix those blown down or fallen, with the bulk, they spoil the sample and reduce the price, as they are invariably bruised, cracked, and dirty, and either contain worms, as well as other filth, which are detrimental to the production of sound sweet cider.

The apples having been gathered and carted to the mill, they are first crushed or ground into a pulp (which is called pomace) the finer the better. This is best done by passing them through rollers, which are placed over a large wooden tub, so that none of the juice is lost or wasted. The rollers could either be driven by an oil engine, horse or other power. The pulp is then pressed. This also can best be done by power. One single line of shafting will be sufficient to work both the rollers and the press, or the press if a small one can be worked by hand.

The best presses are made of iron, square in shape, the sides being perforated to allow the juice to escape as the pressure is increased. First, a frame, made of laths, about ¾-inch thick, and placed two inches apart, is placed inside the press; over this is spread a coarse, strong, strainer cloth, as large again as the lath frame. The pulp is then shovelled on to the cloth until a layer or thickness has been spread, sufficient for the spare parts of the cloth to completely cover; on this is placed another lath and cloth, and so on, until the inside of the press is filled level with the sides. The cover is then lowered very slowly and gradually. Great care must be taken in the management of the press, as, if the pressure is put on too quickly, it will cause the juice to squirt out of the holes inside of the press and fall clear of the iron stand on which the press is fixed and be wasted. The juice is at once either run or bucketed into the fermenting casks, which should hold about 100 gallons each. The best casks are fresh-emptied wine pipes (sherry for choice, as there is then no risk of colouring the cider). These casks are seasoned, light yet strongly made, and are easy to handle.

FERMENTATION.—Cider is produced from apple juice by fermentation. The skins of ripe apples contain germs, which commence to grow in the juice and convert the sugar present in the juice into alcohol; if the fermentation is checked before all the sugar is converted, a sweet cider is produced, while if all the sugar is converted, a dry cider results. Further fermentation would convert the alcohol wholly or partly into acid (vinegar).

There are many different "ferments" existing, both in the soil and in the air, and to produce good, sound cider, it is necessary to exclude all improper ferments—

(1.) By keeping the apples and all utensils absolutely clean (this is most important);

(2.) By avoiding unnecessary exposure of the cider to the air. Also in order to keep the fermentation, regular, the temperature of the cider cellar should be as uniform as possible. To keep the apples as clean as possible, they should be kept off the ground by hurdling (two hurdles being driven in the ground and one fastened across at the bottom, the hurdles being covered with straw or wire netting to prevent apples falling through) or on boards raised above the ground.

As soon as possible after a cask is emptied, it should be "chained," *i.e.*, a chain and some hot water should be placed in it and well shaken about so as to clean off all the deposit. To make sure the cask is quite sweet it is desirable to use what is called a "dry match." The best match is a piece of brown paper about three inches by eighteen inches which has been dipped into melted sulphur; this is let into the cask and held by a piece of stick or wire inside the cask until burnt out, the cask being afterwards turned bung down with either bung or tap hole left open for ventilation.

To provide for the escape of gas given off during fermentation (carbonic acid gas) the bung is sometimes left out, but it is better to use a bent glass tube, inserting one end just through a hole made in the bung and allowing the other end to dip under water in a bottle or other vessel—the joint between the bung and the tube can be made air-tight with sealing wax—this allows the gas to pass out but prevents air passing in. As the alcohol is produced from the sugar in the cider the strength of the cider depends on the amount of sugar present in the juice; the amount of sugar can be ascertained with sufficient accuracy by taking the specific gravity of the juice with a hydrometer or a saccharometer. The sugar is produced in the apples in the process of ripening, and apples should therefore be thoroughly ripe before they are used. Fully ripened apples may contain 12 per cent. of sugar, when unripe they contain only about 6 per cent. As I have said before, the juice should at once be put into the cask as soon as it leaves the press; the cask should be thoroughly dry and ought to be matched as described; it ought to be filled up to within about three inches from the bung hole, but not more, to prevent the cider working over and wasting. When a head arises and enough gas comes off to extinguish a lighted taper or match held in the bung hole, rack off into a clean cask, previously matched, filling the cask nearly full as before, care must be taken in drawing off the cider not to disturb the cask, and on no account must it be tilted. If the cider is allowed to remain without racking until it boils through the head, the head sinks and the cider is injured. It will generally be· found that two rackings are sufficient to stop the fermentation, if not a third must be given using two matches; the dregs should be removed after *each* racking and put into a conical holland bag, to hold 10 or 12 gallons, supported over a bucket on a frame. This cider should be mixed in small quantities, with cider just started to ferment, and on no account be mixed with the cider that has finished working.

Racking and Fining.—When all fermentation has ceased rack off into a clean cask, adding to each hogshead one pint of finings (juice and pulp of apples saved for the purpose, boiled soft, and squeezed through a sieve to remove the core and skins), and bung down after filling the cask.

Final Racking.—After a fortnight rack again into a clean cask, thoroughly *dry* and *sweet*, which has been well chained and washed; fill nearly full, and bung down for keeping.

To make a sweeter cider you must use what is termed in the trade a "Wet Match," so as to check the fermentation as soon as it reaches the stage when a lighted match placed in the bung hole is extinguished. The same kind of sulphur match is used as in the dry process, but in using it 10 gallons or thereabouts of cider are drawn off from the cask which is ready to rack, and placed in an empty cask, which is left for the purpose. The match is then lighted and put into the cask, and the bung tightly driven in so as to keep in all the fumes. When the match has burnt out, which will be in about a minute, the cask should be rocked and rolled for about 15 minutes, so that all the fumes may be absorbed by the cider.

The remainder of the cider is then racked off, poured into the cask so as to nearly fill it, and the bung left out, the dregs being drawn off and put into bags to filter.

This operation must be repeated every time the gas is given off in large enough quantities to put out a lighted taper or match.

If the cider remains for 14 days without giving off enough gas to put out a lighted match, it should be racked off into a clean and dry cask without matching, but leaving the dregs. When all fermentation has ceased this cider is fined in the same manner as dry matched cider. It is the best plan when storing the finished cider to place all the casks on their sides, bung upwards, on pieces of quartering, to keep the belly of the cask just clear of the ground, and to allow a current of air to pass under the cask, and so prevent the staves rotting. Another reason, if the casks are placed on their sides, the head is not liable to become loose, and the dregs are deposited in the belly of the cask, where they are more easily cleaned off by "chaining."

ENCOURAGEMENT OF HORSE-BREEDING.

Paper by Mr. G. L. THROSSELL.

The following interesting paper on "The System and Encouragement of Horse-breeding," was read by Mr. G. L. Throssell, before the Northam Agricultural Society, at a recent meeting:—

The views I desire to express upon this subject are, as you are aware, by no means based upon my own practical experience, but rather gleaned from every day observations, and from opinions expressed by others who have made the matter a study, and whose opinions are, therefore, worthy of consideration.

Now the assertion that the horse is degenerating is both a "negative" and a "positive" statement, for if we refer to most remote records of this useful animal, we find that the horse was at one time a five-toed animal with a long tail like that of a rat. Following on, we find the evolution of the horse, due in some degree to change of the conditions of life, in which nature had to adapt itself to circumstances. Very gradual, no doubt, these changes were continued, covering many centuries, until to-day it is almost incredible that the noble animals we have had in any way descended from a species such as I have briefly mentioned. Bearing in mind the antecedents of the horse and what he is to-day, reads like an emphatic denial that the horse is degenerating. That part of this subject we have to accept on the authority of scientists. Now we come to the question of to-day. Is the horse of to-day degenerating? and to the reply that it is, I wish to draw your attention, giving my reasons why and suggesting some means whereby this may be remedied. Under this category I do not wish to include quite so strongly the heavier breeds, but more particularly those of the lighter breeds of every day use. It will be within the recollection of most that in years gone by considerable trade was carried on in the exportation of horses, not only from this State and district, but also from Australia generally. It will not be difficult to remember the class of animals then exported, and that it was by no means a difficult matter to obtain, at fairly short notice, a shipment of 50 or 100 "Indian market" horses as they were called. Horses 15.2 and 16 hands were not uncommon, and those required for police service were purchased from here. These were sold at about £20 to £25, but where are they to-day? Could they be procured within three months at double the figure. I say no. Some may probably reply, "The country was all open then, not cut up into farms, and horses had many miles of country to range over which they have not now." Admitting that the deficiency in number may be accounted for, but surely this does not account for the almost total disappearance of that stamp of horses. I am also willing to admit the low prices then obtained were not sufficiently encouraging, but to my mind these are only minor causes, and the sole reason to which I attribute is the unwise selection of the sires. Then one is faced with the question, surely among all the stallions imported into this State during the last 10 or 15 years, and also the increased demand for horses, that suitable stallions have been introduced and the necessary encouragement given? To the former I reply no, and the fault in no small degree lies with the race clubs, and these (notwithstanding all their beautiful improvements and in their desire to make their courses and appurtenances thereto attractive) have done more to bring about the degeneration of the useful horse than can well be imagined.

In years gone by horses were to be found that, without all the many months of pampering and preparation, ran, at not only country meetings, but also the most important places, heats of 1½ and two miles, carrying their 10 and 11 stone, and a breakdown was seldom heard of. Then again, races like the "Queen's Plate," on Perth course, over three miles, brought out the horses with stamina, bone, and muscle. Where are these horses to-day? They are not to be found, and why? Simply because the race clubs have eliminated from their programmes all the longer races, substituting flutters over four to seven furlongs, thereby encouraging horses of an entirely different class. These horses are bred from the fastest flyers, merely with the object of producing a "time record breaker" over a short distance, and as these break down for want of proper stamina in most cases, occasionally from accident, they find their way to the stud, the consequence being that to-day, instead of having horses like those of a quarter of a century ago, we are breeding from inferior horses, and therefore encouraging their degeneration. In support of this I would refer you to the evidence given by a well-known horse-owner and trainer in Perth, who for many years previously exported horses regularly to India, but who had to abandon it because the class of horses were now unprocurable. I refer to Mr. T. Haywood. Before the Royal Commission then taking evidence, he said he considered the cause of the falling off of the most lucrative export was entirely due to the great attention paid to the breeding of sprinters, caused by the race clubs' programmes being confined exclusively to short races. What stronger evidence is required than that of a man who has followed both callings. Now, having referred to the cause and the effect, we must look for the remedy, and having laid a certain amount of blame upon the shoulders of the race clubs, it is there I should first apply the treatment, and that would be by compelling, by Act of Parliament, that all race programmes should include a certain percentage of longer races, and gradually increase the distances of the present flutters until in time they should be as much in the minority as the longer ones are at present. My reasons for compelling this by Act of Parliament is because I consider the breeding of horses is an industry of national importance. The trade we once had in our hands has for the time being slipped from us. The demand is ten times greater than ever before, exclusive of local requirements, for we have only to look at the trade ever increasing with India and now Japan. Last year the Indian Government purchased no less than 4,000 unbroken horses for army purposes, at £45 per head, landed in India; but it is now a fact that Australia is no longer able to supply the requirements, consequently India is turning her attention to North America, Argentine, and Hungary. Japan is also a buyer on a very large scale. Therefore, as we are sure of a good market, with an ever-increasing demand, and having the country that will breed them, as has been most conclusively proved, it behoves the Government to take steps. It also behoves this and all other societies who have their welfare and the welfare of their districts and State at heart to do their utmost to establish, on the surest and best foundations, this most lucrative industry. Our geographical position is unique for capturing the trade with the countries named. The Government of Victoria, recognising the importance of this, have placed upon the Estimates the sum of £5,000 towards the improvement of horses throughout their State —a precedent that our Government might well follow.

The system adopted by all the great horse-breeding countries of Europe is—

1. To impose a tax upon all stallions, and that none be allowed to cover without having first passed examination by a duly qualified Government official.

2. To offer a premium to the best sire in each district, the winning horse to undergo the strictest examination and to serve a limited number of mares in that particular district at a nominal fee.

3. The Government to provide stallions to serve at a nominal fee.

The argument used by some against the licensing of stallions—that it would interfere with small men—is one that will not bear investigation, for I believe that if a man did for the time being suffer through his horse not coming up to the required standard, and his services therefore deprived him, he would in a few years be more than compensated by having had the services of the best horse in the district at a nominal fee, whether it was a "premium" horse of a private individual or of the State Government. The result of this system would be that in the course of a few years the stamp of horses would be materially improved, and the scrubbers that are now to be seen throughout the country would be replaced by a horse that would find a ready market both for local requirements and exportation. In this direction agricultural societies can do a very great deal, for at present we have a Government anxious and willing to develop agricultural pursuits in all its branches, and we have as Minister controlling that department our own member, an enthusiastic horseman; so it only remains for our society to rouse itself and bring before the Government our willingness and ardent desire to do our part towards encouraging and improving the system of horse-breeding, thereby adding to the wealth of our State.

HONORARY MINISTER'S VIEWS.

Mr. J. Mitchell (the Honorary Minister administering the Department of Agriculture) said the importance of this question was obvious, when they remembered that there were 95,000 horses in the country, and improved methods of breeding might have put £10 per head on to the value of them. He thought as much money could be made out of horses as out of cattle, and that it did not matter much what kind of horse one bred so long as they were true to type. Either cart-horses, carriage-horses, thoroughbreds, or ponies could be profitably raised. There was a very great opening for anyone who liked to embark in the draught-horse industry. He preferred the Clydesdale, as coming to maturity quickly and being quick in action. The difficulty was to get good mares. Mr. Throssell had said that the thoroughbred was deteriorating, and that that was due to the number of short distance races, but he would point out that the horses that used to run in the three and four mile heats of some years back could not go nearly as fast as the racehorses of to-day. It was the big strong horse that won the short distance races. Canteen, Sir Rupert Clarke's horse, was up to the weight of a 16-stone man, and the same could be said of Wairiki and several other Australian racehorses of to-day. They were beautiful horses, and suitable for any purpose. It must be remembered that of Canteen's stock not 20 per cent. would develop into racehorses, and the other 80 per cent. would be available for other purposes. Positano was another horse that would carry any two men in the room, and run down kangaroos all day long, and Simmer, the N.S.W. horse, was another of the same type. He admitted that a good deal of trouble was caused by racing horses too young. In connection with the horses bred in the State years ago, it had been noticed that the horses bred from English thoroughbreds were the best. This he attributed to the sires having been well selected, and being better for having been bred in a cold country. Of course, in those days it was all open country, and the horses had plenty of run, but the conditions that obtained in Northam 25 years ago obtained in the districts further East. The Government of Victoria was spending £5,000 to encourage horse-breeding, and he believed the Government of this State would be willing to do at least as much if there was a prospect of anything resulting. The German Government was spending a tremendous amount on horse-breeding, and the Russian Government recently gave £10,000 for an Australian racing stallion for stud purposes. That did not look as though the racehorses were deteriorating. He suggested that the agricultural societies might help to stimulate the industry by offering a bonus for the most successful stallion in each class, provided he travelled in the district at a reasonable fee. They must also get better mares. A great percentage of the mares in the district now were only fit for mule breeding, in which they might be profitably employed.

Mr. George Throssell moved, "That in the opinion of this society the Government should, in the best interests of the State, import suitable stallions to travel the various agricultural districts."

Mr. Mitchell was quite in accord with the motion. The Government should import stallions, and charge moderately for their services. He was strongly opposed to the importation of roadster stallions. It would take Western Australia a long time to undo the harm the roadster stallions had done.

The motion was carried.

The President (Mr. T. H. Wilding) gave notice that at the next meeting of the society he would move, "That in the opinion of this society it is desirable that a tax of £20 per head be placed on all stallions, and that the amount thus realised be pooled and offered as premiums to the best horses standing in the district at reasonable fees."—*Northam Advertiser.*

POULTRY NOTES.

By FRANK H. ROBERTSON.

THE EGG-LAYING COMPETITIONS.

The second Egg-laying Competition was commenced on the 1st July, under favourable conditions in every respect, the locality chosen, viz., the Department's Quarantine Area at Subiaco, is admirably suited for the purpose, being in a well sheltered spot owing to the good breakwind of native tree and scrub surrounding it, sandy soil, and of easy access to visitors from the metropolis.

The houses and runs, which were erected by the Public Works Department, are of a very strong and substantial nature, and if any fault can be found with them it would be that they are too good, but that certainly is erring on the right side, and as competitions are likely to run for some years to come, judging by the great interest manifested in them, both by the large body of persons interested in poultry-raising, and the general public, these houses and runs will stand the test of wind and weather for many years, and little short of an earthquake would do them any injury. The size of the runs is the same as at Narrogin, viz., 16ft. x 40ft.; they are enclosed by 1¼in. 6ft. wire-netting, the bottom fastened to 6in. x 1in. jarrah planking, no top rail or wire is used, the houses are all of corrugated iron, with the woodwork outside, each placed separate in the centre 5ft. from the front gate and standing sideways in the pens facing the east, to which they are quite open. The buildings are extra large, viz.:—6ft. by 6ft., the perch is in the back portion of each house, occupying about 2½ft.; the remainder of the space is enclosed by iron 12in. in heighth, to be used as a scratching shed. There is not quite as much tree shelter as one would like, still shade can be obtained at any time owing to the fowls being able to get right round the houses. Some of the pens are just perfect as regards protection from the sun, especially the ones last erected. Forty-eight was the number first put up, but the rejected breeders felt their disappointment so keenly (especially as several of them had previously been balloted out of the Narrogin competition) that the Department acceded to their importunate solicitations and hurriedly erected 16 more pens, and eventually all were satisfied; the final numbers being 64 fowl runs of six hens each, and 22 duck of four each. These latter are built in two rows and are very small, only 12ft. square, made of 2-ft. wire-netting, protected from south and west by two sheets of 6-ft. iron, and one sheet of 6-ft. iron placed in the corner forms the shelter shed. All these pens are, unfortunately, quite devoid of tree shelter, but this will have to be artificially provided for during the summer. A later issue will give views of the houses and runs both at Narrogin and Subiaco.

Visitors may inspect the Subiaco pens every Wednesday and Saturday from noon until 6 p.m. The grounds are situated midway between Karrakatta and Subiaco stations, and face the railway line; cabs are in attendance at the Subiaco station and run to the grounds at moderate charges. If the grounds are to be reached by road take the main Karrakatta road, and the third crossing over the railway line from Subiaco station.

The Narrogin Competition is at the State Farm, four miles from the town, and is open for inspection at any time; but Tuesday is the recognised visiting day, a trap being in readiness to drive visitors out on the arrival of the train at 2·15 p.m. In addition to the egg-laying competition there, a poultry farm is carried on, where all farmers are particularly invited to call. Poultry raising is carried on in all its branches, and an object-lesson thus provided for all seeking information on the subject. Eggs and stock of some of the most useful varieties of poultry are for sale in season. Both the competitions and the Narrogin Farm poultry are in charge of the writer, who has competent assistants at both places, viz., T. Pryce, a former student at Narrogin, and G. Allman, a well-known Perth breeder, at Subiaco.

The following is the list of competitors at the Subiaco Competition for 12 months:—

Pen No.
1. White Leghorns, Sunnyhurst Farm, South Australia.
2. White Wyandottes, A. S. B. Craig, North Fremantle.
3. White Leghorns, S. Craig, Belmont.
4. Black Orpingtons, F. T. Rowe, North Fremantle.
5. White Leghorns, J. D. Smith, Albany.
6. Silver Wyandottes, A. Coombs, Albany.
7. Brown Leghorns, Bungalow Yard, Woodlupine.
8. Silver Wyandottes, W. Snowden, Smith's Mill.
9. White Leghorns, C. R. Roberts, Moora.
10. Brown Leghorns, W. Snowden, Smith's Mill.
11. Silver Wyandottes, C. L. Braddock, Claremont.
12. Brown Leghorns, J. R. Parkes, Bunbury.
13. Black Orpingtons, C. Crawley, Cottesloe.
14. White Leghorns, Ryan Bros., East Perth.
15. Minorcas, A. R. Keesing, West Perth.
16. White Wyandottes, R. G. Smith, Claremont.
17. White Leghorns, Jas. W. Buttsworth, Cottesloe.
18. Golden Wyandottes, L. Matchem, Osborne Park.
19. White Leghorns, G. M. Buttsworth, Cottesloe.
20. Silver Wyandottes, J. E. Redman, Trafalgar.
21. White Leghorns, E. A. Newton, Welshpool.
22. Golden Wyandottes, Glendonald Yards, Highgate.
23. White Leghorns, A. H. Padman, South Australia.
24. Silver Wyandottes, B. Jones, Subiaco.
25. Silver Wyandottes, J. W. Buttsworth, Cottesloe.
26. White Leghorns, Bungalow Yards, Woodlupine.
27. Silver Wyandottes, J. B. Pettit, Busselton.
28. White Leghorns, C. W. Johnson, Osborne Park.
29. Silver Wyandottes, A. H. Padman, South Australia.

30. Brown Leghorns, A. Snell, Bunbury.
31. Golden Wyandottes. H. H. Wegg, Subiaco.
32. Black Orpingtons, Ericville Yards, Belmont.
33. Golden Wyandottes, J. Kirk, Cottesloe Beach.
34. White Wyandottes, Mrs. J. McGree, Claremont.
35. White Leghorns, Ericville Farm, Belmont.
36. Black Orpingtons, G. Bolger, Colin Street.
37. White Leghorns, E. E. Palmerston, Trafalgar.
38. Brown Leghorns, J. White, Trafalgar.
39. White Leghorns, F. Mason, Claremont.
40. Rose-Comb Brown Leghorns, Mrs. Hughes, Subiaco.
41. Black Orpingtons, O.K. Yard, Subiaco.
42. White Leghorns, F. Whitfield, Boulder.
43. Golden Wyandottes, H. M. Kelly, Subiaco.
44. White Leghorns, Mrs. J. McGree, Claremont.
45. Black Orpingtons, H. M. Kelly, Subiaco.
46. White Leghorns, R. G. Flynn, Leederville.
47. Partridge Wyandottes, A. F. Farrant, Claremont.
48. Brown Leghorns, F. Whitfield, Boulder.
49. White Leghorns, Herman S. Jones, Gingin.
50. Silver Wyandottes, J. S. Miller, Leederville.
51. White Leghorns, W. Wade, William Street.
52. Brown Leghorns, M. J. Clark, Subiaco.
53. White Leghorns, F. Piaggio, West Guildford.
54. Silver Wyandottes, C. Attwell, Coogee.
55. Minorcas, E. Hutchinson, Victoria Park.
56. White Leghorns, Perth Farm, Victoria Park.
57. White Leghorns, G. W. G. Lizars, James Street.
58. White Leghorns, E. Garbett, Wooroloo.
59. White Leghorns, Austin & Thomas, Subiaco.
60. Minorcas, A. Savage, Subiaco.
61. White Leghorns, E. Fitzgerald, Albany.
62. White Leghorns, Bon-Accord Yard, Woodlupine.
63. White Leghorns, Adelaide Yard, Gingin.
64. Rose-Comb White Leghorns, Honnor & Forbes, Fremantle.

DUCKS.

1. Indian Runners, F. T. Rowe, N. Fremantle.
2. Do. S. Craig, Belmont.
3. Buff Orpingtons, Ericville Yards, Belmont.
4. Indian Runners, Aveley Farm, Woodlupine.
5. Buff Orpingtons, Sargenfri Yard, South Australia.
6. Indian Runners, J. R. Parkes, Bunbury.
7. Buff Orpingtons, W. Snowden, Smith's Mill.
8. Indian Runners, G. Stead, Cannington.
9. Buff Orpingtons, Bon-Accord, Woodlupine.
10. Do. C. E. Close, Coolup.
11. Do. F. Piaggio, West Guildford.
12. Indian Runners, J. B. Pettit, Busselton.
13. Do. E. A. Newton, Welshpool.
14. Buff Orpingtons, Perth Farm, Victoria Park.
15. Indian Runners, C. W. Johnson, Osborne Park.
16. Do. Mrs. L. Mellew, Claremont.
17. Do. R. A. Dusting, Leederville.
18. Do. Austin & Thomas, Subiaco.
19. Do. A. Snell, Bunbury.
20. Do. Miss E. Parker, Woodlupine.
21. Do. D. F. Vincent, Leederville.
22. Do. Adelaide Yards, Gingin.

Eggs from some of the hens at the Subiaco Competition will be for sale about the middle of August, applications for which should be addressed to the Manager of Egg-Laying Competition, Subiaco.

NARROGIN COMPETITION.

The output of eggs at Narrogin shows a large increase over the first month, viz., 782 for May, against 1,496 for June.

The records are as follows:—

For month ending 30th June.

Breed.	Owner.	Total for Month.	Total to Date.
White Leghorn	Mrs. A. Bristow	113	217
Do.	C. W. Johnson	98	161
Buff Orpington	A. H. Hilton...	84	160
Silver Wyandotte	Miss Buttsworth	51	153
Brown Leghorn	E. E. Ranford	100	152
White Leghorn	G. Oneto	77	125
Do.	F. Piaggio	78	123
Silver Wyandotte	G. W. G. Lizars	73	120
Do.	A. M. Neitschke	76	92
Rose-Comb Brown Leghorn...	Adelaide Yards	56	91
Brown Leghorn	J. D. Wilson...	23	83
Black Orpington	Sparks & Binnington	62	81
White Leghorn	John Handley	77	79
Do.	Miss M. Parker	64	77
Brown Leghorn	Mrs. R. A. Dusting.., ...	59	75
White Leghorn	A. F. Spencer	55	74
Do.	Aveley Yards	37	69
Do.	R. G. Flynn	46	61
Black Orpington	Perth Yards	59	59
Rose-Comb Brown Leghorn...	E. Krachler	48	48
White Leghorn	F. J. Williams	41	41
Do.	J. E. Tull	26	40
White Wyandotte	Mrs. S. J. Hood	34	34
White Leghorn	O. C. Rath	29	38
Golden Wyandotte	W. J. Craig	30	30

THE EXPORT OF APPLES.

THE COMPETITIVE SHIPMENT TO GERMANY.

By the mail which arrived in Perth on Tuesday Messrs. H. G. Barker & Co. received particulars of the sale in Bremen, Germany, on the 22nd ult., of the 120 cases of Western Australian apples constituting the competitive shipment for the Government prize of £10, and shipped by them on account of twelve growers of this State by the s.s. "Bremen," of the North German Lloyd line, on April 11 last. It will be seen from the following extracts from letters that the three judges appointed by the Agent General for Western Australia (Mr. Walter James, K.C.) unanimously decided to recommend that the prize for the shipment which, on being opened up in

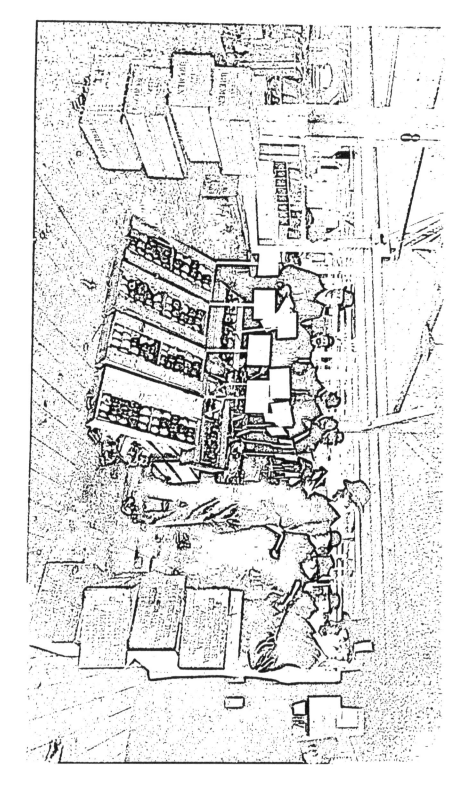

Bremen, was adjudged to have been the best packed for the Continental market, should be awarded to the growers of the ten cases apples marked " S. & J." These growers are Messrs. Teesdale Smith and Johnson, of Mt. Barker, who sent five cases of Jonathans and five cases of Dunn's Seedlings. Of the former the judges, in their notes on the various consignments, remark that they were "excellent in every respect," and of the latter, that they were "nearly as good." The Jonathan apples fetched 23 marks 25 pfennigs, equal to 22s. 3d. per small case, and the Dunn's Seedlings 21 marks 50 pfennigs (21s. 6d.) per small case. Mr. Rutherford's (Torbay) consignment is noted as "very good—second best lot, next to lot 393 (S. & J.)." His 10 cases of Cleopatra apples realised 18 marks 75 pfennigs (18s. 9d.) per small case. Messrs. Norie and Watkins, of Jarrahdale, appear to have obtained the next highest price for their Dunn's Seedling apples, which fetched 17 marks per small case, and are noted as "very good in quality." The following growers are specially commended for the grading of their apples:—Messrs. Smith and Johnson, Mt. Barker; Mr. J. Wheatley, Bridgetown; Mr. G. G. E. Warburton, Cranbrook; and Mr. C. C. W. Russel, of Blackwood Park. For packing, the following are commended, in addition to the above:—Mr. J. Allnut, Bridgetown, and Mr. W. W. Mitchell, Mt. Barker. At the foot of their marked catalogue the judges remark: "Out of the whole 120 cases there was scarcely one apple which was not sound or showed spots."

Extract from letter from Bremen brokers to the Agent General:—"We have the honour to inform you that, in accordance with your letter dated May 10, we appointed a committee of three judges. These three gentlemen, viz., Mr. Max Hassen-Kamp, Mr. Wigand Devous, and Mr. Gustav Scipio, were kind enough to accept the appointment, and kindly judged and reported as hereunder on the shipment of 120 cases apples ex s.s. "Bremen," sold at the auction of the Fruit Company on May 22."

JUDGES' REPORT.

" (1.) Condition on arrival as far as transit is concerned, and whether in sound condition, and therefore well cared for on the steamer.—All cases arrived intact, and in proper order, and the cooling and ventilation on board the N.D.L. s.s. "Bremen" must have been well attended to, as every apple arrived sound, and not a single rotten one was found.

" (2.) Packing.—With the exception of a single case in the lot, ' T. Allnut, Bridgetown,' all apples were packed in ' flat ' cases, with a partition board in the centre. We consider this kind of packing very good, especially for large apples, as they are less apt to be bruised, and they show up better when opened. The timber used varied, but we consider all sorts as equally good. In the lot ' J. Allnut, Bridgetown,' a few cases had been packed with wood shavings, and for primest apples we strongly recommend this. The marking of the cases must be attended to in most cases better, and ought only to be done with stencil plates in even-size letters, showing the variety in full letters, and an initial or name of the grower or packer, and, if different sizes are sent, the grades.

" (3.) Grading.—In general, the sorting was good. Specially well attended to were the lots ' S. & J.,' Mt. Barker; ' J.W.,' Bridgetown; ' G.W.,' Yeriminup; and ' C. C. W. Russel,' Blackwood Park.

" (4.) Best Sizes and Qualities for German Market.—The experience of the undersigned in the Australian apple trade is that only clean-skinned. large to medium apples should be exported to Germany. This for the reason that, in view of the heavy transport charges and of the German import duty on apples, which the buyer must pay, other and inferior sorts will not give a sufficient return. The Australian apple will always be a delicacy for the wealthy in Germany, and, therefore, only superior apples command good prices. We most emphatically recommend restricting shipments to only a few varieties, as only by this means can a regular trade from the coastal towns (Bremen and Hamburg) with the interior of Germany, Austria, Russia, etc., be relied upon. The sorts already well known and much appreciated in the German markets are Cleopatra, Dunn's Seedling, and Jonathan.

"Summing up, we three judges are unanimously of opinion that the lot ' S. and J., Mount Barker,' is the most suitable for the German market, and we recommend the growers of this lot for the prize."

JUDGES' REMARKS ON CATALOGUE.

Lot 370, mark E.H.D.S., Perth : 10 cases (Yates).—"Good, but rather irregular in size."

371-3, J. Walters, London Orchard : 10 cases (chiefly Cleopatra).— "Good yellow, but packing could be better."

374-82, J. Allnut, Bridgetown : 10 cases (assorted).—" Very good ; packing excellent."

383, C. C. W. Russell, Blackwood Park : 10 cases (Blenheim Orange). —" Well packed, but irregular in size."

384-6, G.W., Yeriminup : 10 cases (chiefly. Rome Beauty).—" Well packed ; good appearance."

387, J.H., Mt. Barker : 10 cases (Cleopatra).—" Not ripe ; too irregular in size."

388-9, N. and W., Jarrahdale : 10 cases (5 Cleopatra, 5 Dunn's Seedling).—" Very good in quality."

390-1, W.W.M., Mt. Barker : 10 cases (Spitzenberg and Perfection).— " Rather small, but well packed."

392, Rutherwood, Torbay : 10 cases (Cleopatra).—" Very good ; second best lot, next to 393."

393-4, S. and J., Mt. Barker : 10 cases (5 Jonathan, 5 Dunn's Seedling). —" Jonathans excellent in every respect; Dunn's Seedling nearly as good."

395, W. Sounness and Sons, Mount Barker : 10 cases (Rome Beauty).— " Small and too green."

396-7, J.W., Bridgetown : 10 cases (5 Jonathan, 5 Rome Beauty).— " Jonathan very good, but somewhat irregular in size; Rome Beauty rather green."

"Out of the whole 120 cases there was scarcely one apple which was not sound or showed spots."

BROKERS' COMMENTS.

Extract from the Bremen Brokers' letter to Messrs. H. G. Barker and Co., dated Bremen, 30th May, 1906.—" We want to compliment you on the splendid selection of these 120 cases West Australian apples. This collection has been the best fruit we have seen this year from Australia, the packing, grading, etc., having been done more carefully than that of any other shipment to the Continent. We are glad to report that, on the average, the apples realised very satisfactory prices, up to 23¼ marks for a few cases, which is exceedingly high, when allowance is made for the small cases in which the apples were shipped. Other lots in your shipment which were not so well selected nor so showy sold comparatively cheaper, which was due to the slack market for Australian fruit in general, but even these lots fetched good prices compared with shipments from South Australia and Victoria. This proves again that really good fruit is always saleable, and even in a slow market fetches prices which leave a good margin for the grower. We want you to keep this in mind for next season. We are able to sell any quantity of fruit like the Bremen shipment in our market, and hope that this trial shipment may lead to larger business next year. But you cannot impress upon the growers too strongly to pay the utmost attention to the selection, grading, and packing. If they keep up this now established standard, West Australian fruit will soon have the name of being the best shipped from the colonies. We forward, under separate cover, a photo. which was taken on the day of the sale. In front you will see some West Australian cases opened for inspection."

THE "MONGOLIA" CONSIGNMENT.

COST OF SHIPPING.

In the comments on the trial shipment of apples by the s.s. "Mongolia," in the *West Australian* of 25th May, it was stated that "the average price realised was 13s. 8d. a case," which, after deducting the average expenses from Adelaide or Melbourne (including 4½d. for railage), would leave about 8s. per case in the orchard." This statement was considered fair, because it was known that the expenses of this trial shipment were unduly heavy, and varied in the case of each shipper. The following from the *Blackwood Chronicle*, of 13th June, however, shows that all were apparently not satisfied :—

EXPORTATION: WILL IT PAY.

"Occasionally it is urged upon the farmers of the Blackwood district that exportation of apples is a matter to which they should direct the keenest attention. The proposal is urged with some show of reason and many quotations as to prices realised. Mr. G. W. Hester was so impressed by various statements that he resolved to make the experiment. Accordingly, he selected nine cases of the finest apples, and one of pears. These were carefully packed, carted to the Bridgetown station, and, after passing through many hands, finally reached their destination. The pears, on arrival in London, were found to be valueless; the apples realised a sum of £7 1s. The grower might fairly have expected that he had made a satisfactory deal. The following list of charges throws another light on the matter. It must be understood, however, that the consignment was made through the medium of the W.A. Producers' Co-operative Union :—

LONDON ACCOUNT.

		£	s.	d.
By 2 cases Jonathans, 12s.		1	4	0
„ 3 cases Dunn's Seedling, 15s.		2	5	0
„ 4 cases Cleopatra, 18s.		3	12	0
		7	1	0

	£ s. d.	
To ordinary size packages	0 5 10	
„ packages on show	0 1 6	
„ brokerage and guarantee	0 2 9	
		0 10 1
Balance		6 10 11

PRODUCERS' UNION ACCOUNT.

To proceeds London		6 10 11
By freight, Perth	1 3 2	
„ packing paper	0 14 9	
„ freight, Fremantle	0 6 10	
„ shipping charges	0 7 6	
„ freight and insurance	1 7 9	
		4 0 0
Balance		2 10 11

GROWER'S ACCOUNT.

To Union cheque		2 10 11
By tissue paper	0 5 0	
„ 10 special boxes as prescribed	1 13 4	
„ cost packing	0 5 0	
„ freight to Bridgetown	0 7 6	
		2 10 10
Balance		0 0 1

"The above accounts speak for themselves. Although the apples realised the sum of £7 1s. in London, charges and other items reduced the net profit to 1d. No account is taken of the expenditure of capital and labour necessary to grow the fruit. It is only fair to add that a larger shipment may have reduced the percentage of cost, but in any event the result of Mr. Hester's experiment can only be taken as instructive—it was scarcely profitable."

The matter being one of some public interest and importance, the management of the Western Australian Producers' Co-operative Union, Ltd., was asked to comment on the statements made by Mr. Hester, and has supplied the following report :—

COMMENTS ON MR. GODFREY HESTER'S ACCOUNT SALES RE APPLES EXPORTED.

"Mr. Hester seems to have duplicated several items, and wrongly debited others to the cost of shipping, and though it is admitted that the charges are unduly excessive in many instances, yet the net return to Mr.

Hester would have been higher than the cheque actually received by him —£2 10s. 11d.—if he had not included the case of pears in his consignment. The item 'Producers' Union account,' marked by Mr. Hester for 'freight to Perth, £1 3s. 2d.,' also includes the cost of the cases, as well as railage of the empty cases to Bridgetown. The item 'packing paper' includes tissue wrapping, white paper for lining the cases, and wood wool—total cost, 14s. 9d. ' The item marked 'freight, Fremantle, 6s. 10d.,' is the freight from Bridgetown to Fremantle of the 10 cases of fruit. The shipping charges— 7s. 6d.—also include cold storage. The item under 'grower's account,' marked for tissue paper 5s., should not appear, this being included in the item 'packing paper.' The '10 special cases as prescribed, £1 13s. 4d.,' have been already charged for in the item £1 3s. 2d., which includes cost of cases and railage of cases to Bridgetown. The 'cost of packing' is one always incidental to orchard operations, and is not rightly charged against the shipment. The item 'freight to Bridgetown' is apparently charged by Mr. Hester for cartage from the orchard to the railway station, and under ordinary conditions of export should not be anything like the amount mentioned. The apples would have to be so carted whether for Perth market or for export. The cost of cases was unduly heavy. It should not have been more than 10s., but owing to circumstances for which those having charge of the shipment were not responsible, local cases had to be procured of the standard export bushel capacity, and these were not only double the cost of cases which could have been procured from Tasmania or Adelaide if a larger shipment was being handled, but were so weak that it was found necessary to double-wire each case at Fremantle before they were placed on board the Mongolia. This charge is included in the shipping charges, and will not recur.

"Another item which will not recur was for cartage from the Fremantle station to the cold store, and cartage from cold store back to the ship. This will be avoided by arranging for the transport of export apples in truck loads to be run directly into the cold store siding, and finally from cold store to wharf alongside ship in the truck. As the shipment consisted of 13 small lots, arriving at different times, some by passenger train and some by goods train, this could not, in this instance, be arranged. It has also to be remembered that packing paper, tissue paper, and wood wool were bought in very small quantities for the shipment, a bale of wood wool having to be specially imported for the purpose. All these three items would be very materially reduced if bought in large quantities, which will be done when serious exportation commences.

" Mr. Hester, to be fair, should also have given credit for a quantity of lining paper and wood wool which he has on hand, estimated to value 4s. 10d., and his account would have looked considerably better had he followed instructions and shipped only apples. His inclusion of a case of pears, which turned out to be worthless, considerably decreases his return. Had he sent a case of Cleopatras, the account would have been 18s. more to the good.

" In the London charges also the item 'ordinary size packages, 5s. 10d.; packages on show, 1s. 6d.' are apparently charges that will not recur, as they appear to have been caused in the preparation for the exhibition that was made by the Agent General, and should really have been disbursed by him.

"Mr. Hester's net return is £2 18s. 3d., made up as follows:—

	£	s.	d.
By net proceeds, London	6	10	11
Plus amount paid towards cost of arranging for competition for Government prize	0	7	4
	6	18	3

	£	s.	d.			
Cases and railage	1	3	2			
Packing paper and wood wool	0	14	9			
Railage	0	6	10			
Shipping charges	0	7	6			
Freight and insurance	1	7	9	4	0	0
				£2	18	3

"To this we should add the extra return, had apples been sent instead of the case of pears, 18s.; making £3 16s. 3d.—or equal to 7s. 7½d. per case at Bridgetown railway station.

"The following deductions should be made for charges that will not recur:—

	£	s.	d.
Reduced cost of cases by, say, 1s. 4d. each, including railage to Bridgetown, and making	0	13	4
Cartages	0	2	4
Shipping agents' charges, reduction on quantity, say, 1d. per case	0	0	10
Saving on lining paper, wood wool and freight of same if dealt with in greater quantity, say, 1d. per case ...	0	0	10
	£4	13	7

"Therefore, had the shipment been made on a larger scale, and with the knowledge that we now possess of the difficulties that have to be overcome, and avoided, Mr. Hester's net return, had he sent 10 cases of apples, would probably have amounted to £4 13s. 7d.—or equal to 9s. 4¼d. per case at Bridgetown, delivered at the railway station.

"In any case, even if the return were *nil*, it is only a very slight loss for a large apple-grower like Mr. Hester to make to enable him to establish—as has been done satisfactorily—the value of his products in the London market. A good many growers have in past years made these tests, and to do so have contributed not only the fruit free, but have also paid all expenses in connection with the shipment, and did not consider that the money so spent had been at all wasted.

"Of course, it is clear to everyone that in a first shipment on a commercial scale, a good many difficulties present themselves which could not be anticipated and provided for, and the undertaking of this shipment has caused a good deal of trouble and expense to the Producers' Union, but it will be noted that in no instance has any profit or commission been made by the Union. The cases and material were all charged to the grower at actual cost, and no commission was charged. Under all the circumstances, we think a large grower participating in the shipment has reason to be well satisfied with the results. We hope to make a shipment on a larger scale should the crops prove good—as is likely to be the case—next season, and with the experience already gained, the cost of shipment will in all probability be no higher than that obtaining in South Australia and Victoria."

We publish a very interesting illustration of the sale rooms, taken on the morning of the sale. The photograph was received by Mr. H. G. Barker, and was reproduced by the *Western Mail*, to whom we are indebted for the loan of the block.

KIMBERLEY DISEASE IN HORSES.

In July of last year the report of the Committees inquiring into the Kimberley disease in horses was published in the *Journal*, the outcome of which was a visit of the Government Veterinary Surgeon, Mr. R. E. Weir, to the district for the purpose of studying the matter locally. Mr. Weir, after some months' absence, has just returned and submitted the following report to the Hon. the Minister for Agriculture:—

After completing my inspection work in East I returned *viâ* West Kimberley to Derby for the purpose of making further inquiries *re* the Kimberley diseases in horses.

It was originally my intention to travel over the Fitzroy Road, as the majority of the stations are in that vicinity, but on being advised at the crossing that both feed and water were scarce in that direction, I decided upon taking the telegraph route, where travelling conditions were of a more favourable character.

From information gathered, it appears that a somewhat heavy mortality occurred from this complaint some three years ago, but since that period the seasons have been drier and the feed less rank; also, provision has been made by many for paddock accommodation where grasses of a finer character exist; hence, a material decrease in mortality, and in some cases a complete cessation of the complaint has occurred. The latter welcome result has been secured by the management of the Oscar Range Station, where, acting on the advice supplied consequent on my investigations made in 1897, preventive measures were immediately inaugurated, and with such good effect that instead of the then customary average decrease in numbers, successful breeding has been established.

The disease is undoubtedly due to depasturing for too long a period on the coarse herbage common to the district. This results in impaction of the stomach, followed by complete paralysis of the organ. It is the opinion of some that parasites are the sole cause, but as these are not always present on *post mortem*, it can only be assumed that their presence is chiefly due to disordered digestion. The complaint is more prevalent on stations near the coast, where the pasture is of a coarser character than in the more inland parts, and the difficulty in securing grasses of a suitable nature will always result in a recurrence of the disease.

At the Meeda Station I met a Mr. Perry, who had successfully treated a few cases previous to my arrival, and as he is staying in the district for some considerable time, he is hopeful of rendering good service in coping with the complaint.

Successful treatment is usually possible when applied in the early stages, but with later developments it is difficult to effect a cure. Preventive measures are chiefly such as securing paddocks where the finer grasses prevail, also the growing of green fodder for use during the dry season, and where this is impossible, bran mashes should be given as a substitute. Mild aperients require to be administered at regular intervals, especially before any rapid change in a season.

R. E. WEIR, V.S.,

10th July, 1906.   Chief Inspector of Stock.

THE LABOUR BUREAU.

JUNE REPORT.

The following is the official report of the operations of the Labour Bureau for the month of June, as also for the half-year ending June 30, 1906 :—

PERTH.

Registrations.—The total number of men who called during the month in search of work was 622. Of this number 293 were new registrations, and 329 renewals, i.e., men who called who had been registered during the year prior to the month of June. The trades or occupations of the 622 applicants were as follows: Labourers 176, handy men 75, handy boys 56, farm hands 39, cooks 30, carpenters 23, bushmen 17, grooms 14, horse drivers 12, firemen 11, miners 10, gardeners 10, bakers 9, yardmen 8, engine-drivers 7, painters 7, blacksmiths, carpenters (rough), hotel hands, engineers, and survey hands 6 of each, fitters 5, clerks, drivers, masons, and plumbers 4 of each, and 67 miscellaneous.

Engagements.—The engagements for the month numbered 147. The classification of work found was as follows:—Labourers 51, farm hands 15, bushmen 7, cooks, 7, handy boys, 6, handy men 6, gardeners 5, grooms 5, carpenters 4, woodcutters 4, cube-dressers 3, yardmen 3, boys for farms 3, and 28 miscellaneous.

FREMANTLE.

Registrations.—The applicants for work numbered 82. There were 45 new registrations, and 37 renewals.

Engagements.—The engagements were 6, classified as follows:—Labourers 4, attendants 1, and handy man 1.

The female servants who called numbered 2. There were no engagements.

KALGOORLIE.

Registrations.—The new registrations for the month were 52, and the renewals 47.

Engagements.—There were 18 engagements, classified as follows:—Labourers, 12; fitters, 2; and clerks, cooks, drivers and miners, one of each.

The female servants who called numbered 45. The new registrations were 17, and the renewals 28. There was one engagement—a general.

WOMEN'S BRANCH, PERTH.

Registrations.—There were 228 women called, 133 being new registrations and 95 renewals. The classification was as follows:—Laundress-charwomen, 36; generals, 35; housemaids, 28; cooks, 28; light generals, 24; housekeepers, 21; waitresses, 18; useful girls, 13; cook-laundress, 6; lady helps, 4; nursemaids, 4; and 11 miscellaneous.

Engagements.—The engagements were 67, classified as follows:—Generals, 20; laundress-charwomen, 13; useful girls, 7; light generals, 6; nursemaids, 4; housemaids, 3; and 14 miscellaneous.

GENERAL REMARKS.

The number of individual men who registered for work at Perth during the past six months was 3,133, as against 3,332, or 199 less than that for the corresponding period of last year. The engagements for the half-year were 1,337. There were 1,222 by private persons, this being one in excess of the total for the first six months of last year, and 115 from Government Departments, which is 20 short of the number for the same period of 1905. The engagements for the country districts totalled 903, and the town 434.

At the Women's Branch, Perth, the number of women who called during the period under review was 756, as against 878, or 122 short of the total for the first six months of last year. The engagements were 464, being 80 short of that for the corresponding period of 1905.

At Fremantle the registrations for the half-year were 653, and the engagements 118, being 677 and 40, respectively, short of the total for the same period of 1905. Of the engagements, 34 were by private persons, and 84 were given work on the railway station improvements. The females who called at this office numbered 31, and the engagements 4 for the half-year.

At Kalgoorlie the registrations during the half-year totalled 410, and the engagements 80, being 266 and 34, respectively, short of the total for the same period of 1905. The woman who registered during the six months numbered 157, being three more than for the same period of 1905, and the engagements were 29, this being 19 in excess of the number of last year.

The branch at Cue will be closed, and the books and other papers removed to Northam, where it has been arranged to open in a few days a branch of the Bureau in charge of the land agent there.

THE LABOUR MARKET.

The reports received from various sources show that although there has been a decided slackness in the building trades during the past six months, there are welcome signs of a considerable revival. General labourers are not much in demand. There is always an inclination on the part of those working in the country to make for town, if any public works are under construction. A good many have already reached Perth in search of work on the sewerage scheme, and when work was not obtainable they had to be assisted to get back again to where they came from. At Kalgoorlie employment is somewhat scarce, and there are a good many men looking for work. The mines are employing about the same number of men as formerly, but there does not appear to be any likelihood of an increase. Outside the mines, comparatively speaking, few men are employed, although some are prospecting in the district with very fair success.

RAILWAY PASSES.

At the Central Office, Perth, there were 239 men assisted by railway passes to employment, and 45 at Kalgoorlie branch, at a cost of £217 9s. 7d. Of this amount, £116 13s. 4d., or 53½ per cent., has been refunded. Further refunds will be received, there being a number of agreements for fares not yet due. An additional sum of £27 1s. 2d. was received as a refund for passes issued prior to the year, the total amount refunded during the six months being £143 14s. 6d. There were also 51 men and 38 women sent to work whose fares were forwarded by employers, the amount totalling £77 9s. 5d. The total number of persons supplied with railway tickets, either provided by the Government or employers, was 373, at a total cost of £294 19s.

TESTS OF MILK COWS IN AYRSHIRE.

Some interesting details as to the quality and quantity of milk given by Ayrshire cows were given by Mr. J. Speir, Newton Farm, Glasgow, in a lecture at Cumnock on "Tests of Milk Cows in Ayrshire." He said that for three years the Highland and Agricultural Society have been doing good work in the endeavour to encourage the owners of herds of Ayrshires to systematically record the produce, in regard to both quality and quantity, for the whole of their milking period. During the season 1905 they had 815 cows under continuous supervision in the districts of Cumnock and Fenwick. The result of this testing is the most conclusive yet carried out by the society of the value of selecting cows and bulls for breeding purposes only from mothers which have proved themselves good milkers. From the records of the past year it is seen that among the Ayrshires there are many better milking animals than even the most ardent advocates of the merits of the breed ever anticipated. What, however, much reduces the value of the breed for dairy purposes is the great irregularity in milk yield of many families.

It has long been proved that the ability of a cow to yield a large quantity of milk is an inherited qualification, just as much as any of the other items of the nature of each individual animal. Food, provided it is in moderate quantity, has little to do with it, as is shown by the records at Cumnock, where the farms are all very much of one class. There, out of 372 cows under test, the ten heaviest milking cows were all in one herd. At one time it was supposed that a rich quality of milk must necessarily follow the use of rich food. Repeated experiments during the past fifteen years have demonstrated that quality in milk can be little altered by feeding. These tests clearly indicate the same, as cows of the same age, going on the same pasture, and in other respects treated alike, yielded milk from 50 to 60 per cent. richer in fat than others of a different family. The same applies to the animals when in the house, where the food was more under control than in the field. Under these circumstances many of the heaviest fed stocks gave not only the poorest milk, but least of it.

In Fenwick, where the records were carried on during the whole year, out of 443 cows, there were nine, or 2 per cent., which yielded over £30 in milk; 37, or 8 per cent., which yielded over £25 in milk; and 137, or 31 per cent., which yielded over £20 in milk. Against that there was a considerable number which yielded only from £8 to £11 of milk in the year, the milk being valued at 5d. per gallon for milk of 3 per cent. of fat.

In Cumnock, the supervision of the herds was only continued for thirty-four weeks, and while the milk yield for the period was just as good as in Fenwick, it does not total up to such a large figure. In that period one cow yielded on the grass milk of a total value of £26 7s. 11d., and another ten of upwards of £20. Among the heifers tested at Cumnock were some particularly good ones, about a dozen having yielded milk of a value of from £14 to £16 10s. in thirty-four weeks, with, in many cases, a very large quantity not only before testing began, but after it ceased. When these results are compared with the milk yield of others, which only had a value of from £6 10s. to £9 10s. during the season, the value of the method suggested for the selection of cows for breeding purposes is at once seen.

A very instructive wall diagram was exhibited showing the yield and value of 10 per cent. of the best and worst of the cows of each herd. Out of 372 cows, there were 35 which yielded milk of an average value of £17 4s. 2d., while there was an equal number, the milk of which was only of the value of £10 19s. 2d. The difference is £6 5s. between these two lots of cows in thirty-four weeks, which for the whole milking period might probably be £8 or £10, as when the testing stopped many of the best milking cows were giving a considerable quantity of milk, or had already done so, while the poor ones were mostly dry. It was also worthy of note that the best and heaviest milking cows usually gave the richest milk. In an odd instance or two this did not occur, but as a rule it did so.

As showing the popularity of this work, on which the Highland and Agricultural Society is spending about £200 each year, it may be stated that there are a great many inquiries from buyers of bulls, who wish them out of cows which can be certified to have given a certain quantity and quality of milk. Each farm has a book with the details of each cow, so that the owners of the good ones can easily show a buyer their record, while those having cows giving a low yield are not penalised by their names being published. During the present year there are five milk record societies at work under the Highland and Agricultural Society's scheme, which for this season will control about 2,000 cows.

CROP AND STOCK RETURNS.

Herewith is published in brief outline the totals of the various crops and stock in this State. The returns are up to the 31st of December last. A glance at the stock returns which are given for the years 1896, 1904, and 1905, shows a wonderful increase all round. In the matter of crops the one item that calls for more than passing notice is the very small area given to maize. When it is considered how well adapted this State is for the cultivation of this crop, and the enormous quantities imported, it is hard to understand that more is not grown.

A full report will be published in the next issue of the *Journal*.

Crop Returns to 31st December, 1905.

	Area.	Production.	Average.
	acres.	bushels.	per acre.
Wheat	195,071	2,293,333	11·8
Maize	43	428	10·0
Oats	15,713	283,987	18·1
Barley, Malting	1,436	19,385	13·5
Do. other	2,229	30,113	13·5
Rye	518	4,353	8·4
Peas and Beans	920	10,049	10·9
		tons.	tons.
Hay, Wheaten	99,629	115,283	1·2
Do. Oaten	23,910	22,673	0·9
Do. other kinds	1,367	1,460	1·1
Total Hay Crop	124,906	139,380	1·1
Potatoes	2,145	6,297	2·9
Onions	101	317	3·1
Other Root Crops	146	834	5·1
Grape Vines	3,541	...	...
Fruit Trees	11,026	...	...
Kitchen and Market Gardens	4,605	...	...

Stock Returns to 31st December, 1905.

	31st December, 1905.	31st December, 1904.	31st December, 1896.
	No.	No.	No.
Horses	97,397	90,102	57,527
Cattle	631,825	560,914	199,793
Sheep	3,120,603	2,856,290	2,248,976
Pigs	74,567	69,960	31,154
Goats	21,139	17,212	4,027

BRANDING SHEEP.

Bradford correspondents are incessantly complaining about the method of branding sheep on the fleece. As this has ever been the custom in Australia, and as the only improving result of agitation for years past has been to substitute some other marking material to tar, it seems strange that so little notice has been taken of so much protest. However, several of the Chambers of Commerce in France have taken a hand in discussing the evil, and in generally trying to mitigate the difficulties which are undoubtedly caused by the presence in wool of various foreign substances used for branding sheep. The Chambers of Commerce of Orleans and Rheims have considered various remedies for the difficulties which are reputedly growing greater. In Australia the law awards the ownership of sheep to the possessor, unless the real owner can identify his property by some distinctive mark. Branding takes place after shearing, and the difficulty arises from using tar, paint, and other materials that remain in the wool, and give great trouble during the actual process of manufacturing the goods.

Two remedies have been suggested in the discussion before these French Chambers of Commerce. One of them is the use of a material for marking that will dissolve under the action of certain alkalies or acids used in scouring the wool. The other remedy is to brand the sheep on the nose, or rely for purposes of identification on the earmark alone. The first method offers no guarantee that any ordinary branding fluid will remain on as long as it is needed; its position alone exposes it to much extra wear and tear. The Frenchman places the choice of remedies between these methods, and seems to be of opinion that if the buyer in the home markets insists that the wool shall be free from objectionable marking material, it will soon become the business of the sheep-farmer to decide which method shall be used.

Some of the Chambers are inclined to adopt the view that such rigid rules are impracticable, and will be rendered null and void by the general refusal of the wool trade to adopt them. Wool-combers doubtless feel that by everlastingly pegging away at this grievance matters will be remedied, and it is very evident that much of this complaining falls on deaf ears. Few sheep farmers fully recognise the serious trouble and loss which are entailed by this evil. Custom is a hard obstacle to overcome, and grows no lighter with age.

But if the wool-buyer considers that he has a live grievance, what about the buyer of hides, and the leather merchants? To see the best part of a side of leather completely ruined with a huge fire-brand must be very exasperating. One cattle owner up North did once rise to the occasion, and commence to brand all his cattle on the cheek, but could never ascertain that they commanded even a shilling per head better price than his neighbours' stock, which sometimes bore the appearance of being all brand; and as, in course of time, he received a severe reprimand from the Chief Inspector of Stock for improperly branding, in that he was placing his brand in a position which was not registered, this reformer returned to his old methods.

It is a difficult question, and ever will remain so as long as there are beings in this world who render such disfigurement of wool or hide necessary, owing to a faulty interpretation of the difference between *meum* and *uum.—Elder's Review*.

DAIRY CALVES.

SOMETHING ABOUT THE COST OF REARING THEM.

What is the cost of raising calves, or what should the cost be, is a question of general farm interest which the Department of Agriculture of the United States attempts to answer in a farmers' bulletin. No little prominence is given to the result of an exhaustive experiment made at the New Hampshire station for the purpose of determining the average cost of raising a dairy cow from calfhood to maturity under various methods of feeding.

For a considerable period records were kept of the food consumed and the cost of the gains made by 13 heifer calves from the time they were weaned until 16 months old. The calves were taken from the cows as soon as the latters' milk was fit for creamery use and were fed whole milk. This was gradually replaced by skim milk, until by the end of the second week only separator milk, which was almost free from fat, was fed. To replace the fat, ground flaxseed cooked to a jelly in water (one pound of flaxseed to four quarts of water) was added to the milk. Seven to ten quarts of skim milk and one to two quarts of the flaxseed mixture were fed daily per head in two feeds. During part of the time middlings was substituted for flaxseed. As soon as possible the animals were encouraged to eat grain and hay. The amount of these feeding-stuffs was increased as the animals increased in size and weight, while the skim milk and flaxseed remained nearly constant until they were discontinued, when the calves were six to eight months old and were turned out to pasture.

Some of the calves were taught to drink from a pail, but most of them were fed by means of a "calf feeder," which greatly lessened the work of feeding. A careful watch was maintained to note any indigestion. Diarrhœa or scouring was stopped by reducing the amount of food and adding limewater to the milk.

In discussing the cost of the gains made, the different feeding stuffs are rated at 100 pounds as follows:—Milk, 4s. 2d.; skim milk, 10d.; flaxseed, 13s. 6d.; middlings, 3s. 4d.; bran, 3s.; linseed meal, 5s.; oats, 4s. 2d.; atena, 2s. 8d.; mixed grain (middlings, oat feed and linseed meal 2 : 2 : 1), 3s. 9d.; hay, 2s. 1d., and green barley fodder, 7½d. It is stated that little difficulty was experienced in keeping up a steady growth in size and gain in weight. Differences were always noticeable between individual animals in the rate of growth and the amount of food consumed. Large animals invariably required more feed to maintain their condition than small ones.

It was found that eight calves under five weeks old made an average weekly gain of 7·6 pounds, at a cost of 1s. 8¼d.; from five to nine weeks, the average weekly gain was 9·1 pounds and the cost 1s. 6½d. The same number of calves from nine to thirteen weeks old made an average weekly gain of 11·8 pounds at an average cost of 1s. 10d. Eight calves from thirteen to twenty weeks old gained per week on an average 10 pounds, at a cost of 2s. 2¼d.; six calves from four to eight months old made an average weekly gain of 11·1 pounds, at a cost of 2s. 7½d.; two calves from eight to thirteen months old made an average weekly gain of 5·25 pounds, at a cost of 2s. 5½d.; four heifers thirteen to sixteen months old made an average weekly gain of 6·12 pounds, at a cost of 2s. 8½d. per week; four of the heifers were maintained on pasture from July 24th to October 26th and the total gain in weight of the four animals was 313 pounds.

In conclusion, it is stated that high-priced feeds, such as whole milk, flaxseed, linseed meal and oats, will cause the cost of the weekly ration to increase out of proportion to the gain, if fed freely. They cannot be used with economy except in earlier stages, and whole milk should be discontinued as soon as possible.

THE CONTENTED PIG.

Under the above title, a writer in the *Sydney Morning Herald* has some very original and trite observations to make on the domestic pig. In contrast to ordinary humanity, the pig is to be regarded as quite a reasonable animal, provided it is allowed to have its own way in everything. Some creatures, however, notably those of the human species, preferably the female, are not satisfied when no opposition is offered to their demands. To allow a man everything which he can think to ask for is to create a sense of injury; whilst to apply the same method of reasoning to a woman is to create an insatiable demand for the unattainable. Not so the sensible pig. Give it the best of food every time it suggests that it is hungry, warm bedding, and shelter as a protection from cold, and nice cool shade when heat threatens, and the animal will lie down and let a child play with it. The pig never wants to get out of a stye or out of a paddock when once convinced that it can neither root under nor jump over the fence. It will accept the position with equanimity. If it ever displays an aptitude towards being unreasonable it is on the question of foreign travel. To attempt to drive the pig in a given direction is a problem long since solved by the Irishman of fable—let it assume that you wish it to go in an exactly opposite direction. The pig is prone to be seized with a conviction that its personal interests on such occasions will be best served by a sprint straight ahead to nowhere in particular. The remedy is quite simple, and consists merely in preventing the pig from beginning to run. The beginning is the crucial stage, because once the animal begins to run along a road, or through a standing crop, only two courses are open to a sensible man, either (1) to go about some other business and forget that the pig is at large, or (2) to procure a responsible shooting-iron and terminate all further argument.

The basic principle for creating a thorough understanding between the pig and its owner lies in anticipating a few of the animal's leading requirements. The appetite of the pig is very general as well as generous. It binds no man down to hard-and-fast rules concerning its diet, and if meal and milk of the best are not at hand it will do its utmost to make pork out of any oddments which may happen along. The beginner on a farm soon learns that the pig will eat anything there is to spare, and after that he discovers that the same animal does not stand on ceremony, but will save its attendant the trouble of conveying meals to it if its enclosure be anything slighter than the walls of the Stockade.

One cannot gainsay the fact that there are times when the pig makes loud and unnecessarily shrill remarks, and refuses to be satisfied. When, as a result of the exercise of much ingenuity and no little strategy, the pig has been effectually warded off from the wheat field, or when the harvest is finished, the pig will lift up its voice morning, noon, and night. But reflection will show that the pig is not to blame. Something has been wanting to convert it into the contented pig. Supply that something, and the trouble, to say nothing of the din, ceases.

Commencing at infancy, the tiny sucker never grumbles so long as its mother treats the family to even-handed justice; and, again, when beyond the sucker stage, the small pig utters no complaint, provided the diminishing sustenance it draws from its dam is augmented by supplies of milk and meal. Even at weaning time the amiable youngster makes us no protest if the trough is nicely filled, as the hour for the morning or evening meal comes round. At the usually difficult stage of weaning, the mother pig usually makes more fuss than the youngster, and if she happens to be separated from her family in the open, may develop a habit of charging the person responsible for removing the small members of her family. As it is bad management to allow the lady pig to adopt such an aggressive attitude, the best way to convince her that rushing is bad policy is to allow her to run her snout against a long-handled sharp-bladed spade. Some nerve is required to face an infuriated sow when she is charging, but no right-thinking man should ever dream of attempting to shirk his duty to a pig, and this is one of them. A few attacks on the edge of the spade will complete the lesson.

The whole management of the pig consists of preventing the animal from desiring that which it should not be allowed to compass by its own forceful and persistent methods. Buy good roomy sows of a healthy kind, and mate them with well-bred sires, and you will have young pigs that will not develop the habit of making poor use of their food. Build strong fences round paddocks and sties, and the pigs will not try to get out after they find that it is impossible to do so. Feed the pigs well, and they will not address loud remarks to you concerning your neglect, and in all that appertains to their comfort consider them. In short, allow the pig no cause for complaint, and you will evolve one of the most profitable animals on the farm. And, above all, if ever in doubt as to the cause of any apparent discontent, remember Mrs. Brown's estimable method of dispersing the clouds from her husband's brow, and "feed the brute."

MARKETING WHEAT.

THE STORAGE QUESTION.

At a recent meeting of the Parkerville (S.A.) Agricultural Bureau, the following paper was read by Mr. O'Grady :—

" The time has now arrived when farmers must seriously consider, with a view to bettering the present system of marketing our staple product— wheat. The farmer taking his wheat straight from the field to the nearest market, and selling, is not affected, because he has an open market to deal in, and can command the best price then ruling amongst the various competitors. But on the present system of storing wheat with the merchants, with the object of obtaining a better price later, he wished to enlist the attention of thoughtful producers, to whom, if they gave the question the slightest consideration, it must be apparent that to a great extent it defeats its object. It is hardly likely that a merchant will be disposed to raise the price of an article in order to become the purchaser when he is already enjoying the use of that article free. The person storing with the merchant has to depend too much on his honour, which, as he knew to his cost, was not always to be relied upon. The question was not of so much consequence in the past as now, and he was sure, with a continuance of good seasons, it would assume even greater importance in the future. In the past but a few farmers were in a position to hold over or store their wheat to await better prices; but now most of them, if so disposed, can do so, with the result that a very considerable quantity is stored with the merchants, and acts like a dead weight to drag the price of wheat down.

" Then the question arises, 'What else can be done with it?' To this he would reply, 'Store it at home.' But look at the damage and waste by mice. Build proper barns and stack your wheat in the proper way, and more will be gained by increase of weight than will be lost through mice, etc. He had wheat stacked for nearly a year in normal seasons (that is, when there was not a plague of mice), and had scarcely had a bag cut by them. He had weighed bags of wheat into barn in summer, and weighed them out after winter, with the result of a gain of 8lb. each. Now, as to what a proper barn for storing wheat should be :—Stone, with an iron roof; but there should be plenty of ventilation without actual wet. Such moisture as would come in the air will do no harm; in fact, it will increase the weight. But no rain should be allowed to get in. Plenty of air holes should be left in the wall low down, near the level of the floor. They could be on the same principle as the narrow slits left in the wall of a stable or loose-box, but should have perforated zinc built in across them to prevent mice, etc., making use of them for an entrance. If the doors of barns were made to fit closely, so that mice could not run straight in as is generally the case, there would be fewer mice to deal with, and with proper stacking a few good cats would keep such a barn almost free of mice. The right way to stack wheat is to do it in as open order as possible. His system was to start, say, along the back end wall, place the bags on their edges with the bottoms about 6 inches or a foot from wall, keeping them in pairs. A little space between each pair would be all the better, but the stack will not be so solid or upright as if the bags all touched. This can be carried on right across the end, or as far as desired. A better way, perhaps, would be to leave a narrow passage down the centre of barn. To do this the pair that should be in the centre should be omitted. On each pair of these bags, then, put another two bags, but crosswise, and continue this right up as high as desired, always putting each pair across the pair beneath. Wheat stacked like this, and in a barn such as described, will not be liable to get weevily, unless reaped very green or damp. But the principal advantage is that the mice cannot find any place secluded and cosy enough to establish a home, and the space between each tier, besides leaving a free ventilation for air, gives a right of way for cats.

"There was a good deal in this, Mr. Wehr thought, if it could be carried out, as there was no doubt that the farmers would get a better price for their wheat if they kept it at home until ready for sale than storing it with the merchants; but bad roads very often made it difficult to cart in the winter. Mr. H. F. Koch said it was almost impossible to keep mice out of a barn unless it was built on trestles with mice-proof legs. Mr. T. H. Price found placing plenty of paper amongst the bags a great protection, as the mice did not cut them near so much, using the paper for nesting. In reply, Mr. O'Grady said he was positive that by working on the lines indicated by him the loss by mice would not be worth mentioning; and as to the difficulty of carting in winter, where one was not a great distance from market, it would always be possible to get it away within a reasonable time, even if it were necessary to load lightly. Putting paper amongst the bags seemed offering assistance to the mice to make themselves at home. When a lad he had witnessed a great mess made of a stack of wheat through following somebody's fad. It was to put cockie chaff and mallee leaves amongst the wheat stack to fill up all crevices. This was done, with the result that the bags were cut to pieces by mice, and weevil was so bad that between the two pests very little of the interior of the stack was saleable at any price."

VALUE OF COW PEAS.

Few farmers can supply enough stable manure to furnish the soil with the necessary humus, and planters in the south learned that the quickest way to secure humus is to plant cow peas. This leguminous crop gathers the unused nitrogen from the atmosphere and unlocks with its roots the dormant potash and phosphoric acid in the subsoil. If, when the peas are sowed they are given the necessary amount of phosphoric acid and potash in a fertiliser, the nitrogenous power of the pea will be increased, and when the stubble and roots are ploughed under, much of the mineral elements will remain in the soil ready to be taken up by the next crop. Commercial fertilisers when used alone act as a temporary stimulus, but when used in connection with this legume, prepare the soil for a rotation of crops; say oats or wheat, next year corn with cow peas, next castor beans, supplying with each crop the fertiliser best suited to its needs. As the cow pea will not grow profitably on very poor soil it must be given the fertilisers it requires. Let us see then what the cow pea will do for the farmer in return for the mineral fertilisers. It shades the soil and supplies the nitrogen. It goes deep in the soil and brings up the water and mineral matter needed by the plant. If sown thickly it will smother all the weeds and clean the ground for the next year's crop. It prepares the soil for every crop the farmer can plant. It will grow in every kind of soil and in any climate where corn, wheat, or oats will mature in the north, and will flourish wonderfully far down in the tropics. It thrives in the long, warm summer, and by continued planting will bring worn out lands back to their virgin condition. There are many varities of the cow pea and in planting them we must select the kind needed for the use to which we wish to put them. If we want pea hay we must plant the Clay pea, Whippoorwill, or Unknown. If our object is to pasture the pea field, then we must plant the Unknown pea, the Black pea, and the Red Ripper pea. If we want peas for stock or poultry feed, plant the Black pea, Clay, Crowder, or Unknown. For table use there is the large and small Lady pea and the Sugar and the Buckeye. Peas can be planted in line with the corn at second working, but this is not desirable as it binds up the corn injuriously. The best and commonest way is to sow them between the rows and plough them in at the last cultivation of the corn. In this way the crop costs only the seed and the sowing. Of course these vines cannot be cut for hay, but the peas can be gathered for feed, or if the Black pea or Red Ripper are used, they will lie on the ground until the corn is gathered and the pigs can be fattened or the cattle pastured on them. For pea hay use the vines when the first peas begin to ripen, otherwise the stalks will become too woody. Mow the vines after the morning dew is off. Let it wilt until afternoon, and then haul them into the barn. If you wish to stack your pea hay in the field, cut three forked poles the size of a man's arm and about 8ft. long. In trimming leave the prongs 10 to 12 inches long. Make a tripod of the poles, locking them firmly together with their forks. As soon as the hay is mowed, haul to these poles and throw the vines on them, keeping them some two feet from the ground. When finished cover the stack with a cap of canvas or long grass to protect it from rain. The pea is unsurpassed as a renovator of apple, pear, and peach orchards. With trees planted in any ground suitable for an orchard, no fertiliser will ever be needed other than cow peas. Sow broadcast every year, gathering the peas and letting the whole vine die on the ground. These vines cover the ground during winter, prevent washing of the soil, and by spring are converted by the rain and snow into perfect food for the tree and its crop of fruit. The cow pea can be sowed from May to July, is a valuable food for man and beast and the land on which it is grown, and no matter in what way it may be used it will return with profit every cent. invested in its cultivation.

GARDEN NOTES FOR AUGUST.

By Percy G. Wicken.

As soon as the heaviest of the winter rains have passed over, and the weather becomes a little warmer, preparations should be made to plant as many of the summer vegetables as possible. In most of our country districts where water for irrigation is not available the success of the crop depends on the plants making an early start and getting a root-hold of the ground before the weather becomes hot, consequently all the spring-sown plants should be planted in the various districts as soon as danger from frost is over. In the Geraldton district many plants can be grown all the winter which cannot be planted in the more southern districts until September, and settlers in this district are enabled to secure the early markets and also obtain the best prices. In the more southern districts, where it is not possible to obtain the early crops, it will often be found profitable to wait and delay the sowing as late as possible, so as to have the crop coming in late when the rush of supplies is over. Vegetables sent to market in the middle of the season, when there is a surplus of supplies, often fail to yield profitable returns. Those who are attempting to grow peas or beans on a poor soil would do well to obtain a packet of the nitrogenous bacteria, which can now be purchased in Perth, and inoculate the seeds with it. Although this bacteria has not done all that was claimed for it, it has in many instances, on poorer soils, given a greatly increased crop; but in soils already well supplied with nitrogen it has had but little effect.

Well-rotted manure should be dug into the ground so as to be prepared for planting out from the seed-beds whenever the plants are ready. A rotation of crops is as necessary in the garden as on the farm, and the same plants should not be sown on the same ground for two seasons running.

Asparagus.—As soon as the plants begin to shoot they should be planted out in land that has been previously prepared by digging about 30 inches deep and well mixed with stable manure. All damaged parts of the root should be cut off before planting, and the roots well spread out in the soil, and not bunched up together; cover with fine soil so that the crown of the plant is about two inches below the surface. Where beds are already established they should be covered to a depth of six inches with well-rotted stable manure, and give the bed a good supply of liquid manure; this will cause a fresh growth of thick white shoots.

Artichokes (Globe).—Plant out any suckers or young plants from the seed-bed. They require a rich or well-manured soil.

Artichokes (Jerusalem) can be planted freely this month. They are hardy, are a good wholesome vegetable, and if there is a surplus supply they are excellent for pigs. Plant in drills three feet apart, and about 18 inches apart in the drills.

Beans (French or Kidney).—In the warmer districts the plants will be well forward. They can be planted anywhere as soon as danger from frost is over. Obtain seed of good varieties, and plant out in rows 30 inches to 36 inches apart in land that has been well manured, and supply a little superphosphate with the seed.

BEET (Red).—Sow a little seed of the Globe variety to keep up a supply. The seed is better soaked for a few hours before sowing. Sow in drills about 18 inches apart, and cover the seed with fine soil. When they come up, thin plants out to one foot apart.

BEET (Silver).—May be sown the same as red beet, but only the leaves of this plant are used. This plant stands the dry weather well and yields a good number of leaves. The outside leaves are used as required.

CABBAGE.—Put out as many plants as possible and sow a little seed for a further supply. Plant out in richly-manured land, as they require plenty of food.

CARROTS.—Sow a supply of seed in land which has been well manured for the previous crop. Sow in drills about 18 inches apart, and thin out when plants come up. The short-rooted varieties are the best to grow.

CELERY.—Sow a little seed to keep up a supply. Plant out forward plants from the seed-bed in well prepared trenches. As the plants grow they should be earthed up to cause them to become white.

CUCUMBERS AND MELONS.—In warmer localities where there is no danger from frosts seeds may be sown in the open; but in cooler parts they will have to be raised under shelter.

LEEKS.—Sow a little seed to keep up a supply, and plant out any seedlings that are available.

LETTUCE.—Plant out all seedlings in well-manured beds, and give an occasional application of liquid manure to force them along; a little more seed may be sown.

ONION.—Plant out all the young plants you have available. The land should have been previously well manured and worked up to a fine tilth. Onion beds must be kept free from weeds, or the young plants soon die off. Sow a supply of seed for future use. Large quantities of onions are imported, and they always command a good price.

PARSNIP.—Sow a few rows of seed to keep up a supply, and thin out those already up.

PEAS.—Sow largely of this vegetable so as to keep up a supply. Sow running varieties in drills 3 to 4 feet apart, and the dwarf kinds 18 inches apart, and about 4 inches apart in the rows. The running varieties will require to be staked so as to keep them off the ground.

POTATOES should be planted extensively as soon as danger of frost is over. Particular attention should be paid to the seed that it is good and free from disease. As soon as the tops are a few inches high they should be sprayed with Bordeaux mixture, as this will help to keep the grubs in check. It is no use waiting until the crop is attacked before spraying, as it may then be too late. The losses from the attacks of the potato-moth grub are very serious.

SWEET POTATOES.—Prepare a seed-bed by taking off the top four inches of soil, then lay a number of tubers in this space and place the soil back again. In a few weeks' time the tubers will send out a large number of shoots, and these are broken off and planted out in prepared land. The land should be got ready for the shoots, and the best results will be obtained if they are planted on hills.

TOMATOES.—In warmer localities plants that have been raised in a seed-bed may be planted out, but farther south they will have to be kept under shelter. Seed may be planted in beds to put out later on. Only the best smooth-skinned varieties should be sown, as these always command a ready sale.

FARM.—The season has been a much later one than last year, and all vegetation is very much later than it was this time last year. This may not affect the general yield, as so much depends on how the rain lasts into the summer. A large increase was made last year in the wheat crop over the previous year, viz., 280,096 bushels, and this increase will no doubt be maintained. August is a somewhat slack month on a farm—in most farms fallowing land for next season will be the principal operation, and no doubt a good deal of burning-off will be carried out. Advantage should be taken of any slack time to get the fences repaired, and all odd jobs about the buildings fixed up, and to improve the accommodation provided for the live stock, etc. Crops of potatoes should be planted during the month. Last year we imported potatoes to the value of £91,256, and these might all have been raised in the State. Every farm should grow sufficient potatoes to meet their own requirements instead of having to use imported potatoes. Mangels and sugar beets can be sown this month; they are both crops that stand dry weather well, and will provide a supply of food for the pigs and cattle; they should be sliced or pulped before giving to stock. Hungarian millet is a quick-growing spring crop, and can be either cut for hay or used as green feed; it can be sown as soon as danger from frost is over, and will soon yield a supply of green feed. Jerusalem artichokes and arrowroot can both be planted this month to provide feed for pigs.

Grass seeds are better sown in the autumn, but seeds of *Paspalum dilatatum* and Rhodes grass may be sown this month if not already in. Such summer crops as cow-peas, lima beans, melons, and pumpkins may be sown in the warmer localities; they require deeply-worked ground, as they are all deep-rooted plants and require a good depth of soil for the roots to obtain moisture in during the hot weather.

LOCAL MARKETS' REPORTS.

MESSRS. H. J. WIGMORE & Co.'s REPORT.

H. J. Wigmore & Co, of Fremantle, Perth, Kalgoorlie, and Northam, report as follows in connection with their daily auction sales of chaff and grain at Perth Railway Yards for month ending Saturday, 7th inst.:—

Chaff.—The market this month closes somewhat easier than as reported in our last, although, taken on the whole, our predictions of a regular market have been realised. The easier tone, which we regret now to have to report, has only set in during the last week, and is due almost solely to much heavier quantities of South Australian chaff being offered at the daily auctions, and this chaff has been sold at £4 10s. down to as low as £4 2s. 6d., leaving the importers with a distinct loss, and thus proving that they are unable to find sufficient outlets for even their imported stocks. Another factor also which has undoubtedly had its effect on the market is the publication recently of the hay yield in this State by the Government Statist, and which all farmers will have no doubt noticed in the daily papers of a week or two ago. The yield, as stated, is about 20 per cent. higher than last year Naturally, while the heavy importation of chaff continues, prices cannot reasonably be expected to improve to any extent, and farmers must remember that many contracts have been entered into for South Australian chaff right up to the end of September. Altogether, and looking at the position broadly, we do not expect prices to reach much over £5 this season, and certainly, on the other hand, do not anticipate a further fall of importance. We report closing values for the month as follows:—Prime green wheaten, £4 12s. 6d., and possibly £4 15s. for an extra choice sample; f.a.q. wheaten, £4 7s. 6d. to £4 10s.; good medium wheaten, £4 5s.; medium wheaten, £4 2s. 6d.; cow chaff, £3 2s. 6d. upwards; prime oaten, £4 15s., and, on account of its scarcity, possibly for an extra bright sample £4 17s. 6d. would be realised; f.a.q. oaten, £4 10s. to £4 12s. 6d. Of course, present values for local chaff would have been infinitely higher had the South Australian chaff not come on to the market. Supplies during the month have been drawn principally from Northam and surrounding districts, the Midland and Great Southern lines' consignments being comparatively few. Our Kalgoorlie office has had a very busy month, and supplies to that centre recently have been considerably in excess of the demand. Many trucks have of necessity been stored in that centre to relieve the congestion, and present value for the primest chaff may be stated at £5 12s. 6d. to £5 15s., and even these prices are not possible upon heavy yardings. We do not recommend consignments to Kalgoorlie of any chaff under fair average quality.

Wheat.—Markets in the Eastern States remain practically as last reported. Adelaide wheat continues dull of sale at 3s. 3d. to 3s. 4d., Melbourne being slightly firmer at 3s. 4d. to 3s. 4½d., f.o.b. for f.a.q. samples. On spot the market has also experienced little fluctuation, and few consignments have come forward. The demand in Perth, however, is almost solely for fowl feed purposes, and buyers are not prepared to pay above 3s. 8½d. as we write. If the recent Government statistics are even approximately correct, there is no doubt that large quantities are still in the hands of farmers, and we should not be surprised if the total quantity should be anything from 50 to 80,000 bags. Although there are six months of the year still to go before the new wheat can be reaped, those farmers holding would do well to consider carefully the position. We have buying orders for several thousand bags of wheat, and would be pleased to hear from holders as to quantities and prices required, etc.

Oats.—Algerians have continued to rule high in the Eastern States, and latest quotes available are 2s. 8d. to 2s. 8½d. f.o.b. Melbourne for good feeds. Very little business is passing, however, as prices on spot leave no margin for the importer, spot quotes being 3s. 1d. to 3s. 1½d. whole and 1d. extra for crushed. Stout and white oats also remain at very high prices, with little indenting going on.

Flour.—·We have made our usual heavy sales of Thomas's Adelaide and Northam "Standard" during the month, particularly of the latter, which is becoming very popular with bakers here. We continue to quote on rails Northam £8 sacks, £8 5s. quarters; f.o.b. Port Adelaide £7 10s. sacks, £7 15s. quarters.

Bran and Pollard.—As anticipated, these commodities have eased during the month, and we made heavy sales of bran f.o.b. Melbourne at 10¼d., and Sydney at 9½d. f.o.b. These figures are not obtainable now, however, sellers in Melbourne now asking 10½d., and even up to 10¾d., whilst our Sydney principals telegraph us that they have refused business for South Africa at 10d. Latest quotes from Adelaide are 11d. for bran and 10¾d. for pollard f.o.b. It looks to us now as if offal will firm still further.

Baled Straw.—Not much business has been passing in this line. We quote nominal value for truck lots £3 to £3 5s.

Jute Goods.—Latest advices from Calcutta still indicate very high prices, and few purchases are being made. On spot bran bags are worth 5s. to 5s. 3d.

THE CLIMATE OF WESTERN AUSTRALIA DURING JUNE, 1906.

The weather was very stormy in South-West districts, especially between Perth, Cape Leeuwin, and Albany. A series of storms of the regular winter type swept along the Southern Ocean from West to East, and the whole region from Cape Leeuwin to Tasmania was subjected to a succession of violent storms. The anemometer at the Leeuwin recorded 1,090 miles for the previous 24 hours on the morning of the 4th; 1,232 on the 21st; and over 1,100 on the 25th, and the barometer fell below 29 in Tasmania on the 26th. One "high" interrupted to some extent this series of "lows." As it passed us, it was only a small affair, but it gained considerably in intensity as it moved Eastward, reaching the neighbourhood of Adelaide on the 9th. In fact, on that day the pressure increased greatly over the whole of Australia. On the 11th, the barometer read 30·73 in Victoria. Succeeding this, came such a vigorous and extensive "low" that on the 20th there were strong West to North-West winds and gales throughout the entire Southern portion of Australia, extending all South of a line joining Shark Bay, on the West coast, to Sydney on the East.

The long spell of wintry weather broke up rather suddenly in this State on the 27th, when a "high" came over our South-West district, remaining there for a few days and gaining in intensity until barometers rose to over 30·6, when it commenced to move Eastwards. During its prevalence fine, bright weather prevailed, with frosts and heavy dews at night.

A heavy rain storm visited North-West districts on the 1st and 2nd, and the fall for the month was considerably in excess of the average for previous years between the coast and Marble Bar. It was also excessive between Perth, Leeuwin, and Albany. Elsewhere it was scanty and below the average for previous years.

The atmospheric pressure was, on the whole, about normal in the Western and below normal in the Eastern portions of the State. Temperature was normal in the South-West during the day time, but unusually high at night. Elsewhere it was generally above the average for previous years, especially in the Tropics.

Frosts were only general during the last few days of the month, and then only in South-West districts, inland. The following table shows the mean and absolute lowest readings of a minimum thermometer placed on the surface of the ground at several stations:—

Station.	Mean.	Lowest.	Date.
Peak Hill	43·0	29·0	25
Cue	43·5	32·5	15
Coolgardie	40·0	29·9	28
Southern Cross	37·8	27·0	23, 29
Walebing	36·9	28·0	29
York	40·7	29·5	13
Perth Observatory ...	48·8	33·4	28
Wandering	35·9	24·0	30
Bridgetown	40·1	33·1	30
Karridale	46·5	39·0	12
Katanning	38·1	27·0	28
Mount Barker	41·1	34·8	10, 15, 30

W. E. COOKE,
Government Astronomer.
per E. A. W.

The Climate of Western Australia during June, 1906.

Locality	Barometer (corrected and reduced to sea-level).				Shade Temperatures.									Rainfall.		
					June, 1906.					Average for previous Years.						
	Mean of 9 a.m. and 3 p.m.	Average for previous years.	Highest for Month.	Lowest for Month.	Mean Max.	Mean Min.	Mean of Month.	Highest Max.	Lowest Min.	Mean Max.	Mean Min.	Highest ever recorded.	Lowest ever recorded.	Points (100 to inch) in Month.	Wet Days.	Total Points since Jan. 1.
NORTH-WEST AND NORTH COAST:																
Wyndham	29·994	30·010	...	...	89·6	73·0	81·3	94·0	66·0	86·8	67·1	96·0	54·0	Nil	...	1,383
Derby	29·994	30·009	9·125	29·886	90·6	67·4	79·0	93·2	52·2	85·2	61·3	96·0	48·0	Nil	...	1,017
Broome	29·994	30·026	9·118	29·887	88·5	9·8	76·6	93·2	90	82·1	60·1	96·9	48·4	Nil	...	961
Condon	30·018	30·053	9·173	29·890	81·8	57·5	69·6	86·5	47·0	77·8	53·3	87·0	38·8	295	2	515
Cossack	30·086	30·060	9·178	29·888	81·2	60·0	70·6	92·0	52·0	76·2	57·2	88·8	47·6	288	2	898
Haw	30·045	30·047	63	29·862	80·9	56·7	68·8	86·4	47·0	76·7	55·1	87·0	38·5	99	3	191
Winning Pool	30·072	...	98	29·889	79·1	6·1	67·6	87·0	90	...	...	...	...	119	4	206
Carnarvon	30·076	30·071	30·259	29·884	75·1	55·9	65·5	85·8	45·0	72·9	52·8	83·9	38·2	35	6	72
Minilya Bol	...	30·078	30·350	29·868	70·8	52·7	61·8	77·4	43·0	69·5	51·7	79·8	36·2	55	9	94
Geraldton	90	30·080	30·481	29·843	70·8	55·0	62·9	79·9	41·8	69·3	52·6	79·2	34·7	372	13	683
INLAND:																
Hall's Creek	30·066	30·090	30·244	29·873	85·2	56·6	70·9	95·0	8·0	80·0	50·8	88·5	33·1	Nil	...	395
Marble Bar	...	...	...	...	82·9	57·7	70·3	87·6	47·0	79·4	53·6	92·0	40·5	357	2	841
Nullagine	...	30·090	30·319	...	91	55·2	67·2	87·1	35·6	74·7	48·0	89·8	32·7	157	3	654
Peak Hill	30·110	30·120	30·350	29·870	70·0	19·0	59·5	79·0	39·0	65·9	47·7	77·8	37·5	84	4	108
Wiluna	30·104	30·149	30·421	29·844	68·6	45·6	58·2	79·0	32·6	65·7	43·4	78·7	31·5	82	5	353
Cue	30·068	30·120	30·461	...	68·9	47·4	58·8	84·4	39·5	65·5	46·8	78·0	34·0	65	5	209
Murgoo	...	...	...	...	70·0	47·7	58·8	82·0	40·0	...	...	...	...	107	3	148
Yalgoo	30·078	30·101	30·477	29·781	67·9	47·3	57·6	80·9	39·0	65·0	46·2	79·9	32·9	147	7	388
Lawlers	30·048	30·127	30·500	29·798	67·8	46·3	57·0	78·8	33·2	63·3	45·0	76·2	33·7	54	3	402
Laverton	30·068	30·175	30·513	29·789	66·3	44·9	55·6	79·0	32·4	63·2	42·8	91	29·4	96	3	435
Menzies	30·088	...	30·521	29·739	65·5	44·8	55·2	78·0	33·0	62·0	45·2	75·6	33·8	90	3	437
Kanowna	...	...	...	...	65·5	43·0	54·2	76·0	34·5	...	...	...	...	120	6	426
Kalgoorlie	30·094	30·110	30·548	29·727	64·7	45·7	55·2	76·3	36·0	61·5	45·7	76·4	34·0	131	7	349
Coolgardie	30·083	30·108	30·547	29·691	63·6	44·6	54·1	75·9	36·0	61·3	44·4	78·3	31·5	131	6	414
Southern Cross	30·096	30·080	30·582	29·720	63·4	43·7	53·0	74·0	31·6	62·2	42·6	79·0	28·0	99	9	430
Kellerberrin	...	...	...	...	63·1	43·6	53·4	75·2	35·0	...	...	...	...	240	10	420
Walebing	...	...	...	...	64·6	44·5	54·6	73·8	32·5	62·9	43·4	73·5	30·0	358	18	899
Northam	...	...	...	...	64·4	45·2	54·8	73·0	34·0	63·8	40·4	31	29·6	85	17	605
York	30·062	30·064	30·641	29·686	65·8	49·3	57·3	74·6	37·6	63·2	42·8	76·0	30·4	313	18	584
Guildford	...	...	...	...	...	...	...	...	...	65·0	45·5	72·0	30·2	67	22	1,431

The Climate of Western Australia during June, 1906—continued.

Locality	Barometer (corrected and reduced to sea-level)				Shade Temperatures, June, 1906					Average for previous Years				Rainfall		
	Mean of 9 a.m. and 3 p.m.	Average for previous years	Highest for Month	Lowest for Month	Mean Max.	Mean Min.	Mean of Month.	Highest Max.	Lowest Min.	Mean Max.	Mean Min.	Highest ever recorded.	Lowest ever recorded.	Points (100 to inch) in Month.	Total Points since Jan. 1.	Wet Days.
Perth Gardens ...	...	...	...	...	63·8	50·0	57·9	71·0	40·8	64·2	47·3	...	37·4	648	1591	21
Perth Observatory	30·063	30·094	30·625	29·726	64·4	52·0	58·2	72·2	41·0	63·6	49·1	72·6	36·9	662	1550	22
...le	30·078	30·070	30·637	29·717	64·6	55·3	60·0	72·2	44·0	64·1	51·8	73·2	40·0	577	1140	22
Rottnest	30·055	30·060	30·627	29·765	64·0	57·0	60·5	69·8	50·0	63·3	54·2	78·0	42·4	379	1019	20
Mandurah	...	30·046	30·606	29·746	63·9	51·1	57·5	...	37·7	64·3	46·6	71·0	33·4	1246	2165	21
Marradong	...	...	...	...	...	...	...	...	...	...	...	...	...	711	1161	15
Wandering *	...	...	...	...	61·5	41·0	51·8	69·0	29·0	61·5	38·1	70·0	28·5	544	983	18
Narrogin	...	...	...	...	...	...	...	...	...	...	...	...	...	552	954	15
Collie	...	...	...	...	61·0	43·7	52·4	68·3	32·0	60·9	37·8	68·0	37·6	1098	1761	21
Donnybrook	30·026	30·056	30·644	29·660	64·0	45·8	54·1	69·3	33·4	62·4	42·6	69·2	31·0	1244	1963	22
Bunbury	...	...	...	...	64·2	51·4	57·8	70·4	37·0	63·9	46·2	73·7	35·2	878	1490	23
Busselton	29·992	...	30·621	29·636	62·9	48·0	55·4	67·2	38·0	62·6	45·6	71·0	31·0	891	1649	25
...pe ...raliste	...	...	...	...	61·8	53·0	57·4	69·2	41·0	61·4	39·4	69·2	26·6	666	1573	24
Bridgetown	29·979	30·025	30·560	29·510	60·8	43·8	53·0	69·0	35·7	62·5	47·9	76·0	31·6	954	1692	25
Karridale	29·928	29·978	30·640	29·496	63·0	51·0	57·0	69·7	43·0	23·0	53·5	70·2	46·4	848	1869	24
...e Leeuwin	30·030	30·054	30·635	29·648	59·2	49·0	58·9	70·0	37·7	59·2	42·4	71·5	29·5	650	1667	25
Katanning	...	...	...	...	60·4	44·8	52·6	68·0	35·2	...	...	...	...	328	765	16
Mt. Barker	...	30·003	30·690	29·535	58·5	44·9	51·7	69·4	37·6	61·5	46·2	73·5	35·4	451	956	24
Albany	29·952	30·011	30·664	29·508	61·6	49·3	55·0	69·2	41·2	60·2	46·0	72·4	41·0	772	1825	25
Breaksea ...	29·956	30·044	30·573	29·604	60·7	51·7	56·2	75·0	41·0	63·7	47·7	78·9	36·5	763	1552	26
Esperance	29·998	30·129	30·512	29·729	65·0	49·8	57·4	73·0	41·0	26·0	13·2	75·0	29·8	519	1141	15
Balladonia	30·060	30·097	30·424	29·616	64·0	44·9	54·4	80·4	35·0	64·5	46·5	78·6	29·0	136	893	6
Eyre ...	30·020	...	...	...	68·2	47·5	57·8	...	39·2	...	...	...	...	60	461	8
INTERSTATE.																
Perth ...	30·063	30·070	30·637	29·717	64·4	52·0	58·2	72·2	41·0	63·6	49·1	73·2	36·9	662	1550	22
Adelaide	30·088	30·124	30·651	29·458	62·7	50·1	56·4	70·0	44·5	60·3	46·7	76·0	32·5	518	1054	16
Melbourne	30·053	29·995	30·722	29·343	59·6	46·7	53·2	69·0	33·7	56·9	43·9	68·1	28·0	151	...	...
Sydney	30·170	30·036	30·640	29·610	62·0	50·0	56·0	69·0	43·0	60·4	48·2	74·7	38·1	183	1689	...

SOUTH-WEST AND SOUTH COAST:

* Average for the eggs only.

The Observatory, Perth, June, 1906.

W. E. COOKE, Government Astronomer.

RAINFALL for May, 1906 (completed as far as possible), and for June, 1906 (principally from Telegraphic Reports).

STATIONS.	MAY. No. of points 100 = 1in.	MAY. No. of wet days.	JUNE. No. of points 100 = 1in.	JUNE. No. of wet days.	STATIONS.	MAY. No. of points 100 = 1in.	MAY. No. of wet days.	JUNE. No. of points 100 = 1in.	JUNE. No. of wet days.
EAST KIMBERLEY:					N.W. COAST—cont.				
Wyndham	Nil	...	Nil	...	Balla Balla	...	...	...	...
6-Mile	Nil	...	...	...	Whim Creek	Nil	...	351	2
Carlton	Nil	...	...	...	Mallina	...	...	...	...
The Stud Station	...	...	...	...	Croydon	Nil	...	...	...
Argyle Downs	Nil	...	...	...	Sherlock	...	...	...	...
Rosewood Downs	...	...	...	...	Woodbrooke	Nil	...	...	...
Lisadell	...	...	...	...	Cooyapooya	Nil	...	...	...
Turkey Creek	Nil	...	Nil	...	Roebourne	Nil	...	391	3
Ord River	...	...	...	...	Cossack	Nil	...	288	2
Alice Downs	...	...	...	...	Fortescue	Nil	...	126	2
Flora Valley	...	...	...	...	Mardie	...	...	...	...
Hall's Creek	Nil	...	Nil	...	Chinginarra	...	...	...	...
Nicholson Plains	...	...	...	...	Yarraloola	Nil	...	...	...
Ruby Plains	...	...	...	...	Peedamullah	Nil	...	...	...
Denison Downs	...	...	...	...	Onslow	1	1	99	3
					Point Cloates	...	...	...	...
WEST KIMBERLEY:									
Mt. Barnett	...	...	...	...	N.W. INLAND:				
Corvendine	...	...	...	...	Warrawagine	Nil	...	...	...
Leopold Downs	Nil	...	...	...	Eel Creek	Nil	...	305	2
Fitzroy Crossing (P.O.)	Nil	...	Nil	...	Muccan	...	...	...	...
Fitzroy Station	...	...	...	...	Ettrick	...	...	...	...
Bohemia Downs	Nil	...	...	...	Mulgie	Nil	...	...	...
Quanbun	...	...	...	...	Warralong	...	...	...	...
Nookanbah	...	...	...	...	Coongon	Nil	...	...	...
Upper Liveringa	Nil	...	...	...	Talga	...	...	...	...
Yeeda	...	...	...	...	Bamboo Creek	Nil	...	450	2
Derby	Nil	...	Nil	...	Moolyella	...	...	...	...
Pt. Torment	...	...	Nil	...	Marble Bar	Nil	...	357	2
Obagama	...	...	Nil	...	Warrawoona	Nil	...	258	3
Beagle Bay	...	...	...	...	Corunna Downs	...	...	...	...
Roebuck Downs	...	...	...	...	Mt. Edgar	...	...	...	...
Kimberley Downs	...	...	...	...	Nullagine	Nil	...	157	2
Broome	Nil	...	Nil	...	Middle Creek	...	...	...	...
Thangoo	...	...	...	...	Mosquito Creek	...	...	...	...
La Grange Bay	...	...	...	...	Roy Hill	...	...	...	...
					Bamboo Springs	...	...	...	...
					Kerdiadary	...	...	...	...
					Woodstock	Nil	...	...	...
N.W. COAST:					Yandyarra	Nil	...	...	...
Wallal	Nil	...	145	2	Station Peak	...	...	...	...
Pardoo	Nil	...	...	...	Mulga Downs	Nil	...	...	...
Condon	Nil	...	295	2	Mt. Florence	Nil	...	...	...
DeGrey River	...	...	...	...	Tambrey	Nil	...	...	...
Port Hedland	Nil	...	350	3	Millstream	...	...	...	...
Boodarie	...	...	...	...	Red Hill	Nil	...	...	...

RAINFALL—*continued*.

STATIONS.	MAY. No. of points. 100 = 1in.	MAY. No. of wet days.	JUNE. No. of points. 100 = 1in.	JUNE. No. of wet days.	STATIONS.	MAY. No. of points. 100 = 1in.	MAY. No. of wet days.	JUNE. No. of points. 100 = 1in.	JUNE. No. of wet days.
N.W. INLAND—*cont.*					YALGOO DISTRICT—*contd.*				
Mt. Stewart	Nil	...	...	...	Tallyrang	144	4	...	...
Peake Station	Nil	...	...	...	Mullewa	219	7	139	10
Nanutarra	Nil	...	...	...	Kockatea	290	7	116	6
Yanrey	Nil	...	...	...	Barnong	143	5	72	4
Wogoola	...	...	...	...	Gullewa	135	5	...	...
Towera	...	...	...	...	Gullewa House	163	6	98	11
					Gabyon	175	5	160	8
GASCOYNE:					Mellenbye	213	7	100	8
Winning Pool	14	1	119	4	Wearagaminda	165	4	99	8
Coordalia	...	...	...	...	Yalgoo	187	5	147	7
Wandagee	Nil	...	...	...	Wagga Wagga	95	3	...	...
Williambury	...	...	...	...	Muralgarra	104	4	...	...
Yanyeareddy	...	...	...	...	Burnerbinmah	125	6	78	6
Maroonah	50	1	...	...	Nalbara	76	7	79	7
Ullawarra	...	...	...	...	Wydgee	89	4	90	8
Mt. Mortimer	...	...	...	...	Field's Find	128	5	91	7
Edmunds	2	1	...	...	Rothesay	...	...	...	...
Minnie Creek	...	...	...	...	Ninghan	240	7	...	...
Gifford Creek	Nil	...	...	...	Condingnow	166	6	...	...
Bangemall	...	...	...	...	163-Mile	65	3	94	5
Mt. Augustus	...	...	...	...	Palaga Rocks	57	3	80	4
Upper Clifton Downs	4	2	...	...	126-Mile	122	4	157	7
Clifton Downs	...	...	...	...	90-Mile	250	4	224	6
Dairy Creek	10	2	...	...	Mt. Jackson	141	4	...	...
Mearerbundie	14	2	...	...					
Byro	6	1	...	...	MURCHISON:				
Meedo	28	1	...	...	Wale	...	...	...	...
Mungarra	Nil	...	...	...	Yallalonga	...	...	...	...
Bintholya	...	...	...	...	Billabalong	28	2	...	...
Lyons River	1	1	...	...	Twin Peaks	...	...	...	...
Booloogooroo	...	...	...	...	Murgoo	23	2	107	3
Doorawarrah	20	1	...	...	Mt. Wittenoom	17	1	...	...
Brick House	...	...	...	...	Meka	22	2	82	3
Boolathana	1	1	...	...	Wooleane	27	2	...	...
Carnarvon	7	2	63	5	Boolardy	4	1	...	...
Dirk Hartog	—	...	184	—	Woogorong	30	2	...	...
Shark Bay	52	2	151	8	Manfred	6	3	...	...
Wooramel	43	2	31	5	Yarra Yarra	...	...	...	...
Hamelin Pool	37	4	55	9	Milly Milly	13	2	...	...
Kararang	88	4	...	...	Berringarra	17	2	...	...
Tamala	140	3	...	...	Miloura	4	1	...	...
					Mt. Gould	Nil	...	...	...
					Moorarie	Ni	...	...	...
YALGOO DISTRICT:					Wandary	...	...	...	...
Woolgorong	69	4	...	...	Peak Hill	2	1	84	3
New Forest	47	3	...	...	Mt. Fraser	...	...	...	...
Yuin	134	3	84	5	Minderos	Nil	...	...	...
Pindathuna	93	4	110	6	Abbotts	10	1	31	1
					Belele	...	...	...	...

RAINFALL—continued.

STATIONS.	MAY. No. of points. 100 = 1in.	MAY. No. of wet days.	JUNE. No. of points. 100 = 1in.	JUNE. No. of wet days.	STATIONS.	MAY. No. of points. 100 = 1in.	MAY. No. of wet days.	JUNE. No. of points. 100 = 1in.	JUNE. No. of wet days.
MURCHISON—contd.					COOLGARDIE GOLD-FIELDS:				
Meekatharra ...	...	...	...	...	Waverley ...	140	4	88	4
Star of the East	15	1	38	1	Bardoc	105	3	92	5
Nannine... ...	10	1	22	1	Broad Arrow ...	140	4	132	7
Annean	12	1	...	...	Kanowna ...	145	5	120	6
Tuckanarra ...	...	...	...	...	Kurnalpi' ...	97	3	129	6
Coodardy ...	17	2	25	2	Bulong	135	8	125	6
Cue	20	2	65	5	Kalgoorlie ...	130	4	131	7
Day Dawn ...	3	1	72	2	Coolgardie ...	149	4	131	6
Lake Austin ...	38	2	93	8	Burbanks ...	140	8	145	6
Lennonville ...	25	3	122	7	Bulla Bulling ...	155	6	128	6
Mt. Magnet ...	17	1	74	4	Woolubar ...	188	4	114	5
Youeragabbie ...	41	2	38	2	Waterdale ...	210	4	118	6
Murrum... ...	70	3	55	2	Widgiemooltha...	192	5	149	5
Challa	53	3	76	8	50-Mile	159	8	85	4
Nunngarra ...	42	3	72	2	Norseman ...	130	...	101	7
					Lake View ...	143	7	74	8
					Frazer Range ...	198	6	...	...
EAST MURCHISON:					Southern Hills ...	...	...	...	...
Gum Creek ...	Nil	...	100	2					
Dural	Nil	...	...	...					
Wiluna	5	1	82	4					
Mt. Sir Samuel ...	2	1	115	3	YILGARN GOLD-FIELDS:				
Leinster G.M. ...	...	...	...	...	129-Mile... ...	95	7	...	...
Lawlers	10	3	54	3	Emu Rocks ...	139	11	137	9
Lake Darlôt ...	1	1	...	...	56-Mile	300	8	100	7
Darda	2	2	...	...	Glenelg Rocks ...	96	9	115	12
Salt Soak ...	1	1	117	4	Burracoppin ...	161	4	119	5
Duketon ...	Nil	...	197	2	Bodallin ...	109	3	37	3
					Parker's Road ...	214	3	...	...
					Southern Cross...	225	7	99	9
NORTH COOLGARDIE GOLDFIELDS:					Parker's Range...	194	6	93	12
Burtville ...	...	...	...	...	Yellowdine ...	199	5	108	7
Laverton ...	Nil	...	96	3	Karalee	180	4	180	5
Mt. Morgans ...	1	1	75	2	Koorarawalyee..	210	3	130	4
Murrin Murrin...	18	2	42	3	Boorabbin ...	289	5	127	7
Mt. Malcolm ...	36	2	39	1	Boondi	315	6	135	6
Mt. Leonora ...	17	8	71	8					
Tampa	14	2	68	2					
Kookynie ...	32	8	69	2					
Niagara	37	4	75	2	SOUTH-WEST (NORTHERN DIVISION):				
Yerilla	...	...	...	...	Murchison House	293	5	192	10
Yundamindera ..	26	2	52	2	Mt. View ...	217	2	79	6
Mt. Celia ...	29	2	80	8	Mumby	313	7	240	10
Edjudina ...	35	1	65	1	Northampton ...	320	8	342	12
Quandinnie ...	52	2	135	2	Chapman Experimental Farm	262	4	204	9
Menzies	51	3	90	8	Narra Tarra ...	259	4	...	...
Mulline	70	3	94	3					
Mulwarrie ...	127	5	183	7					
Goongarrie ...	73	3	118	5					

RAINFALL—continued.

STATIONS.	MAY. No. of points. 100 = 1in.	No. of wet days.	JUNE. No. of points. 100 = 1in.	No. of wet days.	STATIONS.	MAY. No. of points. 100 = 1in.	No. of wet days.	JUNE. No. of points. 100 = 1in.	No. of wet days.
SOUTH - WEST (NORTHERN DIVISION)—contd.					SOUTH-WEST (METROPOLITAN)—cont.				
Oakabella ...	306	5	...	...	Rottnest	570	16	379	20
White Peak ...	306	6	...	...	Rockingham ...	505	14	715	20
Geraldton ...	247	7	372	13	Jandakot ...	630	12	824	19
Hinton Farm ...	236	6	...	...	Armadale ...	843	13	713	22
Tibradden ...	295	6	296	15	Mundijong ...	551	14	856	20
Myaree ...	241	7	...	...	Jarrahdale ...	590	15	1139	20
Sand Springs ...	282	5	...	...	Jarrahdale (Norie)	513	15	1164	24
Nangetty	...	...	...	...	Serpentine ...	436	15	969	18
Greenough ...	272	8	304	11					
Bokara ...	288	5	380	12					
Dongara ...	213	8	466	14					
Strawberry ...	169	8	321	15	EXTREME SOUTH-WEST:				
Yaragadee ...	186	3	141	10					
Urella ...	...	...	...	...	Mandurah ...	719	13	1246	21
Opawa ...	172	4	184	14	Pinjarra (Blythewood)	490	16	1201	23
Mingenew ...	182	6	234	15	Pinjarra	574	14	1213	20
Yandenooka ...	193	4	213	15	Upper Murray ...	600	18	1436	23
Carnamah ...	204	7	284	16	Yarloop	485	15	1000	24
Watheroo ...	165	7	269	14	Harvey	626	17	1076	25
Nergaminon ...	...	...	...	...	Brunswick ...	401	9	1022	21
Dandaragan ...	228	10	454	13	Collie	353	15	1093	21
Yatheroo ...	269	9	445	13	Glen Mervyn ...	264	14	1035	21
Moora	104	6	507	13	Donnybrook ...	328	12	1244	22
Walebing ...	240	11	358	18	Boyanup · ...	326	10	1255	26
Round Hill ...	179	9	280	15	Bunbury ...	371	12	878	23
New Norcia ...	199	12	373	19	Busselton ...	571	15	891	25
Wongon Hills ...	182	14	261	16	Quindalup ...	682	17	835	24
Wannamel ...	353	13	617	17	Cape Naturaliste	625	15	666	24
Gingin	510	12	693	15	Glen Lossie ...	614	15	930	25
					Karridale ...	544	19	848	24
					Cape Leeuwin ...	543	22	650	25
					Lower Blackwood	524	14	928	18
SOUTH-WEST (METROPOLITAN):					Ferndale ...	421	11	1178	23
Wanneroo ...	642	14	...	...	Greenbushes ...	250	9	...	...
Belvoir ...	622	16	610	17	Cooeearup ...	411	23	946	21
Wandu	532	19	677	22	Bridgetown ...	463	17	954	25
Mundaring ...	594	11	905	21	Hilton ...	413	9	770	16
Canning Waterworks	640	13	...	...	Greenfields ...	242	11	927	17
Kalbyamba ...	647	14	674	18	Cundinup ...	240	11	536	18
Guildford ...	586	14	697	22	Wilgarrup ...	597	17	922	24
Perth Gardens ...	711	17	648	21	Balbarrup ...	652	9	824	16
Perth Observatory	675	18	662	22	Bidellia ...	783	21	821	15
Highgate Hill ...	668	15	675	21	The Warren ...	...	...	...	...
Subiaco ...	771	15	579	22	Westbourne ...	368	16	680	18
Claremont ...	725	13	...	...	Deeside ...	692	16	712	21
Fremantle ...	466	15	577	22	Riverside ...	612	15	708	25
					Mordalup ...	640	17	702	18
					Lake Muir ...	584	15	770	21

RAINFALL—*continued.*

STATIONS.	MAY. No. of points. 100 = 1in.	MAY. No. of wet days.	JUNE. No. of points. 100 = 1in.	JUNE. No. of wet days.	STATIONS.	MAY. No. of points. 100 = 1in.	MAY. No. of wet days.	JUNE. No. of points. 100 = 1in.	JUNE. No. of wet days.
EASTERN AGRICULTURAL DISTRICTS:					**GREAT SOUTHERN RAILWAY LINE—** *contd.*				
Emungin ...	270	15	221	15	Woodyarrup ...	199	10	269	11
Dowerin ...	144	10	244	12	Pallinup ...	176	9	230	10
Warramuggin ...	...	...	...	...	Tambellup ...	225	12	274	14
Oak Hill... ...	218	7	...	...	Toolbrunup ...	226	9	274	11
Hatherley ...	...	...	...	...	Cranbrook ...	326	12	382	22
Momberkine ...	208	13	305	12	Stirling View ...	337	15	374	19
Eumalga ...	396	14	468	16	Kendenup ...	328	15	459	22
Newcastle ...	251	10	407	17	Woogenellup ...	329	13	...	...
Craiglands ...	698	14	656	18	Wattle Hill ...	346	19	349	22
Eadine	251	13	366	17	St. Werburgh's...	325	15	490	20
Northam ...	226	13	335	17	Mt. Barker ...	325	18	451	24
Grass Valley ...	...	...	...	...					
Cobham	248	12	357	20					
York	180	12	318	18					
Burrayocking ...	150	12	336	12					
Meckering ...	111	11	242	12					
Cunderdin ...	119	7	261	10	**WEST OF GREAT SOUTHERN RAILWAY LINE:**				
Doongin... ...	109	9	...	...	Talbot House ...	252	11	283	15
Whitehaven ...	147	5	346	11	Jelcobine ...	301	10	357	12
Mt. Caroline ...	111	6	263	8	Bannister ...	351	12	582	18
Cutenning ...	92	8	205	11	Wandering ...	278	8	544	18
Kellerberrin ...	106	11	228	10	Glen Ern ...	221	10	292	18
Cardonia ...	114	10	188	10	Marradong ...	344	11	711	15
Baandee ...	85	5	170	9	Wonnaminta ...	187	13	...	...
Nangeenan ...	113	5	96	7	Williams ...	131	8	367	12
Merredin ...	165	5	143	9	Rifle Downs ...	224	8	691	15
Codg-Codgen ...	156	10	144	11	Darkan	186	7	...	...
Noongarin ...	163	5	...	...	Arthur River ...	239	9	336	13
Mangowine ...	177	4	118	11	Gainsborough ...	132	5	257	13
Yarragin ...	...	...	...	...	Glenorchy · ...	249	7	526	12
Wattoning ...	...	...	...	...	Kojonup ...	287	10	538	14
					Blackwattle ...	336	6	...	...
					Warriup ...	343	12	411	22
GREAT SOUTHERN RAILWAY LINE:					Forest Hill ...	442	16	756	25
Dalebridge ...	239	11	295	17					
Beverley ...	243	11	339	16					
Brookton ...	328	10	322	12	**EAST OF GREAT SOUTHERN RAILWAY LINE:**				
Sunning Hill ...	228	12	317	18	Sunset Hills ...	171	11	...	...
Pingelly ...	180	7	302	15	Oakdale	213	12	...	...
Yornaning ...	197	11	370	18	Barrington ...	168	11	...	...
Narrogin ...	176	11	406	14	Bally Bally ...	236	13	235	17
Narrogin Experimental Farm	306	10	552	15	Stock Hill ...	258	8	308	12
Wagin	156	8	309	17	Qualin	202	12	223	9
Katanning ...	205	10	328	16	Woodgreen ...	91	11	...	...
Sunnyside ...	217	13	313	20	Gillimanning ...	189	11	...	...
Broomehill ...	191	10	291	16					

RAINFALL—continued.

STATIONS.	MAY. No. of Points 100 = 1in.	MAY. No. of wet days.	JUNE. No. of points 100 = 1in.	JUNE. No. of wet days.
EAST OF GREAT SOUTHERN RAILWAY LINE—cont.				
Wickepin ...	238	11	...	...
Crooked Pool ...	...	...	...	...
Bunking ...	82	5	249	10
Bullock Hills ...	154	8	267	12
Dyliabing ...	128	11	268	15
Glencove ...	136	8	386	16
Cherillalup ...	86	6	...	...
Mianelup ...	195	12	252	17
Woolganup ...	213	10	296	17
Chillinup ...	119	4	...	...
Jarramongup ...	296	9	...	...
SOUTH COAST:				
Wilson's Inlet ...	667	20	...	...
Grasmere ...	659	21	819	23
King River ...	461	14	586	21
Albany ...	579	22	772	25
Point King ...	482	18	668	20
Breaksea ...	372	22	763	26
Cape Riche ...	210	6	...	...

STATIONS.	MAY. No. of points 100 = 1in.	MAY. No. of wet days.	JUNE. No. of Points 100 = 1in.	JUNE. No. of wet days.
SOUTH COAST—cont.				
Peppermint Grove	505	14	162	15
Bremer Bay ...	298	12	165	14
Coconarup ...	113	9	183	8
Ravensthorpe ...	150	10	177	13
Cowjanup ...	210	9	...	...
Hopetoun ...	306	7	187	8
Fanny's Cove ...	312	10	279	11
Park Farm ...	183	11	...	...
Grass Patch ...	75	5	...	...
Swan Lagoon ...	178	6	...	...
30-Mile ...	137	6	...	...
Gibson's Soak ...	116	7	247	15
Myrup ...	200	13	294	13
Esperance ...	427	13	519	15
Boyatup ...	276	10	458	16
Lynburn ...	...	...	...	...
Middle Island ...	50	6	428	12
Point Malcolm ...	101	3	...	...
Israelite Bay ...	68	11	137	9
Balbinia ...	104	8	161	7
Balladonia ...	144	5	136	6
Eyre ...	134	7	60	8
Mundrabella ...	...	...	...	...
Eucla ...	151	6	87	7

The Observatory, Perth,
11th July, 1906.

W. E. COOKE,
Government Astronomer.

By Authority: FRED WM. SIMPSON, Government Printer, Perth.

[Registered at the General Post Office for transmission by Post as a Newspaper.]

JOURNAL

OF THE

DEPARTMENT OF AGRICULTURE

OF

WESTERN AUSTRALIA.

By Direction of

The HON. THE MINISTER OF AGRICULTURE.

PUBLISHED MONTHLY.

Vol. XIV.—Part 2.

AUGUST, 1906.

PERTH:
BY AUTHORITY/FREE; WM. SIMPSON, GOVERNMENT PRINTER.

1906.

WESTERN AUSTRALIAN GOVERNMENT.

IMMIGRATION.

Nominated Passages.

Persons having friends and relatives in the United Kingdom who are desirous of emigrating to Western Australia may obtain passages at half the ordinary fares by nominating them to the Hon. Colonial Secretary in Perth.

Fares from £6 10s. to £14 10s.

Clerks, artizans, and mechanics will not be accepted.

Advanced Passages.

Working men and others resident in the State may obtain an advance of passage money, including railway fares from port of arrival to destination, to bring their wives and families from the Eastern States and New Zealand to this State.

Such advances to be repaid within six or twelve months, according to the amount advanced.

A responsible guarantor must be provided.

Special Concessions are provided for Settlers taking up Land.

Full particulars can be obtained upon application to the Under Secretary, Colonial Secretary's Department, Perth.

By order,

F. D. NORTH,

Under Secretary.

JOURNAL

OF THE

𝔇epartment of 𝔄griculture

OF

WESTERN AUSTRALIA.

| Vol. XIV. | AUGUST 20, 1906. | Part 2. |

EDITOR'S NOTES.

BLACK-BOY GUM.—In reply to inquiries made as to the commercial value of clean gum from black-boys, the highest price at present obtainable is about £2 per ton, delivered in bags at Fremantle. It is very doubtful if at this price anyone can make tucker at collecting and cleaning it.

OATEN v. WHEATEN CHAFF.—A settler wishes to know which is the best chaff to feed, oaten or wheaten. From an analysis made of the two, oaten chaff has proved to contain more nutritive value than the wheaten, both on account of the number of food units, its nutritive ratio, and its digestibility.

SHOW TRACKS.—In New South Wales considerable success has been obtained by the spreading of oil on the tracks. Dust has been kept down, and in other instances where, on previous occasions, the tracks were all cut up and made into mud, little or no damage has been done, the tracks retaining their normal condition throughout.

BEES AND LUCERNE.—Lucerne growers will be interested in knowing that where plants are grown from seed, bees have been proved to have been the best means of conveying the pollen from one flower to the pistil of another. In districts where bees are absent, the crop, as a seed one, is often a failure, while in other districts where bees are kept seed is obtained in abundance.

NEW CATALOGUES :—During the month we have received from Messrs. Law, Somner, & Co., through their agent, Mr. A. J. Tijou, Fremantle, their catalogues of fruit trees, vegetable, farm, and flower seeds. A special feature is made of their now famous Victory and Coronation potatoes. We have also received Messrs. Rossiter & Co.'s catalogue, containing some 80 pages, considerable space being devoted to useful hints and instructions to the grower.

———

SPRAYING.—In our last issue, the urgency of winter spraying was brought under the notice of our readers, and it is pleasing to note that the orchard inspector's report that most of the growers are busy spraying their fruit trees, using the lime, sulphur, and salt for San José scale, while a few are following this up by a second spraying of vacuum oil emulsion. Those who have neglected this important matter are urged to lose no further time but to spray at once.

———

IMPORTATION OF SEED POTATOES.—For the information of a subscriber and readers, we publish the following particulars re importation of seed potatoes :—All potatoes sent out from Europe for seed purposes are carefully packed in boxes in alternate layers with charcoal ; they are conveyed as ordinary cargo, and during transit they generally commence sprouting, arriving in good condition for immediate planting. It behoves importers, therefore to so time their orders that the arrival of seed catch the planting season.

———

TAX ON STALLIONS :—At a recent meeting of the Northam Agricultural Society, the following resolution was tabled, " That, in the opinion of this Society, it is desirable that a tax of £20 per head be placed on all stallions, and the amount realised be pooled and offered as a premium to the best horses selected by a qualified officer ; these horses to stand at a nominal fee of £1 per head." A number of the members spoke strongly in support of the matter, and it was ultimately decided to adjourn the discussion to the next meeting of the society.

———

THE USE OF FERTILISERS.—Many of our farmers have the idea that chemical fertilisers can be used in much the same way as they have been in the habit of using farmyard or stable manure. This is a grave mistake, as many have found to their cost. Chemical fertilisers, being highly concentrated compounds, must be used with great care and caution in order to get the best result. A too liberal use often results in the loss of a crop. In the use of any standard formula the exact quantities set down should never be exceeded.

———

VALUE OF CORN STALKS.—It is estimated that there are at least 400,000 acres annually cultivated for corn crops, which produce an average of two tons of stalks per acre. Up to the present time, however, no one as yet has come forward to suggest the utilisation of them. In the United States of

America these stalks are valued at 12s. 6d. per ton, so that 800,000 tons mean a loss to the Commonwealth of £500,000 per annum. As a rule, the stalks are not even ploughed in, but literally thrown away. When properly treated, it makes splendid silage. Where this has been tried, an increase of from eighth to tenth of milk more per cow per day has been gained. In America the stalks are used for making cellulose, a constituent of smokeless powder, varnish, kodak films, linoleum, paper, and very many other things.

RUSTS IN WHEAT.—A copy of a book of a very valuable nature, entitled "The Rusts of Australia," by D. McAlpine, Government Vegetable Pathologist of Victoria, has been received. The subject matter shows that a long and most careful study has been made of the matter by the author. Some 210 closely printed pages contain the letterpress proper, while 44 full-page plates (a large number coloured) illustrate the article. The price is 10s. per copy, and should a sufficient number be applied for, the Department of Agriculture in this State will procure a parcel of the books for sale amongst our own farmers.

CURING A JIBBER.—When a young horse dislikes the collar and threatens to become a jibber, a tandem will reassure the horse, and probably cure him of the objectionable habit. Such a horse should be put in the shafts behind a good sharp leader, which latter will start the load, and when once set going the horse with shy shoulders will often do more than his share of the work. If the whip be used, or any violence practised, the jibbing horse will not be cured. He must be coaxed and treated with every kindness, and then he will gradually understand that there is nothing uncomfortable or exacting in harness, and he will settle down to steady work. To those who keep a plurality of nag horses, there is no expense in tandem driving, except the purchase of harness, and more than half of that is available for single driving.

FIBRE PLANTS.—In spite of the enormous amount of cordage made from iron and other metals, says an exchange, there is a continuous and increasing demand for fibres of vegetable origin. New Zealand flax is well worthy of cultivation, as it is a valuable plant for the farmer's own use, and well deserving of a place for selling purposes. In drier localities sisal and other aloes thrive well and promise to become important sources of fibre and of rope making material. There are several Australian plants worthy of a trial as fibre producers, notably some shrubs. The blacks used to make fishing-lines, dilly-bags, etc., of the inner bark of the brush "kurrajong," a small tree, from which the inner bark six feet long or more could be stripped, and from this the most durable cordage we ever saw was made, its strength being phenomenal. It grows like a weed, and would be equally valuable for paper making.

SUPERPHOSPHATE: IS IT INJURIOUS?—There are many who hold the opinion that the present methods of using superphosphates in connection with the growing of cereals, while undoubtedly very successful for a time, are not likely to continue so, and that the land on which their use is continuous will eventually become " sick," and cease to give satisfactory response to the treatment. But while this may be so under some circumstances, on the other hand, according to the *Field*, Mr. W. A. Prout, of Scarbridgworth, England, has carried on wheat-growing for forty years continuously on the same soil without the aid of live stock either for consuming the crop on the farm or for making manure, and practically without variation in the crops produced. The manurial treatment of Mr. Prout's farm has consisted throughout of annual dressings of 4cwt. per acre of superphosphates and 1½cwt. of nitrate of soda, and, with these applications, the land has become richer and more productive, instead of having deteriorated in any respect.

RUBBER CULTIVATION.—Hardly any product is exciting so much attention at the present time as the cultivation of rubber. Plantations are springing up in every locality that is considered at all suitable. Hundreds of thousands of plants are being planted out, while hundreds of pounds of seed are being sown annually. Literature in the shape of pamphlets, magazines, etc., are being published ; the last, if not the best, of its kind has just reached us in the form of a 36 page quarto, entitled *Fiscus Elastica*, by E. M. Coventry, Deputy Conservator of Forests, Calcutta. It is illustrated with many very fine plates that are instructive as well as being very good specimens of the book illustrator's art. The information is highly valuable, containing as it does instructions as to how, when, and where a plantation should be started and cared for. To those who intend to go in for this industry, we would strongly advise them to apply to the Government Printer, Calcutta, for a copy.

WHITE ANT PREVENTATIVE.—According to a report issued by Consul Liefield, of Freiburg, Germany, says an exchange, a new and simple process has been discovered for rendering soft woods proof against the attacks of white ants. This is accomplished by boiling the timber in a saccharine solution, which extracts the air and coagulates the albumen in the sap. In cooling, the air spaces are filled with saccharine matter, which in a large measure is analogous to the fibre of the timber. The timber is then rapidly dried in heated chambers, and emerges in a compact and homogeneous form which does not expand, contract, warp, or split. Should this process succeed, which appears probable, it will revolutionise the timber trade in the tropics and termite infested countries. The necessary material for treatment abounding in northern Australia soft woods will, in a large measure, replace the more expensive hard woods, and the cost of construction be materially reduced, while the difficulties attending the ravages of the white out will be abolished.

ROOTS FOR SHEEP.—It is generally conceded that sheep raising in England is carried on more successfully than it is elsewhere. Those informed concerning methods of sheep feeding in England claim that it is due largely to the fact that the English farmer is a heavy feeder of root crops, such as turnips, mangles, sugar beets, etc. A short time ago a feeding experiment was carried on in England for the purpose of testing the value of turnips when fed in connection with oil meal and clover hay to fatten wethers, as compared with oil meal and clover hay without succulent food. The sheep receiving roots made gains of 42 lbs., while those fed on dry feed alone made gains in the same time of only 26 lbs. per head. This experiment, therefore, demonstrates the value of roots as food for sheep. It is not likely that under our conditions roots can be fed economically in as large quantities as they can in England, but it is certain that more attention should be paid to raising roots, rape, cabbage, and other succulent foods to be fed to lambs and breeding ewes during the winter months. Such foods keep the digestion of sheep in a healthy and vigorous condition, and thereby aid in warding off disease.

MIXED FARMING.—The following valuable return on "Big things on little Farms" was recently published in the *Sydney Daily Telegraph*, the information being supplied by Mr. Thos. Daly, owner of a farm in the Shoalhaven district in New South Wales. The farm consists of 151 acres, and is divided into 21 paddocks. Mr. Daley has a milking herd of 45 Shorthorn cows, and the following is a return for nine months:—

	£
Milk sold	471
Calves sold	121
Profit on Pigs	57
Fat cows sold	41
Maize grown	40
Potatoes	8
Poultry sold	11
Profit on horses	10
Increased value on young horses	20
Calves on hand	22
Total for nine months	£801

Mr. Daly anticipates that for the remaining three months of the year, another £300 will be realised. The whole of the work has been done by his own family, no labour having been employed until a month ago.

WATER-CRESS.—Water-cress may be successfully grown on ordinary garden soil without the aid of running water. When water is laid on from pipes, water-cress will thrive as well as in a running stream. To cultivate on ordinary soil, prepare a bed of good mould about 6 inches deep. Smooth and water it in the evening, and next day reduce the soil to a fine tilth. Mix the seed with fine sand, and sow as evenly as possible, and cover very lightly with a thin layer of mould. Press the seed down, water, and cover with matting. When the seed has sprouted, replace the matting with a shade of branches, and keep the soil quite moist. The plants soon grow; by and by they flower, when a new covering of mould is given them, leaving the plants about 1 inch above ground. Then water freely. Ten days later shoots will appear springing from the roots, which, when 2 or 3 inches high, are removed, and pricked out 3 or 4 inches apart in a new bed. A fortnight later the cress will be 6 inches high, when cropping may begin and continue right up to the first frosts, cutting every fortnight. Care must be taken to give copious waterings every evening. The seed should be sown in spring.—*Queensland Agricultural Journal.*

STOCK ENSILAGE.—A successful experiment in making stock-ensilage has enabled Mr. C. McKay, of Waroona, to generously feed his dairy herd of 13 head right through the winter. Last autumn he cut three acres of sorghum, yielding 15 tons of greenstuff, and stacked same under weights. The stack was kept in shape by the simple method of making a frame of hardwood to prevent the stuff from spreading. Early in May a first cutting was made from it and was found to be a good, sweet ensilage, which, when chaffed, was eagerly eaten by the cows. In colour and fibre it resembled tobacco leaf undergoing sweating, and it gave off a very pleasant and aromatic odour. The chaff was mixed with half its bulk of sorghum hay, a sprinkling of bran being added. The milk supply was kept well up to the average. Mr. McKay states that in making ensilage it is necessary to watch that the top pressure shall be allowed to fall freely and follow the shrinkage and solidifying of the stack, the heads of the plants being laid towards the centre, thus making the sides a trifle higher than the centre, which will so feel the pressure that all air is excluded. "I could not," says Mr. McKay, "continue dairying through the winter if it were not for my ensilage stack." Considering the small amount of labour required, it is a wonder that more farmers do not follow Mr. McKay's example.

PLANT FOOD.—At a recent meeting of the Wesley Young Men's Club, Northam, a lecture on "Plant Food" was delivered by Mr. Wicken, field officer of the Agricultural Department. There was a large attendance, and the lecture was followed with great interest. Mr. Wicken started by explaining how plants obtained their food, and the different elements they secure from the air, from the soil, and by the means of fertilisers. He also explained the wonderful provision of nature by which animals and human beings inhale oxygen and exhale carbon; vegetation, on the other hand, inhaling carbon and exhaling oxygen, thereby keeping up the supply of air in its natural state. He next explained the functions of nitrogen, potash, phosphoric acid, and lime in nature, showing how nitrogen is necessary for the growth of leaf and stem, phosphoric acid to give stamina and help in the formation of seed for further reproduction, potash to give colour to the flowers and flavour to the fruit, and lime to assist in enabling the other elements to pass through the plant cells in the form of protoplasm. Views were shown of different plants, and their varying requirements in the shape of food were explained, and how they could be supplied. The lecturer then dealt with the subject of leguminous crops, and explained how, by another of the wonderful provisions of nature, these plants possess the power of obtaining nitrogen from the atmosphere and returning it to the soil—a power possessed by no other plants. This was a provision of nature for replenishing soil with the necessary amount of nitrogen, which is the most expensive of fertilisers to purchase. By growing a crop of cow peas, soy beans, and such plants, as much nitrogen can be returned to the soil as could be purchased for £5 per acre in the form of artificial fertilisers.—*Northam Advertiser.*

REFRIGERATORS AND MILK.—A case that has recently been investigated at the Midland Dairy Institute contains a valuable hint to dairy farmers. A certain farmer's milk was returned on the ground that it developed a peculiar flavour which purchasers objected to. The milk kept sweet enough, and did not turn sour more quickly than an ordinary sample, but the flavour was bad. Investigation showed that the trouble arose from the use of an old, worn-out refrigerator, and that the copper of the same was giving a bad taste to the milk. It is rather surprising that this does not happen more often, for worn refrigerators are quite common. The corrugated cooling part of a refrigerator is made of thin sheet copper covered with tin, and the thinner the sheet and its coat the better does the cold water on one side cool the milk on the other. On the other hand, if the coating of tin is thin it will wear off quickly, and the wearing off will be very quick indeed if the metal is "scoured" with ash or bath-brick, as some dairymen or maids very foolishly do. It is quite usual to see, in going into a farmer's dairy, the apparatus worn and dented and the copper shining through all over, but now, with the above particular instance before us, it is evident that such a state of matters is risky, no matter how clean the apparatus is kept. A new refrigerator is expensive—too expensive those of us who go to buy think—and makers do not seem to attempt remaking old refrigerators. If some of these would lay themselves out to re-tin and do up partly worn apparatus at a moderate charge they would probably do a good trade. The worn refrigerator does harm, but it is expensive to buy a new one, and it is difficult to get an old one done up.

ANALYSIS OF HONEY.—As some discussion has arisen at different times recently as to the relative value of English and Colonial honey, seven samples of honey were obtained from apiaries situated in different parts of this State, also a sample of English honey, and the whole forwarded to the Government Analyst. Mr. Mann made exhaustive tests, and in his report he states:—"The samples comply chemically with the standard for pure honey. Any choice between them must therefore be purely a matter of taste, on which I do not profess to be an expert. The English sample was rather less candied than the local, though both were more or less crystalline when received. This difference corresponds to the quantity of moisture each contains." The following average was made from the analysis of the seven samples of West Australian honey. The figures given represent percentage:—

	Average sample.	Best sample.
Direct polarisation	9·5 ...	12
Invert „	9·90 ...	11·66
Sucrose (Clerget)	·41 ...	·25
Invert sugar	73·83 ...	75·30
Water	10·40 ...	10·29
Ash	·43 ...	·39

CUTTING SEED POTATOES.—The evidence is accumulating that for seed purposes it is a mistake to cut potatoes into sett size. It has never been the custom in some districts to thus divide potatoes, but in others it has been the practice for generations. The idea in the past has been to prefer good sized tubers, and to divide them into two or three pieces, each with at least two eyes, on the principle that the large seed would be the most vigorous and yield the best crop, and also because it saved the weight of seed per acre. On the other hand, the dividing of a potato severs the fibres, which ramify in its substance, from each eyes, and thus weakens the initial growth—perhaps more than the original size of the potatoes strengthen the same. Again the cut surfaces start bleeding, and there is a waste of sap, and an entry made for fungoid enemies, even where lime is dusted over them. It is being found that moderately sized seed planted whole give the most satisfactory results over even fairly-large seed, and where it takes a ton or over to plant an acre. A friend of the writer who "boxes" a lot of his seed finds that even small tubers if boxed a long time—as early as last July—and thoroughly "greened" in the intervening months gives the best results, and greater freedom from disease. It is rather curious that the small immature tubers do not disease so readily as the bigger ones, and out of a rotten heap one may pick many small potatoes quite untouched. Cutting is done, of course with the sole object of saving seed, and in the olden time, before the days of the potato disease, the eyes were actually gouged out and the "buds" only planted, but all experiments in these late years go to show that a whole fair sized sett gives the best all round results.

BRIDGETOWN FRUIT EXPORT.—The following comparative table showing the export of fruit from Bridgetown, says an exchange, should be of interest as showing the manner in which the fruit industry of the Nelson and Blackwood districts is growing :—

				1905. Cases.		1906. Cases.
January	...	...	...	2,133	...	2,659
February	...	...	...	1,978	...	2,634
March	...	...	...	3,207	...	4,536
April	...	...	...	3,218	...	4,591
May	...	...	...	3,468	...	5,131
June	...	...	...	1,887	...	2,052
Total	...	...	...	15,891	...	21,603

The year 1904 saw an increase over the previous year of 5,016 cases. Last year the increase over the previous year was 3,505 cases, and this yeaf promises a handsome record increase, judging by the above figures. Already the returns show an increase over the corresponding period of last year of 5,712 cases. Of course the six months to come comprise the slack period or the year from a fruit exporting point of view.

WYNDHAM.

THROUGH THE KIMBERLEY.

By R. E. WEIR, M.R.C.V.S, C.G.S.I.

On the early morning of Tuesday, April 10, I found myself a solitary passenger on board the s.s. *Mildura*, which was slowly steaming out of the Fremantle harbour on one of her many journeys to Wyndham for the purpose of conveying fat cattle from Kimberley.

This particular vessel which is practically new to the trade was originally constructed for the carriage of fruit in tropical countries, but on a more profitable charter being obtained from the firm of Connor, Doherty, and Durack, she was brought to these waters. The suitability of this ship for the cattle trade has been clearly demonstrated by the number of successful trips made between Fremantle and the Northern port; as showing the difference between the old time vessels and the new, the mortalitity on board has been reduced some 20 per cent., and the cattle are landed in much better order. Ventilation, which is a chief factor in this particular trade, is well provided for. Cleanliness is also considered, as after the holds are steamed at Fremantle a thorough white-washing of all the fittings, including the water troughs, is done during the voyage North, and thus a very necessary precaution against the spread of disease is taken. In the run to North-West Cape the weather conditions closely resemble those usually prevailing at Fremantle, but from that point on to Wyndham the sea is usually as calm as the proverbial mill pond, and the voyage might be considered ideal were it not for the heat, which is somewhat trying on entering the tropics. Passenger accommodation on board is limited, but provision can always be made for one or two, and as the greatest courtesy is usually shown by the officers the journey can be made very pleasant. After losing sight of the North-West Cape the mainland is not again visible until nearing Cambridge Gulf, which was sighted on the morning of the 17th, exactly one week out from port. As we were then close to land the outlook appeared specially interesting; shallow inlets fringed by white sandy beaches formed a pretty foreground, small hills intersected by valleys rise abruptly near the coast, while away in the background may be seen higher ranges stretching towards the interior. As the entrance to the Gulf was approached, Lacrosse Island, made famous by the marvellous stories of De Rougemont, came in view. This island, situated to the left as the entrance is made, is a good land mark for navigators, and provides shelter during stormy weather. A run of 50 miles, which must be made during full tide (bars of sand block the passage at low water), brings the vessel to Wyndham. This little township, situated at the base of a prominent hill which, owing to its bare and rugged appearance, is not particularly inviting. The vessel is brought alongside a small jetty which appears to be slowly but surely succumbing to the depredations of the teredo beneath water lines, whilst white ants are attacking the upper parts. The latter pests are a serious menace to woodwork in that part of Western Australia, making their home in most unsuspected places and often doing serious damage before their presence is discovered. Various remedies have been tried to compass their destruction, but so far without success. This is not surprising if the following story is true:—A few years ago the patentee of a white ant exterminator was deputed by the Government to visit the district with a view of eradicating the pest from Government and other buildings, but on the mixture proving ineffective a quantity was stored in one of the buildings. An examination some time later revealed the fact that the greater portion of the supposed deadly poison had been consumed by white ants without any apparent injury to their health.

Owing to the ravages of this pest it is almost impossible to grow fruit and many other varieties of trees not indigenous to the locality with any degree of success. The trees may thrive very well for a time, but without any apparent cause they wither and die off. An examination generally reveals the fact that the roots have been attacked by white ants. The business portion of the township is chiefly in the hands of Connor, Doherty, and Durack, who secured a footing in the early days of the Kimberley rush, when Wyndham was the principal provisioning depôt for the mines. In addition to a store, where a good business is still being done with the various cattle stations, a two-storey hotel is owned by the same firm and commands a good situation immediately opposite the jetty, where good accommodation may be obtained, but the catering leaves much to be desired. A post office, court house, and gaol practically comprise the remainder of the buildings, though, at no distant date, the material prosperity of the place is likely to be advanced by the establishment of chilling and other works connected with the cattle industry. To a stranger, the most striking object is the number of native prisoners who may be seen chained together on their way to and from their work. Two large gangs were employed road-making, which appears a very sensible method of utilising their time whilst under detention by the authorities. The climatic conditions of Wyndham and vicinity usually receive a fair share of uncomplimentary comments, but my short stay of one day was seasoned by a cool breeze and was, therefore, not unpleasant. However, I was not sorry, after obtaining a supply of provisions and other necessaries, to find myself seated next to Inspector Haly in a strong buckboard, with four useful horses attached, and the long overland journey to Sturt Creek begun. The road, which is practically macadamised to within a short distance of the Three-Mile, runs along the base of the mount and through low lying swamp land, frequently covered over by an overflow from the Gulf at high spring tides. The greater proportion of this swamp land is devoid of herbage and, consequently, presents a barren appearance. As the Three-Mile is approached, a pleasant change occurs; an elevated plain of basaltic country comes into view. Here we find another small township, consisting of hotel, store, etc., which is surrounded by green herbage, and, for this reason, is much used as a camping ground. The place is most convenient for shippers, but the facilities for watering stock are very inadequate. The water is brackish, and the trough is erected too high above the level of the ground for the cattle to drink with any degree of comfort; good water is, however, obtainable at a spot three miles distant, and known as the Six-Mile, though the supply may give out towards the end of a dry season. From the Three-Mile to Goose Hill, the road runs along flat alluvium country, interspersed here and there with little ponds or lakes, where wild fowl abound in large numbers, particularly ducks and geese, though from frequent disturbance they are almost unapproachable. Goose Hill was reached late in the evening, and the following day was spent in examining the cattle dip, yards, etc. This somewhat expensive work was constructed in 1904, but with the exception of a few hundred head of store cattle which were treated last year, it has remained in complete disuse. Attached to Goose Hill is a reserve of about 11,000 acres, the greater portion comprising plain country, covered with a coarse species of Mitchell grass. This reserve is used largely by drovers and teamsters, to whom it is of great convenience. In the event of the Government experimenting at some future date in the growing of tropical products, a sufficient area suitable for that purpose could be selected. Cotton, for instance, can undoubtedly be grown successfully in that locality, but the great difficulty in the development of an industry of that nature would be the high cost of ordinary labour. With proper appliances and provision for the growth of green fodder, such as sorghum, maize, etc., for which the climate and soil is suitable. The dairying industry could be profitably established, as, independent of an export trade, good values for dairy produce can be obtained locally.

(To be continued.)

THE CULTIVATION OF SUGAR BEETS.

By Percy G. Wicken.

Inquiries are being made as to the method of cultivating sugar beets, and a quantity of seed has been imported from France by the Department of Agriculture, and is now available for distribution. It will grow well in most of our coastal districts, and, the same as mangel-wurzels, will produce a quantity of good fodder suitable for both cattle and pigs.

The beet belongs to the order *Chenopodiaceæ* or *Salsolaceæ*, an order of plants which include among them many of the native saltbushes. The sugar beet *(Beta vulgaris crassa)* is supposed to have been developed from the wild beet *(Beta vulgaris maritim)*, which is indigenous to the countries along the coast of Southern Europe.

The beet is a biennial plant—that is, of two years' duration. The first year it produces a full-sized root; the second year it produces its seed, and then dies off. In some instances plants produce seed the first year, but this is only when they are sown out of season or when the conditions are unfavourable to their growth. The most suitable conditions for the successful cultivation of sugar beets are a deep, well-drained, loamy soil. A good chocolate soil made of decomposed basalt will produce good samples of sugar beet; a light subsoil is also desirable, so as to enable the superfluous water to drain away and the air to penetrate and sweeten the soil. The beet will not grow where stagnant water is to be found during the wet season.

The climatic conditions have a great influence upon the value of the beet for sugar production.

The most favourable conditions are a medium temperature, ranging from 65° to 70° during the summer months, a rainy summer, and a fairly high altitude above the sea. Districts such as the New England tableland in New South Wales and Gippsland in Victoria are well adapted for the cultivation of the sugar beet; while in this State places along the Darling Range and the hills north of Albany would no doubt prove suitable for its production. In the eastern districts the soil is suitable, but the lack of rain during the summer months would not allow the crop to become a success. Swamp land such as found in our south-west coastal districts would grow beets to a large size, suitable for stock feed, but would only contain a very low percentage of sugar.

To obtain beets having a high percentage of sugar they must be kept small in size, and to do this must be planted close together. As the results of analysis we have found that after the roots exceed two pounds in weight the percentage rapidly becomes lower.

Preparation of the Soil.—To prepare land for the cultivation of sugar beets a start should be made in the autumn. If good, clean, well-shaped roots are required the plants must have a good depth of soil to grow in; nothing is so likely to cause forked roots as shallow cultivation. As soon as the roots of the plant strike a hard subsoil, and find they cannot get down any deeper, they begin to send out side roots, and as these become thicker a forked root is the result. To prevent this the best thing that can be done is to subsoil the land, and this will allow the tap-root of the plant to go straight down, and a well-shaped beet is the result. The best way to subsoil land is by using two ploughs following one another, the second plough having the mould-board removed. The first plough should turn a furrow as deep as possible, the second plough, without the mould-board, follows along in the same furrow and breaks up the subsoil to a further depth of 8 to 10 inches, according to the condition of the soil, and does not bring the subsoil to the surface. The subsoiling should be done to a depth of not less than 15 inches, and this will allow plenty of depth for the average-sized beet.

The land should be left in this rough condition during the winter months, and in the early spring it should again be ploughed lightly if necessary and then worked up to a fine tilth by means of disc harrows, rollers, or whatever other implements are available, so as to obtain a good depth of finely-worked soil and a good seed-bed on the surface.

Seed.—The selection of seed is an important question, and only a variety well-known for its percentage of sugar contents should be selected. The two varieties recently obtained by the department are Vilmorin's Improved A and Vilmorin's Improved B; another well-known good variety is De Klein Wanzlebein; other new and improved varieties are being continually brought out. As the production of beet sugar forms such a large industry in Europe, the experimentalists in these countries are constantly trying to improve the sugar contents of the beet; an increase of one per cent. in the yield of sugar means an immense sum to the industry.

The best time for planting the seed is during the end of August or September. The seed is similar in appearance to that of the mangel-wurzel and cannot be distinguished from it. Small size seed should be selected, as

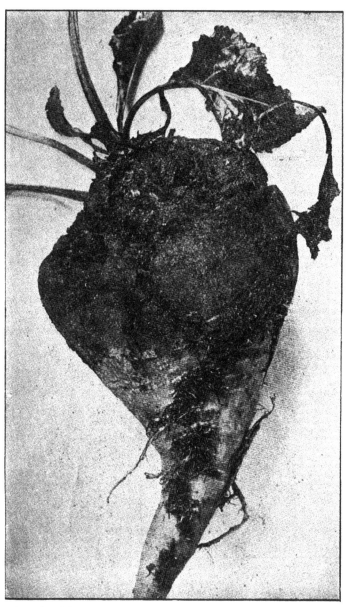

Fig. I.—A late stage of Beetroot Rot, showing the cracking and the rotting of the Root.

experiments conducted in France demonstrate that a small size seed is more likely to produce a small-sized root, and large roots are not wanted owing to their deficiency in sugar contents. The seed is somewhat slow in germinating, and it should be soaked for 24 to 36 hours in a solution of one part rain-water and one part urine at a temperature of from 100 to 120 degrees F. The seeds will absorb about their own weight of the mixture; after the liquid is poured off the seeds should be mixed with some fine wood ashes, and they are then ready for sowing. If the soil is sufficiently warm and moist, the young plants will appear in about eight or ten days. The seeds require a total degree of average temperature equal to 650 degrees F. before they germinate. Therefore, if the average temperature is 65 degrees F. ten days would be required for germination. Experience has proved that a small-sized beet contains a very much higher percentage of sugar than a large one. The best size for the sugar factory is from $1\frac{1}{2}$ to 2lbs. Many factories refuse to receive beets over 3lbs. in weight as the expense of treating low-grade roots is too great to allow a profit to be made. As small beets are required this fact must be kept in mind when sowing the seed. Where beets are grown for the purpose of sugar-making they should be sown in drills 18 inches apart and thinned out to about eight inches apart in the rows. This gives about 48,000 plants to the acre, and, allowing for only half of them to reach a weight of $1\frac{1}{2}$lbs., would give a yield of 16 tons per acre. It is only by a system of close sowing that a crop of small beets can be assured. If the seed is sown at this distance apart it will take from 15 to 20lbs. to sow an acre. If the crop is only sown for purposes of feeding stock, half this quantity of seed is sufficient, and the drills can be placed much further apart.

Sowing the Seed.—If only a small area of land is required to be sown, rows can be marked out by a hoe and the seed dropped by hand and covered with a rake; or a Planet, Jun., hand seed-drill may be used, the fertiliser having been previously sown by a drill. If a large area is to be sown there are special machines made for sowing beet or mangel seed, either on ridges or on level ground. In a wet climate it is best to sow on ridges, but in drier districts they do well on level ground. When the plants begin to show about four small leaves it is time to thin out all surplus plants; this can either be done by hand or by a small turnip-thinning hoe, care being taken to leave the healthiest plants to grow, cutting out all the others, and leaving one plant about every eight inches in the rows. There is a machine specially constructed for thinning out turnips and other plants grown in rows, which will cut out all plants growing between the fixed distances, but this still leaves any clumps of plants to be thinned by hand; also the machine cannot be set to work between drills so close together as 18 inches. When the operations of thinning the plants in the rows is carried out any spaces that have missed may be filled by transplanting some of the surplus plants from other rows.

After the thinning has been carried out the subsequent cultivation consists in keeping the soil between the rows constantly stirred and free from weeds. Where beets are planted for sugar production, and the drills are only 18 inches apart, the work requires a steady horse, who will walk between the rows, and a Planet, Jun., cultivator, which has narrow teeth, and will close up to a narrow width. As the tops of the plant begin to shade the ground this cultivation need not be performed so often.

Fertilising.—The question of fertilising this crop is an important one. Beets, the same as mangels, are a gross feeding crop, and by the application of heavy quantities of fertiliser can be made to grow to a large size. Strong nitrogenous fertilisers increase the size of the roots considerably, but in this instance large beets are not required, and also nitrogenous fertilisers impair the sugar-producing qualities of the root; consequently nitrogenous fertilisers should be avoided.

The best way to adopt for fertilising beets is to use land that has been heavily manured with stable manure for the previous crop, and then, at the time of sowing the crop, a dressing of fertiliser consisting of bone-dust, superphosphate, and sulphate of potash, mixed together in equal quantities and applied at the rate of three cwt. per acre, should give satisfactory results.

The results of analysis tell us that a crop of 15 tons of beets to the acre removes from the soil :—

	Roots. lbs.		Leaves. lbs.		Total. lbs.
Nitrogen	,59·4	...	26·4	...	85·8
Potash	132·9	...	52·8	...	184·8
Phosphoric Acid ...	26·4	...	11·0	...	37·4

The fertiliser mentioned above contains the full amount of phosphoric acid required by the crop, but only a percentage of the nitrogen and potash, leaving the balance to be obtained from the fertiliser applied the previous season. The crop would respond to the increased application of nitrogen, but only at the expense of the sugar contents of the roots.

Harvesting.—The roots should not be pulled until they are fully ripe, and this should be about the end of February or March. The general indication of ripeness is when the leaves turn yellow and mottled. A good indication as to whether the root is ripe or not may be obtained by cutting a root in two with a knife; if the newly-cut surfaces rapidly change colour on exposure to the air the roots are not sufficiently ripe; if they remain white or only turn slightly reddish, they are fit for harvest.

There are several methods of harvesting which may be adopted. Some pull the roots by hand, cut the tops off with a sharp knife, and leave the roots in heaps ready for carting; others cut the tops off with a hoe as they grow in the field, then turn up the roots with a plough, and load into carts. Whichever method is adopted, care must be taken that the roots are not cut or injured below the neck, as fermentation soon sets in, and the roots are then useless for making sugar.

Some time ago the writer carried out an experiment with 17 varieties of sugar beet, which were analysed to ascertain their sugar contents. The percentage of sugar varied from 17·1 to 4·5, and the weight of the beets from 4½ozs. to 55ozs. The 4½-oz. beets gave the highest percentage, and the 55-oz. roots the lowest percentage of sugar. The average yield per acre was 6 tons 5cwt.; the average weight of roots 20ozs., and the average percentage of sugar 12·6.

Diseases.—The principal diseases that attack the sugar beets are the beetroot rot, the leaf-spot fungus, and the beet scab.

The illustration in Fig. 1 shows a root affected by the beetroot rot. This disease first attacks the roots when they are about half-grown, and the roots gradually rot away. The rot is caused by a fungus disease, which attacks the roots and spreads very rapidly. When the crop is once attacked nothing can be done to the affected roots. They should be pulled up and burnt, so as to stay the spread of the disease. The land on which the affected crop was grown should be given a heavy dressing of lime, and beets should not be

FIG. II.—A Beet Leaf, showing the early stages of injury due to the Leaf
Spot Fungus.

sown on the same ground for some time, but a rotation of crops should be carried out, so as not to provide food for the bacteria to live on. This disease does not attack a cereal crop, which may therefore be sown to follow the beet with safety. Fig. 2 shows an illustration of a leaf of the beet suffering from the early attacks of the leaf-spot fungus, a disease which attacks the leaf of the plant. It begins as a small brown spot with a reddish-purple margin. The spots gradually become grey in the centre, and they gradually present a dried-up or withered appearance. The most effective remedy is to spray the plants with Bordeaux mixture, which is composed of sulphate of copper (bluestone), 4lbs.; quick-lime, 4lbs.; molasses, 4lbs.; water, 20 gallons.

1. Dissolve 4lbs. of sulphate of copper in 4 gallons of water in a wooden or enamelled vessel.

2. Then slack 3 to 4 lbs. quick-lime in another vessel in 2 gallons of water, and stir in the molasses; when cool, mix 1 and 2 together and add water to make up to 20 gallons. Two ounces of Paris green made into a paste and added to this mixture is very effective for any leaf-eating insects which may be attacking the plants.

The above mixture, if used in the early stages of growth, is a good preventative against any of the diseases which attack sugar beets.

Fig. 3 is an illustration of a root attacked by the beet scab, which is very similar to the scab which attacks the potato crop. The disease is caused by a fungus growth which attacks the roots. If the fungus spores are in the ground as the result of the disease having been in some previous crop, very little can be done to save the roots; a spraying of Bordeaux miture may help to keep it in check, but the only remedy is to plant other crops in the affected ground until the fungus dies for want of crops which supply the food necessary for the conditions of its life.

Manufacture.—The total production of sugar in the world for the year 1904-05 was 9,483,976 tons, of this total 4,890,722 tons were beet sugar and 4,593,254 cane sugar; from this it will be seen that rather more than half the total supply of sugar is made from beets. Of the 4,890,722 tons of beet sugar produced 4,681,000 tons were produced in Europe, and 209,722 tons in U.S.A. The total quantity of beet sugar produced has decreased during the year; the total produced during the year 1903-4 being 6,083,103 tons. The reason is not stated, but is no doubt due to the beet crop on the continent not being up to the average.

The following notes, taken from the *Year Book* of the U.S. Department of Agriculture, furnish some interesting particulars as to the sugar beet industry in the U.S.A. There are at the present time 54 factories, which have cost, approximately, 40,000,000 dollars, or an average cost each of £150,000, and have a daily capacity to produce, approximately, 4,800 tons of refined sugar from 42,300 tons of beets. The gross return to the farmer from the area cultivated last year was 42 dollars, or £8 15s. per acre, which had to provide the cost of growing the beet and delivering to the factory. The average yield of roots for the entire U.S.A. was 8·4 tons per acre. The reported average extraction of sugar was 11·5 per cent., or 230lbs. of commercial sugar from each ton of roots.

The only instance we have in Australia of a sugar beet factory is that at Maffra, in Gippsland, Victoria, and the results obtained there were not such as to encourage any extension of the industry. From an account of the operations published in the July number of the *Journal of Agriculture* in Victoria, I extract the following, which may be of value to those interested in the proposal to establish a sugar beet factory in this State. The complete article points out many of the causes of failure, and how they may be prevented in the future, and is well worth perusal by those interested in this matter. The article states:—" The factory premises, situated in a compact block of 30 acres, are within 200 yards of the Maffra railway station, and are connected therewith by two lines, with switches; one for unloading beets at the receiving bins, and the other for the despatch of manufactured sugar. A railway weighbridge facilitates the weighing of beets arriving by rail. The factory building is of bold design, and was built with sufficient room for future expansion. The complete plant, comprising washing, elevating, slicing, diffusion, purification, evaporation, sulphitation, boiling, and centrifugal machines, was supplied by the Brunswick Machinery Company (Germany) at a cost of £33,419. The capacity of the plant is guaranteed to 350 tons per day, but the plant can on emergency treat over 400 tons of beet in 24 hours. So far as can be gathered from the reports of professional engineers, the plant is in every way capable of performing the work put upon it, and little of the past failure can be ascribed to the working of the plant or the quality of the sugar produced. It might be mentioned that the selling price of the Maffra beet sugar on the Melbourne market was £22 per ton, a sufficient guarantee that the quality was all that could be desired."

The factory was worked during the years 1898 and 1899, and has since been closed down owing to the supply of beets not being sufficient to keep the machinery running. The total quantity of beets delivered was 8,758 tons in 1898 and 6,317 tons in 1899. The greatest quantity delivered in one day was 261 tons, and the smallest 13 tons; as the capacity of the machinery was 350 tons per day it will be seen that it was never fully employed, and as steam has to be kept up all the time, the working expenses were unduly heavy. Three-fifths of the total supply of beets came from syndicates formed by the company and the small balance only was supplied by the farmers.

Presuming a factory for the treatment of sugar beets was established, the question as to whether the cultivation of the crop would prove profitable or not is one that must be decided by each settler, and depends on the situation of his land and the yield per acre he is likely to obtain. The article above referred to gives the cost of producing an acre of sugar beets in the Maffra district, as follows:—

	£	s.	d.
Rent of land	1	0	0
Winter ploughing	0	15	0
Harrowing three times, 1s. ...	0	3	0
Rolling once	0	1	0
Cost of seed, 12lbs. at 8d. ...	0	8	0
Cost of sowing	0	1	6
Thinning	1	5	0
Hoeing twice, 6s.	0	12	0
Ploughing out	0	5	0
Topping 12 tons at 2s. 6d. ...	1	10	0
Carting three miles by wagon ...	1	10	0
	£7	10	6

Fig. III.—Beet Scab.

It will be noticed that in the cost of raising the crop there is no allowance made for fertiliser : in most of our soils this would be necessary.

It is stated that an average yield of 12 tons of beets per acre may be expected, but I am inclined to think this is too high, as it is considerably above the average yields obtained elsewhere.

An attempt is now being made to induce settlers to grow beets so as to enable the factory to recommence operations, and, as a special inducement, the authorities are offering for the first year 16s. per ton for beets containing not less than 12 per cent. of sugar, with a reduction of 1s. for each percentage below this amount; in addition they propose to give a bonus should the profits warrant it.

Before a small factory could successfully start operations it would be necessary to have a guarantee that at least 3,000 acres would be planted with sugar beet, and this would provide about three months' work for the factory.

Another advantage to be derived from a beet sugar factory is that the surrounding settlers are able to obtain large quantities of the pulp at a very low rate, and as this makes an excellent food for both cattle and pigs, settlers using the pulp would be able to considerably increase their returns by feeding dairy cattle on this by-product. As an attempt is to be made to reopen the Maffra factory it will be interesting to see how it succeeds before advocating settlers to grow beet in this State on an extensive scale.

The plots of beets planted this season will enable us to form an idea as to the yields per acre likely to be obtained, and also the percentage of sugar contained, and we can then form an idea as to the future prospects of making beet sugar.

VEGETABLE GROWING.

By G. CHITTY BAKER.

One of the most striking features on a settler's homestead in this State is the absence of any attempt to form a kitchen or vegetable garden. A whole day may be spent in passing from one place to another without being able to find any efforts being put forth to grow a few vegetables for home consumption. At one place, visited some months ago, I noticed that there was an ideal piece of land alongside of a running creek that ought to grow anything and would make a splendid kitchen garden. I asked the owner why he did not use it. He replied that he had no time and could not be bothered growing vegetables. Yet, before leaving I found that this man actually bought canned vegetables in town for the use of his own family, when at the same time he could have the best that could be grown by devoting, say, one half-day a week, which should be quite sufficient to keep an average family in all vegetables required throughout the year.

In order to maintain good health, it is important that plenty of wholesome vegetables should be always obtainable. It is in the hope that more attention will be paid to the importance of vegetable growing that this article is written. The preparation of the ground, sowing, cultivating, harvesting the crop, and fertilising; giving the kind and quantity each crop requires will be dealt with, so that by careful observance to the various points elucidated, there should be no reason why a supply of good succulent green food for the table should not be had for at least eight months in the year, and, in the more favourable parts, the whole year round.

SIZE OF GARDEN.

Of course, the size of a kitchen garden depends on the quantity of suitable ground available and the requirements, whether for private use only or for marketing. If for private use, then half an acre will be found ample, when properly cultivated, to grow sufficient for the needs of an ordinary family of eight to ten persons. A garden of this size should be easily made on any homestead; but when it is intended to supply the market, then a great deal depends on the labour available, the demands and proximity of the market. As, however, it is the establishment of the home garden that we are at present more interested in considering, the bigger question of a market garden can be left over for another article.

Much difference of opinion exists on the question of gardening; yet there is only one rule to be recognised, viz., to aim at securing "perfection in all you do." The greatest error committed in the average kitchen or house garden is the desire to grow something of everything, which generally results in not growing anything well. The aim of all gardeners, whether the occupation is followed for pleasure or profit, should be to grow the best of each kind, to perfection. The time taken in sowing and cultivating is the same for good sorts as for bad, and, as a matter of fact, bad seed or inferior plants require more coddling and attention than good ones.

In very small gardens, only those things requiring little space and which will grow quickly should be attempted, such as salading, etc.; but to those who can afford to devote at least half an acre, then almost all kinds may be tried.

PREPARING THE GROUND.

Too much care cannot be taken in the first preparation of the ground. The best results can only be obtained by deep cultivation or trenching. Trenching is, of course, the best and more lasting, and it will be supposed that the reader of this article is going to make his first attempt at gardening, and for that reason he will be taken step by step through the whole process. By trenching is meant the displacing of soil in layers, strips of ground 12 to 18 inches wide and nine inches deep being taken off one place and thrown on the top of another. In gardening, however, care must be taken that each layer retains the same relative position after trenching as it did before being removed, and in no case must the top soil be buried, or the subsoil be brought to the top. The proper way to commence is to first divide the ground down the centre, which we will suppose is of an oblong shape. This will give you two strips, which we will call A and B. With a marker strike lines across A 18 inches apart. Next take a spit of nine inches off the top soil of the first two rows, or, as they are termed in trenching, "benches," and wheel it into the top of "B." Now take another spit off bench 1 and place in a heap on "B" alongside, but not with that already removed. "A" will now have the first bench 18 inches deep, the second one nine inches deep. The bottom of the first bench should then be treated to a good dressing—any vegetable matter, weeds, corn-stalks, or anything that will rot. This should be dug in, turning up the bottom of No. 1 bench another spit. Then remove the second spit from No. 2 bench, throwing it into No. 1, working in any good rotten stuff you may have, to form humus in the soil, after which treat the bottom of No. 2 bench the same as you did No. 1. You then commence on No. 3 bench, throwing the top spit on to No. 1, and the second spit on No· 2, turning up the third spit. You then have bench No 1 completed, bench No. 2 without top soil, and bench No. 3 with the bottom only turned up. This operation is continued until you reach the bottom of strip "A", when the soil required to finish must be taken from the bottom of strip "B," working back on this strip until you can reach the place where the soil from strip "A" was placed, and you will find that this when filled in will complete this most important work. The whole should present a level appearance, ready for planting.

It is surprising what a quantity of stuff can be used up in trenching, rakings of yards, sweepings, clippings, and prunings, all of the coarser sorts being dug in with the bottom spit, and the more easily decomposed matter mixed with the second spit ; the richer kinds, such as cleanings from the fowl yards, stables, and manure heaps being used for mixing with the top spit. If this is done properly, not only does it thoroughly enrich the soil by decomposition, but by loosening it the air is enabled to penetrate and sweeten to a very much greater depth than under ordinary circumstances, and above all, the adding of humus to the soil not only loosens stiff clay ground and solidifies loose soils, but it retains the moisture so that garden operations can be continued much longer in the summer than could be done when this system is not adopted.

GARDEN OPERATIONS.

I know of no better advice to be given than that of recommending the keeping of a diary of all work done in the garden. For the last 25 years a sheet account has been kept of the sowing, planting, cultivating, cropping and results of everything grown in our garden, with the result that it is known exactly when to sow, what to sow, when it will be fit to crop, and probable yield. A table has been prepared of these particulars which will be published later on.

· Knowledge and forethought is absolutely essential with regard to the proper time for sowing and planting and the quantity to grow, for it is a great pity to see some things run to seed by reason of being sown too early ; and in the other case, the ground being taken up with crops that cannot be used quick enough while there are no others coming on. Once find out the quantity required, then just that space necessary to grow the number of plants may be sown, the next piece of ground being prepared for a successional sowing.

Besides a diary being kept, for which an ordinary school exercise book will answer admirably, a second one should be used for the purpose of keeping a detailed account of sowing, etc. In this book the tables given in this article should be copied on the front pages. On the first page the times for sowing, remembering that south of Bunbury is later and north of Geraldton earlier than the district on which the time in these tables are based. On the second page copy the quantities and name of fertilisers each kind requires, when and how applied. The third page could be devoted to a plan of the garden, which should be divided into parallelograms of about 100 feet long by 20 feet wide, marking each square so that it may be easily identified. In the book itself a double page should be given to each kind of vegetable; across the opening the following particulars should appear:—

Date of sowing.	Out of ground.	In flower.	Picked, cut, or pulled.	Total quantity obtained.	Name of seed and seller.	Remarks.

In the case of cabbages, lettuce, cauliflowers, etc., instead of using the words "in flower," "planted out" could be substituted, while in root crops it could be left out altogether.

The great value of such a record, correctly kept for a few years, is hard to estimate. The bottom lines of each paper should be devoted to a review of the plantings, giving special note to the best crops, the name of seed, where purchased, the time taken to mature, and the crop secured, so that at the second year's planting, the best results may be followed in order to verify the previous ones. It was five years before I came across a cauliflower that would grow to perfection with me. It is advisable, therefore, for the first year or two to purchase only small quantities of seed of different varieties until it is proved which does best in your particular case.

Sowing.

Having prepared the ground, sowing may be at once commenced, always bearing in mind that it is a continuous cropping that is required for family use, not the sowing of the whole of the patch at one time, growing a great deal more than can be used, and then waiting until the next crop is ready. For a family of eight or ten persons, two rows of peas or beans 20 feet long, followed by sowings at an interval of a fortnight, will provide continuous pickings to the end of the season. A strip 20 feet long and 12 inches wide for carrots, beet, radish, onions, parsnips, and turnips, followed by continuous sowings, will be found to be ample. Seed beds two feet square, for cabbage, cauliflower, silver beet, lettuce, etc., will supply all the plants required. The sowing of seed should be regulated by the season, laying it down as a rule that seed should be at a depth equal to three times its circumference; in winter or on wet ground somewhat less, while in summer and on open soils a little deeper will be found to act advantageously.

In sowing small seed such as cabbage, onions, leek, radish, lettuce, turnips, carrots, and the like, it is well to first get the ground firm and level, sprinkle the seed lightly, and then slightly cover with fine soil, firming all with blows from the back of the spade. I have averaged 97 per cent. of plants from seed sown this way.

Cultivation.

Next to good seeds, properly sown, nothing is so important as cultivation while the crop is growing. Cultivation is necessary, for two important reasons: first, for the purpose of killing all weeds; and, secondly, by keeping the top of the soil loose, evaporation is checked by destroying the capillary tubes before reaching the surface. A loose surface also allows the air and sun to penetrate to a greater depth, thus assisting considerably in the growth of the young plant.

(To be continued.)

POULTRY NOTES.

By Frank H. Robertson.

THE EGG-LAYING COMPETITIONS.

The Egg-laying Competitions are making very satisfactory progress, and their existence cannot but have the effect of acting as a great impetus to the poultry industry in this State, and from this onwards I predict that our egg importations will show a steady decline. More people are taking up poultry-raising, and the dessemination of the heavy-laying strains of fowls all over the State will certainly result in a more bountiful supply of eggs.

There are pessimists who openly state that our markets are glutted and that eggs will shortly be down to non-paying prices. Any who give utterance to such statements are quite ignorant of the correct state of affairs; as a matter of fact the local egg sales are too small to attract the best buyers, so the orders to South Australia continue.

From the appended list of the Subiaco Competition it will be seen that the pen owned by the Sunnyhurst Farm, of South Australia, has started off with a good lead, and their record of 139 eggs is remarkable when one considers the great disadvantage they were under of having to make the sea voyage from Adelaide. The other oversea White Leghorns, sent by A. H. Padman, are also doing remarkably well; these birds were slower in making a start, but at time of writing were laying quite as well as the leaders. Mr. Padman's Silver Wyandottes are also coming along nicely. The leading local birds have put up a first class record, but as was to be expected many pens have made a poor start; in several instances birds which laid a few eggs at first went into a partial moult and almost ceased laying; the change from extra warm quarters to the iron competition houses and more exposed runs no doubt accounted for the poor results.

The ducks as a whole made a very bad start, the change of abode causing a general casting of feathers and a consequent poor egg yield. The leading pen (Durting's) are a notable exception, and have started off with a very satisfactory lead.

As to quality and general typical appearance the fowls taken all round are a really fine lot, sent in splendid condition and present a very pleasing picture and a valuable object lesson to the large body of visitors who attend on every occasion when permitted, viz., on each Wednesday and Saturday afternoon. The following is the record for the first month:—

FIRST MONTH OF SUBIACO COMPETITION.

Fowls.

Six hens in each pen.

						Eggs Laid.
1. W. Leghorn, Sunnyhurst (S.A.)	...	...	...	...		139
2. Silver Wyandotte, C. Attwell	...	...	...	...		123
3. Do. B. Jones	...	...	...	..	...	120

FOWLS—*continued.*

		Eggs Laid.
4. W. Leghorn, S. Craig		118
5. Do. J. D. Smith		118
6. W. Wyandotte, A. S. B. Craig		110
7. Black Orpington, F. T. Rowe		103
8. S. Wyandotte, E. F. Braddock		100
9. W. Leghorn, J. W. Buttsworth		99
10. Do. A. H. Padman (S.A.)		98
11. Do. E. Garbet		96
12. G. Wyandotte, L. Meatchem		92
13. W. Leghorn, C. W. Johnson		87
14. Do. Ericville Farm		87
15. Brown Leghorn, Bungalow Farm		85
16. W. Leghorn, Mrs. McGree		85
17. S. Wyandotte, A. H. Padman		84
18. Brown Leghorn, A. Snell		83
19. W. Leghorn, G. W. G. Lizars		84
20. Brown Leghorn, W. G. Clark		82
21. Partridge Wyandotte, A. F. Farrant		82
22. S. Wyandotte, W. Snowden		80
23. W. Leghorn, Ryan Bros.		76
24. Do. R. G. Flynn		74
25. S. Wyandotte, J. W. Buttsworth		72
26. Black Orpington, Ericville Farm		72
27. W. Leghorn, F. Witfield		70
28. Do. Bungalow Farm		68
29. Do. Austin and Thomas		65
30. Do. G. M. Buttsworth		64
31. S. Wyandotte, A. Coombs		64
32. Black Orpington, G. Bolger		63
33. W. Leghorn, E. Fitzgerald		61
34. Brown Leghorn, J. R. Parkes		59
35. Do. F. Whitfield		59
36. W. Leghorn, F. Piaggio		57
37. Black Orpington, O. K. Yards		52
38. W. Leghorn, Bon Accord Yard		52
39. G. Wyandotte, Glen Donald Yards		50
40. W. Leghorn, H. Jones		50
41. Do. F. Mason		50
42. Do. Adelaide Yards		49
43. Do. W. Wade		48
44. Minorca, E. Hutchinson		47
45. W. Leghorn, E. Palmerston		42
46. G. Wyandotte, H. H. Wegg		40
47. Do. J. Kirk		39
48. Brown Leghorn, W. Snowden		39
49. R. C. Brown Leghorn, Mrs. Hughes		37
50. W. Wyandotte, R. G. Smith		35
51. W. Leghorn, C. R. Roberts		34
52. R. C. W. Leghorn, Honnor and Forbes		34
53. Minorca, A. R. Keesing		32
54. W. Leghorn, E. A. Newton		32
55. Do. Perth Yard		32
56. G. Wyandotte, H. M. Kelley		27
57. S. Wyandotte, J. E. Redman		12
58. W. Wyandotte, Mrs. McGree		11
59. S. Wyandotte, J. S. Miller		5
60. B. Leghorn, J. White		5
61. S. Wyandotte, J. B. Pettit		5
62. B. Orpington, C. Crawley		0
63. Do. H. M. Kelley		0
64. Minorca, A. Savage		0

DUCKS.

Four Ducks in each Pen.

Eggs Laid.

			Eggs Laid
1.	Indian Runner, R. A. Dusting	... ...	64
2.	Do Mrs. L. Melien...		47
3.	Do. G. Steed		47
4.	Do. E. A. Newton		41
5.	Do. Austin and Thomas		31
6.	Buff Orpington, W. Snowden		26
7.	Do. Bon Accord Yard		22
8.	Do. Ericville Farm		22
9.	Do. Perth Poultry Farm		21
10.	Indian Runner, A. Snell		20
11.	Buff Orpington, F. Piaggio		14
12.	Indian Runner, Miss E. Parker		12
13.	Do. S. Craig		2
14.	Do. C. W. Johnson		2
15.	Do. F. D. Vincent		2
16.	Do. F. T. Rowe		1
17.	Do. Aveley Yard		0
18.	Buff Orpington, Sargenfri (S.A.)		0
19.	Indian Runner, J. R. Parkes		0
20.	Do. C. E. Close		0
21.	Do. J. B. Pettit		0
22.	Do. Adelaide Yards		0

Male birds will be placed in many of the pens, from which eggs will be for sale for breeding purposes. Application for same must be made to the manager of the competition at Subiaco.

THE NARROGIN COMPETITION.

The end of July completed the third month of this competition, and has resulted in a very satisfactory output. More than half of the pens yielded over 100 eggs each, the best (131) being from W. J. Craig's Golden Wyandottes, which had previously laid poorly. Several other backward pens have also come on wonderfully during the month. The total output for each month shows a very large increase, viz., May 782, June 1,496, July 2,401. The general health of the fowls continues excellent; there has been no sickness, but several of the Orpingtons and Wyandottes have had several fits of broodiness which, however, is of short duration.

The average takers of the first three months (winter test) has resulted as follows:—

1st Prize £3—Mrs. A. Bristow, Armadale, White Leghorns.
2nd Prize £2—Mr. E. E. Ranford, 100 Carr Street, West Perth, Brown Leghorns.
3rd Prize £1—Mr. E. W. Johnson, Osborne Park, Leederville, White Leghorns.

Results of Narrogin Competition for July; three months gone, nine to go :—

	Breed.	Owner.	Total for Month.	Total for Date.
1.	White Leghorn	Mrs. A. Bristow	112	329
2.	Brown do.	E. E. Ranford	115	267
3.	White do.	E. W. Johnson	100	261
4.	Silver Wyandottes ...	Miss Buttsworth	103	256
5.	Buff Orpington	A. H. Hilton	92	252
6.	White Leghorn	F. Piaggio	125	248
7.	Do. do.	J. Handley	130	209
8.	Silver Wyandottes ...	W. G. Lizars	86	206
9.	Do. do. ...	A. M. Nitschk	110	202
10.	White Leghorns ...	G. Oneto	72	197
11.	Brown do. ...	R. A. Dusting	122	197
12.	White do. ...	A. F. Spencer	121	195
13.	Do. do. ...	Miss M. Parker	97	174
14.	Black Orpington	Sparks & Binnington	85	166
15.	Golden Wyandottes ...	W. J. Craig	131	161
16.	Black Orphington ...	Perth Poultry Yards	101	160
17.	R.C.B. Leghorns ...	Adelaide Yards	69	160
18.	Do. do. ...	E. Krachler	108	156
19.	White Wyandottes ...	Mrs. L. J. Hood	119	153
20.	Do Leghorns ...	J. E. Tull	99	139
21.	Do. do. ...	Aveley Yard	70	139
22.	Brown do. ...	J. D. Wilson	50	133
23.	White do. ...	R. J. Flynn	71	132
24.	Do. do. ...	F. J. Williams	79	120
45.	Do. do. ...	O. C. Rath	34	67
		Totals	2,401	4,679

THE POULTRY AT NARROGIN.

The poultry on the Narrogin Farm are all in perfect health, and a very good egg yield is being obtained from the young hens, the old birds not laying well yet. Turkeys, ducks, and geese are also starting to lay well, and eggs are being set and placed in incubators; over 100 head of strong young birds are now running about.

Some good, useful White Leghorn and Silver Wyandotte cockerels are still for sale, also some choice Bronze Gobblers. Among them are two very massive and good-coloured second season birds, one of which won 1st prize at the last Royal Agricultural Show.

Eggs are now for sale from the following varieties, viz., White and Brown Leghorns, Silver Wyandottes, and Plymouth Rocks, price 12s. 6d. per setting, carefully packed and railage paid to any part of the State. Satisfactory results are guaranteed, but should a poor result be obtained, fresh eggs will be forwarded, provided the eggs not hatching are returned, railage paid, to the Poultry Expert at the farm. Incubator lots of eggs supplied at lower rates.

The invitation to inspect the farm and competition fowls has been largely availed of, as several visitors have called, and found much interest in the practical illustration of poultry-raising there afforded them.

STATE FARM HAMEL.

By G. F. Berthoud.

Cotton, (*Gossypium herbaceum*).—Seeds of the following seven varieties were sown on the 16th November, 1905, 4ft. x 3ft. feet apart, allowing six seeds per hill. The young plants were thinned out to one or two of the strongest of each set. Early American sorts are the best for culture here. The Egyptian and Caravonica varieties although they make strong growth do not bloom and set bolls until too late for maturing before the wet season sets in. The cotton plant is a perennial; here the long wet winter kills the plants therefore they must be treated as annuals only. The chief difficulty is in getting a variety early enough to mature a full crop before the middle of May. Owing to the past Autumn being warm and dry the results are the best yet obtained with this crop here.

Soil.—Low land, light and peaty, tilled to the depth of one foot, which retained fair moisture throughout the summer months.

Manure.—Complete fertiliser, same as used for the potato crop, applied in the soil below the seed, at the rate of about six cwts. per acre.

Cultivation.—The plants were hilled up twice, and the plots hoed and kept free from weeds. The plants generally made fair growth, and were clean, free from insects and other injurious pests. The only damage done was by the high east winds which prevail here in summer, breaking branches and otherwise damaging some plants.

Shine's Early Prolific.—American seed; about one quarter failed to germinate. Growth slow but healthy; habit stocky and well branched; height, four feet; flowers creamy white fading to pale rose; bolls large and well filled, 40 to 60 per plant. The first of these ripened 23rd March. The lint is pure white, silky, and of excellent quality. About two-thirds of the bolls matured properly, the balance were spoiled by rain in May. Yield rate per acre:—Clean lint, 350lbs.; seed, half-a-ton, equal to 16 gallons of oil and 300lbs. of oil cake. Early and good variety.

Louisiana Prolific.—American seed. Germination even and good. Growth free; habit dwarf; height to three feet; plant shrubby and hardy; flowers creamy white, fading deep rose; bolls round, of fair size and well filled, four lobed—40 to 60 per plant, half of which matured. First ripe on 5th April; short staple; lint pure white; yield fair, rather below Shine's Early, Hardy and good early variety.

Ambassy.—Egyptian variety. Local saved seed. Germination very even and strong; growth fair but rather slim and delicate; height to three feet; requires a warmer climate; flowers yellow; bolls long and pointed, about 30 per plant; only a few of these matured during first week in June; staple long and silky; yield very light; failure; late and not suitable for culture here.

Upland.—American seed. Germination fairly even; growth slow; plant of weak habit; height, 2ft. to 2ft. 6in.; flower, pale pink; bolls of medium size, about 20 per plant; late variety; only a few matured **late** in April. Yield poor. Not desirable in this locality.

King's Improved.—American seed. Germination fair; growth good, but rather uneven; height to three feet, freely branched; flowers creamy white, fading to pink; bolls large, and well filled, 30 to 50 per plant; first ripe on 1st April; good staple and colour. Yield fair, but lighter than the two first named. Fair, second early.

Yannovich.—Egyptian variety. Germination uneven; about one-third failed; growth vigorous and tall; height to 4ft. 6in.; flowers yellow; bolls long and pointed, about 50 per plant; a few only matured; late, 9th June; staple long and fine, but spoiled by rain. Yield, failure. Late, not desirable.

Fruitt's Big Boll.—American seed. Germination very good; growth fairly even and strong; habit low set, even, and well branched; height three feet; flowers creamy white, fading to a rose colour; bolls large and good. 30 to 50 on each plant, half of which matured; first lot ripe 7th April; lint of good quality and fair length. Yield fair. A good second early variety.

SWEET POTATO.

Ipomœa Batatas.

Yellow Spanish Cuttings.—Set out 4 feet x 3 feet. Growth moderate; runners five feet long; taken up 12th June; tubers of nice even size, set fairly close to the stalk; shape, various, round to oblong; skin yellow; good quality. Yield 11 tons per acre.

Rosella Cuttings.—Growth fair; runners six feet long; foliage pale green; taken up 12th June; tubers medium size, long; set on long roots away from the stalks, and rather difficult to dig; colour of skin, pale pink; good cooking quality. Yield, seven tons per acre.

White Maltese Cuttings.—Set out 4 feet x 3 feet; growth very vigorous and healthy; vines eight feet long; taken up 12th June; tubers very long, medium size; skin white; rather hard to dig owing to tubers being very brittle; late, hardy and prolific variety. Yield, 14 tons per acre.

Spanish Giant.—Planted 4 feet by 3 feet. Growth healthy, strong, and compact; vines six feet long; leaves round; taken up 12th June; fairly matured; tubers large and pointed; skin pale yellow, flushed pink; set fairly close to stalk; weight up to 4lbs 4oz. each. Good main crop variety. Yield, 17 tons per acre.

The four varieties mentioned in reports were introduced by tuber from Queensland. These were set in boxes of sandy soil, under glass, in September. The cuttings were planted rather late, viz., 21st of November, four feet by three feet apart.

Soil.—Low land, peaty and light, fairly moist.

Manure.—Complete fertiliser, 6 cwt. per acre applied to and well mixed with soil below the sets. Although this class of soil is not the most suitable—a well drained deep and sandy loam is better for this crop—the results obtained were good.

This valuable plant should be more generally grown by agriculturists. The tubers of most kinds are excellent for table use, being more nutritious than the ordinary potato. The vines and tubers make first-class feed for milch cows and other live stock. The plants are healthy, very free from the ravages of injurious insects and leaf blights. Cultivation is easy, providing the land is well tilled and clean at the time of planting. The vines soon over-run and cover the whole surface, thus keeping down the weeds.

NARROGIN STATE FARM.

REPORT FOR THE MONTH OF JUNE.

By R. C. BAIRD.

During the month, seeding operations have been carried on, and we have now almost completed the sowing of cereal crops for the year. Having only one seed drill on the farm, the work of drilling could not be carried on as rapidly as I should have liked.

Owing to the lateness of the Autumn rains and the hardness of the ground in consequence, ploughing was proceeded with very slowly, and the sowing season has been unduly protracted.

The total rainfall for the month was 552 points. The weather has been exceedingly mild, and not favourable to the growth of the crops.

We are now busy drilling at Nash's farm, and expect to finish there in a few days. The area under crop on the new farm will be about 150 acres.

The balance of the cleared land will be ploughed and prepared for summer fodder crops.

On the old farm the early sown crops are making fair growth, and with the beneficial rains we are having, together with mild weather, should make good progress during the winter months. The natural pastures, although looking green, are very backward for this season of the year.

The stock on the farm are in fair condition, but the cattle have to be fed morning and night.

The sheep are in rather low condition; this applies chiefly to the old ewes; the younger sheep being in fair condition.

The ordinary flock ewes have almost finished lambing, and the lambs will be marked shortly. The Shropshire ewes have not yet dropped any lambs.

The work of clearing on blocks 59 and 60 has been completed, 200 acres have been cleared ready for the plough.

Clearing is now being done around the new building site.

The contractors have started the new buildings, and appear to be making good progress.

[This report was received too late for the July issue of the *Journal.*— ED. *Journal.*]

REPORT FOR THE MONTH OF JULY.

During the past month we have experienced some wintry weather with several frosty nights. The rainfall for the month totalled 5·03 inches, and the fields have, in consequence, become very boggy in places.

The crops, although rather late, are looking healthy, except in some of the low-lying spots, where the frosts have touched them.

Ploughing for summer fodder crops has been carried out, and 70 acres have been turned over. Owing to the heavy rains towards the end of the month this work had to be suspended for a time.

A piece of land has been prepared for trial grass plots, the seeds of which will be sown immediately.

Grubbing and clearing is being done at the new farm buildings, and I hope to start fencing there in a few weeks' time.

The erection of the new buildings is being proceeded with rapidly and the contractors expect to have them ready in about six weeks' time.

Poison grubbing in Paddock No. 39 is carried out by students. This paddock is badly infested with poison plants, and not having been previously grubbed, the work is slow and tedious.

The stock are in fair condition, considering the cold weather and the shortage of grass. The ewes and lambs are looking well and have improved in condition during the month.

The working horses having been hard at work ploughing, etc., for some months, are in good working condition.

CHAPMAN EXPERIMENTAL FARM.

REPORT FOR THE MONTH OF JULY.

By J. KEATS.

The planting of orchard with oranges, mandarines, lemons, peaches, plums, apricots, and nectarines was completed on 18th inst.; also the blanks in vineyard were filled up with rooted vines, the principal varieties planted were: Wortley Hall, White Nice, Almeria, Centennial, Muscat, Doradillo, Flame Tokay, Black Muscat, Black Prince, and Waltham Cross. A drain on one side of the orchard has been completed to carry of the storm water from the surrounding hills. Fifty ornamental trees—Kurrajong, Pepper, and Pride of India have been planted around yards and guards erected around them for protection. The trees planted last year have made excellent growth.

We have improved and divided some of the pig styes to accommodate the increasing herd of swine. The largest increase is with the Large Black breed of sows, they are very prolific as compared to the Berkshire, and on that point alone are a very profitable pig for breeders.

The rainfall for month was 467 points. A new 30-acre cultivation paddock has been fenced during the month, and 60 acres of scrub cut in 17B paddock.

Eighty-eight per cent. of lambs were marked from crossbred ewes, and six per cent. tailed of pure bred Shropshires. All the stock on farm are in fair condition.

Satisfactory sales of goats, pigs, and other stock continue to be made.

PEAR AND CHERRY TREE SLUG.

(Selandria cerasi.)

By Inspector L. J. Newman.

The Chief Inspector under the Insect Pests Act (Mr. T. Hooper) reports that the pear and cherry slug has been found in a few orchards this autumn. As this pest reappears in the spring of the year, it behoves all orchardists and fruitgrowers to keep a sharp lookout for it, and, if found, to at once report the matter to the Department of Agriculture. Now is the time for all growers to take concerted action to try and stamp out this pest, which has proved itself to be very serious in the Eastern States, New Zealand, and America. The principal trees liable to attack are the pear, cherry, quince, and hawthorn.

Pear Slug-worm (*a* enlarged) and its Saw fly.

This most destructive insect passes the winter in the pupa state underground; the flies, the progenitors of the spring brood of slugs, emerging from their hibernation as soon as the weather is sufficiently warm.

The fly is of a glossy black colour, with four transparent wings, the veins in the wings being brownish, and the legs dull yellow with black thighs. The female fly is about one-fifth of an inch in length, the male being slightly smaller.

These flies are commonly called saw-flies, from the fact that the females are provided with a saw-like ovipositor at the end of the body, by which slits are cut in the leaves of the trees or plants on which the larvæ feeds, in which slits the eggs are deposited on the under side, and hatch from 10 days to 14, according to the warmth of the weather. As many as 19 eggs have been found deposited on one leaf.

When first hatched the larvæ is of a whitish appearance, but within a few hours after hatching they exude through their skin a slimy matter, which gives them the slimy blackish slug-like appearance, hence their common name (Pear and Cherry Slug). During the life of this insect (which is about four weeks) there are four moulting periods, when the insect would be full grown. After the fourth and final moult, the slug's skin has the appearance of a clear yellowish colour. It then leaves the tree, and crawls or falls to the ground, where it buries itself from one to four inches, undergoing its transformations from larvæ to pupa, and pupa to fly, which it accomplishes in from 14 to 18 days, and sets to work laying eggs for another batch of slugs, and so fresh broods keep coming as long as the weather is warm enough. The damage done by this slug is mainly to the leaves (sometimes as many as 20 slugs being found on a single leaf), which they destroy by eating the upper surface, leaving the lower portion, as a rule, untouched. This, of course, is very injurious, especially during the heat of summer, as the trees are forced to make a new growth, thereby in a great measure destroying the prospects of next year's crop, or else the hot rays of the sun are allowed to penetrate to the centre of the tree, scald the fruit and bark, and also fermenting the sap and producing a stunted growth.

REMEDIES.--(1.) *Dry air-slacked lime*, sprinkled from a perforated tin vessel, or from a bag of some open material, attached to a pole, is very effective.

It has been stated that throwing dust or ashes on the slugs is just as beneficial, but this is an error, as the dust only makes the slug uncomfortable for a while, but on shedding its skin it soon gets rid of it and is none the worse, while the lime kills it.

2. *White Hellebore*, which is a powerful insecticide, is of a light greenish-yellow colour. (This powder at times causes violent sneezing when taken into the nostrils, therefore care should be taken in handling it). The best method of applying this is to take 1oz. of the powder, place in a bowl or dish, holding a quart or more. Gradually add boiling water, stirring all the time to make sure that the powder is thoroughly wetted, then add more boiling water until you have a quart, then add seven quarts of cold water (in all two gallons), stir well and apply.

3. *Paris Green*, applied in the same manner, in the proportion of a teaspoonful to two gallons of water, or 1oz. to 12 gallons of water, has proved very successful.

4. *Kerosene Emulsion.*--As a material for spraying when the fruit is not on the trees, one part emulsion to 25 parts of water, and sprayed whilst hot, is a good check.

5. *Benzole Spray.*--This spray may be used when the fruit is on the trees without any danger, and has been found very effective. Equal parts of benzole and water, to be kept thoroughly stirred when using.

6. *Bordeaux Mixture.*--Adding 1oz. Paris green to every 12 gallons of mixture is very strongly recommended.

7. Disturb the soil for some distance round the trunk of the trees, or treat with lime, to destroy the cocoons in the ground.

8. *Quibell's mixture* watered into the ground is also very effective.

9. *Sulphate of iron*, 1oz. to the gallon of water, is a good ground mixture.

A very minute parasite fly is said to exist in some parts of America, which lays its eggs within the eggs of this saw-fly and from its tiny egg a little maggot is hatched which lives within the egg of the saw-fly and consumes it, thereby keeping it in check.

FERTILISERS AND ENSILAGE.

Mr. Wicken, field officer of the Agricultural Department, recently delivered an illustrated lecture on the subject of fertilisers and ensilage-making, at the Mechanics' Institute, Northam. Mr. G. L. Throssell presided, and the attendance was small, the weather being very much against a large gathering.

The lecture proved a very interesting one, and could not fail to be of great practical value to anyone engaged in agricultural pursuits. Mr. Wicken illustrated his remarks with lantern slides, which made it very easy for his listeners to follow his arguments. The first portion of the address dealt with fertilisers and illustrated the requirements of the land for the purpose of wheat-growing, the constituents of the different manures on the market, the results obtained from the use of complete and incomplete fertilisers respectively, and the unit values of fertilisers. A proper conception of this phase of the subject would seem to be absolutely essential to success, and those who heard Mr. Wicken's lecture could readily appreciate the service the department is doing to the agricultural industry in this respect. But for the efforts of the department the farmers might be preyed upon unceasingly by unscrupulous merchants, but under existing conditions it is clearly the fault of the farmer himself if he does not get value for his money. There are now some fifty brands of manures registered with the department and the constituents of these are announced. By applying the formula of unit values as illustrated by Mr. Wicken in his lecture, any farmer can make sure of getting just what his land wants at the lowest possible price. Mr. Wicken made it very clear to his hearers that bulk counted for very little in the buying of manures, what the farmer should really pay for was the manurial constituent that he required, and without an intelligent application of the unit value system it would be impossible for anyone to say whether a manure costing £5 per ton was cheaper or dearer than one costing £20. The slides dealing with the subject of ensilage-making were equally interesting, and at the close of the lecture Mr. Wicken showed some milking machines, several hundreds of which are in successful operation in Victoria at the present time. Altogether the lecture was very keenly appreciated, and regret was expressed that more practical farmers were not present to hear it.—*Northam Advertiser.*

AUSTRALIAN APPLES FOR SOUTH AFRICA.

WARNING TO SHIPPERS.

In April last a consignment of apples was sent from one of the Eastern States to Cape Town, South Africa. On its arrival they were found to be infected with *fusicladium* fungus, known as " Black Spot " or, sometimes, " Scab." The Minister of Agriculture immediately cabled that consignments so affected would not be allowed to land, and wrote to the Minister for Trade for the Commonwealth on the matter as follows:—

DEPARTMENT OF AGRICULTURE,
Office of the Director of Agriculture,
Capetown, 21st May, 1906.

PLANT IMPORT REGULATIONS OF THE CAPE OF GOOD HOPE RE
AUSTRALIAN APPLES.

Sir,—In pursuance of my cablegram of the 20th May, 1905, relative to consignments of Australian apples for this colony, I am directed to invite your attention to the necessity of the fruit being free from diseases and insect pests, as it is anticipated that several thousand ,cases of Australian apples will be landed at our ports during the ensuing season.

The common "Black Spot" of Australia (*Fusicladium dendriticum*) has been found on apples in South Africa, but is very limited in its distribution. It does not occur at all in our most important fruit-growing districts, and there is every reason to believe that if it got established it would cause considerable loss here during the rainy months. In consequence, our fruitgrowers are very anxious lest new centres of infection should be established, and this Department apprehends danger from the exposal for sale of infected fruit in the shops. Another disease of Australian apples, and one which was found to be common on the fruit sent to this country last year, is "Fly Spot" (*Leptothyrium pomi*). This disease does not occur, so far as is known, anywhere in South Africa, and this Department is naturally very anxious that it should not be introduced.

The Secretary for Agriculture feels that importers have been given quite enough warning, and that if consignments materially affected by these or other fungus diseases or by codlin moth arrive, he would be fully justified in ordering their confiscation or immediate shipment to some port outside South Africa. He would, however, request your Government to kindly warn shippers, as was done a year ago, and thus minimise the risk of loss from our refusal to receive shipments.

I may mention that it is expected that all consignments of apples sent to our ports from Canada hereafter will be examined by Government inspectors before their despatch, with the view of eliminating parcels which would not be acceptable here.

I have, etc.,
(Sgd.)   D. HUTCHEON,
Acting Director of Agriculture.

STATUTORY RULES.
1906, No. 52.

PROVISIONAL REGULATIONS UNDER THE COMMERCE (TRADE DESCRIPTIONS) ACT, 1905.

I, the Governor General in and over the Commonwealth of Australia, acting with the advise of the Federal Executive Council, hereby certify that the following Regulations under the *Commerce (Trade Descriptions) Act, 1905* should, on account of urgency, be immediately made, to come into operation on the first day of October, One thousand nine hundred and six, except as to Part II., and to come into operation as to Part II. on the first day of January, One thousand nine hundred and seven, and make the said Regulations to come into operation accordingly.

Dated this 20th day of July, one thousand nine hundred and six.

NORTHCOTE,
By His Excellency's Command.   Governor General.
WILLIAM JOHN LYNE.

PART I.—INTRODUCTORY.

1. These regulations may be cited as the Commerce Regulations, 1906.
2. These regulations are divided into parts, as follows :—

Part   I.—Introductory.
Part   II.—Trade Descriptions of Imports.
Part III.—Trade Descriptions of Exports.
Part IV.—Examination of Exports.
Part   V.—Classification and Certification on request
Part VI.—Miscellaneous.

3. In these regulations, unless the contrary intention clearly appears,—

"Appointed place" means a place appointed by the Minister, by notice in the *Gazette*, as a place where goods for export may be inspected and examined.

"Approved stamp" means a stamp approved by the Minister.

"Coverings" includes the principal coverings in which goods are to be sold either wholesale or retail.

"Butter fat" means the fat of cows' milk.

"Creamery butter" means butter made from centifugally-separated cream.

"Disease," in relation to fruit, plants, seeds, maize, onions, or potatoes, means any abnormal condition of or in such goods, whether consisting of the presence of or caused by or due to the operations, development, growth, or decay of any insect or fungus, and also includes the condition known as "Bitter Pit."

"Disease," in relation to meat, includes pleuro-pneumonia, tuber-culosis, anthrax, swine fever, trichinosis, cancer, and any disease in stock declared by the Governor General by proclamation to be included in this definition; and also includes any defect or inferiority in the condition of the meat which renders it unfit for human food.

"Meat" means meat intended for human consumption, whether fresh or preserved.

"Manures" includes all articles for use as fertilisers of the soil, except farm-yard or stable manures, and crude materials for the manufacture of manures.

"Pasteurised," in relation to liquids, means subjected to heat in such a manner as to destroy fully-developed micro-organisms, but not necessarily the spores thereof.

"Preservative" means boric acid, salicylic acid, sulphurous acid, formic aldehyde, and any preparation of any of those sub-stances used as a preservative agent, and any substances declared by proclamation to be a preservative.

"Registered brand" means a brand registered in the Department of Trade and Customs, in pursuance of these regulations.

"Sound" and "Soundness" have relation to freedom from disease.

4. These regulations shall not apply to goods brought to Australia or shipped in Australia as ships' stores.

PART II.—TRADE DESCRIPTIONS OF IMPORTS.

5. (1.) The importation of the goods enumerated in this regulation is prohibited, unless there is applied to the goods a trade description in accordance with this Part..

(2.) The goods to which this regulation applies are as follows:—

(a.) Articles used for food or drink by man or used in the manufacture or preparation of articles used for food or drink by man;

(b.) Medicines or medicinal preparations for internal or external use;

(c.) Manures;

(d.) Apparel (including boots and shoes), and the materials from which such apparel is manufactured;

(e.) Jewellery;

(f.) Agricultural seeds; and plants.

6. (1.) The trade description to be applied in accordance with this Part shall comply with the following provisions:—

(a) It shall be in the form of a label or brand affixed in a prominent position to the goods, or to the coverings containing the goods; and

(b) The label or brand shall set out in legible characters a true description of the goods, and the name of the country or place in which the goods were made or produced; and

(c) In cases where any weight or quantity is set out, the label or brand shall specify whether the weight or quantity so set out is gross or net.

(2.) In the case of the following goods, the trade description shall, in addition, comply with the following provisions:—

(a.) In the case of medicines prepared ready for use, and containing 10 per cent. or more of ethel alcohol, if the average dose recommended exceed one teaspoonful (60 minims), the trade description shall set out the proportion or quantity of alcohol in the medicine.

(b.) In the case of medicines prepared ready for use, and containing any of the following drugs (or the salts or derivatives thereof), viz.:—Opium, morphine, cocaine, heroine, stramonium, nux vomica, cannibis indica, bromides, sulphonal, trional, veronal, paraldehyde, or any synthetic hypnotic substance, phenazonum, phenacetinum, or acetanilidum, or any allied synthetic substance, chloral, hydrate, belladonna, cotton root, ergot, or any abortifacient, the trade description shall set out the names of all such drugs so contained.

(c.) In the case of manures, the trade description shall set forth the principal active constituent thereof.

(d.) In the case of articles of apparel the trade description shall state the nature of the principal material from which the article is made; and the term "wool," or any term implying that the material is all wool shall not be applied to any such material unless it contains at least 90 per cent of pure wool. If the material contains wool, but less than 90 per cent. of pure wool, the description shall also state the other substances contained in the material.

(e.) In the case of articles of apparel manufactured from materials containing wool, but not containing as much as 90 per cent. of wool, the trade description shall set out the substances contained in the materials.

(f.) In the case of boots and shoes, the trade description shall set out the principal material from which they are made, and unless the soles are solid leather, without admixture or addition, the description shall state the fact, and nature of the admixture or addition.

(g.) In the case of leather containing any loading of any material or other weighting substance, the trade description shall state the name of the loading or other weighting substance contained in the leather, and the percentage thereof.

(h.) In the case of articles described as gold, the description shall state the carat number indicating the proportion of pure gold in the article.

(i.) In the case of agricultural seeds, the description shall state the name of the seeds and their condition as to soundness, cleanness, and freshness.

(*j.*) In the case of plants, the description shall state the names of the plants and their condition as to freedom from or affection by any disease or pest.

(*k.*) In the case of milk, the description shall describe the milk as Condensed Milk, Concentrated Milk, Dried Milk, or Condensed Skimmed Milk, as the case requires.

(3.) This regulation shall not apply to small packets of seeds sent by post or to seeds imported otherwise than as merchandise.

PART III.--TRADE DESCRIPTIONS OF EXPORTS.

7. (1.) The export of the goods enumerated in this regulation shall be prohibited unless there is applied to the goods a trade description in accordance with this Part.

(2.) The goods to which this regulation applies are:—

Butter, Canned Meat, Cheese, Condensed or Concentrated Milk, Condensed Skimmed Milk, Dried Milk, Fruit, Hares, Honey, Jam, Leather, Maize, Meat (other than rabbits and hares), Meat Extract or Meat Essence, Plants, Potatoes, Preserved Fruit, Rabbits, Seeds.

8. (1.) The trade description to be applied in accordance with this Part shall comply with the following provisions:—

(*a.*) It shall be in the form of a label or brand attached or affixed in a prominent position to the goods, or to the coverings containing the goods ; and

(*b.*) The label or brand shall set out in legible characters a true description of the goods, the word Australia, and the name of the State in which the goods were made or produced; and

(*c.*) The label or brand shall specify the net weight or quantity of the goods except in the case of carcases of meat : Provided that in the case of tinned goods, if the net contents fall short of any number of pounds by less than half a pound, the weight may be described as under that number of pounds.

(*d.*) The label or brand shall include either the name of the manufacturer or exporter or his registered brand.

(2.) In the case of butter (not packed in tins) the trade description shall specify whether the butter is pure Creamery Butter, Pastry Butter, or Milled Butter, as the case requires, and shall be indelibly impressed on the outer covering.

(3.) In the case of the following goods, the trade description shall, in addition, unless the goods have been classified or certified by an officer, and marked by him with an approved stamp, comply with the following provisions :—

(*a.*) In the case of butter (however packed), the trade description shall set out the name and percentage of any preservative contained in the butter, together with the percentages of casein, water, and colouring matter.

(*b.*) In the case of cheese, the trade description shall set out the quantity of rennet and the quantity and nature of the colouring matter (if any), together with the percentage of any preservative or foreign matter contained in the cheese. .

(*c.*) In the case of Meat, Canned Meat, and Meat Extract or Meat Essence, the trade description shall specify its condition as to soundness and suitability for human consumption.

(*d.*) In the case of Fruit and Potatoes, the trade description shall specify their condition as to soundness.

(*e.*) In the case of Leather containing any loading of any mineral or other weighting substance, the trade description shall state the name of the loading or other weighting substance contained in the leather and the percentage thereof.

(*f.*) In the cases of Maize, Seeds, and Plants, the trade description shall specify their condition as to soundness, cleanness, and freshness.

(4.) The trade description specified in paragraphs (*a*) and (*b*) of sub-section (3) of this regulation, in the case of butter and cheese, may, instead of being contained in the label or brand, be set out in a certificate signed by the exporter, and delivered to the examining officer at the appointed place, to which the butter and cheese are sent for inspection and examination.

9. The export of all goods of the kind specified in the First Schedule which do not comply with the standards therein set out is prohibited, unless the trade description applied to the goods either contains the words "Below standard" or states fully the matters in which, and the extent to which, the goods do not comply with the standards.

10. The trade description applied to goods in pursuance of this Part shall have relation to the condition of the goods as at the time of shipment.

11. Where the goods have been inspected by an officer, and a certificate has been issued by him in accordance with these regulations, the goods may be marked with an approved stamp applied to the outer covering or to a label or tag securely fastened to the goods.

12. In the case of any goods mentioned in these regulations exported for consumption in China, Japan, Philippine Islands, and adjacent islands, Singapore, the Straits Settlements, or other parts adjacent thereto, but to the east of India, it shall suffice if the trade description is applied to the outer coverings only.

13. These regulations shall not apply to unfrozen butter exported as ordinary cargo to any of the South Sea Islands.

PART IV.—INSPECTION OF EXPORTS.

14. Where by the law of any State any goods are required to be inspected and approved by a State Authority before export, and the Minister is satisfied that such inspection and approval are as efficient as inspection and marking under these regulations, the Minister may direct that such inspection and approval shall be accepted in lieu of examination and marking under these regulations.

15. The Minister may, by a notice in the *Gazette*, appoint places where any goods mentioned in these regulations intended for export may be inspected and examined by an officer.

16. (1.) All butter (other than tinned butter) intended for export shall be sent to the appointed place at least three days before shipment.

(2.) Goods (other than butter) specified in these regulations intended for export shall be sent to the appointed place in sufficient time before shipment to enable an officer to inspect and examine them.

(3.) The Comptroller-General may permit the inspection and examination of goods to be made in places other than appointed places.

17. The exporter shall give to the officer any information desired by him as to the date of churning of any butter, or the date of killing any meat, submitted to him for inspection.

18. Every person who intends to export any butter (other than tinned butter) shall give written notice to the Customs in Form 1 in the Second Schedule, at least three clear working days before the proposed date of shipment.

19. For all other goods mentioned in these regulations one clear working day's notice in Form 2 in the Second Schedule shall be sufficient.

20. Notwithstanding anything contained in these regulations, the notice to the Customs of intention to export any goods mentioned in these regulations may be for any stated period, and shall state the estimated quantity of such goods to be exported within that period. The notice under this regulation shall be in Form 3 or 4 in the Second Schedule, as the case requires.

21. A declaration by the exporter shall accompany the notice of intention to export condensed milk, concentrated milk, dried milk, leather, maize, seeds, plants, fruit, or potatoes, stating—

(a.) In the case of condensed milk, concentrated milk or dried milk—the extent to which it conforms to or differs from the standard in the First Schedule;

(b.) In the case of leather—the extent to which it contains any loading of any mineral or other weighting substance, and if it contains any such substance, the name of such substance, and the percentage thereof;

(c.) In the case of maize, seeds, or plants, their condition as to soundness, cleanness, and freshness; and

(d.) In the case of fruit or potatoes, their condition as to soundness.

PART V.—CLASSIFICATION AND CERTIFICATION ON REQUEST.

22. The intending exporter may, when giving notice of intention to export, give written notice to the Customs in Form 5, in the Second Schedule, that he requests the Customs to classify, certify, and mark the goods with an approved stamp, in accordance with these regulations; and where such request has been made, the following provisions of this Part shall apply.

23. The officer shall classify butter as follows:—

First Class, Superfine.—Pure creamery butter, containing not more than 14 per cent. of water, and classified at 94 points or over.

First Class.—Pure creamery butter, classified at 86 to 93 points.

Second Class.—Pure butter, classified at 75 to 85 points.

Third Class.—Pure butter, classified at less than 75 points.

24.   The officer shall classify cheese as follows :—

First Class, Superfine.—Pure cheese, classified at 94 points or over.

First Class.—Pure cheese, classified at 86 to 93 points.

Second Class.—Pure cheese, classified at 75 to 85 points.

Third Class.—Pure cheese, classified at less than 75 points.

25.   The officer shall not classify any impure butter or cheese.

26.   In classifying butter and cheese the officer shall take into consideration the flavour and aroma, texture, and condition of the butter ; and the maximum points to be awarded in respect of those matters shall be as follows :—

Flavour and aroma, 50 points.

Texture, including body, grain, and moisture, 30 points.

Condition, including colour, salting, packing, and covering, 20 points.

27.   Butter shall only be examined when its temperature is not higher than 70 degrees Fahrenheit, and is not lower than 40 degrees Fahrenheit.

28.   The officer shall classify hares and rabbits as follows :—

Hares.

First Class.—Hares, each weighing 7lbs. or over.

Second Class.—Hares, each weighing under 7lbs. and not less than 6lbs.

Hares not in prime condition shall not be classified.

Rabbits.

First Class.—Rabbits in prime condition.

Second Class.—Rabbits in good condition, but not in prime condition.

Skinned Rabbits.—Skinned rabbits in prime or good condition.

29.   (1.) The officer, after inspecting and examining any goods for export mentioned in these regulations, may issue a certificate in such one of the forms 6, 7, 8, 9, 9A, 9B, 9C, 10, 10A, 10B, 10C, 11, 11A, or 11B, in the Second Schedule, as is appropriate in the case.

(2.) Where goods are classified, the certificates for the different classes shall be coloured differently.

(3.) The officer shall mark the outer coverings of any goods in respect of which a certificate has been issued by him with an approved stamp, or impress the approved stamp to a tag or label, and securely fasten it to the goods.

(4.) Every certificate issued by an officer shall be in triplicate, and one part shall be given to the exporter, one to the manufacturer of the goods (if any), and the other or others retained by the Customs or dealt with as the Minister directs.

30. When butter or meat has been inspected and marked in accordance with these regulations, it shall be placed in a cool store at an approved place, at a temperature not exceeding 30 degrees Fahrenheit in the case of butter (except in the case of butter intended for consumption in South Africa, when the temperature may be not more than 40 degrees Fahrenheit) and 20 degrees Fahrenheit in the case of meat, within 12 hours after such examination and marking, and shall not be removed therefrom without the authority of an officer.

31. If the refrigerating machinery in any appointed place is rendered inoperative from any cause, and the temperature of the place thereby rises beyond the prescribed temperature, notice shall immediately be given to the examining officer, who may, if necessary, make a fresh examination of the butter or meat, cancel the certificate already given and the approved stamp applied to the goods, and issue a new certificate and apply another approved stamp to the goods.

32. The Comptroller General may allow any goods mentioned in these regulations which have been examined by an officer for export to be removed from the appointed place to be consumed within the Commonwealth.

33. If an officer have reasonable cause to think that the condition, quality, or class of any goods examined and certified to under these regulations has changed since the examination from the condition, quality, or class mentioned in the certificate, he may re-examine the goods, and, if necessary, cancel the certificate already given and the approved stamp applied to the goods, issue a fresh certificate, and apply another approved stamp to the goods.

34. The approved stamp shall only be applied to goods by an officer and as authorised by these regulations, and all goods bearing or having applied to them an unauthorised impression of an approved stamp or any impression of a stamp so nearly resembling an approved stamp as to be likely to deceive shall be deemed to have applied to them a false trade description.

PART VI.—MISCELLANEOUS.

35. (1.) The Minister may appoint any qualified persons to be analysts under the *Commerce (Trade Descriptions) Act, 1905.*

(2.) All Customs Analysts shall be deemed to be analysts under the Act.

36. Any sample taken by an officer, and submitted for analysis, shall be delivered to an analyst, who shall analyse it, and give a certificate of the result of the analysis to the Collector of Customs for the State.

37. Every certificate of the result of an analysis shall be *prima facie* evidence of the facts therein stated.

38. A copy of any certificate of analysis of butter or cheese given under these regulations may be furnished by the Collector of Customs of the State in which the analysed butter or cheese was made, to the manufacturer thereof, upon payment of one shilling.

39. A register of brands used by owners for any goods specified in these regulations, intended for export, shall be kept by the Comptroller General.

40. Applications for registration of brands shall be made by the owners in Form 12 in the Schedule, which shall be accompanied by seven copies of each brand which it is desired shall be registered.

41. No brand shall be registered by the Comptroller General unless it is registered as a trade mark under a Commonwealth or State Act.

42. A separate registration number shall be allotted to each owner of a registered brand, and the number so allotted may be applied to goods in conjunction with the brand.

43. If a trade mark which is registered as a brand is transferred, notice of the transfer shall be given by the transferree to the Comptroller General.

If a trade mark which is registered as a brand ceases to be registered as a trade mark, its registration as a brand under these regulations shall cease.

A MORAL FROM RECENT SHIPMENT OF APPLES TO ENGLAND.

TO THE EDITOR.

Sir,

I have waited for some recognised authority to point out the obvious (to me) deduction to be made from the fact that a considerable proportion of the fruit in this shipment was seriously affected with fungoid diseases.

I notice that the horticultural expert commenting on the fact recommends elaborate spraying in order to check these diseases. I venture to disagree with him, and I ask you to submit my ideas on the subject to your readers.

I will preface these by stating that for the last two years I have been warning local apple-growers that if they do not drain their orchards they will find, when the time comes for exporting, that their fruit will reach England in an unmarketable condition through the development of the fungoid diseases. I have all along realised the danger which these diseases constituted to the industry; but I submit that prevention is better than cure.

I do not grow many apples, but the experience which I have had with grapes is quite on parallel lines. Starting with no practical knowledge, I read in the textbooks that vines could be profitably grown on poor soil and required little or no manure. Acting upon this, I found that diseases increased in virulence annually. The vines became yearly less vigorous, and the crop was utterly unremunerative.

Judging then that the local conditions, which made it imperative that manure should be poured on to even the best-looking soil, in order that it might become productive, applied equally to horticulture, I started to pour it into the vineyard, and when I thought it necessary I drained it. The result is that I now obtain 10 tons of grapes of first-class quality where I previously secured one ton of inferior, and there is little disease.

The moral is, secure perfect conditions in the orchard or vineyard, and produce vigorous trees, and the result will be less predisposition to disease. Of course where diseases exist, spraying must be done ; but I found spraying quite ineffectual while my vines were unnurtured with manure; and I endorse the expert's opinion, that the best all-round spray is the sulphur, lime, and salt.

I believe that the credit is due to my wife of introducing this remedy into this State. At all events, having tried various specifics—bordeaux mixture for fungoid diseases, sulphate of iron for anthracnose, and a fresh preparation for each malady as prescribed in the *Calendar*—I have eventually decided for simplicity, and I spray every deciduous tree and vine with the cure which she found for me in a Californian paper.

But woe betide all unfortunates who handle it carelessly. If the expert is going to advise this spray for general use, let him in mercy warn his pupils to use it carefully. I have had every finger cut deep into the flesh in the course of one morning through ignorance; and I shall be glad to give away my dearly-bought experience to save others the same cost, if any wish for it.   I am, etc.,

                                                                      J. N. COX.

SOIL ANALYSES.

(Notes on table on opposite page.)

The principal features of these analyses are :—
   (1.) The large number of "acid" soils.
   (2.) The frequent deficiency in lime.
   (3.) The generally low percentage of total fertilising constituents. This deficiency is often made up by mechanical conditions favourable for the free penetration of the root system.
   (4.) The relatively large proportion of "available" to "total" phosphoric acid and potash in some instances.
   (5.) The lack of humus.

It is now pretty generally conceded that a soil must be judged as to its fertility, not so much by its total fertilising constituents, as by the proportion of these which are available for plant life.

Dr. Bernard Dyer, in his Lawes Trust Lectures, in America, stated as a result of the Rothamstead experiments, conducted over a period of 50 years, the following definite conclusions could be drawn, viz. :—That a soil containing as low as ·01 per cent. of phosphoric acid "available" required phosphatic manuring, but when the proportion reached ·03 per cent. that necessity no longer existed. The corresponding limits for potash he placed at about ·005 per cent. and ·01 per cent., respectively. Judged by this standard, many of the soils included in this list have to be considered as containing sufficient potash, although the "total" amount of this present is very small.

This opens up a very interesting field of speculation as regards our soils, in the light of the results which have often been obtained with what were in appearance very poor soils.

SOIL ANALYSES (ON FINE SOIL).
E. A. MANN.

Figures represent Percentage.

Numbers	Locality	Description and Character of Soil, Timber, etc., as supplied with Samples	Reaction	lbs. of CaO to correct acid. (lb per acre)	Fine Soil %	Stones %	Total Phosphoric Acid .15	Available Phosphoric Acid	Total Potash 2	Available Potash	Total Nitrogen Kjeldahl Method .25	Total Lime .4	Chlorine
1	Chapman Experimental Farm—River Flat	Reddish brown sandy loam, virgin soil, big wattle	Slightly acid	1,120	100·	...	·016	·0011	·183	·052	·059	·088	·001
2	Do. do.	Virgin soil big wattle	do.	700	100·	...	·027	·0026	·119	·021	·05	·054	Nil
3	Do. Sand Plain	Virgin soil red, light clay subsoil, low scrub	do.	700	99·73	·27	·015	·0005	·118	·038	·039	·051	·001
4	Do. Home Paddock	Virgin soil, dark clay subsoil, wattle and jam	Neutral		97·48	2·53	·107	·014	·583	·08	·09	1·086	Nil
5	Bridgetown—Slope of Hill	Gritted land unmanured, gravelly subsoil, jarrah and red gum	Slightly acid	1,960	76·93	23·07	·064	·041	·073	·023	·332	·582	·004
6	Do. From Flat	Cultived land unmanured, whitish clay subsoil, jarrah and red gum	Acid	3,080	97·78	2·22	·009	·0045	·038	·018	·251	·221	·008
7	Do. Slope of Hill	Virgin soil, red clay subsoil, blackbutt	do.	2,380	87·8	12·3	·024	·003	·128	·02	·179	·98	·003
8	Hamel, S.W.R., State Farm	do. 9in. deep, flooded gum, banksia, blackboy	do.	840	96·66	3·34	·026	·04	·072	·011	·245	·136	·005
9	Denmark (J. Rutherford, Torbay)	harri, red gum, and wattle scrub	Alkaline	...	91·44	8·56	·015	·0037	·047	·006	·129	·284	·003
10	Mt. Barker, 18 miles West (G. Mullens)	red gum and jarrah	Acid	840	37·38	62·62	·021	·003	·085	·014	·133	·192	·001
11	Mt. Barker (W. Thomas)	white gum	Slightly acid	560	91·76	18·24	·08	·0023	·052	·024	·191	·225	·006
12	Do. West (W. Sounness)	jarrah	Acid	700	98·34	1·66	·015	·014	·016	·0058	·071	·072	·001
13	S.W.R. Coolup Agricultural Area	Virgin red gum and blackboy	do.	1,260	86·92	13·08	·005	Trace	·033	·013	·075	·043	·002
14	Narrogin (Poison Country)	Yellowish white clay loam, 12in.	Slightly acid	560	87·43	12·57	·028	·001	·04	·026	·05	·098	·001
15	Do.	Subsoil 12in.—24in.	do.	560	90·	10·	·015	Trace	·057	·0007	·027	·05·	·002
16	Do.	6d 1 3/4rn km, 12in., orig. red gum, white gum, and jam	do.	840	84·56	15·44	·092	·0028	·055	·0113	·119	·211	·003
17	Do.	Subsoil 12in.—24in.	Neutral	...	88·12	11·88	·019	·0009	·032	·014	·05	·098	·002
18	Do.	Subsoil 12in.—24in.	do.		97·38	2·62	·012	·0005	·038	·014	·027	·11	·002
19	Do.	Soil, sandy loam from flats near Creek's surface	do.		94·89	5·11	·008	Trace	·08	·005	·063	·043	·001
20	Do. (From Granite Hills)	Stiff red day km, subsoil on granite rock	Slightly acid	280	20·2	20·8	·015	·0045	·025	·008	·078	·17	·04
21	Do.	Loose sandy loam, 12in.	do.	420	97·56	2·44	·007	·0007	·098	·002	·077	·077	·008
22	Do.	Subsoil 12in.—24in.	do.	560	44·99	55·01	·017	·0005	·08	·0017	·089	·088	·003
23	Do.	Rich sandy loam, 12in.	do.	700	98·28	1·72	·025	·0035	·025	·0123	·089	·153	Nil
24	Do.	Subsoil 12in.—24in.	do.	420	94·79	5·21	·012	·0015	·024	·001	·048	·058	·002
25	Chidlow's Well	Chocolate clayey loam	Slightly acid	470	96·13	187	·017	·001	·022	·005	·071	·048	·002
26	Do.	Dark brown, stiff clayey loam	Neutral		99·3	·7	·017	·0016	·07	·018	·157	·321	·002
27	Do.	Brown clayey loam	do.		83·	17·	·045	·421	·179	·021	·175	·343	·001
28	Do.	Red chocolate clayey loam	do.		93·38	6·62	·031	·001	·106	·02	·061	·404	·008
29	Do.	Drab stiff clayey loam	Slightly acid	392	89·45	10·55	·028	·0002	·273	·009	·105	·251	·004
30	Do.	Brown sandy loam	do.	392	84·	16·	·024	·0008	·112	·01	·092	·22	·003

Bold figures in heading denote standard for a good soil.

TURKEY RAISING.

So far but very little has been done in regard to turkey raising on a large scale in this State. At a few stations considerable flocks have been raised, which have proved very profitable to those engaged in the undertaking. They do very well in most parts of the country, the dryer localities suiting them best. They cannot be raised profitably in or near towns, as abundant scrub and unlimited range is essential. To those contemplating a start, it has been recommended that a two-year gobler and about eight second seasons' hens will form the best nucleus for a flock.

The birds are easily reared, and if allowed sufficient country for them to ramble over they will feed themselves, and can be brought to a marketable condition at very little expense, and the price obtained is always remunerative. Some excellent stud birds are now in this State, no expense having been spared by breeders in obtaining the best birds of the bronze varieties from the United States of America and elsewhere. Anyone engaged in this industry should pay particular attention to securing a good gobbler, as he will soon improve the quality of the flock, whereas with an inferior bird the flock soon deteriorates, and it is only the best birds that obtain the highest prices, and they cost no more to rear than the inferior ones. Plate I. shows a flock of bronze turkeys at Mr. McKenzie Grant's Newmarracarra estate, in the Geraldton district, where turkey raising has been extensively entered upon. The birds are allowed to roam all over the country and to lay their eggs where they like, and in due course they return home with their young ones, the losses being very few. During the past season about 1,000 young turkeys have been raised on this estate.

The bronze turkey is in most respects superior to any other kind (so says an American exchange), a statement with which we agree. The writer goes on to say: "This breed being hardier is more likely to live when very young, and when once grown up it is beautiful and very large. The same amount of food, in fact, will produce in it as much as double the weight possible to be obtained in the ordinary turkey. For example, mammoth bronze male turkeys have been reared upon farms before now, which only one year old weighed 40 pounds and over apiece—a weight exceeding that of the ordinary kinds, under like conditions, from 20 to 25 pounds. Indeed it is no great trouble to get young bronze turkeys to weigh from 20 to 25 pounds, and frequently as high as 35 pounds each, by Thanksgiving or Christmas, in which case they will command in the market a ready sale at prices also better than those paid for the smaller varieties. The most essential point, remember, is to get them started right. A turkey generally lays as many as 25 to 30 eggs before she thinks of incubating; therefore the first dozen ought to be removed from her nest and set under a hen. Why? Because this leaves the turkey about what she can cover and hatch out nicely.

"Then when the little birds are hatched, each of them, as a precaution against vermin and the like, should be greased with some sweet cream on the top of its head, down its throat, and under its wings. Next a large, roomy, movable coop should be prepared, in which to keep the mother and

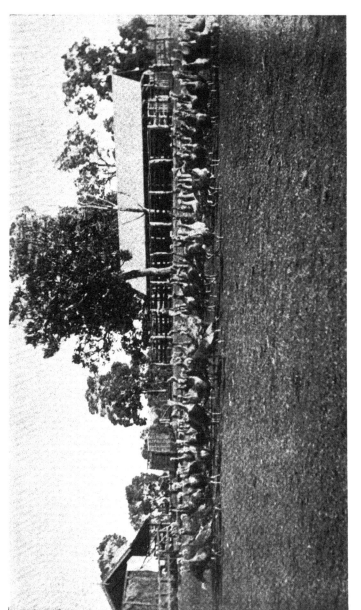

Flock of Bronze Turkeys at Newmarracarra.

her brood until the latter has grown and gained strength, for if allowed to roam at large with them she is liable to wander so far that her little ones will be worn out and unable to return with her. And on what should they be fed? Why, the best things at first are hard-boiled eggs mixed with bread crumbs. Soon a change of diet is necessary, however, and then oat-meal and boiled rice should be given, and later on wheat. Young onions, if chopped fine, will also be greatly enjoyed, and as these are wholesome, the feeding of them, where practicable, should never be neglected. Still, it will not do to overfeed young turkeys (nor old ones, either, for that matter), since that might prove not only a drawback to their growth, but even in reducing the weight previously gained. Furthermore, the disarrangement sustained by the digestive organs, in their being overtaxed, might bring on some one of the many diseases which are so common among poultry, and which, if once firmly established, are very hard to break up and successfully eradicate. Young turkeys, therefore, should be fed regularly, and as the food in their crops digest very quickly, they should be fed quite often and not too much at a time.

" When they get old enough they should be allowed to run at will, and not be restricted, except that they should roost indoors at night and not be left out in any cold, severe storms. The time of winter markets once beginning to draw near, however, they should for several days prior to disposal be deprived of their daily expeditions, confined in narrow quarters, and there fed on purely fattening foods; in other words, given no green material whatever, but rather an abundance of corn, wheat, and similar flesh-producing eatables, care being exercised that none is left after meals to sour and spoil, for this is liable to take away the birds' appetites, and then next to nothing can be done with them. Feed, therefore, regularly and often, and to help fatten them give them more or less milk to drink. Thus dealt with the flesh produced will be more tender and juicy than could be obtained in any other way. This is a fact, for even the flesh of an old gobbler, if only fattened in this manner, will be found tender and juicy— nearly as much so as that of young birds. If you doubt, just make the experiment some time for your own satisfaction."

In reply to questions asked by correspondents, Mr. Baird, late manager of the Government Experimental Farm at Chapman, supplies the following particulars of the flock kept on the farm while he was there:—

The breeding stock kept was about 15 hens and two gobblers.

The young stock bred from them would number from 100 to 120 each year. The birds during the winter and spring roamed over a large area, sometimes going a distance of 2¼ miles away and keeping chiefly amongst the scrub. After the crops are harvested the turkeys confine their attention to the stubble fields.

The birds were not artificially fed at any time.

As the hens laid away in the scrub a record of eggs laid could not be kept. The birds hatched early in the season, and have a hard time of it through exposure, many of the hens returning home without a chick.

The birds were not supplied with grit.

The birds were only penned for culling at the commencement of the breeding season, when a number would be kept penned up for a few weeks.

The netting fence was 6ft. high, but it was necessary to cut one wing to prevent them flying over. The young birds reared in the pens do not attempt to fly over.

Birds are ready for market when about six months old.

In ordinary scrub land from 300 to 500 head could be run on about 1,000 acres of land together with other stock.

PASPALUM GRASS.

The following very interesting letter was recently received by Mr. Teesdale Smith from Mr. B. Harrison, a gentleman residing at Burringbar, Tweed River, and has been handed in for publication :—

"I have just read in the *Western Australian* of December 23rd of the projected relinquishment of the timber industry by your company in the Denmark region, where 'Agricola' says 'there are thousands of acres of land of first-class quality, consisting of a red loamy formation resting on a clay subsoil,' and 'your company's line of railway, 29 miles in length, also affords access to additional immense areas of Crown lands of a similarly satisfactory character.' I have read the article which I have just quoted, with great interest, more especially as I know from many years' experience what immense profits and progress your company could make if it embarked in the dairying industry and stock raising, profits from which very few of your landowners in Western Australia have but a faint idea.

"This will be readily apparent to you after the perusal of my circular, a copy of which I enclose, and I also forward you a small sample of seed. I feel confident that the marvellous paspalum grass would do well in the Denmark district, and in conjunction with the dairying industry would return greater profits than would ever be possible with the timber industry.

"The paspalum grass has proved a mine of wealth to the North Coast; it grows in all classes of soil, even on barren sand, and preserves its verdue through summer and winter. Any land on which this grass is established is worth £10 to £20 per acre, and in this district has reached the reserve price of £32 per acre, and the annual rent for paspalum pasture varies from £1 to £1 10s. per acre.

"A creamery could be erected for £10,000 or £15,000 and if one was erected I feel certain that your land would soon be settled with a large population of thriving farmers.

"It is unnecessary to say more on this subject just now, as my circular and letter will amply prove the truth of my suggestion, which I trust you will carefully consider, and in the meantime I beg to subscribe myself.

PASPALUM DILATATUM.

"P.S.—I would feel pleased if you would kindly send reply, and I will give any further information on this subject at any time. Paspalum grass is already growing well in several places in Western Australia, and Mr. W. C. Grasby, of the *Western Mail*, says it gives greater promise of success than any grass yet introduced into that State."

The following letter was written by Mr. Harrison and published in the Press on this subject:—

"Would you kindly permit me to give your readers a little information about this celebrated grass which is already growing in many places in your State, and which will, I feel certain, prove of inestimable value to the farmers of Western Australia when they become acquainted with its excellent qualities. The great want in your State, judging from all I have heard and read, is a good and abundant summer grass, and paspalum is the fodder plant for this purpose. Mr. C. F. Julius, secretary of the Dairymen's Union, Bucca Creek, N.S.W., says in the *Agricultural* (Government) *Gazette* :—'This remarkable plant is quickly coming to the forefront as a grass peculiarly adapted to our uncertain climate. Being a deep-rooter, its properties as a drought-resister alone proclaim it invaluable, and while throughout the warmer seasons of the year it surpasses all other grasses in the rapidity and abundance of its growth, the severest of our frosts, although retarding its growth, fails to subdue its evergreen state.' It is most efficacious in subduing and preventing noxious growth—a great point in its favour in Western Australia particularly, where the poison plant is so prevalent and proves so injurious to stock. The *Agricultural Gazette* also says:—'A pasture of paspalum generally thrives so vigorously as to take complete possession of the ground to the extermination of all the other growth.' This is the favourite grass with the stockowners and dairy farmers on the North Coast of New South Wales, to whom it has proved a mine of wealth, as it is unequalled, not only for its abundant yield and its adaptability to grow well in all classes of country, but also for its fattening and butter-yielding qualities. The Byron Bay Butter Factory, which was established by our farmers about ten years ago, now pays away annually about £36,000 per month to its suppliers for cream and pork, and the cows from which the milk for this factory is obtained are almost exclusively grazed on paspalum, and very few of them are either hand-fed or housed during the winter months. I feel certain if the farmers and stock-raisers of Western Australia were acquainted with the great value of this marvellous grass they would not delay in cultivating it extensively, which, when once established, remains permanent and enriches the soil in which it is grown, and in Western Australia should carry a bullock per one acre and a half. In the Tweed district it carries more than one head per acre, but the soil is richer here and the rainfall greater than in your State. I need not state the different varieties of soil in which it grows, except to say it thrives best in a moist situation, although it grows well even on the hard bare ridges and soils where other artificial grasses would prove a complete failure. The *Agricultural Gazette* writers also say, 'Our experience goes to prove that paspalum will grow well and yield abundantly on poor soils in dry areas.' Mr. Grasby, writing in the *Western Mail* of the 6th January, quoted many instances of its successful growth in Western Australia, and he also says that there are local varieties which cause the market gardener some trouble to eradicate. This fact alone would prove that this celebrated grass would do well in many places, as similar conditions would suit the cultivated variety. In purchasing seed, great care should be exercised, as much of that obtained from seedsmen is of very poor quality, and judging from the correspondence I have received from people in the other States, very little, if any, of the seed they have purchased has germinated, thereby causing dissatisfaction and much loss. At the Hawkesbury College only about 2 per cent. of the seed would germinate, although the grass grew well.   Mr. Jas. King, president of the Tweed River Dairymen's Union, says :—' Seed that is grown in this (the Tweed) district is generally well developed.   Indeed, if properly harvested, almost every seed will grow.'   This should be borne in mind by those desirous of obtaining good seed, and would prevent both loss and disappointment.   Land laid down with paspalum (after being sown with seed at the rate of 15 or 20 lbs. per acre) should be worth from £10 to £15 per acre.   I noticed in the *Western Mail* that at Wagin there are 3,000 acres of timber felled and ready to be burnt off or fired shortly.   If this ground was sown with paspalum and a co-operative butter factory erected it would prove an object lesson to the farmers of Western Australia, who do not appear to have an idea of the immense profits to be made from dairy-farming.   Mr. G. H. Varley, editor of the *Clarence and Richmond Examiner*, is well known, and this is what he says of ' Paspalum in the North ' :—' In a letter on the North Coast Railway proposition, Mr. G. H. Varley, of Grafton, made several references to the virtues of *Paspalum dilatatum*, which shows what wonderful fodder that grass supplies.   Having mentioned the preponderance of forest ridge country, he says, "Critics will probably suggest that this class of country is of little value for grazing dairy cattle.   But in this connection they may not understand the wonderful adaptability of paspalum to this variety of country.   It is a wonderful fodder plant.   Given a sufficiency of moisture, it will flourish in all classes of soil.   I have seen it luxuriating in the swamps, with water over its crown ; in the Big Scrub in its glory ; but nowhere have I seen it grow with greater luxuriance than on the forest ridges.   A few years ago the Richmond was threatened by a weed called the Mullumbimby Couch.   Cattle fell away on it, and many died.   Since the introduction of paspalum this weed has had notice to quit.   As in quality, so in growth, as compared with other grasses—it is paspalum first, the rest nowhere.   It is only the construction of this railway and the throwing open of these reserves which will attract settlement.   Under these conditions an energetic man, backed up by *Paspalum dilatatum* and cows, is almost sure of success.   Take the "big scrub" of the Richmond as a case in point.   Fifteen years ago this magnificent tract of country was practically in its primeval state.   It was equally provided then, as now, with steam communication to Sydney.   No point of it was more remote than 15 miles from water carriage.   Yet no progress was visible.   Five years later the railway from Lismore to the Tweed was opened.   From that day the jungle began to disappear, and to-day the whole face of the country is altered, paspalum dilatatum being substituted for scrub, and dairy cows for paddymelons.   One butter factory alone, which opened with the advent of the railway, has increased its output from one ton a month to 350 tons a month.   A herd of cows will easily average £10 per head per annum.   One farmer (resident in the Coramba district) published his receipts for one year, which showed a credit balance of £600.   His area was only 160 acres.'

" Mr. H. Munsey, of Dundas, N.S.W., says : ' Paspalum is the grass that has revolutionised the dairying industry on the North Coast.   Scores of instances can be quoted showing that the capacity of farms has been doubled and trebled, and it forms a dense mass of succulent forage. Having spent over a month going through farms where this grass has been sown, I can safely recommend its planting on a large scale. I have seen farms where 100 head of dairy cattle have been kept all the year round on less than 100 acres of land, giving splendid returns in milk and butter. This grass, if enclosed for a short period during the autumn, will provide a good supply of feed for the winter. Its value at this stage cannot be expressed in thousands of pounds. In conclusion, I need only say, as Mr. Jas. King (President of Tweed River Dairymen's Union) says, "that to write of the merits of paspalum would require a newspaper." '

"In conclusion, Mr. Editor, I must apologise for trespassing at such length on your valuable space, and I most sincerely hope that what I have written may prove of great benefit and value to the farmers in your State, who should not hesitate or delay in bringing about an era of prosperity by establishing good and abundant pasture—the first step towards founding dairy factories which have proved such a great boon to the settlers in the other States. I will be only too pleased to give any further information to anyone, providing they forward stamps for reply, and thanking you in anticipation,

I am, etc.,

Burringbar, Tweed River, N.S.W.   B. HARRISON."

THE LABOUR BUREAU.

REPORT FOR JULY.

The report of the operations of the Labour Bureau for the month of July, 1906, is as follows :—

PERTH.

The total number of individual men who called during the month in search of work was 608. Of this number, 306 were new registrations and 302 renewals—i.e., men who called who had been registered during the year prior to the month of July.

The engagements for the month numbered 140. The classification of work found was as follows :—Labourers, 28 ; farm hands, 23 ; handy boys, 13 ; handy men, 11 ; wood cutters, 8 ; bushmen, 7 ; grooms, 7 ; gardeners, 6 ; yardmen, 5 ; cooks, 4 ; boys for farms, 3 ; bridge hands, 3 ; carpenters, 3 ; dairymen, horse-drivers, shepherds, teamsters, 2 of each, and 11 miscellaneous.

KALGOORLIE.

The applicants for work numbered 96. There were 55 new registrations and 41 renewals.

Work was found for 25 men, classified as follows:—Labourers, 12; handy youths, 3; batterymen, cooks, and miners, 2 of each; butchers, boilermakers, engine-drivers, and handy men, 1 of each. The female applicants for work were 37. There were 16 new registrations and 21 renewals. The engagements were 2—viz., barmaid and general.

WOMEN'S BRANCH, PERTH.

There were in connection with the women's branch, Perth, 96 new registrations and 103 renewals. The engagements numbered 60, classified as follows :—Laundress-charwomen, 21; generals, 14; light generals, 10; cook-laundresses, 4; useful girls, 4; housemaids, 3; nursemaids, 2; cook, 1; waitress, I.

GENERAL REMARKS.

The number of individual men who 'called at the central office, Perth, during the month was 608. This is 14 short of the number for June, and 150 less than that for July last year. The engagements were 140, being seven short of the total for June, and 56 less than that for July last year. At Kalgoorlie branch the applicants for work numbered 96, as against 99 for the previous month, and 191 for the month of July, 1905. The engagements were 25, as against 18 for June, and 16 for July, 1905. At the women's branch, Perth, 199 women called during the month. As compared with the previous month that number is 29 short, and also 29 for that of July last year. The engagements were 60, as against 67 for June, and 76 for July 1905. At Kalgoorlie the women who called numbered 37, as against 45 for June, and 82 for July, 1905. The engagements were two, as against one for June, and 12 for July last year.

In a few days a branch of the bureau will be opened at Northam, in charge of the land agent. It will deal largely with agricultural workers, and it is to be hoped may be the means of assisting farmers in that and the the surrounding districts to find suitable employees. The Northam branch will be worked in conjunction with the central office, and vacancies which cannot be filled in the one office will, where possible, be filled from the other.

FOR SALE.

3 PURE BRED Middle YORKSHIRE BOARS,

Recently imported from Victoria.

Apply

The Manager,

State Farm, Narrogin.

HORSES' FEET.

Probably more horses are deteriorated in value through bad shoeing than by any other means. It is not only in the horses which are temporarily or permanently lamed or crippled that the evil is so conspicuous as in those which are spoiled through being shortened in their action and losing that free elasticity which does so much to make a pleasant hack or really first-class driving horse. The habit of stumbling is also largely a result of bad shoeing. The common error of inferior smiths is to interfere too much with the natural formation of the hoof. In this matter, as in most others, the wise course to follow is that which, as far as possible, leaves Nature alone. Indeed, when subject to entirely natural conditions it is better to leave the hoof in its original condition. Hard roads, however, and even constant riding over hard, grassed land, such as is so common in Australia, are not natural work for the equine foot, and, therefore, certain artificial aids are necessary ; but it should be borne in mind that such aids are useful only when they protect the natural growth and help the natural functions. Take, for instance, the frog of the foot. It acts as a soft buffer between the weight of the animal and the ground, so as to deaden the force of of contact, and help the great numbers of small joints in the pastern joint to withstand the shock which accompanies every step. The frog of the foot prevents windgalls and preserves the elasticity of the limb, besides protecting the foot itself. Yet it is no uncommon practice for smiths to leave the heel of the foot so high that when the shoe is placed on it, the frog is far removed from the field of possible contact with the ground. The inevitable consequence is that the organ, deprived of its natural function, dwindles, and the heel contracts. If the foot does not become afflicted with some definite pathological condition it at any rate grows so distorted that it strains the leg, which in turn gives way, and the work of the inferior smith is then complete. Every unshod horse walks largely on his frog. Examine the foot of a colt which has never had a shoe on him, and you will see a great big frog covering half the sole. You will see that when the foot is put to the ground the sole carries the weight before the toe is laid flat. If you find an old horse which has never been shod, you will find an ever-bigger frog ; you will also discover that it is tough and elastic. The frog on a long-shod and badly-shod horse is hard, like a piece of the wall of the hoof. "But," the prejudiced smith will argue, "if I rasp away the wall of the hoof at the heel and let the frog on to the ground, it will become bruised, and your horse will then be lame perhaps for three months, while he is growing a new frog." But this argument is mostly wrong and altogether misleading. If a horse has been shod in the wrong way for many years, and the frog has lost its power of functionising, and has grown hard, and quite incapable of forming a cushion, then, of course, contact with the ground may cause bruising. But then that is only another fact against the practice of throwing the frog out of use. If the horse had been shod in the right way from the commencement, it would not have been so easy to bruise the foot by correct shoeing at a later date. Of course, when a horse has to work with regularity on a hard metal road, there is reason for giving more protection to the frog than would be warranted under conditions more similar to those which are natural. Work on a paved road is altogether unnatural, and the preparation for an unnatural strain must necessarily be of an artificial character. But it is, of course, notorious that horses used on metal roads break down in the legs much quicker than those which run on softer tracks; and the reason of this, I think, mostly is that the former have of necessity to be shod in a way which does not protect the foot from abnormal growth, nor the joints above from jar. But even for work on metal roads, experience will show that the business of protecting the frog is overdone. It is not necessary to have the frog a full inch from the area of contact. On the contrary, it would be beneficial to have it just level with the shoe, not protruding below the shoe, so that it would be bruised and injured, but low enough to give it slight concussion so as to keep it in health and expanded. Sometimes the fault does not lie solely with the smith, for people often think a horse is not properly shod unless his heels are high and both frog and sole cut away with a knife. The two ideas are equally wrong. —Port Lincoln *Recorder.*

THE JERSEY COW AT HOME.

The following article, written by C. Stein, for *The Live Stock Journal*, may prove of interest to our readers :—

We have all been long familiar with the appearance of Jersey cattle in English fields and parks, and have appreciated the picturesquely graceful contrast that they offer to the home-reared " milky mothers of the herd ; " but many of us have only indefinite notions as to their origin and life history. True, there has been a Jersey Cattle Society in England since 1878, but though we are familiar with it and the good work that it is doing, we have still something to learn about its *raison d'être*, and of the characteristics of the animals in which it interests itself. Some notes made by a casual visitor to Jersey, who has had the honour and great privilege to meet many gentlemen most intimately connected with the interests of the Island breed of cattle, may give a modicum of additional information on the subject, even though the visitor himself can only claim the most distant bowing acquaintance with the ethics of flocks and herds in general.

The first thing that strikes even the most casual observer who strolls along a Jersey road is that the cattle in view everywhere are not, as in England, turned into a pasture and allowed to graze at liberty where they will. No; every animal is tethered by a chain passing round the base of the horns, is confined to a very moderate radius from the picket peg, and is left to make the best it can of the herbage that it can find. Its ground is shifted from time to time, but not until it has pretty thoroughly accounted for the pasture within its reach. And there are excellent and convincing reasons for this. Most important is the economical gain. It is to be remembered that the grazing area in the island is very limited, and that it is essential that no scrap of possible food should be wasted. There is here no question of "three acres and a cow," and the proportion is more like a cow to half an acre. We all know how dainty are English cattle in their choice of grass, and how they persistently ignore and spoil much that is perfectly wholesome and nourishing, confining their attention to that which best tickles their palate. Much good and useful herbage therefore dies down without its existence being of profit to anyone. But a Jersey cow is, as a rule, by no means habituated to luxury at home, and will make a meal on vegetation at which an English cow would turn up its nose. And, compared with an English meadow, even the best pasturage in Jersey seems poor. It is sometimes almost incredible how the Island cattle find enough to eat on which to maintain their condition. The writer has even seen, though this is, of course, an extreme case, cows grazing contentedly, and apparently with profit to themselves, on spots near the coast, where there was little growing but gorse and heather. Certainly, for economy's sake, and to avoid unnecessary pampering, the tethering system has very marked advantages, and its results are that the Jersey cow, in its natural condition, will live and thrive where an English cow would be near starvation. In this the relation between the two animals resembles that between a pure-bred Arab, which will eat the roughest of provender, and an English horse, which is unhappy unless it is provided with the best of everything. Then, again, in small holdings one field may have a portion devoted to grazing and the rest carrying roots, or perhaps two different other crops. If on the grazing portion the cows were not tethered they would naturally invade the rest of the field, doing themselves no good, and ruining the cultivation. Finally, when cows of any breed are at complete liberty, there is always a possibility that they may develop a quarrelsome nature, or at least indulge in rough play, sometimes, as it were, running amok among their comrades, breaking horns or otherwise doing irremediable harm.

Wherever one goes in Jersey, no essential variety is to be noticed in the type of animals on the many holdings, and nothing like the heterogeneous mixture to be found on most English farms anywhere meets the eye. One feels as if one was walking through the domains of a breeder who devoted all his energies to produce a single type of animal, and that alone. And this is practically the case. The island is small (only about 28,700 acres), and can easily and completely be controlled by the local government, aided and supported, of course, by the good sense of the people. It is devoted to the interests of its own characteristic breed of cattle, and will have nothing to do with any other. No individuals of any strange breed are admitted within its precincts, no possible risk is run of an admixture of outside blood, and for many generations the breed has remained pure and uncontaminated. Precaution is carried so far that no animal which has once quitted the island is permitted to return, and one example is recorded of the strict way in which this regulation is enforced. Some cattle were, on one occasion, being shipped to England, but, a heavy gale coming on, their vessel was driven back to port, and it was necessary to have a special Act hurriedly passed by the States before they could be allowed to disembark on the quay until the weather moderated.   Without this legalised concession they must have been there and then slaughtered.

The Jersey cattle are supposed by some to have sprung from far distant progenitors in Normandy, by others that their ancestry was Breton; but none have any certain data for their theories, and after all the matter is of little real importance.   Undoubtedly, many long ' years ago, their character had already been altered, improved, and confirmed into a special type by time and care, by the influence of natural surroundings, and by complete isolation.   Even in the early part of the eighteenth century it was recorded that the Island cattle may do very well in Jersey, of the neighbouring districts in France, and this superiority has been accentuated by constant legislation since that time.   The first of several Acts of the States of Jersey prohibiting the import of cattle into the Island was passed in 1763, and this, with the others, has never been relaxed.   It is true that there was one exception, when, about 60 years ago, some Shorthorns and Ayrshires were introduced with the intention of improving the Island breed; but the crosses turned out so badly that all the foreigners were quickly turned into beef.   Only on that occasion has the perfect purity of the Jersey type ever been tampered with, and practically for now nigh 150 years it has been most jealously guarded.

A word may here be said about the cognate breeds of cattle in Guernsey and Alderney.   There are very well marked differences between them and the Jersey cattle, but the points of difference would take too long to describe.   It is sufficient to note that the Alderneys resemble the Guernseys, though they are of a more refined type.   It is said, indeed, that if Guernsey cattle are moved to Alderney, in very few generations they fine down to the Alderney size and character.   The peculiar features of both, therefore, must probably be due to unidentified surrounding conditions.   The distant origin of all the cattle in the Channel Islands is very probably identical, but, whether this is the case or not, the Jerseys have now been formed by a long train of circumstances into an unmistakably distinct race.

It may be permitted to an outsider to think that, in some important respects, size, character of head, richness of milk, and general hardiness of appetite and constitution, the Jersey cow has some affinity with the Kerry, and it may also be noticed that in our Indian Empire the once famous Amrit Mahal cattle*, which were peculiar to Mysore in the last century, have very much the same physical appearance, though as they were peculiarly valuable as draught oxen, the milking powers of their cows have not been much considered.   They have the same deer-like head, clean limbs, and generally aristocratic air as are to be found in the Jersey herds, and when, as in the West Indies, they have been imported to improve the larger and grosser breeds, the influence of their blood has been of most marked value.

The number of cattle in Jersey is now about 11,000, and it may be taken that though, of course, there are great varieties of merit in individuals, there is no single animal in the Island in whose veins does not flow the

---

* The Amrit Mahal cattle were the wonderful draught animals that dragged the artillery of Hyder Ali in his campaigns with the English, and afterwards that of General Wellesley (the great Duke) during the Mahratta war.   The unexpected celerity of Hyder's movement on Bednore, and his good fortune in saving his guns after his disastrous defeat by Sir Eyre Coote at Porto Novo were entirely due to the staunchness and activity of his gun bullocks, which moved his batteries at a quicker pace even than the march of his infantry.

perfectly pure blood of the race, and that is not entitled to call itself a relation of the animals bearing the most distinguished names in the Herd Book, much as the humblest Scottish clansman in old times could always proudly reckon himself a kinsman of his chief. And the mention of the Herd Book leads one to remember with how much zeal and self-devotion the Royal Jersey Agricultural Society, founded in 1833, has worked to maintain in its highest development the breed of cattle forming the glory of the chief among the Channel Islands. In 1866 a Herd Book was established under its auspices, and the conditions of registration in this Herd Book are so stringent and so closely adhered to that the appearance of an animal's name in its pages is a guarantee not only of blood, but of personal merit. In England every calf that is born, the names of whose sire and dam appear in a Herd Book, is *de facto* entitled at its birth to registration in the same Herd Book without any consideration of its individual quality, and the result is that the Herd Books contain many names of little credit. In Jersey quite another system is pursued. The birth of a calf may, indeed, be immediately officially registered, but entry in the Herd Book is a matter for the future, and is only accomplished after the animal has been inspected and criticised by a committee of inspectors, three in number. Committees, whose members are constantly changing, visit the various districts of the Island at intervals, and then adjudicate upon the worthiness of the young stock that are brought before them by the breeders, and they give or withhold the imprimatur of entry in the Herd Book. There are many rules and regulations by which they are guided, but the principal among them seem to be (1) that every bull calf, to be seen as a yearling, must be accompanied by its dam, so that the character of the latter may be weighed in considering the merit of its offspring; and (2) that no heifer, whatever her pedigree, will be looked at until she has borne a calf, as then only can her capacity as a milk-producer be observed. After passing the judging committee each animal receives a certificate of qualification, and must be either commended or highly commended, so that the breeder, without the trouble and expense of exhibiting at an agricultural show, is able to obtain the soundest and best opinion as to the comparative merits of his young stock. Of course such a system is only possible in a small and easily organised island like Jersey, and would be quite impracticable in England; but, none the less, it is a monument to the clear sightedness of its originators, and a credit to the zeal and energy of those who still carry it out.

It might possibly be supposed that a breed of animals so long and so closely hedged round by precautions against outside influences might show deterioration from in-and-in-breeding, but practically this is found to be by no means the case; in fact, it is with good grounds believed that the type of animals is constantly improving. Beyond the experience on this point, gathered within recent memory, there are in existence in Jersey pictures of cows drawn more than 100 years ago, representing animals whose shape and general character would now be considered very defective; and these pictures thus prove that careful mating and the advance of scientific knowledge in the management of stock have attained the ends that were desired in the improvement of the race, without suffering any drawbacks from the deprivation of an admixture of fresh blood. The truth is that, though the island is small, it is quite large enough to allow considerable distances between breeders' farms, and though a total of 11,000 head seems no great number, it is sufficient for the existence of many absolutely distinct families. One thing is certain—there is no endemic disease among Jersey cattle. Tuberculosis is quite unknown, and so marked and irrefutably established is its absence that Jersey enjoys the privilege of exporting cattle to America without their previous examination for this disease, a privilege conceded by the United States to no other country. Other complaints—anthrax, redwater, etc.—unfortunately so rife elsewhere, have never made their appearance in this happy land, and it is therefore abundantly evident that there is no delicacy in the constitutions of its cattle.

The Jersey cattle are essentially milk and butter producers, but as beef producers they are of very small value. In their own particular sphere of usefulness they are, if the English agricultural world would only believe it, pre-eminent. But long as the breed has been familiar in our islands, and great as has been the advance in that familiarity during the last 20 years, thanks to the exertions of 'the English Jersey Cattle Society, many people at home, to whom the knowledge of a Jersey cow's good qualities should be of the greatest practical value, remain ignorant of them, or at least unaccountably apathetic in profiting by them. Other nations have recognised long ago their own best interests, and have come to the little island in the Channel for the means of strengthening and improving their dairy farms. Very large numbers of animals have been exported to the United States; and Denmark, which takes a premier position in Europe as a butter-producing country, buys hundreds of cows yearly. In England alone there is no general demand among dairy farmers for these unequalled milkers, and it is notorious that, when a member of the Jersey Cattle Society wishes to sell any of his stock, first rate as it may be, he can rarely find a buyer except in the ranks of the society itself, and is confronted with the fact that his wares are generally contemned and ignored. Let us examine the matter for ourselves and see what the qualities of a Jersey cow really are. When she is two years old she will, on an average, yield about 450 gallons of milk in the year, and when she comes to maturity this yield will probably increase by degrees to an amount of from 60 to 650 gallons. At six years old the yield is generally at its maximum. When the small live weight of the animal is taken into consideration, and also the proportionately small quantity of food that she requires to keep her in health, this must be considered to be quite a satisfactory performance, even with regard to quantity alone, as compared with the yield of cows belonging to the larger breeds which are popular in England. But the quantity of milk is not the only criterion. Its quality is a more really important matter. And here we meet the somewhat startling fact that the Jersey cow's milk is richer in butter-fat than that of cows belonging to any other breed of dairy cattle. In order to produce one pound of butter only two gallons of milk are required *on an average* (the average number of gallons derived from British cows that is required to make a pound of butter is three), though this proportion is very frequently much improved upon and it is by no means uncommon to produce one pound of butter from one gallon of milk. Here it is worth while to note the officially certified record lately published of a Jersey cow's yield in Denmark during one year. The cow produced in the year 10,327lbs. of milk (10lbs. equal one gallon), and from that milk was made 878lbs. of butter. It was calculated that the net profit for the year earned by the cow was about £30, and when it is remembered that the careful Danes give the lowest possible prices for cows, and that the cow in question had certainly not cost more than £15 at the outside, this return must be considered to be handsome indeed. Of course it is not to be hoped for that this performance can often be equalled, but it indicates very clearly what are the potential capabilities of a Jersey cow. Another characteristic of Jersey cows is that they continue in milk almost indefinitely. They very frequently go on yielding till within a fortnight of calving, and cows have been known to give milk for two, or even three years without intermission. This is naturally bad and exhausting for the individual cows, and it becomes necessary to take measures for arresting this natural lavishness of production.

What, then, are the conclusions that must force themselves upon the mind of an unprejudiced observer, who has had an opportunity of seeing the Jersey cow at home, has heard its life conditions described by the people most interested in its welfare, and has some slight knowledge of the general position of the dairy industry in England? We know at any rate, that in our country this industry is very far from being prosperous and satisfactory. The largest proportion of the butter here consumed is imported, and not only is it imported, but it is of far higher average quality than that of home production. Despite the many admirable agencies that have been for some years working to improve English dairy produce—dairy schools, butter factories, co-operative dairies, etc,—the fact remains that that produce lags terribly in the rear, and that it has made no really effective efforts to overtake the success which is to be found elsewhere. May not one of the reasons for this national shortcoming be found in a lack of system in providing the milk itself? The British farmer, in procuring the cows that are to supply his churns, is under the influence of an idea so long cherished that it has almost become a fixed principle. He wants to have animals that, in the first place yielding milk, will also have such physical proportions as to bear calves profitable for sale as meat, and that will themselves fetch a good butcher's price, if they become barren. The two ends are practically incompatible, and between two stools the farmer falls to the ground; his milk supply is not what it should be, and his loss in this respect is by no means out-weighed, or even balanced, by a profit on dead meat. He cannot, for very many obvious reasons, alter the whole constitution of his herd ; but why should he not, more often than is now the case, do something to improve the general quality of his milk, by invoking the assistance of a Jersey cow or two? In the first place, a proportion of Jersey cow's milk, being as it is of such a rich description, does, when mixed with other milk, improve the standard of the whole, and guarantees that it can always and easily stand the Government test. In the second place, the admixture of a milk containing the greatest known proportion of large fat globules is highly advantageous in increasing the yield of cream and butter by assimilating the smaller globules of other kinds of milk, and making them more profitable for producing butter than they would be otherwise. The milk of a Jersey cow, in fact, exercises a special influence for good in a mixture of milks quite apart from the superior qualities which it individually contributes. All this has long been recognised in the United States and Denmark, where butter-making is scientifically conducted, with results that are patent to the world. Why should English dairy farmers, as a rule, ignore an obvious truth, reject a certain source of profit, and allow themselves to be outstripped in an industry which ought to be peculiarly their own ? If an improved dairy system was followed, the consumer of butter in England would also be a gainer, for more and better butter would be produced in the country, and he would begin to know the luxury of really fresh butter. At present, comparatively very few people, even among the well-to-do, have ever tasted fresh butter. The imported article, however good it may be in quality, must inevitably have been made a long time

before it comes into the market, and must have lost something of its pristine
freshness and flavour.

An apparently strong form of argument against the value of Jersey
cows is frequently brought forward in England—that the Island cattle were
much superior to those, but that when they are brought across the Channel
they are not really adapted to our country and climate, and do not therefore
fill a useful place as compared with our home breeds.   Evidently a very
sufficient answer may be given by pointing to their glowing reputation in
the United States and Denmark.   It certainly cannot be said that in North
America or North Europe is the climate milder, more equable, or more
identical with that of the Channel Islands than is the climate of Britain,
and yet, in both regions, the Jersey cattle have found a sufficiently congenial
home, and have asserted their peculiar excellence.   And in addition, it may
be pointed out that some dairy-farmers in England (though, unfortunately,
a small percentage of the whole class) have used Jersey cows to improve the
general quality of their milk, on the lines indicated on a preceding page,
and have found their profit in so doing.

It would have been presumptuous in a casual observer to offer a
personal opinion upon the various debatable points connected with Jersey
cattle, which have been touched upon.   He has only recorded the impressions
made upon his mind by the apparently very cogent arguments on the subject
which he has been privileged to hear from those who are exceptionally
qualified to speak.

GARDEN NOTES FOR SEPTEMBER.

By PERCY G. WICKEN.

September may be considered the spring month of the year, the soil
becomes warmer, plants begin to make growth, and it should be a busy time
in the garden, as most kinds of summer vegetables can be sown during this
month.   In addition to planting seasonable seeds, the ground must be kept
free from weeds and well worked up to conserve the moisture, while any
land not required for immediate use should be dug over so as to bury all the
weeds and prevent them from maturing their seeds.   As the weather
becomes warmer, a look out must be kept for grubs and other insect
enemies, as at this time of the year they do an immense amount of injury
to the young plants, which are more susceptable to attack than when they
become more matured.   For caterpillars and grubs, the plants should be
sprayed with Paris Green made up in the proportion of one ounce of Paris

Green to 10 gallons of water; first make the Paris Green into a paste, and then add the water. Keep well stirred while using, and remember that it is an arsenical poison and should not be used on vegetables ready for market.

For most other pests, Bordeaux mixture is about the best remedy. In districts where fungus diseases or scale are likely to appear, the young plants should be sprayed as soon as they are a few inches high. It is better to prevent the attack than have to combat the pest when it has become established.

All ground which it is intended to use for summer crops should be well broken up, as deeply as possible; trenching or subsoiling will be found to pay for the labour expended. For plants to grow and mature during the dry weather, the roots must be able to penetrate deeply into the soil.

Stable manure, nightsoil, bonedust, blood manure, and such like fertilisers should be dug into the ground some time before the crop is sown, the more soluble fertilisers should be applied when the seed is planted; or as a top dressing later on when the plant is several inches high. The time to plant most of the spring vegetables is governed by the likelihood of frost. If the more delicate plants come above ground while frosts occur and means are not taken to protect them they will be killed, and the beds will require resowing; as soon as danger from frost is over in the different localities, planting should be proceeded with.

Asparagus.—If the crowns have not already been planted out, they should be moved at once, before the shoots begin to make any growth. The land should have been previously trenched and well mixed with rotted stable manure.

Artichokes (Jerusalem) should be planted out this month; the tubers should be cut into small pieces and planted out the same as potatoes. They are very hardy and will grow in sandy soil and stand a lot of dry weather. They should be planted out in rows three feet apart, and about two feet apart in the rows. The top of the plant is similar in appearance to a sunflower. The tuber is valuable both as a vegetable and as a food for stock.

Arrowroot is well worth cultivating; it is both ornamental and useful. The *Canna edulis* is similar to the flowering Canna in appearance, but yields large quantity of bulbs, which are valuable for pig feed or for making arrowroot or starch. The best arrowroot is made from a plant, *Maranta arundinacea*, which grows in warmer localities and does not grow as large as the *Canna edulis*.

Beans (French and Kidney) are one of the most popular and easily grown vegetables. The ground should be well worked and fertilisers containing potash, phosphoric acid, and lime should be supplied. Those containing nitrogen are not required for this crop. Sow the seed in drills three feet apart and one foot apart in the rows. The Butter Bean and Wax Bean are good varieties to grow, as they are less stringy than some of the older sorts.

Beet (Red).—A few rows may be sown to keep up a supply. The seed should be soaked before planting, as this will help it to germinate quickly.

Beet (Silver).—Put out all the young plants you have of this vegetable or a little seed may be sown in rows. It is a splendid vegetable for the dry weather, as it gives a supply of green leaves when vegetables are scarce.

Cabbage.—Plant out any young plants that are available. Give them plenty of fertiliser to force their growth. Liquid manure or 1oz. of nitrate of soda dissolved in one gallon of water will help them along.

Carrots.—A few more rows may be sown; the ground should be dug deeply and manured some time before the crop is sown. Sow in drills two feet apart and about four to six inches apart in the rows.

Celery.—Plant out all well-grown young plants, and earth up those more forward, so as to cause them to bleach.

Cucumbers.—In nearly all parts seed may be sown in the open, and young plants raised in beds may be planted out. While any danger of frost remains, the plants should be protected at night; a few bushes laid over the bed will answer the purpose. The plants or seeds should be planted on hills slightly raised above the surface, the soil having been previously worked deeply and well mixed with stable manure. The hills should be from six to eight feet apart each way, and from four to six plants should be left in each hill. Put in double this number of seeds and thin the plants out when they come up.

Leeks.—Sow a little seed to keep up a supply, and plant out all young plants that are available.

Lettuce.—Sow either in a seed bed or direct into drills, and thin out as soon as the plants are a few inches high.

Onion.—Plant out seedlings in ground that has been well manured with rotted stable dung, and work the surface soil as finely as possible. Blood manure and bonedust should be liberally supplied and well worked into the surface soil. Plant in drills from six inches to two feet apart, according to variety, and about four to six inches apart in the drills. Keep the drills free from weeds and the land between the rows well hoed.

Melons.—Both rock, water, and preserving melons can be planted during September. Holes should be deeply worked to at least a depth of two feet and stable manure well mixed with the soil; the roots penetrate deeply into the soil to enable them to withstand the hot weather. The holes should be hilled up slightly, so as to bring them about one inch above the surrounding ground. For strong running vines the holes should be 12 feet apart each way, but for the smaller vines they need only be half that distance. The land between the holes should be kept free from weeds. Water and preserving melons should not be planted near to each other, as they cross-fertilise, and both varieties are useless. A handful of superphosphate worked into each hole will help the plants along.

Peas.—In cooler localities a few rows of the quick-growing varieties may be sown. The earlier sown ones that have commenced to run will require to be staked.

Potatoes.—In most parts the potato crop has been sown, but there are many localities in the South-West where planting can be carried out for some time. On some of the swamp land potatoes can be planted all the summer. Potatoes require to be manured with a complete fertiliser, and one containing a good supply of potash.

Pumpkins and Squashes should be largely sown during this month. They should be prepared and the seed sown as previously described for melons. The bush varieties do not take up so much room, and yield very early fruit. The "white bush" marrow and the "custard squash" are some of the earliest.

Sweet Potatoes.—If not already planted, put out in seed beds as described last month. Those that were planted early will soon be sending out shoots, that should be planted out into the field as early as possible. They succeed best when planted in ridges. The ridges should be about three feet apart, and the shoots or cuttings should be planted about 18 inches apart in the ridges. They require ground that has been deeply worked.

Tomatoes.—Those who put out early plants in sheltered beds or under glass should now have forward plants, while many who go in for intense culture will no doubt have forward plants growing in the open. In the Geraldton District the plants should be well established, while further South they will not yet be ready for transplanting. Put the plants out in rows about three feet apart, and as they grow tie them up to stakes and keep the fruit off the ground. Give the ground a liberal supply of fertiliser, and spray the plants with Bordeaux mixture as a preventative against disease.

Farm.—In the drier districts, fallowing will be almost completed, but where the ground has become too wet to carry the teams ploughing operations will have to be postponed until the spring. Where it has not been possible to fallow the land for next year's crop before the heavy rains set in, the work should be carried out as soon as possible after the land is in a fit state to be worked. The land should be ploughed before it becomes dry, and the surface harrowed so as to conserve as much moisture in the ground as possible. If the ploughing has to be done after the ground has become hard, the disc ploughs can be used to advantage.

Large areas of fallow ground are often left idle, which might be turned to much better advantage by growing such crops as rape, mustard, kale, etc. These crops can be fed off by sheep, and the bulk of the crop returned to the ground in the droppings of the sheep. After the crop has been fed off, the land can be ploughed again and will yield a much better crop than if allowed to lie idle.

Land should be ploughed as deeply as possible, and prepared for sowing summer crops, most of which can be sown in September, and will provide valuable fodder for the stock on the farm during the dry months. Pumpkins and squashes, melons, buckwheat, sunflowers, mangels, sugar beets, maize, sorghums, broom millet, Hungarian millet, French millet, and chicory, etc., can all be sown, especially in the cooler districts. As these are all summer crops, and have to stand a lot of dry weather, they should be sown in drills from 30 to 36 inches apart, and the cultivator should be kept constantly going between the rows, so as to keep the surface soil well stirred.

The success or failure of summer crops depends largely on the amount of cultivation given to the soil, and as these crops will provide fodder at a time when fodder is scarce, they should be given special attention.

The Bush Fires Act prohibits burning off in the Eastern districts after October 1st, consequently the work should be pushed forward during September so as to get the work in hand finished by the end of the month.

In the earlier districts, haymaking is often carried out at the end of September, and although this year it may be somewhat later than usual, all farmers should get their harvesting machinery in readiness and secure such duplicate parts as are likely to be required, so that no delay may occur when harvesting operations commence.

LOCAL MARKETS' REPORTS.

Messrs. H. J. WIGMORE & Co.'s REPORT.

Messrs. H. J. Wigmore & Co., of Fremantle, Perth, Kalgoorlie, and Northam, report as follows for month ending Wednesday, 8th inst. :—

Chaff.—Supplies from the country during the month have been fairly well maintained, an average of about 100 trucks per week having come forward. During the past week, however, consignments have fallen off very considerably, and we are pleased to advise that the market closes much firmer than has prevailed for some time. We secured £5 this morning at auction on a yarding of only four trucks for f.a.q. to prime wheaten, and, given a continuance of normal supplies, we see no cause for any depreciation in values, which close as follow :—Prime green wheaten, £4 17s. 6d. to £5 ; f.a.q. wheaten, £4 12s. 6d. to £4 15s. ; good medium wheaten, £4 7s. 6d. to £4 10s.; medium and inferior rades correspondingly lower. We sold cow chaff at yesterday's sales at £4 2s. 6d., but this price must not be accepted as market value. Prime oaten chaff is worth £4 12s. 6d. to £4 15s.; good medium to! f.a.q. oaten, £4 7s. 6d. to £4 10s. Importations of South Australian chaff continue to arrive in considerable quantities by various steamers from Adelaide, and last week over 600 tons were landed at Fremantle. Very little of this, however, has been placed on the Perth market for auction, and this fact, coupled with the recent exceptionally small arrivals of local chaff, has been instrumental in avoiding an easier tendency in local values. We learn that cancellations of heavy contracts of South Australian chaff have been effected by importers [here, and these cancellations will also, no doubt, act beneficially towards hardening values locally. By no means the last of the shipments of South Australian chaff have come forward, however, and farmers must remember that nearly all Perth and Fremantle produce merchants have their stores full of the imported article, and will not bid at auction prices above imported equivalent. Altogether, we again advise farmers that high prices cannot reasonably be expected, and we anticipate that the market will continue to remain in the vicinity of £5 to perhaps £5 5s. until the new season. Producers must also take into consideration that there are now practically only two clear months in which to market before new season opens, and that it is by no means a certainty that a considerable quantity of chaff will not be carried over this season, while, on the other hand, there was no carry-over last season. We are advised of cutting operations now being commenced in various country centres, and probably the ensuing month will see local chaff arriving more freely and regularly to Perth market. In conclusion, we may mention that a considerable proportion of the chaff now coming forward is damaged by rain in transit, and we cannot too strongly urge farmers to see that their trucks are always carefully and completely covered with sound sheets.

Wheat.—Since we last reported to this *Journal* this commodity has eased considerably, and at the moment absolutely highest market value in Perth for prime milling sorts is 3s. 6d. to 3s. 6½d. This fall has been due to somewhat heavy arrivals, and this month farmers generally appear to have been more anxious to market their wheat, apparently fearing a further decline, which has eventuated. Very few of the mills are purchasing, being, as a rule, fully stocked, and the demand in Perth, being almost solely for fowl feed, is necessarily small. Unfortunately we cannot see any prospect of improvement in this market, and are rather inclined to the opinion that prices will ease still further with even normal consignments forward.

Markets in the Eastern States are quiet, and little business is passing. Adelaide quotes 3s. 4½d. to 3s. 5d. for f.a.q. aboard, and Melbourne slightly easier at 3s. 3½d. to 3s. 4½d. f.o.b. South Africa has been enquiring recently, and we understand that good business is expected from Adelaide at above figures.

Oats.—Algerians have eased somewhat during the month, and good feeds are now quoted at 2s. 7d. f.o.b. Melbourne. A firmer market, however, is quite possible in the near future. On spot sales have been made of Algerians whole at 3s. and crushed at 3s. 0½d., these prices allowing no margin for the importer at present Melbourne cost f.o.b.

Stouts.—We have very little alteration to report. Spot sales have been made at 3s. 6d. to 3s. 7d.

Flour.—Business during the month has been limited. For Thomas & Co.'s "Standard" flour we continue to quote £7 10s. f.o.b. Port Adelaide for sacks, quarters £7 15s.; on rails Northam £8 and £8 5s. sacks and quarters respectively.

Bran and Pollard.—Sales on spot have been made at £5 7s. 6d. to £5 10s. for each commodity. Very little alteration to report in the Eastern States, latest quote being 9¼d. to 9⅜d. f.o.b. Sydney for bran, and 9¼d. to 9½d. for pollard. Bran 10d. Adelaide.

Potatoes.—Inquiries are now coming to hand for seed potatoes, and we have made considerable sales both f.o.b. and on spot for the popular varieties, such as Early Rose, Vermonts, Beauty of Hebrons, Up-to-Dates, Carmens, and Sutton's Flour Balls. We shall be pleased to supply farmers requiring with either of these varieties.

Jute Goods have somewhat eased. We hold stocks to arrive from Calcutta of both bran bags and corn sacks, and will be pleased to quote farmers requiring.

KALGOORLIE CHAFF MARKET.

This market closes firm at £5 10s. to £5 12s. 6d. for prime green wheaten, and £5 7s. 6d. for f.a.q. wheaten. As usual, other grades are difficult to quit at satisfactory prices, and we can only recommend consignments to this centre of best quality chaff.

NOTES ON THE CLIMATE FOR JULY, 1906.

Judging by the climatological returns the month has been on the whole a fairly seasonable one, though the prevailing impression seems to be that this month, and in fact the winter generally, has been unusually wet. In West and South districts it was colder than usual, but in North and East portions the temperature was considerably in excess of the average for previous years.

The total rainfall was heavier than usual throughout the Central and Southern agricultural districts and on the Goldfields, elsewhere it was about normal, though, judging by personal sensations, the rain appeared to be more persistent than usual.

The heavy fall above mentioned was due to a "low" which approached Geraldton from the Indian Ocean on the 9th, and then passed overland to Esperance, reaching the latter place on the morning of the 10th. This is worthy of record, as the winter storms generally keep south of our coast. Another species of disturbance is worthy of being placed on record, because it probably belongs to a type which frequently brings general rain and plays an important part in our climatology, though on the present occasion only a few light showers fell. It consists of the passage of cloudy threatening weather from the N.W. coast throughout our Murchison and Goldfields districts and on to South Australia, leaving the S.W. portions fine and clear. This occurred between the 1st and 3rd of the month. The conditions appeared to resemble a summer monsoon, but barometers were very high, and surface winds easterly throughout. It is on such an occasion as this that well-made observations in the upper regions of the atmosphere would doubtless prove both interesting and valuable.

On the morning of the 19th the lowest shade temperature ever recorded at the observatory was reached, viz., 36·5°. This seems to have been one of the coldest nights ever experienced in the State, as many stations recorded a minimum lower than any previous reading. The temperature on the surface of the ground fell to 21° at Southern Cross and Walebing. Frost was occasionally reported during the month, but does not appear to have been very severe. The following table shows the average and absolute minimum temperature recorded by a thermometer placed upon the surface of the ground:—

Station.	Mean.	Lowest.	Date.
Peak Hill	40·0	29·0	31
Cue	41·0	27·0	19
Coolgardie	36·9	26·0	20
Southern Cross	35·4	21·2	19
Walebing	31·6	21·0	19
York	35·6	27·0	2
Perth Observatory	42·4	83·0	19
Wandering	31·6	22·3	1
Bridgetown	35·6	27·0	2
Karridale	41·0	26·0	3
Katanning	34·8	25·0	3
Mount Barker	37·8	29·4	29

The Climate of Western Australia during July, 1908.

Locality	Barometer (corrected and reduced to sea-level)				Shade Temperatures July, 1908					Average for previous yrs.				Rainfall		
	Mean of 9 a.m. and 3 p.m.	Average for previous years.	Highest for Month.	Lowest for Month.	Mean Max.	Mean Min.	Mean of Month.	Highest Max.	Lowest Min.	Mean Max.	Mean Min.	Highest ever recorded.	Lowest ever recorded.	Points (100 to inch) in Month.	Wet Days.	Total Points since Jan. 1.
NORTH-WEST AND NORTH COAST:																
Wyndham	29·981	30·035	30·147	29·812	88·5	70·5	79·5	93·0	66·2	85·0	65·2	94·8	50·0	Nil	..	1,383
Derby	29·986	30·036	30·171	29·857	88·6	69·3	79·0	93·8	51·0	84·9	58·6	94·0	42·0	102	3	1,119
Broome	29·982	30·039	30·168	29·843	84·7	62·1	73·4	92·8	51·2	81·2	57·9	92·5	40·2	11	2	972
Roebourne	30·018	30·088	30·250	29·844	77·6	55·1	66·4	88·5	42·8	76·1	50·1	88·8	38·0	41	2	556
Cossack	30·015	30·099	30·290	29·830	78·0	57·0	67·5	90·0	47·0	74·7	54·7	92·0	43·7	111	2	504
Onslow	30·034	30·090	30·334	29·810	78·1	55·0	66·6	88·8	42·8	75·5	51·9	88·0	44·0	52	4	243
Winning Pool	30·043	..	30·331	29·790	75·1	52·9	64·0	87·0	45·0	..	..	..	..	219	8	425
Carnarvon	30·052	30·132	30·354	29·803	69·7	52·3	61·0	82·0	42·8	71·2	49·6	81·7	40·5	234	8	306
Hamelin Pool	30·084	30·139	30·438	29·766	68·5	49·0	58·8	77·0	42·8	68·5	47·7	77·2	35·6	106	9	200
Geraldton	30·102	30·154	30·486	29·672	66·6	50·7	58·6	76·2	40·0	68·5	49·7	81·0	34·9	454	12	1,137
Hall's Creek	30·082	30·114	30·287	29·834	85·6	56·0	70·8	93·0	44·0	78·3	47·9	92·0	35·0	Nil	..	395
INLAND:																
Marble Bar	30·067	30·136	30·373	29·720	81·0	54·2	67·6	91·0	43·0	78·8	52·6	88·0	38·0	93	3	934
Nullagine	30·085	30·172	30·470	29·730	77·6	50·8	64·2	89·4	32·2	72·2	44·4	82·0	28·9	28	1	682
Peak Hill	30·081	30·160	30·499	29·674	67·0	47·0	57·0	82·0	38·0	63·9	43·9	78·3	34·0	147	7	255
Wiluna	30·115	30·190	30·530	29·740	66·3	44·2	55·2	84·0	32·0	63·5	39·2	77·4	28·9	82	6	435
Cue	..	..	..	..	66·0	45·0	55·5	80·0	32·0	65·0	43·8	78·2	33·2	129	8	338
Murgoo	30·108	30·174	30·511	29·684	64·6	45·3	55·0	78·0	36·5	..	..	..	..	203	7	351
Yalgoo	..	30·200	..	..	63·2	43·7	53·6	78·5	31·8	64·4	42·0	78·0	30·7	211	9	604
Lawlers	30·120	30·222	30·611	29·648	63·9	44·9	54·4	83·6	29·8	62·7	41·4	78·0	31·4	108	6	510
Laverton	30·112	30·198	30·610	29·652	64·7	42·6	53·6	86·0	28·0	61·8	39·4	76·8	29·0	84	8	522
Menzies	..	..	..	..	62·1	43·0	52·0	82·0	30·0	61·6	41·7	77·0	31·2	134	5	571
Kanowna	30·072	30·192	30·3	29·561	61·0	41·3	51·2	76·0	30·0	..	..	..	..	140	8	566
Kalgoorlie	30·093	30·180	30·655	29·556	60·8	43·5	52·2	80·0	31·0	61·5	42·4	76·2	31·7	125	9	474
Coolgardie	30·099	30·170	30·666	29·572	59·8	41·9	50·8	78·9	30·1	61·0	41·2	75·3	31·9	88	10	502
Southern Cross	..	..	..	..	59·8	39·5	49·6	75·2	25·0	61·8	38·6	79·0	25·0	193	12	628
Kellerberrin	..	..	..	..	59·1	38·2	48·6	70·3	28·2	..	..	..	..	299	11	719
Walebing	..	..	..	..	60·9	40·0	50·4	70·8	28·5	59·8	39·8	71·7	28·2	522	15	1,421
Northam	..	..	..	..	60·4	39·0	49·7	71·0	29·8	61·2	39·6	72·0	30·2	438	14	1,043
York	30·086	30·162	30·676	29·501	62·0	43·0	52·5	78·0	32·8	62·0	40·5	71·2	27·6	405	14	939
Guildford	..	..	..	..	..	..	..	..	..	63·1	43·5	73·3	31·5	639	16	2,070

The Climate of Western Australia during July, 1906—continued.

Locality.	Barometer (corrected and reduced to sea-level). Mean of 9 a.m. and 3 p.m.	Average for previous years.	Highest for Month.	Lowest for Month.	Shade Temperatures. July, 1906. Mean Max.	Mean Min.	Mean of Month.	Highest Max.	Lowest Min.	Average for previous Years. Mean Max.	Mean Min.	Highest ever recorded.	Lowest ever recorded.	Rainfall. Points (100 to inch) in Month.	Wet Days.	Total Points since Jan. 1.
Perth Gardens ...	30·072	30·144	30·620	29·441	61·3	46·5	53·9	69·6	37·0	63·2	46·0	72·6	34·0	581	18	2172
Perth Observatory	30·086	30·150	30·657	29·452	61·0	43	53·6	69·2	36·5	62·8	47·5	73·8	37·9	603	17	2153
Fremantle ...	30·101	30·134	30·656	29·504	61·0	5·1	65·0	69·0	39·0	62·6	0·3	78·4	41·0	471	17	1611
Rottnest ...	30·087	30·120	30·644	29·466	60·0	51·9	56·0	67·2	45·0	62·0	52·9	70·0	40·4	417	20	436
Mandurah ...	...	...	...	...	61·1	43·5	52·3	65·6	33·4	62·3	45·0	70·6	31·3	596	20	2761
Marradong ...	...	...	...	...	...	...	...	...	...	...	...	...	...	585	14	1746
Wandering * ...	...	...	...	...	57·9	36·9	47·4	67·1	28·0	58·6	39·1	68·0	27·8	689	17	1622
Narrogin ...	...	...	...	...	...	...	...	...	...	...	...	...	...	508	17	1857
Collie ...	...	...	...	...	58·0	37·7	47·8	67·2	28·0	59·0	38·4	68·7	26·9	782	20	2493
Donnybrook ...	30·061	30·126	30·676	29·411	57·4	38·4	47·9	65·0	30·0	60·5	41·2	0·3	30·6	668	19	2621
Bunbury ...	...	...	...	...	60·3	45·8	53·0	65·2	36·2	62·7	46·5	72·2	35·9	628	19	2118
Busselton ...	30·080	...	30·630	29·390	59·6	43·2	51·4	77·4	34·0	60·6	43·8	66·5	32·5	588	24	2237
Cape Naturaliste	...	...	...	...	58·0	49·0	53·5	67·0	42·0	...	...	...	...	588	22	2161
Bridgetown ...	30·065	30·102	30·600	29·250	58·2	37·7	48·0	67·1	28·9	59·5	38·3	6·1	25·9	557	20	2249
Karridale ...	29·990	30·059	30·670	29·215	59·7	51·2	55·4	61·0	41·0	61·2	46·6	70·8	30·6	738	25	2607
Cape Leeuwin ...	30·060	30·133	30·669	29·477	56·9	40·6	48·8	60·8	44·2	61·2	52·5	70·6	43·0	538	26	2200
Katanning ...	...	...	...	...	55·4	41·1	48·2	66·5	32·0	58·4	40·4	62	25·0	343	16	1108
Mt. Barker ...	30·000	30·084	30·679	29·334	58·7	44·5	51·6	66·2	33·8	60·8	44·8	73·5	33·5	379	22	1835
Albany ...	29·990	30·074	30·668	29·296	57·4	43·5	53·0	69·0	35·5	59·3	49·3	71·8	40·0	534	22	2859
Breaksea ...	...	...	...	...	61·1	45·3	53·2	68·8	39·0	62·6	44·8	77·8	33·0	479	22	2031
Esperance ...	30·022	30·128	30·641	29·443	61·0	41·7	51·4	77·5	36·0	61·2	40·2	76·5	26·2	422	18	563
Balladonia ...	30·065	30·162	30·632	29·522	64·8	45·8	55·3	81·2	34·0	62·1	41·6	78·1	27·2	78	13	471
Eyre ...	30·025	30·174	30·550	29·506	...	...	...	89·0	34·5	...	...	...	...	184	14	645

INTERSTATE.

Perth ...	30·066	30·150	30·657	29·452	61·0	46·3	53·6	69·2	36·5	62·8	47·5	73·8	37·9	603	17	2153
Adelaide ...	30·042	30·168	30·641	29·320	60·0	46·2	53·1	74·0	39·3	58·7	44·3	72·5	32·7	287	...	1341
Melbourne ...	29·966	30·025	30·471	29·234	56·4	44·2	48	64·9	33·0	55·5	41·4	68·4	27·0	134	...	...
Sydney ...	30·050	30·115	30·880	29·580	62·0	46·0	54·0	72·0	38·0	58·9	45·7	74·9	35·9	20	1	1709

SOUTH-WEST AND SOUTH COAST

* Averages for three years only.

The Observatory, Perth, August, 1906.

W. E. COOKE, Government Astronomer.

RAINFALL for June, 1906 (completed as far as possible), and for July, 1906 (principally from Telegraphic Reports).

Stations.	June. No. of points 100 = 1in.	June. No. of wet days.	July. No. of points 100 = 1in.	July. No. of wet days.	Stations.	June. No. of points 100 = 1in.	June. No. of wet days.	July. No. of points 100 = 1in.	July. No. of wet days.
EAST KIMBERLEY:					N.W. COAST—cont.				
Wyndham	Nil	...	Nil	...	Balla Balla	...	...	...	...
6-Mile	Nil	...	...	...	Whim Creek	351	2	58	2
Carlton	Nil	...	...	...	Mallina	...	...	...	...
The Stud Station	Nil	...	...	...	Croydon	262	2	...	...
Argyle Downs	...	...	...	...	Sherlock	...	...	...	...
Rosewood Downs	...	...	...	...	Woodbrooke	350	2	...	...
Lisadell	...	...	...	...	Cooyapooya	...	...	...	...
Turkey Creek	Nil	...	Nil	...	Roebourne	391	3	86	4
Ord River	...	...	...	...	Cossack	288	2	111	2
Alice Downs	...	...	...	...	Fortescue	126	2	51	2
Flora Valley	...	...	...	..	Mardie	148	2	...	...
Hall's Creek	Nil	...	Nil	...	Chinginarra	150	2	...	...
Nicholson Plains	...	...	...	...	Yarraloola	...	...	...	...
Ruby Plains	...	...	...	...	Peedamullah	136	2	...	...
Denison Downs	...	...	...	...	Onslow	99	3	52	4
					Point Cloates	98	3	...	...
WEST KIMBERLEY:									
Mt. Barnett	...	...	...	...	N.W. INLAND:				
Corvendine	...	...	...	...	Warrawagine	...	...	...	...
Leopold Downs	Nil	...	...	...	Eel Creek	305	2	...	...
Fitzroy Crossing (P.O.)	Nil	...	5	2	Muccan	...	...	...	...
					Ettrick	480	2	...	...
Cherrabun	Nil	...	...	...	Mulgie	...	...	...	...
Bohemia Downs	Nil	...	...	...	Warralong	...	...	...	...
Quanbun	...	...	...	...	Coongon	295	2	...	...
Nookanbah	...	...	...	...	Talga	346	2	...	...
Upper Liveringa	...	...	Nil	...	Bamboo Creek	450	2	47	3
Yeeda	...	...	...	...	Moolyella	...	...	...	...
Derby	Nil	...	102	3	Marble Bar	357	2	93	3
Pt. Torment	Nil	...	...	...	Warrawoona	258	3	84	1
Obagama	Nil	...	...	...	Corunna Downs	...	...	...	...
Beagle Bay	Nil	...	...	...	Mt. Edgar	...	...	...	...
Roebuck Downs	...	...	...	...	Nullagine	157	2	28	1
Kimberley Downs	...	...	...	...	Middle Creek	186	2	...	...
Broome	Nil	...	11	2	Mosquito Creek	240	2	...	...
Thangoo	...	...	...	...	Roy Hill	166	2	...	...
La Grange Bay	19	1	17	5	Bamboo Springs	...	...	...	...
					Kerdiadary	Nil	...	...	...
					Woodstock	...	...	...	...
N.W. COAST:					Yandyarra	...	...	...	...
Wallal	145	2	2	1	Station Peak	...	...	...	...
Pardoo	...	...	...	...	Mulga Downs	Nil	...	...	...
Condon	295	5	41	2	Mt. Florence	...	...	...	...
DeGrey River	446	2	...	...	Tambrey	...	...	...	...
Port Hedland	350	3	52	3	Millstream	140	2	...	...
Boodarie	255	2	35	2	Red Hill	...	...	...	...

RAINFALL—continued.

STATIONS.	JUNE. No. of points. 100 = 1in.	JUNE. No. of wet days.	JULY. No. of points. 100 = 1in.	JULY. No. of wet days.	STATIONS.	JUNE. No. of points. 100 = 1in.	JUNE. No. of wet days.	JULY. No. of points. 100 = 1in.	JULY. No. of wet days.
N.W. INLAND—cont.					**YALGOO DISTRICT**—contd.				
Mt. Stewart	...	...	...	...	Mullewa	139	10	362	10
Peake Station	...	...	...	...	Kockatea	116	6	...	...
Nanutarra	...	...	...	...	Barnong	72	4	221	3
Yanrey	...	...	...	...	Gullewa	...	...	...	...
Wogoola	99	4	...	...	Gullewa House	98	11	295	8
Towera	90	4	...	...	Gabyon	166	8	...	...
					Mellenbye	100	8	258	9
GASCOYNE:					Wearagaminda	99	8	234	10
Winning Pool	119	4	219	8	Yalgoo	147	7	211	9
Coordalia	...	...	...	...	Wagga Wagga	95	6	186	7
Wandagee	...	...	...	...	Muralgarra	...	...	181	9
Williambury	...	...	...	...	Burnerbinmah	78	6	191	8
Yanyeareddy	...	...	...	...	Nalbara	79	7	139	10
Maroonah	...	...	...	...	Wydgee	91	8	...	...
Ullawarra	...	...	...	...	Field's Find	91	7	153	6
Mt. Mortimer	...	...	...	...	Rothesay	...	...	...	...
Edmunds	66	4	...	...	Ninghan	171	9	227	8
Minnie Creek	117	3	...	...	Condingnow	178	9	214	10
Gifford Creek	...	...	...	...	163-Mile	94	5	...	...
Bangemall	40	2	...	...	Palaga Rocks	80	4	...	...
Mt. Augustus	...	...	...	...	126-Mile	157	7	...	...
Upper Clifton Downs	77	3	...	...	90-Mile	224	6	...	...
Clifton Downs	2	1	...	...	Mt. Jackson	260	9	130	8
Dairy Creek	45	3	...	...					
Mearerbundie	28	5	...	...					
Byro	...	.	...	...	**MURCHISON:**				
Meedo	27	2	...	...	Wale	111	3	...	...
Mungarra	41	3	...	...	Yallalonga	140	5	...	...
Bintholya	...	...	...	...	Billabalong	...	...	...	...
Lyons River	...	...	...	...	Twin Peaks	146	6	...	...
Booloogooroo	...	...	...	...	Murgoo	107	3	203	7
Doorawarrah	13	3	...	...	Mt. Wittenoom	98	5	...	...
Brick House	...	...	...	...	Meka	82	3	...	...
Boolathana	24	4	...	...	Wooleane	57	4	...	...
Carnarvon	63	5	234	8	Boolardy	27	3	...	...
Dirk Hartog	184	14	333	...	Woogorong	73	4	...	...
Shark Bay	151	8	134	7	Manfred	20	4	...	...
Wooramel	32	5	133	8	Yarra Yarra	28	3	...	...
Hamelin Pool	55	9	106	9	Milly Milly	35	1	...	...
Kararang	201	11	...	...	Berringarra	49	2	...	...
Tamala	252	10	...	...	Miloura	69	5	...	...
					Mt. Gould	...	...	...	...
					Moorarie	16	2	...	...
YALGOO DISTRICT:					Wandary	...	...	...	...
Woolgorong	136	6	...	...	Peak Hill	84	3	147	7
New Forest	161	8	...	..	Mt. Fraser	...	...	...	...
Yuin	84	5	189	7	Minderoo	45	2	...	...
Pindathuna	110	6	...	...	Abbotts	31	1	84	3
Tallyrang	103	5	...	...	Belele	23	1	93	3

RAINFALL—*continued.*

Stations.	June. No. of points. 100 = 1in.	June. No. of wet days.	July. No. of points. 100 = 1in.	July. No. of wet days.	Stations.	June. No. of points. 100 = 1in.	June. No. of wet days.	July. No. of points. 100 = 1in.	July. No. of wet days.
MURCHISON—*contd.*					COOLGARDIE GOLD-FIELDS:				
Meekatharra	...	...	...	...	Waverley	88	4	124	5
Star of the East	38	1	100	2	Bardoc	92	5	128	5
Nannine	22	1	103	2	Broad Arrow	132	7	136	6
Annean	62	2	...	...	Kanowna	120	6	140	8
Tuckanarra	Nil	...	...	...	Kurnalpi	129	6	156	9
Coodardy	25	2	...	...	Bulong	125	6	125	7
Cue	65	5	129	8	Kalgoorlie	131	7	125	9
Day Dawn	72	2	86	5	Coolgardie	131	6	88	10
Lake Austin	93	3	125	5	Burbanks	145	6	77	6
Lennonville	122	7	117	8	Bulla Bulling	128	6	125	10
Mt. Magnet	74	4	100	8	Woolubar	114	5	107	6
Youeragabbie	38	2	...	...	Waterdale	163	6	92	7
Murrum	55	2	146	5	Widgiemooltha	149	5	74	11
Challa	76	3	146	7	50-Mile	85	4	83	9
Nunngarra	72	2	...	...	Norseman	101	7	91	10
					Lake View	74	8	95	15
					Frazer Range	153	7	...	...
EAST MURCHISON:					Southern Hills	133	4	...	...
Gum Creek	100	2	...	...					
Dural	60	3	...	...					
Wiluna	82	4	82	6					
Mt. Sir Samuel	115	3	139	5	YILGARN GOLD-FIELDS:				
Leinster G.M.	...	...	...	...	129-Mile	150	6	...	...
Lawlers	54	3	108	6	Emu Rocks	137	9	...	...
Lake Darlôt	101	3	...	...	56-Mile	100	7	...	...
Darda	91	2	...	...	Glenelg Rocks	115	12	...	...
Salt Soak	117	2	...	...	Burracoppin	119	5	277	6
Duketon	197	2	...	...	Bodallin	37	3	241	4
					Parker's Road	86	6	218	4
NORTH COOLGARDIE GOLDFIELDS:					Southern Cross	99	9	193	12
Burtville	...	...	...	...	Parker's Range	93	12	232	11
Laverton	96	3	84	8	Yellowdine	108	7	194	10
Mt. Morgans	75	2	82	7	Karalee	180	5	200	5
Murrin Murrin	42	3	57	4	Koorarawalyee	130	4	230	8
Mt. Malcolm	39	1	42	2	Boorabbin	127	7	168	8
Mt. Leonora	71	3	65	3	Boondi	135	6	165	9
Tampa	68	2	87	3					
Kookynie	61	2	120	7					
Niagara	75	2	107	7	SOUTH-WEST (NORTHERN DIVISION):				
Yerilla	100	2	...	...	Murchison House	192	10	...	...
Yundamindera	52	2	105	5	Mt. View	79	6	...	...
Mt. Celia	80	3	58	8	Mumby	240	10	414	9
Edjudina	65	1	82	8	Northampton	342	12	595	10
Quandinnie	135	2	...	...	Chapman Experimental Farm	204	9	467	7
Menzies	90	3	134	7	Narra Tarra	269	10	...	...
Mulline	94	3	143	6					
Mulwarrie	183	7	196	8					
Goongarrie	118	5	123	8					

RAINFALL—continued.

Stations.	June. No. of points 100 = 1in.	June. No. of wet days.	July. No. of points 100 = 1in.	July. No. of wet days.
SOUTH-WEST (NORTHERN DIVISION)—contd.				
Oakabella ...	252	11	...	...
White Peak ...	355	10	457	10
Geraldton ...	372	13	454	12
Hinton Farm ...	274	11	542	11
Tibradden ...	296	15	547	13
Myaree ...	229	14	...	...
Sand Springs ...	...	...	...	...
Nangetty ...	...	...	...	...
Greenough ...	304	11	42	11
Bokara ...	380	12	451	11
Dongara ...	466	14	504	12
Strawberry ...	321	15	661	13
Yaragadee ...	141	10	...	...
Urella ...	150	4	448	3
Opawa ...	184	14	365	10
Mingenew ...	234	15	485	10
Yandenooka ...	213	15	481	11
Carnamah ...	284	16	384	10
Watheroo ...	269	14	427	14
Nergaminon ...	...	...	...	...
Dandaragan ...	454	13	734	12
Yatheroo ...	445	13	...	...
Moora ...	507	13	618	12
Walebing ...	358	18	522	15
Round Hill ...	280	15	499	14
New Norcia ...	373	19	607	19
Wongon Hills ...	261	16	...	...
Wannamel ...	617	17	740	15
Gingin ...	693	15	716	15
SOUTH-WEST (METROPOLITAN):				
Wanneroo ...	680	21	588	16
Belvoir ...	610	17	635	17
Wandu ...	677	22	678	19
Mundaring ...	905	21	860	17
Canning Waterworks	888	19	774	19
Kalbyamba ...	674	18	608	13
Guildford ...	697	22	639	18
Perth Gardens ...	648	21	581	18
Perth Observatory	662	22	603	17
Highgate Hill ...	675	21	589	17
Subiaco ...	579	22	537	18
Claremont ...	612	18	521	15
Fremantle ...	577	22	471	15
SOUTH-WEST (METROPOLITAN)—cont.				
Rottnest ...	379	20	417	20
Rockingham ...	715	20	336	13
Jandakot ...	824	19	528	15
Armadale ...	713	22	587	16
Mundijong ...	856	20	561	17
Jarrahdale ...	1139	20	738	17
Jarrahdale (Norie)	1164	24	693	17
Serpentine ...	969	18	632	17
EXTREME SOUTH-WEST:				
Mandurah ...	1246	21	596	20
Pinjarra (Blythewood)	1201	23	467	16
Pinjarra ...	1213	20	437	19
Upper Murray ...	1436	23	626	17
Yarloop ...	1000	24	689	20
Harvey ...	1076	25	753	17
Brunswick ...	1022	21	660	18
Collie ...	1098	21	732	18
Glen Mervyn ...	1035	21	551	12
Donnybrook ...	1244	22	658	19
Boyanup ...	1255	26	749	21
Bunbury ...	878	23	628	19
Elgin ...	...	...	612	21
Busselton ...	891	25	588	24
Quindalup ...	835	24	653	22
Cape Naturaliste	666	24	588	22
Glen Lossie ...	930	25	...	...
Karridale ...	848	24	738	25
Cape Leeuwin ...	650	25	533	26
Lower Blackwood	928	18	639	22
Ferndale ...	1178	23	632	18
Greenbushes ...	956	16	722	12
Cooeearup ...	946	21	512	21
Bridgetown ...	954	25	557	20
Hilton ...	770	16	440	8
Greenfields ...	927	17	445	13
Cundinup ...	530	18	324	15
Wilgarrup ...	922	24	502	22
Balbarrup ...	824	16	565	14
Bidellia ...	821	15	740	16
The Warren ...	...	...	...	...
Westbourne ...	680	18	397	19
Deeside ...	712	21	472	17
Riverside ...	708	25	547	21
Mordalup ...	702	18	278	19
Lake Muir ...	770	21	...	...

RAINFALL—*continued*.

STATIONS.	June. No. of points. 100 = 1in.	June. No. of wet days.	July. No. of points. 100 = 1in.	July. No. of wet days.	STATIONS.	June. No. of points. 100 = 1in.	June. No. of wet days.	July. No. of points. 100 = 1in.	July. No. of wet days.
EASTERN AGRICULTURAL DISTRICTS:					GREAT SOUTHERN RAILWAY LINE—*contd.*				
Emungin ...	221	15	311	15	Woodyarrup ...	269	11	331	12
Dowerin ...	244	12	338	10	Pallinup ...	230	10	378	11
Oak Hill ...	...	...	...	...	Tambellup ...	274	14	284	15
Hatherley ...	277	10	370	11	Toolbrunup ...	274	11	318	11
Momberkine ...	305	12	452	11	Cranbrook ...	382	22	354	21
Bolgart	...	...	555	16	Stirling View ...	374	19	307	17
Eumalga ...	468	16	700	13	Kendenup ...	459	22	384	21
Newcastle ...	407	17	565	15	Woogenellup ...	303	20	...	...
Craiglands ...	656	18	762	18	Wattle Hill ...	349	22	415	21
Eadine	366	17	561	17	St. Werburgh's...	490	20	..	...
Northam ...	335	17	438	14	Mt. Barker ...	451	24	379	22
Grass Valley ...	...	...	...	...					
Cobham	357	20	493	15					
York	313	18	405	14					
Burrayocking ...	336	12	391	15					
Meckering ...	242	12	345	11					
Cunderdin ...	261	10	366	9	WEST OF GREAT SOUTHERN RAILWAY LINE:				
Doongin ...	266	10	288	9					
Whitehaven ...	346	11	...	...	Talbot House ...	283	15	444	14
Mt. Caroline ...	263	8	370	9	Jelcobine ...	357	12	473	15
Cutenning ...	205	11	296	7	Bannister ...	582	18	...	...
Kellerberrin ...	228	10	299	11	Wandering ...	544	18	689	17
Cardonia ...	183	10	...	...	Glen Ern ...	292	18	511	14
Baandee ...	170	9	344	8	Marradong ...	711	15	585	14
Nangeenan ...	96	7	340	8	Wonnaminta ...	433	20	502	16
Merredin ...	143	9	328	8	Williams ...	396	14	464	13
Codg-Codgen ...	144	11	...	...	Rifle Downs ...	691	15	631	9
Noongarin ...	115	9	...	...	Darkan	...	...	...	...
Mangowine ...	118	11	327	9	Arthur River ...	388	13	467	10
Yarragin ...	150	8	315	11	Glenorchy ...	526	12	437	12
Wattoning ...	...	..	...	...	Gainsborough ...	257	13	356	13
					Kojonup ...	538	14	365	10
					Blackwattle ...	633	12	...	...
					Warriup ...	411	22	413	21
GREAT SOUTHERN RAILWAY LINE:					Forest Hill ...	756	25	397	21
Dalebridge ...	295	17	448	16					
Beverley ...	339	16	510	13					
Brookton ...	322	12	368	14	EAST OF GREAT SOUTHERN RAILWAY LINE:				
Sunning Hill ...	317	18	409	17					
Pingelly ...	302	15	454	11					
Yornaning ...	370	18	446	17	Sunset Hills ...	263	11	393	14
Narrogin ...	406	14	455	13	Oakdale	293	19	402	16
Narrogin Experimental Farm	552	15	503	17	Barrington ...	254	14	...	...
					Bally Bally ...	235	17	405	15
Wagin	309	17	430	13	Stock Hill ...	308	12	412	10
Katanning ...	328	16	343	16	Qualin	223	9	383	10
Sunnyside ...	313	20	315	18	Woodgreen ...	161	10	269	16
Broomehill ...	291	16	329	15	Gillimanning ...	270	14	...	...

RAINFALL—*continued.*

STATIONS.	JUNE.		JULY.		STATIONS.	JUNE.		JULY.	
	No. of Points. 100 = 1in.	No. of wet days.	No. of points. 100 = 1in.	No. of wet days.		No. of points. 100 = 1in.	No. of wet days.	No. of Points. 100 = 1in.	No. of wet days.
EAST OF GREAT SOUTHERN RAILWAY LINE—*cont.*					SOUTH COAST—*cont.*				
					Peppermint Grove	162	15	495	16
					Bremer Bay ...	165	14	455	12
Wickepin ...	371	16	531	15	Coconarup	183	8	352	14
Crooked Pool ...	302	14	407	12	Ravensthorpe ...	177	13	367	16
Bunking ...	249	10	...	...	Cowjanup ...	143	11	...	...
Bullock Hills ...	267	12	403	13	Hopetoun ...	187	8	426	9
Dyliabing ...	268	15	309	16	Fanny's Cove ...	279	11	...	...
Glencove ...	389	16	319	17	Park Farm ...	277	12	339	13
Cherillalup ...	289	15	331	9	Grass Patch ...	136	6	220	13
Mianelup ...	252	17	305	19	Swan Lagoon ...	159	11	...	...
Woolaanup ...	296	17	230	12	30-Mile	196	13	...	...
Chillinup ...	210	4	250	2	Gibson's Soak ...	247	15	423	19
Jarramongup ...	222	12	...	...	Myrup ...	294	13	...	...
					Esperance ...	519	15	422	18
					Boyatup...	458	16	...	...
					Lynburn ...	172	12	...	...
SOUTH COAST:					Middle Island ...	428	12	...	...
Wilson's Inlet ...	...	...	553	23	Point Malcolm ...	173	12	...	...
Grasmere ...	819	23	560	19	Israelite Bay ...	137	9	151	14
King River ...	586	21	522	16	Balbinia... ...	161	7	740	16
Albany	772	25	534	22	Balladonia ...	136	6	78	3
Point King ...	668	20	477	16	Eyre	60	8	184	14
Breaksea ...	763	26	479	22	Mundrabella ...	...	·7·	...	...
Cape Riche ...	221	7	288	2	Eucla	87	7	131	12

The Observatory, Perth,
    August 11th, 1906.

W. E. COOKE,
Government Astronomer.

[Registered at the General Post Office for transmission by Post as a Newspaper.]

JOURNAL

OF THE

DEPARTMENT OF AGRICULTURE

OF

WESTERN AUSTRALIA.

By Direction of

The HON. THE MINISTER OF AGRICULTURE.

PUBLISHED MONTHLY.

Vol. XIV.—Part 3.

SEPTEMBER, 1906.

PERTH:
BY AUTHORITY: FRED. WM. SIMPSON, GOVERNMENT PRINTER.

1906.

WESTERN AUSTRALIAN GOVERNMENT.

IMMIGRATION.

Nominated Passages.

Persons having friends and relatives in the United Kingdom who

Advanced Passages.

Working men and others resident in the State may obtain an advance of passage money, including railway fares from port of arrival to destination, to bring their wives and families from the Eastern States and New Zealand to this State.

Such advances to be repaid within six or twelve months, according to the amount advanced.

A responsible guarantor must be provided.

Special Concessions are provided for Settlers taking up Land.

Full particulars can be obtained upon application to the Under Secretary, Colonial Secretary's Department, Perth.

By order,

F. D. NORTH,

Under Secretary.

JOURNAL

OF THE

𝔇epartment of 𝔄griculture

OF

WESTERN AUSTRALIA.

ERRATA.

Line 24, page 179: 38° F. should *read* 28° F.

represented. All particulars may be obtained by writing to the Secretary Fruitgrowers' Federal Conference, 12 Spring Street, Sydney.

SNAKE BITE REMEDY.—Mr. A. J. Tilly, Chemist, Hay Street, has forwarded to the Hon. the Minister for Agriculture a pocket instrument for use in case of snake bite. The instrument consists of a small lancet and a few grains of pure crystals of permanganate of potash contained in a small case 2½ inches long. It is the outcome of a suggestion made by Sir Lauder Brunton, and is extensively used throughout India. It may be obtained from Mr. Tilly at the low cost of one shilling.

SHEEP MANURE.—The manure from sheep is worth more than that derived from any other animal; next, that from the hog, and then from the horse, manure from cattle being less valuable than that from other animals. But in quantity produced cattle come first, then horses, next hogs, with sheep last. The value of manure does not depend altogether upon the animal producing it, however, as the character of the food consumed largely influences the manure, and even the manure from the same animal varies in quality and quantity daily.

COTTON GROWING.—In a recent report on cotton growing received from Mr. G. Berthoud, of the State Farm, Hamel, we take the following particulars:—"From field experiences gained here at Hamel by experiments extending over a period of several years, during which I have cultivated about 30 varieties, comprising American, Chinese, Egyptian, Indian, and Caravonica, I can confidently say that the American sorts are those most suitable for culture in the temperate parts of this State. Shine's Early Prolific and Louisiana Prolific are the two best I know of, and in every way far ahead of the Egyptians for this part.

SULPHUR FOR FUMIGATING.—There have been frequent inquiries in this State for a first-class sulphur for fumigation purposes in vineyards, and complaints are made that the ordinary (Sicilian) sulphur imported here is not always sufficiently volatile to be fully effective against oidium. Arrangements have in consequence been made by the W.A. Producers' Co-operative Union for a small shipment of the " Crown " brand sulphur, which is largely used in European vineyards. It is very light, 1cwt. occupying nearly as much bulk as 2cwt. of the ordinary kind. It is anticipated that the cost will not exceed 16s. per cwt.

IRRITATION IN HORSE'S COAT.—A correspondent writes asking for advice how to relieve a horse that is continually rubbing itself against the sides of the stable, walls, posts, etc. The matter being referred to the Government Veterinary Surgeon, Mr. Weir states that the irritation may result from many causes, but it is likely that the horse referred to is suffering from the presence of a mange parasite. To effect a cure it is necessary that the posts, etc., that the horse use to rub against should be disinfected by washing with a twenty per cent. solution of carbolic. Every part of the animal's body must be washed with soft soap and hot water, the affected parts afterwards to be dressed daily for a week or ten days with the following : creolin, 3 parts ; soft soap, 1 part ; water, 100 parts.

SUNFLOWERS.—According to the *Pharmaceutical Journal*, the best known antidote for malarial district fevers in different countries of South America has long been practised and taken advantage of by the growth of sunflowers, not only as a certain prevention of yellow fever, but also as a lucrative article of commerce. Everyone should take pains to have them in their gardens. They are valuable because they are not only healthy plants to grow near dwellings, but the blossom is exceedingly handsome, they are rich in nectar, and bees work eagerly on them ; the seeds are eaten by poultry, the stalks and leaves are eaten by horses and cattle. Surely a plant of such all-round value is worth growing in our gardens, if not important enough for a field crop.

CAMPBELL'S SYSTEM OF SOIL CULTURE.—We have just received a copy of the work written by Professor H. W. Campbell on the cultivation of the soil. This work has become so popular in the Western States of America that the principles advocated have earned for themselves the title of "Campbell's System of Soil Culture." In a future issue extracts will be made from it for the use of our readers. Briefly, however, the system may be termed, one for use in dry or arid districts. It consists in the proper working of the soil, ploughing deep, and afterwards thoroughly packing the soil the better to receive and retain any rains that may fall, followed by frequent stirring of the top soil to the depth of two or three inches, thus preventing the evaporation of the moisture previously collected in the soil.

How to Feed.— While well balanced rations count for much in feeding cattle for profit, special care should be taken to study the nature of every beast. Cattle are not all made alike, and the quantity of food which one animal would find barely sufficient might, in the case of another beast, be superfluous. The peculiarities of every individual beast should therefore be studied if the results are to realise anticipations. Another point of importance is regularity. Without this, even the best laid plans with regard to successful stock feeding are apt to "gang aft agley," but with it there is bound to be satisfaction. These are two of the points that help towards the attainment of perfection, and farmers would, therefore, do well to see them duly attended to.

Weed Extermination.—A new use has been found for a weed exterminator introduced into this State by Mr. A. Tijou, of Fremantle. It is that of clearing all ground around hives in apiaries. By this means many valuable queens are saved. At swarming times, in those cases where the queen's wing has been cut, when she emerges with the swarm, being unable to fly, she crawls on to a tuft of grass, where it often happens she is over-looked and stood upon. By using the exterminator the ground is made perfectly bare, and this enables the queen to be found at once. The basis of the liquid is composed of carbolic acid, which has a soothing effect on the bees and unlike most other weed destroyers, which have a very strong, unpleasant smell that irritates the bees and make it risky to go near them after it has been used.

Date Palms.—Favourable reports continue to come to hand from those stations around Roebourne, Port Hedland, and Beagle Bay, where some suckers of Algerian date palm, imported by the Department last year, were sent. As a further illustration of the suitableness of the North-West of Western Australia for the production of the commercial date, some excellent specimens of the fruit were submitted to this Department by Messrs. Meares and Cusack, of Tambray Station, in the basin of the Fortescue, and not far from Roebourne. The dates were from a seedling grown on the station. It is one of three date palms which for some years past have fruited there; as regards shape, size, and flavour, each one is somewhat different from the others, although the three are excellent in quality. Great possibilities seem to await date palm culture in the warmer parts of Western Australia.

Poultry-breeding.—If there is one mistake more likely to be made than another by the novice in poultry-raising it is the tendency to keep several breeds. The expert can do this with more or less profit because he understands how to keep them separated or, if he wishes to cross them, understands this as well. The novice, on the other hand, is too often inclined to experiment. He thinks the crossing of two certain breeds ought to give him the finest fowl on earth, and keeps at it until the blood is pretty well mixed, and finds, to his dismay, that the cross is not so good as the poorest of the clean breeds. Again, he tries Rocks one year, and then becomes enamoured of the Wyandottes and gets a few; the next year the Leghorn appeals to him, and so on until he has the time of his life keeping them separated or, as in the first case, becomes involved in a hopeless mixture. Look well into the subject and ascertain as nearly as possible which breed meets the requirements, then get that breed and stick to it through thick and thin until you prove it valuable or worthless.

DAIRY COWS.—Every dairyman should make up his mind as to the class of cow to keep. There are many cows on our farms that do not give more than 3,000 to 4,000lbs. of milk per year; this is not nearly good enough, and the aim should be to weed out all those yielding less than 6,000lbs. with a good four per cent. A weekly or monthly test is not of much value for the purpose of judging, unless the tests are continued for a whole year. A cow when first coming in may give 10 quarts or 12 quarts at a milking, and is immediately set down as one well worth keeping. She may or may not be so. A writer well says, lazy men are noted for doing big things in a short time, and this principle applies to cows. Some cows will give a large amount of milk for a short time; others, a small amount for a very long time; some yield very rich milk; others very poor; whilst most give a medium quantity of medium quality. When the capacity of every cow in the herd is known we have reliable data on which to base a system of feeding and management; without such knowledge, we are to a great extent working in the dark.

ANALYSIS OF STOCK FOOD.—An interesting analysis of the value of several well-known fodders has just been issued by the Queensland Agricultural Chemist, Mr. J. C. Brunnich, in relation to their possession of proteids, the recognised basis of animal tissue, and albuminoids that build up the flesh. The experiments were made at the Biggenden State Farm, and the analyses were compiled according to the latest methods. They may be serviceable to stock owners. Paspalum dilatatum contains as grass, 2·98 proteids, 1 albuminoids; as hay, 5·97 proteids, 10·8 albuminoids. Rhodes grass contains as grass, 3·57 proteids and 1 albuminoids; as hay, 7·13 proteids and 8·4 albuminoids. Golden Nugget maize, green, 1·79 proteids, 1 albuminoids; as dry chaff, 6·40 proteids and 12·7 albuminoids. Mazzagua, the new African fodder plant, as grass, 2·08 proteids, 1 albuminoids; as chaff, 7·39 proteids, 10·2 albuminoids. If these figures are carefully noted it will be seen that Mazzagua and Rhodes grass contain the most animal sustenance and nutrition, and may prove the most serviceable to the dairy farmer and to the stock breeder for the market. These results of the analysis of stock fodders will doubtless be a useful item of information, as the building up of a vigorous herd, whether for dairying or market purposes, naturally depends upon the quality of the food supplied.

VALUABLE GYPSUM DEPOSITS.—Samples of gypsum taken from extensive deposits about the Cowcowing Lake were recently received by the Department, and sent on to the Government Analyst to be tested. Mr. Mann found that the analysis gave a return of 69 per cent. gypsum, and as a result the hon. the Minister for Lands has approved of the site of the deposit being temporarily reserved from selection with a view to preventing the big body of gypsum on the shores of the lake being monopolised by private individuals. Settlers are to have access to this sulphate of lime under liberal conditions, and the Lands Department will give effect to this recommendation. Mr. Despeissis, in a minute to the Hon. Minister of Agriculture on the find, says:—" The distance to the railway line is now a difficulty that will stand in the way of the working of the deposits, but with the possible advance of the railway in the direction of the lake, it should be possible to place the gypsum on trucks at a very small cost. A good dressing for land would be from 5cwt. to 10cwt. The freight is one penny per ton per mile in 4-ton trucks. There is no burning required, and the crushing and sifting would cost very little. Gypsum acts as an agent which sets free potash present in the soil in a more insoluble form than plants can readily assimilate and also promotes the growth of the sweeter grasses, and especially plants of the pea and clover family."

REARING OF DUCKLINGS.—Writing on the subject of the rearing of ducks, the *Réveil Agricole* says:—The breeding of palmipeds, when carried out intelligently, may be made more lucrative than is thought in many circles. Fowl breeding on an extensive scale necessitates experience which the beginner does not always possess. The rearing of palmipeds—and especially that of the duck—is likely to give more satisfaction to the beginner or to anybody who desires to reap good profits in a short time. The duck is undoubtedly the most precocious of the poultry-yard host, and is, moreover, less liable to contract disease. When ducklings have been located on the banks of a stream to find those insects which are so indispensable to them when young, it will be found that success is more easily assured. When sixty days old a duck is fit for the table. It is therefore apparent that the breeding of this bird is very quickly finished. True he is a big eater, but it is not necessary to overfeed him on corn during his two months' existence to secure a good bird. The duck will eat almost anything, and very acceptable meals can be obtained by preparing what comes from the kitchen, along with vegetables and raw or cooked fruit which would otherwise be thrown away. During this time the duck grows but does not fatten. This, however, is of no consequence; for in order to bring ducks to proper condition by the time they are wanted for the market, it is only necessary to give them a fortnight's good feeding prior to the period when they are to be killed. Pastes of flour, barley, maize, maize-grains, potatoes, etc., should then be given at the rate of two good meals daily. The ducklings should be kept by themselves and given free access to water—not for swimming, but for drinking purposes. It is preferable to give them the grains in water. This simple and economical method of rearing ducklings insures the birds being fleshy without being too fat.

THE SADDLE HORSE.—Riding on horseback has never been so popular as it is now in all the large American cities. Prices have never been so high for finished saddle horses, and it follows of course that the supply of saddle-bred animals falls far short of meeting the demand. Horses of all kinds of breeding have been pressed into saddle service and for those which have proved apt pupils very good values have been realised. The history of the world proves that the older a nation becomes the greater is the inclination to take equestrian exercise. We believe (writes the *Breeders' Gazette*) that the present popularity of the saddler is one of the most important signs of the times that can be listed. Association with the saddle horse breeds manliness in man. It is a bad horse indeed that has not some good qualities, and these good qualities invariably find reciprocation in the rider. It is not recorded which of the American humorists first called attention to the "storm deck of a horse," but the one who first made the phrase did better than probably he knew at the time. It is something of a trick to stay on the back of a good horse. No one likes to be put down ignominiously, and the effort of brain and muscle that is required to keep from parting company with one's mount must of sheer necessity be good for the rider. This is getting down to first principles and we will venture the assertion that there never yet was a good boy who would not have been a better one had he been early on pony-back, and the boy is father to the man. There are black sheep in every flock and there are men on whom the influence of the horse has only been for bad, but such are the exceptions. That the influence of the horse saddle is more for good than that of the other members of the equine family finds abundant proof in the affection displayed by men and women for the horses they ride as compared with those they drive or work. From Alexander to Lord Roberts the men who have made history and builded empires have been horsemen.

GOATS' MILK AS A FOOD.--At the Annual meeting of the Women's Agricultural and Horticultural International Union, held in the Museum of the Royal Botanic Society, London, Dr. Thos. Dutton gave an address on the value of goats' milk as a food for infants and invalids. After a general reference to the milks of the cow, the ass, and the sheep, all of which were used for human consumption in different countries, he said it was reserved to the goat, which had from time immemorial served the purposes of man as a milk-supply, to give the most satisfactory results as a substitute for the mother's milk in the diet of children. He instanced a case in which a child took its nourishment direct from the animal itself, the foster mother evincing the greatest affection for the infant, He advised, however, that when given to very young children it should be sufficiently diluted with water on account of the extra richness of this milk as compared with that of the cow or of the human species. At the close of the address the Lady President alluded to goat-keeping as a suitable and profitable occupation for ladies in conjunction with bee-keeping and poultry-keeping. Mr. Holmes Pegler commented on the observations of Dr. Dutton, and remarked that the success of goat-keeping as a profitable commercial undertaking depended largely on the recommendation of the medical profession; and as all goat-keepers had practical experience of the value of the milk for infants, it had always been a surprise to him that medical men did not recommend this article more generally than they do. He called attention to the valuable remarks of Sir William Broadbent in his address on the prevention of consumption and other forms of tuberculosis, delivered some years ago at the Technical College, Huddersfield, in which he said: "It is interesting to note that goats do not suffer from tuberculosis, and to bear in mind that the shrewd physicians of past days used to order goats' milk for persons threatened with consumption." Mr. Holmes Pegler expressed the pleasure it gave him to find that ladies were taking up goat-keeping as a profitable pursuit. During the last thirty years this had been the special object of members of the British Goat Society, the most prominent of whom was, and had been from the first, the Baroness Burdett-Coutts, who had thus set so good an example to ladies in general.

THROUGH THE KIMBERLEYS.

By R. E. WEIR, M.R.C.V.S, C.G.S.I.

(*Continued.*)

Adjoining Goose Hill Reserve on the Ord River road, is Connor, Doherty, and Durack's Ivanhoe Station. A drive of 28 miles brought us to the homestead. Conveniently situated near a large dam of water which provides a plentiful supply throughout the year, the dwelling-house, a prettily-designed structure built on lines which provide the greatest degree of comfort, whilst ventilation has been specially considered—an important matter in building in the tropics. The property, comprising some 700,000 acres, was originally taken up and stocked by the late Mr. Durack in 1892, and since that period, has been used chiefly as a stud station. The herbage over the greater proportion of the run is of a coarse character, Mitchell and Kangaroo grass predominating. The latter grows from a height of from six to ten feet and, at a distance, has the appearance of an immense wheatfield. Grasses of a finer character flourish in the home paddock, and for this reason this portion of the run is chiefly used for the grazing of some 500 head of stud cattle. In utilising the run as a stud station, the firm had in view the rearing of a sufficient number of young bulls to supply their out-stations. This is a very commendable course to follow, as the animals will become acclimatised and not subject to disorders common to those imported from outside. The greatest care and judgment has been exercised in the establishment of the herd. The cows were originally selected from one of the best shorthorn herds in Queensland, and the bulls (chiefly of the Bates' and Booth's strains) were imported from England, South Australia, and Victoria. Being acquainted with these facts, I was not surprised to find that the herd as a whole were a particularly good lot, and that a few of the choicer animals would compare favourably with the best of our Royal exhibits. The firm may be congratulated on the efforts they have put forth, for the development in those parts of an industry which, although originally intended solely for their own requirements, will ultimately be for the mutual benefit of the stock-owners of Kimberley. In addition, there is a superior flock of Angora goats kept on the station and are proving a lucrative speculation their annual clip of mohair continues to command good prices on the London market. Their mutton is also much appreciated for station use. It is a pleasing picture to see them camped at nights on the side of a hill near the homestead, where they quietly repose until morning. An experiment has also recently been tried with sheep—some 20 Shrops. were secured last year, and the results have been most satisfactory. In addition to a good lambing, they have improved in condition to the extent of obesity. They chiefly graze about the homestead, where the conditions of living are of a favourable character; but owing to the coarse nature of the herbage on other parts of the run, their development beyond a limited number is not likely to be realised. The station is intelligently and capably managed by Mr. McCauley, who, like the majority of those associated with the cattle business in Kimberley, has originally obtained his experience in

Queensland. Both Mrs. McCauley and he are most hospitable, and for this reason our short stay has been productive of the most pleasant reminiscences.

After leaving Ivanhoe homestead, the road traverses good plain country to Carlton Reach, where we arrived at noon on the 22nd.   Here we find what people travelling in tropical parts most desire, when a long morning's journey has been completed, namely, good shade and a plentiful supply of water.   Such was our experience after getting underneath the well foliaged trees which line the banks of the Ord at this spot, and one could gaze on the beautiful expanse of water which meets the view.   My thoughts wandered to the possibilities which would occur if this expanse of water permeated the whole course of the Ord, and the river were made navigable, which would revolutionise the whole trade of the Kimberleys, besides making the country a pleasant abode.   From this peaceful resting place our journey was continued to Pandamus Springs, where a good camping ground, including water, was obtainable.   The situation was a circumscribed valley surrounded by high rangy country, which tended to increase the already sultry condition of the atmosphere, thus causing us a restless night. This, however did not deter us from rising early next morning, and after a light breakfast of the usual corned beef and damper we were once more on the track.   A drive of some eight miles over scrubby plain country brought us to the foot of the range, over which we had to climb with no little difficulty until we surmounted its utmost height, from whence a magnificent view of the surrounding country is obtained.   Away to the west lies an interminable range of hills, with here and there smoke ascending from native fires; whilst to the east a beautiful expanse of plain country as far as the eye can reach, and comprising what is known as the Argyle Station.   To descend to the valley beneath it is necessary to travel over a precipitous cutting carved out of the face of the hill.   This we safely accomplished by means of fastening a good large tree to the axle of our trap, to act as a supplement to the break. This cutting, which was formed at no small expense, is known as "Durack's Folly," so named from the reason that Mr. M. Durack was the instigator of getting the work accomplished.   The scheme was first propounded as a means of obviating the difficulties which attended travelling by the old road— which at this particular part consisted of heavy sand—and also to save a distance of 15 miles in travelling.   Were the grade considerably reduced, the object for which it was constructed would be accomplished by making the road possible for heavy traffic, but unfortunately a considerable further expense will have to be incurred before this is realised.   From this point we found the distance too great to reach Argyle homestead on the same evening, but we arrived there early on the following morning, and were made very welcome by the manager, Mr. Durack, and his sister.   The former, a cousin of the owner of the property, has had the management of the station for the past few years, and the proficiency with which he carries out his duties is fully equal to the reputation which this station has held in the past as being the best managed in Kimberley.   The private dwelling and yards attached are of a character requisite to so valuable a holding, and a distinct improvement on the general condition of homesteads in Kimberley.   This property was originally stocked in 1886 by the late Mr. Durack, who after a long and tedious overland journey from Queensland, chose this particular locality as his abiding place.   With the nucleus of a shorthorn herd which he brought over with him, he began a career, which within the space of a few years, brought about a very happy condition of affluence.   Much of his success was undoubtedly due to his own inherited knowledge of cattle, and more par-

Fig. 2.—Carlton Reach, Kimberley.

Fig. 1.—Ivanhoe Homestead.

ticularly to the wisdom exercised in paying special care to improved breeding. So apparent has this been made to the present proprietors that they have carefully followed in the same wise course until to-day they own a herd of 33,000 head of cattle which would compare favourably with any in Australia. This station annually supplies about 1,500 head of bullocks shipped to Fremantle, which are always looked forward to by local buyers, who do not demur to pay an increased rate for the privilege of securing these prime animals. Recently an experiment has been tried by crossing a limited number of cows with the red poll bull, and from the model-like appearance of the progeny the trial has been a success. Yet although this is at first possible, if the system is continued for any length of time a slow but sure deterioration of the herd will occur, until the improvements effected in the past will have been altogether effaced. Special attention has also been paid to horse-breeding, and, contrary to many parts of Kimberley, very satisfactory results have been obtained. At present there are about 700 head on the run, the majority being of the thoroughbred or hackney class, the remainder medium draughts. A large mob were yarded during my visit, amongst them being some promising young thoroughbreds which are likely to gain renown in local racing. The medium draughts are of a class suitable for station requirements, for which good values are always obtainable.

(To be continued.)

HOW TO MAKE OLIVE OIL.

A correspondent writes asking how to convert a large quantity of olives into oil. Mr. Despeissis gives the following information :—

The olives should be picked when ripe, *i.e.*, when they have turned a dark brown or a purplish colour, according to varieties. If picked too early the oil is of a greenish colour and is slightly bitter ; if late the yield of the oil will increase a little, but the quality will deteriorate at the same time.

The oil is not all contained in the pulp ; the kernel also contains 5 to 8 per cent., and the whole berry should for that reason be reduced to a paste before pressing. This is done in special oil mills. The pulp is, in the South of Europe, placed in specially made straw bags, which are heaped up one on top of the other and placed under the press.

The first oil coming from the first pressing is called virgin oil, and sells at a higher price. The pressure is then slackened, the cake broken up and moistened with hot water, put in bags again, and pressed afresh. This oil is kept separate from the virgin or cold drawn oil. The marc or refuse is valuable for its nutritious constituents and fed to pigs and fowls. After pressing, the raw oil is run into a vessel two-thirds filled with water, in which the oil washes. There the impurities sink and settle down, while the oil floats and is carried through an overflow pipe into jars, in which it is allowed to stand in order to clear. From these jars it is decanted off and run through a filtering paper inside a funnel and bottled and corked down, wrapped up in blue paper, and cased. Sunlight affects its colour.

Report on a possible new Commercial source of Alcohol to be found in the Grass-tree (Blackboy)

(*Xanthorrhœa preissii*).

By E. A. MANN,

Government Analyst and Chemist to the Department of Agriculture.

The following report has been submitted to the Hon. the Minister for Agriculture by the Government Analyst:—

I have the honour to submit the following report of the result of certain investigations which I have been making during the past few months on the plant commonly but erroneously known in this State as the Blackboy (*Xanthorrhœa preissii*). A preliminary report was furnished to the Director of Agriculture on 12th October, 1905, but further investigations have since been made, and I will here summarise all that has been done so that this will cancel all previous reports:—

The plant here dealt with is that which has been known throughout Australia for many years as the Grass-tree. This latter name has in Western Australia been applied to another species of the same genus (the *Kingia*) which does not occur in the other States, but I have the authority of the Government Botanist for stating that it properly belongs to the *Xanthorrhœa*, and I use it accordingly in this report. It is classed by Baron von Müller among the *Liliaceæ* (Lillies), but by Bentham among the *Juncaceæ* (Rushes). It is widely distributed throughout the Eastern States of Australia and also over the entire coastal districts of this State South of Champion Bay.

From its peculiar character and appearance, which forms a striking feature of our bush scenery, it is a plant which naturally excites curiosity and interest. Apparently useless, it nevertheless occupies large tracts of country, in the clearing of which it has, in the past, been ruthlessly destroyed, and it is hardly surprising therefore that attempts have been made from time to time to ascertain whether it could not be turned to some practical use.

There is little doubt that much future wealth in this State will be gained by making use of what have been regarded as our waste products, and it is hoped that the investigation here reported may be of some service in this direction.

Amongst other lines of inquiry which have been followed up with regard to this plant, it has been said to have been used as a source of picric acid, but I have been unable to find any reliable references on this subject. Again, it is of a very resinous nature, and it has been thought that the natural exudations of the plant might be turned to good account in the manufacture of varnish. Though I have not been able to find any official records, I have been informed that samples of this resin have from time to time been sent to England to ascertain their value in this respect, but the reports have not

GRASS TREE.

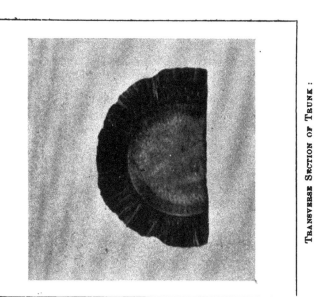

TRANSVERSE SECTION OF TRUNK:
Showing radial character of Core and outer layer of longitudinal fibres next to the shell.

LONGITUDINAL SECTION OF TRUNK:
Showing outer Shell and Core. The latter exhibits a layer of longitudinal fibres next to the outer shell. Average diameter of Core, 8¼in.

been altogether satisfactory. The resin is said to lack " body," and to be of no value except for the cheaper and inferior classes of varnish. On the other hand, it is said to have been successfully used in Queensland.

A much more interesting attempt to turn it to practical account is that which has been made by Mr. Charles Harper, of Guildford, and which led largely to my own investigation. Mr. Harper, in endeavouring to produce from the grass-tree a fodder for cattle, prepared from the interior core of the stem of the plant a meal which I believe has been used on stock with encouraging results.

In September, 1905, Mr. Harper submitted a sample of this fodder to me for analysis, when I obtained the following results :—

		Per cent.
Moisture	... ...	9·19
Fat	... ...	·78
Albuminoids	... ...	2·83
Carbohydrates (by difference) ...	... ...	50·87
Fibre	... ...	35·93
Ash	... ...	·40
	Total	100·00

This large proportion of carbohydrates at once attracted my attention and led me to make a fuller investigation to ascertain how much of this was in the form of sugar, when I obtained the following results :—

		Per cent.
Moisture	... ...	9·19
Fat	... ...	·78
Albuminoids	... ...	8·28
Reducing sugar (calculated as glucose)	...	10·25
Non-reducing sugar (calculated as cane sugar)		15·86
Other carbohydrates (by difference) ...	...	24·76
Fibre	... ...	35·93
Ash ...	... ...	·4
	Total	100·00

The sugars in the above analysis were estimated by the reduction affected on salts of copper. There are other substances besides sugar which affect this reduction, and therefore it is highly probable that there is really less than the 25 per cent. of sugar indicated. It was evident, therefore, that there were two kinds of sugar present, namely, reducing and non-reducing, and that the latter was readily "inverted" and changed into the reducing sugar. I endeavoured to separate the sugars in a pure form by crystallisation, but this was found to be impossible owing to the large amount of resinous and glutinous substances present, which rendered crystallisation very difficult if not impossible.

At first I had hoped that the meal might prove a source of ordinary cane sugar, and this point may still be worth investigating by experts, but as the sugars could not be readily separated and definitely identified I turned my investigation in another direction.

It occurred to me that if these sugars could be fermented they might be made a commercial source of alcohol ; accordingly on the 7th November 350 grammes of the meal (approximately ¾lb.) were almost completely extracted with boiling water and the wash thus obtained was fermented with yeast. Fermentation proceeded vigorously. After the activity of the yeast had subsided it was found that the sugars had been practically all fermented and the resulting alcohol was separated by distillation, with the following results : —

From 350 grammes were obtained 300 cubic centimetres of an alcoholic solution containing 8·34 per cent. of absolute alcohol by weight, or equivalent to 18·3 per cent. of sugar in the original meal. This return was equivalent to 1·24 gallons proof spirit per bushel (60lbs.) of the meal ; as good malt is generally supposed to give about 2 gallons per bushel this return seemed very good.

You will see, therefore, whereas by the copper reduction method 25 per cent. of sugar was indicated, by fermentation only 18·31 per cent. was obtained. This difference might have been due to either (1) variation in composition of successive samples of meal, or (2) the presence of other substances which might have reduced the copper. In consequence of my report of the above facts I was instructed by the Government to conduct trials on a larger scale, and with the very kind assistance of Mr. Despeissis and Mr. Ferguson, who placed the resources of the Santa Rosa and Houghton vineyards at my disposal, the following test was made :—

Six hundredweight of grass-tree core was sliced in a chaff cutter, and placed in a large fermentation vat with 105 gallons of water. It was then heated by a cask steamer to sterilise it, but it was not boiled or extracted by steam, and this, as events have shown, was an unfortunate omission. After sterilisation yeast and mineral yeast-foods were added to the vat containing the mixture of slices of core and water, as it was thought that the fermentation would proceed satisfactorily under these conditions. A certain amount of fermentation did occur, but only of a partial character, even after a second addition of yeast, and on drawing off the wash and distilling it, a very disappointing result was obtained. The alcohol recovered was only equivalent to 4·3 gallons of proof spirit in the whole of the 105 gallons of wash. Subsequent examination of the residue of the grass-tree core and the wash itself, showed that neither the extraction nor the fermentation of the sugar had been complete. In consequence of this, further experiments were carried out in my laboratory on a small scale, but under similar conditions to those employed at Guildford. Without giving details of these tests, I may say that each successive attempt to recover any appreciable quantity of alcohol was abortive, and the results were always similar to those obtained on the large scale, and not like that obtained in the first laboratory test. It was, however, certain that the sugar was there and that it was fermentable, and accordingly the conditions of the first laboratory test were repeated as follows : —

Six pounds of core was extracted with steam, and thus the sugar was concentrated in about two gallons of solution and was at the same time entirely inverted. This wash, when treated with yeast and a mixture of mineral yeast foods according to Pasteur's formula, fermented vigorously and persistently for five days, and on distilling, yielded alcohol equivalent to ·8 gallons of proof spirit per bushel. Only small quantities of sugar were left unfermented.

This yield of alcohol was equivalent to ¾lb. of sugar or 11·4 per cent. on the original core. It was evident therefore that the best results were obtained by extracting with steam or boiling with water so as to simultaneously extract the sugar and invert the non-reducing sugar originally present. An attempt to obtain a concentrated solution by cold extraction was only partially successful, probably on account of the presence of gummy or resinous matters whose influence was removed by the application of heat.

This last experiment was made in February. Owing to delays of various kinds it was found impossible to conduct another experiment on a large scale until last month (June), when the following further trial was was made:—

Five hundredweight of grass-tree core was completely extracted with the aid of heat partly by steaming and partly by boiling in water. On account of the size of the still available the wash was divided into two, and half of it concentrated by further boiling to 24 gallons, which, when tested by the copper reduction method, showed sugar equivalent to 10·5 per cent. of the original core. This wash when distilled yielded three gallons, containing 67·8 per cent. of proof spirit, equal to two proof gallons in all, or ·5 proof gallon per bushel. This represents 7·5 per cent. of sugar. The best figures therefore which have been obtained may be summarised thus:—

> September, 1905.—Laboratory test, 1·24 proof gallons per bushel.   Equal to 18·1 per cent. sugar.
>
> February, 1906.—Laboratory test, ·8 gallons per bushel.   Equal to 11·4 per cent. sugar.
>
> June 1906.—Bulk test, ·5 gallons per bushel.   Equal to 7·5 per cent. sugar.

It will be seen at once that the results varied in value at different periods of the year, the maximum result corresponding with the spring when the grass-tree was likely to have its maximum content of sugar, and it is to be expected that very much better results with such trials would be obtained in the spring than in any other season of the year.

The make-shift arrangements with which such experiments had necessarily to be conducted on a large scale of course told against the results, and with appropriate plant there is little doubt that better results could be obtained.

I would not, however, recommend that any further experiments of this nature be made at present, as I think those already conducted are quite sufficient to prove that the grass-tree core is at any rate at certain seasons of the year a possible source of alcohol; and considering the large quantities of material obtainable and the ease with which it could be collected and treated, it would seem that this discovery should be commercially valuable.

The following tables of comparison may be of interest:—

Percentage of Sugar in Sugar Cane	12 — 18*
„ „ Beet	9 — 15
„ „ Grass-tree Core ...	7½ — 18

In this comparison it must be remembered that in the grass-tree the percentage is reckoned on the *core* only, of which good sized trees will yield about a hundredweight each.   In the cane and beet the percentage is on the entire plant, but the higher figures given for cane is exceptional.

In the above experiments with the grass-tree where the " sugar " has been calculated from the alcohol produced, the theoretical factor has been

---

* Average extraction in sugar manufacture about 10 per cent.

used, but as the theoretical yield is never obtained the percentages of sugar given must be considerably below the truth. By theory pure sugar should yield 51 per cent. of alcohol, but the average yield is probably about one proof gallon for 10lbs. of sugar. Recalculated on this basis the results on page 9 would become :—

Date of Test.	Proof Gallons per bushel.	Equivalent percentage of sugar in original core.
September, 1905	1·24	20·6
February, 1906	·8	13·3
June, 1906	·5	10·0

which are much nearer the figures obtained by analysis.

The yield of alcohol from other materials may be stated as follows, compared with grass-tree core as tested :—

	Yield in proof gallons per bushel (60 lbs.). %
Pure starch	4·68
Wheat, rye, barley, oats, buckwheat, maize (average)	2·06
Malt	2·00
Potatoes (containing 21% starch)	1·26
Sugar cane (containing 12% sugar) ...	·72
Beet (containing 10% sugar)	·60
Grass-tree core	·5 to 1·25

In such substances, as potatoes, in which the original source of the alcohol is "starch," this has first to be converted into sugars before fermentation can take place. This process is avoided in the case of the last three materials in the above list, and they are therefore more comparable among themselves.

It is interesting to learn, as I have been informed, that in the early days of this colony this property of the plant was known to the convicts then employed here, and it was a common thing for them when working in the country districts to brew from the grass-tree a spirituous liquor which served them as a substitute for beer.

I forward herewith a sample of the alcohol obtained from my last experiment, which has only been further rectified by one direct distillation in glass and which has now a strength of about 48 degrees over proof. It is hardly necessary for me to dwell extensively upon the uses to which alcohol may be put, but I may say that for the manufacture of methylated spirit and for use in internal combustion engines (probably the most important application of alcohol of the future), this spirit seems to be admirably adapted.

I would suggest that if the Government consider this discovery worth publishing, as I personally think it is, the best way to have it turned to practical account would be by offering a bonus to the first person producing a given quantity of spirit from this source.   The further treatment of the subject both in its commercial and technical aspects is one, I would suggest, rather for private enterprise, and the means at my disposal in this laboratory do not render it possible for me to carry the matter further.

Incidentally I may mention that there are certain side issues which might be worth pursuing at the same time if the manufacture of spirit from the grass-tree were taken up on a large scale.

(1.) The resin present in the outer shell or covering of the trunk could probably be utilised for making cheap varnishes as already indicated; grass-tree spirit itself being used as a solvent.

(2.) The outer strippings of the trunks could be used as an excellent fuel for raising heat in connection with the extraction and distillation.

(3.) The whole core contains a large percentage of fibre, which is short and already in a suitable condition for use, and it has been suggested to me by Dr. Ince that this could be used to advantage in the manufacture of strawboard and rough paper.

(4.) The green leaves of the plant have a certain value as fodder for stock.

The plants are easily gathered, as they can be knocked over readily, and the outer scaley protective covering or shell is easily removed.   The core could then be sliced and extracted with steam, and the wash so obtained fermented in vats.   Thus the entire process should be simple and inexpensive.

An examination of the *Kingia Australis* * has also been made to see whether this could be similarly used, but the character of the plant and its small sugar content excluded it from any such application.

In this investigation Dr. Ince and Mr. T. I. Wallas have given me valuable assistance, and Mr. Despeissis and Mr. Ferguson have also been most kind in their help, the former incurring considerable trouble and expense in carrying out tests at Guildford, and the latter affording the assistance of his still and conducting the distillation.   I should like here to acknowledge my indebtedness to these gentlemen.

In the accompanying photographs are shown longitudinal and transverse sections of the trunk of the grass-tree, in which the very curious and interesting arrangement of the fibres in the core can be distinguished.   From the centre fibres, radiate to the circumference, and are interlaced by longitudinal fibres passing down through the core.   The latter are specially accumulated in an outer layer next the surrounding outer shell, composed of dead leaf bases.   Between these interlacing fibres is contained the "*meal*" which contains the sugar.

* Erroneously named the " Grass-tree " in this State only.

DEEP-ROOTED GRASSES FOR SUMMER GROWTH.

By PERCY G. WICKEN.

Owing to the long period of dry weather experienced in this State during the summer months, the question of obtaining grasses or fodder plants that will yield a supply of green feed during this period is one of considerable interest to settlers. During eight months of the year supplies of grass and other fodders are easily obtained, but during the remaining period the plants that will be likely to provide green food are very limited. I have no doubt that, with proper cultivation, on land that has been fallowed the previous autumn, the quantity of fodder plants grown could be very considerably extended. Most settlers, however, require a grass that when once sown will give them no further trouble, as the growing of crops does, but will continue to supply green feed for several seasons. Whether such a grass can be obtained still remains to be seen, but inquiries have been made from all sources and all parts of the world by the Agricultural Departments of this and the other States; and, although nothing has yet been obtained which will answer the requirements in all parts, a number of valuable, deep-rooted, drought-resisting grasses have been obtained, which, if sown in well-worked soil, will supply an amount of green feed at a time when it is required.

The following are a few notes on some of these grasses;—

Paspalum dilatatum.

This grass is also known as "Golden Crown Grass" and "Large Water Grass," but is generally spoken of as paspalum. Although there are numerous varieties of paspalum, many of them very good grasses, the paspalum dilatatum has proved itself most adaptable to the Australian climate, and can be found growing in nearly all parts of Australia, from dry inland districts to the highly fertile river flats. Although it cannot be expected to give the same results in the arid districts as it does in a well watered and fertile district, it has nevertheless proved a valuable fodder in nearly all parts.

It is a somewhat coarse leafy perennial, and grows in clumps. It is probably a native of South America. It will flourish in nearly all tropical and semi-tropical localities provided there is a sufficient rainfall, and has proved itself to be one of the most valuable fodder plants yet introduced into Australia.

Although somewhat slow in making a growth in the spring, as the weather becomes warmer it makes a rapid growth, and under favourable conditions will reach to a height of between four and five feet, while during the winter months, although it only grows slowly it provides a small amount of green feed very suitable for sheep. Several people claim having introduced this grass into Australia; but Mr. E. Seccombe, of Wollongbar, on the Richmond River, New South Wales, was the first man to plant any area and to make the grass known. This was about the year 1892, and since then the grass has been tried with more or less success in all parts of Australia. Mr. Seccombe was very anxious to improve the pastures on his dairy farm, and for

Paspalum dilatatum grown by Mr. A. W. Edgar at Gingin.

this purpose obtained seeds from all parts, and found the paspalum dilatatum do better than any other grass he was able to obtain. He became a great advocate for this grass for dairy purposes, and on the Richmond River some wonderful results have been obtained from feeding stock on this grass. The Richmond River district is a highly fertile one, and has plenty of summer rain, conditions that are not found in the greater part of the agricultural areas of this State. Although not perhaps flourishing to the same extent as on the Richmond River, paspalum dilatatum has done very well in many parts of this State. In the South-West district, about Bunbury and all along the South-Western settlement, there are here and there some splendid patches of this grass. On the Midland Line, as far as Koojan, the grass is growing well. On the Southern Line, right through from Beverley to Albany, there are small areas that promise to give excellent results. In the Eastern districts, where the conditions are drier, this grass will not grow to the same extent, but where it has become established it has stood the dry summer months as well as any grass that we have yet found.

Considerable difficulty is often experienced in growing this grass from seed, but this can, I think, be put down to two causes, both of which may be avoided, viz., insufficient cultivation of the soil, and immature and badly selected seed. The ground for sowing grass seed requires to be brought to a fine tilth ; the seed, being small and light, requires to be covered very lightly, and if the soil is rough and covered with clods as we so often see it, it is impossible for the young seed to obtain a roothold. The ground cannot be too finely worked to sow grass seed ; it requires to be harrowed, cross-harrowed, disced and rolled, until a fine level surface is obtained. It is no use to say it is too much trouble, or it will not pay; if it is worth doing at all it is worth doing well, and it is better to run a harrow or roller over the ground a few extra times than to find your labour and seed all lost, and then put the blame on the seedsman or anybody except yourself. If the ground is well worked the seed may be sown broadcast and simply rolled in ; if sown in this way it is better to mix the seed with cocksfoot grass seed, as the cocksfoot does well in the winter, and is at its best when the paspalum dilatatum is at its worst. By this means a good pasture may be obtained which will carry a great number of stock all the year around.

Quantities of immature seed have been sold in this market, and this has been the cause of so many complaints as to the seed failing to grow. The seed ripens unevenly, part of the seed head being quite yellow, and the other part green. The best way to harvest a small quantity is by hand, to go along and pick off all the yellow seeds, but if any quantity has to be harvested this method will be found to be too slow and expensive. The best way to harvest a large quantity is to cut down the grass and tie into sheaves and remove them to the shed, and then shake the sheaves over the floor, the seeds that come off first will be mostly good plump seeds, with very little green seed among it, and will nearly all germinate. After this is done, the sheaves may be kept and shaken several times, or put into a heap and thrashed out with a flail, but the seed is only of a second quality, and the germinating power is small. The first quality of seed fetches the best price, and is well worth the extra as it is troublesome to obtain. The second quality is sold for any price that can be obtained, and is the dearest in the end as it often fails to germinate at all.

In the drier districts the seed should be sown during the autumn months but in the moister districts may be sown in the spring, say, September. The plant does not make much growth until the weather becomes warm. About 10lbs. of seed are required to sow an acre, and the seed may now be purchased in Perth from 1s. 6d. to 2s. per lb. A good way to plant out this grass in small areas is by subdivision of the roots; the plant grows to a large clump which may be dug up and the roots divided and planted out in rows. A single clump often gives several hundred cuttings. The largest of the roots should be cut off, and also the long stalks of grass. The divided roots can then be placed in the ground and the earth well pressed round them. An acre planted in this way, the plants being three feet apart each way, would require 4,840 plants. The roots may be obtained from any seedsman in Perth. The price varies according to the quantity required.

The analysis of hay made from paspalum dilatatum grass in New South Wales was as follows:— .

Moisture	...	...	...	...	10·55
Soluble albumenoids	...	...	...	...	1·38
Insoluble albumenoids		...	...	...	8·93
Digestible fibre	...	..	...	...	29·96
Woody fibre	...	...	...	...	27·95
Soluble ash	...	...	...	...	4·32
Insoluble ash	...	...	..	...	2·05
Amide compounds		...	...	...	14·86

This analysis shows that the total amounts of albumenoids and of digestible fibre, which are the chief factors in determining the feeding value of the hay, are fully equal to the hay made from the English meadow grasses.

In the last issue of the JOURNAL a letter was published from Mr. B. Harrison, of the Tweed River, New South Wales, giving some particulars of the results obtained there from the growth of this grass, and should have proved of interest to those who have this grass under cultivation. He gives instances of 100 head of dairy cattle being kept all the year round on 100 acres of paspalum dilatatum grass, and giving splendid returns; and the writer has seen paddocks in the same locality where similar results have been obtained.

The illustration shows the growth of the paspalum dilatatum grass on Mr. A. Edgar's Strathalbyn Estate at Gingin. Mr. Edgar has been very successful with this grass and has found it give excellent results from a stockbreeder's point of view.

Paspalum virgatum.

This grass belongs to the same species as the paspalum dilatatum, and is a very strong growing variety and at the Hamel State farm has reached over 9 feet in height after a few months' growth. The grass is more upright in habit of growth than the paspalum dilatatum. It is a deep-rooted grass, spreads rapidly, and gives a heavy yield of fodder. It is not of nearly such good feeding value as paspalum dilatatum and stock do not eat it so readily, in many cases they do not eat it while there is any other green food available. It is suitable for poor soil and a dry climate, but should not be allowed to spread in good soil. As it can be grown where very few other grasses will succeed, a small area put out on land not likely to be required for any other purpose might prove of value at a time when feed is short. It can be either raised from seed or by division of roots, and both seed and roots can be obtained from Perth seedsmen. Seed should be sown either in the autumn or early spring, about 10lbs. being required for an acre.

PLATE. I.—*Paspalum virgatum* grown at Hamel Experimental Plots.

The illustration shows a row of paspalum virgatum grass grown at the Hamel farm.

Panicum spectabile.

Kuown in this State as "African Wonder Grass."

Baron Von Müeller in his work on Select Extra-Tropical Plants, states in regard to this plant:—

"The 'Coapem' of Angola. From West Africa, transferred to many other tropical countries. A rather succulent, very fattening grass, famed not only in its native land, but also long since in Brazil. This grass, which was, with the help of the great Kew establishment, first obtained by the author for Australia and Polynesia, is, according to Mr. R. L. Holmes, "the wonder of all beholders in Fiji, strangling by its running roots almost anything in its course. At its original starting point, forming a mass of the richest green foliage, over six feet high, gradually lowering to the outer border, where a network of shoots or runners cover the ground; it roots at the joints and sends up then a mass of the softest and most luscious fodder." In Fiji, it runs over the soil at the rate of 10 feet in three months. Readily propagated by pieces of the procumbent stem, which roots freely at each joint. Spoken of also in high praise, on account of its astonishing growth, by Mr. Edgar, of Rockhampton Botanical Gardens, Queensland. Requires to be well fed down. It may be assumed that at present about 300 well defined species of Panicum are well-known, chiefly tropical and sub-tropical; very few extending naturally to Europe or the United States of North America, Japan, or the southern part of Australia. Though mostly from the hot zones, these grasses endure the cooler clime in many instances, and some of them would prove great acquisitions, particularly the perennial species. Numerous good kinds occur spontaneously in Queensland and North Australia. Panicum is the genus richest in species amongst grasses."

This grass has been grown at the Hamel State farm, the Narrogin and Chapman farms, and has given most promising results; in fact, it seems to stand the dry weather better than any grass that we have yet had growing. A large number of the roots were distributed last season, and from the reports received it appears to be doing equally well in sandy and clayey land and also in dry places. At the Subiaco Depôt last year this grass grew well and kept green on a patch of loose sand on which everything else was dried up. All the plants raised last year have been divided up and transplanted so as to increase the area under this grass for next season.

Unfortunately the grass has not yet seeded in the south-west of the State as the weather does not seem hot enough to mature the seed; consequently the seed must be obtained from a more tropical climate or else the plant can be propagated by the division of roots. The Department has been trying to obtain a supply of the seed but has not yet succeeded. The plant grows most luxuriantly, and as well as the upright growth sends out long lateral stems which form fresh roots at the nodules and cause the grass to spread quickly.

The roots should be planted in early spring and should be put in rows three feet apart, and the roots two feet apart in the rows. Under favourable circumstances they will cover the ground the first season.

The accompanying illustration shows four and a half months' growth of this grass at the Hamel plots.

Panicum prolutum.

Known as "Rigid Panick Grass." Is a native of Australia. Mr. F Turner, F.L.S., in his work on Australian Grasses, states:—

"This erect, rather rigid, perennial species is found growing principally in the interior.of New South Wales, Victoria, Queensland, and South Australia, and in some situations it is moderately plentiful. It is generally found growing on good land that is liable to periodical inundations, and as it makes most of its growth during the summer months, it is a valuable standby for stock when other grasses are somewhat scarce. It is a valuable addition to other herbage, and under ordinary circumstances will retain its greenness far into the autumn months. It is not considered a good grass to make hay of, as its stems and leaves are too rigid when fully developed, but as a pasture grass in the interior it is much valued. Before the aborigines tasted the sweets of civilisation they used to collect the seeds of this grass in large quantities and use them as an article of food, after grinding them between two stones, which converted them into a kind of meal. The Rigid Panick Grass is well worth conserving where it is already grown, and disseminating in suitable districts where it does not already exist. There would be no difficulty in collecting seeds of this grass, for under ordinary circumstances it produces an abundance, which ripens in the summer and autumn months. As much seed as would sow several acres could be collected in a few hours in a reserved area within the railway enclosures."

Baron Von Müeller states this grass is indigenous to South-Eastern Australia, and flourishes in the hottest weather.

This grass has been grown at the Hamel plots during the last two years, and has proved an excellent grass for withstanding the dry weather. It is deep-rooted, and when young makes an excellent food for stock, but gets rather coarse if not fed down. So far the grass has only been grown on a small scale, but the manager of the Hamel farm hopes to shortly plant a larger area so as to test it under different conditions. At present we can only say that it is a grass that promises well.

The illustration is taken from Mr. F. Turner's work on Australian Grasses.

Chloris virgata.

Known as Rhodes Grass. Is a grass that has been introduced from South Africa, where it has a great reputation as a drought resister. In places where it has been tried in Australia it has given a good account of itself and has stood the dry season very well. At present the cultivation of any extensive area has been prevented by the high price of seed, but as plots become more plentiful the price of seed will no doubt come down. At present the best means to plant the grass is to obtain a small sample packet, which can be purchased for a shilling. If this seed is sown under favourable conditions sufficient plants will soon be obtainable to divide up, and thereby increase the area from which a supply of seed may be obtained the following year. The habit of growth is very similar to that of the couch grass; the plant sends out long runners which root at each joint and form a fresh plant. When grazed on by stock before the plant is well grown these long runners are pulled up and prevented from rooting and the plant receives a great check in growth. To prevent this the stock should be kept off the grass until it becomes well established.

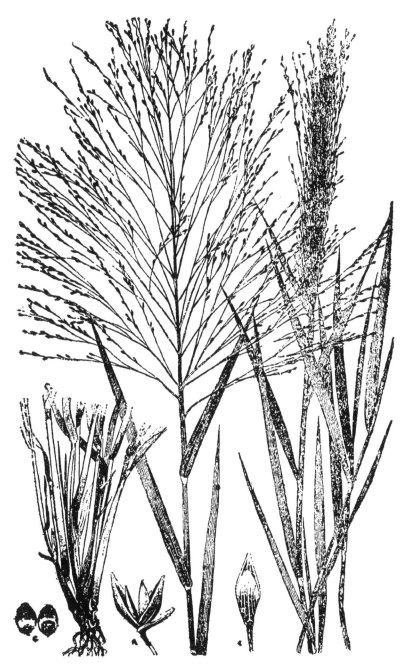

Panicum prolutum, F.V.M., by Turner.

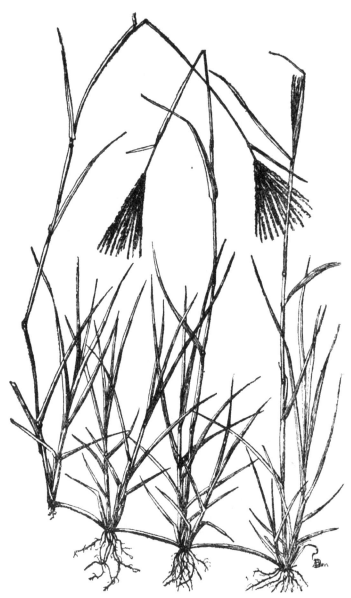

Rhodes Grass (*Chloris virgata*).

Small areas of this grass have been tried at Hamel, Narrogin, and Chapman State farms. At Hamel, in a moist situation, the grass made a wonderful growth. At Narrogin and Chapman the grass made a fair growth, but the results are not decisive enough to draw conclusions from. At the Subiaco Depôt it was tried in a dry sandy soil, and although it did fairly well, it did not resist the dry weather to the same extent as the African Wonder grass, sown at the same time, neither did it yield nearly such a supply of green fodder. The seed should be sown in the early autumn, or, if not obtainable then, in the early spring; but, under the climatic conditions in this State, the autumn-sown grass is likely to give the best result. Although the plant will not make much growth during the winter, it will obtain a good root-hold of the soil, and it is this property which enables it to withstand the dry summer months. If roots are planted, they should be put in about three feet apart each way. To plant a square chain of land at this distance will require 480 plants, and these can be purchased from the Perth seedsmen at the rate of 10s. per 100, or at a reduced rate for larger quantities.

The illustration of Rhodes Grass is taken from the JOURNAL issued by the Transvaal Department of Agriculture, from whom the Department of Agriculture in this State has just obtained a quantity of seed of this grass, which will be sown at the State farms in this State.

Among other grasses and plants now being tried, which have deep rooting qualities, and that are likely to prove valuable for our summer climate are—*Gymnothrix candata*, a perennial grass, the seed of which was recently obtained from Japan, where it is highly spoken of; *Eragrostis* or *Agrostis pilosa*, said to be a native of Australia; Bokhara Clover, a very deeply-rooted plant of the leguminæ tribe, which grows well during the summer; the *Lathyrus sylvestris*, another strong-growing plant of the same order. These grasses are now all growing at the Hamel plots, and some notes on their growth will be published in a future article.

INTRODUCTION OF PARASITES.

REPORT OF COMMITTEE.

Final report of the Advisory Board upon an inquiry into the allegations made by Mr. Lowe, late Assistant Entomologist, as to the non-efficacy of the endeavours of the Department of Agriculture to cope with insect pests by means of their natural parasites.

The interim report authorised to be presented to the Hon. the Minister for Agriculture, and forwarded by the Secretary, was considered necessary and sufficient to justify the continuation of Mr. Compére's researches, and was made with the object of leaving him free, should the Minister decide to instruct him to proceed on his travels.

As the scheme of parasitisation of insect pests has been the subject of controversy for some years past, the Board is of opinion that it is desirable, in the public interest, that whatever evidence may be available on either side should be clearly set out for the impartial judgment of those concerned.

Speaking generally, it may be said that the conflicting opinions in this field appear to be, on the one side, those of the professional museum-trained entomologist, who mainly concerns himself with the identification and description of insects in general, irrespective of their places in the economy of nature. Success with him is measured by the degree of completeness in the collection under his charge.

This view of the parasitical theory was placed before the Board by Mr. Lowe (a disciple of Mr. Theobald, by whom he was recommended to the Government), in effect, in the following words :—

> "This is an old abandoned scheme, founded on unnatural and impossible working principles, making a vain attempt to force nature to overreach immutable laws contrived and welded by an allwise and beneficent Creator.

> "Our present day naturalists versed in this knowledge declare this precious scheme to be diametrically opposed to the working of the sublime laws of nature."

On the other side are the practical entomologists, who hear the agriculturists calling for aid against the ravaging hosts of minute foes, and who say, "We are not concerned as to what the insect is; we want to know what it does. If it is a fighter on the side of the agriculturist, we want him in millions ; other insects we have no time for " ; and so they go on their way searching for the farmer's friends, heedless of the thousands of forms useless to him, each one of which, however, would claim attention in turn from the academic entomologist.

It is unfortunate for Mr. Lowe that the statement of the case as put forward by him on behalf of the museum-trained scientists, was distinctly at variance with his own expressed opinion published only a short time previously, as follows :—

> "The importation into this State from other parts of the world of species of insects that destroy other kinds of insects and are known as parasites, with the sole object in view of their assisting growers to contend against the destructiveness of harmful insects, called pests in their orchards, is a subject that arrests the attention of every enlightened citizen of the State. For are we not all, either directly or indirectly, interested in the welfare and development of our fruit growing industry, and, consequently, in every real endeavour that is made to foster and raise it to the proud position it aspires to, of the first and best fruit producer of the State of the Australian Commonwealth ?

> "The whole scheme of opposing insects that attack cultivated vegetation by their insect enemies, which assist to hold them in check on uncultivated vegetation, is founded on the philosophical statement made after a calm, contemplative view of nature's method. This statement " no insect is a pest in a country where it is indigenous" is proved only in relation to time and things in nature. It was made years ago, before its present advocates were born, and gives an excellent illustration of the survival of the fittest, the war of species, which has raged, and will continue to do so, while things exist.

African Wonder Grass (*Panicum spectabile*).   Four and a-half months' growth.

"A strong colony would prove themselves capable of doing the work in one year, without orders, supervision, or wages, that had previously kept a man engaged for the spraying season. He would be able, instead, to give his time to another part of the orchard work.

"To grasp the full significance of the benefits the utilisation of these natural checks would confer, we should consider not only the large direct lost from the depredations of the insect, but also the annual cost growers had formerly been put to of combatting insect pests by the use of spray-pump and kerosene. Again the worry of carrying out tiresome, time-wasting directions for spraying. A great argument in favour of the attempt to adopt this rational method of treatment is the cost of the elaborate plant required for spraying and keeping it in repair. (Page 305, October number, Vol. XII. of the AGRICULTURAL JOURNAL, 1905.)

It is furthermore important that the change of view admitted in his evidence by Mr. Lowe, should have been almost concurrent with his disagreement with Mr. Compère, and his knowledge of the probability of his salary being omitted from the annual estimates to be placed before Parliament. His culminating misfortune, however, occurred when the witnesses nominated by himself with emphatic unanimity testified to the excellent work done by parasites collected and introduced by Mr. Compère.

Under these circumstances the Board had no option but to register the failure of Mr. Lowe to substantiate his allegations. The Board is of opinion, however, that it would be failing in its full duty, were it to omit to direct attention to some of the more important deductions suggested by a close analysis of the evidence placed before it.

It may be fairly claimed that the birth of the science of the utilisation of the services of insignificant friends in the insect world dates from the widespread devastation of citrus growers in California and Cape Colony in the eighties, and in the marvellous reproduction of the *Icerya purchasi* as recorded in the history of Californian horticulture, and described by Mr. Compère in the following words:—

"We did not keep down the Cottony cushion scale, though we tried to do so. Ten times as much was spent on sprays as the orchards were worth in the endeavours to clean out the scale by spraying."

From that time this proposition has forced its recognition upon a limited world; limited, because though this pest was subjugated as rapidly as it arose by its arch enemy the *Vedalia*, the nature of the lesson has been only partially recognised. California has found it possible to subdue many of its foreign foes by foreign friends. Hawaii freed its sugar plantations from devastation by the Meally bug through the aid of an Australian lady-bird. Satisfactory progress has been made in this State as the evidence attached discloses. It is not uncommon, however, to find persons who, when first attracted by the probabilities suggested, rushed to the conclusion that all that is necessary is to turn loose a colony of parasites and the work is done. These are disappointed if no immediate result follows, and at once condemn the system.

A most useful lesson in this connection may be gathered from the evidence attached hereto. A few years ago the orchards and gardens of this State were grossly infected with the Black scale and the Soft-brown scale. To-day it seems they are in subjection. But this condition was not reached until no less than 11 distinct enemies of the scale had been introduced as follows:—

BLACK SCALE.

From	Variety Parasite.	Date of Arrival.	Number Liberated.
New South Wales ...	*Dilophogaster Californica*	16– 4–02	45
Do. ...	*Hemencyotus Crawii* ...	28– 4–02	11
New South Wales and Queensland	*Myiocneme Comperi* ...	12– 6–02	938
South Africa	*Scutellista Cyanea* ...	28–10–02	30
New South Wales and Queensland	1 unnamed	12– 6–03	60
South Africa	2 unnamed ... · ...	17– 9–03	85
Brazil	1 unnamed	2– 7–04	60
California	2 unnamed	12– 7–04	19
China	*Red Scutellista*	1–11–05	3

The above have been established. There were many more species sent in which may have established themselves but have not yet been identified.

This would seem to suggest that the fullest measure of immunity from any pest is only to be obtained by procuring every variety of insect which may be found preying upon the pest.

With the success of the past in evidence before us, coupled with the so far well-sustained contention that "no insect is a pest in a country where it is indigenous," it would seem an act of wanton disregard for the immense potentialities possible to the State were we to lapse into the do-nothing policy of some other States. The longer they continue on that course the better the start secured by our growers, and the greater will be the attraction we can offer to settlers from oversea.

In conclusion, the Board desire to express their recognition of the good work being done by the inspectors, as shown in their evidence, and especially of the earnest enthusiasm shown by Mr. Newman in the work of observation of the imported parasite. It would further suggest that much more of Mr. Compère's time could be given to collecting were it arranged that he could be met from time to time at Colombo or other convenient port by an officer from the Department who would be competent to take charge and convey home whatever "desirable aliens" may have been secured. By this means probably twice the work would be accomplished within a given time.

(Sgd.) CHAS. HARPER,
Chairman.

EGG CROP.

By G. Chitty Baker.

The present season may be termed the egg harvest of the poultry yard, more eggs being layed during the Spring of the year than any other time. The natural consequence is reduction in the selling price, and those who go in for egg production on a large scale must, when they have to buy feed, find but very little profit in the industry, for it is also at this time of the year that the price of grain hardens, so that we are faced with the unsatisfactory state that as the price for our eggs becomes less the cost of feed increases.

This condition of affairs would be somewhat disheartening if it were not for the fact that science has enabled us to adjust matters by regulating the market, and storing the surplus crop of eggs until better prices are ruling.

There are several ways of preserving eggs. The small man can use silicate of soda, sold under a variety of names, as water-glass, etc., etc., yet it cannot be controverted that the best and safest way to keep eggs is that of cold storage. Not only does it keep the eggs in a much better state, but so little does it affect the natural conditions, that the germ has been brought into life after several months of cold storage. This has been proved by an experiment made for hatching purposes in April last, and reported in the June issue of the Journal, as follows :—" An experimenth as just been made by an officer of the Department of Agriculture to test the hatching properties of eggs that had been kept in cold storage. Eggs were obtained in November of last year, and placed in cold storage by Mr. Cairns at the Government Refrigerating Works on the 1st of December. They were subjected to a very severe test. At times the temperature was shown as low as 38°F. In April, a clutch was taken out and placed under a hen. On the fourth day the eggs were tested, when seven were found to contain live germs, three had just started germination, and died, and the remaining three eggs were infertile. On the seventh day two more were found to contain dead germs; the five remaining ones continued to die off, only one chick being fully developed, but had not stamina enough to emerge from the shell. Although the experiment can hardly be claimed a success, yet the main point, i.e., that the germ is not destroyed by cold storage, opens up a big field for experiments for the safe transit of valuable eggs over long distances."

This result, unsatisfactory in a sense as it is, could never be obtained from eggs treated in any other manner for the purpose of preserving them ; at the same time it establishes the advantages of cool storage.

It has often been a matter of surprise that while endless pains have been taken in order to increase egg production, very little trouble has been gone to to get the best kind of egg for keeping. A bad keeping egg is not only worthless in itself but has a very injurious effect on all others that it comes in contact with. The best egg for cold storage is that from a yard where no male bird is allowed to run, having a close, firm, and dense shell. For the latter purpose it will be found to be of great commercial value if poultry keepers were to breed up for this purpose. It is a phase of the question that has not attracted the amount of attention it deserves ; a thin porous shell allows a too rapid change to the egg matter, either decomposition sets in earlier or too great evaporation takes place, in either case the keeping qualities are far away inferior to that of the egg that has a thick close shell; a good keeping egg can always be told by holding it up to the light when it will have an even opaque appearance, while with the thin and very porous egg, when submitted to this test, will have the appearance of being spotted all over, sometimes in blotches. These should always be rejected when filling up a case for storage.

Selecting Eggs and Packing.—As previously stated, the best eggs are from yards in which hens only are kept eggs; to have a close thick shell, of medium and uniform size, selecting clean to soiled ones. On no account must eggs intended for cold storage be washed, dipped in any solution, or rubbed, but packed direct from the nest. The reason of this is that when an egg is laid it has a microscopically thin film over it, which is easily removed, while its retention is a great assistance to its being kept in a fresh con-

Egg Box, for Transit or Cold Storage.

dition. One of the best kind of packing cases is here illustrated. It consists of an ordinary kerosene case with patent cardboard fillers, that may be obtained in sets at a cost of about one shilling, and would pack 25 dozen eggs. The sets may be purchased from the makers, Messrs. Sands & McDougall, Perth, to whom we are indebted for the use of the illustration. For cold storage it is necessary to take off a half inch slip from the top and bottom sides of the front and back of the case to ensure a complete circulation of air. The following points are worth remembering when cold storage is used : Collect from nests and pack direct; don't wash eggs ; select clean ones; give preference to thick shells; have all eggs in one case of an even size ; do not attempt in any way to treat with preservatives.

ENTOMOLOGISTS' CONFERENCE.

We have just received, through the courtesy of the Minister of Agriculture of New South Wales, a copy of the proceedings of the Conference of States' Entomologists recently held in Sydney. From this we gather that valuable work has been done. The reports on the Codlin Moth and Fruit provides particularly interesting reading, and are here reproduced.

REPORT OF CODLIN MOTH SUB-COMMITTEE.

That for the suppression of Codlin Moth in the Australian States, this Conference is of the opinion that no more effective means than the following have been yet proved in Australia :—

1. That the distribution of the insect or of fruits which have been affected thereby should be prohibited by a clearly worded law, which should be strictly enforced.

2. In the orchard the following measures have proved effective to the extent of saving up to 90 per cent. of the fruit when consistently applied in accordance with the breeding habits of the insects in the respective localities :—

   (a.) Spraying from three to six times after the setting of the fruits with arsenite of soda (Kedzie's formula), or Paris Green of standard quality.

   (b.) Clearing away all natural refuge for the caterpillars, such as rough bark, knot-holes, stakes, rubbish, etc.

   (c.) Using bandage traps around the stems of the trees, which in turn are frequently cleansed.

   (d.) Making all fruit stores moth-tight, and destroying the winged insects as they emerge from time to time.

   (e.) All infested and fallen fruits collected from the trees and ground as frequently as possible, and destroyed by boiling.

   (f.) The use of second-hand fruit cases or bags for handling fruit without their being efficiently disinfected should be discouraged.

Moved by Mr. Froggatt, seconded by Mr. French—That the report be adopted. Carried unanimously.

11. Restrictions necessary to secure States in which fruit flies are not established against infestation by those of New South Wales, Queensland, West Australia. and elsewhere.

Motion 21.—That, in the opinion of this Conference, it is not desirable in order to exclude the fruit flies of New South Wales, Queensland, and West Australia, to prohibit the fruit from other States being imported into Victoria, Tasmania, and South Australia respectively, until improved methods of inspection have been tried and have proven ineffectual.

Moved by Mr. C. French (Victoria), seconded by Mr. A. M. Lea (Tasmania).

The Chairman, in introducing the discussion, stated that the consideration of the means to be adopted for the protection of the orchards of the Southern States of Australia from infestation by Fruit Flies (*Tephritidæ*), that occurred in Queensland, New South Wales, and Western Australia, was one of the most important subjects that the Conference had to deal with. Those who were familiar with the ravages of fruit fly maggots knew what their presence in the orchard might mean to its proprietor. The question, moreover, would receive additional importance should the measures for protection advocated seriously interfere with the prime industries and commerce of the Commonwealth. He alluded to a recent movement in Victoria aiming at the prohibition of the importation of bananas, citrus, pineapples, and other fruits from States where the pests alluded to were already established.

He would dwell upon this matter from a Queensland point of view, leaving his colleague of New South Wales to speak with reference to it from his own standpoint.

Such an embargo as that to which he alluded as being proposed would involve a loss in trade to the northern State of at least £50,000 per annum, a loss which would have very far-reaching effects. This embargo would in a great measure apply to that constituted by that important food product, the banana, that served now as the principal motive for the visits to the ports of north-east Australia of the large steamers engaged in the shipping industry.

The Chairman stated that even if bananas received this exceptional consideration this State exported large quantities of citrus and other fruits to Victoria—nearly 32,000 cases of the former having been directly shipped thereto in the interval 1st January to 15th June of the present year alone; and as for pine-apples and cucumbers and the extension of the prohibition to them, he had never met with anyone in his State who had these fruits to be fly-maggot infested, nor had his own personal investigations led to any such discovery.

The true fruit flies of Queensland affecting cultivated plants were two in number, viz :—(1), the so-called Queensland Fruit Fly (*Tephritis Tryoni*, Froggatt); (2), the Spotted Fruit Fly (*Tephritis psidii*, Froggatt); but in this connection he would refer to a third since it had been stated to occur in Queensland fruit by Mr. C. French—the so-called Mediterranean Fruit Fly (*Ceratitis capitata*, Wiedemann); the words "so-called" being used advisedly, since the Mediterranean Fruit Fly was *Ceratitis hispanica*, Breme.

The second of these (*Tephritis psidii*), he would not further allude to, as his remarks concerning Tryon's fruit fly might be applied to it; and since it appeared never to have been encountered in fruit at the Southern ports, and even had not hitherto been recorded in Australia.

He continued that, so far as regarded the Queensland Fruit Fly (*Tephritis Tryoni*, Froggatt), he was of opinion that it would never become established in the fruit-growing districts of the Southern States of Australia. That the facts that had led him to arrive at this conclusion, and that had been already submitted to the Government of Victoria, were as follow :—

(1.) That, during the twenty years since he had studied the insect, he had never found that it had extended its range of permanent occurrence.

(2.) That its occurrence in Queensland exhibited two features—

(a.) There were districts in which it was permanently endemic;

(b.) There were others to which from time to time it got transported by wind or human agency, but in which it did not permanently subsist.

(3.) That, notwithstanding, a vast trade in fruit subject to the attack of the fruit-maggot fly had existed between Queensland and the Southern States, and between it and Victoria, especially, for years before any inspection had been insisted upon or exercised; and that, since these procedures had been followed, maggot-infested fruit had been found within the markets and shops of these States, or in Victoria, at least, as admitted by Mr. French. No single instance has been brought to light of the insect's having established itself even temporarily in any Southern orchard or garden. In Southern New South Wales, again, it had no permanent existence, or was absent therefrom.

(4.) That it was a feature connected with several fruit flies that they did not extend their range of occurrence, being apparently hindered in this by climatic barriers. A remark applicable to species of these insects that were native ones, such as the one under consideration.

Secondly, and with reference to the so-called Mediterranean fly (*Ceratitis capitata*, Wied):—

(1.) He had no personal evidence of its occurrence in Queensland, although a special locality search had been instituted in a in which its presence had been suggested, involving a close scrutiny of fruit emanating therefrom, as soon as this suggestion had been received; but he was prepared to accept Mr. French's statement that he had, on the other hand, found it in oranges, contained in Queensland fruit-cases, exposed for sale; two instances of which had been brought under the notice of the Queensland Department of Agriculture.

(2.) That the occurrence of the insect under these conditions did not necessarily prove its existence in the orchards of his State, as was capable of being explained by practices of the trade.

The trade practices he alluded to were,—

(1.) One brought personally under his notice by a well-known fruit exporter of New South Wales, who, amongst others, received these Queensland oranges, and repacked them for the Southern States and elsewhere. He, on the previous day, whilst bringing under his notice some defects in the packing of Queensland oranges, referred to neglect to fully fill the boxes, the latter thus requiring the addition of fruit before they could be despatched, the deficiency—often amounting to 8 per cent.—being supplied by the local product.

(2.) The unscrupulous procedure of using the designation (? cases) of Queensland fruit to sell New South Wales inferior lines that had been referred to by a Victorian agent of the Queensland Citrus-growers' Association when in Brisbane. Of course, the wide occurrence of *Ceratitis capitata* in New South Wales orangeries was well established.

(3.) That even if the insect existed in West Australia, New South Wales, and Queensland, and so became transported to the Southern States, and although it might thereby become established in the orchards, the probability of this happening could not be inferred from the known range of occurrence of the Mediterranean Fruit Fly, since the Australian insect (*Ceratitis capitata*) and the Mediterranean one (*Ceratitis hispanica*) were distinct species, as held by Breme, Guerm Meneville, Macquart, Rondani, Targioni, Penzig, Lunardoni, Continental entomologists, to whose writings he referred.

(4.) That in some of the European countries was it found necessary to place an embargo on fruit fly infested fruit from the Mediterranean region, or by that infested by the fly now under consideration, although, as stated by Macleay as early as 1829, such was exposed for sale in the streets of their cities. Macleay makes special reference to tender and diseased fruit there emanating from the Azores.

(5.) That the question of prohibiting the introduction of citrus and other fruit from the Mediterranean region, the headquarters of the true Mediterranean Fruit Fly, had not been mooted.

The Chairman then briefly alluded to the history of the movement in Victoria from the issue of a circular by the Government Entomologist to the meeting of fruit-growers at Doncaster, giving Mr. French credit for the solicitude for Victoria's interests, as regards the fruit-growing industry, that he had displayed.

In conclusion, he stated that Queensland was in full sympathy with Victoria in its desire to keep its orchards free from the presence of these fruit fly pests, but he was of opinion that there was no urgent necessity for adopting the extreme measure directed in part towards an important industry of that State that had been alluded to.

Mr. W. W. Froggatt (New South Wales) generally concurred in the points elaborated by the Chairman so far as they had reference to the fruit flies common to both States, and especially with Mr. Tryon's reference to the limitations characterising the range of the Queensland Fruit Fly.

Mr. French (Victoria) stated, on the assumption that the fruit flies would not thrive in Victoria—as suggested by Mr. Tryon so far as regarded the Queensland Fruit Fly—the value of inspection might be questioned. He was of opinion that they would, and they had had an instance of a Victorian orchard being infested by the Mediterranean species. He then referred generally to the circumstances under which he had found the latter insect in fruit in Queensland fruit cases.

Mr. Lea (Tasmania) stated that as regards the Queensland Fruit Fly (*Tephritis Tryoni*) he was opinion that it would not thrive in Tasmania or in Victoria, but, speaking for Tasmania, it would not be safe, he considered, to allow maggotty fruit to come in. However, the so-called

"Mediterranean Fruit Fly" (*Ceratitis capitata*) would thrive both in Victoria and Tasmania, as had been proved in two instances of infestation that had been promptly stamped out. And that the Government of Tasmania would not relax in any way the measures that it had taken to prevent the introduction of the injurious insects under consideration. As for prohibition of fruit importation from fruit-fly infested States and countries, he had heard the suggestion spoken of amongst Tasmanian orchardists, and in this matter if the question came up for consideration he would follow the procedure adopted by Victoria.

The Chairman stated that the fact that local infestation had taken place in two instances and the fly had disappeared either supported the view that the Mediterranean Fruit Fly would not thrive in Victoria or Tasmania, or that if local infestation took place it could be successfully coped with.

Mr. G. Quinn (South Australia) commended Mr. French on the part taken by him, as animadverted upon by the Chairman, in taking initiatory measures in urging on Victoria the prosecution of the strongest measures to secure the exclusion of fruit flies. It was expected of the Government Entomologist that he should be the watchdog of the interests of his State in a matter of this kind.

In South Australia the question of the expediency of prohibiting fruit-exports from fly-infested States and countries had been early raised, and debated even in the Legislative Chamber; but on full consideration it had been decided that it was unnecessary, Personally, he was averse to pro-hibition. But the alternative procedure that it had been recognised as being neceessary was the most thorough inspection and the rejection of diseased fruit or even fruit presumably so, and he was not aware that any fruit fly had escaped the scrutiny of his officers on whom this devolved. He had mentioned this matter of close inspection because the charges for inspection had been commented upon, but thorough inspection involved a more than nominal outlay. He was of opinion that South Australia pos-sessed districts were the climate approximated to that of those districts of Western Australia where the Mediterranean Fruit Fly was disastrously prevalent.

Mr. A. M. Lea referred to the great destruction of fruit occasioned by the insect referred to in the orchards of Western Australia, as noted by him personally. He also was in accord with Mr. Quinn's statement regarding the climatic conditions of West Australia and South Australia respectively.

The motion after this thorough discussion was put to the meeting and carried unanimously.

Motion 22.—While not considering this alone to be a sufficient safe-guard, this Conference desires to emphasise the value of the system of inspecting fruit at the ports of shipment, as in the extension of this system, combined with a critical examination at the port of entry ,lies the hope of preventing the spread of fruit flies to the States still uninfested by them.

Moved by Mr. G. Quinn, seconded by Mr. W. W. Froggart.

This motion was carried unanimously, and without discussion.

Motion 23.—That, in the opinion of this Conference, rigid inspection of all fruits liable to carry fruit flies in any stages should be made; and that, when any fruits are seen to be affected by such pests, the whole of the same, together with the packages containing them, should be destroyed by boiling or burning, as the case may require.

Moved by Mr. A. M. Lea (Tasmania), seconded by Mr. G. Quinn (S.A.).

Carried unanimously.

FRUIT FLIES.

Measures for Adoption in States wherein Fruit Flies are established.

Motion 26.—That for the suppression of fruit flies in the Australian States the Conference is of opinion that no more effective means than the following have been yet proved:—

All infested and fallen fruits should be gathered and destroyed at least once a week, either by boiling or burning. The fruit of valuable trees may be economically protected from fly infestation by being covered in hessian, cotton netting, or other suitable fabric.

The recommendation covering the destruction of maggot-infested fruit should especially contemplate measures of this kind carried out early in the season, before the fruit fly in the course of natural production has become especially numerous.

Neglected and abandoned orchards should be destroyed.

Where the pest has first appeared in an orchard or district, the ground under the fruit trees should be sprayed with kerosene or other mineral oil, and all fruit picked and destroyed.

Rigid inspection of markets should be made, and infested fruit seized and at once destroyed.

Success can only be expected against fruit flies by uniform and compulsory action.

All market refuse, being liable to comprise fly-infested fruit, should be regarded as disease-infested, and treated accordingly.

We are aware in making these recommendations that no evidence has been placed before the Conference to show that these precautionary measures have yet been fully put into practice with anything approaching combined and thorough action in any district, much less in any State.

No contact insecticide so far is known to be effective against fruit flies.

Bandages, as for codlin moth, are useless against fruit flies.

COW MANURE.

A correspondent writes asking the value and uses of cow dung as a manure. The matter was referred to Mr. Despeissis, who states that cow manure is called " cold " manure when compared with horse or sheep manures which are " hot " manures, as it decomposes much more slowly.

Its value as a fertilising material, apart from the care taken in conserving it, is influenced by the age and class of animals; manure for instance from growing animals and milk cows being poorer than that from grown-up steers and fat beasts.

The best plan of utilising the manure referred to, which presumably has been more or less exposed to the elements, is to turn it into a rich compost, by mixing with it some phosphatic fertilisers and ashes or potash fertilisers; build it up on a piece of non-absorbent ground and after a few weeks cut it across and rebuild it, or cart it out on to the field.

Half a cwt. of super or Abrolhos guano and the same quantity of kainit per ton of cow manure would add to its manurial value very materially.

In grazing countries, cow manure is greatly used for top-dressing grass land. Reinforced in the manner suggested it would answer, when well rotted, for all kinds of gardening or for growing potatoes, or any crop at all.

POULTRY NOTES.

By Frank H. Robertson.

THE EGG-LAYING COMPETITIONS.

These events are now the all absorbing topic to anyone who takes an interest in poultry, and the progress of events are being watched very keenly.

The following are the records for August of the Subiaco birds:—

Fowls.

Six hens in each pen.

Owner and Breed.					Aug.	Total.
1. Sunnyhurst (S.A.), W. Leghorn	...	...	...	...	140	279
2. J. D. Smith, W. Leghorn	...	...	...	...	133	251
3. C. Attwell, S. Wyandotte	...	...	...	...	122	245
4. A. F. Farrant, Partridge Wyandotte			...	...	159	241
5. B. Jones, S. Wyandotte...	...	...	...	...	120	240
6. S. Craig, W. Leghorn ...	...	...	...	...	121	239

FOWLS—*continued.*

Owner and Breed.	Aug.	Total.
7. A. H. Padman (S.A.), W. Leghorn	139	237
8. L. Meatchem, G. Wyandotte	141	233
9. A. S. B. Craig, W. Wyandotte	120	230
10. E. Garbett, W. Leghorn	131	227
11. F. T. Rowe, Black Orpington	121	224
12. Ericville Farm, W. Leghorn	134	221
13. A. H. Padman (S.A.), S. Wyandotte	133	217
14. Mrs. McGree, W. Leghorn	128	213
15. W. J. Clarke, Brown Leghorn	131	213
16. E. F. Braddock, S. Wyandotte	107	207
17. C. W. Johnson, W. Leghorn	120	207
18. Bungalow Yard, Brown Leghorn	120	205
19. G. W. G. Lizars, W. Leghorn	116	200
20. R. G. Flynn, W. Leghorn	123	197
21. F. Whitfield, W. Leghorn	126	196
22. Ryan Bros., W. Leghorn	120	196
23. J. W. Buttsworth, W. Leghorn	95	194
24. F. Whitfield, Brown Leghorn	134	193
25. E. Fitzgerald, W. Leghorn	132	193
26. A. Snell, Brown Leghorn	110	193
27. J. W. Buttsworth, S. Wyandotte	120	192
28. Bungalow Farm, W. Leghorn	122	190
29. W. Snowden, S. Wyandotte	108	188
30. F. Piaggio, W. Leghorn	127	184
31. G. M. Buttsworth, W. Leghorn	120	184
32. A. Coombs, S. Wyandotte	117	181
33. Ericville Yard, Black Orpington	106	178
34. J. R. Parkes, Brown Leghorn	118	177
35. Geo. Bolger, Black Orpington	113	176
36. H. Jones, W. Leghorn	123	173
37. Austin and Thomas, W. Leghorn	105	170
38. O. K. Yard, Black Orpington	117	169
39. Adelaide Yard, W. Leghorn	119	168
40. E. Hutchinson, Minorca	120	167
41. E. Palmerston, W. Leghorn	124	166
42. Glen Donald Yard, G. Wyandotte	115	165
43. Bon Accord Yard, W. Leghorn	107	159
44. Perth Yard, W. Leghorn	126	158
45. A. R. Keesing, Minorca	124	156
46. F. Mason, W. Leghorn	102	152
47. Honnor and Forbes, R. C., W. Leghorn	115	149
48. H. M. Kelly, G. Wyandotte	121	148
49. C. R. Roberts, W. Leghorn	112	146
50. W. Wade, W. Leghorn	97	145
51. E. G. Smith, W. Wyandotte	109	144
52. W. Snowden, Brown Leghorn	102	141
53. Mrs. Hughes, R. C. Brown Leghorn	100	137
54. E. A. Newton, W. Leghorn	102	134
55. Jas. Kirk, G. Wyandotte	87	126
56. H. H. Wegg, G. Wyandotte	79	119
57. Mrs. McGree, W. Wyandotte	105	116
58. C. Crawley, Black Orpington	106	106
59. J. E. Redman, S. Wyandotte	91	103
60. J. White, Brown Leghorn	97	102
61. J. B. Pettit, S. Wyandotte	87	92
62. J. S. Miller, S. Wyandotte	82	87
63. H. M. Kelly, Black Orpington	85	85
64. A. Savage, Minorca	80	80
Total for the month		7,366

DUCKS.

Four in each Pen.

Owner and Breed.		Aug.	Total.
1. R. A. Dusting, Indian Runner	... ...	116	180
2. E. A. Newton do.	... ...	116	157
3. Mrs. Mellen do.	... ...	106	153
4. Austin and Thomas, Indian Runner ...	... ...	102	133
5. G. Stead, Indian Runner	... ...	85	132
6. A. Snell do.	... ...	97	117
7. W. Snowden, Buff Orpington ...	... ...	83	109
8. Bon Accord do.	... ...	76	98
9. Ericville do.	... ...	71	93
10. Miss Parker, Indian Runner ...	... ...	75	87
11. F. T. Rowe do.	... ...	85	86
12. C. E. Close do.	... ...	85	85
13. Perth Poultry Yard, Buff Orpington	... ...	63	84
14. Adelaide Poultry Yard, Indian Runner	... ...	74	74
15. J. R. Parkes, Indian Runner ...	... ...	39	39
16. Sargenfri (S.A.), Buff Orpington	... ...	30	30
17. S. Craig, Indian Runner	... ...	27	29
18. F. Piaggio, Buff Orpington ...	... ...	0	14
19. F. D. Vincent, Indian Runner	... ...	8	10
20. C. W. Johnson do.	... ...	5	7
21. Aveley Poultry Yard, Indian Runner	... ' ...	2	2
22. J. B. Pettit, Indian Runner ...	... ...	0	0

Total eggs laid for month 1,345

From the above list it will be seen that the laying was very good and uniform throughout, only 10 pens producing less than 100 eggs each. The Sunnyhurst pen, from South Australia, which had the lead for the first month (July), still head the list. These birds come from a yard which has already made a great name in laying competitions in the Eastern States, and their foremost position in our competition affords striking evidence as to the reliability of proved egg-laying strains to maintain their reputations for productiveness.

The variety of breeds represented is a popular collection; still there are some good varieties absent which would have added to the interest of the competition, viz., Buff Orpingtons, Plymouth Rocks, Langshans, Andalusians, and Hamburghs. Of Minorcas, there are only three pens, and one of them is so far last. It is, however, by no means uncommon to find this splendid breed occupying very backward positions in competitions. Too much attention to fancy points has undoubtedly been the cause of decadence of these one-time great layers, but strains of great prolificacy do still exist, as was proved by the splendid record put up by Minorcas at the recent Rockdale competition, where they came third, with a magnificent record of 237 eggs per bird for the 12 months. There are too many small eggs to be seen at our markets, and as the Minorca is the bird which stands out as a producer of the largest eggs, its presence is urgently required among our flocks to attain the desired end. The writer, recognising the necessity of remedying matters in this direction, is taking steps to re-introduce the breed at the Narrogin Poultry Farm, and would recommend poultry keepers to again take up the breed and develop its latent great egg-laying qualities.

The Subiaco competition serves to bring one of the newer breeds into prominence, viz., the Partridge Wyandotte, a pen having] been entered by Mr. Farrant of Claremont. They laid 82 eggs during the first month, and for July made the magnificent yield of 159, which was stated to have been a record, but such is however not the case, having been exceeded by a pen of R.C. White Leghorns at the last Rockdale competition, which for October 1905 laid 167 eggs; Brown Leghorns also laid 168, Langshans 165, and White Leghorns 166.

The ducks have also laid well, and the two leading pens, both Indian Runners, each produced 116 eggs out of a possible 124. All of the waterfowl have quite got over the moult, and a greatly increased output can shortly be looked for.

It is rather a pity that only two breeds of ducks should have entered. Other good varieties that would have been acceptable are Rouens, Aylesburys, and Pekins, the last-named in particular, because strains of Pekins are celebrated for their laying qualities; such, however, are not to be found among the mammoth show type of this favourite variety, but among the medium sized and more active specimens.

THE FEEDING OF THE FOWLS.

Many inquiries are made as to what the birds are fed on, as persons who get poor results from their own birds think that some special feeding is employed to get so good a supply of eggs from birds at competitions; such, however, is not the case; plain fare is the order of the day, given regularly and in a common sense manner. Animal food and green stuff, of course they have. If nothing but bran and pollard and wheat were given, and the birds stuffed to their fullest extent all the year round, the egg yield would not be a big one. The mode of feeding is to give, at 7 a.m., a mash composed of pollard, steamed lucerne, chaff, and a little bran three times a week, a little oil cake is added, also boiled liver, or the soup of same; cut fresh bone is given at midday, the mash is mixed crumbly, and as much as the birds will eat is given to them; if any remains in the pens it is taken away. Green stuff is given at mid-day; Cape weed at present is the chief supply; it is not cut up but is thrown into the pens whole, and employment is thus found the birds in picking it to pieces. The evening feed is generally wheat, occasionally varied with crushed maize, barley, or stout oats, the general allowance being about six handsful to each pen, but this is reduced or increased as the judgment of the feeder dictates, which means according to the appetites of the fowls; this is where care is necessary, and in this respect the feeder who studies his birds soon learns to know what is the correct quantity; the appearance of the crop is one good indication, another is whether the fowls eat with avidity or not, then again some birds are more prone to put 'on flesh than others; all these little points are attained by experience easily learnt by anyone who takes an interest in their fowls, but given the best of feed, if injudiciously applied, a good egg supply will not follow. This is just where the mistake so often occurs, it is not so much what the food is, but how it is given. The hard feed is scattered on the ground. As the pens are clean, the scratching shed will be used later on for grain feeding.

A liberal supply of shell and crushed blue metal is always kept in the pens, and it is surprising the amount consumed, especially at this time of year, when a heavy egg yield is being obtained. The grit is not kept in tins at present, but is left on the ground at the back end of each run.

The ducks are fed entirely on mash made much the same as for the fowls, except that more bran and oilcake are added; the birds are given as much as they can eat, a supply of grit is always before them. The water is kept in kerosene tins, one side only half cut away, so that the birds can drink in comfort, at the same time not large enough to let the birds into it. Large square water tins are kept outside the runs, and the ducks allowed out of the runs one lot at a time, where they can get a good wash.

Male birds have been placed in about half of the pens. Eggs from same are for sale at parcels ranging from 10s. 6d. to £2 2s. per setting. Anyone requiring eggs should apply to the manager, at Subiaco.

THE NARROGIN COMPETITION.

The following is the record of eggs laid at the above contest, by which it will be seen that the egg yield was not so good as at Subiaco, which is probably owing to the cold and wet experienced during the past month. A much larger yield will no doubt be obtained for September.

	Breed.	Owner.	Total for Month.	Total to Date.
1.	White Leghorns	Mrs. A. Bristow	108	437
2.	Brown do.	E. E. Ranford	111	378
3.	Buff Orpingtons	A. H. Hilton	120	372
4.	Silver Wyandottes	Miss Buttsworth	111	367
5.	White Leghorns	C. W. Johnson	83	344
6.	Do. do.	F. Piaggio	96	344
7.	Silver Wyandottes	A. M. Neitschke	133	335
8.	Brown Leghorns	Mrs. R. A. Dusting	111	308
9.	Silver Wyandottes	G. W. G. Lizars	96	302
10.	White Leghorns	J. Handley	76	285
11.	Do. do.	A. F. Spencer	88	283
12.	Do. do.	Miss M. Parker	99	273
13.	Black Orpingtons	Sparks & Binnington	94	260
14.	White Wyandottes	Mrs. S. J. Hood	103	256
15.	R.C. Brown Leghorns	Adelaide Yards	94	254
16.	Golden Wyandottes	W. J. Craig	92	253
17.	R.C. Brown Leghorns	E. Krachler	82	238
18.	White do.	G. Oneto	38	235
19.	Do. do.	F. J. Williams	109	229
20.	Black Orpingtons	Perth Yard	62	222
21.	Brown Leghorns	J. D. Wilson	89	222
22.	Do. do.	Aveley Yard	81	220
23.	White do.	J. E. Tull	75	214
24.	Do. do.	R. G. Flynn	62	194
25.	Do. do.	O. C. Roth	69	136
		Totals	2,282	6,961

THE POULTRY AT NARROGIN FARM.

The poultry are all looking well and laying well. Chicken raising is in full swing; at the present time over 200 youngsters have so far been hatched, and losses are almost *nil*.

There still remain some birds for sale. viz.; Silver Wyandotte Cockerels and Bronze Turkey Gobblers, some very fine specimens among the latter.

Eggs are for sale of the following varieties, viz.: White Leghorns, Brown Leghorns, Plymouth Rocks, Pekin Ducks, and Indian Runner Ducks, all at 12s. 6d. per dozen, carefully packed and railage paid to all parts of the State; anyone having poor results can be supplied with a fresh lot of eggs provided the old ones are returned to the farm. This is an exceedingly liberal arrangement, as it practically means a guarantee of a live chick for every egg; such, as anyone knows, is unusual, and it is not likely that any purchaser of eggs who gets from 8 to 10 chicks would feel dissatisfied with the result, still, there is the guarantee, as it is determined that all purchasers of eggs must receive full satisfaction.

A limited number of Toulouse Geese eggs are also for sale at 30s. per dozen or 10s. for a hen sitting of four. A few Bronze Turkey eggs are also for sale at 20s. per dozen, but a guarantee could not be given to replace these two varieties on account of the limited supply available.

A Decrease in Egg Importations.

From the Government Statistician's Office it is pleasing to learn that there has been a decrease in the importation of eggs of £10,000 worth for the year 1905.

The following figures give the value of the importations from 1895:—

1895.	1896.	1897.	1898.	1899.	1900.	1901.	1902.	1903.	1904.	1905.
£	£	£	£	£	£	£	£	£	£	£
11,920	33,389	51,429	52,667	50,682	60,465	57,430	71,885	73,538	80,055	70,528

The decrease is substantial, and has every prospect of being a permanent and ever-increasing one; it is certainly to be hoped that such is the case. Next year's figures will be awaited with interest for confirmation on the point.

Poultry Importations.

This State is not even able to supply its own requirements in poultry, as we still import, but to a very small extent in comparison with eggs. The greater number of poultry arrive in a frozen condition, as shown by the figures hereunder :—

1904—Frozen poultry, £3,227; live poultry, £1,785. Total, £5,012.
1905—Frozen poultry, £4,040; live poultry, £1,068. Total. £5,108.

The above figures show a trifling increase for 1905. The whole amount of £5,000 odd is not large, but it serves to prove that we are still backward in the matter of raising table poultry, when it pays people to go to the expense of incurring all the shipping charges and land poultry here at a profit. There are, of course, many persons who consider that prices both for poultry and eggs are already too low to produce them at a profit, and particularly at this time of the year, when eggs in the wholesale markets recede to 1s. per dozen, and even as low as 10d. It certainly is a low price, but it must be remembered that eggs, in common with other products of the farm, have their periods of glut, also their times of scarcity. What is required is to regulate the market, and this can assuredly be done by making use of

Cold Storage.

By this means eggs are kept fresh for an indefinite period, provided, of course that they are perfectly good when placed in the stores, for be it remembered that perishable products cannot possibly be improved in quality by semi-refrigeration; all it can do is to arrest decay, and hold in suspension the degenerating powers that would otherwise assert themselves. It therefore means that fresh eggs, placed in the cool stores now, are available for sale during the scarce period from February to June at prices which will show a handsome profit after paying all expenses. The writer placed a few cases of eggs in the Government cold stores last November. The eggs were bought at 1s. a dozen in the wholesale auction rooms, and some were sold during the month of May by auction at 2s. per dozen, and an unlimited quantity could have been disposed of at that price. The remainder of the eggs still remain in the cool stores for further experiment. The writer this day ate some for breakfast and found them excellent. Cold storage of eggs is not a particularly new idea, as it has been largely availed of in other parts of the world, particularly in the United States of America; in Victoria it has now attained large dimensions. In conversation the other day with a Melbourne manufacturing stationer, he informed me that his firm annually makes tons of the cardboard fillers for packing eggs for cold storage. The cardboard divisions made for this purpose fit kerosene cases to allow of 25 dozen eggs being held in each case. This is the best way of packing eggs for cold storage. A few auger holes should be bored in the sides of the boxes to allow the cold air free egress. The expenses incurred are, say, 3d. per kerosene case; fillers, 9½d. the set for 25 dozen eggs; storage charges, 3d. a case per week. The other usual charges would occur, viz., railage, cartage, and auctioneers' commission. Allowing for all these, it would not exceed 6d. a dozen even to a farmer residing 150 miles from Perth, but the price realised in six months' time from now would at least double the present market prices, and thus result in a 50 per cent. better price for a producer. The writer has now commenced to place eggs from the farm and competitions into cold storage, and trusts later on to show actual results as to what can be done in this respect.

EXPORT OF FRUIT.

REQUIREMENTS OF LONDON MARKET.

The following interesting report on the requirements of the London fruit market has been supplied to the Press by Mr. Alex. Crawford. In dealing with exportation of fruits from this State he says:—

"There should be a good market for Navel oranges—Washington Navels. I saw them sold in Regent-street and Bond-street as a special seedless orange marked up at 4s. 6d. and 5s. per dozen. I only saw them in three or four shops altogether, and in none were they labelled 'Navel' or 'Washington Navel.' One shop had them marked 'New seedless orange, finest quality, 2s. 6d. per basket'—and on it were fine, good-sized Navel oranges. I was told by one salesman that he had obtained as high as 4s. per dozen for them at auction. This salesman was very particular to point out that in sending oranges to the London market the utmost care should be taken in grading them, and each one in a case should resemble the rest like pennies. All sizes, to small medium, are saleable, but for the highest class trade with clubs and best hotels there is always a demand for extra large ones. 'That market,' he remarked, 'would be easily overdone, as the demand even in London is limited. In fact,' he said, 'there is always a good market here (London) for anything out of the way good in the fruit line.' Questioned on the subject of

MANDARINS

being sent home, he was doubtful if they would pay unless they could be shipped at a very low cost. There was but little demand for them, and the few that came did not find ready sale. I saw some in a shop window, and bought some at 3d. per dozen, and if they were a fair sample of what goes there, I do not wonder at their not finding a ready sale, or any sale at all. I sampled one or two other lots at Covent Garden, but they were little better, and I could not help wondering what success a 'Jupp's' or 'Lauder's' mandarin would have if put on the English market in good condition. As regards the ordinary run of oranges, that is, medium and small-sized, I do not think there will ever be a market for them. I bought very fair medium-sized oranges at the retail price of three for 1d. That meant, wholesale, probably, not 2d. per dozen, and I scarcely think it will ever pay to send them there at the price. Of course, this was at a time when they were most plentiful, but the market seems to be fully supplied the year through with this class of orange, not only from Europe, but from Africa and the Islands.

LEMONS

can be bought at from 3d. to 4d. per dozen in the smaller retail shops, and from the hawkers' barrows. Of course, in the shops in the better localities the prices are much higher, but the wholesale price for the ordinary Lisbon lemon was about 2d. per dozen. Some I saw brought equal to about 4d. per dozen. At a show I visited there was a fine display of fruit from Australia, South Africa, and West Indies. From all the Australian States, South Africa, and West Indies the fruit had been sent over especially for the show, and only the choicest specimens of the various fruits were in evidence. They were packed with the greatest care in soft wood shavings and silk paper, and not the sign of a bruise or a flaw of any kind was to be seen. About 70 varieties of apples were exhibited, five of each variety on a plate, with a small card bearing the name of the variety neatly. The exhibits attracted much attention, and were a credit to the various States. The Western Australian looked very mean in comparison with some of the others. There were only three varieties, and scarcely one but was more or less seriously damaged. Some of them had been packed so tightly in the cases that they were almost cubes in shapes, four sides flattened in, almost square, and no names sent, the only fruit that could be identified being Jonathans. The exhibit of

PEARS FROM TASMANIA.

was magnificent, and consisted of about thirty varieties in splendid condition. Amongst them were the following varieties:—Wedale's St. Germain, Buerre Clairgeau, Giblin, Edgewood, Winter Nelis, Chaumontel, Easter Beurre, Beurre Diel, Crassane, Passe Colmans, Black Pear of Worcester, l'Inconnue, Easter Bergamot, Madame Cole, Beurre Capiamont, Josephine de Maline, Vicar of Wakefield, Angon Fiorelle, Conseiller, Beurre Rose, Thompson's

Vicar of Winkfield, Doncaster Seedling. and Glen Morceau. In examining the general packing I found that in some instances the fruit was packed in boxes divided with cardboard, like those used for packing valuable eggs in. The fruit was surrounded with fine shavings of soft wood, having first been wrapped in several sheets of fine silk paper. Others were packed in trays, well wrapped in silk paper, and protected with silk paper or soft wood shavings. Although the pears looked so well they were singularly devoid of flavour, and such as I was able to sample had a very wooden taste with a little juice. I saw pears from South Africa sold by auction at 3s. per dozen, and I saw similar ones for sale in a Bond-street fruiterer's marked 12s a dozen. Several commission merchants who handle these goods told me that not withstanding the

High Prices often Obtained

the loss is so heavy that they did not think that pears ever paid the shippers.

Amongst the exhibits at the West Indian Court were sweet potatoes, but for size and quality they were not to be compared with those grown in Western Australia. Questioning the salesmen about these I found that some were of opinion that there would be a fair market for them, whilst others thought they would not pay to ship.

Grapes in considerable quantity are sent from South Africa, and reach London at a time when there are but few on the market, except the high-priced home-grown hot-house grapes. Although the grapes arrive in fair condition they, from all reports, can scarcely be said to be much of a success, owing to a want of care in sending other than those of finest quality, and through the not thinning of the bunches when they are growing. One of the largest buyers told me that it was worse than useless to send grapes to the London market unless they had been carefully thinned when growing, so that every grape had room to thoroughly develop. Unless this is done, as a rule the grapes begin to go bad in the centre of the cluster where they are tightly jammed together, and when once decay is started the grapes are almost unsaleable, except to hawkers at a nominal price. It would seem that there would be a fair market for

A High-class Grape,

well thinned, preferably purple in colour, to arrive at the end of March, April, or May; after that it would be too late. If white grapes are sent, the French White Muscat would be preferred. In good condition the grapes might bring anything from 6d. to 2s 6d. a pound, the price being very variable. Extra fine ones arriving about Christmas might realise high prices, but the market at that season is unreliable, and none of the salesmen recommend sending them. All the salesmen practically agree that the best method of packing grapes is in cork dust. I saw some casks of Almira grapes from Spain, opened up in a sale-room, which had been in store in the cellar for six months. They were sound and in good order, only looking a little sunken. The temperature of the cellar was about 50deg. F. Out of 20 bunches taken from one cask only one bunch showed any signs of decay, and from 15 bunches taken from another cask there was no sign of decay.

What Salesmen Recommend.

One salesman—one of the largest handlers of colonial fruit—gave me the following :—" Leave pears alone ; they do not pay for the trouble, and

there is generally a loss on the consignments.   Impress upon your people the
necessity of thoroughly grading all apples sent.   You can send all kinds,
extra large, large, medium, and small, to suit all classes of buyers, but they
must be carefully graded, only one size to a case.   They should all be
wrapped in paper and packed on their sides.   If oranges are sent, the best
time for them to arrive is in August, September, October, and November. It
is even more important that these should be graded than apples.   They
should be all exactly the same size in a case.   Each one should be wrapped
in paper, and a case should contain exactly one of the following numbers of
oranges : 80, 120, 150, or 250—the larger sizes of cases preferred.   There
would probably be a fair market for new potatoes to arrive in England about
the beginning or middle of December.   Kidneys are the only variety that
would be saleable, and they would need to be packed in cases, carefully
graded, and small.   Large tubers would be unsaleable."   Almost all the
salesmen impressed upon me that all cases in which fruit is packed should
be planed up, and made as neat as possible.   The better the case looks the
better chance there is of getting a good price.   No matter how good the
fruit may be, if in rough cases, it will not bring anything like as good a
price as if the case is nice-looking.   It is almost incredible how much the
appearance of the case has to do with the price realised.

VEGETABLE GROWING.

By G. Chitty Baker.

(Continued.)

Transplanting.

It is always advisable to raise the plants of cabbages, lettuce, cauliflowers, celery, onions, Cape goosberries, tomatoes and herbs in small seed
plots for planting out after the young seedlings have made a fair growth.
Exception to this rule, however, is made with regard to lettuce, during the
late spring and summer months ; the seed must be sown in drills where the
plant is to remain, and thinned out to the proper distances apart.   The
reason for this is that lettuce plants, if sown in seed beds at this time and
then transplanted, are very apt to run to seed.

In transplanting, care must be taken that the plants receive little or no
check.   Dull weather is always the best to select for this, and the operations
carried out towards the close of the day.   If the ground is at all dry, a good
plan is to first open the rows and apply a liberal amount of water.   The
plants should be taken up carefully from the seed bed, and put into
a bucket containing water, to which has been added half an ounce
of sulphate of ammonia, and the same quantity of sulphate of potash and
superphosphate to each gallon of water.   In cases where these fertilisers

Nam	Time required for Crop to Mature.	Fertilisers required per square rod.		
		Super-phosphate.	Sulphate of Ammonia.	Sulphate of Potash.
Asparag	to 3 years from seed	7 lbs.	3 lbs.	1 lb.
Beans,	mopths	9 ,,	1 ,,	$\frac{3}{4}$,,
,,	to 5 months ...	9 ,,	1 ,,	$\frac{3}{4}$,,
Beetroot	to 5 ,, ...	2 ,,	$\frac{1}{2}$,,	$\frac{1}{4}$,,
Cabbage	to 6 ,, ...	$2\frac{1}{2}$,,	$1\frac{1}{2}$,,	$\frac{3}{4}$,,
Carrots	to 3 ,, ...	2 ,,	1 ,,	$\frac{3}{4}$,,
Cauliflo	to 6 ,, ...	$2\frac{1}{2}$,,	$1\frac{1}{2}$,,	$\frac{3}{4}$,,
Celery ..	to 5 ,, ...	7 ,,	3 ,,	1 ,,
Cucumb	to 4 ,, ...	2 ,,	$1\frac{1}{2}$,,	$\frac{3}{4}$,,
Lettuce	0 to 13 weeks ...	$2\frac{1}{2}$,,	$1\frac{1}{2}$,,	$\frac{1}{4}$,,
Melon,	to 4 months ...	2 ,,	$1\frac{1}{2}$,,	$\frac{3}{4}$,,
,,	to 4 ,, ...	2 ,,	$1\frac{1}{2}$,,	$\frac{3}{4}$,,
Onion ..	to 4 ,, ...	$\frac{1}{4}$,,	$\frac{1}{4}$,,	1 oz.
Parsnip	to 4 ,, ...	$2\frac{1}{2}$,,	1 ,,	$\frac{3}{4}$ lb.
Peas ..	to 4 ,, ...	9 ,,	1 ,,	$\frac{3}{4}$,,
Potato ..	to 4 ,, ...	7 ,,	1 ,,	$1\frac{1}{4}$,,
Pumpki	to 4 ,, ...	2 ,,	$1\frac{1}{2}$,,	$\frac{3}{4}$,,
Radish	to 6 weeks ...	$2\frac{1}{2}$,,	$\frac{1}{2}$,,	$\frac{1}{4}$,,
Sea Ka	to 4 months ...	$2\frac{1}{2}$,,	$1\frac{1}{2}$,,	$\frac{3}{4}$,,
Silver	to 3	$2\frac{1}{2}$,,	$1\frac{1}{2}$,,	$\frac{3}{4}$,,
Sprouts	to 6	$2\frac{1}{2}$,,	$1\frac{1}{2}$,,	$\frac{3}{4}$,,
Spinac	to 3	$2\frac{1}{2}$,,	$1\frac{1}{2}$,,	$\frac{3}{4}$,,
Squash	to 4 ..			$\frac{3}{4}$,,
Tomato	to 5 ,,			$\frac{1}{2}$,,
Turnip	to 13 weeks ...			$\frac{1}{4}$,,

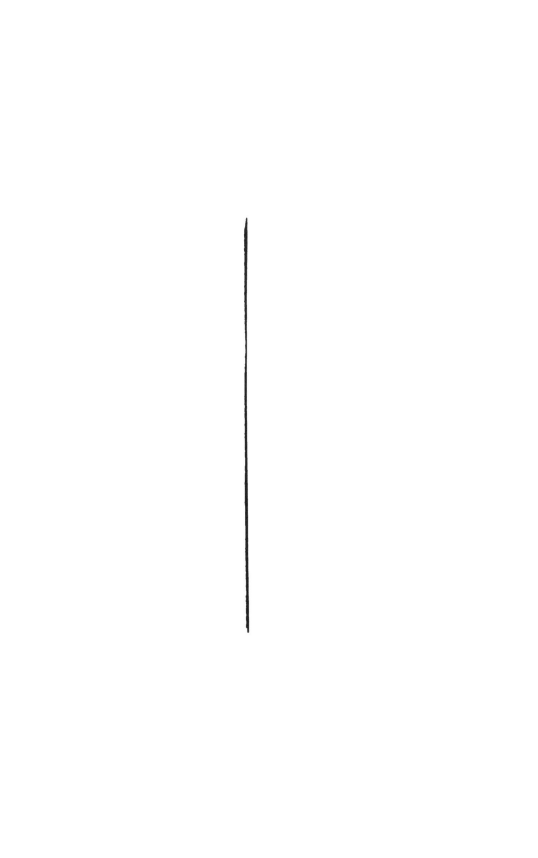

are not available a little liquid fowl or other manure may be used. For cabbages and cauliflowers, a good protection from aphis, etc., is to soak the seedlings in some good, strong, warm soap suds for a few minutes before planting out.

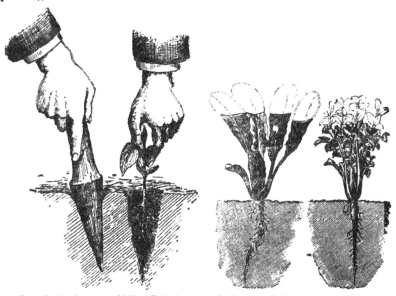

Transplanting by means of dibber (Bailey).   Cutting tops off plants when transplanting (Bailey).

In warm and dry weather it will be found to be a very great advantage if the tops of the leaves are cut or sheared off as shown in the illustration above. This prevents too great an evaporation, which the roots are unable to meet until they become established in their new position.

FERTILISING.

As most crops require different quantities of fertilisers, to treat all vegetables alike would be absurd; neither is it advisable to generalise the subject. In the chart published with this article the quantities of fertilisers required for each crop are given. The area dealt with is one rod, 30¼ square yards or 5½ yards square, this being about the amount of space required for a crop for an ordinary sized family. The particular manner of when and how to apply is given as each vegetable is dealt with further on. As a general rule it may be laid down that such fertilisers as sulphate of ammonia, sulphate of potash, and nitrate of soda are best applied during the growth of a plant, as by reason of these fertilisers being so soluble there is always the risk of a portion being leached out and loss to the plants before being sufficiently grown to avail themselves of it.

(To be continued.)

SOIL ANALYSIS.

HAMEL SETTLEMENT.

(By E. A. MANN, Government Analyst.)

According to a promise made by the Hon. the Premier to the settlers at Hamel recently, the Department has had nine samples of soil taken from various blocks and submitted for analysis, with the following result.

The samples taken were as follows :—

(1.) Power's Block.
(2.) Hallam's Block (Virgin).
(3.) Hallam's Block (Fallow).
(4.) Hallam's Block (Swamp).
(5.) Owen's Block.
(6.) Skilling's Block.
(7.) Ryan's Block.
(8.) Ryan's Block.
(9.) O'Grady's Block.

No. of Sample.	Percentage of Fine Soil. (Passed by 2 m.m. Sieve.)	Percentage of Roots and Stone. (Retained by 2 m.m. Sieve.)	Reaction of Soil.
1	95·72	4·28	Acid
2	97·86	2·14	Faintly Acid
3	97·15	2·85	„ „
4	97·15	2·85	Acid „
5	95·78	4·22	„
6	94·74	5·26	„
7	94·21	5·79	Faintly Acid
8	88·68	11·32	Acid
9	93·17	6·83	„

Analysis of Soil.

—	1.	2.	3.	4.	5.	6.	7.	8.	9.
Phosphoric Acid (total) ...	·017	·006	·005	·022	·018	·013	·016	·020	·041
Phosphoric Acid (available)	·0056	·0014	·0005	·0033	·0031	·0020	·0028	·0052	·0064
Potash (total)	·062	·033	·106	·055	·056	·031	·056	·044	·039
Potash (available)... ...	·0065	·0065	·0083	·0012	·0008	·0017	·0033	·0027	·0065
Lime	·050	·055	·039	·042	·070	·056	·052	·060	·063
Nitrogen	·269	·162	·145	·263	·269	·201	·252	·252	·482
Chlorine	·015	·009	·005	·018	·011	·010	·012	·010	·029

"Total" represents percentage soluble in strong acid.

"Available" represents percentage soluble in 1 per cent. citric acid in seven days (Dyer).

Fertiliser requirements and remarks :—

The soils generally are of poor quality.
Nos. 1, 2, 4, 5, 6, 7, 8, and 9 are deficient in potash, phosphoric acid, and lime.
No. 3 is deficient in phosphoric acid and lime.

The principal features of these analyses are :—

(1.) The large number of "acid" soils.

(2.) The frequent deficiency in lime.

(3.) The generally low percentage of total fertilising constituents. This deficiency is often made up by mechanical conditions favourable for the free penetration of the root system.

(4.) The relatively large proportion of "available" to "total" phosphoric acid and potash in some instances.

(5.) The lack of humus.

It is now pretty generally conceded that a soil must be judged as to its fertility, not so much by its total fertilising constituents as by the proportion of these which are available for plant life.

Dr. Bernard Dyer, in his Lawes Trust Lectures, in America, stated as a result of the Rothamstead experiments, conducted over a period of 50 years, the following definite conclusions could be drawn, viz. :—That a soil containing as low as ·01 per cent. of phosphoric acid "available" required phosphatic manuring, but when the proportion reached ·08 per cent. that necessity no longer existed. The corresponding limits for potash he placed at about ·005 per cent., and ·01 per cent., respectively. Judged by this standard, many of the soils included in this list have to be considered as containing sufficient potash, although the "total" amount of this present is very small.

This opens up a very interesting field of speculation as regards our soils, in the light of the results which have often been obtained with what were in appearance very poor soils.

[With reference to the foregoing analysis, Mr. Despeissis recommends that a good liming would neutralise the acidity of the soil, and prepare the crops to better utilise any fertilisers which may be applied to the land. Phosphates, more especially, are needed, with a little potash for such crops as belong to the pea and clover family, as well as potatoes.—Ed. JOURNAL.]

ALGARROBILLA.

(*Balsamo-carpon brevifolium* Clos. and *Cæsalpinia brevifolia*, Bentham.)

Dr. Thorp, of Perth, who is an enthusiast in arbor culture, recently wrote to the British Consul at Chili for particulars of the cultivation and habits of Algarrobilla, the pods of which, according to Von Müeller, are extraordinarily rich in tannic acid, from 67 to 68½ per cent. being found in the husks. The tanning with this preparation is accomplished in one-third of the time required for leather from oak-bark. This material is also specially valuable as giving a bloom to the leather. In response to his queries Dr. Thorp has received the following:—

" The shrub is indigenous in Chili, in the northern half of the Province of Coquimbo and southern half of the Province of Atacama. It grows nowhere else in Chili nor in any other part of the world.

" The country where it grows is a dry desert where nothing else useful grows. It does not grow continuous over the country, but in clumps in the small valleys sheltered from the wind by the spurs of the hills.

" The rainfall does not average more than two inches annually. The shrub needs very little moisture, but it must have some, or it will not flower. During some periods there is no rain for three or four years in succession, when the shrub does not flower, and it loses most of its small leaves, but it does not die; it just waits for better times.

" Some of the country is owned by private owners, who protect the crop of Algarrobilla and claim a tribute from the gatherers, but most of the land belongs to the State, where anyone may gather it.

" The climate in the home of the Algarrobilla during the summer is delightful, and the gathering is a favourite holiday for miners and their families. They camp out amongst the hills for weeks, and have a healthful and enjoyable holiday."

ANSWERS TO QUESTIONS IN DR. THORP'S LETTER.

1. The soil is calcareous and very dry; rainfall about two inches per annum. Atmosphere is dry and clear. There are 300 sunny days in a year. It does not grow nearer the coast than 30 miles. The best zone is 3,000ft. above sea level, and 50 to 60 miles inland.

2. It is used locally in Chili for tanning hides, but only in a very limited extent. The pods are gathered principally for export to all foreign countries for making ink, dye stuffs, and tanning.

3. I do not know its comparative price, but it sells in England at from £10 to £15 per ton.

4. It is a thorny shrub or bush, from two to six feet high; very slow growing.

5. It is not cultivated at all owing to the want of water where it grows best. I do not know how old it is before it begins to bear, it appears to live indefinitely.

6. January to April. It only requires to be dried and kept dry and put into good wheat bags for transport. Its weight is about the same as barley.

7. The plant has no other use.

8. A small parcel of 10 to 20 pounds could be sent by post from Chili, quite enough for a trial. Dr. Thorp should get new seed direct from Chili because the seed generally contains the egg of a fly, which is hatched out in some way within a year. The grub eats out the inside of the pea and destroys the seed.

" I think that the climate of Western Australia has too much rainfall. Probably the bush might grow, but I do not think that it would give fruit.

" One essential condition, however, is that there must be no rain after the pod is formed, for the pod consists of gum, soft at first, then it dries when ripe. It is held together by a network of fine fibres. The pods are friable and the gum is easily rubbed into powder in the hand. It is soluble in water, and owing to this it must not be rained upon when growing; an occasional slight shower might not hurt it but much rain would ruin it.

" After it is in sacks it should be kept dry or it runs and cements itself into a solid lump, but when dried again it is quite good.

" I tried some years ago to cultivate a few bushes in a garden at one of the island railway stations where there is water for the locomotives, pumped from a deep well. The bushes grew well and flowered for some years but they never gave any fruit. I concluded that it was because the bushes got water in the garden amongst the other plants all the year round, which was unseasonable for them.

" If the plants had been planted at a distance from the garden and watered only in June, July, and August I think they would have produced fruit.

" Although I do not think that West Australia has a suitable climate, possibly some of the other States on the Australian Continent would suit. It is a valuable crop and well worth an extended trial.

" It has the advantage of growing well with almost no rain and where nothing else will grow for want of water. South Africa will not do because the rainy season is in summer. It needs heat and a dry atmosphere to ripen it properly."

(Sgd.) JOHN KING, British Vice Consul.

Carrizal Bajo, 24th May, 1906.

STATE FARM HAMEL.

By G. F. Berthoud.

POTATO EXPERIMENTS.

The following results have been obtained from a number of new varieties of potatoes lately imported from England and America. Owing to the late planting, which was done in the middle of May, followed by heavy rains and cold weather, the yields are light. The tubers, which were dug on the 13th August, were rather small, but sound. They should, however, make excellent seed for the larger trial plots in the summer. All sets were manured with complete fertilisers at the rate of 6cwt. per acre.

Southern Queen.—Growth, healthy and vigorous, the foliage being wide and smooth, slightly frosted. Tubers, kidney-shaped, with shallow eyes; a good, promising, second early variety. Yield, average 2¼ tons per acre.

Early Bird.—The growth of these dwarf and weak; the tubers very small, round, and with white skin; eyes shallow; an early variety. Yield very light.

Bright Eyes.—A second early variety; medium-sized, round tubers, with white skin and pink eyes. Yield moderate.

Peckover.—The growth of this variety was poor and weak; small oblong tubers, with white skin and shallow eyes; a main crop variety. Light yield.

Highlander.—This variety also proved to be of a weak growth, with small pebble-shaped tubers, white skin, and shallow eyes. Yield very light. Main crop variety.

Midlothian (Dobbie).—Growth quick, healthy, and good, with wide, smooth leaves; tubers of nice even size, pebble shape, white skin, with shallow eyes. A very promising early variety. Yield, average three tons per acre.

Royal Purple.—The growth showed stalks of moderate height, healthy foliage, dug before fully matured, tubers of fair size, kidney shape, of a light purple colour. Fair yield. Main crop variety.

Table Talk.—Growth fair and healthy, dug too soon, tubers medium size, round, white skin, with shallow eyes; a promising variety and should prove a good main crop variety. Yield fair.

From the data collected the following are considered the best in this trial, and may prove to be valuable introductions:—Midlothian Early; Southern Queen, and Table Talk.

DISTRICT NOTES.

NORTHAMPTON.

By T. Hooper, C.I.

I beg to report that on my journey to Northampton recently I noticed the wheat crops along the Midland line were looking very well; the growth seemed very even and the colour was that of a good healthy green. The land along this line is of a red sandy loam. In comparison with the Great Southern line the soil is not so heavy and the rainfall less, want of drainage therefore would not be felt to the same extent. Arriving at Northampton at midday I proceeded in the afternoon to Spring Vale, some 20 miles distant. M last visit to this neighbourhood was four years ago, and I could see ymany clearings under wheat which at my previous visit was covered with scrub. A great deal of the land around Northampton is capable of producing good wheat. At Sandy Gully, 10 miles from North-ampton, Messrs Boyd & Box have a splendid piece of wheat land 90 acres in extent, and I was informed by them that last year the portion of this land then tilled returned them an average of 24 bushels to the acre.

From Sandy Gully to Spring Vale is mostly a big sand plain, out of which every few miles rises the table-topped hills peculiar to this part of the country. Spring Vale is a valley running between two low ranges of hills. The soil here is a rich, black vegetable loam, of great depth and admirably adapted to the culture of citrus fruits. There is a small creek running through this valley of great value to the four or five orchardists which are settled there. But in its wilder moods during winter, it plays great havoc with the trees and vegetable crops, but I consider it could be effectually curbed if the settlers threw up a bank at the head of their orchards and widened and deepened the channel of the creek.

With regard to citrus fruits, I have never seen finer young trees or fruit in the State. Certain peaches, such as Briggs' Red May, China Flat, and Shanghai, do remarkably well here. The Elberta and other varieties which do well South of Perth, do not thrive in this district. It is well here to note that while good soil is the first essential of an orchard, other factors such as temperature, rainfall, wind, etc., must be taken into consideration. As evidence of this, apples, I may say, do not thrive here, the Rome Beauty being a strong grower, making about the best growth, the reason being the temperature during the summer is too high for them. On the other hand, Queensland bananas tried in this particular valley, are cut by the frost.

Messrs. Boyd and Box also have on trial some pine apples procured from this Department. The plants, which are looking well and making fine growth, bid fair to be a success.

At one time the Black and Brown Scales were severe pests in these orchards, but the introduction of parasites have thoroughly cleaned the trees, also the surrounding bush plants that were infected.

On my return to Northampton I saw a fine field of potatoes, about eight acres in extent, belonging to Mr. Hipper. I think if they had been planted a little earlier on account of future lack of rain, it would have been better for this particular field.

From Northampton I went to Norman's Well, and inspected Mr. J. Smith's orchard. This orchard, since Mr. Smith has had it, about two years, has much improved. Judicious pruning and cultivation have made the difference.

In conclusion, I may state that the Government experimental farm at Chapman having shown what this district can produce, has given an impetus to farming around Northampton.

FRUIT INDUSTRY AT BRIDGETOWN.

By GEO. W. WICKENS.

As the fruit season, 1905-1906, is now practically finished, a few notes on the progress of the industry in Bridgetown district may be of interest to readers of THE JOURNAL.

Although most portions of this State, as well as our Eastern neighbours, were suffering from a shortage in fruit production during the past season, the Blackwood district again demonstrated the suitableness of its soil and climate for apple-growing, and shows an advance on the previous season's output of over 5,000 cases.

Prices in our own markets have been very satisfactory from the growers' point of view, and this, taken in conjunction with the success of the trial shipments to England and Germany, has given orchardists great encouragement to extend the acreage already under fruit, while the newer settlers are busy clearing their holdings, and planting out young orchards in the hope of having at least a few years of fair prices in this State before general exportation comes along, and come it will, inevitably and speedily, at the present rate of planting.

The three varieties of apples that are likely to give best results for export purposes are:—"Jonathan," "Dunn's Seedling," and "Cleopatra." Each variety is a regular and heavy cropper and comes into bearing while the tree is comparatively young.

If growers prefer planting only two varieties, I would recommend "Jonathan" and "Dunn's Seedling," for although "Cleopatra" is superior in quality to either of the others, its liability to bitter pit, especially on young vigorous trees, renders it of less value for export, particularly as the disease often cannot be detected when the apples are gathered, but appears after they have been stored for some little time. I may mention that I have frequently noticed trees planted in high, well-drained land outgrow this disease as the vigour of growth lessens and the crop becomes more abundant, but where drainage is bad Cleopatras will always "spot."

Jonathans "spot" slightly, Dunn's Seedling scarcely at all. All benefit from a thorough winter spraying of lime, sulphur, and salt.

A puzzling thing in this district is the comparative non-success attending the efforts of those who are trying to grow early stone fruits.

Apricots are shy bearers in almost all situations.

Cherries are so long coming into bearing that orchardists are afraid to take the risk of planting them.

Early peaches (Briggs' Red May and varieties ripening at that season) shed a great quantity of their buds just before bursting, and trees which at the time of winter pruning promised an abundant crop set only a few fruits. When I noticed this, two seasons ago, I thought perhaps it was owing to something exceptional in the season, and would not recur regularly, but last year the same thing occurred, and in going through the orchards during the past fortnight I found all varieties of early peaches again dropping their buds. Quite a number of orchardists are talking of working over their early varieties with later ones, the later ones, as a general rule, setting their fruit well.

In pruning early peach trees, it is becoming common to leave the trees until the fruit has set, then the limbs that have shed their buds are cut back for wood for next season, while those carrying fruit are left severely alone, the fruit nearly always being at the tips. The result is a weird looking tree, for shape is entirely sacrificed to fruit, but it really seems the only way to be sure of a payable crop.

It is worthy of note that while early peaches were light last year, apricots and cherries cropped more heavily than they have been known to do previously. Quite a number of apricot trees of a fair age bore for the first time, and people who had begun to look upon their cherry trees as "ornamental," were surprised to find they had cherries for sale.

The stationmaster at Bridgetown has courteously supplied me with the record of fruit sent from Bridgetown railway station during the past four seasons. It will be noticed there is a slight decrease for the months of July and August in 1906, as compared with the same months in 1905; this is owing to the number of orchardists who, early in the season, sold right out to wholesale dealers, the fruit being railed as it was gathered and the purchaser taking the risk of storage.

It must be remembered that the record given below does not represent all the fruit produced in the Blackwood district; but only of that portion lying around Bridgetown, and also most of what is grown as the Warren.

Fruit grown at Upper and Lower Blackwood is railed at stations nearer Perth.

Fruit Record from Bridgetown.

Month.	Season 1902-3.	Season 1903-4.	Season 1904-5.	Season 1905-6.
	cases.	cases.	cases.	cases.
January	1,350	1,404	2,133	2,659
February	1,373	1,803	1,978	2,634
March	1,542	2,833	8,207	4,536
April	2,390	3,092	3,218	4,591
May	1,686	2,808	3,468	5,131
June	784	1,600	1,887	2,052
July	258	639	1,257	1,158
August	170	305	619	571*
September	38	89	168	...
October	...	37	12	...
November	...	...	...	...
December	111	108	276	...
	9,702	14,718	18,223	23,332
Increase	...	5,016	3,505	5,109

* To 27th August.

A MACHINE FOR PICKING COTTON.

By WILLIAM DALE.

Since the invention of the mower, reaper, and binder operated by animal power and steam engines, the idea of utilising mechanical means for harvesting the American cotton crop has been agitated. The revolution which was caused in agriculture by the modern methods of gathering the cereal crops indicated the saving in time and labour which could be effected in the Southern cotton fields if a machine were perfected which would harvest the ripe cotton more expeditiously than the negro farm hand.

A number of devices has been invented to take the place of hand labour in gathering the cotton crop. With one exception, however, all of these have proved failures. The principal defect has been that the machines would harvest the immature as well as mature cotton. Those familiar with this branch of agriculture know that a field must be covered several times after the bolls begin to open, as, unlike grain, the cotton does not ripen with any uniformity. During the last harvesting season, however, a machine was employed in several of the Southern States, which proved to be not only a decided improvement over the ordinary hand method, but by its means only the ripe cotton was picked, the other plants being untouched.

Part of the Field Picked and Unripe Bolls left on the Plants.

The Cotton-Picking Machine at Work.

As the photographs show, this picker is notab'e for the simplicity of its construction. Power is obtained from an ordinary gasoline engine such as is utilised in automobiles of the smaller types. In fact, the engine installed in connection with the picker utilised in the field trials was taken from an Oldsmobile and developed but 8 horse-power. In moving the picker over the ground, gearing is employed as in traction engines. Sprocket chains pass around sprocket wheels on the rear axle, thence upward and around the driving shaft. The engine, which is mounted on the rear of the truck frame, as indicated in the photographs, is employed not only to move the picker over the field but to operate the mechanism by which the cotton is harvested and placed in the storage receptacles. There are four of the latter attached to the sides of the machine. They consist merely of cloth cylinders which are open at the top, the bottom ends being held together by strings so that when the cotton is to be removed it is only necessary to loosen the end by pulling the string, when the contents of the receptacle will fall out.

The lint is conveyed to the receptacles by tubes which are attached to the series of picking devices. The lower portions of these tubes, which are made of thin sheet iron, terminate in steel conduits of the same diameter inside. Each conduit or pipe contains a fan which serves two purposes. It "doffs" or cleans the cotton, blowing out any bits of leaves, casing, or other foreign matter which may have been caught up with the lint by the picker arm, and drives the lint through the tube into the receptacle with which it is connected, by air pressure.

The picker arms are dirigible in design and comprise eight in all, four attached to the forward section of the machine and four to the rear section, all of course being connected with the tubing leading to the cotton receivers and working in connection with fans. The picker arms are fastened to the conduits by means of hinged joints, and as the illustrations show, each consists of a case enclosing an endless belt which revolves upon pulleys placed at either end. This belt is provided with a series of curved teeth. At its outer end the upper part of the casing is cut away, so that the belt is exposed for several inches. When the cotton is to be removed from a boll the operator directs the outer end of the picking arm in such a position that the teeth engage the lint. As fast as it is stripped from the boll it is carried by the endless conveyor to the blower casing, as it is called, doffed, and forced through the tube into the receiving bag. The picking head, as it might be called, is provided with a shield intended to prevent hulls, leaves, and twigs from being drawn into the picker, but, as already stated, any small particles of foreign matter are removed by fans.

The means for actuating the picker belts and doffer fan consist of a light shaft running longitudinally of the machine and parallel to the fore and aft extension tubings. This shaft is geared to the engine through the medium of gears and friction clutch, the lever of the clutch being arranged convenient to the driver. This shaft has a constant speed and is independent of the motion of the machine through the field. Power is applied to the picker belt and doffer fan from this shaft through an arrangement of light sprocket wheels and chains, which permit the dirigibility of the picking arms without in the least interfering with their flexibility.

There are seats provided on the machine to carry four operators, and each operator is provided with two picking arms, one for each hand. The arrangements of seats and picking arms is such that when facing in the direction in which the machine is travelling over the field, the two rear operators face to the right, one picking one side of the centre row and the other picking one side of the left outside row. Thus all of the centre row and one-half of each of the outside rows, in all equal to two rows, are picked.

During the trials which were made in the cotton fields in North Carolina and Alabama, it was found that eight horse-power was ample to give the machine necessary momentum with its force of hands, also to operate the picking and transferring mechanism. The rate of speed in the fields varies of course according to the amount of cotton to be picked. Where a large proportion of the bolls are open the field is covered in less time than where a small quantity of cotton is ready to be gathered, but it is obvious that with devices which can be guided as described, only the mature cotton need be gathered. As the picking belts revolve at the rate of about 350 feet per minute and eight of the pickers are in continuous operation, the capacity of the machine is much greater than where expert negro labour is employed. During the tests in Alabama the machine moved at the rate of 31 feet per minute, picking three rows of plants simultaneously. In a day of 10 hours it covered nearly five acres. The operators were young negro boys, constituting all of the manual labour with the exception of the engineer. In this trial the machine harvested 3,000 pounds of cotton in a day at a total cost of 4·75 dols., including fuel and wages. At the usual price paid for cotton picking in this State the expense for harvesting the same quantity would be 15 dols., while the machine covered a given area in one-sixth of the time which would have been required by six expert cotton pickers. In harvesting cotton in North Carolina the same results were obtained.

While the general design of the cotton picker allows three rows of plants to be harvested at one time, it can be readily enlarged to take in four or possibly five rows, and it is probable that with other improvements its capacity can be greatly increased, just as the harvester and binder of the wheat field has been radically changed since it was first introduced on the farms of the West. The inventor of the cotton picker, Mr. George A. Lowry, is now experimenting with several additional devices which are intended to further increase its speed and efficiency.—*Scientific American.*

THE SECRETION OF MILK.

By A. MEEK.

The structural facts relating to milk secretion have been investigated by various histologists, and the conclusions of Heidenhain, modified and extended by the work of Michaelis, have been recently corroborated by Brouha.

Brouha's researches were made on the mole, bat, and cat, and showed that the succession of events during one period of suckling in these animals was as follows:—

The acini and the ducts are gorged with milk just prior to suckling, and the epithelium of each acinus becomes almost pavement-like in flatness, approximating in appearance to that which clothes the ducts. This is due to the distension of the alveoli by the milk, and the pressure is sufficient to compress the blood capillaries, so that in this state the secretory activity of the cells is suspended.

As soon as suckling commences the acinus is emptied, and the pressure upon the capillaries is released. The blood begins to flow freely around the acinus, the cells gradually regain the cylindrical shape which characterises their active phase, and the elaboration of milk commences. The growth of the cells inwards is irregular. While remaining closely attached at their bases they become free internally, and project into the cavity of the acinus-like papillæ. At the same time fat globules appear in the cells in the form of minute drops, accumulating especially, however, in the projecting free inner parts of the cells. The nucleus may also be divided. The free portion of the cell with its contents is now detached, and the cytoplasm dissolves in the acinus, liberating the fatty contents, and a nucleus if such be present.

The secreting cells, after undergoing this change, continue to secrete fat globules of various sizes, which gradually approach the free surface, and are projected into the cavity of the acinus by cytoplasmic contraction. In this case, however, there is no sacrifice of the protoplasmic structure. The liquid portions of the milk are also added to the alveolar contents. This goes on until the ducts, and finally the acini, become once more gorged with milk, and the secretion in consequence gradually ceases with the increase of alveolar tension. The cells become stretched and flattened, the flow of blood is lessened, and the acinus ceases to function until it is emptied again.

In such a secretion period there is therefore (1) a short phase, when the cells are preparing for their function, which is consummated with a sacrifice of their free borders; and (2) a long phase, which lasts until the gland is filled with milk, and during which no further loss of protoplasm takes place. The activity of each cell during the period of secretion may be expressed by a curve of a wave-like shape, the anterior side of which, after gradually leaving the horizontal, rises rapidly to the crest, the posterior descending more leisurely to the base line.

If these may be taken to be the conditions which accompany the successive secretions in the cow, it may be said that a certain part at all events of the albumenoid constituents of milk are contributed by the early breaking down of the cell. It may also be concluded that colustrum is due to an intensification of the first phase at the beginning of the milking period.

It is a well-known fact that in the cow and other animals the last-drawn milk, the "strippings," is richer in fat than that first removed. It has been usual to explain this as being due to a process of creaming in the udder. It has also been suggested that the more fluid portions would descend more readily than the fat. Such explanations, however, are not convincing, but with these morphological considerations before us it is possible to re-state the problem, and to indicate its solution.

An average cow yields, say, 1¼ gallons at each milking, or say, 1,400 c.c. from each quarter. It has, however, been computed that the total capacity of the udder is only 3,000 c.c., or 750 c.c. per quarter. This would mean that during the process of one milking as much again is added to the milk contained in the quarter at the commencement of milking. The process of milking one quarter, however, does not take longer than two and a-half to three minutes. It may, therefore, be concluded that the calculation of the distended capacity of the udder is erroneous. If it be the fact that milk secretion begins at this astounding rate so soon after milking has commenced, then it would be impossible to strip the udder of its contents, and milking might be presumed to go on continuously. It is, however, well known that the milk can be practically completely removed, and that no further milk can be withdrawn until some time has elapsed. Furthermore, it is manifestly impossible for the secretory cells to regain in the short time of milking a condition of activity which would account for an appreciable portion of the supply which is yielded. The capacity of the udder may therefore be said to be measured by the quantity of milk which may be removed at a single milking.

If this be the case, then, that the act of milking removes simply the milk which has accumulated since the previous milking, it is at once plain that the richness of the stripping is due to a re-absorption by the lymphatics of the liquid or watery constituents in the acini when the latter are in a state of distension.

It is more difficult to attempt an explanation of the reported diurnal variation in the quality and quantity of milk. The evening milk is usually richer than the morning, but experimental results are not in agreement with regard to the point. The investigations made by Ingle seemed to prove that when cows are milked at six-hour intervals the watery constituents are much increased between 11 p.m. and 5 a.m. An exactly opposite result was obtained at Offerton in the case of cows milked at twelve-hour intervals. The experiments, which were described by Bryner Jones, showed that a richer milk was obtained in the morning, and a greater quantity in the evening, even exceeding that got after a period of fourteen hours. Were the results of experiments more in agreement, it might be possible to suggest, for example, that the general effect which is believed to be true from the experience of dairy farmers, is due to nervous change during the hours of darkness. But further experiments are evidently necessary before the problem can even be stated.—*Board of Agriculture Journal*, England.

HOW TO REAR BROODER CHICKS.

It isn't a difficult matter to get plenty of chickens hatched, either by the natural method or the incubator. The rules are easily learned. It is keeping the big per cent. of them alive when safely out of the shell. So many women put up the plaint: "The chicks taken from the hen and raised by hand, as it were, do so much better for me than those hatched by the incubator. Incubator chicks are decidedly weakly." I admit that some incubators do nearly cook the chicks when they come out; but you must watch this, and when you see them panting for breath get them out, as I do the chicks liable to be crushed. If you do not overcrowd, and the breeding stock was healthy, your incubator chicks have equal chance—should have better—with the hen-hatched.

I have learned long ago that, all things being equal, it is absolute cleanliness that keeps the chicks alive, allied with the right kind of first feed. After from 24 to 36 hours of comfortably getting used to the world they have come into, I scatter very fine, clean gravel on some well-scalded boards for the chicks to pick at. The first water they get is water that has been boiled and cooled, and sometimes they get nothing for several days but weak store tea. With the gravel I give rolled oats, pin head oats or crushed crackers, if the oats are not handy; sometimes it is almost impossible to get pinhead oats in the towns about us, and whatever I give is rolled in the raw yolk of an egg. I feed very sparingly, but every two hours through the day for the first few days. After the first day I alternate the egg food with some form of dry chick food such as are advertised in your columns.

Of late years I find the chick foods pay best to start the chicks upon, and as the weather gets warmer I often start the chicks from the very first on this dry food. I find also that with this dry mode of feeding I raise most chickens if I keep not more than 25 together, either in the home-made brooders I construct for them, or even less under the hen. Especially in the spring should the hen be given fewer chicks than this. There isn't a hen in existence that can warm over 15 or 16 small chicks, and as they grow she fails to keep this many as warm as is necessary during the cold nights that stay well into late spring. To help her out, I have tight brood coops and give her fresh straw and plenty of it every night or two. One thing I never neglect, and that is meat scraps every day or two for the chicks. Sometimes the chick foods have these in. If not, chop up bits for them.

'Lack of cleanliness in the brood coops or brooder is the cause of the little chick cholera, or infectious leukaemia, its proper name by the scientists. This disease is caused from dirty floors. The chicks can take it in a box placed in the kitchen, the brooder or from the brood-coop floors, anywhere that you allow the droppings to accumulate and get heated. The heat somehow starts a rod-like intestinal germ to multiplying rapidly in the droppings, the chicks take the disease and die. It is most dangerous if you place the chicks on boards. It does not get so bad if you keep clean sand spread on the floor and chaff above, but this must be taken out often and the floor scalded off, for chicks will die of it at any age; although the first few days of their life are most susceptible to it. Paper spread upon the floor of the brooders is nearly as dangerous as the bare boards.

The chicks do not take the disease from each other, I have found, but from taking the germs into the mouth. The first symptoms are a dull drowsiness, the chick is very hot to the touch; the discharge, if the chick does not die in a few hours, is watery and sometimes white. It will clean out a brooder full of chicks in a few days.

I have learned how to guard against this disease. I get ready for it, and the first sign of it among the wee chicks sees the sick ones—no use to fool with doctoring them—put out of their misery, as their droppings only make the germs more numerous. The well chicks are removed to new quarters and the old thoroughly cleaned, scalded, and disinfected. There was a time when I lost chickens by it, the worst loss once being among chicks three weeks old and over. It was in the brood coops, caused by the filth in the grounds about them from chickens raised there the year before. The warmer the weather became the greater the mortality among these chicks. I lost them by the dozens and dozens. I had a fashion then of putting 60 and more together. So many helped create a greater heat at night. At last it was borne in upon me what I had to deal with.   I destroyed the coops that were old, disinfected the new, sprayed the grounds with a strong disinfectant, placed the chicks in small bunches and looked after keeping the coop floors well scalded, well sanded, and nót only stopped the disease, but have raised hundreds of chickens on the same spot since.

Chicks kept with hens get the disease also.   These chicks of mine were with hens.   If one can avoid this disease for the chicks and keep them strong for the first two weeks of life, the biggest end of the battle is over, although I never give wet food and mashes to any extent until I am sure they are beyond the perils of indigestion.   You seldom see a chick clog behind that is fed small grains with plenty of grit.   It is those chickens that are fed too much corn meal, clabber cheese, etc., that show up this trouble. They need a variety from the very first is my experience after losing them by thousands through lack of knowing how to care for them to better profit.   Corn meal I never give the little chicks nowadays.   Later on they can have it when they get so strong they can digest anything they can gobble down.

I am always on the lookout for the big head vermin.   Sometimes they are thick on the hens in the spring; although hot weather is their time to multiply.   I dust the hens well with insect powder when setting them, but never within ten days of the chick's hatching.   Insect powder will kill the young chicks.   This I know by dire experience.   If I find one of these big fellows lurking on the chick's head, the hen gets an extra good greasing with lard.   That is sufficient; to put sulphur in it makes sores on the chicks and stunts their growth, and it takes very little coal oil to kill them—as I know too well, also.

The chicks not with the hens in early spring must have heat.   The brooders have their own heat provided, but I have some other ways of keeping the chicks in the home-made brooders warm.   Jugs of hot water around which the chicks huddle is one, another is a lamp placed safe from overthrow, another way is bringing in the chicks in smaller boxes than the day quarters and turning the gas on in an old stove at night.   One can improvise heat for them both day and night, but the regular brooders are handiest in the long run.

TESTING SEED.

When it is considered that over 20,000,000 acres are annually under crop in the Dominion, something of the importance of good vital seed to sow this amount of land can be grasped.   What is 50c. or $1 per 100 pounds more than the ordinary price for good seed grain when compared with the results that are sure to follow the use of good seed of known vitality?   Yet it is all too true that thousands of bushels of grain and grass seeds are annually sown in lottery fashion.   Comparatively little of the seed is subjected to any test whatever.

During the last two or three years there has been quite an awakening among the farmers to have their seed corn tested, owing to the number of failures to get a stand of corn, which was largely the outcome of planting seed of poor vitality. Through the efforts of the seed branch in the Dominion Department of Agriculture, the scales have fallen from many a farmer's eyes. He has seen very great differences in the quality of clover and grass seeds he has been in the habit of buying without question. Not only have many farmers purchased seed of low vitality, the result of having been kept over a season and not properly cared for in many cases, but they have bought seeds with many kinds of noxious weed seeds.

In order to awaken an interest in the importance of good seed, a seed laboratory was established in 1902 by Prof. Robertson, who was at that time Commissioner of Agriculture and Dairying. Forty-five years ago the first testing station was established at Tharand, in Germany. Germany now maintains no less than 39 such stations. The Scandinavian countries have 24. In Austria-Hungary they have 16 stations, and a compulsory guarantee system. In the other countries mentioned they have a voluntary guarantee system, else they could not do business.

In the United States during 1896, at a convention held in Washington, the Association of American Agricultural Colleges and Experimental Stations appointed a committee to devise and adopt a standard form of seed-testing apparatus and methods of procedure for all the American stations.

The standard adopted by the Americans is the Canadian standard, as there is only the one station for seed testing in Canada, which is the one mentioned above.

The permanent staff in the seed laboratory at Ottawa consists of an expert in charge and six assistants. The work has increased so much of late that a temporary staff has been added, and still it is not enough to keep pace with the samples coming in for examination. Already this year over 1000 samples have been sent in. This increase in the work is largely due to the Seed Control Act, 1905, coming in force on the 1st of September last, and the interest taken by those handling seeds in their desire to live up to the requirements of the bill. In seed testing there are two lines of work: First, the examination of the seeds for purity, and, second, the germination test. To carry on the purity work the laboratory is equipped with two pairs of sensitive balances, two sets of sieves designed for the work, an apparatus for separating seed by means of regulated air currents, a number of wide field magnifying glasses, a microscope with its accessories, an herbarium reference collection of seeds and filing cabinets for keeping samples of the seeds which have been tested.

In testing the seeds for purity in the laboratory the sample sent is thoroughly mixed. A certain amount is weighed carefully (from 2 grams to 50 grams, according to the size of the seeds), and if any foreign matter smaller than the seeds under examination be present it is screened out with the sieves. The sample is then spread out on a table before the operator, who examines it seed by seed, and separates the absolutely pure seeds from the rest. The foreign matter is then classified as: (1.) Inert matter, broken seeds, sand, dirt, sticks, and chaff; and (2) foreign seeds (a) seeds of useful or harmless grasses, (b) weed seeds which are subdivided as noxious and other weed seed. The pure seed is then weighed, and the difference between that weight and the original weight represents the percentage of foreign matter. Sheets are filled out according to the finding, and this constitutes the report on purity. A copy is kept for reference, and the report goes to the sender of the sample accompanied by a printed sheet on seed testing of Timothy, alsike, and red clover.

Of the 1,000 samples tested so far this year the general average has been much better than during previous years. Many of the samples are entirely free from any of the twenty-three weed seeds mentioned in the Seed Control Act, and very few other weed seeds are found. The samples of Timothy seed on the whole have been particularly good. Some of the alsike and red clover samples have not been so good. For instance, a sample of alsike was examined a short time ago and in the 2-gram sample under examination there were 61 noxious seeds, and 12 other weed seeds not mentioned in the Act. This would mean that in one pound of alsike seed of the sample referred to there would be 17,520 weed seeds, of which 85 per cent. would be seed of weeds mentioned in the act. Such seed is prohibited from being sold for seeding purposes in Canada. Section six of the Act sets the minimum standard at five noxious weed seeds per 1,000. One sample of red clover seed contained 94 weed seeds in the five grams examined, nearly 80 per cent. being the noxious weeds mentioned in the act. This would mean that in one pound of red clover there would be about 8,924 weed seeds. Such seed would be prohibited for sale for seeding purposes in Canada.

How Farmers may test their Seeds.

In buying grass and clover seeds it is a good plan to wet the finger and place it on a sample of seed in the palm of the hand and note what foreign seeds are present. Often by rubbing the dry seeds between the thump and fingers the vitality of the seed is indicated. Usually old seed of low vitality has a dead, dry touch, while vital seed has an oily, lifelike touch. It always will pay the purchaser of seeds to take a fair sample and spread it out thinly on a white sheet of paper and go over it carefully with a knife, with the aid of a small magnifying glass. This will show whether it is very pure or not. If it is sold as seed of first quality, and there is any suspicion in the matter, then a representative sample of the package may be taken at least within seven days after the purchase of the seed, and if the seed be bought in a sealed package then it must be taken on the breaking of the seal. The sample must be taken in the presence of the seller or in the presence of two disinterested persons, put in a package and send to the Dominion Seed Analyst. If the report shows that it will not grade No. 1 there is ground of action against the seller, and the report of the analyst is *prima facie* evidence in the case. It should be remembered that all samples of seeds and letters pertaining thereto, if directed to the Seed Branch, Department of Agriculture, Ottawa, need no postage. O.H.M.S. will take its place. Further, it should be remembered that samples will be tested for farmers, seed merchants, and seed vendors free of charge.

All seeds may be tested for germination, where the room is kept moderately warm in soil or between moistened folds of blotting paper or flannel. A good way to test the vitality of corn is to take a shallow box, put in some sand, put a piece of cotton marked off in small squares and moistened, over the moistened sand. If the corn be in the ear as it should be, each ear to be tested should have a number and the kernel taken from near each end and the centre to the number of six should be placed on the square with the corresponding number of the ear. When filled up put a piece of cotton over the corn, and on it a thin layer of sand moistened. In four or five days, if vital, it will sprout and the percentage of vitality may be obtained.

As the advantages of testing seeds are better known, more of it will be done, and good results are sure to follow. It means dollars [and cents to the farmers of Canada.

GOVERNMENT LABOUR BUREAU.

AUGUST REPORT.

The Superintendent of the Government Labour Bureau reports as follows for last month :—

PERTH.

Registrations.—The total number of individual men who called during the month in search of work was 817. Of this number 436 were new registrations and 381 renewals, *i.e.*, men who called who had been registered during the year prior to the month of August. The trades or occupations of the 817 applicants were as follow :—Labourers, 317; handy men, 69; handy lads, 67; farm hands, 42; carpenters, 83; cooks, 32; grooms, 17; blacksmiths, 13; gardeners, 13; miners, 13; engine-drivers, 12; bushmen, 11; hotel hands, 10; horse-drivers, 10; yardmen, 10; bakers, 8; fitters, 7; bricklayers, 6; clerks, 6; carpenters (rough), 6; kitchenmen, 6; painters, 6; sawmill hands, 6; brickmakers, 5; firemen, 5; boilermakers, grocers, storemen, and station hands, 4 of each; dairymen, engineers, sailors, shearers, strikers, seamen, wheelwrights, and wiremen, 3 of each; and 47 miscellaneous.

Engagements.—The engagements for the month numbered 294. The classification of work found was as follows :—Labourers, 131; bushmen, 31; farm hands, 23; sailors, 10; handy men, 9; boys for farms, 7; cooks, 7; gardeners, 7; handy lads, 7; woodcutters, 7; yardmen, 6; carpenters, 5; dairymen, 5; groom-gardeners, painters, and sawmill hands, 4 of each; brickmakers, 3; blacksmiths, firemen, horse-drivers, kitchenmen, orchardists, and shearers, 2 of each; and 12 miscellaneous.

KALGOORLIE.

Registrations.—The applicants for work numbered 88. The new registrations numbered 46, and there were 42 renewals. The classification was as follows :—Labourers 29, handy men 17, handy youths 8, engine-drivers 5, cooks 5, clerks 4, fitters 4, blacksmiths 3, and 13 miscellaneous.

Engagements.—There were 8 engagements, classified as follow :— Labourers, miners, and yardmen, 2 of each; handymen and kitchenmen, 1 of each.

The female servants who called numbered 40. The new registrations were 16 and the renewals 24. The classification was as follows:—Generals 10, cooks 7, waitresses 7, useful girls 4, housemaids 4, and 8 miscellaneous. There were 5 engagements, viz.:—3 generals, I cook, 1 barmaid.

WOMEN'S BRANCH, PERTH.

Registrations.—The new registrations for the month were 92, and the renewals 109. The classification was as follows:—Generals 42, cooks 32, laundress-charwomen 25, housemaids 24, light generals 20, useful girls '16, housekeepers 11, waitresses 9, cook-laundresses 8, nursemaids 4, ladyhelps 4, and 6 miscellaneous.

Engagements.—There were 74 engagements, classified as follows:— Generals 18, laundress-charwomen 15, cook-laundresses 7, housemaids 7, useful girls 6, light generals 4, waitresses 4, housekeepers 3, nursemaids 3, and 7 miscellaneous.

GENERAL REMARKS.

The number of individual men who called at the central office, Perth during the month was 817. This is 209 in excess of the number for July, and 121 less than that for the month of August last year. The engagements were 294, being 154 in excess of the total for July, and 43 more than the number for August last year. Of the 294 engagements, 214 were by private employers, which is the seventh highest monthly total since the inauguration of the Bureau in 1898. The engagements for country districts were 213, being the second highest monthly total since the Bureau was established, this total only being exceeded in March of this year.

It may be interesting to note that there were 40 men wanted by the Government for the Collie-Narrogin line. For these positions 120 men applied. The names were received a few days prior to the day of selection. On the day fixed for selecting, due notice of which had been given, it was found that only 34 responded when their names were called. Of this number six were not selected. The remaining 12 were chosen from those who had been registered only for a day or two, and nine out of the 28 had been registered for less than a week. The fact that many of the men who had applied for this work may have felt that they were incapable of performing it satisfactorily, and probably would not have been selected, is the only reason that can be given to account for so many absentees when work was actually offered.

At Northam a branch of the Labour Bureau was opened on 30th August, which is in charge of the Land Agent.

At Kalgoorlie branch the applicants for work numbered 88, as against 96 for July, and 187 for August last year. The engagements were 8, as against 25 for July, and 19 for August last year. At the women's branch. Perth, 201 women called during the month, as against 199 for July, and 227 for August last year. There were 74 engagements, as against 60 for the previous month, and 73 for the month of August last year.

PROTECTING THE POTATOES.

At the present time no crop presents a fairer appearance than the popular esculent. If, however, we have a superabundance of moisture and a deficiency of sunshine, its very existence may be seriously threatened by disease. On this account the precaution of spraying is one which should never be neglected by those who wish to make the potato crop prove remunerative. No crop so well repays the trouble and slight expense which the operation entails, and as we are now on the eve of the month when the fungus is usually most active, a word as to methods of spraying may not be out of place.

Properly applied, "Bordeaux" mixture not only reduces risk of disease to a minimum, but preserves the vigour of the haulm and benefits the growth of the tubers to such an extent that a substantial increase of crop is secured. The spraying should be begun before the attacks of the "spores" or "germs" can take place, that is, as soon as there is a fair development of haulm. It should be repeated about three weeks later, and, in some cases, a third application should be given after the lapse of another two or three weeks. The plants should be sprayed from beneath as well as from above, and the application will be most effective when applied as a fine spray rather than as a rain.

"Bordeaux" mixture should be thoroughly well made of pure materials. The ordinary formula is well known, and need not be repeated here. Recommendation, however, is made of an improved and effective "Bordeaux" mixture, which has not only proved itself highly satisfactory, but has the advantage of being a solution, instead of containing a sediment, of the copper compound.

IMPROVED "BORDEAUX" MIXTURE.

Copper sulphate (bluestone)	1lb.
Lime (fresh and quick)	1lb.
Agricultural treacle	1lb.
Water	10gals.

Dissolve the "bluestone" in 10 gallons of (preferably) rain water, and boil the lime and the treacle together with a quart of water for half-an-hour. When the "bluestone" has all dissolved, and the lime and treacle liquid is fairly cool, pour the latter into the "bluestone" liquid, stir well, and it is ready for use. This mixture will keep for months if covered so that air is not allowed free access to the surface. A thin film of oil—paraffin—carefully floated on the surface of the liquid, will secure this. The paraffin can be skimmed off when the solution is required for use. Metallic vessels must not be used for mixing or storing the solution, which also is poisonous. In appearance, this differs from ordinary "Bordeaux" mixture in that instead of being a mixture containing a blue sediment, it is a greenish-coloured liquid containing a chemical compound of copper and treacle. When sprayed on a plant, the carbonic acid in the air rapidly turns the solution into a blue powder, which becomes firmly and intimately fixed to the surface of the foliage. The success attending the spraying of "Bordeaux" mixture lies wholly in anticipating attacks of disease, and maintaining a protective coating so long as danger of infection lasts. It must, therefore, be used for what it is—the preventive which is better than cure.—*Exchange.*

THE CARE OF STRAWBERRIES.

After the fruit is picked the plants should be mowed off and burned, as this retards runners from forming and also kills many troublesome insects. Top dress liberally with fine stable manure or chicken droppings. Cultivate often, and cut off runners when they begin to appear, because a crop of runners is detrimental to a large crop of berries the following spring. I spray at least four times with Bordeaux mixture, adding two grains white arsenic to each gallon. The arsenic is made soluble by boiling in water one part white arsenic and four parts salsoda. Plants that are well cultivated, liberally top-dressed after the fruit is picked, with runners closely cut, keep on improving with age for at least five years.

Crowns form rapidly, and the plants grow to be six or eight inches in diameter, measured without leaves, and have 100 or more fruit stools, which will yield from two to three gallons choice fruit from each plant. The better cultivation and care the plants have after the fruit is picked the better the crop will be the next season.

Plants from runners can be made to bear a good crop of fruit next season by raising a a crop of peas and harvesting in August. Apply a heavy dressing of well rotted barnyard manure, working it in deeply, and set plants not latter than September 1st. Spray, cut all runners, but above all cultivate shallow every day, if possible, when the ground is dry enough to work. In this way a good crop can be obtained the first year. But for those who cannot get plants in the early fall—by September 1st—I would recommend planting them in spring, for the plants are then more mature, and can be handled with less care and considerable work saved in cultivating and cutting runners. In that case there will be but little fruit the first season. I think it a decided mistake to pick off blossoms to stop fruiting. Let blossoms stay the first year, but keep off the runners, for these detract from following berry crops.

In selecting for future plants mark the choicest plants at picking time, then remove a number of them to a place apart from the others, into soil which has been prepared by being put in the best of condition. Cultivate until runners start, pick off all blossoms, and save the runners from these plants only. Some varieties are better suited to some localities than others. Select a few kinds for trial, setting at least fifty feet apart, for pollen will mix within that range. Select the kind which gives the best satisfaction, discarding the rest, and success is assured.

I find no difficulty whatever in producing at the rate of over 1,000 bushels of choice strawberries to the acre, but in order to do so the plants must have all necessary attention in care and cultivation, particularly a double dose of the latter. Remember it must be very shallow and very often.—*Exchange.*

GARDEN NOTES FOR OCTOBER.

By PERCY G. WICKEN.

Last month should have seen a large quantity of garden stuff sown, as seeds sown last month are enabled to obtain sufficient roothold of the ground before the weather becomes too warm. Only in the more Southern districts, where moist land is available all the year round, can much be done in the way of planting vegetables at the present time. The principal work in the garden this month will be keeping the ground free from weeds, the soil well stirred, and insect pests in check.

All kinds of plants may be put out in the open, and if it is not possible to plant out in showery weather, they must be shaded from the sun until they become firmly established, when the shade may be removed. This should be done on a cloudy day, as the hot sun striking on the delicate plant will probably wilt them so that they will not recover. All weeds should be cut down before the seeds have an opportunity of ripening, as by this means their spread is prevented. Many weeds will ripen their seeds after being cut down if the seed heads are allowed to form before cutting.

In a small garden the weeding must be done by a hand hoe, but where a large area is under cultivation the work can be carried out by means of the Planet Junior horse hoe.

Cut worms will most likely be troublesome, and they are capable of doing great damage. They generally hide in the ground round the stem of the plant during the daytime, and at night eat round the stem of the plant, which then breaks off or wilts away. By disturbing the ground round the stem of the plants these grubs can generally be found.

The best remedy is to lay a small quantity of bait, composed of Paris Green, mixed with a little bran, round where the grubs are troublesome, they will eat this and it will poison them. Care must be taken that fowls or other domestic animals do not get at this bait. as it is an arsenical poison, and will poison them.

As a general rule all fungus diseases of plants should be sprayed with Bordeaux mixture, and all leaf or stem-eating insects with Paris green and water, but this should not be applied for some weeks before the vegetables are fit to send to market.

Any backward plants may be stimulated into more active growth by the application of liquid manure, in the proportion of 1oz. of nitrate of soda dissolved in one gallon of water, or, in the case of a field crop a top dressing of nitrate of soda or sulphate of ammonia applied broadcast along the rows at the rate of 1 cwt. per acre and hoed into the soil will have an almost immediate effect.

Artichokes (Jerusalem).—May still be sown this month, although those sown earlier will probably yield best. The tubers should be cut into pieces the same as potatoes and planted in rows 3 feet apart, and 18 inches in the drills.

Arrowroot.—A few bulbs of the Canna Edulis may be planted out this month, the plant is both ornamental and useful, as a large supply of bulbs can be obtained for pig feed.

Beans.—French, kidney, scarlet runners, haricot, snake beans, wax beans, butter beans, etc., may all be planted out in large quantities this month where the ground is moist. Beans can be grown in the coastal districts nearly all the year round. The main crops should be planted in September or early in October. Plant in rows three feet apart, and manure well with superphosphate and sulphate of potash, and cultivate well so as to keep the ground moist.

Beans, Lima.—Should be sown in large quantities during the month, as they are an excellent bean for table use. There are many varieties, some climbers and others dwarf varieties. The climbing varieties require a trellis or poles to grow on, as they are prolific growers. The dwarf varieties should be planted 3 feet apart each way, and the climbing varieties about 4 feet.

Beet (Red).—Sow a few rows to keep up a supply.

Beet (Silver).—Is valuable for the supply of green leaves during the dry weather. Plant out any young seedlings you have ready. A little seed may be sown.

Cabbage.—Plant out any healthy plants you may have on hand, and top-dress any plants not doing well with liquid manure.

Carrot.—A few rows may be planted to keep up a supply. Weed the rows, and thin out plants from the rows already up.

Celery.—Plant out all forward plants in trenches, and hill up those making growth so as to cause them to bleach.

Cucumbers.—Seed may be planted in all parts. The hills should be worked deeply, and well rotted stable manure should be mixed with the soil. Plant about eight seeds in each hill, and thin out when plants come up.

Egg Plants.—Plant out all young plants, and sow a little more seed.

Leeks.—A little seed may be sown.

Lettuce.—Plant out any young plants available, and a little more seed may be sown.

Melons.—All kinds of melons may be sown this month. The holes should be deeply worked, as the roots penetrate deeply into the soil. The land between the hills should be ploughed or well scarified before the vines begin to run. Any very long runners should be pinched off, as this will often cause the fruit to set.

Onions.—In moist localities a further supply of seedlings can be planted out. Those already up should be kept free from weeds, and the surface soil should not be allowed to cake.

Parsnips.—A few rows may be sown to keep up a supply.

Peas.—In moist localities a few rows may be sown.

Potatoes.—If not already sown, potatoes should be planted at once. They will only be successful in moist localities if sown at the present time.

Pumpkins and Squashes can be planted out largely this month, but the ground should be deeply worked. This is a very profitable crop to grow, as the pumpkins can be stored and kept until required for use. Plant in hills about 12ft. apart each way.

Sweet Potatoes.—There should now be available for planting out plenty of shoots from the tubers sown in beds last month. As soon as the shoots are three inches above the ground, the tubers should be lifted and the shoots broken off and planted out in rows three feet apart and about 18 inches apart in the rows.

Tomatoes.—In the northern districts the early-sown plants should be ripening their fruit. The early, fruit always fetches a good price, and the object of the grower should be to produce ripe tomatoes as early as possible in the season. In all parts of the State seedlings may be planted out in the open this month; as many plants as possible should be put out, as there is always a demand for this vegetable. As the plants begin to make a good growth they should be tied up to stakes so as to keep the fruit off the ground. A little seed may be sown in moist localities for planting out later on.

Tumeric.—A useful plant used for flavouring soups, etc. Grows somewhat similar in appearance to ginger. Pieces of the root may be planted in the same manner as potatoes.

Farm.—In the extreme eastern farming areas the hay harvest will commence early this month, but in most of the wheat-growing areas it will be somewhat later, according as to how the season turns out. Reapers and binders should be looked to and put in order to commence work whenever required, and duplicate parts obtained to replace any breakages. When cutting for hay, it is a good plan to cut a stripround all the paddocks to be kept for grain, and plough up this strip. It will then act as a fire-break, and may possibly save the crop from destruction should a fire break out in the vicinity.

The agricultural societies will be holding their annual shows during October and November, and it is the duty of all farmers to support their local society by exhibiting any stock or produce that they have that is likely to be creditable to the district. Apart from the money distributed as prizes, a good agricultural show does much to advertise a district, as it brings before those interested the capabilities of the soil in the locality, and thereby induces settlement.

As the grass becomes dry the York Road poison plant sends out green shoots, and it is at this time that it is so dangerous to stock. A sharp look-out should be kept in paddocks likely to be infected, and any plants that can be found should be grubbed out.

In the cooler and moister districts such crops as 90-day maize, melons, pumpkins, sorghum, cow peas, soy beans, mangels, sugar beets, and pearl millet may be sown in well-prepared soil. They should all be sown in drills, so that the cultivator may be kept going between the drills.

As dealers are now canvassing the country districts to secure orders for fertilisers for next season, settlers should bear in mind the fact that the Fertiliser and Feeding Stuffs Act is now in force. This Act makes it compulsory on all vendors of fertilisers to register their brands and the contents thereof with the Department of Agriculture in Perth.

Before purchasing any fertiliser ,one should ascertain whether it is a registered brand, and in the case of vendors trying to sell an unregistered brand, should report the fact to the Department of Agriculture, so that steps may be taken in the matter.

In addition to registering the brand of the fertiliser the vendor has to supply an invoice certificate stating the percentage of nitrogen, potash, and phosphoric acid contained in the fertiliser, and samples of the fertiliser are taken from time to time by the Inspector of Fertilisers, to see that they are up to the registered standard.

LOCAL MARKETS' REPORTS.

Messrs. H. J. WIGMORE & Co.'s REPORT.

Messrs. H. J. Wigmore & Co., of Fremantle, Perth, Kalgoorlie, and Northam, report as follows for month ending Saturday, 8th inst.:—

Chaff.—As anticipated in our last monthly report, supplies from the country during month ended to-day have been extremely heavy. This fact, in conjunction with the large quantities of imported chaff in store at Perth and Fremantle, has naturally had a depressing effect on the market. During the past week, however, consignments have fallen off considerably, and the market closes with a somewhat firmer tendency, although by no means on an equivalent with rates prevailing last month. Whereas prime green wheaten was readily bringing £4 17s. 6d. to £5 during July and early August, it is now a matter of difficulty to secure £4 10s. for the same quality. The following closing rates will give an indication of the market:—Prime green wheaten £4 10s., with perhaps £4 12s. 6d. for an occasional exceptionally bright, well-cut sample; f.a.q. wheaten, £4 5s. to £4 7s. 6d.; good medium wheaten, £4 2s. 6d.; medium and irregular wheaten, of which descriptions a heavy proportion is coming forward, £3 to £4 according to quality and condition. Inferior varieties are, as a rule, selling considerably below proportionate value to prime. Prime oaten would probably realise £4 10s., while f.a.q. oaten is worth £4 to £4 5s. Unfortunately, we cannot advise farmers of any likelihood of a rise of any importance on present values, simply on account of the quantity of imported chaff available already mentioned, and owing to the heavy supplies that are undoubtedly still in farmers' hands, and which must necessarily come forward to market before the influx of new season's chaff, as, of course, with every prospect of an excellent season during coming year, it would be most unwise, in our opinion, for any holders to carry over their chaff. The weather in the country continues very satisfactory from a farmer's point of view, and the recent rains have no doubt helped crops along, our advices from the agricultural areas being to the effect that crops generally are looking very well. We should not be at all surprised, in spite of many opinions held to the contrary, to see fair quantities of new season's chaff coming forward to market towards the end of next month, and altogether we maintain the wise course for farmers to follow is to forward their chaff regularly to the market now.

Our Kalgoorlie office also reports a weaker market, in sympathy with Perth, and arrivals to that centre have also been fairly copious. Month under review closes with prime green wheaten worth £5 2s. 6d. to perhaps £5 5s., while f.a.q. wheaten has been sold at £4 10s. to £4 15s. Lower grades are impossible to quit at satisfactory rates.

Wheat continues dull of sale in the Eastern States, and both Adelaide and Melbourne have eased considerably, the former quoting 3s. 1d. to 3s. 2d. f.o.b., and the latter 3s. 3d. to 3s. 4d. f.o.b. for shipping parcels. On spot the local market is also extremely dull, and very little wheat has been arriving for auction. Present value is about 3s. 5½d. to 3s. 6d. on rails, Perth, for prime milling. Millers, as a rule, hold large stocks of flour, and are not purchasing, thus reducing the demand almost solely to fowl feed. As we see no possible chance of an improvement in the wheat market, we again recommend farmers to consider the advisability of disposing of stocks held by them.

Oats have eased somewhat in Melbourne, and Good Feed Algerians have been quoted at 2s. 5d. to 2s. 5½d. f.o.b., in sound sacks. We have sold considerably at these figures. On spot the market remains practically the same, and sales continue to be made at 3s. to 3s. 0½d. on rails. Our sales as above have been mostly for shipment at the end of this month, in order to avoid payment of duty, which expires on the 8th October for all Commonwealth goods, and little business for prompt shipment from Melbourne is passing. This is natural, as of course merchants are endeavouring to get rid of spot stocks before the elimination of the duty next month.

Bran and Pollard.—During the month we have made heavy sales of both bran and pollard, f.o.b. Sydney, at 8¼d., but this market is now slightly firmer at 8¾d to 9d. f.o.b., for bran, while pollard remains cheapest from Sydney at 8¼d. On spot £5 to £5 2s. 6d. is being asked for bran, and £5 5s. to £5 7s. 6d. for pollard. We can quote a limited quantity of pollard free on Rails Northam, and invite inquiries.

Flour.—We have to report an easier tendency in the Eastern States, in sympathy with wheat. We can now quote Thomas' Adelaide "Standard" at £7 5s. f.o.b. sacks, £7 10s. quarters. On rails Northam, we can book at £8 and £8 5s., sacks and quarters respectively.

Potatoes.—F.o.b. Melbourne, £7 10s. for prime redskins in new bags. On spot, £9 5s. to £9 10s. rails Fremantle.

Onions.—£8 for Levien's best, and £7 5s. to £7 10s. f.o.b. Melbourne, for ordinary Spot lines are quoted at £9 10s.

Jute Goods.—Remain firm, and somewhat heavy indent orders have been placed from Calcutta. We still recommend farmers to buy at least half their requirements now, in order to secure themselves in case of emergency, and will be pleased to receive inquiries. We are also prepared to supply quantities of second-hand bran bags and corn sacks, guaranteed sound; prices on application. For farmers' information we may say that we put up our second-hand bran bags in bundles of 100, and second-hand cornsacks in bundles of 51.

NOTES ON THE CLIMATE FOR AUGUST, 1906.

The principal feature of the weather during the month was the unusually heavy general rainfall in the early part, the finest general downpour ever recorded in the State. On Thursday morning (2nd) a "high" which had been traversing the Southern parts of this State was well on its way to South Australia, and there were vague indications of a "low" approaching our Western coast from the Indian Ocean. On Saturday morning (4th) the barometer at Geraldton (29·72) was the lowest in Australia, and rain had commenced to fall on the North-West and West coast. The "low" then passed down the coast and round the Leeuwin, where the barometer fell to 29·10 next morning, but the rain extended right through the Murchison and Coolgardie Fields, as well as in the South-West districts. In fact, the heaviest fall was between the Murchison and North-West coast, where from three to nearly five inches were generally recorded. Elsewhere from one to two and a-half inches fell. Special attention is called to this disturbance because the indications point so unmistakably to the fact that it first approached the North-West coast from the Indian Ocean, and did not come up from the Antarctic low.   Three times again during the month did unsettled weather visit the interior, but under different conditions.   In all these cases a "high" barometer was slowly passing eastward across the Southern parts of the State, with strong easterly winds, but in the upper atmosphere a disturbance seems to have passed from the North-West coast across the interior in a more or less South-Easterly direction towards South Australia.   On the 13th and 14th moderate to heavy rain fell on the North-West coast and passed South-Eastwards, just missing the goldfields, but bringing general rains throughout South Australia all South of Alice Springs, and as far West as Eucla.   The rain was recorded on the South-West coast of South Australia on the morning of the 16th, and next morning it was general.   The third of these disturbances brought rain on the North-West coast on the night of the 18th, and throughout the Coolgardie Fields next night.

During the latter part of the month a "high" of great intensity passed slowly across Southern districts from West to East, giving a spell of fine dry weather, with strong unpleasant Easterly winds.   This was followed by a "low," which brought moderate to heavy rain in South-West districts on the 30th.

On the whole, the pressure was about normal in the Northern half of the State, but higher than usual in the Southern, especially in the South-East, where the excess amounted to one-tenth of an inch and upwards.   .

Temperature was generally below the normal, especially on the Eastern Goldfields, where the defect amounted to 4 or 5 degrees for the mean daily maximum.

Rainfall was rather less than usual in the extreme South-West coastal section South of latitude 30 degrees, but elsewhere, except in the extreme North and North-East, it was very heavy, and far in excess of the average for previous years.   Frosts were occasionally experienced in Southern portions of the State, but they do not appear to have been very severe.   The following table shows the mean and absolute readings of a minimum thermometer placed on the surface of the ground and read daily.

Station.	Mean.	Lowest.	Date.
Peak Hill	44·0	38·0	1
Cue	44·8	36·3	31
Coolgardie	40·4	30·1	2
Southern Cross	38·0	29·0	2
Walebing	35·0	28·0	14
York	37·9	32·0	27
Perth Observatory ...	44·8	35·0	9
Wandering	...	...	...
Narrogin	...	...	...
Bridgetown	35·6	25·0	26
Karridale	39·0	26·0	27
Katanning	32·7	24·0	25
Mount Barker	37·7	30·8	13

The Climate of Western Australia during August, 1906.

Locality	Barometer (corrected and reduced to sea-level).				Shade Temperatures.									Rainfall.		
	Mean of 9 a.m. and 3 p.m.	Average for previous years.	Highest for Month.	Lowest for Month.	August, 1906.					Average for previous Years.				Points (100 to inch) in Month.	Wet Days.	Total Points since Jan. 1.
					Mean Max.	Mean Min.	Mean of Month.	Highest Max.	Lowest M.	Mean Max.	Mean Min.	Highest ever recorded.	Lowest ever recorded.			
NORTH-WEST AND NORTH COAST:																
Wyndham	30·006	30·008	30·172	29·839	88·5	71·6	80·0	97·8	56·0	9·3	69·1	97·7	56·2	Nil	...	1388
Derby	30·012	30·008	·86	29·861	89·2	6·4	76·8	95·8	49·4	89·0	59·7	98·0	45·2	38	1	1157
Broome	29·993	30·019	6·34	29·859	85·8	6·1	76·0	96·2	49·5	86·0	59·1	98·8	43·0	44	2	1016
Condon	30·036	30 66	30·228	29·926	91	59·5	69·8	90·5	46·0	80·8	52·8	95·2	37·0	107	2	663
Cossack	30·035	98	30·270	29·900	78·0	60·0	69·0	91·0	53·0	80·7	56·4	92·8	45·8	501	7	1003
Onslow	30·046	30·073	30·296	29·872	77·6	59·2	68·4	87·0	41·8	79·3	52·7	92·9	40·0	366	8	609
Winning Pool	30·051	...	30·302	29·888	76·1	57·0	66·6	84·6	43·6	...	...	...	...	479	5	904
Carnarvon	30·122	30·118	30·392	29·821	71·2	54·9	63·0	83·0	45·2	73·0	52·2	90·2	39·8	85	10	661
Hamelin Pool	30·095	6·113	30·405	29·734	71·8	52·9	61·8	79·0	40·0	71·5	48·1	83·0	35·7	34	9	534
Geraldton	30·141	6·139	30·464	29·670	68·5	51·4	60·0	77·0	42·8	69·2	50·3	84·8	37·3	601	7	1738
INLAND:																
Hall's Rk	30·046	30·060	30·318	29·838	86·9	56·5	71·7	95·0	36·8	85·7	51·2	95·2	32·8	Nil	...	395
Marble Bar	30·142	30·096	30·317	...	83·3	58·2	70·8	96·2	48·0	85·5	55·7	90·2	39·0	135	6	1089
Nullagine	30·130	30·120	30·420	29·850	76·8	52·7	64·8	94·0	37·0	79·4	47·5	9·5	30·1	238	8	910
Peak Hill	30·153	30·134	30·470	29·790	68·0	49·0	57·5	79·0	42·0	61	46·9	83·8	36·4	621	8	876
Wiluna	30·170	30·144	30·478	29·777	64·2	46·3	55·5	78·2	41	69·3	42·1	85·8	29·3	250	9	685
Cue	...	...	...	...	65·5	47·0	56·2	74·0	39·0	69·0	45·5	86·0	31·0	69	8	837
Murgoo	30·143	30·135	30·497	29·704	65·3	48·0	56·6	75·0	37·5	...	...	...	...	351	8	702
Yalgoo	30·168	30·142	30·523	29·739	62·9	45·8	54·4	74·5	61	6·1	44·0	85·3	31·5	284	6	888
Lawlers	30·218	30·167	30·619	29·859	63·7	46·2	55·0	76·0	38·6	67·6	44·3	85·2	28·2	81	7	691
Laverton	...	30·142	...	...	65·0	45·8	55·4	75·4	34·8	67·6	42·6	81	27·0	220	8	742
Menzies	...	...	...	...	60·9	44·7	52·8	72·5	34·0	65·4	44·0	88·8	29·7	232	...	803
Kanowna	30·230	30·144	30·625	29·549	6·1	43·6	51·8	70	37·2	...	...	...	...	319	9	885
Kalgoorlie	30·211	30·142	30·606	29·543	59·5	45·0	53·0	71·0	37·5	65·0	44·1	82·0	34·0	318	6	792
Coolgardie	30·215	30·124	30·560	29·560	62·0	43·5	6·5	70·6	36·0	64·7	42·9	81·0	31·2	327	8	829
Southern Cross	...	...	...	...	...	...	...	...	...	65·0	40·6	82·0	25·0	199	8	822
Kellerberrin	...	...	...	...	61·7	42·4	52·0	73·0	30·0	63·7	41·0	78·9	31·4	305	11	901
Walebing	...	...	...	...	62·8	42·8	52·8	72·8	34·5	63·7	41·0	78·9	31·4	305	11	1626
Northam	30·210	30·140	30·519	29·542	62·3	42·4	52·4	69·3	34·2	65·0	39·8	6·1	31·2	243	10	1286
York	...	...	...	...	6·2	46·7	55·0	61	40·0	61	41·1	91	29·8	238	10	1177
Guildford	...	...	...	...	...	...	...	...	...	66·2	44·5	81·6	30·2	417	12	2487

The Climate of Western Australia during August, 1906—continued.

Locality	Barometer (corrected and reduced to sea-level)				Shade Temperatures									Rain fall		
					August, 1906					Average for previous Years						
	Mean of 9 a.m. and 3 p.m.	Average for previous years	Highest for Month	Lowest for Month	Mean Max.	Mean Min.	Mean of Month	Highest Max.	Lowest Min.	Mean Max.	Mean Min.	Highest ever recorded	Lowest ever recorded	Hits (100 to inch) in Month	Wet Days	Total fall since Jan. 1
SOUTH-WEST AND SOUTH COAST:																
Perth Gardens ...	30·176	30·138	30·518	29·510	63·9	49·3	56·6	69·0	41·2	65·1	51	79·7	33·6	67	11	2679
Perth ...tory	30·188	30·134	30·528	29·515	63·3	48·4	55·8	69·7	41·0	64·0	47·8	80·4	37·5	53	13	2706
...lle ...	30·205	30·120	30·544	29·515	6·7	50·5	57·1	71·0	43·5	63·5	50·7	77·3	41·0	424	12	2035
...t ...	...	30·108	...	...	...	...	...	...	...	...	...	...	...	...	...	...
Mandurah	...	...	...	...	6·2	45·7	54·4	68·6	36·2	62·9	53·2	76·2	32·7	51	13	3343
Marradong	...	...	...	...	...	...	...	...	...	64·3	44·8	76·2	...	30	10	2176
Wandering *	...	...	...	...	...	37·5	...	68·9	29·0	61·5	37·1	72·9	28·2	83	11	85
Narrogin	...	...	...	...	...	...	...	...	...	...	...	...	...	...	...	...
Collie ...	...	...	...	...	60·4	42·9	51·6	67·5	32·0	61·8	37·6	75·7	27·5	69	13	2852
Donnybrook	...	30·124	...	29·418	62·6	42·3	52·4	70·0	34·0	63·4	43·6	74·2	29·4	482	11	2103
Br.nbury	...	...	...	...	63·6	47·3	55·4	68·9	39·8	63·8	46·7	75·5	33·2	26	14	2464
Busselton	30·188	...	30·553	...	61·4	44·5	53·0	68·4	6·1	62·4	44·7	73·8	33·6	54	14	2781
Cape Naturaliste	30·155	...	30·520	29·370	60·0	50·0	55·0	64·0	41·0	...	...	...	...	88	14	2549
Bridgetown	...	30·101	...	...	61·5	39·0	50·0	69·0	30·0	62·0	39·2	75·9	28·2	418	16	2667
Karridale	30·130	30·061	30·550	29·100	62·0	4·0	53·0	68·0	34·0	61·8	46·5	74·4	32·5	91	16	2998
Cape Leeuwin	30·203	30·112	30·595	29·416	61·0	52·0	56·0	66·0	44·0	61·6	52·5	72·3	43·8	43	22	2633
Katanning	30·172	30·076	30·618	29·177	61	44·2	51·6	68·2	31·0	60·0	41·1	51	30·4	196	13	1804
Mt. Barker	30·165	30·070	30·610	28·30	59·0	41·0	50·0	68·0	34·0	...	...	...	...	36	17	1671
Albany	30·204	30·059	30·631	29·98	61·1	46·5	53·8	70·0	36·5	61·5	45·6	77·5	34·3	421	16	2760
Breaksea...	30·253	30·156	30·671	29·50	59·0	50·0	4·5	66·0	42·0	59·5	49·7	74·8	34·5	44	16	2465
Esperance	30·288	30·135	30·614	29·601	63·4	47·4	55·4	73·0	38·0	63·7	46·3	82·8	33·8	266	17	29
Balladonia	...	...	...	...	60·6	42·0	51·3	71·0	31·2	64·7	40·6	88·0	28·0	100	8	571
Eyre ...	...	...	...	...	63·4	45·7	54·6	76·2	29·9	64·9	43·6	88·7	29·1	40	18	85
INTERSTATE.																
Perth ...	30·188	30·134	30·528	29·55	6·3	49·4	55·8	69·7	41·0	64·0	47·8	80·4	37·5	53	13	2706
Adelaide	30·265	30·125	30·558	29·90	0·2	45·8	53·0	67·0	36·1	62·0	46·8	82·0	32·3	99	6	1740
Melbourne	30·214	29·981	30·520	29·681	57·0	43·0	50·0	67·6	41·1	58·8	43·2	77·0	28·3	173	14	...
Sydney	30·280	30·108	30·520	29·740	62·0	48·0	55·0	73·0	41·0	62·2	47·5	82·0	36·8	64	11	2278

* Averages for three years only.

The Observatory, Perth, 5th September, 1906.

W. E. COOKE, Government Astronomer.

RAINFALL for July, 1906 (completed as far as possible), and for August, 1906 (principally from Telegraphic Reports).

Stations.	July No. of points 100 = 1in.	July No. of wet days.	August No. of points 100 = 1in.	August No. of wet days.
EAST KIMBERLEY:				
Wyndham	Nil	...	Nil	...
6-Mile	...	...	...	...
Carlton	Nil	...	...	...
The Stud Station	...	...	...	...
Argyle Downs	Nil	...	...	...
Rosewood Downs	Nil	...	...	...
Lisadell	...	...	...	...
Turkey Creek	Nil	...	Nil	...
Ord River	...	...	...	...
Alice Downs	...	...	...	...
Flora Valley	...	...	...	...
Hall's Creek	Nil	...	Nil	...
Nicholson Plains	...	...	...	...
Ruby Plains	...	...	...	...
Denison Downs	...	...	...	...
WEST KIMBERLEY:				
Mt. Barnett	...	...	...	...
Corvendine	...	...	...	...
Leopold Downs	10	1	...	...
Fitzroy Crossing (P.O.)	5	2	Nil	...
Cherrabun	52	2	...	...
Bohemia Downs	Nil	...	...	...
Quanbun	...	...	...	...
Nookanbah	...	...	...	...
Upper Liveringa	46	1	...	...
Yeeda	44	2	...	...
Derby	102	3	38	1
Pt. Torment	68	1	...	...
Obagama	...	...	...	...
Beagle Bay	132	4	...	...
Roebuck Downs	...	...	...	...
Kimberley Downs	74	...	...	...
Broome	11	2	44	2
Thangoo	...	...	...	...
La Grange Bay	17	5	40	2
N.W. COAST:				
Wallal	2	1	45	2
Pardoo	75	2	...	...
Condon	41	2	107	2
DeGrey River	36	1	...	...
Port Hedland	52	3	126	6
Boodarie	35	2	...	...

Stations.	July No. of points 100 = 1in.	July No. of wet days.	August No. of points 100 = 1in.	August No. of wet days.
N.W. COAST—cont.				
Balla Balla	...	...	...	...
Whim Creek	67	3	410	7
Mallina	186	3	...	...
Croydon	81	3	...	...
Sherlock	...	...	...	...
Woodbrooke	101	4	...	...
Cooyapooya	83	3	...	...
Roebourne	86	4	385	7
Cossack	111	2	501	7
Fortescue	51	2	396	5
Mardie	70	1	...	...
Chinginarra	50	1	...	...
Yarraloola	21	1	...	...
Peedamullah	110	2	...	...
Onslow	52	4	366	8
Point Cloates	...	...	...	...
N.W. INLAND:				
Warrawagine	50	2	...	...
Eel Creek	75	1	...	...
Muccan	...	...	...	...
Ettrick	25	1	...	...
Mulgie	62	1	...	...
Streely	70	3	...	...
Warralong	77	1	...	...
Coongon	51	1	...	...
Talga	...	...	...	...
Bamboo Creek	47	3	-170	4
Moolyella	...	...	...	...
Marble Bar	93	3	135	6
Warrawoona	84	1	178	5
Corunna Downs	56	1	...	...
Mt. Edgar	...	...	...	...
Nullagine	28	1	228	6
Middle Creek	49	1	...	...
Mosquito Creek	85	1	...	...
Roy Hill	...	...	...	...
Bamboo Springs	...	...	...	...
Kerdiadary	Nil	...	...	...
Woodstock	65	1	...	...
Yandyarra	...	...	...	...
Station Peak	...	...	...	...
Mulga Downs	117	2	...	...
Mt. Florence	72	2	...	...
Tambrey	97	4	...	...
Millstream	59	2	...	...

RAINFALL—continued.

STATIONS.	JULY. No. of points. 100 = 1in.	JULY. No. of wet days.	AUGUST. No. of points. 100 = 1in.	AUGUST. No. of wet days.	STATIONS.	JULY. No. of points. 100 = 1in.	JULY. No. of wet days.	AUGUST. No. of points. 100 = 1in.	AUGUST. No. of wet days.
N.W. INLAND—cont.					YALGOO DISTRICT— contd.				
Red Hill ...	67	2	...	...	Mullewa ...	362	10	269	7
Mt. Stewart ...	...	...	...	...	Kockatea ...	387	8	241	6
Peake Station ...	23	1	...	...	Barnong ...	221	8	266	4
Nanutarra ...	Nil	...	...	...	Gullewa ...	...	...	207	6
Yanrey ...	82	4	...	...	Gullewa House...	295	8	233	5
Wogoola ...	125	9	256	...	Gabyon ...	235	10	...	...
Towera ...	138	8	...	...	Mellenbye ...	258	9	...	...
					Wearagaminda...	234	10	225	8
GASCOYNE :					Yalgoo ...	211	9	284	6
Winning Pool ...	219	8	479	5	Wagga Wagga ...	186	7	...	...
Coordalia ...	...	...	...	...	Muralgarra ...	181	9	...	...
Wandagee ...	...	...	...	...	Burnerbinmah ...	191	8	232	6
Williambury ...	162	7	...	...	Nalbara ...	139	10	...	...
Yanyeareddy ...	152	5	...	...	Wydgee ...	229	8	354	6
Maroonah ...	90	1	...	...	Field's Find ...	153	6	266	6
Ullawarra ...	8	2	...	...	Rothesay ...	...	...	208	6
Mt. Mortimer ...	...	...	...	...	Ninghan ...	227	8	292	6
Edmunds ...	105	6	...	...	Condingnow ...	214	10	...	...
Gifford Creek ...	...	...	...	...	163-Mile ...	214	8	312	5
Bangemall ...	...	...	...	...	Palaga Rocks ...	175	8	337	5
Mt. Augustus ...	...	...	...	...	126-Mile ...	171	9	...	..
Upper Clifton Downs	77	3	...	...	90-Mile ...	233	5	...	...
Clifton Downs ...	168	4	425	...	Mt. Jackson ...	130	8	...	...
Dairy Creek ...	190	6	...	...					
Mearerbundie ...	142	8	...	...					
Byro ...	164	7	...	...	MURCHISON :				
Meedo ...	154	5	...	...	Wale ...	...	...	...	...
Mungarra ...	...	...	...	...	Yallalonga ...	...	...	...	...
Bintholya ...	...	...	...	...	Billabalong ...	68	4	...	...
Lyons River ...	2¡1	6	...	...	Twin Peaks ...	163	7	...	...
Booloogooroo ...	...	...	...	...	Murgoo ...	203	7	351	8
Doorawarrah ...	...	...	...	...	Mt. Wittenoom ..	157	4	...	...
Brick House ...	264	8	...	...	Meka ...	179	6	...	...
Boolathana ...	221	8	...	...	Woolesne ...	168	7	...	...
Carnarvon ...	234	8	355	10	Boolardy ...	...	...	...	...
Dirk Hartog ...	333	...	482	...	Woogorong ...	...	...	...	...
Shark Bay ...	134	7	357	7	Manfred ...	145	5	...	...
Wooramel ...	133	8	245	7	Yarra Yarra ...	167	6	...	...
Hamelin Pool ...	106	9	334	9	Milly Milly ...	82	1	...	...
Kararang ...	199	10	...	...	Berringarra ...	93	3	...	...
Tamala ...	271	11	...	...	Miloura ...	99	6	...	...
					Mt. Gould ...	95	6	...	...
					Moorarie ...	99	4	...	...
YALGOO DISTRICT :					Wandary ...	...	...	...	...
Woolgorong ...	175	6	...	...	Peak Hill ...	147	7	621	8
New Forest ...	192	9	...	...	Mt. Fraser ...	...	...	...	...
Yuin ...	189	7	...	...	Minderoo ...	85	2	...	...
Pindathuna ...	160	4	...	...	Abbotts ...	84	3	318	4
Tallyrang ...	252	11	...	...	Belele ...	93	3	...	..

RAINFALL—*continued.*

Stations.	July. No. of points. 100 = 1in.	July. No. of wet days.	August. No. of points. 100 = 1in.	August. No. of wet days.	Stations.	July. No. of points. 100 = 1in.	July. No. of wet days.	August. No. of points. 100 = 1in.	August. No. of wet days.
Murchison—contd.					**Coolgardie Gold-**				
Meekatharra ...	...	3	...	...	**fields:**				
Nannine ...	108	2	351	5	Waverley ...	124	5	...	...
Annean ...	88	2	...	...	Bardoc ...	128	5	330	6
Tuckanarra ...	...	...	...	...	Broad Arrow ...	136	6	219	6
Coodardy ...	...	...	...	...	Kanowna ...	140	8	319	9
Cue ...	135	8	499	8	Kurnalpi ...	156	9	295	5
Gabanintha ...	100	2	339	5	Bulong ...	125	7	316	8
Day Dawn ...	86	5	437	6	Kalgoorlie ...	125	7	318	6
Lake Austin ...	125	5	545	6	Coolgardie ...	88	10	327	8
Lennonville ...	117	8	347	7	Burbanks ...	77	6	300	7
Mt. Magnet ...	100	8	361	7	Bulla Bulling ...	125	10	333	5
Youeragabbie ...	155	7	...	...	Woolubar ...	107	6	...	...
Murrum ...	146	5	...	...	Waterdale ...	92	7	...	...
Challa ...	146	7	...	...	Widgiemooltha...	74	11	272	9
Nunngarra ...	102	5	...	...	50-Mile ...	83	9	...	...
Birrigrin ...	118	6	...	...	Norseman ...	91	10	225	8
					Lake View ...	95	15	...	...
					Frazer Range ...	101	10	...	...
East Murchison:					Southern Hills ...	106	5	...	...
Gum Creek ...	105	2	...	...					
Dural ...	75	4	...	...					
Wiluna ...	82	6	250	9					
Mt. Sir Samuel ...	139	5	236	6	**Yilgarn Gold-**				
Leinster G.M. ...	...	...	...	...	**fields:**				
Lawlers ...	108	6	181	7	129-Mile...	365	9	...	...
Poison Creek ...	90	4	...	...	Emu Rocks ...	322	10	...	...
Lake Darlôt ...	...	...	...	...	56-Mile ...	194	6	...	...
Darda ...	57	3	...	...	Glenelg Rocks ...	355	11	...	...
Salt Soak ...	35	6	...	...	Burracoppin ...	277	6	...	...
Duketon ...	27	3	...	...	Bodallin ...	241	4	...	...
					Parker's Road ...	218	4	184	7
					Southern Cross ...	193	12	199	8
North Coolgardie					Parker's Range...	232	11	...	...
Goldfields:					Yellowdine ...	194	10	201	4
Burtville ...	...	...	...	...	Karalee ...	205	5	205	2
Laverton ...	84	8	220	8	Koorarawalyee..	230	8	201	5
Mt. Morgans ...	82	7	232	5	Boorabbin ...	168	8	240	7
Murrin Murrin...	57	4	256	8	Boondi ...	165	9	226	8
Mt. Malcolm ...	42	2	226	7					
Mt. Leonora ...	65	3	275	7					
Tampa ...	87	3	...	...	**South - West**				
Kookynie ...	120	7	302	8	**(Northern Divi-**				
Niagara ...	107	7	287	6	**sion):**				
Yundamindera ...	105	5	394	10	Murchison House	320	12	...	...
Mt. Celia ...	58	8	...	...	Mt. View ...	342	8	285	4
Edjudina ...	82	8	...	...	Mumby ...	414	9	393	9
Quandinnie ...	105	7	...	...	Northampton ...	595	10	444	7
Menzies ...	134	7	232	6	Chapman Experi-	467	7	...	...
Mulline ...	143	6	414	10	mental Farm				
Mulwarrie ...	196	8	348	8	Narra Tarra ...	...	...	...	...
Goongarrie ...	128	8	307	7					

RAINFALL—*continued.*

STATIONS.	JULY. No. of points 100 = 1in.	JULY. No. of wet days.	AUGUST. No. of points 100 = 1in.	AUGUST. No. of wet days.	STATIONS.	JULY. No. of points 100 = 1in.	JULY. No. of wet days.	AUGUST. No. of points 100 = 1in.	AUGUST. No. of wet days.
SOUTH - WEST (NORTHERN DIVISION)—*contd.*					SOUTH-WEST (METROPOLITAN)—*cont.*				
Oakabella ...	376	11	...	...	Rottnest ...	417	20	...	...
White Peak ...	457	10	...	...	Rockingham ...	426	14	522	11
Geraldton ...	454	12	601	7	Jandakot ...	528	15	554	12
Hinton Farm ...	542	11	...	...	Armadale ...	587	16	...	...
Tibradden ...	547	13	...	...	Mundijong ...	561	17	515	11
Myaree ...	564	11	312	7	Jarrahdale ...	738	17	744	13
Sand Springs ...	466	9	405	7	Jarrahdale (Norie)	693	19	724	13
Nangetty ...	428	10	247	7	Serpentine ...	632	13	600	12
Greenough ...	426	11	465	8					
Bokara ...	451	11	370	8					
Dongara ...	504	12	464	7	EXTREME SOUTH-WEST:				
Strawberry ...	661	13	378	6	Mandurah ...	596	20	581	13
Yaragadee ...	371	8	230	4	Pinjarra (Blythe-wood)	467	16	533	14
Urella ...	448	3	234	5	Pinjarra ...	437	19	575	10
Opawa ...	365	10	318	7	Upper Murray ...	626	17	755	13
Mingenew ...	485	10	377	7	Yarloop ...	689	20	626	12
Yandenooka ...	481	11	370	9	Harvey ...	753	17	...	...
Carnamah ...	384	10	462	9	Brunswick ...	660	18	...	...
Watheroo ...	427	14	270	9	Collie ...	732	18	459	13
Nergaminon ...	...	...	...	...	Glen Mervyn ...	551	12	...	...
Dandaragan ...	734	12	276	8	Donnybrook ...	658	19	482	11
Yatheroo ...	705	16	...	...	Boyanup ...	749	21	453	14
Moora ...	618	12	275	7	Bunbury ...	628	19	346	14
Walebing ...	522	15	305	11	Elgin ...	612	21	440	15
Round Hill ...	499	14	271	9	Busselton ...	588	24	554	13
New Norcia ...	607	19	280	11	Quindalup ...	653	22	...	...
Wongon Hills ...	385	15	...	...	Cape Naturaliste	588	22	388	14
Wannamel ...	740	15	379	11	Glen Lossie ...	554	18	...	...
Gingin ...	716	15	362	11	Karridale ...	738	25	391	13
					Cape Leeuwin ...	533	26	433	22
					Lower Blackwood	639	22	497	15
					Ferndale ...	632	18	460	11
					Greenbushes ...	702	13	414	14
SOUTH-WEST (METROPOLITAN):					Cooeearup ...	512	21	432	14
Wanneroo ...	588	16	342	11	Bridgetown ...	557	20	418	16
Belvoir ...	635	17	420	12	Hilton ...	440	8	332	8
Wandu ...	678	19	480	13	Greenfields ...	445	13	...	...
Mundaring ...	860	17	651	13	Cundinup ...	324	15	...	...
Canning Water-works	774	17	...	...	Wilgarrup ...	502	22	372	14
Kalbyamba ...	608	13	...	...	Balbarrup ...	565	14	424	8
Guildford ...	639	16	417	12	Bidellia ...	740	16	...	...
Perth Gardens ...	581	18	507	11	The Warren ...	...	...	...	...
Perth Observatory	603	17	553	13	Westbourne ...	397	19	379	15
Highgate Hill ...	589	17	505	12	Deeside ...	472	17	...	...
Subiaco ...	537	18	512	12	Riverside ...	547	21	...	...
Claremont ...	521	15	...	...	Mordalup ...	278	19	...	...
Fremantle ...	471	15	424	12	Lake Muir ...	486	18	...	...

RAINFALL—continued.

Stations.	July. No. of points 100 = 1in.	July. No. of wet days.	August. No. of points 100 = 1in.	August. No. of wet days.	Stations.	July. No. of points 100 = 1in.	July. No. of wet days.	August. No. of points 100 = 1in.	August. No of wet days.
EASTERN AGRICULTURAL DISTRICTS:					**GREAT SOUTHERN RAILWAY LINE—** *contd.*				
Emungin	311	15	...	...	Woodyarrup	331	12	189	10
Dowerin	338	10	...	...	Pallinup	378	11	158	7
Oak Hill	...	...	...	...	Tambellup	284	15	209	8
Hatherley	370	11	...	...	Toolbrunup	318	11	...	...
Momberkine	452	11	...	...	Cranbrook	354	21	...	...
Bolgart	556	16	249	10	Stirling View	307	17	226	11
Eumalga	700	13	312	11	Kendenup	384	21	316	11
Newcastle	565	15	323	11	Woogenellup	396	19	...	...
Craiglands	762	18	336	9	Wattle Hill	415	21	262	15
Eadine	561	17	...	...	St. Werburgh's	341	20	...	...
Northam	438	14	243	10	Mt. Barker	379	22	336	17
Grass Valley	418	7	...	...					
Cobham	493	15	...	...					
York	405	14	238	10					
Burrayocking	391	15	223	11					
Meckering	345	11	169	7					
Cunderdin	366	9	...	...	**WEST OF GREAT SOUTHERN RAILWAY LINE:**				
Doongin	288	9	...	...	Talbot House	444	14	...	...
Whitehaven	490	10	...	...	Jelcobine	473	15	...	...
Mt. Caroline	370	9	155	5	Bannister	499	14	...	...
Cutenning	296	7	...	...	Wandering	688	17	343	11
Kellerberrin	299	11	182	8	Glen Ern	511	14	...	...
Cardonia	272	10	...	...	Marradong	585	14	430	10
Baandee	344	8	178	3	Wonnaminta	502	16	...	...
Nangeenan	340	8	...	...	Williams	464	13	311	9
Merredin	328	8	...	...	Rifle Downs	631	9	...	...
Codg-Codgen	319	10	...	...	Darkan	...	...	...	...
Noongarin	333	10	...	...	Arthur River	467	10	292	8
Mangowine	327	9	...	...	Gainsborough	356	13	229	9
Yarragin	315	11	...	...	Glenorchy	437	13	...	...
Wattoning	290	5	...	...	Kojonup	365	10	260	9
					Blackwattle	348	11	...	...
					Warriup	413	21	...	...
GREAT SOUTHERN RAILWAY LINE:					Forest Hill	397	21	443	16
Dalebridge	448	16	...	...					
Beverley	510	13	289	8					
Brookton	568	14	289	7					
Sunning Hill	409	17	...	...	**EAST OF GREAT SOUTHERN RAILWAY LINE:**				
Pingelly	454	11	234	8	Sunset Hills	393	14	...	...
Yornaning	446	16	213	10	Oakdale	402	16	241	9
Narrogin	455	14	239	12	Barrington	373	15	191	5
Narrogin Experimental Farm	503	17	...	...	Bally Bally	405	15	...	...
Wagin	439	13	260	10	Stock Hill	412	10	267	7
Katanning	343	16	196	13	Qualin	383	10	215	5
Sunnyside	315	18	233	15	Woodgreen	269	16	...	...
Broomehill	329	15	232	11	Gillimanning	357	14	...	...

RAINFALL—*continued.*

STATIONS.	JULY. No. of Points 100 = 1in.	JULY. No. of wet days.	AUGUST. No. of points 100 = 1in.	AUGUST. No. of wet days.	STATIONS.	JULY. No. of points 100 = 1in.	JULY. No. of wet days.	AUGUST. No. of Points 100 = 1in.	AUGUST. No. of wet days.
EAST OF GREAT SOUTHERN RAILWAY LINE—*cont.*					SOUTH COAST—*cont.*				
					Peppermint Grove	497	16	250	13
Wickepin ...	531	15	...	...	Bremer Bay ...	455	12	211	15
Crooked Pool ...	407	12	217	6	Coconarup ...	352	14	152	12
Bunking ...	408	8	...	...	Ravensthorpe ...	367	16	178	13
Bullock Hills ...	403	13	...	...	Cowjanup ...	371	15	...	...
Dyliabing ...	309	16	...	...	Hopetoun ...	426	9	256	7
Glencoove ...	319	17	...	...	Fanny's Cove ...	374	9	...	...
Cherillalup ...	331	9	252	8	Park Farm ...	339	13	218	14
Mianelup ...	305	19	172	10	Grass Patch ...	220	13	...	...
Woolganup ...	230	12	152	8	Swan Lagoon ...	248	13	...	...
Chillinup ...	250	2	...	...	30-Mile ...	317	14	...	...
Jarramongup ...	362	17	...	...	Gibson's Soak ...	423	19	260	11
					Myrup ...	406	18	305	18
					Esperance ...	422	18	266	17
					Boyatup...	397	13	...	...
					Lynburn ...	284	15	...	...
SOUTH COAST:					Middle Island ...	350	17	138	15
Wilson's Inlet ...	553	23	...	...	Point Malcolm ...	184	14	...	...
Grasmere ...	560	19	325	14	Israelite Bay ...	151	14	117	11
King River ...	522	16	282	10	Balbinia...	740	16	...	...
Albany ...	534	22	421	16	Balladonia ...	78	3	100	8
Point King ...	477	16	855	11	Eyre ...	184	14	140	13
Breaksea ...	479	22	434	16	Mundrabella ...	76	3	...	...
Cape Riche ...	288	2	...	...	Eucla ...	131	12	228	14

The Observatory, Perth,
    5th September 1906.

W. E. COOKE,
Government Astronomer.

By Authority: FRED WM. SIMPSON, Government Printer, Perth.

JOURNAL

OF THE

Department of Agriculture

OF

WESTERN AUSTRALIA.

| Vol. XIV. | OCTOBER 20, 1906. | Part 4. |

EDITOR'S NOTES.

SYRACUSE PLOUGHS.—We have just received a catalogue of the famous "Syracuse Ploughs" from Messrs. Foy & Gibson, who notify that a large selection of these implements will be on exhibit at the forthcoming Royal Show.

SHEEP ON EVERY FARM.—Some sheep could be profitably kept on nearly every farm. They not only serve to keep the pastures free from weeds, but they also prove excellent scavengers for cleaning up the stubble fields after harvest. If well cared for they yield a handsome profit on the investment, as well as providing the most wholesome kind of fresh meat.

PIG BREEDING.—Of late considerable discussion has taken place over the best age to use a boar for breeding purposes. Authorities agree that in no case is it wise to use a boar under the age of nine or ten months. The best age, however, is when the boar is from three to five years old; mated to a sow of similar age, the result is the most prolific, and produces vigorous and perfect offspring.

EXPORTATION OF BUTTER:—The Australasian butter export to Great Britain is a trade of twenty years only. In 1886 two tons were received from Australia and five from New Zealand, and up to 30th April, 1906, the total quantity of butter from Australasia handled in Europe from the beginning of the trade amounted to 283,895 tons, a very respectable addition to the Old Country's food supply, representing, at a very rough estimate of value, say, £27,000,000, of which sum a good proportion has gone to develop the colonial dairying and general agricultural interests.

PASPALUM.—In an article published last month, entitled "Deep-rooted Grasses," a description and illustrations were given of Paspalum. The one supposed to represent *Paspalum virgatum*, facing page 170, was inserted in error, as this plate really represents the "Teosinte" plant. The two plants are so very different to each other, that anyone with only a slight knowledge of these grasses must know that a mistake had been made.

APPLE CULTURE.—Out of a total area of 11,026 acres under fruit in this State at the end of 1905, nearly one half, or 5,049, were under apples; as the basis of computation is 100 trees to the acre this means 504,900 trees. During the present planting season this number has been increased by some thousands. The time when exporting fruit in order to get rid of surplus crops, is now not far distant, so far as apples are concerned.

FREIGHT ON LIME.—The Commissioner for Railways has notified that the following reductions in the freight on agricultural lime came into force on 1st September:—Lime for Agricultural purposes (must be so declared on consignment note); minimum, 5 tons per wagon, owner's risk—

Up to 10 miles	... ...	Class M, 2s. per ton.
11 to 75 miles	... ...	½d. per ton per mile added to the rate for ten miles.
Over 75 miles	... ...	½d. per ton per mile added to the rate for 75 miles.

FRUIT GROWING ON THE GOLDFIELDS.—An illustration appears in this issue of a garden at Kurrawang, belonging to Mr. Leslie, the particular feature of which is the luxuriant growth of the peach trees which were planted only two years ago. The soil is the ordinary loam prevailing all over the Eastern Goldfields. They have not so far received any special treatment, but their general appearance promises well for the extension of orchards into these districts. We shall be interested to know how they bear, the quality and quantity of fruit maturing, as, after all, this is the main point.

WOOD WOOL.—We have received a sample of wood wool from Messrs. Saunders & Stuart who states that it is their intention to exhibit a machine at work making wood-wool at the annual show of the Royal Agricultural Society. The value of wood-wool as a packing for fruit has for some time been approved of in the export fruit trade of the Channel Islands to Great Britain. There is no reason that we can see, why this substance should not be of any great value to our fruitgrowers, and we would suggest that every orchardist should experiment with it, this coming season and note the results.

PEDIGREE AYRSHIRE BULL.—An opportunity rarely occurring is now presented to dairymen by Mr. H. Hamersley, who is offering his splendid Ayrshire bull "Artist of Oakbank" for sale. Mr. Hamersley has bred some splendid stock from this sire and is now selling him in order to replace with a change of blood. The bull is brown and white, was calved in November, 1898, bred by William McNab & Bros., Victoria, sire "Jamie of Oakbank," 184 A.H.B. of A., dam "Adeline," 27 A.H.B. of A. Both the sire and dam took a number of firsts and champions prizes. Further particulars may be obtained by writing to Mr. Hamersley, Guildford.

FRUIT GROWING ON THE GOLDFIELDS.

Peach Trees, two years' growth, Mr. Leslie's garden, Kurrawang.

HONEY YIELD.—According to statistics in the Handel's Museum, Germany leads in the production of honey among European countries with 1,910,000 beehives, furnishing 20,000 tons of honey. Spain is next with 1,690,000 hives and 19,000 tons of honey. Austria-Hungary is third with 1,550,000 hives and 18,000 tons of honey. The other European States are far behind. France produces 10,000 tons, Holland 2,500, Belgium 2,000, Greece 1,400, Russia and Denmark 900 tons each. In these statistics the effect of climatic conditions is noteworthy, especially when comparing Russia and Greece. The latter has only 30,000 beehives, yielding 1,400 tons of honey, while the former with 110,000 hives, produces only 900 tons.

INSECTS AND FUNGI.—We are in receipt of a copy of "Insects and Fungi, Injurious to Plants," Part II., By G. F. Strawson, also " Standard Fungicides and Insecticides in Agriculture " by the same author. Both of these books are of the greatest value to agriculturists, and should be on the book-shelf of every homestead. By making one's self familiar with the various pests and the signs of disease, early remedial and preventative measures can be used, which would result in the saving of many pounds. The books are well illustrated, and written in plain simple language, scientific terms being dispensed with as much as possible. The books are published at 3s. 6d. and 1s. 6d. respectively, and may be obtained from the author, 71A Queen Victoria Street, London, E.C.

THE OVERRUN EXPLAINED.—One pound of butter fat will make about one and one-sixth pounds of butter. During the process of butter making, the slight loss of fat in the skim-milk and butter-milk is more than compensated for by the added water, caseine, and salt in the butter. The additional butter made from a pound of butter fat is called the overrun— that is, the extent to which the churn overruns the test. The amount of overrunning depends upon the completeness of skimming, thoroughness of churning, and the way in which the butter is handled. A butter maker can readily determine the amount of overrun by dividing the total number of pounds of butter produced for a given time by the number of pounds of fat in the milk delivered to the creamery during that period.

SCALE ON COUCH GRASS.—During the last few weeks several reports have been received by the Department of couch grass being attacked and sometimes killed, leaving the places bare of all growth. The work of investigating into this trouble was placed in the hands of Mr. L. J. Newman, who has charge of the Entomological Laboratory, and he found, on examination of the grass attacked, that the roots were covered with a small scale. Specimens forwarded to Mr. A. M. Lea, the Tasmanian Entomologist, for identification, brought the following reply:—" The scale on the grass received belongs to the genus *Odonaspis*, and Green (the authority on scale insects), of Ceylon, has determined it as a new species, for which he proposes the name of *Odonaspis Australiensis*, but the description has not yet been published. So far the experiments tend to show that it can be destroyed by the liberal use of a strong decoction of tobacco or quassia chips."

IMPORTED STOCK.—A fine shipment of stud rams, ewes, and horses arrived at Fremantle on the 30th ult., consigned to Messrs. Dalgety & Co., on behalf of clients. The principal consignments were rams and ewes from

Mr. John Murray, Rhine Park, S.A., and Mr. A. F. Murray, of the same State. The shipment included 164 rams from Rhine Park, many of them ranging in value from 18 to 100 guineas; three stud rams at 80, 53, and 43 guineas, from Mr. A. F. Murray, and rams from other stations; also 500 stud ewes from Dutton & Melrose, North Booboorowie, 320 ewes from Rhine Park, and 15 horses from various breeders. Two special stud rams, one costing 80 guineas and the other 53 guineas, were landed at Albany for Mr. James Munro, of Pallinup. The 100-guineas special stud ram is for Mr. W. B. Sewell, of Geraldton. The 500 selected merino ewes landed here are for Mr. G. J. Gooch, of Gingin, and the same owner receives 100 selected merino rams. The horses and remainder of the merinos go to various land-owners. This valuable consignment is further evidence of the care now being exercised in improving the local stock. Other shipments are expected to follow shortly.

———

SUFFOLK SHEEP.—The Suffolk is the outcome of a cross between the old Norfolk horned sheep and the Southdown, and a type with which very few are familiar in this State. Its merits should commend the strain to practical exploitation at an early date. It has black face and legs, but has lost its horns, and its general appearance is that of the Hampshire Down. Its chief features are:—Hardiness, early maturity, prolificacy, and good quality of meat. The following are the points of the type:—Head, horn-less; face, black and long, with fine muzzle, and with a small quantity of clean white wool on the forehead; ears of medium length, black, and fine; eyes, bright and full; neck, of moderate length, with a good crest in the case of the rams; shoulders broad and oblique; chest, deep and wide; back and loin, long, level, and well covered with meat and muscle; tail, broad and well set-up; ribs, long and well-sprung, with full flank; legs and feet, straight and black, with fine flat bone; woolled to knees and hocks, clean below; forelegs well apart; hindlegs well filled with mutton: belly covered with wool; fleece moderately short, close, and fine, without any tendency to mat together, and not shading off into wool or hair; skin fine, soft, and pink.—*Exchange.*

———

HOW TO THROW A HORSE.—To thoroughly take the conceit out of a horse there is no better way than to throw him. It certainly requires pluck and determination to throw a horse single-handed, but if done, your horse is virtually conquered for good and all. To do this, put a good, strong halter on your horse, take a strap with a ring in it and buckle it round the horse's off foreleg below the fetlock joint; take a rope eight feet long and tie it to this strap; place a surcingle round the horse's body; take up your position on the right side of the horse, bring the rope over the horse's back from the off side; take hold of the rope and pull his foot to his body; take a firm hold of his foot, holding it in that position; then take hold of the horse's halter with the left hand, pull his head to you and press against his body with your elbow, using the words, "Lie down." The majority of horses can be thrown in this way in under a minute, while others, of course, may fight longer. As soon as the animal has been thrown, take the rope that is underneath him; bring it in under the surcingle, and pass it through the ring of the halter, and back under the surcingle again, and thus you have the rope in position to bring his head over his shoulder. Make him put his head on the ground, and if he makes any attempt to get up pull his head up immediately, which will prevent him from rising. This will give him thoroughly to understand that you are master. Once a horse realises your power over him he will do almost anything a horse can do.—" Horseman."

RIPE WHEAT.—When is the wheat ready for cutting? is a question every farmer is asking himself. Put shortly, it is ready as soon as the straw begins to turn yellow. This change means that circulation of food stuff from the root has ceased, and that any further changes will be within the plant itself. The process of growth comprises, first, the storing up of the nutrient bodies in the stem and leaves, then the transference of these to the young seed, and lastly, in part, from the seed to its coverings—such as the hulls, bran, etc. The most suitable time to cut, in order to get the greater food value out of both straw and grain, is just before the straw is completely yellow. The process of ripening will go on after the stalk is separated from the soil, until it is thoroughly dried for stacking. All this, however, is subject to certain limitations. In a dry, hot time, there will be no ripening after cutting, while the ordinary ripening before cutting go on so quickly that we must cut early in any case, or else there will be a lot of seed shed from over-ripeness. Another consideration is whether the grain is required for seed or for food purposes. Dead-ripe grain is the best for seed, because the shells have been developed and hardened, but then in ordinary work, if the seed is ripe it gets knocked off in handling, so it must not be allowed to get too ripe. The moral of the whole is to cut a little before ripeness arrives in the case of all our grain crops. By this means we harvest a little earlier, prevent the grain from shelling out, and get the best quality in both grain and straw.

THE CARE OF PIGS.—If there is any good reason why pigs on some farms are given their feed in the form of a thin slop we would like to be enlightened. We do not refer to milk, nor to kitchen slops. We refer to the practice of adding so much water to the mill feeds or ground feeds that the feed is lost in the water. There is enough feed in the water to colour the slop and make the pigs drink it greedily, but what benefit comes from forcing the pigs to drink so much water that they may get their feed? So far as we have been able to observe this excessive slopping makes pot-bellied soft pigs, and much disease of the digestive system is due to the filthy slop barrels and wagons. Let us hear from some of those who follow the practice of heavy slopping. There must be some reason for it or they would not do it. If you do not keep your feeding troughs clean; if you have a filthy swill barrel; if you permit the feed to become sour every now and then, don't be surprised if the pigs scour. Keep the feed sweet; keep the barrels and troughs clean; don't feed more at any one time than the pigs will clean up, dip once a month and disinfect the pens and sleeping quarters. If you do these things you will not have much bother with digestive troubles. It does not pay to make the pigs get along with a few baskets of corn thrown over the fence early in a morning and often after dark at night. No amount of care after harvest will make up for the loss caused by neglect just at the time when the pigs need regular feed and attention. When the pig is used as a scavenger it is well enough to let him hustle for a living until winter, and then finish him for market with corn in a dry pen. But pigs in the corn belt are not used as scavengers. They are used to take some of the grain to market in the form of pork, and to do this at the greatest profit they must be kept growing constantly from the time they are farrowed until hauled off.

EGG WEALTH.—Insignificant as egg-production appears to be, yet it is an astonishing fact, and will come as a surprise to many, that egg-production in the United States of America is millions of pounds in value ahead of the great steel industries of that place.   In order to illustrate the amount to be made out of a few laying hens and the use of cool storage, we will take for example that a householder, farmer, fruitgrower, or settler has four dozen fair laying hens, these should in the course of the months of July, August, and September, the principal laying months of the year with us, lay an average of two dozen eggs per bird per month, or a total of 96 dozen per month.   Of these fill three cases, each to contain 25 dozen, as explained in last month's JOURNAL, for cold storage ; the balance (21 dozen) could be used for household purposes.   The cases, as soon as filled, could be lodged in cold storage at a cost of 1s. per case per calendar month.   Assuming that they are kept there for six months from the date of lodging the first cases, then we would have a total cost as follows, allowing 1s. per dozen for eggs, the market price during the months under review :—

	£	s.	d.		£	s.	d.
225 dozen eggs at 1s. dozen	11	5	0	To 225 dozen eggs sold at 2s. per dozen	22	10	0
9 cases, with cardboard separators	0	12	11	Less cost	14	12	11
Storage : 3 cases 6 months	0	18	0				
„ 3 „ 5 „	0	15	0				
„ 3 „ 4 „	0	12	0				
Cartage and incidentals	0	10	0				
	14	12	11	Profit on three months' production	7	17	1

Of course it is understood that even at 1s. per dozen for eggs there is a profit on the production, so that the £8 1s. shown above may be termed additional profit.   Allowance must also be made for freight, breakage, and commission.   How many housewifes to whom it is possible to put this scheme into practice would be very glad to receive such an amount in addition to the ordinary income.   The foregoing is simply the facts of a practical result of what was done in Perth last year.   The women of this State, whether they be the wives of orchardists, settlers, or others, or those who are fighting their own battles without the help or handicap of a husband, should give thought to this possibility of increasing their pin-money in one case or earnings in the other.   Though at one time " Hen-wife " was a term used in somewhat a scornful sense, even within the life of the present generation, it is now synonymous with all that means prosperity, and is equally befitting the wife and daughters of the most refined as it does the humble cottager.

DISEASED POTATOES.—Quite a number of complaints have been received by the Department of bad and unsound seed potatoes having been sent out to customers.   From samples received it is evident that they are affected by " wet rot."   The following particulars of this disease are taken from page 422 of Vol. XIII. of the "JOURNAL":—" Wet Rot."—In damp, warm seasons, the tubers underground may suffer from this malady, which also affects potatoes stored in pits or sheds in which dark, damp, and warm conditions prevail.   The disease begins with the formation of dark patches beneath the skin of the potato, and the whole interior soon becomes affected by a brown, slimy " wet rot."   It is difficult to detect this disease without cutting open the tuber, but the evidence of disease, in the interior, cannot be mistaken. " Seed" derived from crops known to have suffered from " wet rot" should not be used.   The disease, of which there are several forms, is of *bacterial* origin.   It is increased, subsequently, by the attacks of various *fungi* upon the weakened tissue. Suspected tubers should be soaked in a weak solution of "Bordeaux" mixture for an hour, then well dried, dusted with sulphur, and stored in shallow trays. "Seed" showing disease should be destroyed.

FIG. 4.

FIG. 5.

FIG. 4.—The sprouting of a potato suffering from the initial stages of "wet rot."
a, sprouts; bb. indications of the "wet rot."
The sprouts are weak and spindling.   Compare with the adjacent
illustration.

FIG. 5.—The sprouting of a healthy potato.   To be compared with Fig. 4.
aa, Sprouts.

Care should be taken to prevent contaminating clean ground, and it would be wiser to obtain fresh seed rather than plant diseased, or unsound tubers. In places where diseased tubers have been known to grow, a spell of at least two years should be given before using the ground again for this crop.   Mr. Despeissis recommends spraying all crops with either Bordeaux or Burgundy mixtures every two or three weeks from the time the plants are a few inches out of the ground."

RICE MEAL, A NEW DAIRY COW FOOD.—Rice meal, according to the *Scientific American*, is a material which dairy farmers have recently been using in increased quantities as a food for dairy cattle.   The advantages of rice meal, it is stated, are its high percentage of oil, which averages about 12 per cent., some samples containing as much as 15 per cent.   The oil is one that becomes solid at ordinary temperature, possesses a sweet odour and agreeable taste, and is in every way a satisfactory food constituent.   The mild and pleasant flavour of the meal is also an important factor, for obviously it is thus rendered free from any objectionable properties in this respect to dairy produce, while the richness of the ash in phosphoric acid assists in making it well adapted to the preparation of young animals' natural food.   Rice meal contains a comparatively low percentage of nitrogen, which is equal to about 12 per cent. of albuminous substances, but, nevertheless, with the exception of only a small proportion, these consist of albuminoids, and they, as nutrients, are by far the most valuable constituents containing this element.   However, an increase in the quantity present may be made with advantage, and as the percentage of oil is so considerable, it is possible to mix with materials poor in that ingredient and yet obtain a food supplying a satisfactory amount.   For example, by adding beans and peas to rice meal, in the proportion of two-thirds of the latter to one-third of the former, a valuable and digestible feeding stuff may be prepared, for these leguminous seeds, although poor in oil, are very rich in nitrogen.

The value of bran and pollard, as compared with rice meal, has been computed by Mr. Mann, the Government analyst, as follows:—

The following show the food unit values of these materials obtained from references:—

	Rice Meal.	Pollard.	Bran.
Food Units	115·23	107·9	104·34
Nutritive Ratio	1·4	1·6	1·4

	Rice Meal.	" Middlings."*	Bran.
Digestibility—			
Per cent. digestible proteine	62	80	78
Per cent. digestible carbohydrates	92	81	69
Per cent. digestible fat	91	86	68

You will see that the rice meal has a higher digestibility than the others, except in proteine and a higher food value, but its nature is different: being of a carbohydrate nature it is rather of a *heat-forming* than muscle-forming character. Alone it would not meet all requirements, but mixed with more nitrogenous food should be of value.

MOLASCUIT.—"Molascuit," the new food for animals, is prepared entirely from the sugar cane, and the sugar cane is a tropical grass. The process of preparing it is protected by Royal Letters Patent, and is as follows:—The interior of the sugar cane is formed of a number of minute cells, and the cells (after the cane is crushed and the juice expressed) are obtained by disintegration and screening. The product of this operation, known as Megass Meal, consists of 75 per cent. digestible food, and has the remarkable property of absorbing four times its weight of molasses. The original juice, in fact, is replaced by molasses in these cells, and the final dry product arrives in this country in perfect condition. It is a much better food for animals than liquid molasses. It has the advantage that, being a nice dry meal, it can be shipped in bags, as compared with liquid molasses, requiring expensive barrels or puncheons; it is not fit for human consumption, and therefore not so liable to petty theft as ordinary molasses. Dr. Voelcker says in the Journal of the Royal Agricultural Society of England, 1902:— " While the use of beet sugar molasses has been considerably developed in the manufacture of compound feeding cakes and in special preparations, it may be well to mention that recently a handy form for utilising and exporting sugar cane molasses has been found in the absorption of the molasses with inner part or pith of the sugar cane itself. Sugar cane molasses is not open to the objection that may be taken to beet sugar molasses, as it is free from the excessive saline matters which the latter contains, and it has also a much more pleasant taste." The following is an analysis and report by Prof. John Hunter, F.I.C., F.C.S., on a recent shipment of Demerara " Molascuit " to Scotland :—†Albuminous compounds, 2·12 ; oil, 0·32 ; sugar, 61·04 ; digestible cellulose, etc., 10·60 ; indigestible cellulose, 5·56 ; ash, 6·68 ; moisture, 12·68 : 100·00. The learned professor added :—" This is an excellent example of feeding stuffs of its class. If used judiciously it will be found a highly advantageous addition to the ordinary feeding stuffs of the farm." It will be noted from the figures that the feeding value of the article is dependent upon sugars and digestible cellulose. It is not claimed

---

* Figures for " Pollard " not obtainable.　　† Containing Nitrogen 0·34 per cent.

Mr. Kelly's Homestead.

Fat Bullocks on Texas Downs Station.

to be complete food, but will be found a valuable article to mix more or less with all other foods for animals, in proportion to the albuminoids contained in the other foods. It gives to the usual food supplied to animals an especial relish; it improves the digestion; it keeps them in health, which is clearly demonstrated by the improved appearance of the animal. It is recommended for cattle at the rate of about 1 to 2lbs. per day, milch cows 3 to 4lbs., and for horses 1 to 2lbs., according to their work, but for sheep and pigs a less quantity should be given.

THROUGH THE KIMBERLEYS.

By R. E. WEIR, M.R.C.V.S.

(Continued.)

Leaving our kindly host and hostess at Argyle, a run of 30 miles over good plain country, chiefly alluvium flats, brought us to Sugar Springs where we found evidence of artesian boring. It appears that an attempt was made some time ago to put down a bore at this spot, but on account of the plant used being insufficiently powerful to penetrate the desired depth, this very necessary work had to be abandoned. This failure, however, should not deter from further trials being made, as undoubtedly the nature of the country is artesian. Evidence of this is obtained from a spring in the locality which has been opened out and now flows continuously throughout the year. This water is distinctly artesian in character. From this part to the Negri River the country is basaltic, and waterworn boulders strew the road for practically the whole distance of 30 miles; in consequence, vehicular traffic is most arduous for horses and inconvenient to travellers. We had traversed but a short distance before one of the buggy springs gave way, but fortunately we were then nearing the Police Station at Wild Dog, where by reason of kindly assistance rendered by the officers in charge, temporary repairs were effected, and a slow monotonous journey continued to Texas Downs. Here we were welcomed by the proprietor and his wife, Mr. and Mrs. Kelly, under whose genial influence the hardships of the past days' travelling were soon forgotten. We trust, however, that our strong comments on the negligence of the Roads Board for not removing the obstructions, which could be done for a comparatively small expenditure, has resulted in the construction of a road which will be found comparatively smooth for all time. Texas Downs Station, comprising some 50,000 acres, is to a large extent hilly country interspersed by well grassed flats, which are possessed of good fattening properties. This is well borne out by the accompanying photograph of two steers taken at the homestead and which shows the magnificent proportions to which cattle may be raised in that part of the country, and at the same time disposes of the statements so often circulated—that Kimberley pastures are lacking in fattening qualities. That we are often supplied with inferior beef from Kimberley is not due to any defects in the pasturage, but arises chiefly from the fact that a great demand has existed for fat stock during the past few years, and the consequent temptation to ship immature animals, which are liable to rapidly loose condition during transit. As time proceeds the present conditions should alter and our supplies will then be more in accordance with the accompanying photograph. When that desirable period arrives, both owner and consumer will have secured a much needed improvement, which will no doubt be found beneficial to all parties. About two miles from the homestead a deposit of salt is found in the bed of the Ord River. After being freed from impurities the supply, although coarse, is much used locally for domestic and other purposes. A few have a prejudice against its use, for the reason that it is supposed to have a special detrimental action on brain matter, but this is purely supposition and has no foundation in fact. From this on to the Ord River homestead the road traverses good undulating country, which was then showing signs of a long dry season. At the homestead we were met by Mr. Patterson, one of the proprietors, who also represents Messrs. Copley & Co., more particularly with regard to the annual shipments of cattle; a position for which he is specially adapted owing to his past experience in this line of business. The Ord River Station is one of the oldest, and perhaps for such an extent of country (5,000,000 acres), it is one of the best all round properties in this State. At present it has a carrying capacity of 75,000 head, with an annual branding of 18,000, whilst 6,000 fats are annually forwarded from the station for shipment to Fremantle. The property is magnificently watered by the Ord, Nicholson, Turner, Osmond, and Negri Rivers, besides a number of springs which flow continuously throughout the year. The country in parts appears like huge paddocks, with trees fringing the river banks for boundary fences. The grasses are all of a finer nature than those near the coast, and are more rapidly affected by dry seasons. This was very evident at the time of my visit. The effect of two dry seasons was so disastrous that all pasture on the river frontages had completely disappeared for the time being, and for two days after leaving the homestead the country travelled over might be compared to fallow land, and only with difficulty could we secure any form of feed for our horses. Water was also becoming limited, and on occasions we had to search for and clean out soaks to obtain sufficient for our requirements. The country has, however, wonderful recuperative properties, and should good rains be obtained at the end of the year, the land, which at the time of my visit was presenting a barren appearance, will again assume its brightest form, and the stock which had then to travel long distances for a meagre subsistence will again luxuriate in abundant pasture. Leaving the Ord Station at the Turner River, the road passes through a deep rough gorge in the ranges and leads into broken country, where the boulder-strewn beds of several rivers had to be crossed and recrossed. Two days' travelling through country of this nature caused us to hail with joy the pleasant change experienced on entering what may be termed the garden of Kimberley. This is a long narrow strip of country snugly enclosed between the Mt. Edward Ranges, and so well and favourably known by the name of "Flora Valley." A drive of 20 miles over a plain well covered with Mitchell and Flinders grasses brought us to the homestead, where we were most hospitably received and entertained by the Messrs. Gordon Bros., who, together with Mr. Buchanan, are the owners of the station. The Messrs.

Fig. I.—Bokhara Clover: showing root of two year old plant

Fig. III.—Field Pea: showing root system, for purposes of comparison.

Gordon, although men now advancing in years, still retain that youthful cast of mind so often met with in persons who have spent the greater part of their lives in the bush. Although their experience has been chiefly confined to cattle, yet they have an inherent love for horses, and as the country is well adapted for the rearing of these animals they have bestowed a great deal of attention to producing a good stamp of station horse sired by the thoroughbred. These horses are much sought after by station-owners, and consequently have proved a profitable investment. The station was originally stocked in 1893 with 600 head of Shorthorns, and the number has since increased to 7,000, from which a draft of 250 head of fats are disposed of annually. The leasehold comprises 440,000 acres, which includes a plain about 40 miles long by seven miles wide, the remainder being mountainous country, which is of little value for feeding purposes. It is well watered by the Elvire, Fox, and Johnston Rivers, besides a number of creeks and springs. The native question, which is always a vexed one in the Kimberleys, appears to have been solved in a very practical manner on this station. The proprietors have collected the natives together and formed a large camp near the homestead, where they are practically supplied with provisions by the station. The older natives and young children remain in close proximity to the camp, where they may hunt and obtain a portion of their food in the usual native fashion, while the stronger and more able bodied perform the necessary station work and are cared for at the homestead. This humane treatment has engendered the most kindly feeling on the part of the natives towards the Messrs. Gordon Bros., and in consequence they (the natives) have become trustworthy, and perfect order is maintained by moral suasion alone.

DEEP-ROOTED PLANTS FOR SUMMER CULTIVATION.

THE FIELD PEA—A COMPARISON.

By PERCY G. WICKEN.

In the last issue of the JOURNAL an article was published on deep-rooted grasses. The plants mentioned in the present article come under the same heading, and several of them belonging to the leguminous tribe would be suitable for cultivation in conjunction with the grasses already mentioned, as by this means a mixed pasture could be obtained which would be of more value than one composed of one grass only.

The accompanying illustrations are from photographs taken to show the deep nature of the roots, and show, when once established, what a firm hold the roots of these plants are able to obtain of the soil. As they penetrate so deeply, they are enabled to obtain a supply of moisture at a lower depth than are surface-rooting plants, which probably die off as soon as the weather becomes dry.

A comparison of illustrations 1, 2, and 3 will demonstrate the difference. The first two plants are deep-rooted and send their roots between two and three feet into the subsoil, and will stand and grow well during the dry weather. Fig. 3 is a plant of the ordinary field pea, which grows only during the winter months, and whose roots only penetrate about six inches or less into the soil, and which very soon dry up when the weather becomes warm.

BOKHARA CLOVER.
Melilotus leucantha.

Also known as Sweet Clover, is a perennial leguminous plant; it is a very deep-rooted plant, and as such is a good drought-resisting fodder. It is valuable both as a fodder, and as a bee plant and also for green manuring.

The deep searching nature of the roots, which penetrate several feet into the sub-soil, enable the plant to obtain its food supplies from the sub-soil, and when the plant is ploughed in for green manure the leaves, etc. are turned into the surface layer of soil, and as they decompose, add to it a large quantity of valuable plant food.

The plant grows from three to five feet in height, according to soil and locality. The leaves resemble the lucerne plant in appearance, but the flowers are white. Bokhara Clover is said to do well on poor soils, particularly when of a calcareous nature.

Opinions differ very considerably as to its value as a fodder for stock; in some instances sheep and cattle are reported to eat it readily, while in other instances they will not touch it. This is the case with a good many other fodder plants, and to induce stock to take to it they should be put to graze on it at a time when other feed is scarce. If stock are put on it early in the spring before the clovers have made much growth they will often eat it, and when they have once acquired the habit they will eat it at any time afterwards.

The seed may be either sown in the autumn or spring. In the dryer districts the autumn sowing is preferable, the seed being sown so that it will germinate with the first rains, it will then make a good root growth during the winter, and have a firm hold of the soil by the time the weather becomes warm. In the cooler and moister localities the seed is better sown in the spring, as it will not start into growth while the ground is wet and cold.

The seed should be sown in drills three feet apart, and as it is a strong growing plant it soon fills up the ground between the rows. About 10lb. of seed is sufficient for an acre of ground, and the seed can be obtained from almost any seed merchant at a price of from 1s. to 1s. 6d. per lb.

There is another variety of the same plant which has a yellow flower, but it is not considered of such good feeding value.

The accompanying illustration was taken at the Departmental Experimental Plot at Hamel, and shows the root system of a plant two years old. A comparison with the two-foot rule at the side of the plant illustrates the depth the roots penetrate into the ground, and the power it will thus have of withstanding a period of dry weather. The plants at Hamel made an excellent growth during the dry weather, and several cuttings of fodder could be obtained. This is a plant that is worth cultivating for summer fodder. If used to mix with maize or sorghum for the purpose of making silage, it would much improve the feeding qualities of the silage.

FLAT PEA.

Lathyrus sylvestris.

Is often called Wagner's Flat Pea. It is a legumious plant, very similar in appearance to the common garden or sweet pea. In favourable localities it grows into a tangled mass and several cuttings of fodder can be obtained in a season. It can either be made into hay or into silage for the purpose of feeding stock. The same remarks as have been made in the case of Bokhara Clover, re the stock not taking to it in the first instance, apply to this plant, and it is often necessary to keep sheep on the crop for some days before they will take to eating it. The value of the plant is stated to be its ability to grow on light soils, too dry for most other crops, but its disadvantage is that it takes several years to become established. At present, the only experience we have to record of its growth in this State is at the Experimental plots at Hamel, and here, under favourable conditions, it has made an excellent growth. This season the Department of Agriculture have obtained a quantity of seed from Germany and a number of packets have been distributed, and as reports come to hand we shall be able to form farther opinions of its value.

Some years ago the writer grew a quantity of this plant in New South Wales, and although it grew fairly well, the results were not up to expectations. However, the success obtained at Hamel is sufficient to warrant a further trial being made in this State.

The seed should be planted in the early Spring in drills 18in. apart and the seeds about six inches apart in the drills, or the seedlings may be raised in a seed-box and transplanted when they are strong enough. The seeds should be covered from two to three inches deep, according to the nature of the soil; three inches in a light soil, and two inches in a heavier one. As the young plants are slow growing, they will require to be kept free from weeds until they become established. The crop is a splendid one as a renovator of the soil, and if turned under as a green manure will add to the supply of nitrogen in the soil.

The illustration of the plant shows the root system of one of the plants grown at Hamel; during the first season it only makes a few inches' growth, and the plants do not obtain the greatest growth until about three years old. The three plants shown on the photograph are one, two, and three years old respectively, and a comparison with the two-foot rule will show the great development of the root system during that time. The two-year-old plants had roots which penetrated about 3ft. 6in. into the subsoil, and the plant was thus enabled to obtain food and moisture from such a depth as to make it almost independent of surface conditions.

Lathyrus sylvestris will not stand any considerable amount of frost, and in a cold locality the plant becomes cut down every winter. and would want resowing. Under these conditions, owing to its slow-growing habit, it is hardly likely to be profitable to grow; but, under more favourable conditions, and where there is a mild winter, it is well worth a trial.

THE FIELD PEA.

Pisum sativum.

This illustration is shown for the purpose of comparing the root system with that of the Bokhara Clover and *Lathyrus sylvestris.* The Field Pea is only a shallow-rooted plant; it grows only during the winter months, and in this climate dies out as soon as the weather becomes hot. The roots of a large plant are only from 12 to 15 inches in length, and instead of penetrating deeply into the soil, are only to be found running along near the surface. The Field Pea is a very valuable plant for turning into the soil for a green manure and for improving the value of land, but as it only grows at a time when food of all description is plentiful it is not so valuable as a fodder to settlers in the dryer districts as a plant that will grow during the summer months when the supply of green feed is short.

If field peas are allowed to ripen, and when dry are stacked, they will make a valuable fodder during the time when feed is scarce, but for the purpose of grazing the object is to obtain plants that will grow during the dry periods of the year.

Peas or some other variety of leguminous crop should have a place in the rotation whenever a system of mixed farming is carried out.

On looking at the roots of this plant the nodules formed by the nitrogenous bacteria can be plainly seen, and it is by the means of these bacteria that this tribe of plants are enabled to utilise the supply of nitrogen from the air.

VEGETABLE GROWING.

By G. CHITTY BAKER.

(*Continued.*)

In the August issue I dealt with the subject of trenching; and in order to make this matter as plain as the importance of the operation warrants, a sheet of diagrams is herewith published, so that if the letterpress already referred to be read with them, there should be no doubt as to the manner that this work should be carried out.

SAVING SEED.

Those who desire to save their own seed for future sowing will do well to remember that care must be taken that no other variety of the same plants are flowering at the time of those from which it is wished to obtain the seed. In selecting such plants, choose the healthiest, and allow it to ripen its crop; do not pick any off, as those that first set are generally the best; this is

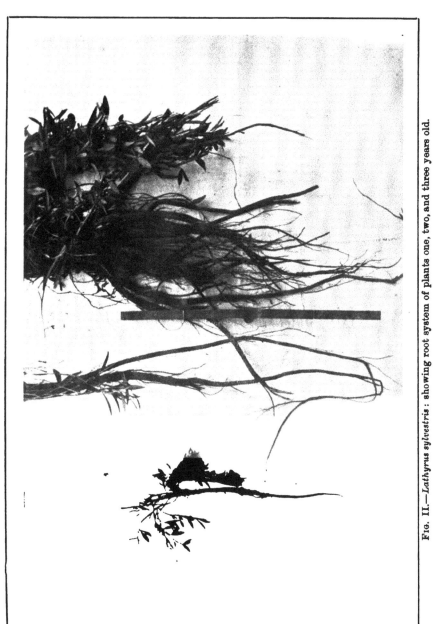

Fig. II.—*Lathyrus sylvestris*: showing root system of plants one, two, and three years old.

applicable to peas, beans, tomatoes, melons, and cucumbers. With respect to all other vegetables, always select the best and quickest growing plant, with any characteristic you may wish to perpetuate. As a rule, however, it is neither profitable nor wise to save seed from small gardens. In any case a change of seed should always be made every third, or, at the longest, every fourth year.

ASPARAGUS (*Asparagus officinalis*).

This plant is not cultivated to the extent it deserves, considering how easy it is to grow, and the ready sale always waiting for it. It is surprising that we do not see more of it in our gardens. Asparagus is best raised from plants, which may be obtained from one to three years old. If seed is used then a season at least is lost. The seed bed should be worked into a fine tilth, and when the "grass" from the seed is about six inches high it should be thinned out so that the plants stand about 12 or 18 inches apart.

To prepare a bed that the plants are to finally occupy, preparations should be commenced in the autumn. Select an open space, trench this about three spits deep, well manuring each spit with good rotten compost. In about a month, do the same work over again, and where it is possible, even a third trenching in early spring will well repay the cost of labour. Asparagus beds that have been thus properly prepared will last from 20 to 30 years. In planting out, the greatest of care must be exercised; on no account must the roots be exposed, even for a little while, as the drying influence of the wind or sun, if allowed to reach them, would seriously injure the plant.

The best soil is a nice sandy loam, thoroughly and deeply worked, enriched with good compost or stable manure, while the worst is a clay or wet pasty loam. Having made the ground even and firm, stretch a line across and take out a trench about four inches deep, keeping the side next the string, even and vertical. Having seen that there are no bruised roots, place the plants in the trench, about 12 inches apart, close to the upright edge, drawing the loose soil round them, at the same time firming it down; rake over and leave an even surface. The rows should be at least 18 inches apart. During the first year a crop of young onions followed by lettuce can be profitably grown on the bed. In growing asparagus on a large scale it will be found better to plant one to two feet apart in drills three to four feet distant, so as cultivation may be made by horse. Only a very few heads should be cut from the first crop, allowing the others to run up, as it is according to the good growth of the tops during the summer that the roots are enabled to start the buds for the following season's crop of heads.

The tops should never be cut down until they have changed colour, when everything from the bed must be cleared up, raked over, and two inches of good rotten stable manure spread over for the use of the coming crop. The application of salt is not altogether necessary, in fact in the early stages it is distinctly injurious. I know of a market gardener at Enfield, near London, who grew asparagus for 40 years and never once used salt, yet he was enabled to produce the finest of heads.

Considerable advantage may be made by occasional waterings during the early stages of growth with a solution containing one ounce of sulphate of ammonia, two ounces of superphosphate, and half an ounce of sulphate of potash to each gallon of water.

BEANS, FRENCH (*Phaseolus vulgaris*).

There is no crop so popular with the private gardener as the dwarf or French bean; it is easy of cultivation, and such sorts as the Canadian Wonder provides a number of pickings from the same plants. Sowing may be commenced in August and continued every fortnight right on to February in those gardens where a good watering can be given. Owing to the enormous growth in the demand on Canadian Wonder, the seed has been allowed sadly to deteriorate. This bean is certainly, when good seed can be obtained, the best variety for general use. Sow the seed in drills about 1¼ inches deep, four inches apart; in fact when plants are given six inches or even eight inches in a row, better crops are obtained. Pale Dun and Golden Butter are also good varieties to grow and form a very pleasant change. An occasional watering with a solution of half an ounce of sulphate of iron to each gallon of water will be found beneficial in most of our soils.

RUNNER BEAN (*Phaseolus multifloras*).

This very popular bean is but seldom grown, owing, it is said, to the trouble entailed in staking them. Where sticks can be obtained, it is certainly unwise not to grow a few plants. One good plan is to sow three seeds in a triangle every six feet on each side of the centre path and well staked. When in flower they add greatly to the appearance of the garden. When planted in rows they should be sown one foot apart in rows of at least four feet distance. Some growers plant them in double rows, of a foot apart, the double rows being six feet apart. As this bean is somewhat longer in maturing it is not advisable to make any sowings later than November; the first may be made in September. Fertilise and cultivate the same as for dwarf kinds.

LIMA BEANS.

This bean is but little known in this State. The growth and cultivation are the same as that given to the other beans; they are, however, more delicate and the first sowings for either the pole or dwarf kinds should not be made until October. They are unlike the French beans as the pods are not used, but the seeds, shelled the same as broad beans, when green are very delicious, equal to the best marrow-fat pea, and when allowed to ripen and dry are used as haricots. The two best varieties are "Challenger" (tall), and Henderson's Bush Lima. When they once start bearing pickings can be made right along to the winter.

BROAD BEANS (*Faba vulgaris*).

This well-known bean grows equally well on heavy land or deep sandy loam; they are rather a long while coming into bearing, five months being the usual time. The first sowing may be made immediately after the first autumn rains, early in April, and continued up to June or July, so as the crop has time to mature before mid-summer. The seed is sown in drills at least a foot apart, the rows being four feet or even more. A good plan is to have the rows at least six feet apart and plant a row of early potatoes between. Keep the ground well cultivated and free from weeds. Fertilise the same as for the other kinds of beans. The best bean I ever grew was Symond's long pod. Some growers advocate pinching the tops off after flowering has commenced; when this is done the tops so picked should be boiled, as they make a very nice vegetable.

BEETROOT (*Bitu vulgaris*).

We do not eat enough of this vegetable. Boiled, allowed to get cold, dressed with vinegar and white pepper, and served with cold meat, it is at once appetising, nutritive, and most easily digested. It is often fried in fritters, and by many preferred to mushrooms, which it sometimes resembles when cooked this way. Beets are most easily cultivated, but when it comes to growing them for exhibition, considerable care is required to insure well-shaped roots. It grows best in a good sandy loam, following a crop that has been well manured. Freshly applied manure tends to create forked, mishapen, and unsightly roots. The ground should be well and deeply worked, the seeds sown about three quarters of an inch deep in drills 18 inches apart. So soon as the plants show above ground thinning must be commenced, keeping all the plants single until they finally stand 6 inches to 8 inches apart in the rows. Hand weeding must be done until well established, when the hoe can be used. Any fertilisers used after the plants have started should be applied in a weak liquid form. Seed may be sown from March to August. Those sown later are liable to run to flower. The long red and turnip are both good sorts, the latter being the earliest and best for summer growing.

Silver Beet, although belonging to the same family, is cultivated for its leaves, the mid-rib of which forms an excellent substitute for asparagus, while the green part is served as spinach. Silver beet is a rank grower, and requires frequent applications of liquid manure, a solution made of 2ozs. of superphosphate, 1oz. of sulphate of ammonia, half ounce of sulphate of potash, and quarter of an ounce of sulphate of iron to each gallon of water will have a decided marked influence on the growth and flavour of the leaves. The leaves should be pulled and never cut, and if, when boiling, a little lemon juice is added, the appearance is improved; this prevents them from turning black. Soda must never be used. A bed of silver-beet, properly cared for, will give pickings for over twelve months. The seed may be sown in beds as for cabbages, etc., from autumn to spring, and planted out when about four to six inches high.

BRUSSELS SPROUTS (*Brassica oleracea bullata gemmifera*).

Brussels sprouts are recognised as one of the best of the cabbage family, but they do not seem to be grown in the quantity they should be. It is very rarely to be seen in the market, yet it is quite as easily grown as any other of the cabbage tribe. One fault I find is that growers are prone to curtail the space required for really good plants. Seed should be sown about the end of November or early in December, sheltering them if the weather is inclined to become too hot. When the young plants have made four or six leaves they should be pricked out in rather good soil, three to four inches apart, and allowed to remain until the first early autumn rains, when they should be carefully lifted, planted two feet apart in rows three feet wide, in well manured ground. The aim in growing Brussels sprouts should be to have sturdy, robust plants, in preference to long stems. Veitch's Exhibition is one of the best in this State.

CABBAGE (*Brassica oleracea capitata*).

The cabbage is the most popular vegetable grown, and takes pre-eminence in the cottage garden of all other kind of vegetables even the potato; on the farm and in large market gardens it often seems to pay the better of the two

At the present time, by looking through the various seedsmen's catalogues such a variety are mentioned that there should be no trouble in selecting that kind that suits both soil and locality the best. By a proper selection cabbages may be obtained all the year round. Seeds can be sown every month in the year excepting May and June. The best rule, however, is to make four sowings, namely, in January, April, July, and October. The seed beds from these four sowings should supply plants for the whole twelve months.

Cabbages will grow in almost any kind of ground, but succeeds best in well worked deep loam. Plants grown in the summer will be greatly benefited by one or two sprayings with Bordeaux mixture, to which a little Paris Green has been added ; this, however, should only be applied in the early stages, before any signs of hearting is shown. When it is necessary to leave young plants in the seed bed they should be thinned out, to stand well clear of each other, in order to induce short sturdy growth.

For private gardens the St. John's Day (early and late varieties) will be found a good all-round cabbage. One of the best for early summer sowing, to come in during autumn and winter, is the Savoy. This gives an abundance of fine sweet greens and may be cut at any stage of its growth. In suitable soil it is a rapid grower, requiring plenty of room—18 inches apart in rows two feet wide. The first sowing for Savoys may be made in December and successive ones during January and February following. A dressing of lime is often very beneficial to all the cabbage tribe ; in dry weather an occasional watering with a solution containing two ounces of sulphate of ammonia and one ounce of sulphate of iron to each gallon of water will greatly help the growth.

CAULIFLOWER (Brassica oleracea botrytis cauliflora).

Cauliflower, to grow to perfection, must have well-tilled rich loam ; no other vegetable will respond more quickly to a liberal use of well-rotted manure than cauliflowers. When plenty of moisture can be obtained cauliflowers may be grown all the year round, while plenty of moisture is essential to quick growth ; stagnant water is very injurious, well drained damp soil is the best. For early autumn use, seed should be sown in December, giving them plenty of room during summer growth, two feet by three feet being a safe distance. In the winter they may be much closer, say 18 inches apart all ways. Continual sowings may be made every month to May. Waterings may be given occasionally with the solution given for cabbages.

CARROTS (Daucus carota).

Carrots require a deep sandy loam following a crop that has been well manured. If manure is added then the ground should be dug at least two spits deep, the manure, which must be well rotted, turned in with the second spit. Seed may be sown at any time between March and September —early sorts in March, medium sorts in June, later sorts in September. Carrots are best sown in drills, as weeding and cultivation is easier. Short Horns are the best for small gardens.

CELERY (Apium graveolens).

Although celery is a most popular vegetable, it is not grown to the perfection that it is seen in the other States. The fault in a great measure can be accounted for by our hot, dry summers. A few hot days give the growing plants a severe check, with a result that it becomes either stringy or bolts. Seed for the main crop may be sown in November or December. When large enough the plants should be carefully raised and placed in their permanent position, watering and sheltering until well established. In gardens where the soil is of a fair depth it is a good plan to dig a trench about one foot deep, applying the manure to the bottom and digging in. Plant the young seedlings in this, and as they grow draw in the earth previously thrown out, firming it round the plants. This will make them grow well with fine white stalks. In colder parts, ordinary drain pipes may be used to bleach the stalks. When, however, the sun is at all hot, earthing will be found to be of more advantage. In earthing up, care must be taken not to cover up too much of the plant at a time, for if any of the soil get between the leaves it is liable to make them rot.

(To be continued.)

PRUNING LATERALS OF APPLE TREES.

By G. W. WICKENS.

While inspecting in the Upper Blackwood district recently I was asked if I knew the reason why a great number of lateral shoots on Jonathan apple trees had died back after pruning, the old wood in some instances literally bristling with dead pegs.

Nearly all orchardists who are familiar with the Jonathan and its characteristic growth know what has caused the shoots to die; but it is evident that a number of growers have not yet noticed that this particular variety needs special treatment, whether pruning is carried out in winter or summer; and I am writing to the JOURNAL hoping that a few notes on the subject may be of use to those who have not yet had sufficient practical experience to note the different habits of the various kinds of apple trees.

The method usually adopted in pruning laterals, either in winter or summer, is to shorten them back to distances, varying, according to the ideas of the pruner, from half an inch to four inches from the leaders. When this is done in the autumn wood growth is checked, and fruit spurs are usually formed. I say "usually" advisedly, for I have in my mind an instance where an orchard was pruned on 10th March, and the laterals of Cleopatra's made over a foot of young growth afterwards, due to the fact that the trees were young and vigorous and the land kept moist by summer working. I also noticed that all the apple trees pruned in the summer pruning contest, held at Bridgetown on 9th February last, grew vigorously afterwards, while trees in other parts of the district pruned at the same time stopped growing and formed fruit buds.

From my experience I think it is quite impossible to lay down any hard and fast rule as to the exact date when summer pruning should commence; this can only be found out by the orchardist himself, for the time will vary according to the vigour of trees, the season being moist or dry, or the land being cultivated or uncultivated.

The point I wish to emphasise, however, is that with some varieties of apples, notably Jonathan's, the length of the lateral must not enter into consideration, but care must be taken that the bud to which it is cut is full and plump.

If the orchardist examines the base of the lateral shoots on Jonathan's he will notice that the buds are invariably sterile, or what are commonly known as "blind buds"; if on this particular variety the laterals are pruned back to these blind buds they will neither develop into wood growth nor fruit spurs, but after remaining dormant for a season will die back to the leaders, hence the dead pegs mentioned above. This will happen either with winter or summer pruning.

Another variety, the only one I know at present, somewhat similar to the Jonathan in this respect is Esopus Spitzenberg.

Personally, in pruning Jonathans I strongly favour leaving all lateral growths (meaning side shoots 12 to 15 inches in length, not wanted to form main limbs) severely alone for the first year. The terminal buds will always fruit the following season. The weight of this fruit bends the laterals, and nearly every bud, with the exception of the "blind" ones at the base, will develop into a fruit spur. If the tree then shows signs of being over-burdened with fruit-bearing laterals, it is a simple matter to shorten them to whatever length is desirable.

It must be remembered that I am advocating the above method for Jonathans only, and I have proved the benefit of it for this vareity.

Cleopatra in its habit of growth is entirely different. No matter how close the laterals are pruned, the buds will always develop either into wood growth or fruit spurs. Summer pruning is usually very successful with this variety, but anywhere in this district it is a good cropper with or without summer pruning.

On the other hand, to get the best results from Rome Beauty summer pruning is essential, for it is one of those varieties commonly known as "tip-bearers," especially while the tree is young, and unless the laterals receive judicious pinching during summer, long unsightly bare stems are noticeable throughout the tree.

I have often been surprised at the number of growers who cannot tell the different varieties of apple trees when the leaves are off during winter. To make a success of winter pruning the orchardist should know the different habits and be able to tell at sight varieties in common use, such as:— Cleopatra, Jonathan, Dunn's Seedling, Rome Beauty, Nickajack, Yates, Rokewood, Sturmer, Stone Pippin, Five Crown, Regmer, and Adams' Pearmain. Each of these has a growth peculiar to itself alone, and it is not a very difficult matter to notice and remember them, and quite repays the labour.

POULTRY NOTES.

By FRANK H. ROBERTSON.

POULTRY IN THE ORCHARD.

In the eyes of many fruit-growers, fowls in the orchard are almost as bad as the proverbial bull in a China shop; they are so afraid of the damage that may be done. At certain times of the year, and among special kinds of fruits, fowls may do some damage, but taken all round they will be of great use and profit to the orchardist, provided they are properly managed. In the first place, under the shade of trees, fowls find comfort, as protection from the sun is one of the first requisites in poultry-raising, and secondly, fallen fruit and insect life furnish valuable food to the birds, at the same time doing good to the trees by keeping down insect pests. If only for this reason alone, it would be well worth the while of fruit-growers to go in more largely for poultry. Even supposing nothing was made out of the fowls, their presence would well repay any trouble or expense in attending to them. Mr. Grant, a well-known Victorian orchardist, in writing to the poultry contributor of a Melbourne weekly says: "We find it absolutely necessary to go in stronger than ever for poultry in the orchard." Mr. Grant has for several years been a large breeder of high-class stock, particularly Wyandottes, and his testimony as to the value of fowls among the fruit trees offers strong evidence as to the successful combination of fruit and eggs.

Poultry under certain conditions would no doubt do much mischief, for instance, if allowed to roam among the grape vines when in full bearing, it is easy to imagine that the fruit would suffer considerably, although I do know of an instance where a farmer allowed the birds to run among the vines, and he considered that the comparatively small amount of fruit destroyed did not much matter; this cannot be reckoned as the usual way of running the combination of fruit-growing and poultry raising, but rather the exception. If fowls are to be run in the vineyard, let them be only very little ones, viz., chickens, and for preference even then in coops, or, if with hens, confine the hen and let the chickens run in and out of same; or ducks could be run in the vineyard provided, of course, that there is a good water supply available. If apples are the fruit grown, the risk of damage being done is much less, at the same time it would not be wise to allow the fowls to roost in apple trees. A good way to work them under such conditions would be on the portable run system, that is by making light, movable houses and wire runs made in sections of light timber and wire netting, so that they can be easily moved from one portion of the orchard to another. Another way of working the portable run system would be to use them for fattening cockerels. The expense of making movable houses and runs is not great, but unfortunately this is just the stumbling block—expense and trouble; the average fruit-grower or farmer says yes, that sounds all right, but look at the cost and the work entailed; it won't pay, I have not got the time, too much work, etc., etc. Just so, what about the vines or the fruit trees; do they not want a lot of looking after if a good crop is to be grown? Yes; any amount of labour, what with prunning, spraying, and keeping the weeds down, one is kept going all the time. Whatever one raises whether it is wheat, fruit, or fowls, work is required.

THE MARKET REQUIREMENTS OF POULTRY.

In going in for poultry-raising it is always wise to consider what branch to take up to best suit the market requirements, because one so often hears of disappointments by persons who have started with full confidence in getting an ample reward for their labour, only to end in bitter disappointment, and an everlasting determination never to pay any attention to poultry-rearing again, having come to the conclusion that there is nothing in it and it cannot be made to. pay, whereas in most instances the failure, when fully gone into, can be traced to wrong methods or bad judgment displayed in producing an article for which there is not a ready sale.   The market requirements must always be considered.   As an instance, the writer met an enthusiast of a year ago who had gone in largely for ducks for the table, but had kept his birds too long, and sent them to auction in poor condition ; the consequence was that birds which should have fetched 6s. a pair sold for half that money.   The grower, disgusted at low prices, ate duck to such an extent that he has had enough of this form of poultry for the rest of his life, and now feels as if he never wanted to see a duck again. The duck market was certainly well supplied last season, and only those who produced the article for which there was a demand, viz., the 10 to 12 weeks-old bird, fat and in good condition, could hope to find a profitable outlet. Then, again, our market is a small one.   In a recent conversation with one of our leading salesmen, he stated that 1,000 pairs of poultry placed in the rooms on a single day makes a complete glut in the market.   The grower requires to study the markets ; and if ducks cannot be produced profitably, go in for something else ; and there is no getting away from the fact that it is chiefly eggs that are most wanted, therefore anyone going in for poultry will always find that egg production is the best to pay chief attention to, notwithstanding the fact that prices are so low at the present moment ; and, as pointed out in last month's notes, cold-storage is to be the means of solving this difficulty.   Then, if fowls for the table are produced, it is well to remember that the best prices are obtained during August and September.   It is not advisable to place too much value on the Christmas market ; there certainly is a big demand at that season of the year, but it has so frequently happened that many people recognise this fact all at the same time, and the Christmas market gets over-supplied.   It is a great mistake to send table poultry a few days before the holidays ; prices are much better a month earlier.   It is always wise to keep in communication with the auctioneers, and take their advice when to sell.   Newspaper reports are to a certain extent misleading, because by the time the fact becomes generally known that prices are good, everyone sends in, and the market is glutted.   What is wanted is to send before it becomes generally known that prices are good, and this can only be done by acting quickly on the advice of salesmen who go to the trouble of promptly advising their clients when the markets are bare.

Geese and turkeys should receive more attention ;   under suitable conditions, they are both easily raised and very profitable, and it is a wonder that they are not more largely produced.   Geese, in particular, as they are so easily reared, and require but little labour ; no housing is wanted, and at the time of the year when they are being reared there is plenty of waste grass land available.   As the grass disappears, the young stock are raised and ready for the table.   The old birds are kept for stock purposes for the following season at but little expense ; they can pick up most of their living on the stubble-fields, thus merely acting as scavengers, and living on stray grain which would be otherwise lost.

EGG-LAYING COMPETITION.

SUBIACO RESULTS—SEPTEMBER.

Appended are the records of eggs laid at the competitions now in progress at Subiaco, viz., one for hens, of which there are six in each pen, and the other of four ducks in each. Both competitions are to run for another nine months. It would therefore be premature yet to consider which will be the ultimate winners, but the very excellent and consistent laying of the Sunnyhurst pen of White Leghorns from South Australia stamps them as having a good prospect. The pen of Partridge Wyandottes, which put up such an excellent record for last month, lost some ground in the early part of the month owing to broodiness affecting them, but at the present time they are going as strong as ever. A very large number of the setting varieties have been affected in a similar manner, which somewhat interfered with their output; but taken all round the laying may be regarded as excellent, and that of the ducks quite out of the ordinary, as three of the pens have laid the full possible compliment, viz., 120 eggs from each pen, being an egg a day from 12 ducks for the month. All the pens of ducks are laying remarkably well, the present daily average being about 84 eggs from the 88 ducks. The following are the prizes so far won :—

Fowls.—Monthly prize of £1.—First month, Sunnyhurst, White Leghorns, 139 eggs; second month, A. F. Farrant, Partridge Wyandottes, 159 eggs; third month, Sunnyhurst, White Leghorns, 150 eggs. *Ducks.*—Monthly prizes of £1.—First month, R. A. Dusting, Indian runners, 64 each; second month, E. A. Newton and R. A. Dusting, equal, Indian Runners, 116 each; third month, R. A. Dusting, C. E. Close, and S. Craig, equal, 120 each.

Prizes for first three months, winter test.—*Fowls.*—1st prize, £3, Sunnyhurst (S.A.), White Leghorns, 429 eggs; 2nd prize, £2, J. D. Smith, White Leghorns, 388 eggs; 3rd prize, £1, A. H. Padman (S.A.), White Leghorns, 380 eggs. *Ducks.*—1st prize, £3, R. A. Dusting, Indian Runners, 300 eggs; 2nd prize, £2, E. A. Newton, Indian Runners, 272 eggs; 3rd prize, £1, Mrs. L. Mellen, Indian Runners, 263 eggs.

FOWLS.
Six hens in each pen.

Owner and Breed.	Sept.	Total for three months.
1. Sunnyhurst (S.A.), *W. Leghorn	150	429
2. J. D. Smith, *W. Leghorn	137	388
3. A. H. Padman (S.A.), *W. Leghorn	143	380
4. A. F. Farrant, Partridge Wyandotte	138	379
5. S. Craig, *W. Leghorn	131	370
6. C. Attwell, *S. Wyandotte	116	361
7. A. H. Padman (S.A.), *S. Wyandotte	143	360
8. G. E. Garbett, W. Leghorn	131	358
9. F. T. Rowe, *Black Orpington	130	354
10. W. J. Clarke, Brown Leghorn	139	352
11. Ericville Farm, *W. Leghorn	131	352
12. B. Jones, *S. Wyandotte	103	343
13. C. W. Johnson, *W. Leghorn	129	336
14. A. S. B. Craig, *W. Wyandotte	105	335
15. Mrs. McGree, *W. Leghorn	122	335

* Male birds in these pens.

FOWLS—*continued.*

Owner and Breed.				Sept.	Total for three months.
16. L. Meatchem, *G. Wyandotte	...	...	...	101	334
17. G. W. G. Lizars, *W. Leghorn	...	...	...	133	333
18. F. Whitfield, Brown Leghorn ...	...	...	...	139	332
19. Bungalow Yard, Brown Leghorn	...	...	...	126	331
20. E. Fitzgerald, W. Leghorn	...	...	...	134	327
21. F. Piaggio, W. Leghorn	...	...	...	140	324
22. F. Whitfield, *W. Leghorn	...	...	...	125	321
23. R. G. Flynn, W. Leghorn	...	...	...	122	319
24. Ryan Bros., *W. Leghorn	..	...	...	120	316
25. G. M. Buttsworth, *W. Leghorn	...	...	...	129	313
26. Bungalow Farm, *W. Leghorn	...	...	...	121	311
27. C. L. Braddock, S. Wyandotte	...	...	...	103	310
28. Austin and Thomas, W. Leghorn	...	...	...	139	309
29. Jas. Buttsworth, S. Wyandotte	...	...	...	113	305
30. J. W. Buttsworth, *W. Leghorn	...	...	...	109	303
31. A. Snell, *Brown Leghorn	...	...	...	109	302
32. J. R. Parkes, Brown Leghorn ...	...	...	...	125	302
33. Adelaide Yard, W. Leghorn	...	...	...	132	300
34. E. Palmerston, W. Leghorn	...	...	...	133	299
35. Ericville Yard, *Black Orpington	...	...	...	121	299
36. H. Jones, W. Leghorn	...	...	...	116	289
37. E. Hutchinson, *Minorcas	...	...	...	121	288
38. W. Snowden, S. Wyandotte	...	...	...	100	288
39. O. K. Yard, *Black Orpington...	...	...	...	116	285
40. Bon Accord Yard, W. Leghorn	...	...	...	125	284
41. A. R. Keesing, Minorcas	...	...	...	127	283
42. Geo. Bolger, *Black Orpington	...	...	...	103	279
43. Perth Yard, W. Leghorn	...	...	...	113	271
44. Glen Donald Yard, G. Wyandette	...	...	...	103	268
45. A. Coombs, S. Wyandotte	...	...	...	84	265
46. W. Snowden, Brown Leghorn ...	...	...	...	121	262
47. F. Mason, W. Leghorn ...	...	...	...	107	259
48. C. R. Roberts, *W. Leghorn	...	...	...	113	259
49. W. Wade, W. Leghorn ...	...	...	...	113	258
50. H. M. Kelly, *G. Wyandotte ...	...	...	...	110	258
51. Honnor and Forbes, R. C., W. Leghorn	...	...	...	107	256
52. Mrs. Hughes, *R. C. B. Leghorn	...	...	...	112	249
53. R. G. Smith, W. Wyandotte ...	...	...	...	103	247
54. E. A. Newton, W. Leghorn	...	...	...	104	238
55. H. H. Wegg, G. Wyandotte ...	...	...	...	105	224
56. Mrs. McGree, W. Wyandotte ...	...	...	...	107	223
57. J. White, Brown Leghorn	...	...	...	120	222
58. Jas. Kirk, G. Wyandotte	...	...	...	96	222
59. C. Crawley, B. Orpington	...	...	...	107	213
60. J. E. Redman, S. Wyandotte ...	...	...	...	108	211
61. A. Savage, Minorca	...	...	...	123	203
62. H. M. Kelly, *B. Orpington	...	...	...	118	203
63. J. S. Miller, S. Wyandotte	...	...	...	118	200
64. J. B. Pettit, S. Wyandotte	...	...	...	93	185
Total for the month	...	...	...	7,610	18,945

DUCKS.

Four in each Pen.

Owner and Breed.				Sept.	Total for three months.
1. R. A. Dusting, *Indian Runner	...	...	...	120	300
2. E. A. Newton * do.	...	...	...	115	272
3. Mrs. Mellen * do.	...	...	...	110	263
4. Austin and Thomas, *Indian Runner	...	...	...	118	251
5. A. Snell *Indian Runner	...	...	...	113	230

* Male birds in these pens.

Docks—*continued.*

Owner and Breed.		Sept.	Total for three months.
6. G. Stead *Indian Runner		98	230
7. W. Snowden, *Buff Orpington		107	216
8. Miss E. Parker, Indian Runner		118	205
9. C. E. Close do.		120	205
10. F. T. Rowe do.		119	205
11. Bon Accord, *Buff Orpington		106	204
12. Ericville * do.		105	198
13. Perth Poultry Yard, *do.		109	193
14. Adelaide Poultry Yard, Indian Runner		118	192
15. S. Craig, Indian Runner		120	140
16. J. R. Parkes, Indian Runner		104	143
17. Sargenfri (S.A.), *Buff Orpington		100	130
18. F. D. Vincent, *Indian Runner		116	126
19. C. W. Johnson * do.		107	114
20. Aveley Poultry Yard, Indian Runner		105	107
21. F. Piaggio, Buff Orpington		62	76
22. J. B. Pettit, Indian Runner		68	68
Total eggs laid for month		2,358	4,077

NARROGIN RESULTS.

	Breed.		Owner.				Total for Month.	Total to Date.
1.	White Leghorns	...	Mrs. A. Bristow	...	...	...	114	551
2.	Brown do.	...	E. E. Ranford	...	...	...	131	509
3.	Buff Orpingtons	...	A. H. Hilton	...	...	...	112	484
4.	Silver Wyandottes	...	A. M. Neitschke	...	...	...	143	478
5.	Do. do.	...	Miss Buttsworth	...	...	...	92	459
6.	White Leghorns	...	C. W. Johnson	...	...	...	102	446
7.	Do. do.	...	F. Piaggio	...	...	...	100	444
8.	Brown Leghorns	...	Mrs. R. A. Dusting	...	...	...	113	421
9.	Silver Wyandottes	...	G. W. G. Lizars	...	...	...	102	404
10.	White Leghorns	...	A. F. Spencer	...	...	...	104	387
11.	Do. do.	...	Miss M. Parker	...	...	...	106	379
12.	Black Orpingtons	...	Sparks & Bonnington	...	...	...	114	374
13.	White Leghorns	...	T. Handley	...	...	...	84	369
14.	White Wyandottes	...	Mrs. L. J. Hood	...	...	...	104	360
15.	R.C. Brown Leghorns	...	Adelaide Yards	...	...	...	98	352
16.	Golden Wyandottes	...	W. G. Craig	...	...	...	99	352
17.	White Leghorns	...	Aveley Yard	...	...	...	119	339
18.	Brown Leghorns	...	J. D. Wilson	...	...	...	111	333
19.	White do.	...	F. G. Williams	...	...	...	100	329
20.	R.C. Brown Leghorns	...	E. Krachler	...	...	...	84	322
21.	Black Orpingtons	...	Perth Yards	...	...	...	99	321
22.	White Leghorns	...	J. E. Tull	...	...	...	104	318
23.	Do. do.	...	R. J. Flynn	...	...	...	106	300
24.	Do. do.	...	J. Oneto	...	...	...	61	296
25.	Do. do.	...	O. C. Rath	...	...	...	105	241
			Totals	...	...	...	2,607	9,568

The above shows a substantial increase on the previous month's output, viz., 375 eggs. Narrogin is a later district than Subiaco, and it is expected that the returns will increase as the season advances.

* Male birds are in these pens, and eggs are obtainable for setting purposes, applications to be addressed to the Manager, Egg-laying Competition, Subiaco.

NARROGIN STATE FARM.

REPORT FOR THE MONTH OF AUGUST.

By R. C. BAIRD.

Cold easterly winds have been frequent during the month, and crops have not made much headway, but towards the end of the month a more vigorous growth was noticeable, and with the advent of warmer weather a marked improvement may be expected.

Ploughing fallow land was carried on till the ground, owing to heavy rains, became so soft that the work had to be suspended.

Up to the present we have ploughed about 90 acres of fallow land, and still have about 200 acres to plough. It is intended to put a portion of this land under fodder crops for summer feed.

Clearing has been continued around the site of the new buildings. Sufficient space has now been cleared for a site for stables, piggeries, milking shed, and other outbuildings, which it is intended to erect at an early date.

Some of the farm buildings at the old homestead will have to be removed to the new farm site. This work will, I expect, be carried out shortly.

During the month the pigs have been turned into one of the small paddocks of barley and rape, and are doing well on it. For young, growing pigs especially it is splendid fodder. Brood sows also do well on it, while it saves the cost of other and more expensive foods.

Several new pigs, imported from Victoria, have been purchased for the farm. They are of the middle white Yorkshire breed, and should prove an acquisition to the swine herd.

The sheep are in very fair condition, and as the growth of grass will now be more vigorous I expect an all round improvement in the flocks. The percentage of lambs marked is 80.

The cattle, although somewhat low in condition, are already showing signs of improvement.

REPORT FOR SEPTEMBER.

During the month a good deal of rain fell, accompanied by hail. The weather was cold and boisterous, and crops in consequence made but little progress. Towards the end of the month a few mild days intervened, and an improvement was noticeable in all cereals and pastures.

Rainfall for the month, 318 points.

The crops sown for ensilage, comprising a mixture of rye, peas, and vetches, have not made good growth. The peas and vetches suffered severely from the effects of the heavy frosts that occurred while the ground was in a wet and sodden state.

The barley and rape mixture sown early has done very well, and has been carrying a number of stock for the past two months, while that sown later is just beginning to make headway, and is now sufficiently advanced to carry stock.

Ploughing for fallow has been carried on when the weather permitted. The paddock we are ploughing is one recently cleared. It is mostly low lying, and owing to the boggy nature of the ground we have not been able to proceed with the ploughing as quickly as I should have liked. With the advent of fine weather I expect to make better progress.

The orchard and vineyard work has been somewhat retarded owing to the heavy rains that have fallen. The underground draining carried out last year in the vineyard has had a marked effect for good. The water is draining off rapidly, and I expect to get the cultivators to work in a few days' time.

Clearing for a small orchard and vineyard at the new quarters is being proceeded with, and will be completed shortly.

The stock are all in fair condition and improving.

The sheep are in very fair condition, and should improve from now on. The lambs, of which 80 per cent. were marked, are doing remarkably well.

CHAPMAN EXPERIMENTAL FARM.

REPORT FOR THE MONTH OF AUGUST,

By J. KEAYS.

Early in the present month five acres of cotton were planted, the first ever tried in this district. The fertiliser used was superphosphates, at the rate of 2cwt. per acre, in drills, and seed sown on top 1½in. deep. The following are the varieties and method of planting and areas of each:—

Carovonica Kidney,	1 acre planted,	7ft. by 7ft.		
,,	II. Silk,	,,	,,	,,	,,
,,	Wool,	,,	,,	,,	,,
Afifi,	¼ acre	,,	4ft. by 1ft.	
Janovitch,	,,	,,	,,	,,
Ashminom,	,,	,,	,,	,,
Abassi,	,,	,,	,,	,,
Sea Island,	1 row	,,	,,	,,

The potatoes are making vigorous growth, and there seems every promise of a good yield. The onion crop is also promising well. We have had a lot of work in keeping the strong growth of weeds in check. For the past few months we have grown a liberal supply of vegetables for farm use.

During the month 20 acres amber cane were sown, also pearl millet and sugar beet. Fallowing is still being pushed on with.

Since the dairy herd have been depasturing on the rape they have given much better results, and have improved considerably in condition. We now separate a quantity of the milk and make butter for farm use.

All the stock on farm are in good condition. The pure Suffolk mare "Blaze" dropped a colt foal by "War-Dance." He is very sturdy, and a fine type of Suffolk.

The rainfall for the month was 348 points, but the weather was very warm and unseasonable, consequently some of the early sown crops are out in ear.

The flooded state of the Chapman River and Rushy Gully caused considerable damage to the fences that cross those streams. We had about 14 chains of fence washed out of line. It is the biggest flood experienced for many years.

REPORT FOR MONTH OF SEPTEMBER.

The rainfall for September was 146 points, making a total since beginning of year of 1,476 points. This is below the average for this district. During the latter part of the month we had some cool, showery weather which will do an immense amount of good to the crops, particularly the late ones. Hay-cutting will be in full swing by the end of October.

The fertilisers on the manurial test plots that are inducing best growth up to the present date are superphosphates (experimental fertiliser), Thomas's phosphate, and a mixture of superphosphates and guano. There is very little difference between those four kinds. In the variety test wheat plots Toby's Luck, Alpha, Australian, and Bred 73 are showing the most vigorous growth.

The lucerne sown in May is now looking well and has apparently established itself well enough to survive the summer months. The small plots of mixed grasses have not done so well; the native grasses have out-grown them in some places.

The Angora goats are in excellent condition and have dropped 16 kids during the month.

By erecting 12 chains of wire netting fence we have subdivided 17s grass paddock. This will be a great convenience, as it gives another handy paddock close to the homestead.

PASPALUM.

To the Editor.

Sir,—The landowners in your State do not as yet appear to realise the great value and productiveness of this really wonderful plant, from which the farmer gets such a quick return and abundant yield, while it proves very effectual in suppressing noxious growth of all kinds, and will thrive in any description of soil, providing there is sufficient moisture. When its many excellent qualities become known in Western Australia it will give a great stimulus to settlement and enterprise, and will create a great demand for the immense area of land, amounting to hundreds of thousands of acres, as yet unoccupied in your State. If these lands and the terms for their acquisition were advertised in the North Coast papers, especially those of the Richmond and Tweed Rivers, I feel certain that it would result in obtaining many desirable settlers with capital, and a good knowledge of dairy farming for your State. The cultivation of Paspalum grass has proved a great factor in promoting the prosperity of these districts, and there has been a great demand for seed in the dairying districts in Queensland, where one firm this season aver they have disposed of 50,000lbs. Last season their sales amounted to only 6,000lbs. This demand for seed is not surprising, especially when we have testimony like the following:—W. S. Campbell, Esq., Director of Agriculture, when interviewed in Sydney, recently said that "he, like others who had visited the Richmond and Tweed Rivers, had returned with a strong impression of the prosperity of the people in that part of the country. The paspalum grass grows with extraordinary luxuriance, and so high is the growth that if it stood up straight, the stock would be quite lost in it. As it is, though bending over by its own weight, in many places only the backs of the cattle are visible. Apparently the cattle are unable to eat it down, and he believed that it would sustain five or six head of stock per acre for several months. Farmers are doing wonderfully well, land is realising high figures, and he thought it would go still higher."

I trust you will excuse me for trespassing so much on your valuable space, but the importance of the subject is my excuse. This is proved by the returns of the North Coast Co-Operative Creamery, which was established in 1895, and which has since that time paid away the immense sum of £1,150,000 7s. 2d. to butter suppliers, and £150,464 14. 7d. to pig suppliers, and has now an annual turnover of about half a million sterling per annum. For the sake of comparision I need only say that if we possessed about a dozen similar institutions, the returns therefrom would equal in value, the whole of the minerals now in this State for the past year, or about 6 million pounds sterling.

Paspalum grass on the Northern rivers, in conjunction with our dairying industry, which has now assumed large proportions, has caused settlement to progress by leaps and bounds, enhanced the value of all property immensely, and the land now available for settlement is scarce and dear, for which the Government is charging selectors £2 and £3 per acre, and imposing all kinds of unreasonable restrictions. Land which some years ago could have been purchased for a few pounds per acre is now bringing from £10 to £30 per acre, and if it were not for the large areas of land available in Queensland on easy terms, the value of property here would have reached a fabulous price. I feel certain that if the W.A. Government advertised their land here, and agreed to erect factories for their settlers, they would be successful in promoting rapid settlement, and would bring about an era of prosperity in Western Australia of which they at present have but a faint idea, and it is a deplorable fact that your legislators exhibit or display such a great lack of interest in agricultural matters which are so deserving of attention, and are of such vital importance.

The dairying industry is at present booming everywhere, and in many localities which a few years ago were considered unsuitable for this purpose, and through the climate being too dry, the settlers are embarking in this business with energy and enthusiasm, with every prospect of success. In Western Australia there are hundreds of thousands of acres unoccupied, which, for dairying purposes, are eminently suitable, and your Government have now a splendid opportunity to attract a most desirable class of settlers, many of whom possess much capital, by advertising judiciously. The tide of prosperity and progress should be takenthe at flood, for never before was there such a favourable opportunity to dispose of land, to attract capital, and develop the agricultural resources of your State.   Wake up Westralia! Apologising for trespassing on your time.

I have, etc.,
B. HARRISON,

13th June, 1906.   Burringbar, Tweed River, N.S.W.

HOW TO IMPROVE THE DAIRY CATTLE.

The following interesting article is taken from a paper by Primrose McConnell, B.Sc., F.G.S., of Essex, and read at the British Dairy Farmers' Conference in England recently.   The article has been published in all the principal papers, and it is to the columns of *The Dairy* that we are indebted for our information :—" Our live stock shows for a couple of generations now have been —nominally at least—devoted to the improvement of our live stock, and in the case of our own British Dairy Farmers' Association, milk cows have been specially looked after.   In nine cases out of ten, however, the method of improvement has been simply one which took notice only of the conformation of the animal, its style, its coat of hair, the set of its horns, the size and shape of the udder and teats, and so on, while the most important point of all— the milking power—has been neglected.   I believe the Milking Trials of the London Dairy Show were the first attempts to encourage and test the milking powers of our cows—organised principally by the late Mr. Tisdall and the late Dr. Voelcker.   For many years these trials have been the most important feature of the show, and the " Inspection Prizes " have to take a back seat.   Prejudice and custom die hard, however, and we seem only beginning to realise the fact that the principal value of a cow depends on the amount and quality of the milk she yields.   The improvement of our dairy cattle resolves itself into two heads :—(1) The improvement of the cow herself, and (2) the improvement of her milk yield. Taking these in this order, we have—

1.—THE IMPROVEMENT OF THE COW.

It is this that our shows and our breeders have hitherto paid most attention to, and the general conformation of the animal has been the subject of our care for a couple of generations, and it is doubtful if we can carry her bodily development much further in some directions. It is for superiority in this line that our "Inspection Prizes" are given at the Dairy Show, and it is because we have done so much in this direction already that there is a tendency to make this subordinate to the testing of the milk yielding capacity of the animal, not only at our own show, but at several others besides. It is not very difficult, however, to point out various matters in which cows could be improved, for our show-yard faddists have gone out of their way in many cases to try to spoil the animal for practical use, and if they would retrace their steps, and try to undo some of the evil they have done, they would confer a benefit on suffering cow-men.

There is, for instance, a tendency in some breeds to have cows with teats of too small a size for comfortable milking. It is not, of course, desirable to have these too large, but there is a medium that ought to be aimed at, and which suits the size of a man's hand in milking. Quite recently a milkman said to me that any fool could milk a shorthorn, she was so easy to do, but a man needed to know something about the job, and have Job's patience, to be able to tackle the cows of another breed which I shall not name. There is no sense in making cows either with teats so thick and long that you cannot grasp them or so small that you need to milk with the thumb and the forefinger. I humbly commend this point, therefore, to breeders and "Inspection" judges; A milk cow—strange as it may appear—is kept for the purpose of yielding milk as well as for looking at, and the development of a teat suitable for milking purposes is worthy of their attention.

Again, of what use are the horns? In a wild state they were, of course, absolutely necessary for defence, but now, under domestication, they are an unmitigated nuisance and a danger. You may get your eye poked out when you tie the animal up in the stall, while she is certain to try to rip up her neighbour whenever she gets a chance. There would be fewer torn hides and ruined milk-bags if the horns were absent, or at least rounded-in like those of the Jersey breed. I therefore am a great advocate of having polled cows as much as possible, though outside the Red Polls I do not know where we are to get them. To use Red Poll bulls may not always suit—at any rate my own attempt to cross the same with Ayrshires and other breeds was a failure. Next to this, however, much might be done by adopting small incurved horns as the type to aim at. As a matter of descent, many of our breeds—the Shorthorn and the Ayrshire, for instance—had originally horns similar to those of the Jersey, and the wide, or straight, or upstanding ones we now see are the result of senseless show-yard fads. If we want to really improve the utility and handiness of our animals we will return to the old form.

It is a matter of opinion as to whether or not we should encourage the beefing faculty in our milking herds. Our American cousins hold that the "dual purpose" cow is an impossibility—that is, one that shall milk well for several years, and can then be fatted off for the butcher. They maintain that an animal must be developed for either milk or beef, but not both together, and point to the results yielded by their Jerseys in competition with their Shorthorns to prove this. We in this country are not so positive about it, as though some of our dairy breeds are not beefers, yet in the case of the milking Shorthorn at least we have an animal that gives very respectable results in both lines, and the aptitude in this direction might be encouraged and developed.

II.—IMPROVEMENT OF THE MILK YIELD.

To my mind you cannot improve the milk yield of cows by feeding any possible combination of rations, as far as the quality of the milk is concerned, though you can, of course, improve the quantity of the same. I believe I was the first to point this out in this country some 13 years ago. I got my information from Professor Heury, of Madison, Wisconsin, and scarcely believed it myself at first, it was so contrary to the opinions usually held. Repeated trials have, however, shown that the food does not influence the the richness—that is, the butter-fat—of the milk. The latest trial of importance was that conducted by Cornell University. A herd of cows which had been underfed was taken over by the experimenters and well fed for two years, and the total result was an average increase of one-fourth of a per cent. of fat, the animals being on the down grade when the experiment closed, so that practically there was no permanent improvement in this line. Another fact that has been brought home to us is that extra food is not always followed by extra yield in the quantity of milk. Repeated tests have shown many cases where high feeding gave poor results at the pail. It would appear that many cows get more food than is good for them, and that over-feeding is very easily done. I have in my own experience on two occasions increased the milk yield as to quantity by reducing the food - especially the concentrated food—the cows were getting, and I have come across various cases of a similar nature.

Another matter I may mention at this stage is the effect that the soil and other characteristics of a farm have on the milk yield, independently of the breeding and feeding of the animals. For instance, the cows in a lime-stone country always yield milk rich in fat, and which keeps well, while the milk from cows on, say, a clay soil, is of a poorer quality, and does not keep so well. This subject is a hobby of mine, but up to the present I have found little definite information on the same, and only mention the matter in passing as one worthy of further investigation. We are now beginning to realise more and more that the milk-yielding power of a cow cannot be permanently altered as far as she herself is concerned, but that by selecting the best cows, and keeping the calves of the same for the making of our future cows, we may gradually raise the standard of a herd.

Our own British Dairy Farmers' Association has made some attempt to develop all our dairy breeds in this way. Some years ago a movement was made to start a register of cows of a certain proved milking capacity. It does not appear that the matter caught on, or that anything more was done, though the milking trials now so largely developed have in effect been a test and an encouragement to find out and breed from the best dairy animals.

The most extensive and thoroughgoing tests and attempt at develop-ment yet made, however, are those which have been conducted by the Highland and Agricultural Society of Scotland with the Ayrshire breed during the last three years. This is so noteworthy that some details may be given. A test of a cow's milk once a fortnight as to quantity and per-centage of fat has been found to be quite sufficient if carried on during the whole of the milking season. Accordingly one person was appointed to go round 12 herds in rotation and weigh and sample each cow's milk a night and a morning at each visit. The results were tabulated and have been published in "Transactions" of the above Society in 1904, 1905, and 1906. The milk is reduced to the "common denominator" of 3 per cent. of fat—that is, the gallons per annum are totalled up and the average of the analyses is taken, and then the proportion is added on which would equal the yield if the milk were "watered down," as it were, to a 3 per cent. basis. This is done by multiplying the total natural gallons by the average percentage of fat and dividing by 3. Thus, a cow yielding 600 gallons of milk with 4 per cent. of fat is reckoned as giving 800 gallons at 3 per cent., while to arrive at comparative money values this 3 per cent. milk is calculated out at 5d. per gallon. By this means we get one figure representing the, combined quantity and quality of the milk yield, and it is amazing to find the differences among cows, even in one herd, where they all appear to be similar and are similarly treated. Thus, taking a single case by way of example, I find in one herd the best cow yields 1,312 at 3·80 per cent. fat, equal to 1,679 gallons, worth £34 19s. 7d., and the worst 481 at 3·20 per cent. fat, equal to 521 gallons, worth £10 17s. 1d., and so on with almost any lot taken at random. Complete records have been made out for about 30 farms in two districts in Ayrshire, and the figures for 1905 show that in one case the best cows were yielding over £10 more produce per head in the season than the worst ones, and in the other case over £6 per head during a part season of 34 weeks. If, therefore, these cows were eliminated, the average of the whole would be very much improved. This has already been done in many cases, and I give in the table below the results from three selected but typical farms, showing the gradual rise in the milk and butter yield obtained during four years since the testing began :—

Years.	No. of Cows.	Natural galls. per head.	Pounds butter per head.
FARM A			
1900	11	663	235
1901	9 .	761	287
1902	11	698	281½
1903	11	809	317¼
Average gain ...	...	146	82¼
FARM B.			
1900	15	693	247
1901	15	708	264
1902	15	721	277
1903	16	750	292½
Average gain ...	...	57	45¼
FARM C.			
1900	71	669	236
1901	69	691	248
1902	70	700	252
1903	73	707	260
Average gain ...	...	38	24

The natural sequence of this is that the farmers whose herds have been so tested are only going to breed from their best cows, and will get rid of the inferior ones or their calves as soon as possible. The work has been under the superintendence of Mr. John Speir, who is well known to our association, and from whom I obtained the above figures.

In a private letter I had from him when preparing this paper he says:— "This year there are somewhere about 4,000 cows being tested. There has been a great demand for the names of certain herds, and several buyers have been round buying up bulls, calves, and heifers out of the best cows. The work is going to boom the Ayrshires in a way that they were never boomed before, and on such a sound basis that buyers have confidence in giving big sums for the progeny of the best cows. Each year is revealing a greater number of good cows among the Ayrshires, but also a great number of useless ones, and if these latter were only got rid of. the breed would be very much more profitable, even without any further improvement in the best of the animals, on which I look for even some improvement. The periodic visit of the tester keeps up a continuous interest in how the cows are doing."

In another letter Mr. Speir adds :—" At the show at Fenwick last week there were two new classes, one for cows giving over 1,000 gallons of natural milk and another for those giving 800 gallons or over. In the first class there were 10 entries, all good cows. There has been quite a rush to buy the calves out of these cows, and many of them are already sold at very good prices.

General Conclusions.

To sum up, therefore, the gist of the whole matter is to test your cows for their milking powers, to keep the progeny of the best animals only to supply the next generation, and to kill off the inferior animals as quickly as you reasonably can.

For trade or registration purposes an official test is the most reliable, to be conducted by a society or an institution, but there is nothing to hinder a number of farmers from joining together and arranging for some one to go round their farms at a regular interval. There is nothing to hinder one farmer from conducting his own test if he wants to breed improved animals by using a weighing machine and a Babcock-Gerber fat tester. It does not follow of course that a good cow will always yield good progeny. One of the best cows ever tested at the London Dairy Show was a Shorthorn, the owner of which I happened to know. I asked him afterwards how her heifer calves turned out, but he said they had all made very ordinary animals. This, of course, is one of the exceptions which prove the rule. As like begets like, we may be sure that in the majority of cases the best cows will yield the best calves, and if we keep on testing and selecting the best, we will gradually raise the milking power of the standard cow in time.

All that has been said applies equally well to bulls. A good milking bull (as the phrase goes) is quite as necessary for the improvement of the milking strain as a good milking cow, and therefore it is necessary to see and know the ancestry of the same ; while a bull calf from a good cow, if he has a satisfactory sire, is worth keeping for herd purposes, or worth a lot more to sell. At our own show, prizes have been offered for several years for bulls from dams which have won a prize or certificate at some milking trial or test. Last year there were 12 exhibits, and 16 in 1904, numbers which may be looked on as fair, but there is likely to be more attention paid to this in future, and more demand for sires of this class.

The amount of milk which individual cows can possibly yield in a day or a year is something enormous, and far beyond what we usually expect at an average. Thus at our own show we have had a Dutch cow yielding over eight gallons in the 24 hours; while as to the total yield per annum, the Holstein test in the United States have repeatedly shown animals yielding up to 3,000 British gallons during the milking year. In our home herds we find a large proportion of animals yielding over 1,000 gallons per annum —I have had several myself showing from 1,200 to 1,400 gallons—though the average of the United Kingdom is computed at 450 gallons per head. It therefore becomes quite feasible to grade our cows up to 1,000 gallons each without reaching the physiological limit probably, and this would, of course, be practically doubling the yield as far as quantity is concerned.

Now as to the quality of the milk. We have had at our show a Jersey which yielded $9\frac{1}{2}$ per cent. of fat, with total solids amounting to $19\frac{1}{4}$ per cent. Compare this with our 3 per cent. "standard" for fat, which we find in many cases very difficult to attain to with the morning yield. In this respect also we do not seem to have approached the possible limit of the cow, and we might develop her still further.

At the present time the judicious selection of and breeding from the heaviest milking cows seems the most feasible way of improving our dairy cattle. It takes time, of course, for while you can make a selection of the cows in hand after one year's test, you require to wait for three years' additional time to realise on and prove the progeny of the same. On the other hand, it does not involve any direct outlay and only a little trouble to test and select and eliminate the inferior cows, by either fatting off or selling for what they will fetch in the market, and thus raise the average yielding power of the herd. It is perfectly certain that many of our cows do not pay for their keep, and the owner has to make his own living out of the profits from a few of his best animals. If by any means we can grade the lot up nearer to the standard of the present best cows, it will be a tremendous advance and a tremendous financial improvement, and enough has been said above to show that it not only can be done, but is being done, and that the principle can be applied to any breed and by either associations or individuals.

COTTON GROWING.

By A. Despeissis.

More than passing attention has of late years been directed towards cotton growing in various parts of the world, and in Australia the matter has been taken up from the Queensland to the West Australian shores.

That industry is still with us in the experimental stage, and we have much yet to learn in regard to cotton culture.

Directions for sowing, cultivating, and harvesting have from time to time been issued, but the volume of inquiries which comes in from would-be growers make it desirable to place before them the experience of others who can speak with authority.

To the courtesy of the British Cotton Growing Association this Department is indebted for a sheaf of literature on the subject, and with the idea of placing before others reliable information, I have culled from Sir D. Morris and Mr. J. R. Bovell's joint notes on Sea Island Cotton in the United States and the West Indies, and in Mr. Samuel Simpson's report to the Government of British Central Africa, much that is presented in the following notes :—

NOTES FROM REPORT ON COTTON GROWING.

Soil.—The question of success in cotton growing does not depend upon soil. The plant grows well in most soils, the best being a lightish loam with a heavier subsoil.

Standing water in the soil is detrimental, whilst vigorous growth cannot be expected in very light sandy soil.

Climate.—Between lines about 40° on each side of the Equator.

The whole question of cotton growing is one of climate, and it is on this point that everything turns.

Cotton is essentially a summer crop.

The three largest cotton producing centres in the world are the United States of America, Egypt, and India.

Rainfall.—In Egypt the rainfall can be neglected for agricultural purposes. All the cotton is grown under a perfect system of irrigation, the water being applied every 20 days, the amount averaging 3in. of rainfall, with 10 to 12 applications of water=30 to 35 inches.

In the Southern section of the United States the average monthly rainfall during the cotton growing period is about 5in., with rain falling about 10 days in the month.

In British Central Africa—average rainfall about 65in. per annum—wet and dry seasons well defined. Winter is dry and cold there, and the crop can be gathered in the dry period. Maize and cassava grow there to perfection.

In Western Australia the Northern part should be more suitable than other portions of the State, chiefly on account of the summer rains, which are absent in the South-Western division.

Labour in British Central Africa, India, and Egypt is both plentiful and willing, but it is not very efficient. Very few implements are used, except the hoe. Wages vary from 4s. to 6s. per month.

Kinds to Grow.—Abbassi—on suitable soil. Ashmonui—well suited to the hot climate of Upper Egypt; smaller than the Affifi, and fibre shorter and not so brown. Affifi—a good kind. The Kidney Cotton—on poorer soils. It is perennial and remains several years in the ground, provided it is cut back annually. American cotton, especially the quick ripening varieties from the Northern parts of the United States cotton lands, and also Caravonica kinds, which are tall shrubs, should do well with us.

Mr. Berthoud recommends amongst other sorts tried at the Hamel Experimental Station:—

Shine's Early Prolific.—American Seed; about one quarter failed to germinate. Growth slow but healthy; habit stocky and well branched; height, four feet; flowers creamy white fading to pale rose; bolls large and well filled, 40 to 60 per plant. The first of these ripened 23rd March. The lint is pure white, silky, and of excellent quality. About two-thirds of the bolls matured properly, the balance were spoiled by rain in May. Yield, rate per acre:—Clean lint, 350lbs.; seed, half-a-ton, equal to 16 gallons of oil and 300lbs. of oil-cake. Early and good variety.

Louisiana Prolific.—American seed. Germination even and good. Growth free; habit dwarf; height to three feet; plant shrubby and hardy; flowers creamy white, fading deep rose; bolls round, of fair size and well filled, four lobed—40 to 60 per plant, half of which matured. First ripe on 5th April; short staple; lint pure white; yield fair, rather below Shine's Early. Hardy and good early variety.

Method of Cultivation.—Cotton is a deep-rooted plant, 'so that the deeper the cultivation the better.

Time of Sowing.—In British Central Africa, as early as possible at the beginning of the rains. This allows the ripening and gathering of the crop in the dry season. October, November, or December are good months to sow.

Method of Sowing.—Done in the ridge. When the climate is dry, sowing is done on the flat to reduce evaporation to a minimum.

Sowing and Planting.—A shallow furrow is first opened 2in. or 3in. deep; the seed is deposited and covered by 1in. or 2in. of soil; for that purpose a "Cotton Planter" is sometimes used. It is similar to a wheelbarrow, provided with a long seed box carried at right angles with the barrow. The implement is drawn by a horse or a mule, and the crank attached to the wheel connected to a lever attached to the seed box opens and closes alternately, the seed outlet in the box thus keeping a constant delivery. Seed is thus economised, and deposited more evenly.

On smaller plantations the planter is not used. A furrow is opened, and the sower drops the seed through a tin tube 5ft. or 6ft. long, with a funnel at the upper end. Into this the seed is fed by hand, a harrow is subsequently drawn to cover the seeds, and sometimes a board is used as a substitute.

Distance Apart.—Varies according to soil and varieties cultivated. For bushy kind 3ft. to 3½ft. is an average, with the plants 15in. to 18in. apart in the rows. If the soil is very rich 4ft. to 5ft. is not too much between the ridges. Distance apart is regulated by the size the plants attain.

Sowing the Seed.—Sow on top of the ridge. The seed is cheap, and should be sown liberally.

Thinning should be done on a wet day, when the plants are about 6in. high; the two best plants being left.

Resowing.—As soon as the plants are visible above the ground the blanks should be filled by means of seeds sown overnight.

Hoeing should be done continually, as long as the workers can get between the rows without damage. It keeps down weeds and conserves the moisture. In America they believe that two such hoeings are equal to one rain.

Topping is not always necessary, except when the plants grow too much wood. As it hastens the ripening of the crop, it is an advantage in countries with a short growing season.

Harvesting.—Picking commences when the crop is ripe. If the boll is not well opened the fibre is weak, because the natural twist which gives strength and is so desirable has not been developed. Cotton should be graded into early, middle, and late pickings; different varieties should be kept separate. Spinners only give price of worst samples to mixed cottons.

Yield of Cotton Lint per Acre.—This is sometimes estimated by averaging the number of bolls on the plants. In the Sea Islands, for every 15 bolls, when the plants are in rows 5ft. x 20in., the yield is usually about 100lbs. of lint per acre. This varies slightly with the variety of cotton. On the average, 300lbs. of lint are obtained from 1,100lbs. to 1,200lbs. of seed cotton. The yield of lint per acre varies considerably with the soil, cultivation, and manuring. It averages 150lbs. to 350lbs. per acre (probably 224lbs.) and 12 bushels (720lbs.) of seeds of 60lbs. each.

Ginning is the name given to the operation whereby the lint is separated from the seed. Freshly picked cotton is easy to gin; it should be well sunned before that operation. This allows the insects to escape and makes the cotton of a more silky texture.

Egyptian cotton merchants, after ginning, spray a little warm water at a temperature of 170deg. Fah. This keeps the strength of the fibre, which has become heated in ginning. Too much water spoils the colour and causes permanent injury.

Gins.—These are both hand and power machines, chiefly of the roller type for long-stapled varieties. The British Cotton Growing Association, which has recently been formed for the purpose of encouraging the growth of cotton in new territories, has taken an active part in providing these gins and other machinery to associations of growers. These appliances are loaned and remain the property of the Association while they are used for the instruction of beginners and use of small settlers.

Baling.—Each country has its standard size and weight of bales. These are pressed, packed, weighed, and marked. The standard size of American bale weighs 500lbs., with a density of about 35lbs. per cubic foot. The Indian bale is the densest, being about 40lbs. to the cubic foot; it weighs about 400lbs. The Egyptian bale is the largest, weighing about 740lbs., whilst the Peruvian and Brazilian only average about 200lbs. each.

Sea Island cotton is baled like a packet of hops, with no iron bands, each weighing about 400lbs.

Factory consists of buildings and machinery. The buildings need not be of an elaborate kind. Stores must be provided, also engine-house, and cement foundation and solid masonry walls for fixing the machinery. These consist of oil engine, shafting, brackets, pulleys, and belting, gins, press; carriers or elevators for seed-cotton and for lint and seed.

Oil Press is a necessary adjunct of a cotton factory. Even for manuring purposes, cotton seed is far better after the oil has been extracted. Such machinery could also be used for treating other oil-producing seeds, such as earth-nut, castor oil, etc.

Cost.—In the Sea Island districts of South Carolina the cost of cultivation and all expenses average $35 per acre, the returns for the lint and for seed $57, leaving a net profit of $22 per acre.

In the West Indies it is reckoned that the total cost of placing cotton in the Liverpool market is 7d. per lb.; best Sea Island cotton fetching 12d. per lb., and there remains a net profit at the rate of £5 per acre. This allows for expenses of cultivation, calculated at the rate of £3 per acre, ½d. per lb. for picking, 1½d. for ginning and baling, and the balance for freight (65s. per ton weight), manure, commission, cartage, and brokerage.

In British Central Africa the cost of cultivation, including clearing land, cost of seed, sowing, subsequent cultivation, harvesting, ginning and baling a crop of 230lbs., freight, commission, dock charges, interest on capital, is reckoned at £3 8s. 10d. per acre.

The price of Sea Island (that is long-staple) cotton is now about 12d. per lb., while Upland (short-staple) cotton is selling at 5d. to 8d. per lb.

HARVEY CITRUS SHOW.

The Annual Show held at Harvey last month provided a most interesting study to the growers of citrus fruits. One feature particularly stands out very prominent, and that is the fact that the oranges which gained first prize had been stored in cold storage. The following report of the Show is taken from the columns of the *Southern Times :—*

" So far as the show itself was concerned it may be termed an unqualified success. As compared with the previous exhibition there was a far greater and distinctly superior display of the various citrus fruits. As may be imagined, the citrus section of the show was the greatest attraction, and the exhibits there were undoubtedly well worthy of the expressions of admiration that were heard all round the room. In the orange section the Washington Navels were easily first, both in quality and in quantity. These oranges have now secured first place in the markets of the world, and, practically speaking, from a commercial standpoint, there are no varieties to compare with them. As regards the exhibits at Harvey, they were undoubtedly all of a first-class order. The exhibit displayed by Mr. R. L. Cowan, of Mundijong, which secured the first prize, was a beautiful type of this favourite orange. The specimens, twelve being the stipulated number, were absolutely uniform in size and quality, and the fruit itself was of a superior quality, the flavour being all that could be desired. It may be mentioned that the fruit shown had been for some time stored in cool storage ; whereas the oranges which were awarded the second prize were only just taken off the trees. The specimens shown by Mr. I. Lowe only missed, by a very small margin, the first prize, the flavour being quite equal to the first exhibit, but lacked the careful grading that distinguished the first prize exhibit. The Valencia oranges, which in point of number were second to the Washington Navels, were fairly well represented, but could not compare in size and quality with the former variety. In this class also Mr. Cowan carried off the honours, being awarded first and second prizes. In the mandarin varieties Harvey scored conspicuously. A magnificent exhibit of ' Beauty of Glen Retreats ' shown by Mr. Roy Hayward, who secured first and second prizes, were much admired, the fruit not only being of most delicious flavour, but being also of the highest quality. The same remarks also applied to other varieties of mandarins, which were a decided feature of the show. The lemon section was a splendid display. There were a large number of entries, and in this collection also Mr. Cowan again scored. His exhibits, which had been carefully cured, were shown in first-class condition, and were an excellent type of the fruit. According to Mr. Hawter, whose experience is undoubted, they were a very excellent representation both in appearance and in flavour of what a first grade lemon should be. The other exhibits were also of a high order, and the difference between the prize takers and the rest was only a small one. Pomeloes were fairly well represented but in this class the old variety could not in any way compare with the newer and better flavoured sorts. In this section Mr. A. V. Goss came in first, although Mr. W. L. Owen's exhibit ran him a close second. There was a fine display of Seville oranges, a fruit of a most useful type for the making of marmalade.

The specimens which secured the prizes were an ideal type of this fruit, and it would be difficult to equal them elsewhere. In addition to the various varieties mentioned previously there were numerous kinds of oranges exhibited, but they only occupied a position from their individul merits as specimens of the particular classes they represented. From a commercial standpoint the Washington Navels have so outclassed all others, that fully, if not more than ninety per cent. of all oranges now planted are of that variety. One small exhibit, which appeared to be of the old St. Michael variety, attracted some attention although not displayed as a prizetaker. They were specimens taken from a tree 45 years old. So far as the individual oranges were concerned, judging from external appearances, they would have taken a prize against all comers.

" Perhaps the most useful exhibits in the show were the cases of packed oranges shown by Mr. R. L. Cowan, of Mundijong. Two exhibits were shown and the one that secured the prize was a marvel of the packer's art, although in the opinion of some of the visitors who claim to have a knowledge of this particular work, his other case should have had preference. In the case of the prize winner, all the oranges were packed on a diagonal plan, and were so arranged that each orange on the top row rested on three in the lower row and *vice versa* if the case was reversed. By this means a larger number can be packed in a case and the fruit will travel without being damaged. In the second case, each fruit on the top row rested on four in the lower row and consequently was still less liable to damage in transit. According to Mr. Cowan, who has had considerable experience in the art of packing, having been for years connected with the growth of citrus fruits in Florida, no auctioneer in New York would even entertain the idea of attempting to dispose of fruit which was packed in a similar manner to the rest of the fruit shown as packed specimens. They not only could not sell them, but they would pass them out of the auction rooms.

"Mr. Cowan, the principal prize winner, it is interesting to note, is an orchardist with considerable experience of the citrus industry in California and Florida. Some eleven or twelve years ago his orange orchard in the latter State was completely destroyed by a blizzard, which in one short night's work ruined the work of eleven years. Disheartened by the blow, Mr. Cowan determined to seek other lands, and finally decided upon settling in Western Australia, whose possibilities as a citrus-growing country at once arrested his attention. Selecting some lands on the Mundijong flats—the fitness of which for orange cultivation was derided by local residents—he commenced anew a career as a citrus grower, and has won an admitted success in the undertaking. The Washington Navels which he exhibited were a very superior fruit, even in size and quality, thin-skinned, and of delicious flavour. As the result of ten years' experience in Western Australia, Mr. Cowan has an optimistic word for its possibilities as a citrus country. It can, he declared, produce oranges second to none in the world, the Washington Navels ranking in quality with the best of California, which have a great reputation. In Florida, it appears, this splendid and favourite orange will not thrive."

HAMEL EXPERIMENTAL FARM.

POTATO TESTS.

A variety of potato has been introduced from France. It originated with M. Labergerie, on his experimental plots at Verriéres, by the careful selection and improvement of *Solanum commersoni*, a wild type of potato which grows naturally in low wet land along the Mercedes River, Uruguay, South America.

The chief merits claimed for this new comer are good quality, remarkable productiveness, and power to thrive vigorously in swampy, wet soils, where other varieties would fail. If these claims prove to be reliable, it will be a valuable acquisition to cultivators in this State.

POTATO "VIOLET" *(Solanum commersoni).*—The tubers reached here sound and in good condition for planting. They were set out on sandy land, well drained, on 25th May.

A part of the tubers were cut into small sets; all these failed to germinate. The whole sets came up well and grew into fairly strong plants. The foliage appears to withstand the injurious effects of cold and wet better than any other variety of potato yet tried here.

The plants were dug up on the 12th September, and yielded a fair return of well-shaped, medium-sized tubers : shape, oblong; skin, smooth; eyes, shallow; colour, bright violet. The next planting of this distinct potato will be done in low wet soil, and we may look forward to getting interesting results.

THE ANGORA GOAT IN AUSTRALASIA.

A branch of pastoral industry which is yet in its earliest stages in this State, but the true value of which is coming to be recognised, is the rearing of angora goats. Except in occasional instances, these animals have hitherto been looked upon in the light of novelties and not as a source of profit, though, thanks to the few individual efforts, the production of mohair may be considered as already established on a firm basis. But our landholders, particularly those who have but lately taken up rural occupations, and have not yet brought into use the whole of their holdings, will do well to fully consider the possibilities—nay, the probabilities—of reward from still further extending the scope of the industry.

INTRODUCTION TO NEW SOUTH WALES.

The pioneer—at any rate, of the present generation—of the angora industry in New South Wales was Mr. Rex N. Blaxland, who, in 1897, brought from

Tasmania some pure-bred animals, of direct descent from importations by the Acclimatisation Society of Victoria to the island State. These progenitors of the Australian angora of to-day came from Asia Minor, the original home of the race, and where the mohair industry has been carried on for generations.

Mr. Blaxland sent his purchases to his father's station, Murinbin, near Singleton. Breeding proceeded there till 1901, when the best of the flock were transferred to Mr. Knox's property, at Wyalong. Further success was achieved there, and photos of some of the animals, particularly of the bucks "Perfection" and "Uncle Sam"—the latter an importation from the United States—show that they are of a fine stamp; while a specimen of the staple from "Perfection" exhibited was soft and silky, and fully 15 inches in length. The fleece was also up to the mark in weight, cutting about 12lbs. of mohair.

In conversation with a *Farmer and Settler* representative, Mr. Blaxland said that the angora first commended itself to him as being adapted to the profitable utilisation of unimproved country, which, to be profitably used for sheep, would require the immediate expenditure of about 4s. or 5s. per acre in ring barking, sucker-knocking, and mattocking the undergrowth. This outlay would extend over, say, three years, during which time only a very nominal return would be secured. But with angoras, practically the whole of such work, except ringing, could be dispensed with, the animals at the same time bringing in half-a-crown's worth of mohair each. And as they may be stocked at an average of two to the acre, the owner has a monetary return of 5s. per acre, instead of a similar expenditure, if the land be prepared for sheep according to the regular plans.

Angoras may be considered as specially suitable to local climatic conditions, as they can stand extremes of heat and cold, though not wet, and they thrive best in dry, warm weather. The Wyalong stud, for instance, went through the long and severe drought of 1902 without loss.

EARLIER EXPERIMENTS.

While Mr. Blaxland is the present day pioneer, as long ago as 1832 a a retired squatter, Mr. Alexander Riley, imported to Sydney a consignment of 13 goats, which had been secured from France at a cost of 1,300 francs. The animals were taken to Raby, near Campbelltown, and to Cavan, on the Murrumbidgee, the prospect of the successful establishment of the new industry being very bright. But on the death of Mr. William E. Riley, who had superintended the introduction of the angoras for his father, the flock was dispersed.

In 1856 the first importations to Victoria took place, seven angoras being brought from Turkey by Mr. Sichel, a Melbourne merchant. In 1873, the flock had increased to 108, the average weight of the fleeces being 2lb. 9ozs. each, after a year's growth. The value of the fleece of six months and 18 days' growth was : bucks, 11s. 0½d., does 7s. 8d., the highest prices for each sex being 18s. 8d. and 15s. 1d. respectively. But in 1878 the major part of the Victorian flock was transferred to West Australia, and is believed to have lost its identity as a pure flock.

The greatest success has been achieved in South Australia, the owner who gained most experience being the late Mr. Kempe, of Peake station. In 1903 he wrote that he considered angoras as a proven paying industry; that the average value of fleece was 4s. to 6s. for all ages and sexes; that the

mutton was palatable, and unobjectionable to taste or smell; that they thrive
on the roughest country in South Australia; and would live on scrub, bushes,
weeds, and plants that horses and cattle do not touch and sheep only
nibble at.

The Question of Fencing.

Perhaps the greatest difficulty appertaining to the introduction of
angoras is the question of fencing, to keep the animals within bounds. Mr.
Blaxland regards this as still in an experimental stage. In some cases a
skeleton fence of seven wires has been found sufficient, provided that they be
kept very tight. He is now trying an eight-wire skeleton fence, and at
present is unwilling to express a decided opinion on the subject.

Making a Start.

For settlers thinking of introducing angoras to their property, with the
intention of breeding, Mr. Blaxland considers that, for a start, it would be
sufficient to mate five ordinary nannies with one mature pure-bred angora
buck, putting them on to about 50 acres of land. From such a commencement, of course, the early returns would be only nominal; but a year or two
should be sufficient to show a decided advance, not only in their value for
preparing the land for grazing, but also in the amount and quality of
mohair secured from shearing.

Angoras or Sheep.

For some years to come, it may be admitted that angoras can attain no
more than the position of auxiliaries to sheep, serving to profitably occupy
land at an earlier period after first settlement than the great wool-producing
flocks. But as the industry becomes more fully established, there is no
reason why the angora fleece should not be of considerable value for mohair
manufacture, it being capable of adaptation to all the usual processes now
applied to wool.

Mohair Finer than Wool.

The manufacture of mohair, said Mr. Blaxland, is still in its infancy.
The difference between it and wool is that the latter has a hollow fibre and a
serrated edge, and it rapidly absorbs both moisture and dust. On the other
hand, mohair has a solid fibre with a smooth surface; and as a result dust
only lies on the top, and may easily be shaken and brushed off.

The advantage of this is easily understood when we remember the
amount of dust accumulated when travelling by road, particularly in motor
cars. And cloaks, rugs, etc., made from mohair should command a ready
sale. Ordinary suits of clothes and neckties, too, may be had in mohair
material. Indeed, such neckties are already in use, and at first sight may
easily be mistaken for silk, so soft and bright is the manufactured article.

Value of the Skins.

The skins of angoras may also be tanned and adapted to ordinary uses,
such as the manufacture of mats and rugs, the present value of imported
rugs made from the skins of two wethers being three or four guineas.
Angora skins ought always to find a ready sale, too, for goat-skin leather,
for which there is at present a tremendous demand.

Another direction in which the angora should prove useful is as a food. Angora mutton is claimed to be not so coarse to the taste as ordinary mutton, and the meat of cross-bred animals between angoras and common goats is said to be really first-class eating. And although there exists in the public mind a prejudice against goat flesh, it is considered to be unfounded; and it may be only a matter of time when it will be broken down.

As to the progress already made in the industry, it was already established in Tasmania and South Australia. But New South Wales buyers purchased largely at the sale of the Kidman and Kempe flock, in Adelaide, in May last; and this fact, combined with some neglect to foster the industry, have been responsible for the dispersal, except in one instance, of flocks in those States, and have given New South Wales the pride of place in production of mohair. The principal stud, of course, is that of Mr. Blaxland at Wyalong; but in the past six months other property owners have taken up the industry, notably near Goulburn, where it is regarded as having a big future.

With regard to foreign countries, the export of mohair from Asia Minor is now valued at about a quarter of a million sterling annually, while a similar value is sent from the United States, and three times as much from Cape Colony. In 1900, the figures were as follow:—Asia Minor, 3,360,000lbs., valued at £200,000; United States, 800,000lbs., worth £430,000; and Cape Colony, 10,780,205lbs., for £576,000.—*The Farmer and Settler.*

BORDEAUX MIXTURE.

HOW TO MAKE IT OF DIFFERENT STRENGTHS.

Bordeaux mixture derives its name from the place of its discovery, Bordeaux, France. It consists of copper sulphate, which is commonly called blue vitriol or bluestone, fresh lime and water.

Formulas used—several strengths of the mixture are used under different conditions:—

I. (2:4:50) copper sulphate, 2lbs.; quicklime, 4lbs.; water, 50 gallons.

II. (3:6:50) copper sulphate, 3lbs.; quicklime, 6lbs.; water, 50 gallons.

III. (4:4:50) copper sulphate, 4lbs.; quicklime, 4lbs.; water, 50 gallons.

IV. (6:6:50) copper sulphate, 6lbs.; quicklime, 6lbs.; water, 50 gallons.

Formula I. is used for very tender foliage, as peach, plum, greenhouse plants, tender seedlings, etc.

Formula II., which is one-half stronger than the preceding, has about the same use, but for slightly less tender leaves.

Formula III. is the formula for general use on apples, pears, asparagus, grapes, tomatoes, melons, strawberries, etc., during the growing season.

Formula IV. is the strongest formula that is often used. It is considered best for potatoes and cranberries. It may be used on grapes, on peaches, apples, and pears before blossoming, and sometimes on other crops. It was once more commonly used, but, except as here noted, it is generally being displaced by Formula III.

How to make Bordeaux Mixture.

First method, made from stock solution and tested. The following method is the one that I consider best :—

First.—Suspend in a barrel of water 1lb. of copper sulphate for each gallon of water. It will dissolve in a day, and will keep indefinitely if covered to prevent evaporation. Stir before using.

Second—Slake good stone lime, after which cover it with water. It will keep indefinitely. Stir before using.

Third—Put five cents' worth of yellow prussiate of potash (potassium ferro-cyanide) in a small bottle (about four ounces) and fill with water. Label poison.

Put as many gallons of 1 in spray tank as you desire pounds of copper sulphate.

Fill the tank nearly full of water.

Add milk of lime (2) till you think you have about enough, pouring it through a strainer. Stir, and then put in a drop of 3. If this yellow solution changes to a dark brick colour add more lime and stir. Continue to add lime till a drop of 3 keeps yellow when it hits the mixture.

To make formulas I. and II. add as much more lime as was required by this test. For formulas III. and IV. add a-half more lime.

Second method, made from stock solutions, but not tested.

1. Same as No. 1 above.

2. Weigh the lime. Measure out as many gallons of water as there are pounds of lime. Slake the lime with as much of this water as is needed. When slaked put into a barrel or tank with the remainder of the water. Stir very thoroughly before using.

Put in spray tank as many gallons of 1 as you desire pounds of copper sulphate. Fill tank nearly full of water, and add as many gallons of milk of lime as you desire pounds of lime, pouring through a strainer.

Third method, no stock solutions.—Weigh out the copper sulphate, dissolve, put in tank and fill nearly full of water. Slake the lime, dilute with some water, and add to the mixture, pouring through a strainer.

Fourth method, stock solutions for small gardens:—

1. Dissolve the copper sulphate in water, using one-half pound to the quart. Keep this in a large jug, bottle, or glass kerosene receptacle. Shake before using.

2. Combine the lime and water in the same proportions (one-half pound to a quart, using part of the water to slack it, and add the remainder later). Keep in a covered pail, jug, or bottle. Shake or stir before using.

For formula I. use four fluid ounces of 1, eight fluid ounces of 2, and six quarts of water.

For formula II. use six ounces of 1, twelve ounces of 2, and six quarts of water.

For formula III. use eight ounces of each to six quarts of water.

For formula IV. use twelve ounces of each to six of water.

It is always better to determine the amount of lime to use by the test given in the first method. Add nearly all the water to the copper sulphate, then strain the lime into it. It may also be prepared according to the third method, reducing the amounts proportionately.—*Exchange.*

SALT FOR LIVE STOCK.

Every now and then we meet a man who declares, and cites his past experience, that livestock have no need whatever of salt. Some go even farther, and say that salt is a poison. This is so entirely contrary to almost universal experience, that farmers are disposed to laugh at the man who, with a straight face, tells them that livestock have no need of salt.

This question of the value of salt as part of the ration of dairy cows was taken up by Professor Babcock in 1889, and the results when written out were so at variance with public opinion regarding the effects of salt that it was thought unwise to publish them until more careful tests had been made. In short, this first experiment seemed to show that the yield of milk and the fat content were practically the same, whether the cows had any salt or not. This was also true of trials of this kind made by other experimenters, such as Professor Roberts, of the Ontario Station; Professor Arnold, author of "American Dairying;" and Boussingault and La Bel, foreign experimenters. It was shown that where cows had been induced to eat a large amount of salt, five to seven ounces a day mixed with their feed, the result had been a marked falling off in the quality of milk, with no increase in yield. Professor Babcock's experiment is now published for the first time, in connection with two others conducted ten years later, and continued for a long period, and with the most thorough and painstaking care, as is usual with experiments conducted at the Wisconsin Station. We give the conclusions in full:—

"In every case the cows exhibited an abnormal appetite for salt, after having been deprived of it for two or three weeks, but in no case did the health of the animal, as shown by the general appearance, the live weight, or the yield of milk, appear to be affected, until a much longer time had elapsed. This period of immunity varied with individual cows from less than one month to more than a year.

" In every case there was finally reached a condition of low vitality, in which a sudden and complete breakdown occurred, from which recovery was rapid if salt was applied. This stage was marked by loss of appetite, a generally haggard appearance, a rough coat, and a very rapid decline in both live weight and yield of milk.

"The breakdown was most likely to occur at calving-time, or immediately after, when the system was weakened and the flow of milk large. In general the cows giving the largest amount of milk were the first to show signs of distress. They all suffered less in pasture than when confined to the stable.

"The behaviour of the cows in these trials indicates that their food contained sufficient chlorine to maintain them in good health, while dry, for an indefinite period, and it seems probable that, under conditions existing in Wisconsin, a dry cow or a steer would suffer no great inconvenience if given no salt except that contained in the usual feed eaten. It is calculated that the ration given in these experiments contained chlorine equivalent to about 0·75 ounces of salt per day, and it is assumed that this is the minimum amount of salt required per 1,000lbs. live weight to sustain an animal that is not producing milk. If this amount is not present in the food it should be supplied directly.

" In addition to this a cow should receive enough salt to compensate for the chlorine contained in the milk produced. In general this will require about 0·6 of an ounce of salt for each twenty pounds of milk given. A slight excess will do no harm, and it is recommended that dairy cows in Wisconsin be given at least one ounce of salt per day. Exceptionally heavy milkers will require more than this.

" The uniform results obtained with all cows employed in these trials indicate beyond question that in Wisconsin and in other regions similarly located salt, in addition to that obtained in the food, is absolutely essential to the continued health of a dairy cow while producing milk.

" It is evident, moreover, that the amount of salt which must be supplied directly will vary greatly in different localities, it being more at high elevations and at places remote from the sea.

"The success of these experiments must be chiefly attributed to the exceptionally long periods during which salt was withheld. In no previous tests, so far as the writer knows, have cows been deprived of salt for more than thirty consecutive days, which period is shown to be entirely inadequate, under conditions which exist at this station. The twenty-three cows that were deprived of salt in our trials all continued for more than sixty days, and several of them for more than six months, before any noticeable effect upon their physical condition or yield of milk occurred.

" The results naturally suggest the question whether the short periods usually employed in feeding experiments have been sufficient to show the physiological effect of any particular. food. In comparatively few feeding experiments have careful observations been continued for more than thirty consecutive days without a change. Most of the knowledge regarding the relative value of the standard feeding stuffs has been derived from trials in which the periods did not exceed two weeks. This is especially true of data concerning the digestibility of foods.

"It seems likely from the behaviour of all the cows in these trials that there are certain reserve forces which enable an animal to adapt itself to adverse conditions, and even to overcome the effect of malnutrition for much longer periods than have hithertofore been considered sufficient.

"It is not intended to throw discredit upon the work already done, but it is suggested that much additional knowledge concerning the physiological influence of foods may be gained, and thereby many of the uncertainties which exist to-day regarding feeding problems be eliminated by greatly extending the experimental periods."

All of which shows that the practice of the farmer who ordinarily salts his cattle regularly every week, or oftener, is based on sound scientific principles. It shows, moreover, the folly of drawing broad general conclusions from the results of one experiment, or from many experiments unless conducted under practically the same conditions and circumstances. — *Elder's Weekly Review.*

RABBIT DESTRUCTION.

THE SOUTH AFRICAN CARNIVOROUS ANT.

The destruction of rabbits may possibly enter on a new phase in the near future, by the introduction into Australia of a flesh-eating ant from South Africa. The interesting letter on this subject, written by Mr. D. Blackburn to Mr. C. U. Kingston, the London manager of the Australian Mortgage, Land, and Finance Company, which we publish, has been submitted to Mr. C. French, the Victorian Government entomologist, for his opinion. In view of the red ant possibly proving a serious trouble, Mr. French has advised caution in the matter. He has written to the Government entomologists of Cape Colony, Natal, and the Orange Colony, for the fullest information respecting the habits of the ant. The following is the letter referred to:—

Mr. C. U. Kingston,—Sir,—Referring to our conversation to-day on this subject, I have thought it might assist you if I embodied in a concise form the points to which I drew your attention, and amplified my letter to Lord Avebury.

About 1896 the scarcity of a cheap form of flesh food for the kaffirs employed on the Rand mines induced me to take up the artificial breeding of rabbits, of which I had had considerable experience in England. I began with about 50 does of any kind available, and later imported from England the Belgian hare for crossing purposes. The result was successful. They bred well, and the does throve; but when the young turned into the enclosures began to breed the results were not so satisfactory.

So long as the rabbits were confined in hutches they throve, but the average of natural increase in the enclosures fell very much. A year later I turned out at Sans Souci, five miles from Johannesburg, about 300 assorted rabbits for sporting purposes. The conditions were apparently perfect, for there was an abundance of green forage and green food in the neighbourhood. We refrained from shooting long enough to enable the stock to have bred, but the ultimate result was very unsatisfactory. The young made a tardy and scanty appearance, and the experiment was abandoned.

Later I was commissioned by the agent of the Saxonwald Estate, Johannesburg, of 10,000 acres, to turn out 700 rabbits for sporting purposes. Within 12 months of the turning-down of the 700, a rabbit was the rarest item in a day's bag.

In 1901 I took up residence in Natal, and with the able assistance and encouragement of the editor of the "Natal (Government) Agricultural Gazette," and Messrs. William Baynes, M.L.A., and C. W. Brooke, J.P., of Loteni, president of the Loteni Farmers' Association, I conducted an elaborate series of rearing and breeding experiments in both the high and low regions of Natal.

At Loteni I had an elaborate, almost scientifically-conducted rabbitry. I bred from imported English Belgians, and crossed them with fine healthy specimens of the common grey. Again the hutches were successful, the enclosures not. Within nine months 110 does produced less than 500 young. According to hutch average they should have numbered nearly 4,000.

Meanwhile, some dozen farmers who had, upon my advice, tried the experiment, were undergoing the same experience—hutches good, enclosures non-productive.

In December, 1902, I was receiving reports from 21 farmers, whose districts practically embraced all Natal and five distant points in the Transvaal and Orange River Colony. All told the same tale.

After about 12 months my enclosed rabbits at Loteni practically ceased to breed. I dug up a number of burrows and found the secret. The newly-born young were covered with red ants. I communicated with all the farmers experimenting. They found the cause of the non-increase was the red ant. I immediately devoted my attention to this discovery, and found that the attacks were made by a species known as the meat-eating ant. Its scientific name I do not know.

The cause of the almost entire absence of small furred animals in red ant infected districts was explained.

I found that the meerkat, the dassie—a species of rabbit—the cane rat, the sprenghaar—a species of hare—were very scarce in red ant areas, and all make their nests in rocky places too hard for the ant to burrow in. It is also noticeable that rats are rare on farms in the veld; also mice. In the towns they swarm. I found in a packing-case at Loteni a large house rat big with young. I confined and fed her in a stable infected with red ants. The young were devoured within 24 hours of birth, and the mother died three days later. I noticed, and the kaffirs confirm the view, that all animals born without hair are subject to the attacks of red ants. At my Krugersdorp farm I have a large red ant area, and run about 150 sheep. I have frequently examined the newly-born lambs, but never saw an ant on them The kaffirs, who are very observant, say the red ant (intutane) will act as scavenger and remove the after-birth of oxen and sheep, but never gets on the animal. My observations confirm this. This red ant is essentially a meat eater and scavenger. By way of experiment I put near their haunts about 100lbs. of offal—intestines of rabbits, sheep, and other animal matter. In eight days nothing was left but such parts as the sun had dried hard. I noticed for months afterwards, until the rains had cleansed the ground, the red ant swarmed over the spot. I also saw several fights on and near the spot between the red ant and other species, in which the meat-eater was always victorious. He is very pugnacious, and judging by the extent to which he swarms all over South Africa, either has very few or feeble enemies. The ant bear destroys the hill of the meat-eater equally with those of other species. Fowls also devour them greedily.

CONCLUSIONS.

Three years' attempts at rearing rabbits in Natal, Transvaal, and Orange River Colony, in various climates, but under apparently perfect conditions as to food supply, have shown nothing but disaster. Two years' close observation of my own and other farmers' experiments have proved that the red meat-eating ant is a ferocious attacker and destroyer of the newly-born rabbit when in the burrow. After a short time the ants found the hutches, and entered and devoured. They were only kept out by raising the hutches on 6-inch posts, surrounded by a 6-inch ring of tar kept moist by the sun and tallow. The tallow had to be abandoned because it attracted the ants, who literally covered the tar and formed a bridge. A report to this effect made by me to the Transvaal Minister of Agriculture was considered so conclusive by him that he refused the request of a farmers' association to prohibit the importation of rabbits as unnecessary, and referred them to my report.

The Ministers of Agriculture of the Orange River Colony and Natal are also sufficiently satisfied with my discovery to refrain from prohibiting rabbit importations.

During 16 years' close observation as a small farmer and a diligent writer on agricultural subjects, I have never seen or heard of any ant, except the destructive white ant, becoming a serious nuisance. On the contrary, the red meat-eater is recognised as a useful scavenger who completes the work of the vultures.

The fact that after 150 years the rabbit is practically unknown in South Africa points to some restraining cause. This is the more significant as thousands are kept in hutches by boys all over the country, and it is unreasonable to suppose that none ever escape.

All fur-bearing animals of the veld, born naked, have their breeding places in spots free from red ants. Meerkats hide and hunt among ant-hills, but never breed near them.

I am personally aware of over 2,000 rabbits that have either been purposely or accidentally turned loose within three months; dogs, guns, and a reward ranging from 6d. to 5s. to kaffirs for each live rabbit captured have been practically ineffective.

I could easily procure all the queen ants required, but as my efforts have been devoted to destroying instead of preserving ants, I do not know how or whether they would bear transport.

(Signed)   DOUGLAS BLACKBURN.

7 April, 1906.

P.S.—I have noticed on many occasions that the doe has died within a few days of the destruction of her young by ants. In no case does she return to the same burrow to litter, and invariably deserts her young when attacked by ants, so that even if the ants did not quite kill the young, they would die from parental neglect.

THE FIELDS OF THE FUTURE.

"The open fields" is to become a phrase of the past. The fields of the future will be covered in with a network of wires which will radiate high tension electricity through the crops beneath and bring them to a fruitfulness such as the old-fashioned sunshine could not possibly bestow.

Such, at any rate, is the potential outcome of experiments which Mr. J. E. Newman, an electrical engineer, is carrying out on a farm at Iron Cross, midway between Evesham and Alcester. Twenty acres of arable land belonging to Messrs. R. and B. Bomford are traversed sixteen feet above the ground, by wires suspended from poles placed at intervals of a hundred yards. The wires are insulated so completely that the current can find its way to the ground only through the air, and consequently through the crops. Unfortunately, there is on the farm no streamlet capable of generating an electric current, and a three-horsepower oil engine is therefore used for the purpose; it drives a dynamo, the current from which is converted to a high tension before transmission to the wires. The engine is run for only a few hours a day, at intervals varying in length according to the state of the weather and the amount of moisture in the soil. When the ground is very dry the current appears to be harmful rather than beneficial, particularly in the case of peas, beans, and clover, when they have once appeared above the surface.

Twelve of the acres included in the experiment have been sown with wheat, seven with barley, and there are small plots of other crops. In the case of almost all of them Mr. Newman confidently expects that germination will be hastened and the yield increased as a result of the discharge of electricity from the wires. In the case of the wheat, he says, he will be disappointed if the yield, both of grain and of straw, be not twenty-five per cent. greater than it would be otherwise, and if there be not such an improvement in the character of the grain as will make it equal for milling purposes to Canadian wheat.

These anticipations are to some extent based on the results of experiments as to the effects of electricity on vegetable growth, which were carried out by the late Prof. Lemstrom, of Helsingfors University, in Germany, and at Durham, and also on previous experiments made by Mr. Newman himself.

Jointly with the experiments in Worcestershire, Mr. Newman is prosecuting researches at Bitton, near Bristol. Last year he obtained very encouraging results from the distribution of current over tomatoes and cucumbers grown indoors, and cabbages, peas, beans, and strawberries grown outside. Especially marked was the enhanced rapidity with which peas under the influence of the current appeared above the ground as compared with those not so stimulated.

In all previous experiments of this kind, however, low tension electricity has been employed, and it is believed that the present trials at Iron Cross are the first in which a high tension current derived from a dynamo has been made use of in this way. In the unsuccessful experiments made in Russia some years ago the current was discharged direct into the soil.

The poles and wires at Iron Cross have been fixed at such a height as to permit of steam ploughing, and they give the fields an extraordinary appearance. People stare in amazement at what seems to be a telegraph system in a tangle. If the nearest rustic be interrogated, the reply, given with a knowing smile, is that "Farmer Bomford thinks he can grow wheat by electricity," and the experiment is regarded locally as a great joke.

That fact, however, by no means disturbs the equanimity of Mr. Newman. It is, indeed, quite within the bounds of possibility, given an adequate supply of electricity at a sufficiently cheap rate, that in the not very distant future Great Britain may once more be able to produce the bulk of the wheat she consumes, and to find employment for a much greater proportion of her sons upon her own soil.— *London Tribune.*

HOW TO USE CEMENT.

The increasing use of cement makes it desirable that farmers should know more about the subject, for they can lay cement walks and floors as well as anybody, and if handy with carpenters' tools, so that they can make the forms, can put in foundations to buildings, retaining walls, and other small structures. Portland cement is so called because first made near Portland, England, or, as some say, by reason of its colour resembling that of a building stone found near that city. At any rate, Portland cement is the trade name for cement made from a mixture of lime and clay and burned in a kiln, wherever made. Formerly nearly all cement made was imported and sold for from $3 to $5 per barrel of about 400 pounds. Now enormous quantities are made in this country, although not enough for our requirements. There is, however, a great difference in the quality of cement. That imported is generally good, because it does not pay to send poor stuff on so long a journey. The difference is in the materials used and in the care with which it is manufactured. It does not pay to use poor cement, although usually a good job can be done with it by increasing the quantity of cement used in the concrete. It will cost no more to use good cement and less of it. The best way for a farmer, who cannot usually be a good judge of cement, is to order of a responsible dealer and hold him responsible for the quality.

In small jobs, where only a few barrels of cement are used, it is safest to buy the best and use plenty of it. Where any considerable quantity is required expert advice should be taken and expert concrete men employed to do the work. Ordinary concrete is made of one part in seven good cement, two parts sharp sand entirely free from loam, and four parts broken hard rock with sharp corners. Creek gravel can be used if broken rock is not available; but the foregoing formula supposes rock broken as evenly as possibly, with no pieces larger than an egg. If creek gravel is used a larger quantity of cement will usually be required, partly because there will be no sharp edges and partly because it will usually be finer than broken rock. The finer the gravel or broken stone the more cement must be used. In making concrete, the sand and gravel are first thoroughly mixed, dry, on a plank platform. It must be thoroughly turned over at least twice, and it is better to do it three or four times. In general, the more labour expended in mixing the better the job. The proper amount of cement is then spread over the pile and again thoroughly mixed by turning the materials over at least twice. It is then ready for use. In making a walk the first requisite is to tamp the ground with a rammer until it is as solid as it can be made. Rammers can be bought in any village. They are simply chunks of cast iron with holes in them to receive the handle, which the farmer can put in himself. The usual sizes are five pounds and seven pounds. Different shaped rammers are made for special work. The ground or the form being ready, the dry concrete is wet, being well mixed as the water is turned on and applied at once. For a walk or floor lay concrete to the depth of four inches and ram down as solid as possible. The more it is rammed the better and more desirable the work. A little experience will show how much water to apply. It is better to have too much than too little, but it is best of all to be just right. With the right amount of water and the right amount of ramming there should be a little film of water on the surface of the finished job. When the first setting has taken place--in from half an hour to an hour—it is ready for the finishing coat, which is two or three parts sharp sand to one of cement—not more than two parts of the job is to be first-class—applied one-half inch thick. Smooth it with a light board three or four feet long, whose edge is perfectly straight and champered as nearly to an edge as is safe to use without danger of chipping off. If you are skilful enough you may follow with a plasterer's trowel, which will leave a perfectly smooth surface—that is if you are really skilful; otherwise it will be a lot of ridges. The writer uses the board and then lets well enough alone. As soon as it has set sufficiently cover it with old sacking and wet it down twice a day for a week. Then take off the sacking and you will have a walk which will last until it is worn through by the feet of some future generation. Slovenly work in mixing or tamping, or failure to keep moist until thoroughly set, will result in depressions, cracks, and such generally bad work as you can see in any city side walk in front of houses made to sell. We are writing here about a good walk made to stay. In laying the forms for the sidewalk place four and one-half inch boards on edge thoroughly staked on the outside to resist the thrust of the cement in tamping. Have the alignment perfect. Fill with concrete to within half an inch of the top, and fill with the finishing coat. The smoothing board should be long enough to rest on the edges of the form boards as it is drawn along. If the ground is solid clay and well tamped four-inch boards will probably answer for forms, but when making a walk it is best, on the form, to give it sufficient body so that you will not fear to drive over it with a wagon if you want to.—Exchange.

SHROPSHIRES.

Although a comparatively recent breed, these valuable sheep are probably more widely distributed at the present time throughout Australia than any other British breed. More especially is such the case in this State, and one has but to glance through the pens at this year's Adelaide show to realise the important part played by the strain among all classes of husbandmen. Although modern in their improved character, the original stocks were the Longmynds of Shropshire and the denizens of Cannock Chase, in Staffordshire. The type is distinctly a Southdown, but larger in size, far more hardy in constitution, and, therefore, suited to colder situations, and most prolific. The increase in all cases is to a certain extent and often materially influenced by the nature of the land, as yielding nourishing or inferior feed. On an average, if the ewes are well cared for before and during the time the ram is with them, fully 50 per cent. of twins may be looked for. And when Shropshire rams are mated with Lincoln ewes the increase is greater. These results have been attained by experience and experiment in the native country of this breed. As to the nature of the increase when the ewe is a Merino, the same proportion should be capable of establishment if due regard be paid to the attendant circumstances of condition.

The Shropshire ewe is a good mother, and can do justice to her offspring, whilst her system is ever responsive to a generous diet. The Shropshire sheep of the present day exhibit much of the quality of the Down, with considerably more size. The features are rather longer, of a uniform dark—but not black—tint, the eye full and large, the forehead moderately flat and well woolled, the ears rather large and thin, standing well out from the head. Much improvement in symmetry has taken place of late years. Formerly the shoulder was frequently upright, the spine not straight, the top far from level, and the forequarters generally light. Now the best-bred sheep are as true-grown as the Downs. The character of the wool is of great importance, especially where the climate is moist. An open condition of wool is to be deprecated; the staple should be fine and close, with which a good weight is quite possible.

The main points are:—Fine masculine head, with neat ears well covered with wool, and dark face, large deep body on short legs, pink skin, and legs the same colour as the face. The yield, both of mutton and wool, is far greater than from the Southdown or other short-wool. The quality of the meat, both from the fineness of the texture, the presence of fat in the tissues, and the rich, dark colour, is fully equal to the best Southdown. In this State they take rank as the most important short-wool breed of the present day, having shot to the front, in keeping with the expansion of the frozen-lamb trade, as one of the most desirable strains to cross with the Merino.

Some time ago a special exhibit was arranged from the State Farm, Bathurst, New South Wales, to show farmers the results of experiments as to what cross with the Merino ewe produced the best freezer. These results brought out at the head of the poll the Shropshire-Merino. Of the lambs

penned for the special purpose of this experiment, the average live weight at
five months old was as follows :—

Shropshire-Merino	...	...	...	...	82 lb.
Border Leicester-Merino		...	...	...	76 lb.
Southdown-Merino	...	...	...	...	74 lb.
English Leicester-Merino		...	...	...	70 lb.
Lincoln-Merino ...	...	...	...	...	67 lb.

The dressed weight on these figures would be about half. In these there is
nothing extraordinary as to the maximum attainment. Many of our local
breeders can surpass the weights at the same age, but the interest lies in the
difference between the various classes. For some reason which has not yet
received any very satisfactory explanation, the Shropshire has gone somewhat out of favour in Victoria. Climate and some alleged difficulty in the
fattening of the cross as a two-tooth are bearing the blame, but to what
degree respectively has never been categorically made clear. Some considerable stir has from time to time been made in and out of the Press regarding
excessive barbering of Shropshires for exhibition purposes. Visitors to our
show could judge for themselves to what extent the practice has been
adopted or avoided here.—*Elder's Weekly Review.*

GARDEN NOTES FOR NOVEMBER.

By PERCY G. WICKEN.

As November approaches we may expect the weather to become warmer.
The crops will be ripening, and in the earlier districts hay-making will be
well advanced.

In the Eastern districts the harvest promises to be a prolific one, and
the farmers expect to obtain a yield somewhat above the average. Gardening
operations will consist chiefly of keeping the soil well stirred between the
rows so as to conserve the moisture. Where no water is available for
garden purposes, the amount of planting which can be done is very limited,
but in the Southern districts there are many varieties of vegetables which
may still be planted out.

As the native grass becomes dry, the danger from bush fires becomes
greater. Where such danger exists a strip should be ploughed round the
homestead. A double line of plough furrows about a chain apart, and then
on a calm day burn the grass between the furrows, will make a good fire-
break, and may be the means of saving the buildings should a fire break out.
If the orchard or garden are kept free from weeds and the headlands kept
cultivated, they are fairly free from danger of fire.

Any plants that it is necessary to plant out during the month should be
well shaded from the wind and sun until they become established.

Any plants that are not looking healthy or not making a satisfactory
growth should be given a little nitrate of soda or sulphate of potash as a
top dressing ; this will probably give them a fresh start. In the drier districts
the growth of vegetables and trees can be helped along by mulching round
the roots any stable manure well rotted, rotten leaves, bush rakings, decom-

posed straw, etc., will answer the purpose. This can be spread over the ground and will help to keep it moist. At the end of the summer it can be worked into the soil and will act as a manure. The mulching should not be allowed to touch the trunk of a tree or the stem of a plant.

Beans.—French and Kidney beans may be sown in any places where there is sufficient moisture to enable the crop to grow. Those already growing should be kept well hoed, and a little sulphate of potash may be applied along the rows and raked in. There are many varieties of both dwarf and climbing habits. One catalogue recently to hand contains a description of no less than 172 varieties of French and Kidney beans. This number should give gardeners plenty of choice as to which variety to grow, and out of such a number some varieties should be found to suit almost any conditions.

Beans.—Lima beans are a native of South America, and suitable to grow in a warm climate. They are highly esteemed in both North and South America, and should be much more used in this State than they are at present. In the Eastern States they are becoming very popular, and there is a steady demand. As they become better known here the demand will increase. There are both dwarf and climbing varietes, and the cultivation can be carried out the same as for French beans. The running varieties are strong climbers, and will soon cover a trellis. The pods are not edible ; it is only the bean that is good for food, and this may be used either in its green state, or after it has been dried. They are heavy bearers, and will stand a lot of hot weather.

Beans (Madagascar) are a perennial plant where the frost does not cut them down in winter. They are great climbers, and yield a large supply of beans in the summer months. The whole pod is eaten, the same as a French bean, but they are somewhat strong in flavour. Seed can be planted this month.

Beet (Red).—A few seeds may be sown to keep up a supply. The Globe variety is the best for summer growth. The seed should be soaked before sowing, and sown in moist land. If the ground is dry do not soak the seed, as the seed in this case often sprouts and then dies off.

Beet (Silver).—This is a splendid vegetable for summer use. If the outside leaves are taken off as required, the plant will continue to give a supply of leaves all through the summer.

Cabbage.—Only in very moist spots or where irrigation is possible will it be any use to plant cabbages out at this time of the year. Any young plants that are commencing to grow should be top dressed with a little nitrate of soda. This should be mixed with sand and spread along the rows, but should not be allowed to touch the leaves of the plants. If grubs are troublesome spray, with Paris green and water, in the proportion of 1oz. Paris green to 10 gallons of water. Make the Paris green into a paste before adding the water.

Carrots.—A few seeds may be sown to keep up a supply.

Celery.—Plants already growing should be earthed up to cause them to bleach. A little seed may be sown in a moist spot.

Choko.—A few of these fruits may be planted ; they will soon sprout in the warm weather ; they will require a trellis, as they are good climbers ; the fruit makes a variety for the table. Work a deep hole and manure well the same as for pumpkins.

Cucumbers.—Early sown plants will now be bearing.   Where sufficient moisture is obtainable a few more seeds may be sown.

Egg Plants.—Plant out any young plants and shade from the sun.   In moist localities a little more seed may be sown.

Maize.—Sweet maize should be more extensively cultivated than it is. It makes a good table vegetable.   If planted in rows, and the cultivator is kept going, it will stand a considerable amount of dry weather.

Melons and Pumpkins.—The cultivator should be kept going between these plants until the vines commence to run over the ground, and further cultivation is not practicable.   In moist localities seed of the bugle pumpkins and pie melons may be sown, but the hills should be well mulched with stable manure.

Okras.—Seeds planted last month should have now produced plants strong enough for transplanting.   The plants will require shading from the sun until the roots obtain a hold of the ground.

Sweet Potatoes.—Shoots and cuttings from vines already planted should now be available for planting out.   The cuttings should be set on ridges three feet apart, and about 18 inches apart in the rows.   Keep the ground cultivated until the vines begin to run.

Tomatoes.—From the early districts fruit will now be coming into market.   In cooler districts plants may still be planted out if shaded from the sun.   If the plants are staked and kept off the ground a much better yield of fruit is obtained, and the plants are kept free from disease.   Only smooth-skinned varieties should be sown, as they are more saleable than the rough-shaped ones.

Farm.—Hay-making will be the principal business on most farms during the month, while in earlier districts the grain will be also ripening. Harvesting operations will therefore occupy all the farmers' time.   At the time of writing there is every indication of the harvest being a good one, but much depends on the weather for the next few weeks.   The season is somewhat late, but this is no disadvantage, especially in the more southern area where the ground often remains soft until the crops are fit to cut; and an early ripening crop sometimes proves a disadvantage owing to the ground not being able to carry the harvesting machinery.   Owing to the interstate duties having lapsed in October, there will no doubt be a great influx of chaff from the Eastern States, and this will tend to keep the price in this State at a lower level.   Growers should take this fact into consideration when deciding as to whether to cut for hay or to keep their crops for grain. As many growers chaff their hay straight from the field they should be careful that it is thoroughly dry, otherwise it is liable to become heated in the bags and to deteriorate in value.

Early in the month such crops as cow peas, soy beans, velvet beans, sorghum and pearl millet, bugle pumpkins, and pie melons may be sown on fallow land, but the land should have been previously deeply worked to enable the roots to penetrate down into the soil.

LOCAL MARKETS' REPORTS.

STOCK AND STATION.

Messrs. John M. Hopkins and Co. report :—Business in the country and the city is more animated than heretofore. All classes of stock, if of right ages, are being eagerly purchased. Sales in the country and at our W.A. Stock Bazaar well attended. On Wednesday, the 3d inst., we sold, in conjunction with Messrs W. H. and J. De B. Morrison, the well-known milking Sorthhorn dairy herd of Mr. James Morrison, of Waterhall, Guildford. Prices for cows in full profit varied from 12½ to 17 guineas. The highest price realised was 18 guineas, paid by Mr. W. J. Butcher, M.L.A., for the well-known prize winner Snowflake. The principal purchasers were Mr. W. J. Butcher, M.L.A., Mr. Jos. Thomson, M.L.C., and Mr. Jas. Munro, of Cottesloe. Fat wethers, shorn, sold to 16s. 6d., the principal buyers being Staff-Captain Heads, of Collie, and Mr. M'Kenzie, of Armadale and Esplanade Hotel, Perth. We sold during the week a nice line of hoggets, wethers, at 16s. 6d. ; ewes at 24s ; lambs at 12s. Horses are in good demand, a line of mediums being placed at £42 per head. Farm mares continue in great demand, and record prices are ruling, varying from £40 to £50 per head. We sold on account of Mr. Sutton, of Mandurah, a line of light horses and ponies at £8 per head. Saturday's sale was well attended, and the bidding spirited. A line of fresh country horses sold at prices slightly in advance of ruling rates. Light delivery, £12 to £14 ; heavier types, from £20 to £24 ; hacks, to £22 10s. One stylish buggy pony reached £20. Aged draughts are hard to place, sales being made from £20 to £25 10s. ; aged mares, £21 10s. to £26. Farms continue in good demand ; properties with good established improvements are eagerly sought for. Cattle.—We sold heifers to £3 15s. ; a mixed line at £4 10s., with better sorts to £5 10s. per head ; Ayrshire bull, £5 10s. Demand for young cattle continues good.

DALGETY'S REPORT.

Messrs. Dalgety and Co., Ltd., report as follows :—

Wheat.—European markets are reported by cable as having slightly improved, and values of Australian wheat at port of call are valued at 29s. 9d., and for steamer shipments 29s. 3d. to 29s. 6d. per quarter of 480lbs. c.i.f. Cargoes for prompt shipment are inquired for, and buyers are prepared to give up to 30s. per quarter. Melbourne notify that the spot markets there remain steady, and to-day's values are given at 3s. 1d. to 3s. 3d. New wheat being sold for forward delivery at 3s. Adelaide report the wheat market there as quiet, parcels being quoted at 3s. 1½d. to 3s. 2d. per quarter.

Local Wheat.—Supplies forward have been in excess of the requirements, which has had the natural result of easing values all round. A heavy proportion of the wheat arriving proves to be affected by weevils, and this, consequently, reduces its value. Farmers now are realising the fact that there is no possibility of any advance in rates, and are quitting their holdings prior to the arrival of the new season's crop. Wheat this year has been far in excess of the requirements, naturally resulting in surplus stocks through the country. The importation of flour from the Eastern States has been very heavy during the season, consequently the demand for wheat has been restricted, flour being landed even with the duty on at the cost of that milled locally. Now that the duty has been abolished a further reduction in the price of wheat is anticipated, and during the coming season there is every possibility of an exceptionally heavy crop, which tends to point to low prices during the season.

Chaff.—The heavy supplies which were arriving during September have decidedly eased, and prices have slightly regained. Prime green wheaten, which has been in small supply, is receiving good attention, but cow chaff and inferior grades are in little or no demand. The tone of the merket is better throughout, but buyers are careful in their purchases, owing to the fact that, in several of the agricultural districts farmers are busy with their hay-cutting operations, and on the Greenough Flats hay has been cut prior to the 1st of the present month. There is every probability that during the course of the coming week a small proportion of the new chaff will be placed on the market, and, consequently, the last season's chaff will secure less attention, although we anticipate an advance of former seasons. We expect a large quantity of the new chaff will come forward in a heated condition, and if farmers are not careful heavy losses will be made. We would advise our clients, during their cutting operations, not to press the chaff too tightly in the bags, and, although bags are at an advanced price, it is better to place a less quantity in to prevent this heating which occurs when pressed too tightly. We would request our clients in general to consider the subject of their new season's chaff prior to its disposal, and remind them that, owing to the abolition of duty, the cheap freights allowed by the interstate steamers, and the enormous surplus of chaff anticipated in South Australia, will absolutely debar any high rates being secured at this centre during the coming season. It would be therefore advisable to secure any high rates if offered, or to place same through the medium of auction when advice is received to that effect. Ruling rates :—Prime green wheaten, £4 2s. 6d., with an occasional £4 5s. for primest grades ; fair average quality, £3 15s. to £3 17s. 6d. ; good sound medium with colour, £3 5s. to £3 7s. 6d. ; inferior, from £2 upwards.

Oaten Chaff.—A few trucks forward, realising £3 15s. per ton. This can be graded as fair average quality. The demand for oaten chaff is light ; small quantity would slump values.

Algerian oats have declined heavily in Melbourne. Stocks on spot are fairly heavy, and the minimum market quotations are 2s. 5½d. and 2s. 6½d. whole and crushed respectively. White oats ranging from 3s. 2d. crushed.

EASTERN AND SOUTHERN DISTRICTS' STOCK MARKET.

Messrs. Dalgety and Co., Ltd., York, report under date of October 10, as follows :—Business during the past week has been brisk, and good sales of stock have been effected. Fat sheep are coming into the markets more freely, whilst fat cattle are still rather scarce, and consequently selling well. Store sheep all round are a bit easier. Good baconers and porkers are in demand and few are offering. Horses are still rather dull of sale.

Pingelly Sale, October 4.—A full yarding of stock came forward, comprising 2,400 sheep, five head of cattle, eight horses, and 20 pigs. A large attendance of farmers and buyers were present, and a most successful sale resulted. We sold as follows :—Thirty-one fat lambs, 12s. 6d. ; 46 shorn fat wethers, 18s. 6d. ; 49 lambs, 12s. ; 20 mixed sheep, 7s. 6d. ; 10 lambs, 8s. ; 102 hoggets, 14s. 9d. ; 74 ewes and lambs, 22s. ; 355 ewes, 15s. 7d. ; 116 hoggets, 18s. 2d. ; 86 ewes, 17s. 9d. ; 45 ewes, 15s. 9d. ; 113 hoggets, 18s. 8d. ; two Shropshire rams, £2 2s. 6d. ; one ram, 30s. ; three old rams, 7s. 6d. ; two good sows, 20s. ; light-weight porkers, 10s. ; bull, £6 10s. ; dairy cows, £6 10s. to £7 ; yearling, 27s. 6d. to 30s. ; draught gelding, £19 10s. Next Pingelly sale, Wednesday, November 7.

York Sale, October 9.—Agents booked a good yarding of sheep, cattle, horses, and pigs. About 2,000 sheep, 10 head of cattle, 40 pigs and 12 horses were offered to a fair attendance of buyers. The yards were cleared with the exception of two small pens of sheep. Our sales were as under :—135 hoggets, 16s. ; 200 wethers, 16s. 6d. : 101 wethers, 16s. 6d. ; 325 wethers, 16s. 6d ; 31 wethers, 14s. 10d. ; 197 ewes, 15s. 3d. ; 102 hoggets, 17s. 3d. ; 100 hoggets, 16s. 10d. ; four fat bullocks, £9 15s. ; two fat steers, £4 15s. ; bull, £5 ; cow, £7 ; horses, draughts £20 to £35, light £5 to £11 10s. Next York sale, Tuesday, November 13.

KALGOORLIE.

Chaff report for week ending 11th October, 1906 :—Since last Saturday, supplies here have been light. On one or two days only a solitary truck reached Kalgoorlie ; yesterday and to-day the total amount was eight or nine trucks of medium quality. During the past week, prices have ranged up to £4 5s. No really prime green chaff has come through, and we consider nominal value of same to be £4 10s., and there is a very good inquiry for same for immediate delivery. Present prices are as follows :—Prime green wheaten, up to £4 10s. ; good wheaten, £4 2s. 6d. ; medium grades, up to £3 17s. 6d.

HIDES, SKINS, TALLOW, ETC.

Messrs. Dalgety and Co., Ltd., report :—

Sheepskins.—A good catalogue was offered to buyers, bidding being animated, and prices were somewhat better than last week's. We quote as under :—Superfine crossbred and merino, three-quarter to full wool, to 7¾d.; red and earthy fine crossbred and merino, 5½d. to 6½d.; good fine crossbred and merino, half to three-quarter wool, 6d. to 7½d.; red and earthy fine crossbred and merino, 5d. to 6d.; good fine crossbred and merino, quarter to half wool, 5d. to 6½d.; red and earthy fine crossbred and merino, 4¾d. to 5½d.; pelts, crossbred and merino, 4¾d. to 5½d. In all cases where pelts of above are sundried, weevil-eaten, torn, or perished, prices are from 1d. to 2d. below quotes.

Hides.—A good offering was forward, the market being firm at last week's quotations, which are :—Heavy special, none forward; medium and light, super condition, 5¾d. to 6d.; medium and light, ordinary, 5¼d. to 5¾d.; medium and light, dirty, 5d. to 5¼d; dry, 4¾d. to 7½d.; damaged and cut, 4½d. to 5¼d.; bulls and stags, 3d. to 4d.; tickies, 5¼d. to 5¾d.

Tallow.—Only a small offering forward, the market for which still remains firm. We quote (nominally) as under :—Super mixed, in casks, to 24s. per cwt.; good mixed, in casks, 20s. to 23s.; inferior mixed, in casks, 18s. to 22s.; medium mixed, tins and oddments, 18s. to 22s. 6d.

Kangaroo Skins.—A good offering of fair quality skins were forward, and last week's prices were fully maintained. ¾lb. to 1½lb. average, 2s. 5d. to 2s. 9d.; 1½lb. to 2lb. average, 1s. 10d. to 2s. 4d.; extra heavy and very light weight, 1s. 4d. to 2s.; damaged lines, 1s. 3d. to 2s. 3d.; brush kangaroo, 1s. 2d. to 1s. 5d.; euro skins, 1s. 3d. to 1s. 8d.; wallaroos, 1s. 6d. to 1s. 9d.

Opossum Skins.—A small offering was forward for to-day's sale, prices remaining about equal to last week's, with the exception of one extra good line of greys, which realised 9s. per dozen. Good greys and reds, to 8s. per dozen average; fair greys and reds, to 7s.; inferior greys and reds, 6s. to 6s. 6d.; blacks, 16s. to 24s.

Horns, Hair, etc.—Offerings have been very small of late, and we quote nominally :—Horns, in fresh condition, to 32s. per 100; horns, in stale condition, to 25s. Horsehair, to 1s. 4d. per lb. Cow hair, to 6½d. per lb. Rough bones, to 3s. 6d. per cwt.

GUTHRIE'S REPORT.

Messrs. Guthrie and Co., Ltd., report as follows in connection with produce markets :—

Wheat.—According to cable advices, the London market is firmer, and Australian wheat is now worth 31s. per quarter of 480lb. c.i.f., this being an improvement during the last 14 days of 1s. 6d. per quarter, and new season's cargoes are quoted at 30s. 6d. to 30s. 9d. per quarter. Adelaide and Melbourne markets are firmer, and business has been done at 3s. 2¾d. to 3s. 3d. per bushel, which is about equal to the present market rate for Western Australian milling wheat free from weevil. The local market is dull, and millers are evidently not buyers for any quantity. There are still moderate parcels in farmers' hands, and holders are now showing much more desire to sell, even on present low rates. During the past week deliveries at loading stations have not been heavy, and only limited quantities of this wheat have found their way to Perth. However, there have been several trucks of wheat rejected by millers placed on the Perth market, and this has had the effect of further weakening values at Perth. At the present time good sound wheat is worth, in Perth yard, 3s. 1½d. per bushel, although a fair quantity of the wheat now being delivered by farmers is more or less weevily. The grain weevil is yearly becoming a source of trouble, and farmers would do well to take precautions now that their sheds are empty, to have same thoroughly drenched with Jeyes's Cyllin before they start to cart new wheat. With regard to new wheat there is little disposition on the part of buyers to purchase, ideas being about 2s. 10d. per bushel at country stations, although, of course, prices will be generally influenced by the yield. The crops have still a critical time to pass through.

Chaff.—Kalgoorlie market has been receiving lighter supplies, and although prices have shown no material improvement, the general tone of the market is firm.

and good feed lines are being more readily quitted, and during the coming week prices should be a little better. At the present time, prime green wheaten chaff is not saleable in Kalgoorlie at anything over £4 5s. per ton. Perth and Fremantle yardings have been on the decrease, and a much better tone prevails, whilst the market is at least 2s. 6d. per ton firmer than at the time of our last report. Of course, a temporary interruption in the chaff arrivals at Perth would have no material effect on prices, as most merchants were during the recent glut able to take advantage of the position, and accumulate plentiful stocks of good chaff at low prices. We consider that during the balance of the present month the value of prime green chaff will be even slightly improved upon. The ruling rates to-day are :—Prime green wheaten, £4 2s. 6. per ton; f.a.q., £3 17s. 6d. per ton; best medium, £3 10s. to £3 12s. 6d. per ton; medium, £3; inferior from £2 per ton upwards. Oaten chaff has been sold at £3 15s. to £3 17s. 6d. per ton. At the present time, Perth supplies are being drawn chiefly from Northam districts. We are advised that already some farmers in the early districts have commenced to cut their new season's hay, so new chaff should be on the market about the end of the current month. Our Kalgoorlie office reports as follows :—For week ending the 10th inst., we have to report particularly light yardings, viz., 15 trucks in all. The arrivals to hand have not been prime green throughout. Every truck that has come to hand has contained a quantity of damaged bags. There is a good demand for a few trucks of really prime green. We have made sales as high as £4 5s., and think there is another 5s. per ton on present market for tip-top quality. The present market rates are :—Prime green, £4 5s. to £4 10s.; f.a.q., £4 per ton.

Algerian Oats.—Melbourne market is in a further state of collapse. Good feed are selling at 1s. 10½d. per bushel Melbourne. On spot stocks are fairly heavy, costing considerably more than present Melbourne parity. Quotations to-day are :— Whole, 2s. 7d.; crushed, 2s. 8d. per bushel on rails Fremantle.

New Zealand Oats.—Market dull, whole 3s. 1½d. per bushel, crushed 3s. 2¼d. per bushel on rails Fremantle.

Bran.—Is weaker in the Eastern States, and is now quoted at 8¼d. per bushel Adelaide. On spot the market is £4 12s. 6d. to £4 15s. per ton.

Pollard.—Also dull on spot, quoted at £4 17s. 6d. per ton.

Potatoes.—Best screened Red skins in new sacks are quoted at £6 10s. per ton aboard Melbourne. Stocks on spot are light, merchants being afraid to import on account of the early advent of local new potatoes. The market is steady at £8 7s. 6d. to £8 10s. per ton.

Onions.—Are much firmer in Melbourne at £7 to £8 per ton. Stocks on spot are absolutely bare. The market is nominally £9 10s. to £10 per ton.

WIGMORE'S REPORT.

Messrs. H. J. Wigmore and Co., of Fremantle, Kalgoorlie, and Northam, report as follows for week ended Friday, 12th inst. :—

Chaff.—Until to-day (Friday) comparatively small yardings have been experienced daily in Perth yards during present week. The total yardings, irrespective of imported chaff, amount to 78 trucks this week, as against 35 last week. We predicted last week that with normal yardings £4 2s. 6d. would probably be secured this week. As a matter of fact, we secured this price on Wednesday last. We consider that £4 2s. 6d. may again be realised during next week, and possibly £4 5s. for an extra prime sample, as it would appear now that very heavy yardings will not be forthcoming for some time, which, of course, is a distinct advantage to the producer. New chaff has not yet been in evidence in Perth yards, although we were advised that some was to have been forward on or about the 10th inst. Doubtless, however, the light rains which have been experienced in several districts in the country are responsible for this non-arrival. We should not be at all surprised, however, to see several trucks in during next week, but of course it all depends upon the weather. Cutting of the new crop is going on in several places, but of course, as a general rule, this will not be available for chaffing for perhaps a fortnight yet. Speaking generally, there is no doubt that the crops are somewhat behind last year. During the present week we have received several letters from farmer clients residing in various districts, pointing to a possible shortness of straw. If this is general, it would appear as if, during the present season, much more relatively will be stripped than during last season. Our advices, however, are not wide enough for us to form a definite opinion on this point. Imported chaff still continues to be forwarded to Perth in small quantities. To-day, for instance, £3 15s. was realised for one truck. This is somewhat higher than other sales this week. Kalgoorlie market, as will be seen from our appended report, is somewhat firmer, owing to lighter arrivals; £4 7s. 6d. is now possible for extra green samples at that centre, but qualities below prime it is still inadvisable to send to the goldfields. Chaff to Perth during the week has been received principally from the following centres:—Meenar, Woodside, York, Pinjarra, Wyola, Grass Valley, Meckering, Spencer's Brook, and Burges' Siding. To-day's yarding consisted of 26 trucks, highest price available being £4, which we secured for a truck of very nice chaff from Burges' Siding. We quote closing prices as follows:—Prime green wheaten, £4, and perhaps £4 2s. 6d. for a choice sample; f.a.q., £3 10s. to £3 15s.; good medium, £3 2s. 6d. to £3 7s. 6d.; medium and inferior qualities, from £2 upwards, according to condition. A larger quantity of oaten chaff than usual has found its way to Perth this week, and, as we anticipated, for prime stuff, £3 15s. was available; f.a.q. oaten is worth £3 2s. 6d. to £3 10s.

Wheat.—London markets continue very depressed, although there is a slight improvement noticeable during the last few days. Adelaide market is now considerably under Melbourne, the relative price for f.a.q. being 3s. 0½d. to 3s. 1½d., and 3s. 2½d. to 3s. 3½d. f.o.b. Melbourne. Considerable speculation, however, has been done for forward delivery of new wheat at prices which rather surprise us. The future of the wheat market, however, generally is by no means satisfactory. Local Wheat.— Very much depressed, owing to abnormal arrivals. If millers were purchasing, the comparatively small quantity received in Perth would soon be consumed, but as a matter of fact very few millers indeed are in the market for wheat, and those who are now prepared to purchase will not do so at present prices. When we refer to "abnormal arrivals" we, of course, mean for fowl-feed purposes only, and, generally speaking, all the wheat now coming into Perth is purchased only for poultry-feeding. As far as any forecast can be given, we should say that local wheat will fall to at least. 3s. in Perth in the near future; 3s. 1½d. wheat ex store is now offering.

Flour.—Nominally £7 15s., Northam, for Thomas' "Standard" and £7 2s. 6d. f.o.b. Adelaide for the same brand, quarter-sacks in each instance 5s. extra. Only small business has been possible during present week.

Oats appear to have steadied, but have touched as low a figure as 1s. 9½d. f.o.b. Melbourne for prime heavies. Our Melbourne advices go to show that the downward tendency has been checked. Spot prices are 2s. 6½d. whole, 2s. 7½d. crushed for good feed in truck lots.

Bran and Pollard.—Ninepence Adelaide, 8½d. Melbourne, and 8d¼. to 8½d. Sydney are ruling prices f.o.b. for bran and pollard. Spot prices have fallen with the remission of duty, and may be quoted at £4 15s. free on rails for bran and £4 17s. 6d for pollard.

Potatoes.—We quote best screened red skins f.o.b. Melbourne in sound sacks £6 5s. On spot we have made sales at £8 to £8 10s. for prime quality.

Onions.—Levien's screened £8 f.o.b. Melbourne; ordinary farmers' onions, £7 f.o.b. On spot onions have been somewhat scarce, and sales have been made at £8 10s., and even higher.

Jutes.—For October-November delivery cornsacks, lower prices are cabled from Calcutta. Bran bags maintain their price, and we again advise those farmers who require for early marketing, and have not already purchased, to do so immediately. So far as cornsacks are concerned, it is possible they may do better by waiting. seeing that October shipments from Calcutta would be in ample time for the grain crop. We invite inquiries about new and second-hand bags.

KALGOORLIE REPORT.

Our Kalgoorlie office reports:—A total of only 17 trucks chaff have arrived at this centre during week ended to-day. The market is 5s. to 7s. 6d. per ton firmer than at end of last week, and ruling price to-day for prime green wheaten is £4 5s. to £4 7s. 6d. We sold ex store at latter figure, and have also been successful in placing fair parcels ex country stations to outside Goldfields buyers at current Northam rates.

NOTES ON THE CLIMATE FOR SEPTEMBER, 1906.

The principal climatological feature of the month was the unseasonably low temperature. With the exception of Wyndham in the far North, the mean temperature at every station was below the average for previous years. At Perth the day temperature was the lowest on record, and at both Cue and Coolgardie, representing the Murchison and Yilgarn fields, it was the lowest, with the single exception of September, 1905.

Pressure was also subnormal, every station recording less than the average for previous years, the deficit in Southern portions being about one-tenth of an inch.

The weather was rather more rainy than usual in South-West districts, but elsewhere mostly fine. There was the usual succession of highs and lows, but special mention may be made of a disturbance which approached the West coast from the Indian Ocean on the 5th, and travelled overland to the Southern Ocean between Esperance and Eyre. It passed just South of Perth and was responsible for moderate to heavy rain in South-Western districts, and cloudy unsettled weather throughout the Southern half of the State.

On the whole the rainfall was about an inch in excess of the average in South-Western coastal districts, diminishing to about normal on the Eastern boundary of the South-Western division; elsewhere it was generally very light, except in the East Kimberly district, where 431 points were recorded at Turkey Creek, and 195 at Hall's Creek. This is the earliest heavy rain on record in that district.

Frost was occasionally reported from inland portions of the South-Western district, but it was never severe. The following table shows the mean and absolute lowest readings of a minimum thermometer placed on the ground's surface at a few typical stations :—

Station.			Mean.		Lowest.		Date.
Peak Hill ...	...	...	46·0	...	39·0	...	14
Cue	...	...	43·6	...	...	...	...
Coolgardie	...	...	38·3	...	30·0	...	12
Southern Cross	...	...	36·6	...	25·0	...	12
Walebing	...	...	33·8	...	25·0	...	11
York	...	...	39·2	...	32·0	...	8
Perth Observatory	...	...	44·4	...	38·6	...	11
Wandering	...	...	31·7	...	22·0	...	11
Bridgetown	...	...	35·9	...	26·0	...	10
Karridale	...	...	41·5	...	28·0	...	8
Katanning	...	...	34·8	...	26·0	...	2
Mount Barker	...	...	41·3	...	32·0	...	21

Observatory,
    Perth, 10th October,, 1906.

W. E. COOKE,
    Government Astronomer.

The Climate of Western Australia during September, 1908.

Locality	Barometer (corrected and reduced to sea-level).				Shade Temperatures.									Rainfall.		
					September, 1908.					Average for previous Years.						
	Mean of 9 a.m. and 3 p.m.	Average for previous years.	Highest for Month.	Lowest for Month.	Mean Max.	Mean Min.	Mean of Month.	Highest Max.	Lowest Min.	Mean Max.	Mean Min.	Highest ever recorded.	Lowest ever recorded.	Points (100 to inch) in Month.	Wet Days.	Total Points since Jan 1.
NORTH-WEST AND NORTH COAST:																
Wyndham	29·872	29·953	30·002	29·812	94·4	76·1	85·2	102·1	60·0	94·6	74·6	104·5	65·0	1	1	1316
Derby	29·984	29·971	30·073	29·810	92·1	64·0	78·0	98·8	49·0	94·2	65·4	108·0	54·5	Nil	...	1147
Broome	29·942	29·980	30·069	29·843	86·0	66·0	76·0	96·8	54·2	88·3	65·2	101·0	54·8	Nil	...	1016
Condon	29·922	30·009	30·097	29·843	82·8	57·1	70·0	90·0	47·2	84·8	56·2	98·8	42·0	12	1	675
Cossack	29·960	30·018	30·110	29·840	81·0	59·0	70·0	90·0	54·0	86·0	60·8	98·2	50·0	8	2	1013
Onslow	29·974	30·030	30·117	29·818	79·5	55·8	67·6	88·4	50·0	83·5	56·1	101·0	43·5	44	5	652
Winning Pool	29·977	...	30·107	29·818	78·4	53·6	66·0	85·6	46·0	...	...	...	...	19	3	928
Carnarvon	30·028	30·081	30·244	29·849	72·3	55·5	63·9	79·8	48·8	74·8	56·4	95·7	43·0	28	5	687
Hamelin Pool	30·016	30·072	30·206	29·848	71·9	51·2	61·6	78·8	44·0	76·6	51·7	96·8	40·0	11	3	546
Geraldton	30·022	30·104	30·246	29·797	68·3	51·0	59·6	77·8	43·8	70·9	51·9	94·0	39·0	246	17	1983
INLAND:																
Hall's Creek	29·913	29·996	30·156	29·738	92·1	62·4	77·2	101·0	37·4	93·2	60·1	100·4	42·2	195	4	587
Marble Bar	29·954	30·012	30·159	29·783	87·9	59·1	73·5	92·0	51·8	91·0	58·7	101·7	42·0	7	1	076
Nullagine	29·970	30·042	30·170	29·750	83·9	52·9	68·4	82·0	43·0	87·0	52·0	98·5	34·7	Nil	...	930
Peak Hill	29·946	30·010	30·210	29·728	73·0	51·0	62·0	84·1	42·0	76·7	48·0	91·0	38·1	15	3	891
Wiluna	29·996	30·076	30·212	29·752	71·8	49·0	59·9	81·0	40·0	75·3	49·6	93·8	33·7	12	1	697
Cue	...	...	...	...	71·3	47·3	59·3	81·0	37·8	75·3	...	93·2	37·0	21	3	874
Murgoo	29·975	30·076	30·201	29·727	70·2	47·1	58·6	81·0	40·0	...	...	...	...	12	2	704
Yalgoo	...	...	...	...	70·0	45·8	57·9	83·0	36·5	74·2	47·3	93·6	35·7	48	2	936
Nungarra	...	...	...	...	68·8	43·3	56·0	81·5	36·0	...	...	...	...	13	1	679
Lawlers	29·950	30·066	30·181	29·729	71·1	46·9	59·0	82·4	38·4	73·8	48·4	95·2	34·7	13	1	704
Laverton	29·969	30·054	30·267	29·679	72·3	46·3	59·3	84·2	36·9	73·3	47·7	94·5	32·3	13·	2	752
Menzies	29·979	30·076	30·231	29·730	69·0	44·1	56·6	80·0	37·0	71·7	47·6	92·1	33·5	Nil	...	903
Kanowna	...	...	...	...	67·1	43·9	55·5	79·2	36·2	...	...	...	...	2	1	887
Kalgoorlie	29·985	30·076	30·266	29·613	68·6	44·7	56·6	79·7	35·5	70·7	47·9	90·8	34·9	2	1	794
Coolgardie	29·968	30·075	30·262	29·606	67·0	43·4	55·2	79·0	33·2	70·3	46·3	92·0	35·0	16	3	845
Southern Cross	29·995	30·064	30·265	29·738	68·6	41·2	54·9	78·6	29·0	70·9	43·8	87·2	31·0	28	5	850
Kellerberrin	...	...	...	...	...	...	...	...	...	...	...	...	...	78	8	979
Walebing	...	...	...	...	63·2	40·6	51·9	75·2	29·5	65·8	43·8	79·9	32·4	241	20	1872
Northam	...	...	...	...	64·7	42·6	53·6	72·4	34·0	67·2	44·8	80·6	32·8	175	18	1661
York	30·002	30·098	30·288	29·740	64·2	42·3	53·2	72·0	34·0	67·8	43·3	84·7	31·8	144	17	1320
Guildford	...	...	...	...	64·6	46·7	55·6	71·8	36·0	67·6	48·9	83·0	37·7	389	17	2876

The Climate of Western Australia during September, 1908—continued.

Locality	Barometer (corrected and reduced to sea-level).				Shade Temperatures.									Rainfall.		
					September, 1906.					Average for previous Years.						
	Mean of 9 a.m. and 3 p.m.	Average for previous years.	Highest for Month.	Lowest for Month.	Mean Max.	Mean Min.	Mean of Month.	Highest Max.	Lowest Min.	Mean Max.	Mean Min.	Highest ever recorded.	Lowest ever recorded.	Points (100 to inch) in Month.	Wet Days.	Total Points since Jan. 1.
Perth Gardens ...	29·986	...	30·258	29·654	64·2	49·1	56·6	70·8	41·8	67·9	98	87·6	38·4	83	18	3022
Perth Observatory	30·000	30·092	30·261	29·645	62·9	48·1	55·5	68·2	40·3	66·0	50·2	86·4	39·0	83	19	3099
Fremantle ...	30·018	30·102	30·282	29·719	62·3	50·8	56·6	68·0	42·8	64·7	52·5	84·0	41·8	352	19	2387
Rottnest ...	29·996	30·097	30·259	29·709	61·6	52·0	56·8	65·8	47·6	64·3	53·6	88·0	42·6	66	16	2066
...h ...	...	30·088	...	...	62·5	46·9	54·7	61	30	65·3	50·0	82·0	35·0	88	19	90
Marradong ...	...	...	...	...	58·8	38·7	48·8	63·0	29·0	...	...	...	...	414	10	2590
Wandering ...	...	...	...	...	57·2	40·0	48·6	64·0	32·0	...	...	...	...	329	13	2294
...in ...	...	...	...	...	61·5	39·8	6·6	64·5	30·2	...	...	...	...	324	12	2142
Collie ...	...	...	...	...	62·4	42·2	51·8	65·9	30·6	63·2	41·9	78·7	29·5	514	17	87
Donnybrook ...	29·984	30·094	30·331	29·696	61·3	47·5	55·0	67·0	36·0	64·4	46·2	79·6	32·5	50	19	2743
Bunbury ...	...	...	...	...	60·8	44·5	52·6	65·0	34·1	65·1	49·2	83·8	32·2	516	20	2880
Busselton ...	29·962	...	30·255	29·649	59·0	47·4	53·2	6·8	43·0	63·9	49·4	78·8	34·2	328	23	2890
Cape ...te ...	...	...	...	...	60·2	40·1	50·2	65·9	32·0	...	...	...	...	328	23	2890
Bridgetown ...	29·935	30·079	30·260	29·530	60·0	41·0	50·5	66·0	34·0	6·6	42·2	79·2	31·5	372	21	3119
Karridale ...	29·915	30·086	30·260	29·490	60·0	51·0	55·6	64·0	46·0	63·3	48·1	82·5	31·5	532	24	3531
Cape Leeuwin ...	29·991	30·078	30·279	29·705	59·5	41·8	50·6	66·2	34·0	62·5	53·4	79·5	43·8	87	26	3070
t...g ...	...	...	...	...	57·4	42·3	49·8	65·2	32·0	63·7	43·4	81·1	29·8	87	14	1646
Mt. Barker ...	29·920	30·049	30·282	29·590	60·7	46·1	53·4	6·8	39·0	63·1	47·3	84·8	34·0	35	22	2243
...lny ...	29·920	30·044	30·279	29·479	57·8	48·4	53·1	69·0	41·5	60·6	50·2	84·2	37·1	451	24	3201
Breakers ...	29·920	30·062	30·272	29·620	64·6	46·0	55·3	6·8	39·5	66·1	47·9	86·6	35·2	380	26	2845
Esperance ...	29·939	30·048	30·271	29·627	67·1	42·3	54·7	82·5	31·4	67·9	43·8	87·2	28·8	305	11	2184
Balladonia ...	29·911	6·076	30·257	29 84	67·4	43·8	55·6	6·7	35·6	67·3	46·4	90·2	29·2	63	8	634
Eyre ...														54	6	839
INTERSTATE.																
Perth ...	30·000	30·102	30·261	29·645	62·9	48·1	55·5	8·2	40·3	66·0	50·2	86·4	39·0	393	19	3099
Adelaide ...	29·970	30·071	30·294	29·617	64·8	47·5	56·2	77·2	36·9	66·5	47·9	90·7	32·7	336	15	2078
Melbourne ...	29·963	29·992	30·385	29·518	62·2	45·7	54·0	76·1	36·0	62·6	45·4	81·8	32·1	384	12	
Sydney ...	30·080	30·045	30·380	29·740	65·0	51·0	58·0	70·0	44·0	66·3	51·4	89·8	40·8	136	12	2409

SOUTH-WEST AND SOUTH COAST:

The Observatory, Perth, 11th October, 1908.　　W. E. COOKE, Government Astronomer.

RAINFALL for August, 1906 (completed as far as possible), and for September, 1906 (principally from Telegraphic Reports).

Stations.	August. No. of points 100 = 1in.	No. of wet days.	September. No. of points 100 = 1in.	No. of wet days.	Stations.	August. No. of points 100 = 1in.	No. of wet days.	September. No. of points 100 = 1in.	No. of wet days.
EAST KIMBERLEY:					N.W. COAST—cont.				
Wyndham	Nil	...	1	1	Balla Balla	...	...	...	...
6-Mile	...	...	...	...	Whim Creek	410	7	11	2
Carlton	Nil	...	...	...	Mallina	353	6	...	2
Ivanhoe	Nil	...	...	...	Croydon	511	7	...	...
The Stud Station	...	...	...	...	Sherlock	...	...	...	...
Argyle Downs	Nil	...	.	...	Woodbrooke	382	5	...	...
Rosewood Downs	...	...	...	...	Cooyapooya	332	6	...	...
Lissdell	...	...	...	...	Roebourne	365	7	6	2
Turkey Creek	Nil	...	431	6	Cossack	501	7	8	2
Ord River	...	...	...	...	Fortescue	396	5	3	1
Alice Downs	...	...	...	...	Mardie	461	6	11	4
Flora Valley	Nil	..'	...	...	Chinginarra	365	5	10	4
Hall's Creek	Nil	...	195	4	Yarraloola	344	4	20	1
Nicholson Plains	...	...	...	...	Peedamullah	346	4	41	3
Ruby Plains	...	...	...	...	Onslow	366	8	44	5
Denison Downs	...	...	...	...	Point Cloates	450	9	...	...
WEST KIMBERLEY:					N.W. INLAND:				
Mt. Barnett	...	...	...	...	Warrawagine	120	1	...	...
Corvendine	...	...	...	...	Eel Creek	145	2	...	...
Leopold Downs	...	...	...	...	Muccan	...	...	...	...
Fitzroy Crossing (P.O.)	Nil	...	1	1	Ettrick	...	...	...	...
Cherrabun	Nil	...	...	...	Mulgie	...	...	...	...
Bohemia Downs	...	...	...	...	Streely	...	...	...	...
Quanbun	63	1	...	...	Warralong	103	3	...	...
Nookanbah	...	...	...	...	Coongon	102	2	...	...
Upper Liveringa	...	...	...	...	Talga	120	2	...	...
Yeeda	24	2	...	...	Bamboo Creek	170	4	10	1
Derby	38	1	Nil	...	Moolyella	...	...	...	...
Pt. Torment	78	1	...	...	Marble Bar	135	6	7	1
Obagama	20	1	...	...	Warrawoona	178	5	10	1
Beagle Bay	...	...	...	...	Corunna Downs	175	6	...	...
Roebuck Downs	...	...	...	...	Mt. Edgar	...	...	...	...
Kimberley Downs	...	...	...	...	Nullagine	228	6	Nil	...
Broome	44	2	Nil	...	Middle Creek	180	6	...	...
Thangoo	...	...	...	...	Mosquito Creek	162	4	...	...
La Grange Bay	40	2	3	1	Roy Hill	389	4	...	...
					Bamboo Springs	...	...	...	...
N.W. COAST:					Kerdiadary	524	5	...	...
Wallal	45	2	30	2	Woodstock	459	6	...	...
Pardoo	...	...	...	...	Yandyarra	449	7	...	...
Condon	107	2	12	1	Station Peak	...	...	...	...
DeGrey River	...	...	...	...	Mulga Downs	426	7	...	...
Port Hedland	126	6	5	1	Mt. Florence	420	6	...	...
Boodarie	187	6	...	...	Tambrey	...	...	...	...
					Millstream	429	6	...	...

RAINFALL—continued.

STATIONS.	AUGUST. No. of points. 100 = 1in.	AUGUST. No. of wet days.	SEPTEMBER. No. of points. 100 = 1in.	SEPTEMBER. No. of wet days.	STATIONS.	AUGUST. No. of points. 100 = 1in.	AUGUST. No. of wet days.	SEPTEMBER. No. of points. 100 = 1in.	SEPTEMBER. No. of wet days.
N.W. INLAND—cont.					**YALGOO DISTRICT**—				
Red Hill	371	8	...	...	contd.				
Mt. Stewart	447	7	...	...	Mullewa	269	7	62	10
Peake Station	...	...	...	...	Kockatea	241	6	...	...
Nanutarra	...	...	...	...	Barnong	266	4	24	1
Yanrey	900	7	...	...	Gullewa	207	6	...	...
Wogoola	585	5	...	...	Gullewa House	233	5	18	1
Towera	440	6	...	...	Gabyon	269	8	42	3
					Mellenbye	195	6	27	7
					Wearagaminda	225	8	...	...
GASCOYNE:					Yalgoo	284	6	48	2
Winning Pool	479	5	19	3	Wagga Wagga	233	7	...	...
Coordalia	...	...	...	...	Muralgarra	227	3	...	...
Wandagee	...	...	...	...	Burnerbinmah	232	6	26	2
Williambury	518	9	...	...	Nalbara	214	6	20	2
Yanyeareddy	...	...	...	...	Wydgee	354	6	...	...
Maroonah	651	4	...	...	Field's Find	266	6	9	4
Ullawarra	...	...	...	...	Thundelarra	...	...	47	4
Mt. Mortimer	...	...	...	...	Rothesay	208	6	59	6
Edmunds	368	7	...	...	Ninghan	292	6	34	3
Gifford Creek	459	7	...	...	Condingnow	244	6	...	...
Bangemall	409	4	...	...	163-Mile	312	5	...	...
Mt. Augustus	...	...	...	...	Palaga Rocks	337	5	...	...
Upper Clifton Downs	430	9	...	...	126-Mile	279	5	57	4
Clifton Downs	594	6	...	...	90-Mile	243	4	49	2
Dairy Creek	510	8	...	...	Mt. Jackson	213	6	38	6
Mearerbundie	465	9	...	...					
Byro	580	7	...	...	**MURCHISON:**				
Meedo	292	7	..	...	Wale	264	6	...	...
Mungarra	515	6	...	...	Yallalonga	254	9	...	...
Bintholya	...	...	...	...	Billabalong	351	8	...	...
Lyons River	606	9	...	...	Twin Peaks	273	9	...	...
Booloogooroo	...	...	...	...	Murgoo	351	8	12	2
Doorawarrah	448	11	...	...	Mt. Wittenoom	284	6	...	...
Brick House	315	8	29	3	Meka	386	8	...	...
Boolathana	341	10	24	3	Wooleane	346	8	...	...
Carnarvon	355	10	26	5	Boolardy	452	9	...	...
Dirk Hartog	482	...	117	1	Woogorong	336	8	...	...
Sharks Bay	357	7	19	2	Manfred	...	...	...	...
Wooramel	234	7	49	4	Yarra Yarra	440	7	...	...
Hamelin Pool	334	9	11	3	Milly Milly	519	7	...	...
Kararang	304	8	...	..	Berringarra	502	7	...	...
Tamala	...	...	...	...	Mileura	394	9	...	...
					Mt. Gould	352	8	...	...
					Moorarie	329	7	...	...
YALGOO DISTRICT:					Wandary	...	...	...	...
Woolgorong	220	6	...	...	Peak Hill	621	8	15	3
New Forest	261	7	...	...	Mt. Fraser	...	...	...	...
Yuin	194	6	25	4	Minderoo	3'0	5	Nil	..
Pindathuna	270	4	...	...	Abbotts	318	4	7	1
Tallyrang	203	5	...	...	Belele	305	7	27	2

RAINFALL—continued.

STATIONS.	AUGUST. No. of points. 100 = 1in.	AUGUST. No. of wet days.	SEPTEMBER. No. of points. 100 = 1in.	SEPTEMBER. No. of wet days.	STATIONS.	AUGUST. No. of points. 100 = 1in.	AUGUST. No. of wet days.	SEPTEMBER. No. of points. 100 = 1in.	SEPTEMBER. No. of wet days.
MURCHISON—contd.					**NORTH COOLGARDIE GOLDFIELDS—contd.**				
Meekatharra ...	...	...	...	...	Goongarrie ...	307	7	17	2
Gabanintha ...	339	5	28	1					
Quinns ...	419	4	...	...	**COOLGARDIE GOLDFIELDS:**				
Nannine ...	351	5	1N	2	Waverley ...	319	6	...	...
Annean ...	346	6	...	...	Bardoo ...	330	6	3	1
Tuckanarra ..	320	3	25	1	Broad Arrow ...	319	6	5	2
Coodardy ..	426	7	Nil	...	Kanowna ...	319	9	2	1
Cue ...	499	8	21	3	Kurnalpi ...	295	5	22	2
Fay Dawn ..	437	6	Nil	...	Bulong ...	316	8	9	3
Lake Austin ..	545	6	22	...	Kalgoorlie ...	318	6	2	1
Lennonville ...	347	7	16	2	Coolgardie ...	327	8	16	8
Mt. Magnet ...	361	7	13	2	Burbanks ...	300	7	26	2
Youeragabbie ...	358	4	7	1	Bulla Bulling ...	332	6	27	3
Murrum ...	226	4	...	...	Woolubar ...	300	4	...	...
Challa ...	351	6	5	1	Waterdale ...	323	6	...	...
Nunngarra ...	426	5	13	1	Widgiemooltha...	272	9	77	9
Birrigrin ...	328	4	21	1	50-Mile ...	278	6	51	7
					Norseman ...	225	8	72	5
EAST MURCHISON:					Lake View ...	218	10	110	11
Gum Creek ...	367	5	Nil	...	Frazer Range ...	171	9	69	6
Dural ...	262	6	...	...	Southern Hills...	144	5	...	...
Wiluna ...	250	9	12	1					
Mt. Sir Samuel ...	236	6	15	2	**YILGARN GOLDFIELDS:**				
Leinster G.M. ...	...	...	...	...	129-Mile... ...	225	8	...	...
Lawlers ...	181	7	13	1	Emu Rocks ...	152	8	97	11
Poison Creek ...	276	8	...	...	56-Mile	215	3	88	2
Wilson's Patch...	...	...	2	1	Glenelg Rocks ...	119	10	101	14
Lake Darlot ..	...	...	...	...	Burracoppin .	114	4	71	6
Darda ...	186	5	11	2	Bodallin ...	115	3	49	2
Salt Soak ...	225	10	17	3	Parker's Road ...	187	4	61	3
Duketon ...	212	6	15	1	Southern Cross ...	199	8	28	5
					Parker's Range...	177	8	65	9
NORTH COOLGARDIE GOLDFIELDS:					Yellowdine ...	201	4	41	2
Burtville ...	...	...	...	...	Karalee	205	2	40	2
Laverton ..	220	8	13	2	Koorarawalyee..	201	5	90	8
Mt. Morgans ..	232	5	8	1	Boorabbin ...	240	7	57	5
Murrin Murrin..	256	8	10	2	Boondi	226	8	24	9
Mt. Malcolm ..	226	7	5	1					
Mt. Leonora ..	275	7	5	1	**SOUTH-WEST (NORTHERN DIVISION):**				
Tampa ...	284	6	Nil	...	Murchison House	390	9	...	...
Kookynie ..	302	7	38	2	Mt. View ...	285	4	...	...
Niagara	287	6	20	1	Mumby	393	9	163	12
Yerilla ...	410	5	20	1	Northampton ...	444	7	200	10
Yundamindera .	394	10	46	2	Chapman Experimental Farm	348	5	146	10
Mt. Celia ...	302	9	45	2	Narra Tarra ...	368	5	251	11
Edjudina ..	305	8	...	...					
Quandinnie ...	374	5	...	...					
Menzies ...	332	6	Nil	...					
Mulline ...	414	10	33	4					
Mulwarrie ..	348	8	41	5					

RAINFALL—continued.

STATIONS.	August. No. of points. 100 = 1in.	August. No. of wet days.	September. No. of points. 100 = 1in.	September. No. of wet days.	STATIONS.	August. No. of points. 100 = 1in.	August. No. of wet days.	September. No. of points. 100 = 1in.	September. No. of wet days.
SOUTH - WEST (NORTHERN DIVISION)—contd.					SOUTH-WEST (METROPOLITAN)—cont.				
Oakabella ...	497	8	238	12	Fremantle ...	424	12	352	19
White Peak ...	...	...	...	...	Rottnest	314	14	308	16
Geraldton ...	601	7	246	17	Rockingham ...	522	11	439	18
Hinton Farm ...	...	...	...	...	Jandakot ...	554	12	417	15
Tibradden ...	414	8	...	...	Armadale ...	549	12	394	22
Myaree	312	7	...	...	Mundijong ...	515	11	330	19
Sand Springs ...	405	7	187	11	Jarrahdale ...	744	13	562	20
Nangetty ...	247	7	121	12	Jarrahdale (Norie)	724	13	505	18
Greenough ...	465	8	127	11	Serpentine ...	600	12	430	17
Bokara	370	8	239	17	EXTREME SOUTH-				
Dongara ...	464	7	245	14	WEST :				
Strawberry ...	378	6	174	13	Mandurah ...	...	...	...	...
Yaragadee ...	230	4	...	...	Pinjarrah (Blythe-	581	13	538	19
Urella	234	5	...	...	wood)	533	14	531	17
Opawa	318	7	88	11	Pinjarrah ...				
Manara	...	...	138	...	Upper Murray ...	575	10	559	18
Mingenew ...	377	7	128	13	Yarloop	755	13	715	21
Yandenooka ...	370	9	168	11	Harvey	626	12	632	19
Arrino	...	...	218	14	Brunswick ...	595	13	515	21
Carnamah ...	462	9	161	13	Collie	539	10	646	14
Jun Jun	...	...	180	15	Glen Mervyn ...	459	13	514	17
Watheroo ...	270	9	234	14	Donnybrook ...	459	13	496	18
Nergaminon ...	...	...	...	...	Boyanup ...	482	11	570	19
Dandaragan ..	276	8	351	16	Bunbury ...	453	14	516	20
Yatheroo ...	290	7	298	13	Elgin	440	15	612	21
Moora	250	8	316	14	Busselton ...	346	14	616	19
Walebing ...	305	11	241	20	Quindalup ...	544	13	423	24
Round Hill ...	271	9	242	16	Cape Naturaliste	547	14	476	17
New Norcia ...	280	11	242	19	Glen Lossie ...	388	14	323	23
Wongon Hills ...	245	9	...	...	Karridale ...	...	...	...	...
Wannamel ...	379	11	373	17	Cape Leeuwin ...	391	13	532	24
Gingin	362	11	397	12	Lower Blackwood	433	22	437	26
					Ferndale ...	497	15	462	23
					Greenbushes ..	460	11	462	12
					The Peninsula ...	412	14	422	14
SOUTH-WEST (METROPOLITAN) :					Cooeearup ...	432	14	...	...
Wanneroo ...	342	11	262	13	Bridgetown ...	418	16	372	21
Belvoir	420	12	291	17	Hilton	332	8	411	8
Wandu	480	13	395	23	Greenfields ...	414	10	484	18
Mundaring ...	651	13	583	18	Cundinup ...	332	9	...	...
Canning Water- works	583	12	485	16	Wilgarrup ...	372	14	404	21
					Balbarrup ...	424	8	500	16
Kalbyamba ...	486	9	413	16	Bidellia ...	...	...	...	...
Guildford ...	417	12	389	17	The Warren ...	...	...	...	...
Perth Gardens ...	507	11	343	18	Westbourne ...	...	...	...	...
Perth Observatory	553	13	393	19	Deeside	879	15	...	...
Highgate Hill ...	505	12	323	18	Riverside ...	295	12	406	...
Subiaco	512	12	395	19	Mordalup ...	316	13	417	20
Claremont ...	441	12	386	17	Lake Muir ...	274	13	356	15

RAINFALL—*continued.*

STATIONS.	August. No. of points. 100 = 1in.	August. No. of wet days.	September. No. of points. 100 = 1in.	September. No. of wet days.	STATIONS.	August. No. of points. 100 = 1in.	August. No. of wet days.	September. No. of points. 100 = 1in.	September. No of wet days.
EASTERN AGRICULTURAL DISTRICTS:					GREAT SOUTHERN RAILWAY LINE—*contd.*				
Emungin ...	182	10	224	17	Woodyarrup ...	189	10	312	11
Dowerin ...	197	6	146	11	Pallinup ...	158	7	253	9
Oak Hill ...	...	...	...	...	Tambellup ...	209	8	...	...
Hatherley ...	166	5	...	...	Toolbrunup ...	210	7	266	13
Momberkine ...	225	7	210	10	Cranbrook ...	242	12	291	17
Eumalga ...	312	11	209	15	Stirling View ...	226	11	362	20
Bolgart ...	249	10	212	12	Kendenup ...	316	11	384	22
Newcastle ...	323	11	191	11	Woogenellup ...	190	12	...	...
Craiglands ...	336	9	342	18	Wattle Hill ...	262	15	378	20
Eadine ...	394	12	...	...	St. Werburgh's ...	244	14	322	22
Northam ...	243	10	175	13	Mt. Barker ...	336	17	345	22
Grass Valley ...	...	...	...	...					
Cobham ...	256	6	162	12					
York ...	238	10	144	17					
Burrayocking ...	223	11	130	13					
Meckering ...	169	7	130	9					
Cunderdin ...	168	8	134	8	WEST OF GREAT SOUTHERN RAILWAY LINE:				
Doongin ...	183	7	106	9	Talbot House ...	258	7	182	10
Whitehaven ...	261	6	...	...	Jelcobine ...	310	7	219	11
Mt. Caroline ...	155	5	128	9	Bannister ...	485	11	...	...
Cutenning ...	...	...	...	...	Wandering ...	343	11	329	13
Kellerberrin ...	182	8	78	8	Glen Ern ...	352	11	244	15
Cardonia ...	138	7	...	...	Marradong ...	430	10	414	10
Baandee ...	178	3	81	6	Wonnaminta ...	319	13	...	...
Nangeenan ...	120	4	144	7	Williams ...	311	9	...	...
Merredin ...	135	7	82	9	Rifle Downs ...	407	8	406	8
Codg-Codgen ...	116	10	...	...	Darkan ...	...	...	...	...
Noongarin ...	137	8	106	8	Arthur River ...	292	7	300	11
Mangowine ...	145	8	...	...	Gainsborough ...	222	9	216	11
Yarragin ...	...	...	...	...	Glenorchy ...	362	8	305	11
Wattoning ...	...	...	...	...	Kojonup ...	260	9	281	7
					Blackwattle ...	202	4	...	...
					Warriup ...	290	16	307	20
GREAT SOUTHERN RAILWAY LINE:					Forest Hill ...	443	16	401	22
Dalebridge ...	273	8	201	15					
Beverley ...	289	8	176	13					
Brookton ...	289	7	183	12	EAST OF GREAT SOUTHERN RAILWAY LINE:				
Sunning Hill ...	319	12	208	19					
Pingelly ...	234	8	188	8	Sunset Hills ...	231	7	...	...
Yornaning ...	213	10	213	14	Oakdale ...	241	9	150	11
Narrogin ...	289	12	268	11	Barrington ...	191	5	139	12
Narrogin Experimental Farm	461	11	324	12	Bally Bally ...	250	9	...	...
Wagin ...	260	10	290	8	Stock Hill ...	267	7	195	10
Katanning ...	196	13	347	14	Qualin ...	215	5	156	11
Sunnyside ...	233	15	281	17	Woodgreen ...	156	7	77	11
Broomehill ...	232	11	291	13	Gillimanning ...	222	8	187	13

RAINFALL—*continued.*

Stations.	August. No. of Points. 100 = 1in.	August. No. of wet days.	September. No. of points. 100 = 1in.	September. No. of wet days.	Stations.	August. No. of points. 100 = 1in.	August. No. of wet days.	September. No. of Points. 100 = 1in.	September. No. of wet days.
EAST OF GREAT SOUTHERN RAILWAY LINE—*cont.*					SOUTH COAST—*cont.*				
					Peppermint Grove	250	13	...	...
					Bremer Bay ...	211	15	341	13
Wickepin ...	226	8	230	14	Coconarup ...	152	12	229	15
Crooked Pool ...	217	6	258	14	Ravensthorpe ...	178	13	249	16
Nalyring ...	...	...	317	13	Cowjanup ...	152	12	235	...
Bunking ...	164	6	252	10	Hopetoun ...	256	7	271	16
Bullock Hills ...	228	9	259	8	Fanny's Cove ...	219	8	...	...
Dyliabing ...	259	11	...	...	Park Farm ...	218	14	...	...
Glencove ...	224	9	268	13	Grass Patch ...	206	18	...	...
Cherillalup ...	252	8	303	16	Swan Lagoon ...	180	8	...	...
Mianelup ...	172	10	265	15	30-Mile ...	191	10	...	...
Woolgaanup ...	152	8	261	11	Gibson's Soak ...	260	11	282	15
Chillinup ...	220	2	251	4	Myrup ...	305	18	...	...
Jarramongup ...	...	...	...	...	Esperance ...	266	17	305	11
					Boyatup ...	253	9	...	...
					Lynburn ...	275	14	...	...
SOUTH COAST:					Middle Island ...	138	15	...	...
Wilson's Inlet ...	423	17	405	24	Point Malcolm ...	187	13	...	...
Grasmere ...	325	14	433	25	Israelite Bay ...	117	11	157	10
King River ...	282	10	430	18	Balbinia ...	...	...	...	...
Albany	421	16	451	24	Balladonia ...	100	8	63	8
Point King ...	355	11	520	17	Eyre	140	13	54	6
Breaksea ...	434	16	380	26	Mundrabella ...	...	...	...	...
Cape Riche ...	242	10	314	7	Eucla	228	14	15	8

The Observatory, Perth,
    10th October, 1906.

W. E. COOKE,
Government Astronomer.

By Authority: FRED. WM. SIMPSON, Government Printer, Perth.

[Registered at the General Post Office for transmission by Post as a Newspaper.]

JOURNAL

OF THE

DEPARTMENT OF AGRICULTURE

OF

WESTERN AUSTRALIA.

By Direction of

The HON. THE MINISTER OF AGRICULTURE.

PUBLISHED MONTHLY.

Vol. XIV.—Part 5.

NOVEMBER, 1906.

PERTH:

BY AUTHORITY: FRED WM. SIMPSON, GOVERNMENT PRINTER

1906.

WESTERN AUSTRALIAN GOVERNMENT.

IMMIGRATION.

Nominated Passages.

Persons having friends and relatives in the United Kingdom who are desirous of emigrating to Western Australia may obtain passages at half the ordinary fares by nominating them to the Hon. Colonial Secretary in Perth.

Fares from £6 10s. to £14 10s.

Clerks, artizans, and mechanics will **not** be accepted.

Advanced Passages.

Working men and others resident in the State may obtain an advance of passage money, including railway fares from port of arrival to destination, to bring their wives and families from the Eastern States and New Zealand to this State.

Such advances to be repaid within six or twelve months, according to the amount advanced.

A responsible guarantor must be provided.

Special Concessions are provided for Settlers taking up Land.

Full particulars can be obtained upon application to the Under Secretary, Colonial Secretary's Department, Perth.

By order,

F. D. NORTH,

Under Secretary.

JOURNAL

OF THE

Department of Agriculture

OF

WESTERN AUSTRALIA.

| Vol. XIV. | NOVEMBER, 1906. | Part 5. |

EDITOR'S NOTES.

VEGETABLE GROWING.—Owing to the Annual Report of the Department of Agriculture being published in this issue the continuation of the article on "Vegetable Growing," together with other useful matter, is unavoidably held over.

PROCESS OF MAKING RUBBER.—A machine has been invented in England for the making of rubber from wheat. It is claimed that a substance in many respects equally as good as the natural rubber can be produced at a very low cost.

FLAX GROWING.—The Department is obtaining a flax-making machine for display at the forthcoming exhibition at Perth, and will be glad to obtain a supply of the linseed fibre for treatment. Persons having any on hand are requested to communicate with the Department of Agriculture, Perth.

COTTON GROWING.—The Department of Agriculture intend to exhibit a ginning machine at the forthcoming Chamber of Manufactures' Exhibition to be held in Perth next month. The Department will be glad to hear of anyone having any cotton bolls on hand, which, if forwarded, will be treated at the Exhibition.

WHEAT GROWING.—From recent exchanges we learn that Canada's progress in wheat-growing is the agricultural phenomenon of the day. The area under wheat in Manitoba in 1906 is officially estimated at 3,141,537 acres, against 2,643,588 in 1905, an increase of 497,949 acres, or about 19 per cent.

HANDLING BEES.—It is not generally known that anyone attending to bees may escape many stings by first thoroughly washing their hands, then rubbing them all over with a little pure beeswax. This prevents any odour from the hands being noticed by the bees. The scent from beeswax attracts a bee's attention very strongly, and seems to deprive them of any exhibition of hostility or bad temper.

SHEEP RAISING.—Considerable interest is being taken amongst our farmers as to the wisdom of feeding sheep on cultivated land. It is claimed that by so doing better feed is supplied, at the same time the ground is considerably improved by the rest and manuring it obtains.. As the system has not been in force long enough in this State to obtain reliable data, we would be glad to hear from any settler who has had any experience in this matter.

BUTTER TESTS.—An interesting report on a series of butter tests with Shorthorn and Jersey cows, carried out on the Experimental Farm of the Somerset County Council in four seasons, has been contributed by Mr. J. H. Burton to the *Journal of the Board of Agriculture*. Ten pedigree Jerseys and six non-pedigree Shorthorns were obtained at starting, and the numbers were substantially the same throughout the trial, vacancies being made good. The treatment of the two lots was in all respects identical, except that the Shorthorns, of course, consumed much more food than the Jerseys. Altogether eighty-six tests were made in the four seasons, and the average butter ratios (pounds of milk per pound of butter) were 27·92 for Shorthorns and 19·09 for Jerseys. The actual quantities of butter obtained in eighty-one tests from 343¼ gallons of milk were 124lbs. 15¾ozs. from Shorthorns, and 180lbs. 9½ozs. from Jerseys.

THE PRICE OF PRODUCE.—Speaking in connection with the ceremony of laying the foundation of the Meckering Agricultural Hall recently, the Hon. the Minister for Agriculture (Mr. James Mitchell) said that wherever he went he heard a certain number of people crying out that the prices were going to be so low that agriculture would not be worth following, but he urged them not to pay too much heed to those to whose interest it was to cry prices down. In Adelaide and Melbourne the present price of wheat was about 3s. per bushel, and chaff was about the same as in Western Australia. Wheat could not be landed from the Eastern States at less than 6d. per bushel. It was easy for the few millers in the State to put their heads together and say they would not give more than a certain price, but the producers should find a means of combining for the protection of their own interests. The farmers should get at least 3s. per bushel, if not more, for their wheat this season. It would soon be necessary for them to go in seriously for exporting, and the Government would have to assist. Some people blamed the Government for reducing the freight on timber for export whilst keeping up the freight on timber for home consumption, but he thought it was a perfectly right thing to do. Something of the sort would have to be done in regard to wheat for export. And the Government would have to recognise that they must place their producers on such a footing that they could compete in the world's markets with the producers of other countries.—*Exchange*.

STOOKING.—In the matter of setting up sheaves after cutting, there are apparently great differences in practice between different parts of the country. It is called thraving in some districts, though one never sees a complete thrave nowadays. Twenty-four sheaves make a thrave, but it is seldom that more than six are put in a stook now. The name thrave has survived long after the time when cutting and tying by hand was let at so much per thrave of 24 sheaves, each sheaf of a certain diameter—which was tested by the farmer or his foreman from time to time. It may seem to some quite unnecessary to give instructions on the art of stooking, but the writer knows of whole districts where farm workers do not know how to "set up." In such places the style followed is for two men to work together, one picks up a sheaf and dumps it down on its end, and waits till his mate dumps the other alongside it. Three couples of sheaves are put down this way, all standing more or less perpendicular on their own bottoms. The result is that a lot of sheaves tumble down before the row is finished, whilst the least wind blows the half of them over, and they do not protect each other from rain. The proper method is for each man to work a row of stooks by himself. He should take a sheaf under each arm, set their butts on the ground, and draw the heads up together. Then the outside couples should be done the same way, and in addition slanted inwards to the middle couple. By following this plan the stook is made to prop itself up, and it will stand any ordinary wind without being blown over, while as the tops are slanted inwards towards a point or a ridge they act like a roof and shed the rain off to an amazing extent.

HALL'S CREEK STOCK ROUTE.—The following telegram has been received by the Secretary for Mines from Hall's Creek, Kimberley. It is dated Thursday, November 1, 1906, and the author is Mr. A. W. Canning, who led an exploring party from Black Range to Hall's Creek with the object of opening up a stock route:—"The route travelled by us was via the east portion of Nabberu, Windich, Pierre, and Weld Springs, thence generally towards North-West and Lake Disappointment, passing several waters and large lake thirty miles from Weld Springs, fair amount good country, and a number of prominent hills. Thence round north end of lake, thence to separation Well. Good feeding country generally to twenty miles west of Well. Patchy, good-looking auriferous country thirty miles west of Separation Well. From Separation, fifty degrees to limestone flat extending west of Lake Auld. Propose to leave Separation Well out of stock route, going via Helen Hill and Auld Lake. Thence along flat easterly and north-easterly to Godfrey Tank, passing several small grassy lakes. Godfrey Tank now dry. Thence a little north of east to lakes west of Sturt's Creek, along watercourse to creek, up Sturt's Creek and Cow Creek to Flora Valley, junction of Elvire and Johnston Rivers. We camped there, borrowed horses from Gordon Bros., came to Hall's Creek, and passed extensive old oak patches. Thirty-five permanent waters sunk, eight wells cleaned out, and sunk on fifteen native wells. Put down two bores; generally sandstone or limestone cement; very little timber required. Natives numerous all along route, and invaluable to us, giving information readily. Party worked splendidly; Trotman particularly useful. If wells stand drawing, as I anticipate, route ought, when finished, be about best watered stock route in colony. A great deal of soft spinifex. Will send written report next mail, which will reach you about Christmas."

ANNUAL REPORT.

DEPARTMENT OF AGRICULTURE.

The Hon. Minister for Agriculture.

SIR,

I have the honour to submit herewith the Annual Report of this Department for the year ending 30th June, 1906, embodying the reports of the various officers in the Professional Division.

The following is a statement of the expenditure for the period under review :—

	Amount on Estimates.	Actual Expenditure.
	£	£
Agriculture	23,454	23,533
Refrigerating Works	3,940	3,312
Stock	3,181	2,951
Rabbits, etc.	20,200	17,514
	50,775	49,310
Less revenue received	...	9,699
Net cost	...	£39,611

We spent, therefore, £1,465 less than was provided in the Estimates.

When I was appointed Acting Under Secretary at the end of the past financial year there was a considerable amount of clerical work in arrears, chiefly in the compilation of the personal files of the various officers. These are now being brought up to date, and when this is done I shall be in a position to say definitely what staff is required, but so far as I can see now, it appears to me that it will be absolutely necessary to increase the clerical staff if the work of the Department is to be carried on with promptness and efficiency.

Since the last annual report was written the offices of Bee Expert, Botanist, and Assistant Entomologist have been abolished, and the services of these officers dispensed with. It is proposed to entrust the custody of the herbarium specimens now on hand to the Perth Museum.

The reading room and library have been freely used by the general public during the past year, but a large amount of the information therein is unavailable owing to the lack of a decent index. This is a matter that should be remedied as early as possible.

Applications for the *Journal* continue to come in freely, and a considerable revenue is now being received from advertisements. On the approval recently given by you, the Acting Sub-Editor (Mr. G. C. Baker) has effected very considerable economies in the printing and publishing of the *Journal*, with the result that at present this publication is being issued at a net cost of about £150 per annum, the figures for September being:—

Cost of printing, postage, etc.	£84	17	8
Less amount received by subscriptions and advertisements	70	15	0
	£14	2	8

The report of the manager of the refrigerating works shows that during the past year the receipts exceeded expenditure by £570. Experiments of an interesting and instructing nature have been carried out during the year in the direction of storing eggs, fruit, etc., in cold store, and the results have been most satisfactory. A considerable increase of business and revenue is anticipated in this direction in the near future.

The officer in charge of the rabbit division reports that a considerable wave of the pests reached the fence during the spring, and no less than 5,115 rabbits were captured during September, October, and November. Besides these large numbers were destroyed by poison, dingoes, etc.

The fence is being kept in good repair, and with the exception of a few repairs where the netting had rotted through the quantity of salt in the soil, or had become damaged by bush fires, gales, etc., the upkeep has not been great.

The suppression of those colonies that had got west of No. 1 fence has been vigorously pursued, and, as Mr. Wilson's report indicates, with good results.

The report shows that in one instance rabbits were found west of No. 2 fence, but active steps were taken to deal with them, and the Inspector's report goes to show that the outbreak was entirely suppressed.

No. 2 fence has now been handed over to the Department and at present we are charged with the maintenance of 1,639 miles of fencing, viz., the whole of No. 2 fence and No 1 fence from the coast to 700 miles west of Burracoppin.

The balance of the work of the Department is fully dealt with by Mr. Despeissis in his report as Acting Director.

I have, etc.,

W. B. HOOPER,
Acting Under Secretary for Agriculture.

9th November, 1906.

Acting Director's Report.

To the Hon. Minister for Agriculture.

SIR,

In presenting this report for the year 1905-6, I feel I can hardly do justice to the work done by the Department, as the position of Acting Director was only conferred upon me in June last, a couple of weeks before the end of the financial year. Brevity must therefore be a necessity.

AGRICULTURAL PROGRESS.

The marked demand for agricultural land which set in a few years ago has been fully sustained, and as a natural consequence the area under cultivation continues to expand with unabated vigour.

				acres.
This year it reaches the total of	...	...	...	364,731
Last year it stood at ...	...	...	...	327,391
Showing an increase of	...	...	...	37,340

The increases in the area under ordinary farm crops are here tabulated :—

	1905.	1906.	Increase.
	acres.	acres.	acres.
Wheat (corn)	182,080	195,071	12,991
Oats	13,864	15,713	1,849
Barley	3,251	3,665	414
Potatoes	1,906	2,145	239
Onions	66	101	35

The estimated total yield of these crops shows as follows :—

	1906.	Increase on 1905.	Average per acre.
Wheat (corn)	2,293,333 bushels	280,090 bushels	11·8 bushels
Oats	283,987 „	57,669 „	18·1 „
Barley	30,113 „	12,165 „	13·5 „
Hay	139,380 tons	25,580 tons	1·1 tons
Potatoes	6,297 „	680 „	2·9 „
Onions	317 „	71 „	3·1 „

The fact that, even with a population increasing at the rate of over 12,000 a year, our importations of flour are steadily on the down grade is a sure indication that in that direction we are gradually overtaking our requirements.

The figures stand as follow :—

1904.	1905.	Decrease.
£85,813	£50,089	£35,726

Much, however, remains to be done to make us independent of foreign markets in the matter of foodstuffs that can easily be produced on our own farms; and the following list of some of the principal items imported into the State during last year shows what would be saved to us were these articles produced locally :—

				£
Wheat	value	...	...	4,054
Flour	,,	...	...	50,089
Bran and Pollard	,,	...	...	54,140
Chaff and Hay	,,	...	...	6,654
Barley	,,	...	...	8,442
Malt	,,	...	...	35,822
Oats	,,	...	...	70,686
Maize	,,	...	...	1,508
Peas and Beans	,,	...	...	2,047
Potatoes	,,	...	...	91,256
Onions	,,	...	...	20,272
Hops	,,	...	...	19,594
Fruit and Vegetables	,,	...	...	185,525
Wines	,,	...	...	34,944
Meats (Salt, Fresh, and Preserved)	,,	...	...	139,844
Bacon and Hams	,,	...	...	116,163
Lard and Dripping	,,	...	...	8,700
Poultry (dead and alive)	,,	...	...	5,108
Eggs	,,	...	...	70,528
Honey	,,	...	...	1,598
Butter	,,	...	...	313,177
Cheese	,,	...	...	34,460
Preserved and Concentrated Milk and Cream	,,	...	...	100,355
Horses	,,	...	...	64,773
Cattle	,,	...	...	36,511
Sheep	,,	...	...	39,274
Pigs	,,	...	...	80
				£1,515,605

It is obvious that, with the progressive reduction in the importation of many of these articles, which total a value of about 1½ millions, as local production increases, so much wealth now lost to the country would remain in circulation within this State. Although a definite period of time cannot be named when we will be independent of the rest of the world for many of the articles enumerated in the above list, yet indications clearly show that we are gradually winning from the land much of that which we now have to import.

STOCK BREEDING.

The Report of the Chief Inspector of Stock is published in full with this Report, and it is here only necessary to place on record the number of stock of different kinds in the State.

The figures as supplied by the Government Statistician show the gradual increase during the last decade of horses, cattle, sheep, pigs, camels, mules, donkeys, and goats, and their distribution throughout the different portions of the State.

Number of Live Stock in Western Australia on the 31st December in each of the Ten Years, 1896 to 1905.

YEAR	HORSES. Total.	CATTLE. Over one year old. Dairy Cows (in milk and dry).	CATTLE. Over one year old. Other Cattle.	CATTLE. Under one year old.	CATTLE. Total.	SHEEP. Total.	PIGS. Total.	Camels.	Mules and Donkeys.	Goats.
	No.	No.	No.	No.	No.	No.	No.	No.	No.	No.
1896	57,527	6,814	148,266	34,713	199,793	2,248,976	3154	3,984	104	4,027
1897	62,222	18,083	192,523	34,365	244,971	2,210,742	809	3,072	219	4,229
1898	63,604	21,252	202,758	45,937	269,947	2,251,548	39,483	3,197	209	265
1899	65,920	21,828	224,632	50,615	297,075	2,282,306	55,963	2,571	218	987
1900	68,253	25,378	261,447	51,765	38,890	2,434,311	61,740	3,246	332	7,220
1901	73,710	34,111	300,320	64,116	847	2,625,855	61,062	2,596	361	8,424
1902	80,158	24,324	334,350	78,462	7,336	2,704,880	52,883	1,519	505	11,522
1903	82,747	27,232	843	77,942	74,617	2,600,633	50,209	2,031	600	14,120
1904	90,225	27,724	433,296	100,470	58,490	2,853,424	70,299	1,958	840	17,980
1905	97,397	5,311	98,781	98,033	63,525	3,120,603	74,587	2,413	1,061	21,139

HORSES.

In a period of ten years the number of horses has barely doubled, and this in spite of the fact that the demand for all kinds of horses has never been brisker or prices higher. Our own market has absorbed all the locally bred horses, besides thousands more, especially draught horses, which have been introduced from the Eastern States and sold at high figures.

With prices for light horses ranging from £10 to £35, and for draughts from £30 to £70, it is hard to explain why so little attention has hitherto been paid to horse breeding. Apart from our own market, we have within a short distance of our shores—in India—a market anxious to supply itself with remounts and artillery horses of the right type. Of these, 3,000 to 4,000 are required annually for the army on a peace footing, the price being about £45 delivered in India. When it is borne in mind that the resultant of all the efforts put forward during the best part of a century by the horse breeding departments in India has been singularly disappointing, we may reasonably look upon that market as one worth catering for; Australian bred horses having gained there a reputation for strength, size, and docility.

The matter of encouraging horse and mule breeding in the State has occupied the attention of agricultural societies as well as of prominent land owners, and it is one of the functions of this Department to help it in every reasonable manner.

CATTLE.

A glance at the stock returns shows how important cattle breeding is becoming in the country. In ten years it has increased threefold. The North and the North-Western portion of the State supports three times as many head of cattle as the rest of the State put together. With the rate of progress made in that part of the State, the burning question is how best to market those cattle. At present the trade is hampered by a long sea voyage, which is not conducive to fat cattle keeping their condition. In fact the mortality during the voyage is at times heavy. This is especially the case with East Kimberley cattle, which come from tick-infested country. On arrival at Robb's Jetty they have to be subjected to the discomfort of dipping and subsequent quarantine under conditions which inflict a hardship, and this, if unavoidable is nevertheless real, before they are liberated and slaughtered. Cattle for the Goldfields' market are trucked through under quarantine.

The possibility of providing an overland stock route from the East Kimberley country to the Eastern Goldfields is now being investigated by a survey party specially sent out by the Government.

The question of providing canning and chilling works at the port of Wyndham is also being considered by private enterprise. Practical support from the Government to attain that end has been sought.

The establishment of a central abattoir near Fremantle is also one which is nearer realisation, and recommends itself both from an economic and a sanitary standpoint.

The returns quoted above point out the slow progress made by dairying, the number of milch cows having just about doubled in ten years in spite of the high price of dairy produce. The South-Western Division takes a long lead over the rest of the State in this industry.

Strong indications are at hand that a welcome change has set in regarding the raising of our requirements in dairy produce. The two butter factories established at Busselton and Perth have helped to advance the industry along the right path to success, and with the delivery of milk or cream at the railway station or the factory, the farmers' trouble now ends. Much of the drudgery of dairying is also in a fair way of being alleviated by the introduction of improved milking machines. In the Eastern States these have of late done much in simplifying the labour problem in its relation to dairying to one which allows of a much more practical solution.

Steps are being taken to show a set of one of these machines at work at the forthcoming Western Australian Manufacturers' Exhibition in Perth, in December and January next.

The increased attention given of late to establishing permanen. pastures, and to the growing and the conservation of fodder crops, is also rapidly removing difficulties which have hitherto stood in the way of maintaining and milking dairy cows right through the most trying part of the year.

SHEEP.

The increase in sheep during the last ten years has been very slow The high prices ruling for meat have prevented any great increase in the flocks. Improvement is, however, noticeable in the class of sheep both as regards weight and quality of wool and of meat.

The number of sheep is about equal both in the North-Western and in the South-Western portions of the State, but the distribution of the flocks affords an interesting comparison. According to the returns for 1904 supplied by the Statistical Department, there were in the South-Western portion of Western Australia 1,444 flocks under 500 sheep each ; 245 flocks of 501 to 1,000 sheep; 109 flocks of 1,001-2,000 ; 60 flocks of 2,001-5,000 ; 21 flocks of 5,001-10,000; and 9 flocks of 10,001 to 20,000 sheep each.

In the Northern and North-Western portion, the figures show fewer flock masters and larger flocks, thus :—47 flocks under 500; 4 flocks, 501-1,000; 8 flocks, 1,001-2,000 : 6 flocks, 2,001-5,000; 21 flocks, 5,001-10,000; 40 flocks, 10,001-20,000; 17 flocks, 20,001-50,000; and 3 flocks, 50,000 to 100,000; these three latter classes comprising half the number of sheep in the division.

In the South-Western Division the lamb-raising industry is being taken up with signal success. For that purpose the Lincoln-Merino cross, mated to the Shropshire ram is becoming very popular, and gratifying results have rewarded those who have built up their flocks on those lines, and have provided for the lambing ewes early sown fields of rape in lieu of the dried-up and scant silver grass of the previous season, which may have escaped the bush fires of the latter part of summer.

PIGS.

Slow progress is also being made in pig raising. The butcher's requirements have in that respect done much in preventing a more rapid increase. The industry, however, is now entering upon a new era. Its development will keep pace with that of dairying. Another important factor, besides, which promises to stimulate pig breeding is the establishment near Fremantle of a large bacon factory provided with the most modern appliances for the curing of ham and bacon.

The enterprise shown in the establishment of that capacious factory by Messrs. Hutton & Co. is one which is calculated to benefit the farmer by providing a market for a class of pigs which he cannot sell to the butcher as " porkers ;" and also by steadying the particularly fluctuating pork market.

The capacity of that up-to-date factory may be gauged when it is said that it is capable of putting through in one year 50,000 pigs, or over one-fourth more than the total number of pigs at present in the State.

The comparatively small capital required, and the quick return realised, place pig farming within the reach of a great many, and when it becomes an adjunct of another agricultural industry which provides by-products suitable as pig feed, it is decidedly profitable.

GOATS.

Within the last few years increased attention has been directed towards the raising of goats in Western Australia.

The fact that the animal is a scrub browser, as compared with the sheep, which is a grass grazer, mark the goat as an animal well adapted for roaming over much of our country. The long periods of dry weather besides, and the vast stretches of country with a scanty supply of surface water, also suit the goat to perfection. Of these there are three classes, all useful, of their kind :—

1. The mohair-producing kind, of which the Angora is the type.

2. The milking goat, which is exemplified in the Maltese, Spanish, and Swiss goats.

3. The meat and basil-producing goats, which are smooth-haired, as are most common goats which represent that class.

The Angora goats have, so far, met with the greatest degree of favour. They have proved themselves to be better adapted to the climatic conditions prevailing on our Chapman farm than those of the Narrogin farm, where the winter season is rather bleak and wet for that class of farm stock.

All the stud bucks raised by the Department have been readily sold, and many more could have been placed.

Inquiries have been made regarding cost and freight of some milking goats from Southern Europe, but the latter have proved so high as to almost prohibit their importation.

For a country like this, however, where a notable portion of the population lives in the interior, the milk goat seems to be an ideal animal. It thrives on the arid country, and, when kept, would oust the imported tinned milk, of which some £100,000 worth is now imported annually.

To show the value set on the mohair industry in other parts of the world it is interesting to note that at the Cape of Good Hope, by Act of Parliament, a duty of £100 is imposed on each Angora buck or ewe exported from that colony, except in the case of export to a South African State or Colony, which shall, by its own Legislature, have imposed a duty of not less than £100.

BEES.

The efforts of our bee-keepers have practically resulted in the requirements of the local market being overtaken. Indeed, the minds of apiarists have been much exercised on the question of how to give relief to a glutted market, and how best to develop our export market.

Several suggestions have been advanced and promises of practical assistance have been made by the Department in order to foster and develop an export trade in honey. Unfortunately, however, the negotiations have for a time been suspended owing to the lack of response on the part of the majority of bee-keepers in coming forward and sharing with those more enterprising members of their Association the responsibilities which the project would entail.

In spite of the full market, some honey is still imported, to the value of £1,500 worth, but this is said to be mostly of an inferior grade ; its cheaper value unfortunately has a disturbing effect on the local market.

WINE INDUSTRY.

With the impending disappearance of the sliding scale of customs dues, the measure of protection which the locally made wine enjoyed will soon be a thing of the past.

During the year special efforts have been put forward by Eastern wine makers to establish a trade for their goods with this country.

These efforts have resulted in abnormally low prices being quoted for some brands of imported wines from the Eastern States, with the result that the market is in anything but a stable condition.

In the meantime, our leading makers have on the other hand endeavoured by means of thorough cultivation and careful handling to both improve the yield of their vineyards and the quality of their wine and bring them up to the standard of the best wines of Australia.

It is recognised that we have climatic advantages equal to any of the best known wine growing countries of the world, that is to say, a wet winter, which gives to the ground a thorough soaking; a moist and genial spring, which insures a good setting; a moderate if dry summer, free from thunderstorms and hailstorms, or from protracted periods of hot, parching winds, and a clear and sufficiently dry autumn, which offers a guarantee of conducting vintage operations under favourable conditions.

To these natural advantages our vineyard proprietors enjoy should be added those they owe to a judicious selection of the choicer kinds of grapes which experience has proved produce the best wine under Australian conditions.

We still suffer a disability in so far as our labour is more costly than in the Eastern States, but with the growing use of machinery this drawback is in a measure alleviated.

The following return shows the quantity of wine made in Western Australia for each of the ten seasons 1897-1906:—

1897	...	...	...	...	75,693 gallons.
1898	...	...	...	...	89,099 ,,
1899	...	...	...	...	113,799 ,,
1900	...	...	...	...	86,802 ,,
1901	...	...	...	...	130,377 ,,
1902	...	...	...	...	185,735 ,,
1903	...	...	...	...	158,853 ,,
1904	...	...	...	...	138,371 ,,
1905	...	...	...	...	185,070 ,,
1906	...	...	...	...	208,911 ,,

This return is satisfactory considering that the area under wine grapes has of late years, owing to the advent of Federation, received a sudden check. Fresh attention, however, is being given to the planting of vineyards for wine making.

There is reason to believe that more liberal treatment will be extended to distillers, judging from the investigation conducted by the Federal Tariff Commission. This, too, should be the means of inducing capital to look for investment in that direction.

FRUIT DRYING.

The teachings of the last two seasons have borne fruit.

During the months of February and March the unheeded rushing of the market with ripe fruit had so lowered prices that not a few left their grapes unpicked on the vines to the uncontrolled depredations of birds, bees, and ants. Frequent remarks were heard about the greed of the middlemen, the excessive freight and charges, the high cost of picking and packing, and the pecuniary losses which crowned the season's operations.

Others set to work differently. When the market was low they kept away from it and busied themselves instead securing, by drying in the sun and turning into raisins, much that would otherwise have been unmarketable fruit. This, more particularly in the case of muscatels, proved remunerative. Instead of selling at a loss, the crop sold readily at a price that represents somewhere about £10 per ton for the fresh grapes.

For some years to come there will be for raisins and currants a ready market to meet the local demand. For the past 10 years £110,000 worth have been imported, and the figure for last year amounted to £13,875, all of which can be produced locally at no great extra cost, and at the same time help to relieve a temporary glut, and turn a probable loss into a satisfactory profit.

Cool Storage of Fruit.

The natural expansion of fruit culture must necessarily result in periodical gluts of the market. Drying affords a ready means of converting into a stable commodity some kinds of perishable fruit, others can, by careful handling, be kept over sufficiently long periods in cool storage. The improvements introduced of late years in that direction permit of keeping until the off season, and at a cost which leaves a fair margin of profit, produce which would otherwise have to be sold at a loss.

With the increase of settlement, fruit planting continues to receive its full share of attention.

The following table, which gives the number of each kind of fruit trees introduced, shows that apples and oranges come easily first. Greater attention is being given to cherry culture, in response to the high price that fruit fetches, and of the improvement in the yield which the trees show as they get older :—

	Per-simon.	Plum.	Quince.	Small Fruits.	Orna-mental.	All others.
Fremantle	106	9,586	1,079	939	78,536	74,062
Albany	...	2,202	...	6,134	223	493
Totals 1905-1906 ..	106	11,788	1,079	7,073	78,759	74,555
Totals 1904-1905 ..	237	7,632	1,098	3,779	31,564	8,999
Increase	...	4,156	...	3,294	47,195	65,556
Decrease	131	...	19	...	...	...

ion of the relative importance of each kind and of the suitableness of one kind
le to the intending planter, and also to the canner and to the packer.

7estern Australia, for the Season ended the 28th February, 1906.

Fruit Trees, etc.								Kitchen Gardens.	Market Gardens.
.pricots.	Peaches.	Plums.	Figs.	Bananas and Plantains.	Other Fruit Trees.	Small Fruit.	Total Fruit Trees, etc.		
acres.	acres.	acres.	acres.	acres.	acres.	acres.	acres.	acres.	acres.
2	11	1	7	1	14	1	85	30	111
3	9	1	21	2	4	3	72	48	43
58	175	78	96	8	·79	56	1,558	168	339
34	66	31	53	...	32	8	459	82	151
36	66	40	43	...	47	10	462	55	14
40	70	46	54	89	56	20	1,056	100	1,286
10	22	4	23	1	23	...	154	14	510
38	65	31	96	2	47	25	979	114	145
52	175	76	55	1	60	13	1,979	67	69
3	9	8	1	...	12	4	80	12	34
18	28	26	16	...	17	15	255	36	17
48	75	74	34	...	94	...	1,008	68	20
14	158	54	12	...	47	4	1,344	68	25
9	30	13	14	...	16	6	241	33	27
30	67	75	8	...	52	5	1,237	65	572
395	1,026	558	533	104	600	170	10,969	960	3,363
...	1	...	3	10	3	2	24	72	70
2	4	1	6	...	10	1	33	23	117
397	1,031	559	542	114	613	173	11,026	1,055	3,550

. The progressive incre[...]

1905.

Year.	G[...] Products For Wine-making.	Other Fruit Trees.	Bananas and Plantains.	Other Fruit Crops. Small fruit.	Total Area Under Vines, Fruit Trees, and small fruit.
	acres.	acres.	acres.	acres.	acres.
1896	938	160	*	120	4,687
1897	1,253	319	*	43	5,577
1898	1,290	381	*	70	6,638
1899	1,400	412	51	44	7,710
1900	1,469	452	84	54	8,621
1901	1,710	496	74	28	9,705
1902	1,660	542	67	24	10,400
1903	1,530	575	104	132	11,362
1904	1,445	542	115	482	13,169
1905	1,385	613	114	786	14,567

lia of late years, the area having trebled itself in ten years, the quantity of

table given below shows that, nevertheless, of apples and oranges we still

to Western Australia, 1905-6.

.oquats.	Oranges.	Lemons.	Pomelos.	Bananas.	Pine Apples.	Passion Fruit.	Goose-berries.	All other Fruits.	Grand Total.
394	20,763¼	8,430¼	69	17,106¼	349	762	1,110	...	98,458
...	778	113	...	366	9	6	48	¿00	2,271
394	21,541¼	8,543¼	69	17,472½	358	768	1,158	100	100,729
2	20,533	9,738	2	22,198	422	1,096¼	1,969	334¼	113,060
392	988¼	...	67	...	...	...	...	...	...
...	...	194¼	...	4,725½	64	328¼	811	234¼	12,321

INSECT PESTS ACT.

The stringent measures taken at an early date against the indiscriminate introduction from abroad of these enemies, which prey on fruit trees and crops, have been the means of keeping out of the country a number of insect pests.

To effect that end two ports only are recognised as ports of entry where fruit and plants can be imported. These, on arrival, are subjected to a close scrutiny on the part of a skilled staff of inspectors, and when necessary they are subjected to disinfection. The two ports of entry are Fremantle and Albany. It has been found advisable to close for that purpose the other ports which a few years ago received a small fraction of the fruit and plants introduced; greater security and greater efficiency are thereby assured.

To fight those pests already introduced, which have found a footing in some of our orchards and gardens, a staff of inspectors, with power under the Insect Pests Act to enter and inspect, and, where necessary, issue instructions for checking or for eradicating pests, administers the Act.

That staff of inspectors has lately been reduced by two. This reduction at a time when the area under orchard increases at the rate of over 1,000 trees a year, causes at times some difficulty in coping with urgent work. Of the two inspectors removed from the administration of that Act, one, Mr. Newman, has been placed in charge of work until lately done by the Assistant Entomologist, and the other, Mr. Bailey, is engaged a good deal of his time in connection with the Fertilisers and Feeding Stuffs Act.

CODLIN MOTH.

The Chief Inspector, Mr. T. Hooper, reported that another serious outbreak of codlin moth had been discovered in some gardens at North Perth.

The first outbreak of the codlin moth recorded in Western Australia dates from 1903, when four gardens were found infested at Albany, and four at North Perth.

In 1904 a wider range of inspection led to eleven more gardens being found slightly infested at Albany, and three more at North Perth.

Drastic measures were taken for the eradication of the pest.

In 1905 the number of infested gardens at Albany was reduced to two only.

In Perth no codlin moth grub was discovered that year, although a diligent inspection of the suspected locality was conducted.

In 1906 no evidence of the presence of the codlin moth was found at Albany.

In Perth two gardens were found slightly affected in the old infested ground, but a fresh outbreak was discovered at West Perth in three adjacent gardens. All apples, pears, and quinces within the infested area were then picked and destroyed; a number of trees too large to treat in the ordinary way were cut down or grubbed out, a few trees only being left, as traps, to carry fruit next season. These trees will be sprayed with arsenical preparations, and the fruit will be picked and destroyed before any codlin grub will have time to come out and continue the trouble. A careful watch will be exercised over Perth, which, for the purpose of dealing promptly if need be, has been declared an infested area under the meaning of the Insect Pests Act.

FRUIT FLY.

That pest, the Chief Inspector reports, was later than the previous year in forcing itself to the attention of fruit growers. It is not unlikely that the care taken the previous season in destroying maggoty fruit helped to delay its early appearance.

One of the best ways of compelling people to pick and destroy their maggoty fruit has been found to follow a close inspection of fruit offered for sale in auction rooms and fruit shops.

The number of cases of fruit seized at auction rooms and shops was 367, or 83 less than the previous year.

Several colonies of predaceous beetles, introduced from Brazil by Mr. Compere, were liberated last summer in some gardens of Perth, but it is too early yet to state whether these friendly beetles have established themselves.

SAN JOSE SCALE.

The inspection of orchards to locate this introduced scale takes place mostly in the winter, when the trees have lost their leaves. The returns to hand show that although 300 more trees were reported to be scaly, yet the number of scales per tree has decreased in a remarkable manner. On many trees it is a hard task to find the scale.

Since this scale was first discovered in Western Australia, 312 orchards have been reported infested. Of these. 180 are now clean and 132 still under treatment; but last year as the trees grew larger, the work of eradication became correspondingly more onerous.

The use of vacuum oil emulsion the last two winters promises to materially reduce the number of scaly trees from now on.

At auction rooms 17 cases of fruit only were seized during the year on account of San José scale, as against 50 cases the year before.

MUSSEL SCALE.

So far, 14 orchards have been found infested with that scale. One of these orchards is now reported clean, and the number of scales on infested trees in the other orchards is decreasing. This pest is one of the worst the Tasmanian apple growers have to contend with, and the work of eradicating it from our orchards will be followed up with every possible care.

Of other fruit pests red mite and woolly aphis give much trouble in some localities. The best method of coping with them is receiving the attention of the Government Entomologist.

ENTOMOLOGICAL WORK.

The work of fighting our insect pests by means of their natural enemies, which was initiated by this Department a few years ago, continues with the same satisfactory results.

An illustration of the popularity of this method of fighting pests is afforded by the number of applications for parasites received from all parts of the State.

During the year 410 applications were registered and 360 supplied, leaving still on the books 50 to be dealt with. These will receive attention in the spring, when insect life becomes more active.

The following, drawn up from our Laboratory register, give a list, with date of introduction, of the several internal parasites or predaceous insects collected by the Government Entomologist during his travels abroad; it also gives the number of the colonies received, and where and when these were liberated :—

APHIDES PARASITES.

Date.	From.	Name.	No. liberated.	Where liberated.	Date.
21/7/02	Queensland	Unnamed	5	Perth Gardens	23/7/02
22/4/02	New South Wales	Do.	40	Perth and Bunbury	23/4/02
21/5/03	Seville	Do.	4	Perth Gardens	22/5/03
21/5/03	Do.	Do.	56	Do.	23/5/03
26/4/06	Algiers	Do.	2	Do.	17/5/06

No less than 14 species of internal parasites (besides a number of ladybirds which feed upon it) have been introduced into this State, and out of these 11 specimens have, to my knowledge, established themselves.

BLACK SCALE.

Date.	From.	Name.	No. liberated.	Where liberated.	Date.
16/4/02	New South Wales	Dilophogaster Californica	11	Perth Gardens	20/4/02
22/4/02	Do.	Do.	34	Guildford	29/4/02
28/4/02	Do.	Hemencyotus Crawii	11	Perth Gardens	7/5/02
12/6/02	Queensland	Myiocneme Comperei	938	51 colonies (various places)	Various
28/10/02	Capetown	Scutellista Cyanea	11	Perth and Coolup	3/1/03
28/10/02	Do.	Microterys sp.	20	Perth Gardens	3/11/02
1/1/03	Hong Kong	Aristolochin	12	Do.	12/1/03
2/1/03	Canton	Unnamed	10	Do.	9/1/03
9/1/03	Hong Kong	Do.	12	Do.	12/1/03
17/9/03	Capetown	Do.	83	7 colonies	Various
3/10/03	Do.	Do.	17	West Perth	14/11/03
22/7/03	California	Scutellista Cyanea	90	8 colonies	Various
1/11/05	Timor	Red Scutellista	3	Government Gardens	6/11/05
1/11/05	China	Unnamed	3	Do.	6/11/05

BROWN SCALE.

Four species of internal parasites of this scale have been introduced into this State and two have so far established themselves; of another, from China, which was liberated last spring, 81 specimens liberated may be expected to show results next season.

Date.	From.	Name.	No. liberated.	Where liberated.	Date.
22/4/02	New South Wales	Unnamed	83	7 colonies	Various
1/11/05	China	Do.	81	10 colonies	do.
1/11/05	Do.	Do.	2	St. George's Terrace	12/11/05
28/4/06	Algiers	Failed to breed out	...	...	...

RED SCALE.

Date.	From.	Name.	No. liberated.	Where liberated.	Date.
19/10/04	Palestine	Jerusalem ladybird	160	10 colonies	Various
8/11/05	China	Unnamed	14	West Perth	8/1/06

These 14 have become established, and several colonies have been collected and sent out.

LECANIUM CYMBIFORME SCALE.

Date.	From.	Name.	No. liberated.	Where liberated.	Date.
21/5/08	France	Unnamed	200	Perth and Claremont	Various

This parasite seems to have disappeared, as no traces of it have been found for the last two seasons, and the scale seems to be on the increase.

LADYBIRDS INTRODUCED.

9/4/02	New South Wales	Cryptolemus Montrouzieri	1,328	13 colonies	Various
16/4/02	Queensland	...		Perth Gardens	24/5/02
28/4/02	Do.				
20/5/02	New South Wales	Unnamed	20		
30/7/02	Do.	...ius Lafertei			
"	Do.	Veronia lincola			
"	Do.	Cryptolemus			
"	Do.	Coccinella ...mia	250	Various orchards	Various
"	Do.	Novius Kobelei			
"	Do.	Novius cardinalis			
"	Do.	...ous chalybeus			
29/10/02	...lia	Leis conformis ...	1,900	14 ...cies	do.
21/5/03	Seville	U ... med ...	300	5 ...cies	do.
"	Marseilles	Do.	10	Perth Gardens	22/5/03
"	Malaga	Do.	50	7 ...cies	V ...nus
19/10/04	Palestine	...am ...byrd	50	10 ...cies	do.
11/11/04	Marseilles	Unnamed	50	Mixed varieties	do.
27/2/06	C ...ifornia	Coccinella ...lia.	28	Perth and ...dijong	do.
			52	do.	do.
26/3/06	Do.	Hippodamia convergens	301	8 ...cies	do.
	Do.	...lla Californica...	471	8 ...cies	do.
2/5/06	Italy	Hippodamia convergens Unnamed	22	1 ...ment	2/5/06

The above 16 sendings of various species of ladybirds (aphide and scale feeders) have in almost every case established themselves, and can be seen feeding in many orchards around Perth.

CABBAGE MOTH.

16/9/02	New South Wales	2 species unnamed	110	Perth district ...	15/10/02
21/5/03	Malaga ...	Do.	25	South and West Perth	12/6/03

The above have both established, and are doing good work.

FRUIT FLY.

Date.	From.	Name.	No. liberated.	Where liberated.	Date.
16/7/04	Brazil	Unnamed	1 pair	Mr. C. W. Ferguson's, Midland Junction	26/7/04
3/8/04	Do.	Do.	1 pair	Mr. Glyde's, Adelaide Terrace	13/8/04
3/8/04	Do.	Staphylinid Beetle ...	12	Mr. S. Burt's, Adelaide Terrace	13/8/04
11/1/05	I dia	Unnamed	10	St. George's Terrace	11/1/05

Nothing has been seen of these parasites since they were liberated.

STAPHYLINID BEETLES,

Date.	From.	Name.	No. liberated.	Where liberated.	Date.
14/7/04	Brazil ...	Staphylinid Beetle	20	Mr. Barrow's, Adelaide Terrace	14/7/04
26/5/05	Do.	Do.	100	Insectary ...	26/5/05

This last lot of beetles increased in the Insectary, but not to the extent that was anticipated—only 375 being available for distribution. These were liberated in specially-constructed bins, wormy fruit being gathered and placed in the bins. Altogether eight colonies have been placed in various orchards, and in two instances they have been found established, but it is too early yet to pronounce definitely as to their value. A fresh colony has been started in the Insectary to supply further colonies next summer.

During the year an investigation was conducted concerning the value of the introduced parasites for checking insect pests.

This investigation was forced upon the Department on account of serious and sweeping charges made against the Government Entomologist and the method of fighting pests advocated by him. The fact that these charges emanated from Mr. F. Lowe, Mr. Compere's late assistant, made it imperative that evidence be called whereby they would be either sustained or disproved.

This task was entrusted to the Advisory Board of the Department, and from the published evidence called and solicited, the Board was able, with no dissentient voice, to report as follows :—

"The contretemps caused by the holding of the investigation referred to was unfortunate both to Western Australia and to California, which by common agreement share in the cost and expense of keeping Mr. Geo. Compere, our Government Entomologist, travelling round the world in search of beneficial parasites of insect pests common in either State or possibly in both."

BOTANICAL BRANCH.

The advice of the Government Botanist was largely availed of by settlers for the purpose of having either noxious or useful plants identified.

Of plants reputed to be poisonous to stock, forty or more are supposed to belong to our State.

To the new and inexperienced settler it is a matter of grave concern whether it is safe to stock some of his paddocks on account of the presence of some suspicious plants in them. On the other hand, much nutritious grass and feed may be going to waste because of the over cautiousness of the owner in not stocking his land for fear of possible loss by poison.

In advising in instances such as these, the authority of the Government Botanist has been helpful to those on the land ; for that reason, it is a matter for regret that it was deemed necessary—if only for a time—to abolish the office.

In the following account of a visit of investigation to the North-West, Dr. Morrison throws some interesting light on that portion of the State :—

"In September last I proceeded to Onslow, on the North-West coast, under instructions to inquire into the cause of death of about 120 cattle, believed to have been brought about by their eating a poisonous plant. From Onslow I travelled by buggy up the Ashburton River, calling at the stations Minderoo, Globe Hill, Uaroo, and Nanutarra. Between Globe Hill and Uaroo the shrub that had caused the damage was found, and also between the latter and Nanutarra, where the cattle had eaten it. Subsequently specimens were also found at Minderoo, and one shrub was observed at Onslow. Those who had seen the cattle affected had no doubt as to this plant having been the cause of the poisoning, and others from districts farther north also recognise it as a poison.

"A critical examination of the plant, which is a small much-branched shrub under two feet in height, showed it to be a species of the genus *Indigofera*, closely resembling in many points *I. Georgei*, recently found at Tammin, on the Eastern railway system. The differences, however, appeared sufficient to constitute it a distinct species, hitherto undescribed, and I accordingly named it *Indigofera boviperda*.

"Near the Uaroo homestead, scattered along the track, were seen a number of the carcases of the bullocks that had dropped out of the mob after having eaten the poisonous shrub the previous night or morning. Among the symptoms of poisoning, as related by Mr. McCarthy of Uaroo, were the following: ' The bullocks could be heard moaning, they went along listlessly and lazily, their eyes staring vacantly, and could not be urged on, or they would run excitedly against anything in front of them without heeding where they were going ; they went off their feed, but at night they would always return to the watering troughs, and had to be driven out of the way ; sometimes they were scoured, passing offensive motions, or, with the abdomen blown up, they would try to raise themselves, turn the head and sink down dead.'

"A bundle of the shrub, which was in an advanced seeding stage, was brought to Perth and handed over to the Government Analyst, Mr. Mann, who, on making a test analysis of it, found that a poisonous alkaloid was present in it. For a complete analysis further supplies have been sought from residents on the Asburton River, should the new season's growth of the plant have taken place.

"As compared with the extra tropical South-West Division of the State, the North-West Division shows many strong contrasts. Timber trees are seen only on and near the banks of the Ashburton River. The four species of eucalyptus observed possess bark of a more or less pure white colour, which serves as a protection against the ardent rays of the sun ; and they look as if they had had applied to their trunks and branches a dense coating of paint. Other trees and shrubs are protected from the heat and drought by the development of a thick corky bark, and the name "cork-bark" is applied to a considerable number of plants differing widely in other respects.

"Another contrast is presented in the development of grasses. The South-West Division of this State, with its predominating sandy soil, is known to botanists as one of the poorest regions of the earth's surface in indigenous grasses ; but in the North-West, as on the flats adjacent to the Ashburton River, their variety and bulky development give to the region its special value for pastoral settlement. A species of ' Spinifex' (*Triodia Cunninghamii*) is predominant where the red sand lies immediately over the stiff clay of the plains, and is a source of trouble to the traveller, while only its flowerstalks can be eaten by cattle; but there are areas of strong red loam in which nutritious grasses grow in the greatest luxuriance, providing in good seasons a massive bulk of forage, more than sufficient for the year's requirements and for storage as hay or ensilage in expectation of future dry years. The grasses on the plains were so far advanced and withered as to be mostly unsuitable for identification, but in the bed of the river or close to it, a number of fresh specimens were found, along with plants of the Saltbush and other families, growing in the mud, sand, or gravel, in which moisture was retained. In all 12 species of grasses were found during the journey, and an equal number of the *Chenopodiaceæ*, or Saltbush order, as here enumerated :—

GRAMINEÆ.

"*Panicum distachyum* (the Two-finger grass), a perennial grass, rooting at the nodes, yielding a large quantity of fodder. Dr. Bancroft states that horses will not leave this grass and that it is also most useful for fresh water marshes and for consolidating river banks; *Setaria viridis*, *Spinifex longifolius* (*on coast as sand binder*), *Triraphis mollis*, *Aristida arenaria Pollinia fulva*, *Triodia Cunninghamii* ('*Spinifex*', *so called*). *Leptochloa subdigitata*, *Sporobolus indicus*, one of the Rat's tail grasses, very resisting and valuable pasture grass; *S. Lindleyi*, *Eragrostis falcata*, said to be one of the best of pasture grasses in arid tracts of subtropical Western Australia, and *E. eriopoda*.

CHENOPODIACEÆ.

"*Rhagodia sp.*, very valuable fodder plants on salt-bush runs; *Chenopodium carinatum*, one of the Blue-bushes, nutritive and wholesome; *Dysphania littoralis*, *D. plantaginella*, *Atriplex halimoides*, one of the best dwarf species for salt-bush pastures, readily raised from seeds of which about 20,000 go to the pound. Where these plants are to be grown permanently the soil must contain a fair proportion of saline matter, especially chloride, either naturally or artificially. A remarkable salt-bush for its productiveness and its drought-resisting power, grows in alkali-impregnated soil better than any other plant; much liked by sheep. *A. semibaccata*, *Anisacantha muricata*, *Selerolama bicornis*, *S. diacantha*, *Bassia astrocarpa*. *Salicornia sp.*, *and Salsola Kali.*

ALEX. MORRISON,
Government Botanist."

11th July, 1906.

SEED DISTRIBUTION.

On this subject the Field Officer, Mr. P. G. Wicken, reports as follows :—

With the idea of encouraging settlers to grow a greater variety of crops, a large quantity of seeds have been distributed during the year. These include such fodder crops as Cow-peas, Lucerne, Maize, *Lathyrus Silvestris*, Rape, Sheeps' Burnett, and Chicory. In addition to the above, over a ton of grass seed has been distributed, in small lots, to settlers in all parts of the country. The grasses include—*Paspalum dilatatum*, Rhodes Grass, Cocksfoot, Timothy, Tall Fescue, Tall Oat Grass, Wallaby Grass, Rib Grass, Hungarian Forage Grass, and White Clover; also a quantity of roots of African Wonder Grass, Rhodes Grass, and *Eragrostis pilosa* have been sent out from the Hamel State Farm.

Although packets of grass seed have been supplied to several hundred applicants, I regret to report that not one per cent. of those receiving seeds ever furnished any report of the results obtained.

So far, the system of supplying seed, and in many cases fertiliser, to settlers for experimental purposes has not given the best results.

Subiaco Depôt.

This depôt, which was originally reserved for the purpose of quarantining imported grape vine cuttings and live stock, necessitates the employment of a caretaker. We have about two acres of cleared land, and twenty of bush paddock. Advantage is taken of this cleared land to grow a few hardy grasses; a number were planted last year, but it was too late before the ground was got ready, and the grasses did not obtain the necessary root hold before the weather became dry and warm. This year small plots of grasses have been planted earlier in the season, and are now making good growth.

Three varieties of Cow-peas (black, white, and whip-poor-will) were grown, and all did fairly well, the black giving the heaviest yield.

Roots of African Wonder Grass, Rhodes Grass, and the native grass *Eragrostis pilosa* were planted in September, and these grasses all grew very well and yielded a large quantity of green feed all through the summer, although they were grown on almost pure white sand. These roots have been divided and transplanted, and we now have about six rows of each of these grasses planted. The African Wonder Grass did the best of the three.

A number of rows of peas and lucerne were planted during August and treated by Dr. Blackburne with the nitrogenous bacteria, but the results were not conclusive. The experiments were conducted with the object of ascertaining whether the bacteria taken from one variety of pea was effective on another variety.

The results of these inoculated seeds did not come up to expectations. Neither did those leguminous seeds similarly inoculated with nitrogen-fixing bacteria which were distributed amongst a number of experimenters.

In poor soil the yield was somewhat increased; but in more fertile soils, presumably better stocked with nitrifying bacteria, the improvement was not apparent.

Fertilisers and Feeding Stuffs Act.

Regarding the administration of this Act, Mr. P. G. Wicken, the Inspector under the Act, reports:—

The Fertiliser Act.

The amendments to the Fertiliser Act were passed by Parliament in December last. In April a start was made to put the Act into force, and notices were published calling on all vendors to register the brands and contents of their fertilisers in conformity with the Act.

A number of these have done so, and the collected samples have been submitted to the Government Analyst for his examination. As soon as this work has been completed the results will be compared with the percentage of fertilising ingredients registered, and the list will be published for general information.

Melbourne Exhibition.

An exhibition was held in Melbourne under the auspices of the Australian Natives' Association during January and February last. This State was represented, and a very good collection was got together, and entrusted to Mr. P. G. Wicken. Agriculture was represented by collections of grains, fodders, grasses, and wild flowers; other exhibits included timbers, minerals, work from the manual training classes at the public schools, curiosities from the Museum, and a large collection of photographs representing all the industries of the State. Statistical signs, showing the imports of agricultural produce, were shown, and a quantity of literature on land settlement was distributed to a number of inquirers thinking of coming to this State. The W.A. Court was the subject of favourable comment. The cost was £105 4s. 5d., which was very little considering the benefit derived by the State.

AGRICULTURAL SHOWS.

During the year a substantial brick pavilion was erected for the Department of Agriculture on the Royal Agricultural Show Ground at Claremont. This building, which measures 60ft. x 40ft. provides ample space for the departmental exhibits, and enabled us to make a display of produce from the State Farms in advance of anything that has yet been attempted in the State. The Narrogin, Chapman, and Hamel Farms were all represented, as well as the different branches of the Department, and the exhibits shown. Hitherto canvas tents have done duty for covering our exhibits. With the steady development of agriculture better things may be expected in the future.

The National Agricultural Show was last lyear held in Bunbury, and the Department also made there a display of the produce from the State Farms.

THE STATE FARMS.

A good deal of developmental work has been done on the three State farms at Narrogin, Chapman, and Hamel.

THE CHAPMAN FARM.

This State farm stands in the centre of a vast stretch of country which lies 25 miles north of Geraldton and 15 miles east of Northampton.

From an administrative point of view, the situation constitutes a disadvantage. Until four or five years ago, the great expanse of country which lies in that locality was given up almost exclusively to grazing, and little or no attempt was made with regard to the cultivation of the soil.

It was mainly to prove the capabilities of that land, and thus to help along its settlement, that the farm was established.

All the available land has since been selected, and settlement has outrun the extent of the area in question. It is recognised that the farm has, in helping the speedy settlement of the land, fulfilled the part it was desired it should. Since then its object has been extended, and it has become the medium whereby practical instruction in farming is provided for intended settlers in quest of a training that will fit them for the task they have set themselves.

The number of students have increased from four to seventeen—the number at present on the farm. They are mostly young Englishmen and Australians; the work they have to do is of a varied character, and the Manager reports that they apply themselves to it with interest and energy.

Several of the ex-students have selected land in the district, while others who have settled in other parts of the State are said to be doing satisfactorily.

The farm, which is well watered by the Chapman River, and also by wells served by windmills, is now securely fenced in and conveniently subdivided. The land is one-third first-class, one-third second-class, and one-third third-class or sand plain and jam and consists of 1,278a, on which stands the homestead. During the year an additional 900 acres have been secured a few miles away. When that land is fenced, ringbarked, and supplied with water, it will constitute a useful run for young and for dry stock, but it is not at present utilised.

The land cleared covers 521 acres, of which 100 acres are sand plain.

The cost of the last clearing contract for 112 acres of ringbarked wattle country was 18s. per acre. The good river flats under green wattle trees can be cleared for 25s. per acre. Of the cleared land, 434 acres are under corn and hay crops, fodder and artificial pasture, and also under potatoes and vegetables, cotton, and orchard. The rest is fallow land for next year's cropping. By reason of the lack of fallow land, the crops were sown rather late last season, and the estimated yield will in consequence suffer.

In the drier agricultural districts of the State well pulverised fallow has been proved to be the keystone of successful farming, as it enables the seed to be sown earlier on clean land still supplied with a notable proportion of the moisture stored up during the previous rainy season.

On that class of land, the rape crop has been a great help in providing fodder for stock, especially lambing ewes, at a time when the natural herbage was still backward, and when other fodder crops were not yet ready.

Field peas promise to rival rape as a serviceable winter fodder crop. Their growth has been so satisfactory that the area allotted to them will be increased next season.

Artificial grasses have not hitherto proved a success at the Chapman Farm, but sheep-burnett and the salt bushes sown early last spring are doing well on the sand plains. The systematic cultivation of these salt bushes promises to bring many of our sand plains under profitable occupation.

The creeping kinds are better liked by sheep, and amongst these some have proved as successful in America, as they are with us for growing on alkaline soils where no other vegetation of any value for stock grazing can be made to grow. In some districts pastoralists do not consider salt bushes of much value, as stock do not eat them at all readily. This, however, seems to be a wise provision of Nature which makes available for use in seasons when other sweeter herbage is scarce a plant whose sustaining and even fattening properties are beyond question.

Lucerne, I was pleased to notice on the occasion of a visit of inspection to the Chapman Farm, is establishing itself with every promise of success on the richer, deeper, and moister wattle flats on the banks of the river. The success of the 12-acre experimental'field in that direction will be of considerable value to many in the district who own land similarly situated. Amongst other experimental crops is a five-acre patch of cotton, of various kinds. The result of this experiment will be carefully noted and reported upon when the crop is more advanced. Hitherto the appearance is not as favourable as was anticipated.

The Manager of the farm reports that the experimental plots of broom corn and amber cane sown last spring did splendidly, showing vigorous growth throughout the summer; four cuttings, of 2ft. high each, were taken off without irrigation during a long dry summer.

Cow-peas did equally well, and are apparently at home in this soil and climate. Of the varieties sown the "whip-poor-will" one did the best.

The cereal crops, remarks the Acting Manager, Mr. F. Keays, were on the whole very fair, considering they were sown late in the season. Better results are anticipated from sowing five or six weeks earlier.

Result of Field Crops.

Variety Wheat.	Date sown.	Manures—rate per acre.	Character of soil.	Yield per acre.	Remarks.
				bushels.	
Aust. X B 77 ...	M'y 19	Superphosphates, 100lbs.	Red loam; second crop	16¼	Early, straw weak, thin grain.
Jade	June 1	Do. ...	Do. ... do.	21	Medium early, strong straw, plump grain.
Jade	,, 29	Thomas's Phos., 100lbs.	Poor sandy soil; first crop	14¼	Do. do.
Toby's Luck ...	,, 26	Superphosphates, 100lbs.	Fair red loam; first crop	22	Strong straw, plump grain.
Lucky Talavera	,, 26	Do.	Do. ... do.	16	Medium early, good grain.
Aust. X B 73 ...	,, 26	Do.	Do. ... do.	19¼	Early, good grain, sheds freely.
Alpha	,, 26	Do.	Do. ... do.	14¼	Early, plump grain.
Aust. X B 100 ...	,, 26	Do.	Do. ... do.	14¼	Early, long straw, sheds freely.
Plover	,, 26	Do.	Rather poor soil; first crop	7	Mid-early, thin.
White Lammas	,, 26	Do.	Do. ... do.	16¼	Mid-early, plump grain.
Tardent's Blue	,, 26	Do.	Do. ... do.	15	Late, good grain.
Gallard's Hybrid	,, 26	Do.	Do. ... do.	4	Very poor, not suitable for this district.

Results of Field Crops.

Variety Oats.	Date Sown.	Manures. Rate per acre.	Character of Soil.	Yield per acre.	Remarks.
				bushels.	
Algerian ...	June 12 ...	Super. 100lbs. ...	Fair loam; third crop	28	Early, fairly plump
G. Fleece ...	July 1 ...	Thomas's Phosphate 100lbs.	Good loam; third crop	19	Fairly plump
W. Siberian ...	,, 12 ...	Thomas's Phosphate 100lbs.	Do. do.	13	Thin and light
Cape Barley ...	June 30 ...	Super. 100lbs. ...	Good red loam; second crop	36	Fair grain, rather smutty

Results of Cropping on Sand Plain.

Variety Wheat.	Date Sown.	Manures, Rate per acre.	Character of Soil.	Yield per acre.	Remarks.
Alpha...	July 18	Guano 120lbs.	Sand plain	bushels. 7¼	Fairly plump, good colour
Rerraf...	,, 19	Do.	Do.	4	Grain small and shotty
Aust. XB 73	,, 19	Do.	Do.	6¼	Grain good bright colour
Steinlee	,, 19	Do.	Do.	5	Grain rather thin

Manure Test Plots on Sand Plain.

No. of Plot.	Date sown.	Manures, Rate per Plot.	Cost of Manure per Plot.	Yield per acre.	Remarks.
			s. d.	bushels.	
No. 1	July 19	Thomas's Phosphate... 66lbs.	2 6	8¾	Straw fair length, grain good
No. 2	,,	Super. ... 48lbs.	2 2	8¾	Fair head, medium straw, good grain
No. 3	,,	Victorian Super. 40lbs.	2 6	8	,, ,, ,, ,, ,,
No. 4	,,	Guano ... 116lbs.	2 11	5¼	Light straw, very small heads
No. 5	,,	No manures	...	1	Exceedingly poor

The area of above plots was 1 rood 28 perches each, and the variety of wheat sown was Australian X.B. 73.

The live stock at the Chapman Farm comprise, amongst others, a'stud of Suffolk Punch horses. Several mares are in foal, and the entire "War Dance," who is available at a low fee for mares belonging to settlers around, is gaining a good name for the class of stock he gets. He had last season almost a full list, and served 48 mares for 30 different owners, and 14 of our own mares. A good percentage of the mares proved in foal.

The cattle consist of a herd of 20 pure and 20 cross Dexter Kerries. These small cattle show their value in keeping up their condition well, and thrive; the cows are quiet; although the milking is done by squads of students changing every few days, they are easy to milk.

Our flock of pure bred Shropshire ewes and rams, imported from Tasmania and South Australia, have now increased to 44. Their stock is much in demand amongst the settlers around.

Angora goats, as reported above, have done particularly well at the Chapman Farm. We have numerous inquiries for both sexes, but now only sell bucks, which are in great demand, mostly for crossing with the common goats.

The herd of pigs now number 100, and consist of pure bred Berkshire and Large Blacks and their cross. They all do well.

Of poultry, only Golden Wyandottes and Silver Grey Dorkings are kept at the Chapman Farm, besides a fine lot of American Bronze Wing Turkeys, which do remarkably well, these birds finding their own food about the yards and the paddocks.

STAFF.

A considerable reduction has been effected in the permanent staff. On the 23rd June last there were, including immigrants, 12 paid hands. That number has now been reduced to six, viz.: two farm foremen, stud groom, cook and assistant, and general servant. All the farm work is done by the students, under the direction of the foremen.

THE NARROGIN FARM.

The initial object of this farm was to demonstrate in a practical manner the advantages of improved cultivation for securing a bigger return from the land; to raise stud stock for the benefit of farmers and also clean seeds for sowing their land; to offer a field for training farmers' sons and others wishing to settle on the land; to only touch on experimental work with caution, making it quite a subsidiary feature of the farm. Operations were first started on 1,726 acres some five miles to the west of Narrogin.

That area was what was left unselected of the wide expanse of State land lying in that direction. A good deal of it is very poor and thickly infested with poison bushes. Some of the land is fair and a small portion very good.

During the year an adjoining farm, measuring 1,100 acres of partly improved land, was purchased; this brings the area of the farm to 2,826 acres. Of these, 604 have been cleared for the plough and most of it is ringbarked. This year 474 acres are under cultivation. The crops comprise wheat for grain and wheat for hay—oats and barley, 305 acres. The balance is under crops for ensilage and green fodder; a small orchard and vineyard and small grass plots complete the acreage under cultivation.

A notable reduction has been effected in the working staff of the farm proper, and this has now been brought down to two foremen who direct the work of the students. The number of these is constantly increasing. From half a dozen students which were on the farm at the beginning of the year, the number had at the end of June reached 15, and it has since come up to 26, while more are on their way out from England.

The students only pay the sum of £2 2s. a year.

To cope with their ever-increasing number, it has been thought advisable to build new quarters capable of putting up 40 students. That new building was erected on the recently purchased farm alongside the new Collie-Narrogin Railway line.

A vigorous policy of reorganisation has been effected on that farm, which should become a self-supporting concern.

Fresh students, however, provide poor farm work, and when their number becomes out of proportion with the extent of the cultivable land they are more a drag than a help to the management.

Hamel State Farm.

Mr. Geo. Berthoud reports on this Experimental Station as follows :—

The total acreage is now 114 acres. That acreage is worked with a ploughman and a general assistant working under the manager. No students are kept at Hamel. A gang of good-conduct prisoners, working under a chief warder, have been engaged opening drains, putting up poultry yards, gates, and fences. The rainfall in the locality amounts to about 50 inches a year, and this, combined with the fact that the brook overflows its banks several times during the winter, does not allow of cropping at that time of the year.

Experimental work only has hitherto been carried out at Hamel, the work consisting chiefly of testing new varieties of grasses and fodder plants, cereals, fruits, and tubers. Mr. Berthoud recommends that seed potatoes should be grown in larger quantities to permit of choice seeds from selected kinds being sold to farmers.

The work carried out there is proving of great interest to visitors. The plots are usually at their best from October till April.

As the area of each plot needs to be restricted, the returns showing the yield of crops are computed by carefully weighing the matured crops gathered on a measured average portion of each plot.

Mr. Berthoud's experience is that on account of the shortness of the season, the crops need more fertilisers than would appear necessary from a casual inspection of the soil. The cost of the complete fertiliser used for potatoes and other crops is at the rate of about 9s. per cwt.

Wheat.—Fifty varieties, including a few new crossbreds, were grown. Excess of damp reduced the yield, which ranged from 8 to 22 bushels and averaged 11 bushels.

Oats.—A few new varieties from Europe and America were sown; the yields averaging 16 bushels, with a range of 8½ to 23 bushels. The best varieties were " Champion Beardless," " Holbran," and " Russian Black."

Rye.—This cereal did better than either wheat or oats, the yields ranging from 8 to 18 bushels with an average of 13 bushels. The best were " Markisoher " and " Summer Saxon."

This season 52 varieties of cereals have been sown, the plots looking better than they did last year.

Field Peas.—Of these the common grey and white "Chilian" did well; they are strong growers and constitute a good cover crop for sowing on old weedy land, they clear off sorrel and improve the land greatly for succeeding crops, and yield an average per acre of 27 bushels of grain which is excellent feed for pigs.

Maize proved a very good crop, yielding from 17 to 81 bushels per acre, with an average of 52 bushels. The seeds of 24 varieties were sown in November on moist peaty soil, with complete fertiliser at the rate of 6cwt. per acre.

The Dent varieties are prolific, giving large grain, floury, and excellent for stock; being tall and vigorous they require a richer and stronger soil than the more hardy "Yellow Flint" of which "Ninety Day" is one of the best.

The Dent corn also requires a longer season; the best early kind proved to be "Pride of the North," and the best late ones "Kansas 4568," "Reid's Yellow," "Funk's Yellow," and "Old Gold."

Potatoes.—Of these, seven plantings were made in August, November, December, January, February, and May. Complete fertilisers at the rate of 8cwt. to the acre were used, and all sets showing signs of disease were rejected.

The early August planting was partly spoilt by heavy rains and flood water. The varieties comprised 6 imported and 180 new seedlings; of these many failed to germinate, and a large number have been rejected; a few only are promising, the stock of which is now being increased. The crop yielded 4 to 12 tons per acre; average, 7 tons.

November planting consisted of 16 imported kinds and of 28 seedlings; of these 6 imported and 21 seedlings were rejected. Crop dug first week in March. Yield, 1 to 25 tons; average, 8 tons. The best were "Early Norton Beauty;" main crop, "Factor" (25 tons per acre), "Pink Blossom," "Radium," and "Duchess of Norfolk."

Early December planting: Eight varieties. Crop dug first week in April. Yield, 9 to 19 tons; average, 14 tons. Best, "Earl Norton Beauty." Main crop, "Pink Blossom," "Radium," "Snowball." The variety "Factor" was not planted in this lot.

Early January planting: All American imported seeds. Crop dug early in April. Yields 8 to 19 tons; average, 12 tons. Best early, "Red River Triumph"; second early, "Clinton" and "Early Rose."

Late January planting: Twelve seedlings selected from No. 1 (August planting). Dug first week in May. Yield, 6 to 14 tons; average, 9 tons. Best seedling, second early, No. 150. Main crop, Nos. 151-140.

February planting: All American seed. Dug 7th May. Yield, 6 to 8¼ tons per acre; average, 7 tons. Best second early, "Rose of Erin," "Red Jacket."

May planting: Same as No. 1 plot. These comprise 11 of the newest sorts from England and France, including "Violet," the new hybrid of Solanum Commersoni. They are all promising.

The potato moths in the grub stage are one of our most serious pests, eating their way into the tubers, thus spoiling them for seed or table use. Under present conditions the keeping of seed in a sound condition is a most difficult thing. A specially built seed store, fitted with shelves to carry the seed trays, and with plastered ceiling and walls and cemented floor and with close fitting frames covered with wire gauze would, by preventing the ingress of moths and by permitting the free circulation of air, prove a valuable means of storing potato seed. Such store would also be useful for storage of maize and other seeds liable to the depredations of mice and weevils.

The Hamel Farm seems to be singularly well adapted for the raising of sound potato seed for sale. Its area is too small to make it a payable concern as a dairy farm. The growing of potato seed on the other hand, which would be sold to farmers at a fair price, would make it self-supporting, and would confer a boon on potato planters who at times find it very difficult to procure sound seed.

The large sum of £91,000 is still sent away annually to the Eastern States for potatoes, and the raising of that crop is worthy of every encouragement.

Sweet Potatoes is also a most profitable crop; the tubers are excellent for the table, and also provide nutritious feed greatly relished by stock.

Four varieties, sprouted in shallow boxes of sandy soil, under glass, supplied rooted slips which were planted out in November. The vines provide in the early winter very good green feed for milk cows. The yield varied from 7 to 17 tons; the average being 12 tons to the acre. "Spanish Yellow" and "White Maltese" are both recommended.

Cotton.—Seven varieties were sown in November. The plants made slow, but fair healthy growth. It is better adapted to districts with moist summers and dry autumns, and for that reason the South-Western Division of this State has not hitherto proved well adapted for cotton growing. The early American sorts gave the best results, yielding seeded lint at the rate of 350lbs. per acre. "Shine's Early Prolific" and "Louisiana Prolific" proved the best. Seeds were, besides, produced at the rate of half a ton to the acre.

Hops.—The variety "Oregon," planted two years ago, is proving a strong and hardy grower. The crop was picked early in March, and sun-dried in shallow trays covered with hessian. A superior sample was produced which was highly praised by both our brewers and experts in England and in the Eastern States. A satisfactory yield at the rate of 2,250lbs. green, cured 600lbs., worth 1s. 3d. per lb., was produced. We import of hops £20,000 worth a year, and, in spite of the costly picking, it promises to become a profitable crop.

Rice.—Sown in November. Two varieties—"Bertone," Italian, and "Yamani," Egyptian. Ripe in April. Results fair.

New Zealand Hemp.—Thrives best along the edge of brooks.

Tomatoes.—Nine varieties of leading new sorts introduced from England and America. Plants set out in November. All fruited well. The choicest and most prolific are: "King Edward VII.," "Magnificent," "Tenderloin."

Pumpkins.—Six varieties. Sown 5th December. All made vigorous growth, yielding heavy crops of sound fruit. "King of the Mammoth" for stock, and "Table Crown" and "Bugle" for home use are the best.

Water Melons.—Sown 7th December. Ten varieties: all grew and bore well. For quality the best are "Halbert Honey," "Seminole," and "Kleckley Sweet;" for market "Rattlesnake" and "Sugarstick" are good carriers.

Mr. Shiel's Farm, Tammin. Wheat crop : estimated yield 12 bushels to the acre.

Rock Melons.—Six varieties, sown 1st December. Cropped fairly. The best are "Irondequoit," "Tip-top," and "Lewis Perfection."

Orchard.—The trees which were planted in 1904 are all growing vigorously, a few of them showing fruit for the first time.

This orchard was established not as a commercial orchard, but for testing the value of new varieties of fruits, two trees each of a number of varieties being planted for that purpose. Full notes regarding each kind will be made available in due course.

In June, 1905, a fig plantation, consisting mainly of the true drying Smyrna figs "Calimyrna" and "Kassaba," with a suitable proportion of wild Capri No. 1 and No. 2, for fertilising purposes, were imported from California. This plantation will be gradually increased, and when bearing, steps will be taken to introduce the specific wasp, which is the active agent of the caprifi.ation of fig trees.

Date Palm suckers from some of the choicest kinds of Sahara were introduced from Algeria, a few of which were planted at Hamel to supply suckers for stocking the warmer districts of the North-West, which has been proved to be well suited for the date palm.

Amongst other plants a few pine-apples, buck yams, and taniers were also raised from introduced plants.

Fodder Plants.—A number of valuable kinds for summer use were tested amongst others.

Cow Peas.—Four varieties sown early in December, when the ground is warm. The most robust kind proved to be the "Black" and the "Iron" cow pea. They all grew luxuriantly, covering the ground with a leafy growth.

Teosinte.—Sown early in December. The plants stooled out remarkably well, and attained the height of 10ft.; requires rich moist soil and a warm climate. The seeds do not mature at the latitude of Hamel.

Mazagarua (Sorghum cernum).—A strong variety of African millet or Dhoura. Sown 22nd November. Stools out freely and makes a remarkably vigorous growth 12ft. high; does not mature its seeds as far South as Hamel. A fresh supply of seeds for sowing in the warmer North-West is expected from Nigeria.

Vetches.—Only 7 out of 28 varieties germinated; these did not make satisfactory growth; they were sown late, 1st of June. Better results would probably be obtained if sown in the autumn, on high and well drained land.

Pearl Millet.—Sown 24th November; growth good; good green feed when cut young. Stools out well; can be cut several times.

Sorghum Saccharatum and Amber Cane.—Sown 7th December; made very good growth, 10ft. high; useful fodder if cut when sweet, late in the autumn.

Giant Millet.—Sown 23rd December; growth tall and even, 5ft.; good for green feed; ripe early in April. Large drooping heads; seeds useful for poultry.

Hungarian Millet.—Sown the same date; very rapid grower, 4ft. high; ripe early in April; heads well filled.

Experimental Grasses.—A large number of small plots were sown in drills during the early part of last winter. Of 70 varieties sown in May,

1905, 26 failed to come up or else died off during the long wet winter. The best are:—Chewing's fescue, sheep's burnett, Canada blue grass, wallaby grass, Festuca teniufolia, cocksfoot, tall fescue, Timothy, tall oat grass, Paspalum dilatatum, Rhodes grass, African wonder grass. These are greatly relished by the cattle. O rye grasses, Pacey's rye grass withstood the heat better and did not die off like the other rye grasses.

Indigenous Grasses.—Of these Mr. Berthoud says:—" There are a large number of valuable grasses and fodder plants worthy of extensive culture; owing to the difficulty of obtaining ripe seeds a few only are grown on these plots. Country residents seldom gather and send seeds; I am always pleased to receive seeds of any useful or ornamental native plant. Of those grown here the following have done well:—Danthonia or Wallaby Grass, several varieties; Mitchell Grass, one variety, good; Kangaroo Grass, one variety; Andropogon, three kinds, all good, and stand heat very well."*

From the foregoing it is easily understood of what practical importance the introduction and trial culture of plants of economic value as staple crop, fodder plants, and grasses have for all interested in the cultivation of the soil and also for the State itself.

No reasonable outlay should be spared in carrying out work of such educational value. Such undertaking is manifestly beyond the means or inclination of the average farmer, and it is one which the State can best take in hand and carry out for the benefit of all.

A. DESPEISSIS, M.R.A.C.,
Acting Director of Agriculture.

Report of the Chief Inspector of Stock.

THE DIRECTOR OF AGRICULTURE.

I have the honour to submit my Report on the working of this section of the past twelve months.

STAFF.

No increase has been made to the staff during the past term. Over twelve months ago I recommended the appointment of an additional Inspector to more thoroughly supervise the markets in the South-West Division, but, although the Hon. the Minister approved, a delay has occurred in consequence of investigations which had to be made by the Public Service Commissioner, and which are evidently not yet concluded. For this reason, a great deal of additional railway travelling had to be done by other Inspectors, and even then the most perfect supervision could not be obtained. In all other respects the staff has performed particularly good service, and I think this is clearly exemplified by the very marked reduction in outbreaks of disease.

---

* A more detailed report of the work done at Hamel by Mr. Berthoud will be published in the next issue of the JOURNAL.

TICK CATTLE.

The old and much discussed tick trouble has once more been brought forcibly into evidence by the recent discovery of ticks on Mr. Morrison's cattle at Waterhall, near Guildford, and the continuous hatching which occurred in the Bayswater District since December of last year. Although both outbreaks were somewhat serious when first discovered, yet the prompt action and care exercised particularly by Mr. Morrison, was the means of a speedy diminution of the pest, and the most recent inspection found the animals perfectly clean. A somewhat similar experience is also being obtained at Bayswater, where, with one exception, the herds are free from the parasite, and there is every appearance of an early eradication. This satisfactory condition is to a great extent due to the altered climatic conditions, which bears out the experience gained with the pest in past years, viz., that successful hatching could occur in this latitude during the summer months, but with the advent of winter vitality becomes impaired, and the tick is ultimately rendered effete. It is therefore apparent that the fear entertained with regard to ticks becoming established in these parts need not be seriously entertained. The winter season should be the means of exterminating them, but although this is now almost an established fact, yet every care is necessary against further infestation, as although no great injury may accrue from fever, yet the presence of the parasite is also a menace, particularly where milking herds are concerned. We must, however, not overlook our beef supplies, as, until such time as our Southern herds meet the local requirements, supplies must be brought from East Kimberley, and any delay which may occur in transit generally creates unfavourable conditions.

As soon as circumstances will allow, the question of slaughtering all tick-infested cattle at Wyndham will have to be considered, and works necessary for the trade established. This will obviate any further trouble regarding the tick in these parts, and relieve the minds of many who are building up valuable herds in our agricultural centres. The continuous dry seasons in East Kimberley have resulted in a further lesson, and no injury has resulted from fever to any of the stock within the infected area. Losses, however, have again taken place in connection with clean cattle travelling through infected country *en route* for shipment at Wyndham, and it was with a view of preventing a recurrence of this trouble that a personal visit had to be made to the district.

The matter is now under consideration by the Government, and it is hoped a solution of the difficulty will be found. The securing of an overland route for tick-infested stores is also a matter of urgency, as many of the smaller stations are becoming overstocked, and no outlet is at present available, unless by the Northern Territory, which occurrence, if possible, should be checked, as it is very much against the interest of the State.

PLEURO-PNEUMONIA.

It is gratifying to be able to report that this disease, which was so prevalent a few years ago, was confined to one outbreak for the year. This occurred amongst a large herd in the Balbarrup District, but its eradication was accomplished without any serious loss occurring, and no further developments have taken place. Two instances were noticeable amongst the early shipments of East Kimberley cattle, but the lesions were of an old standing character, and nothing of an active nature has been discovered.

My own examination of many of the herds in East Kimberley, and the reports to hand from the local inspector were, and are of the most favourable character, and we are of opinion that the disease has been exterminated. As far as is known, therefore, the State may be considered free from this disease.

TUBERCULOSIS.

Instances of this complaint are not infrequently being met with, particularly in the dairy herds, but although the Tuberculin Test has been applied to others of a suspicious nature, it cannot be said that the disease is at all general.

Tuberculosis in pigs.—The complaint has been more pronounced amongst pigs this year. This may be attributed to in-breeding; and with the discovery that a certain strain of stud animals was affected and were transmitting the disease to their progeny, remedial steps were taken. The prompt destruction of these, and more careful attention to breeding, should have the required effect, and prevent a recurrence of the trouble. With this exception, pigs have been exceptionally healthy throughout the State. Three outbreaks only were reported for the year: one at York, diagnosed as pneumonia, became amenable to treatment; the others, at Canning and Fremantle respectively, were considered suspicious of swine fever, though the outbreaks fortunately did not spread beyond the original animals affected, and the premises are now in a satisfactory sanitary condition.

DISEASE.

A disease peculiar to young animals in the midland parts of the State has been investigated during the term, and the complaint was diagnosed as an ulcerated condition of the joints, more particularly the hock and hip. The trouble was often noticeable at birth, but usually became apparent a few weeks after. Weakness of the hind quarters, followed by almost complete paralysis, being especially characteristic. A want of lime salts in the food or nutrition supplied to the young before birth was advanced as the cause, and this theory was borne out by an analysis which was afterwards made of the soil on which the stock had been running. Phosphate of lime more particularly was found to be wanting, and this appears to be the case with nearly all the lands of the State, which element can only be successfully applied where agriculture is being followed.

LIVE STOCK GENERALLY.

Owners of stock throughout the State are to be congratulated on the freedom from disease which at present exists amongst their flocks and herds. Probably in no other country in the world can such favourable conditions be obtained in this direction, and, with careful supervision, there is no reason why the same happy state of immunity should not be maintained. Poison plants and Zamia palms are, unfortunately, still a source of worry to many, but their extermination is slowly but surely being carried out, and this after all is the only practical way of overcoming the trouble. Owing to the dry seasons experienced in the North, a very serious shortage has resulted in fat sheep for the supply of our local markets, and this has necessitated the importation of over 17,000 beyond last year's number.

This is regrettable, as the deficiency might have been avoided had the ruling price of stores been less for the supply to our local farms. Fat cattle from Kimberley are also likely to be affected by the dry conditions prevailing there, but the speedy growth of our Southern herds, which has been taking place during the past few years, may be the means of supplying any want in this direction. However, although the season has not been good throughout the State, it is gratifying to find that the recent statistical returns show a steady increase in the various branches, which means additional wealth for the State, and a happy augury for the future.

HORSES.

In last year's report attention was drawn to the large imports which were being made in horses, particularly draughts, brought from the Eastern States. Therein the necessity was advised for some action being taken to stimulate the breeding of this class of animal. Although a good deal of correspondence has occurred in the matter, nothing of a definite character has apparently been done, and the position unfortunately remains unaltered.

I would suggest that the various agricultural societies take the matter in hand, and with united action inaugurate a scheme which would tend towards the stimulation of the industry in this State.

PASTURES.

Growth was retarded in the Southern parts of the State during the early part of winter, but the recent heavy rains will have the effect of stimulating growth, and a plentiful supply should now be obtainable.

The Ashburton and Gascoyne districts were particularly dry until about two months ago, when a favourable change occurred and rain became general. This also applies to the Lower Murchison, but the upper portion has not been so favoured, and in consequence the losses in lambing will be somewhat serious. Two dry seasons have now been experienced in the Kimberleys. Many of the stations, particularly those inland, are already short of feed, and unless rains are had by the end of the year it will be a difficult matter for many to secure even bare sustenance for their stock.

Inspection fees, stock introduced from Eastern States into Western Australia from 1st July, 1905, to 30th June, 1906.

Horses	...	...	...	...	...	...	1,113	}	1,167
Mares	...	...	...	...	...	...	54		
Cattle	...	...	...	...	...	...	4,817		
Bulls	...	...	...	...	...	...	74	}	5,356
Cows	...	...	...	...	...	...	465		
Sheep	...	...	...	...	...	...	45,587		
Rams	...	...	...	2,328	...	2,369		}	49,859
Ewes	...	...	...	1,868	...	1,903			
Pigs	...	...	...	3	...	...	...		3
Dogs	...	...	...	...	...	...	...		138
Poultry	...	...	...	...	...	...	...		1,042
Camels	...	...	...	103	...	...	...		103
Goats	...	...	...	41	...	...	...		41
Donkey	...	...	...	1	...	...	...		3
Mules	...	...	...	4	...	...	...		13

Inspection fees collected for above, £498 18s. 7d.

Inspection fees, stock introduced from England into Western Australia from 1st July, 1905, to 30th June, 1906.

Horses	...	...	... 9	Dogs	...	...	...	5
Sheep	...	...	... 1	Poultry	...	...	...	3
Rams	...	...	... 1	Camels	...	...	...	2
Pigs	...	...	... 7	Goats	...	...	...	1

Inspection fees collected for above, £6 3s.

Inspection fees for stock exported from Western Australia to Eastern States.

Horses	...	...	... 34	Camels ...	...	...	...	2
Dogs ...	...	...	... 53	Goats ...	...	...	...	2
Sheep...	...	...	... 1	Pig	...	...	...	1
Poultry	...	...	... 52					

Inspection fees collected, £14 0s. 9d.

To South Africa ... 1 horse... 5s. | To England ...2 horses ...7s. 6d.

Export Certificates.

Hides and skins exported from Western Australia to Eastern
States—
    Revenue collected ... ... £32 0s. 0d.

Jetty Dues.

Revenue collected	£122 5s. 3d·
Fines collected for introducing stock into Western Australia without certificates	£10 10s. 0d.
Fees collected for Veterinary Attendance	£8 8s. 0d.
Rent collected for Quarantine Yards, Robb's Jetty	£200 0s. 0d.
Rent collected for Cottages, Robb's Jetty	£33 0s. 0d.
Water Rates collected, Robb's Jetty	£16 16s. 0d.
Dipping Charges, Robb's Jetty	£33 10s. 0d.

Stock landed at Fremantle from North-West Ports from 1st July, 1905, to 31st May, 1906.

Name of Port.	Cattle.	Horses.	Sheep.	Pigs.
Wyndham	7,789	70	...	...
Derby	2,278	...	1,907	...
Port Hedland	248	104	2,183	...
Cossack	...	12	1,940	...
Onslow	...	...	...	43
Carnarvon	2,308	55	25,189	...
Point Sampson	99	...	...	...
TOTALS	12,722	241	31,219	43

R. E. WEIR, M.R.C.V.S.,
Chief Inspector of Stock.

Manager's Report of the Government Refrigerating Works.

The Under Secretary for Agriculture.

I have the honour to forward, herewith, the 9th Annual Report of the Government Refrigerating Works ending 30th June, 1906.

The writer relieved the late manager (Mr. Gresham) on 22nd June last year. After reporting what should be taken in hand to repair and freshen up the building and plant, clients were written to and visited, and all probable and possible sources of business looked up.

The repair work then in progress, taken over from the late manager, was completed, after which all parts of the building insulation were sampled. Out of 24 samples taken, those from the bottom passage floor were found most defective. This floor was repaired, and the whole of the outside of the building was cleaned up, painted, and roof repaired. The machinery overhaul disclosed a well-worn plant, so far as the refrigerating section was concerned.

The vote for repairs coming late, we decided to postpone further work after October till time and opportunity allowed a more thorough overhaul to be schemed out and undertaken. One of the CO_2 condensers punctured and blew out in November, as the summer rise in pressure was beginning to be felt. The other condenser, practically as old, was then responsible for the whole of the work from that date to the present time. This indication that our plant had seen its best days was the subject of a report to you, with the result that a Linde Ammonia Compression and Forced Air system will replace the present worn out apparatus, and the building will be brought up to date as far as possible this year. It goes without saying that this failure of our plant at the beginning of summer spoilt our prospects somewhat, and it was deemed prudent by the Hon. the Minister not to take on too many leases in consequence till we were on surer ground. The gradual decline of the efficiency of this part of the plant showed the wisdom of the course, and our revenue suffered in consequence, not so much for lack of probable business as for lack of power.

As the balance-sheet shows, we did practically as well this year as last, but the amount of ice orders we could not fill would have made a very substantial increase on all previous efforts. Our selling end was considerably ahead of our manufacturing end, and as the latter required continual nursing to keep things together, the former had simply to wait.

Our only hope in this business is to have a good margin of power to make ice while the sun shines, so that experimental work in cold storage products may be paid for by the more remunerative business of supplying ice.

Increasingly keen competition in shipping and handling perishable products militated against operators carrying anything like the stock of former years. Shipping facilities now so regular and well-managed means that cold storage work that might be done here is done in Melbourne or Sydney, where they handle large quantities for their Western Australian clients. This, of course, is to be expected when the margin of profit to the distributor shrinks, and, no matter how well we might be equipped, the best days of storing for imported produce are passing.

A rough estimate made by one of our largest importers is that we now grow and kill three-quarters of our own beef, two-thirds of our own mutton, and four-fifths of our own fresh pork; while there is no reason that we should not draw more heavily on our own stock supplies for local consumption. If stock routes over dry stages are the difficulty, the cold storage man must be brought into requisition as the only practical solution of the fresh meat problem.

Two new lines of imported produce have been added by the local firms to the long list of cold storage commodities brought into the State. We refer to rock oysters, trawled at great depths in New Zealand waters, and frozen into small bottles solid. While this commodity is within the reach only of the fairly well off, the possibility of transporting foodstuffs in this compact form is worthy of imitation in many other lines such as raw fruit, juices, and pulps. The other new line, a shipment of chilled beef and mutton from Melbourne, is of more interest and points to greater possibilities in displacing a great deal of the hard frozen stuff by placing a better article on the table. The first shipment by the " Riverina " we inspected was only a partial success. It was stowed in racks and not hung, and was carried at too high a temperature in an unsuitable chamber with still air and dripping coils overhead. This damp air prevented the *rigor mortis* from giving the " set " that distinguishes well hung chilled meat from ordinary fresh or defrosted meat; it also gave it a bleached and uninviting appearance. Chilled meat, as distinct from frozen or locally-grown fresh meat, now forms a heavy proportion of the oversea supply to Great Britain, and at no distant date we may draw most of our meat from our Northern stock areas for the greater part of the year. It is well to note that U.S.A. and South American chilled meat sells at practically double the price of Australian frozen meat at Glasgow and London.

Wholesale butchers' stores were fairly well occupied during the year, but of course nothing to the extent of a few years ago. The retail butchers are going in for ice-cooled chambers in their own shops. This saves a lot of time in carting as well as expense, and has probably come to stay. To meet this new order of things we must sell more ice, until the demand for cold storage space by the State-grown products displaces the oversea import, and for the next few years at all events it will pay us better to widen the area of ice consumption at a low rate in preference to having a valuable plant standing idle. The ice supplied to the Railway Department for cooling refrigerating cars, though an improvement on previous years, is a long way under what these cars should consume for efficient transport. A refrigerated car being an expensive mass of timber and insulation, when cooled down by ice will give the best possible results, but if the car is loaded with cold storage produce without ice it is then the hottest vehicle on the line.

The mass of hot structure absorbs all the work that the refrigerating machine has put into the produce in transit, to the great detriment of such produce.

The Commissioner in yielding to consignees in this matter, who excuse themselves on the ground of their short journey only to Perth, should reconsider the *time* factor in the case. Consignees will unblushingly talk of claims for damaged stuff in cool stores, even although the stuff arrived damp and soft through lack of consistency on the part of Railway authorities to run these expensive cars as their design and construction demand they should be run. This is the primary cost of most of the losses in beef, mutton, and rabbits. Once the outer film of frost crystallisation thaws, the damp begins and encourages mould and decay; all pretence of restoring the bloom and flavour after a bad trip in a hot car from ship's side or elsewhere is a useless waste of power and money.

If ever cold storage is to be made remunerative in this State the absurdity of loading a so-called refrigerated car with frozen produce probably a hundred degrees F. colder than the car itself must cease, and if the distance to be travelled cannot be adjusted to a payable rate the more vital factor of *time* should be considered. Butter, for example, often reaches us at a temperature of *eighty-four degrees F.*, and runs like oil through the interstices of the cases. Agents who handle this commodity complacently accept this state of affairs with the Railways, while at the same they tell us our freezing charges are too high.

The overhaul work undertaken since last annual report consisted of completing fire service schemed out by previous manager. We also changed the supply of water for the boilers from the sewage to City main, thus substituting a better supply augmented by all steam condensed. This has led to an improved internal condition of the boilers, commented favourably upon by the machinery inspectors. The other work of plant and building repair was wound up in October, for the reason that further tinkering was only a waste of money. We therefore decided to allow the unspent balance of the authority to stand over till something more thorough was schemed out. Our scheme for improving plant and building is embodied in the plans and specifications now ratified.

The Health authorities' mandate, based upon City Engineer's report, "that we abolish the spray from tower nuisance over footpath," was already provided for in our last year's work, but left unfinished for the foregoing reason. The sudden outburst of new-born interest in March last by the City Engineer in our tower, which has been doing the same work for the past nine years, was as unnecessary as the kindergarten methods used in collecting the data for his report.

We would place on record our best thanks to Mr. Cooke, the Government Astronomer, for his valuable assistance in correcting our thermometers and devising an ingenious temperature recorder, whereby the temperature of experimental room is transmitted at will to the office by an electrical current improvement of his own adaptation. This saves door opening, and the consequent inrush of hot as well as the outrush of cold air, and is very useful.

The coupon system for sundries and ice, introduced by us in October, has been a great success in labour saving. Out of 5,300 issued, only two were carelessly or intentionally misplaced. We hold Health Board's certificate for the destruction of the misplaced baskets and our "stuff in" and "stuff out" balances.

We burned close on £1,000 worth of Collie coal during the year, all of which was tested and checked. All the mines have had a turn, and it would be invidious to place any one much ahead of another, as all send damp stuff occasionally. Taking the whole year's workings on the Babcock & Wilcox boilers our evaporation was seldom less than 5lbs. steam per lb. of coal from and at 212° F. for the whole period.

All hands worked well, and there were no absentees from any cause other than annual leave.

The question of improving the approaches to our leading platform, with a view to help business, is now well within reasonable distance of being undertaken.

The rubbish dump has been the centre of discussion for some time, and although somewhat improved by adapting sealed cans for market refuse, nothing short of demolition will abolish a harbour for nuisance by so-called men with the habits of animals.

Our first work on fruit was on sealed packages for the November Show of last year. We held these from June, and supplied thermograph records of temperature of the experimental room during the period of storage. The Press and producers commented favourably on the work, the methods, and the result. We had a great many inquiries for fruit space early in the season, but the shortage and high prices did not favour holding over, and we have stored about a couple of thousand cases for produce dealers, and as these cases have been picked and packed for the auction, bruises, stem punctures, finger nail marks, and other evidences of careless handling and grading were to be expected.

Pears and apples can be seen here after six months' storage, and will speak for themselves. The flavour, weight, and condition will compare well with anything in Australia, so my informants say who have spent their lives in the business.

Next year we hope to be better able to meet the expected surplus with the new plant and system, and have no doubt other plants will be installed here for fruit storage now that the advantages of cool storing are being demonstrated.

Sale-room prices now and in the month of March will give a fair idea of this year's operations. Pears bought at 10s. and 11s. have realised 22s. 6d. The charge of 2d. per case per week is as cheap as anywhere in Australia. It amounts to less than one apple or one pear per week. Each fruit packed carefully free from bruises and skin abrasions means one week's storage for a case. Growers and farmers should have the butt end of this fact in their mind's-eye when writing so ably for reduced rates to the Department. Supervision, system, and thoroughness are all that is required, but growers may rest assured that the average stuff sent to auction rooms would not be fit for cold storage, as 50 per cent. is usually useless through disregard of what they themselves know to be the standard of prime stuff. Agents and produce dealers complain bitterly of the lack of honour on the part of growers to keep to their promises. Stuff opened here, for which 1s. per case over the ruling price rate was paid, disclosed "windfalls" and rubbishy stuff that would discredit a whole district.

We have done considerable experimental work during the year on fruits and eggs, and these observations are still proceeding. Briefly, it may interest producers to know that eggs bought at 10d. per dozen in November sold in the auction room in May at 2s. and 2s. 6d. per dozen. This does not include the probable thirty per cent. selling charge of the retailers on the above figures. The cost covering that period for 100 dozen eggs would be 2s. 6d. per week in one barrel. We can do quantities over ten barrels at the rate of 2s. per week. It is no exaggeration to state that those eggs auctioned in the sale-room at 2s. and 2s. 6d. on the same date that new laid eggs were realising 2s. 10d. to 3s. per dozen, were practically as good as the new laid article. The most expert egg dealer in the sale-room on that date could not tell the difference between the eggs we had stored 25 weeks previously and those laid that morning. Taking the moderate figure of 1s. per dozen as a purchasing price, and 2s. per dozen as a selling price, conditions,we are assured, quite within the next few seasons' possibilities, the margin of profit for the owner of stored eggs is worthy of consideration. We prefer the eggs in pasteboard or wire fillers. This insures better circulation of air, and possesses none of the objectional features of chaff or bran packing in exchanging flavours. These stored eggs are eatable after 14 days' exposure to the sun, a fair limit for every-day business. It may be safely assumed that fresh eggs cool stored by our method will turn out as fresh six months after storing as they were the day they came into our charge.

ABATTOIRS.

The writer begs to report that after an engagement in Queensland he took up the work here on May of last year.

After spending a short time looking at plans already prepared, files dealing with the question and the proposed sites, a report was forwarded recommending certain modifications in plans and site position, which, in the writer's opinion, will improve the cost of handling and supervision of such abattoirs when they are erected.

A report dealing with an abattoir under offer to the Government was forwarded during September.

The proposed Kalgoorlie and Boulder City site was visited and reported upon in April of this year. The writer, in consultation with the Chief Architect's Department, suggested certain alterations to the sketch plans already prepared, with a view to give greater facility in handling fresh and chilled meat for local requirements and conditions. The trade there having been used to the primitive methods generally associated with private abattoirs will naturally take a little time to appreciate the new order of things should the central system be adopted, but there can be no question that a more efficient, cleanly, and better supervised meat supply will follow their advent in this as well as any other town that adopts this system.

Basing the cost of such abattoirs on figures supplied by the best abattoir practice in Australia, we find that a range of from 15s. to 30s. per head of the population supplied by such public abattoirs is about the average all round.

In figuring out £20,000 for the Kalgoorlie-Boulder centre for buildings and plant, we believe that by the use of local materials such as jarrah in the construction, the final cost of the buildings will be within the average. We believe that a type of a strong framed open, airy structure, will serve our purpose just as well or better than the more ponderous stone and brick architectural triumphs of the older States ; provided, always, that the appliances and equipment are well chosen. The question of fencing, roads, or railway sidings are not considered in the above figure. Railway haulage of materials to the sites—always a big item of first cost—will have to be offset by having plain substantial buildings, with a maximum of efficiency in equipment.

While the important question of drainage will be a matter of little difficulty at Fremantle or coastal towns generally, owing to the handiness of fall to the sea outlet, the inland towns will be a more complex problem. Areas for sewage farm cultivation must be considered in the reserves marked off for abattoirs, so that every available source of revenue may be utilised to reduce running costs, even with unsaleable residues from floor washings.

30th June, 1906.

RECEIPTS AND EXPENDITURE AT GOVERNMENT REFRIGERATING WORKS.
1905-1906.

Receipts.

							£	s.	d.
Rents	...	...	...	...	...	...	2,074	2	0
Ice ...	...	...	...	...	...	...	1,055	19	3
Storage	...	...	...	...	...	...	719	18	0
							£3,849	19	3

Expenditure.

			£	s.	d.
Salaries and Wages	... ...	...	1,807	12	5
Coal	... ...	...	557	17	7
Freight	... ...	...	452	14	8
Calcium	... ...	...	65	0	4
Gas	... ...	...	112	3	3
Cartage	... ...	...	34	3	0
Electric Plant Maintenance	... ...	...	62	14	3
Oil and Waste	... ...	...	53	16	0
Packing	... ...	...	2	12	3
Water	... ...	...	83	15	3
Leather	... ...	...	16	14	0
City Council	... ...	...	5	12	8
Miscellaneous Tools, Boiler Requisites, Inspection, etc.			76	0	3
Special Authorities—					
Platform Scales, Thermograph, and Clock	...	...	24	13	5
			£3,355	9	5

		£	s.	d.			
Deposit on Gas Bottles to be returned							
when bottles are returned	... ...	36	0	0			
Value of Materials in Stock	... ...	40	0	0			
					76	0	0
					£3,279	9	5

A. D. CAIRNS.

Manager Government Refrigerating Works.

10th July, 1906.

Report on the Rabbit Department.

The Under Secretary for Agriculture.

In compliance with instructions received, I beg to submit hereunder a review of work, etc., in connection with the Rabbit Branch during the year ending 30th June, 1906, for use in compilation of Annual Report.

The year just closed has, on the whole, been unusually dry, and one therefore not considered favourable to the increase of rabbits; as a matter of fact very little breeding has been noticeable during the latter half of the summer and early autumn. A considerable wave of the pest reached the fence during the spring season, and kept the boundary-riders busy clearing the traps and guarding against burrowing close to the netting. During the months of September, October, and November, no less than 5,115 captures were made in the traps along 465 miles of the fence, and the remains of numbers of others (for which scalps were not recorded) were also found, some destroyed by dingoes, others by the poison plant.

During the excessive heat of December, January, and February, the rabbits kept off the fence clearing, though they appeared to be as numerous as ever back in the shade of the scrub. In December the scalps obtained numbered 775, and during the first quarter of the present calendar year the captures fell away to 607. It would appear as though the rabbits have come to recognise that they have encountered an effectual barrier, and are recoiling somewhat to the Eastward.

Throughout the greater part of the summer the presence of numbers of emu parading up and down the fence interfered very much with the successful working of the small "gin" traps, otherwise many more rabbits might have been caught.

The fence is being kept in perfect order throughout, and wherever any suspicion of weakness asserts itself, steps are at once taken to effect improvement. In this way a deviation was erected during the year at 204 miles north, where it was found that "boodie" holes existed on both sides of the fence for a considerable distance, and as rabbits were taking possession of those on the east side, and an examination showed that some holes passed right under the fence, a new bit of fencing was erected to embrace the whole of the danger area. Near the 250-miles north, where the fence had been subject to undermining, from storm-water off the hills, it was found advisable to safeguard the position by considerable drainage and other earthwork. Somewhat similar work had to be done at several points within twenty miles south of Burracoppin. About twenty miles north, where the fence crosses a narrow saltpan, an examination showed that the netting beneath the surface of the ground had deteriorated very much, and in several places was eaten right through within a couple of inches of the surface. After three years standing in such saline soil this was not unexpected. The bottom strip of netting was renewed over some thirty panels. (The netting in the fence at the south coast end is, as yet, standing the effects of the salt sea air remarkably well.)

Some damage occurred to the fence in places during the summer owing to bush fires; the worst of these destroyed some seventy posts, but the effectiveness of the fence was not interfered with even for a day, as temporary repairs were immediately effected, and the damage soon afterwards made thoroughly good.

The prevalence of gales during the summer also caused a lot of temporary injury to the fence through trees and limbs falling upon same, though not in such a way as to cause a free passage for rabbits, and the boundary-riders at once got to work putting things in order again.

One instance occurred during the year of a gate being left open for fully twenty-four hours. Inquiry pointed to the almost certain conclusion that this was the work of aboriginals.

The conservation of a water supply for fence maintenance purposes between the goldfields railway line and the South coast was completed during the year by the department's two day labourers, and notwithstanding the exceptionally long and hot summer, no inconvenience to speak of was experienced from shortage of water along that portion. Tanks, etc., have been constructed by the Works Department along the 250 miles north of the railway line; a sufficient supply along that portion should therefore be available next summer.

The construction by the Works Department of seven huts along the fence has enabled boundary-riders to live more comfortably, and conduced considerably to their contentment. Buildings, including inspector's cottage, store rooms, cart shed, stable, and the necessary yard accommodation have also been completed at the main depôt (Burracoppin); and a paddock embracing 260 acres has been fenced in for the accommodation of horses or camels; this has been ring-barked, and scrub cut .in same, and is gradually being cleared and sown with grass seed.

At all boundary-riders' camps and other suitable places along the fence line, a trial of artificial grasses has been made. Last year Johnston-grass seed was sown, but the late date of sowing and the dry season which followed probably accounted for only a small proportion of it showing up. This autumn, besides Johnston grass, Wallaby grass, Rape, and a mixture of seeds were planted in good time, and are already showing signs of coming on well. Feed for live stock being very scarce along the fence, these grasses, should the trial be successful, will prove of great benefit to the maintenance staff.

Rain-gauges, to the number of nine, have been installed along about 400 miles of fence line; the rainfall is regularly recorded and returns forwarded monthly to the department and the Government Astronomer. The average rainfall along the fence, commencing 40 miles North of the sea, at Starvation Harbour, and running Northward to a point about 60 miles Eastward of Mount Magnet was—in January 47 points, February 69 points, March $7\frac{1}{2}$ points, April 10 points, May $137\frac{1}{2}$ points, June, 133 points.

An improvement has been effected in the means by which supervision of fence maintenance has been carried out, by the providing the supervising officers with a light buckboard buggy and pair of mules or brumbies. The original plan of examining the fence from the top of a camel was never satisfactory and camels soon became fractious at being compelled to go down so frequently to allow proper inspection to be made. Now that a fair water supply is established along the fence, the use of the former animals has become possible.

The introduction of a light camel wagon for conveying supplies has also proved an advantage over packing the animals; boundary riders and rabbiters' provisions are regularly delivered by this means at depôts along the fence once every two months. During the year the camels formerly in use by the tank-sinking party were passed over to rabbiters and the ration carrier; this enabled the dispensing with one camel driver, and the men who were retained out of the above party for casual work were provided with a dray and pair of horses.

The grubbing of the mallee-butts along the fence clearing between Burracoppin and the sea, by the Public Works Department, has considerably lightened the duties of the boundary-riders on that part during the last few months. The work previously necessary to prevent the growth of suckers near the netting was in some places more than the men were able to overtake. The grubbing has made possible the increasing of most of the lengths, and some reduction of the maintenance staff.

The work of coping with the rabbits which got to the westward of the outer fence line before the barrier was completed has been proceeded with vigorously, especially during the dry summer months.

Although the rabbits between the two fences exist in places far apart, and covering a vast area—from near the coast on the South, to the neighbourhood of Nannine in the North—at no place can it be said they are numerous; and the efforts to destroy them are at present more than keeping pace with the natural increase. Every effort was made during the hot weather to suppress those colonies which had established themselves along the shores of Lakes Carmody, Hurleston, and Varley, and with such good effect that fresh traces of rabbits have become difficult to find in localities previously fairly thickly infested. The arrival of rains has made the examination of country possible which during the summer was inaccessible from want of water; such examination so far has shown that the chain of lakes referred to extends for fully a hundred miles, and traces of a few rabbits are to be seen at different points throughout that distance.

North of the railway line the incursion appears to be still in a more or less migratory stage. At no place are the rabbits established in any numbers; and when any small colony is located and most of its members destroyed, those few that have escaped the traps and poison move off elsewhere.

During the summer three poison distributers were obtained, and used with phosphorised pollard wherever it was found they could be worked to advantage. Unfortunately, the most of the country is too thick with scrub to enable their use at places remote from the fence, but near the latter they did some good work. Camels, however, proved very awkward cattle to work in the shafts of a poison cart among stumps and timber; but owing to the scarcity of water their use had to be resorted to.

The discovery of the presence of rabbits on the West side of No. 2 fence, some 45 miles North of Cunderdin, appeared at first a rather serious matter. On making thorough investigation it was found that very few rabbits (apparently not more than a couple) had got across the fence line at that part before the fence was erected, having evidently come across from Cowcowing Lakes, on the shores of which a small colony had been located at the time the fence was in course of erection. Vigorous steps were taken to stamp out this small incursion; one rabbit was trapped, miles of lines of baits were laid, and soon all signs of fresh traces disappeared. Some hundreds of square miles of country were searched to ascertain whether any rabbits might have escaped farther Westward, but up to the present nothing has been discovered to show that any of the invading rabbits were left alive.

The number of rabbits captured between the two fences, and for which scalps were handed over during the year did not average more than 190 per month; what number were destroyed by poison, the bodies of which were not found in the scrub and holes, it is impossible to estimate.

Acting upon instructions received on the 13th February, I marked off a block of 21 acres in the reserve at 20-mile South, for the purpose of cropping. This has since been cleared and sown—ten acres with wheat, and ten with oats; also about half an acre with a mixture of grass seeds.

In the Burracoppin paddock another ten acres were, in accordance with instructions, cleared and sown with mixed wheat and oats. Both crops were fertilised with 75 pounds of superphosphate to the acre. They are looking remarkably well up to the present, and promise satisfactory yields.

H. M. WILSON,
Rabbit Branch.

Burracoppin, 14th July, 1906.

CROPPING THE EASTERN SAND PLAINS.

By T. W. KIRTON.

Under instructions from the Government Agricultural Chemist I visited some "sand plains" at Tammin towards the end of October to procure specimens of wheat grown on these areas for exhibition at the Royal Agricultural Show, and the following notes as to the condition under which the wheat was grown have been prepared by his direction:—

The "Eastern sand plain" is a term applied to a large tract of semi-arid country lying to the east of Meckering on the Eastern Goldfields line.

At Tammin some interesting trials of this land for agricultural purposes have been made by Mr. W. H. Shields, whose place I visited. The soil on that sand plain is of a grey colour on the surface merging into a yellow sand extending to a depth of 2 feet, and under this a stratum of clay and gravel. The natural vegetation is a short mallee scrub, which is cleared at a cost of 5s. to 10s. an acre.

The average rainfall is 12 inches, which falls very regularly during a period of six months, extending from March to October, when the crops are in possession of the ground.

The fertiliser used on Mr. Shields' land was 150lbs. of superphosphate to the acre, drilled in with the seed. The seed was sown from March to June. The accompanying illustrations will convey a better impression of the results than any verbal description.

Mr. Shiel's Farm, Tammin. General view of the crops of Rye, Wh

Four crops have been planted, viz., 100 acres each of rye, oats, barley, and wheat, the rye being in the centre and the other crops planted in concentric circles around it.

The following is the anticipated average yield of the different crops :—

	Hay per acre.	Grain per acre.
1. Wheat	18 cwts. ...	10 bushels
2. Oats	...	12 „
3. Barley...	. ...	15·5 „
4. Rye	...	15·5 „

Samples of soil were taken as follows and analysed in the Government Laboratory :—

1. Surface soil (to a depth of 9 inches) from four different points on the uncultivated virgin sand plain.

2. Surface soil (to a depth of 9 inches), mixed samples from four parts of experimental area.

3. Subsoil from same places as No. 2 (from 9 inches to 18 inches).

4. Clay substratum.

The following results of the analysis are published here by permission of the Government Analyst :—

MATERIAL: SIX SAMPLES OF SOIL FOR ANALYSIS, TAKEN FROM SAND PLAINS
AT TAMMIN, EASTERN RAILWAY.

Result f Analysis.

	1.	2.	3. .	4.	5.	6.
Percentage of Fine Soil (Passed by 2 mm. sieve) ...	98·91	98·52	91·95	98·72	98·88	98·10
Percentage of stones and roots (Retained by 2 mm. sieve)	1·09	1·48	8·04	1·28	1·12	1·90
Reaction of Soil—	Acid	Faintly Acid	Faintly Acid	Almost Neutral	Alkaline	Alkaline

ANALYSIS OF FINE EARTH—AIR DRIED.

Percentage of Fertilising Ingredients.

	1.	2.	3.	4.	5.	6.
Total Constituents—						
Phosphoric Acid	·019	·014	·014	·01	·018	·028
Potash	·028	·026	·068	·046	·27	·24
Lime	·113	·125	·115	·157	3·38	1·01
Nitrogen	·073	·07	·08	·073	·13	·12
Available Constituents—						
Phosphoric Acid	·0041	·0015	·0006	·0015	·0016	·012
Potash	·0023	·0031	·0062	·0045	·025	·031

Required—

Phosphoric Acid	...	...	...	...	...	·15
Potash	..	...	...	...	...	..	·2
Lime	...	...	...	...	...	...	·4
Nitrogen	...	...	...	...	...	·25

"Total" represents percentage soluble in strong acid.

"Available" represents percentage soluble in 1 per cent. citric acid in 7 days. (Dyer.)

"Required" represents a standard of total constituents for first class soils based on general experience, but to be considered only as a tentative standard to be used as a rough guide. The "available" constituents should be roughly one tenth of those shown in this column.

Fertiliser Requirements and Remarks.

Samples 1, 2, 8, and 4 are all deficient in fertilising constituents, and could certainly not be expected to stand continual cropping. No. 5 is deficient in phosphoric acid, but rich in potash, and No. 6 is well provided with both constituents in an available form. Nos. 5 and 6 are decidedly the best of the samples, and could be classed as good soils. Their proportion of lime is also notable, and probably has much to do with their fertility.

The large proportion of fine earth in all cases permits of the development of a good free root system, which is also of importance.

E. A. MANN,
Government Analyst.

THROUGH THE KIMBERLEYS.

By R. E. WEIR, M.R.C.V.S.

(*Continued.*)

The road from Flora Valley homestead passes over broken country which gradually rises until a fairly high altitude is attained on the border of the Sturt Creek country. From this point a good view is obtained of a large area of well-grassed land, stretching away for miles to the northward, and bearing a striking resemblance to the Queensland Downs. The chief drawback to this pleasing view is the absence of any permanent supply of water; at least two million acres is now practically useless owing to the lack of this necessary adjunct to successful stock-raising. According to a well-known authority, Dr. Jack, the possibility of obtaining an artesian supply is very remote. Taking as an index the growth of isolated trees scattered over the country, there is evidence that at least a moderate supply of water, suitable for stock, could be obtained by sinking wells. If this were done, and windmills erected, there is little doubt that the country might safely be stocked. The immense area of open country suggested the great possibilities of wheat-growing; in fact, the whole landscape reminds one of the description given of the Canadian prairies. A conflict of opinion, however, exists as to whether wheat would flourish under existing conditions in this latitude.

However, its present isolated position settles the question of its profitable growth. The plain gradually dips towards the east, where it meets a low chain of hills running north and south. At the base of the hills a watercourse, or what may be more correctly described as a chain of water holes or small lakes, is formed. Some of these are comparatively small and shallow whilst others are of fairly large dimensions, and should withstand a long period of drought. As this is' the only source of water supply for the Sturt Creek Station, it will be readily understood that during dry periods the question of providing water for stock in the outlying portions of the run is a very serious one, and causes grave anxiety to the management. At the time of my visit all the smaller water holes had become exhausted, and it was necessary to collect the stock and place them on the country adjoining the more permanent supply. As a natural sequence to this, the feed in the immediate vicinity was becoming rapidly consumed, and the serious position of the great distances betwixt feed and water was becoming imminent. This has been overcome, however, by taking up additional country on which permanent springs have been found, thus solving the difficulty with respect to the future operations of this particular station. With a view of inspecting this recent addition to the run and the new supply of water, the manager (Mr. Atkinson) and myself arranged to visit it whilst the station hands were mustering the cattle. We left camp at an early hour of the morning and travelled over ridgy country with intervening well-grassed flats until mid-day, arriving at a small oasis prettily situated in a miniature valley, where we camped for lunch. Here we found a well-shaded spring of clear, cool water, for which we were very grateful. This would prove an ideal spot for a homestead, and as the present position of Sturt Creek Station buildings is distant from the centre of the property, and the surroundings of an uninviting nature, the manager is seriously considering their removal to this locality. Tropical and subtropical fruits, also all kinds of vegetables, could be successfully cultivated. This is a decided advantage in a district where fresh fruit and vegetables are practically unprocurable. The surrounding valleys are particularly fertile and well covered with a species of grass which closely resembles rye grass in appearance and nutritive qualities. I am of opinion that if this grass can be successfully propagated in the more southern portions of the State it would, owing to its fattening qualities, prove a valuable feed for sheep and horses. Continuing our journey through similar country we entered a large valley about 12 miles in breadth, and stretching in a westerly direction as far as the eye could reach. This valley may be described as a waterless tract of country, covered with stunted trees and coarse undergrowth, which provide a fair amount of rough feed for stock. At the northern end of this plain, close to the South Australian border, and near to Mount Brophy, there is a magnificent spring which would provide water for some thousands of stock. We arrived at this locality about dusk, and were very pleased that our long day's journey was over. The spot is an ideal camping ground. Instead of a thick undergrowth, through which we had been travelling for the last 10 miles, we found an open and well-grassed forest which reminded me of the salmon gum country in the eastern districts. This strip of country appeared to extend a long distance east and west. From general indications I am decidedly of opinion that artesian water can be found in the locality. The characteristics of the water supplied by the spring strengthens this opinion. The present flow of water from this spring would give an ample supply for several thousand head of stock, and should be the means of rendering it possible to stock the whole of the surrounding country, which hitherto has remained in complete idleness. This new area of country will undoubtedly prove a valuable addition to the Sturt Creek Station, especially so during dry seasons. Starting on our return journey early on the following morning, an incident occurred which I shall long remember. The manager had occasion to leave me after crossing the plain and entering the broken country, he gave me minute directions how to reach the well where we had camped the previous day at noon, and where he proposed to again meet me. I confidently set off with my pack and saddle horses on the course directed, but after travelling some distance my pack horse ("Tommy") showed a strong tendency to bear in an easterly direction. I was doubtful with regard to our course, but decided that, for a time at least, it would be wiser to trust to Tommy's better knowledge of the locality. Travelling steadily for a considerable distance, I estimated that, judging by the time, we should be nearing our destination. Failing to see any indications of the locality, from what I remembered on the previous day, I became exceedingly doubtful of Tommy's sagacity, and decided to reconsider my position. Being fully satisfied that it was practically impossible for me to find the spring, I made up my mind that my best course was to make direct for Sturt Creek, which I knew must lie in a westerly direction. Having acquainted Tommy with my decision, I persuaded him with some trouble to take the new route, and after travelling for some time, we arrived at the bed of a watercourse which I felt sure must lead to Sturt Creek. Here Tommy showed his local knowledge by taking a perfectly straight line, and avoiding the curves in the watercourse, brought me out to the Sturt Creek country by the shortest possible route from the point where the course was altered. It is needless to mention the intense feeling of relief when I sighted some cattle on the plain, and was confident that water was to be found in the vicinity. About 4 p.m. we arrived at a water hole which I had previously visited, and then I knew I was about 10 miles from the camp. After my own and horses' thirst had been satisfied, and a short rest taken, I set out for the camp, but darkness came on before sighting it. Being unable to see any light to guide me, I had just decided to camp on the open plain for the night, when suddenly a welcome blaze shot up a short distance ahead, and continuing my journey I rode into the camp, much to the surprise and delight of those assembled, including the manager who had arrived about a quarter of an hour before. He was then occupied in relating to the others how I had lost my way, and how he had tracked me for a considerable distance until, losing my trace in thickly-grassed country, he had been compelled to give up the search and make for the camp. My sudden appearance was a matter of general congratulation, and no one was more pleased and thankful than myself on the happy termination of what might have been a serious incident.

DRY FARMING.

By G. Chitty Baker.

During a recent visit to the Eastern Goldfields I was very much struck at the possibilities of growing good crops if a system of dry farming was practised. In America large tracts of desert land have been made to return splendid crops by this style of cultivation. From the name it is evident that the chief difficulty against which the farmer must contend is the limited moisture supply and inability to irrigate. It is evident, then, that those who would gain the highest success in this particular line must get the fullest use of the moisture that is present.

While plants require a large amount of water for growth, some as high as 500 pounds for each pound of dry matter produced, yet when we figure the water required to mature a crop in terms of inches it appears to be very slight. Seven inches precipitation conveys enough water to the earth to grow a good cereal crop. Since the average annual precipitation of the Eastern Goldfields area is not less than ten inches, it is evident that if a portion of this moisture were saved paying crops could be grown.

PREPARATION OF THE SOIL.

In preparing the soil for a dry land crop the first essential is to have a seed bed that will store the maximum amount of water. When land is to be broken for the first time, experience seems to indicate that this can best be done in the spring, or at least not later than December. As to the depth, little definite experimentation has been carried on to determine this, but the general practice is to break from four to six inches deep. The deeper the soil is broken for the first time the greater reservoir of loose earth there will be to hold moisture later. The soil will be harder to work down for a year or two, but better results seem to attend deep breaking eventually.

As the breaking is being done, it is important to keep the land cultivated. A good plan is to disk the part ploughed during the day, before leaving the field in the evening. The land will work down more easily when in this condition than if allowed to remain untouched for a time, and since the disking fills the crevices and forms a mulch on the surface, any moisture that may be present is prevented from escaping. If the furrows are allowed to remain just as the plough leaves them, hard and compressed, with spaces between them such that the air circulates freely, every particle of moisture present, either in the furrows or the underlying soil, escapes. This leaves the soil hard to work into seed bed condition, and since moisture is lacking, the humus or vegetable matter that has been turned under does not decompose.

In this connection good results come from using a land roller or heavy soil compactor of some sort. Such an implement presses the layers of soil together closely and makes conditions for the rise of moisture more favourable. This brings about rapid decomposition of the humus material, prevents the two free admission of air and drying of the soil, and is of value to the growing crop, as it provides a perfect connection for the rise of ·

moisture later.   When the roller is used, however, it should be immediately followed by the harrow or some surface cultivator that will form a dust mulch on the surface of the ground, so that the rising moisture may be arrested before it escapes into the atmosphere.

CULTIVATE THE LAND FREQUENTLY.

After the ploughing and first cultivating have been completed, it is important to cultivate the land frequently.   This works it into a good seed bed and by keeping a mulch on the surface retains the moisture.   It is especially important to cultivate after each rain, in order that the fallen moisture may be imprisoned.   This cultivation may be continued after the crop is sown and until it is up, without seriously injuring it and with profit to the crop later.

When ground that has been broken in the spring has been kept cultivated all the summer it is usually in condition for ploughing and sowing the following autumn.   Of course the ground is frequently so hard that the cost of ploughing may be out of proportion to the advantage gained. Again, in some localities the prevailing high winds cause the soil to blow so as to seriously affect its surface.   The merit in autumn ploughing lies in the fact that autumn and winter moisture is admitted to the soil more frequently when the ground has been opened up.   If the soil is compact the moisture cannot gain admission and so passes off, or evaporated by the sun.

Early spring cultivation ought to follow on land that has been autumn ploughed.   An experiment reported by King, of Wisconsin, in his " Physics of Agriculture," brings out the value of this.   He determined the spring moisture content of a piece of autumn ploughing as soon as the soil was in condition to be cultivated.

He then had a portion of the ground cultivated, while a similar portion was allowed to remain untouched.   Seven days later moisture determinations on the two areas showed that there was a slight gain in the percentage of moisture in the surface foot of the cultivated area, while in the uncultivated area six pounds of moisture, an equivalent of an inch and three-quarters precipitation, had been lost from the surface foot.   When the atmosphere becomes warm enough to evaporate water from the surface, moisture that has been deposited there during the autumn and winter goes very rapidly.

With the soil in a packed condition, as we find it in the spring, water moves through it rapidly from particle to particle.   This movement is from the wet to the drier parts, and as the dry part is at the surface, the water brought to the surface passes off into the atmosphere.   When the surface soil is stirred and the compact condition broken up, the moisture cannot move through and is accumulated in a few inches below the surface.   This accounts for the increase of moisture in the cultivated area in the experiment reported.   When the ploughing is done in the spring, cultivation ought to follow immediately for the same reason as in the case of breaking.

Summer Fallow.—In dry land, farming summer-fallowed land each alternate year makes conditions favourable for the greatest returns.   The objection to this system in localities of greater precipitation, viz., the loss of plant food from leaching, does not apply on the Goldfields.   The advantage gained comes from the additional moisture stored, so that two years' moisture will be at hand to produce one crop.

Since no direct returns are gained the season the land is summer fallowed, it is important that the moisture be accumulated and retained for the succeeding crop. To do this the summer fallow must be kept thoroughly cultivated. This keeps weeds from growing and wasting moisture, and by maintaining a mulch on the surface prevents loss from evaporation. The cultivation of the summer fallow can be done at a very low cost, as the men and the teams necessary on the farm can be utilised in this way during the crop-growing season.

DESTRUCTION OF BRACKEN.

A correspondent from Collie sends the following queries to the Department:—

I am troubled with what appears a most perplexing question in connection with land which I hold in the South-West. I hold about 700 acres of beautiful hilly slopes of loose chocolate soil with blackbutt timber and bracken ferns. It was my intention and hope that I could run sheep on this land, being well watered and plenty of feed and ferns. These ferns were pretty much in evidence before ringbarking, but since ringing are coming up that thick that it is impossible for grass to grow—the more I clear the better they like it, and the sheep do not. Now, sir, I would be exceedingly pleased of any suggestion you can give to improve my grass and not the ferns, apart from ploughing, which, owing to the quantity of land, is impossible.

Sorrell.—Would also be very glad to know the best way of dealing with this towards eradication.

Apologising for trespassing on your valuable time, but the information is of great importance to me, whose experience is limited in these matters.

The matter being referred to Mr. Despeissis, he replied as follows:—

"The problem of clearing out bracken ferns at a small cost on pasture land is one that has not yet been satisfactorily solved in this State, and I can only quote the experience of settlers who have battled with it with more or less success.

"Rolling down the ferns and, after they have been allowed to lay for a while, setting fire to them, has been productive of good results, but this operation is not everywhere practicable, on account of the uneven contours of the country and the timber lying in the way. At all events it will have to be repeated at intervals before any good can be done. Cutting with a scythe and burning would also do some good. Repeat the operation when new fronds appear. It is not unlikely that on suitable land such very spreading grasses like Paspalum or African Wonder grass would in time smother the bracken ferns in such places where the cultivation necessary for the establishment of the grasses would permit the sowing of the seeds.

"Sheep pastured on land sown with grasses would naturally trample down a lot of bracken. From what I have seen of these grasses in spots where they have been growing with great luxuriance, they are quite capable of smothering other vegetation. The experiment is worth trying.

" Scrub exterminator can also be used in some places. Of these the arsenic preparations make the ground barren for some time. Crude carbolic acid diluted with 30 to 50 times its bulk with water is also looked upon as a good scrub exterminator, which is spread over the land by means of a spray pump or watering cans.

" This Department will gladly receive your experience as well as that of those settlers who have successfully mastered the bracken fern. I shall be glad if you will report on the success or otherwise of any of the methods suggested.

"*Sorrell.*—This is readily eaten down by sheep. In orchards and gardens summer cultivation and liming do much to eradicate the weed. In other places the grasses aforementioned sown amongst the sorrel would also assist to smother it out of existence. It answers the double purpose of providing nutritious forage and in ridding the land of the weed."

THE ANALYSIS OF FERTILISERS.

The Fertiliser and Feeding Stuffs Act has now been in force for a few months, and up to date about 120 fertilisers have been registered in accordance with the Act. Of these, over 100 samples have been obtained in the prescribed manner and forwarded by the Inspector of Fertilisers, Mr. P. G. Wicken, to the Government Analyst. The first batch of results have now come to hand, and are published herewith. For the purpose of arriving at the value of these fertilisers the following unit values have been prepared by Mr. E. A. Mann, the Government Analyst, on the basis of the prices at which the fertilisers are sold on trucks at Fremantle. The unit value of a fertiliser is the value of each one per cent. of the different fertilising ingredients contained. Mr. E. A. Mann writes :—

"The following values are based upon the figures obtainable with regard to manures sold in Western Australia during 1906, and are all calculated on the basis of prices on trucks at Fremantle :—

Ingredient.	Form.	Value per unit.	
		s.	d.
Nitrogen	In the form of Nitrates (nitrate of soda)	17	9
Do.	In the form of Sulphates (sulphate of ammonia)	17	6
Do.	In Organic Matter (blood and bone manures) ...	15	3
Potash	As Sulphate	5	10
Do.	As Muriate	4	6
Phosphoric Acid ...	Water Soluble	5	2
Do.	Citrate Soluble	3	6
Do.	Acid Soluble	3	3
Do.	In Thomas's Phosphate, without regard to solubility	3	5

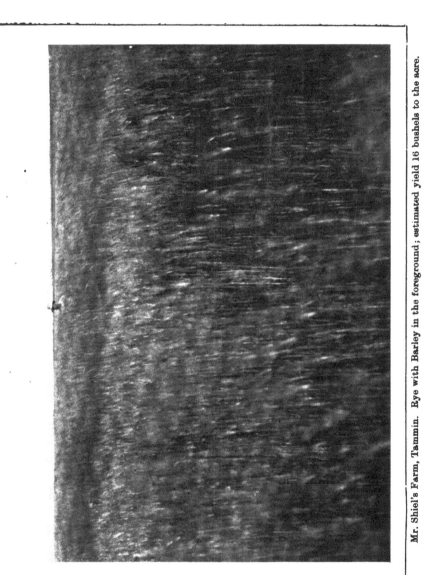

Mr. Shiel's Farm, Tammin. Rye with Barley in the foreground; estimated yield 16 bushels to the acre.

"If the purchaser wishes to put a check upon the price he is paying for a fertiliser he must demand a certificate of analysis, which he proceeds to use as follows:—

"Suppose a bone-dust has been certified as containing—

Nitrogen	2·6 per cent.	
Citrate Soluble Phosphoric Acid	3·4	,,
Total Phosphoric Acid	18·5	,,

The difference between Citrate Soluble and Total, or 15·1 per cent., is the 'Acid Soluble' Phosphoric Acid.

"Read these percentages as units and calculate from the above table of 'unit values' thus:—

			£ s. d.
2·6 Units of Nitrogen at 15s. 3d., are worth			1 19 8
3·4 ,, Citrate Soluble Phosphoric Acid at 3s. 6d., are worth...			0 11 11
15·1 ,, Acid Soluble Phosphoric at 3s. 3d., are worth			2 9 1

Therefore total value of Manure of Composition certified is ... £5 0 8

"This will represent about the value of the manure on trucks at Fremantle and allowance must be made for extra freight, etc., when purchasing elsewhere.

"Or to take another sample:—

A superphosphate is certified to contain—

17·94 per cent. Water Soluble Phosphoric Acid.
2·0 ,, Citrate ,, ,,

	£ s. d.
17·94 Units of Water Soluble Phosphoric Acid at 5s. 2d., are worth	4 12 8
2·0 ,, Citrate ,, ,, 3s. 6d. ,,	0 7 0

Total value of Superphosphate at Fremantle £4 19 8

"The same method can be followed with any class of manure. Thus a purchaser can check the accuracy of the price asked by the vendor, but of course the above prices must be considered as making no allowance for extended payments."

For the purpose of enabling farmers to easily ascertain at a glance the value of the registered fertilisers, the Inspector of Fertilisers has compiled a list showing the registered percentage of the fertilising ingredients in each fertiliser, and also the percentage found by the Government Analyst; these will be found bracketed together, and so as to make these more complete a table has been added showing the value of the fertiliser as registered and as found by the Government Analyst; by referring to this, purchasers will be able to easily ascertain the difference in the money value between the percentage as registered and the percentage found. In some instances the fertilisers are in excess of the registered percentages, and in other below it. The unit value is of service as the means of comparing the value of different fertilisers on a common basis, and does not necessarily mean that it is the price asked, as this depends on several factors, including the quantity purchased, the terms required, and whether taken delivery of from the ship's side or store, etc. Valuing all fertilisers on a common basis according to the contents of fertilising ingredients, the value of the fertilisers per ton is as stated in the unit value column of the following table.

THE ANALYSES OF FERTILISERS.

Number of Sample	Name of Fertiliser		Where obtained	Nitrogen	Water Soluble Phosphoric Acid	Citrate Soluble Phosphoric Acid	Add Soluble Phosphoric Acid	Total Phosphoric Acid	Potash	Value on Unit Basis (£ s. d.)
18	Thomas' phosphate	Guaranteed analysis	G. Wills & Co.	...	...	...	...	14·00	...	2 7 10
18	Do.	Found by Government Analyst	do.	...	...	...	...	17·23	...	2 18 9
7	Thomas' phosphate	Guaranteed analysis	Elder, Shenton, & Co.	...	...	...	...	14·00	...	2 7 10
7	Do.	Found by Government Analyst	do.	...	...	...	...	14·95	...	2 11 0
12	Concentrated superphosphate	Guaranteed analysis	G. Wills & Co.	...	30·00	1·00	...	39·00	...	9 19 10
12	Do.	Found by Government Analyst	do.	...	38·65	5·05	...	44·00	...	11 11 10
26	Superphosphate	Guaranteed analysis	do.	1·25	16·00	...	...	16·0	...	4 2 8
26	Do.	Found by Government Analyst	do.	1·37	17·04	·43	...	17·47	...	4 9 5
1	Nitro superphosphate	Guaranteed analysis	Gardiner Bros.	1·85	8·25	4·28	4·00	17·87	...	4 19 9
1	Do.	Found by Government Analyst	do.	·87	13·50	1·08	4·83	19·44	...	5 13 9
8	Abrolhos guano	Guaranteed analysis	Elder, Shenton, & Co.	...	...	21·31	8·40	29·71	...	5 16 5
8	Do.	Found by Government Analyst	do.	...	...	6·97	17·76	24·73	...	5 15 3
2	Potato manure	Guaranteed analysis	Gardiner Bros.	·53	9·01	8·42	4·22	17·42	5·0	5 15 9
2	Do.	Found by Government Analyst	do.	1·09	11·90	1·09	4·88	18·44	3·15	6 0 0
11	Nitrate of soda	Guaranteed analysis	G. Wills & Co.	16·00	...	...	...	...	...	14 4 4
11	Do.	Found by Government Analyst	do.	15·35	...	...	...	...	...	13 12 4
14	Nitrate of soda	Guaranteed analysis	Gardiner Bros.	15·50	...	...	...	...	...	13 15 9
14	Do.	Found by Government Analyst	do.	15·88	...	...	...	...	...	13 13 9
3	Nitrate of soda	Guaranteed analysis	J. M. Drummond & Co.	12·0	...	...	...	...	...	11 10 9
3	Do.	Found by Government Analyst	do.	15·24	...	...	...	...	...	13 10 6
27	Bone meal	Guaranteed analysis	G. Wills & Co.	2·0	...	7·38	15·54	23·00	...	5 5 8
27	Do.	Found by Government Analyst	do.	4·51	...	...	...	23·87	...	7 4 8
24	Sulphate of potash	Guaranteed analysis	Couche, Calder, & Co.	...	...	...	...	...	50·00	14 11 8
24	Do.	Found by Government Analyst	do.	...	...	...	...	...	49·27	14 7 4
23	Kainit	Guaranteed analysis	Gardiner Bros.	...	...	...	...	...	11·3	3 10
23	Do.	Found by Government Analyst	do.	...	...	...	...	...	10·25	3 52

Guaranteed analysis / Found by Government Analyst	Muriate of potash / Do.	G. Wills & G. / do.
Guaranteed analysis / Found by Government Analyst	Muriate of potash / Do.	Gardner Bros. / do.
Guaranteed analysis / Found by Government Analyst	Sulphate of ammonia / Do.	do. / do.
Guaranteed analysis / Found by Government Analyst	Sulphate of ammonia / Do.	Producers' Union / du.
Guaranteed analysis / Found by Government Analyst	Sulphate of ammonia / Do.	Couche, Calder, & Co. / do.
Guaranteed analysis / Found by Government Analyst	Sulphate of ammonia / Do.	G. Wills & Co. / do.
Guaranteed analysis / Found by Government Analyst	Bone dust / Do.	do. / do.
Guaranteed analysis / Found by Government Analyst	Bone manure / Do.	do. / do.
Guaranteed analysis / Found by Government Analyst	Grass manure / Do.	Gardner Bros. / do.
Guaranteed analysis / Found by Government Analyst	Horticultural manure / Do.	do. / do.
Guaranteed analysis / Found by Government Analyst	Abrolhos Guano / Do.	Elder, Shenton, & Co. / do.
Guaranteed analysis / Found by Government Analyst	Do. / Do.	P. Park, Claremont
Guaranteed analysis / Found by Government Analyst	Superphosphate / Do.	Couche, Calder, & Co. / do.
Guaranteed analysis / Found by Government Analyst	Superphosphate, concentrated / do.	do. / do.
Guaranteed analysis / Found by Government Analyst	Special potato manure / Do.	do. / do.
Guaranteed analysis / Found by Government Analyst	Guano / Do.	do. / do.

a Below registration in nitrogen.   b Below registration in phosphoric acid.   c Below registration in potash.

THE ANALYSES OF FERTILISERS—continued.

Number of Sample	Name of Fertiliser		Where obtained		Nitrogen	Water Soluble Phosphoric Acid	Citrate Soluble Phosphoric Acid	Acid Soluble Phosphoric Acid	Total Phosphoric Acid	Potash	Value on Unit Basis £ s. d.
36	Guano, ammoniacal	Guaranteed analysis	Couche, Calder, & Co.		1·0	…	6·50	16·00	22·5	…	4 10 0
38	Do. do.	Found by Government Analyst	do.		1·23	…	1·56	21·75	23·31	…	4 14 9
57	Thomas' phosphate	Guaranteed analysis	W. Padbury & Co.		…	…	…	…	17·00	…	3 13 1
57	Do.	Found by Government Analyst	do.		…	…	…	…	16·35	…	3 15 10
58	Superphosphate	Guaranteed analysis	do.		…	16·5	1·23	…	16·5	…	4 5 3
58	Do.	Found by Government Analyst	do.		…	16·44		…	17·66	…	4 9 3
62	Nitro superphosphate	Guaranteed analysis	G. Gill (Gardner Bros.' brand)		1·35	8·95	4·32	4·10	17·67	…	4 18 9
62	Do.	Found by Government Analyst	do.		1·17	12·73	1·78	5·64	20·14	…	5 10 9
64	Special fertilizer	Guaranteed analysis	W. B. Haynes & Co.		3·6	…	14·19	4·10	17·4	…	7 10 2
64	Do.	Found by Government Analyst	do.		4·75	…		4·44	18·63	…	7 7
63	Bee fertiliser	Guaranteed analysis	C. A. Lehmann (Oetterby Co. brand)		3·25	…	5·63	9·14	14·75	…	5 6 8
63	Do.	Found by Government Analyst	do.		2·97	…	8·90	3·28	12·18	…	4 12 0
16	Sulphate of potash	Guaranteed analysis	Gardner Bros.		…	…	…	…	…	52·0	15 3 4
16	Do.	Found by Government Analyst	do.		…	…	…	…	…	48·58	14 3 4
4	Kainit	Guaranteed analysis	J. M. Drummond & Co.		…	…	…	…	…	12·0	3 10 0
4	Do.	Found by Government Analyst	do.		…	…	…	…	…	12·91	3 15 3
5	Sulphate of potash	Guaranteed analysis	do.		…	…	…	…	…	51·16	14 18 5
5	Do.	Found by Government Analyst	do.		…	…	…	…	…	51·4	14 19 10
34	Bone-dust	Guaranteed analysis	Couche, Calder, & G.		3·25	…	6·50	13·50	19·0	…	5 12 10
34	Do.	Found by Government Analyst	do.		3·22	…	7·25	14·00	21·25	…	6 0 2
36	Kainit	Guaranteed analysis	do.		…	…	…	…	…	12·0	3 10 5
36	Do.	Found by Government Analyst	do.		…	…	…	…	…	11·91	3 9 5
42	Bone-dust	Guaranteed analysis	Binny & Son		3·75	…	8·90	14·31	18·5	…	5 11
42	Do.	Found by Government Analyst	do.		3·39	…		18·27	18·27	…	5 12 0
43	Nitro bone-dust	Guaranteed analysis	do.		3·9	…	3·64	12·04	40	…	4 2
43	lbs.	Found by Government Analyst	do.		3·77	…			15·64	…	4 14

Guaranteed analysis ... ... Found by Government Analyst ...	44 44	Kainit Do.	... ...	... ...	Producers' Union ... do.	... ...	... ...	... ...	... ...	... ...	... ...	12·0 12·37	3 10 0 3 12 2
Guaranteed analysis ... ... Found by Government Analyst ...	56 56	Do. Do.	... ...	... ...	W. Padbury & Co. ... do.	... ...	... ...	... ...	... ...	... ...	... ...	10·0 13·06	2 13 4 3 16 2
Guaranteed analysis ... ... Found by Government Analyst ...	51 51	B. and B. manure Do.	... ...	... ...	Forrest, Emmanuel, & Co.... do.	... ...	5·19 3·02	... ...	1·16 1·93	5·23 9·02	6·43 10·94	... ...	5 0 6 a4 2 0
Guaranteed analysis ... ... Found by Government Analyst ...	52 52	Bone manure Do.	... ...	... ...	do. do.	... ...	4·03 3·72	... ...	3·86 2·17	13·63 14·68	16·43 16·85	... ...	5 15 7 5 12 0
Guaranteed analysis ... ... Found by Government Analyst ...	55 55	Sulphate of potash Do.	... ...	... ...	W. Padbury & Co. ... do.	... ...	... ...	... ...	... ...	... ...	... ...	39·0 40·6	11 7 6 14 9 4
Guaranteed analysis ... ... Found by Government Analyst ...	54 54	Sulphate of ammonia Do.	... ...	... ...	do. do.	... ...	20·0 19·95	... ...	... ...	... ...	... ...	... ...	17 10 0 17 9 1
Guaranteed analysis ... ... Found by Government Analyst ...	61 61	Muriate of potash Do.	... ...	... ...	G. Gill do.	... ...	... ...	... ...	... ...	... ...	... ...	63·0 58·83	13 19 0 c13 4 6

a Below registration in nitrogen. b Below registration in phosphoric acid. c Below registration in potash.

e Below registration in potash.

NARROGIN STATE FARM.

REPORT FOR THE MONTH OF OCTOBER.

By R. C. BAIRD.

Early in the month the sowing of summer crops was completed. The ground worked for this crop was ploughed in July, and at that time was somewhat boggy in many places. Towards the end of September the ground was sufficiently dry to carry the teams, and the spring-tooth cultivator was set to work to break up and pulverise the soil, thus bringing it to a fine tilth.

The seed drill was used, and super at the rate of 1½cwt. per acre was applied at the time of seeding. In the case of the smaller seeds, such as millets, etc., the seed was mixed with the manure so as to secure an even distribution.

The crops are now above ground and looking well. Forty-seven acres have been put under the various fodder crops, the area of each variety being as follows :—

Ninety Day Maize	...	12 acres	Kaffir Corn	¼ acre
Sorghum Saccharatum ...	4 acres	Hungarian Millet ...	¼ acre
Broom Corn ...	5 acres	Egyptian Millet ...	¼ acre
Planters' Friend ...	4 acres	Siberian Millet	¼ acre
Early Amber Cane ...	18 acres	Japanese Millet ...	¼ acre
Cow Peas	2 acres		

Owing to the dry weather experienced during the month the crops have not made such progress as one would expect at this season of the year. In the experimental plots the early varieties of wheat are far in advance of the later ones ; while those which suffered from the severe frosts in August are still very backward. A good downfall of rain now would greatly benefit all the crops.

Fallowing has been brought to a close for this season, the ground having become too hard for ploughing.

One of the difficulties in fallowing in this district is that during the winter months the ground becomes so wet and sodden that the teams cannot get on to it, and as the spring weather approaches the time during which ploughing can be carried on before the ground becomes dry again is very short. This work should be pushed on with all the available strength of the farm while the soil is in a suitable condition for ploughing.

Shearing operations are being carried on and will be completed in a few days. The sheep are in excellent condition, and are cutting very good fleeces.

The farm horses, with the exception of a few old ones, are in good working condition. Two foals were dropped during the month, making now three so far, with three mares still to foal.

A Holstein cow and twin calves arrived at the end of the month. The cow, with her progeny, was imported from South Australia and should prove a valuable addition to our dairy herd.

The cattle are all healthy and putting on condition now.

CHAPMAN EXPERIMENTAL FARM.

REPORT FOR THE MONTH OF OCTOBER.

By J. KEAYS.

The month set in dry and continued so throughout. Twenty-four points of rain were recorded for the month, making a total of 15 inches since begining of the year. Cereal crops have made fair growth and are filling up well. Hay cutting is now completed and barley cutting is being pushed on with.

Shearing was completed during the month and the results are very favourable. The Angora goats have been shorn twice during the year, in April and October. It is certainly an advantage to shear twice a year, because the hair is not so matted and is cleaner, and none of the goats cast their fleeces, which is so common when only shorn once a year. The only drawbacks to this system are the cost of shearing and the shorter staple, but there is no doubt it pays to shear twice a year.

The potato crop was attacked by the potato moth but were prevented from doing much damage by spraying with Bordeaux mixture and Paris green.

Very satisfactory sales of the Large Black breed of pigs continue to be made, also of Shropshire rams.

The summer fodder crops of maize and amber cane are making excellent growth. The natural pastures are drying off very fast owing to the very warm weather.

AGRICULTURE ON THE EASTERN GOLDFIELDS.

Report by G. CHITTY BAKER.

I beg to report on my visit to the Eastern Goldfields to judge the gardens for the Goldfields Water Supply Administration, a separate report of which is herewith attached.

While travelling I took the opportunity of visiting as many orchards, market gardens, and farms, as possible.

The advent of water on the goldfields has had a marked effect, but still greater results are to be gained if the users would only go to the trouble of obtaining a knowledge as to how and when to use the water, and how best to conserve it in the ground, as well as how to make the best use of the rainfall.

It is a fact that nearly all those engaged in market gardening or fruit-growing are persons who have never had any practical training in these matters, and yet they are making a good living at it. One man assured me that he paid for all the water he used out of the sale of lettuce from a patch of about three square rods.

Vegetables of all kinds do well. The ground seems to be impregnated with nitrogenous bacteria, as a few plants that I pulled up in different districts were very thickly infested with nitrogenous nodules. Onions seem to do particulary well. Silver-beet, peas, beans, cabbages, and lettuce also thrive and grow better than I have seen them do in and around Perth.

Fruit trees come into bearing much earlier than in the coastal districts, maturing finer fruit. Whether they will continue to do so can only be ascertained by time, as up to the present we have no data to go on. Stone fruit seems to do best, pip-fruits making but small growths; while the citrus tribe, although in several places have grown well and borne crops at three and four years old, equal, if not better, than that obtained from trees two or three years older in the coastal districts, yet they already show signs of going off.

Disease to crops is confined to ravages of caterpillars (I was unable to identify), aphis, cut-worms, and black scale. With regard to the aphis, this is kept in check by a native lady-bird, which is swarming in myriads in Kalgoorlie gardens; and although at the time of my visit there was ample evidence of the damage done by the aphis, yet it was very difficult to find any live specimens. In many instances I found remains of aphis that had been parasitised, and was fortunate enough to see a small ichneumon fly hatch out of one of these pests. The trouble seems to be that the recent hot spell hatched the aphis much earlier than the lady-birds or flies, so that considerable damage was done before the beneficial insects could get to work. A gentleman in Kalgoorlie asked me to visit his garden to see the aphis and the destruction they had worked, but a most careful search failed to find a single specimen; numbers of lady-birds and flies, however, were seen everywhere. Fungoid diseases were not seen on the Fields, either in the gardens or orchards.

Rabbits are troublesome, eating all the young twigs and bark off the fruit-trees.

The two most promising orchards are kept—one by Mr. Hy. Borret, of Salisbury Road, and the other by Mr. Curtis, both of Kalgoorlie. The trees in these orchards made wonderful growth for the very short time they have been planted, the majority of them being in the second and third year, and having abundance of fruit well formed. One peculiarity I noticed was the enormous trunks of the fig trees. One I measured, which I was assured was of the ordinary size when planted, that is, about one inch in diameter, now stands, in its third year, with a butt of six inches in diameter. the growth throughout the trees being uniform. Vines also do very well in these places.

The growth of cereals for hay provided a most interesting study. Some six years ago I saw a crop of wheat and oats grown by Mr. Hocking of Kalgoorlie, which gave a very good result. On the present occasion I saw a fine crop of wheat grown by Mr. Scott, of Kalgoorlie, which had been sown in April last at the rate of a bushel and a-half per acre, and which gave a return of from two to three tons of hay to the acre. Another crop on the same homestead sown in June last gave the return of from three to four

GOLDFIELDS FARMING.—Stack of Wheaten Hay, grown by Messrs. Bow Bros., Coolgardie.

tons of green ·feed per acre, no manure of any kind having been used. At Coolgardie Messrs. Bow Bros., were just finishing cutting a fifty-three acre paddock of wheaten hay, forty-five acres being upon fallowed land, sown at the rate of one and a-half bushels to the acre (the remaining eight acres had not been ploughed) the seed, one bushel to the acre being harrowed in. The forty-five acre block grew to two feet high and yielded at the rate of 15 cwt., while the eight acre lot grew to two feet six inches, with much stouter stalks; this lot was sown later than the former, it kept green longer, and was cut a week later. On another patch of thirteen acres a yield of half a ton to the acre was obtained from self-sown seed.

The first attempt to grow hay was made by Messrs. Bow in 1904, when the ground was grubbed and cleared in April of that year, sown in May, and grew to one foot high. On the seventeenth September following no rain having fallen from the date of sowing, horses were turned in to eat it off as it had all withered; on the same night heavy rains fell, flooding the ground, the horses were taken out and in a day or so the crop started to grow again, and on November the first it was cut, yielding over one ton of hay to the acre.

The crop at the Boulder racecourse is a most satisfactory one, the yield of which I was unable to ascertain.

· It is quite evident that with a better knowledge of what is termed dry farming, the Fields will in a year or so be able to grow the most of its own hay.

Taking the successful culture of flowers, together with the other matters related above, it must be admitted that great possibilities have presented themselves on the Eastern Goldfields, the development of which will be watched with much interest and should provide many valuable object lessons.

AWARDING OF PRIZES FOR GOLDFIELDS GARDENS.

Report of Mr. G. CHITTY BAKER to the Secretary of the Goldfields' Water Supply Administration.

I have the honour to report that after a careful examination of the various gardens entered for competition I beg to submit my awards as follows:—

Class " A " (Gardens of an assessed value of over £50).

There was only one entry for this on the Goldfields, viz., Mr. Brennan, of Kalgoorlie

Class " B " (Kalgoorlie).

J. A. Hughes, 799 Vardin Street	...	1st prize
A. G. Lovell, 2339 Lewis Street	...	2nd prize
J. Edis, 958 Lyall Street	...	3rd prize

Class " B " (Boulder).

P. Dawson, 573 Vivian Street	...	1st prize
F. A. Liebeg, 462 Burt Street	...	2nd prize
E. ·Pascoe, 574 Vivian Street	...	3rd prize

Class " B " (Kanowna).

Mrs. Ogilvie, 573 Moran Street ... 1st prize
A. Middleton, 442 Golconda Street 2nd prize

Class " B " (Coolgardie).

A. P. McCormack, Clifton Street ... 1st prize
Mr. Giles, 1101 King Street ... 2nd prize

At Northam there were seven entries in Class " A " and thirteen in Class " B," the awards being as follows :—

Class " A."

G. L. Throssell, Gordon Street ... 1st prize

Class " B."

J. W. Paterson, Gordon Street ... 1st prize

After considerable difficulty was experienced in coming to a satisfactory decision, owing to the fact that several of the competitors had really good gardens, and it was only on my adopting a system of points that I was able to decide.

The points adopted were as follows :—

General appearance	20
Utility	10
Design	10
Variety	10
Lawns	10
Shade	10
Freedom of disease	5
Watering	10
Fencing	5
Preparation of ground	10
Total	100

In arriving at a decision I adopted the plan used by Mr. Despeissis last year, and considered that. in the main, the chief merit of a garden should be a pleasant and useful annex to the house.

I noticed that several of the competitors who had competed the previous year had abandoned all attempts at kitchen gardening. Their gardens were certainly pleasing, and showed great taste, but they failed to score in utility. Another striking feature was the absence, in a good many instances, of any atttempt to form a lawn. Wherever grass had been grown, it added considerably to the appearance, very pleasing to the eye, and an ideal plan to rest on in the cool of the evening.

A number of market and fruit gardens were visited, showing great promise, and I venture to say that a close study of the scientific requirements, together with a judicious use of water, will eventually give great results.

It seems to be the general rule to apply water very lavishly, without any attempt to conserve it in the ground, with a consequence that while the plants utilise a small portion, the greater bulk is evaporated by the sun. Thorough stirring of the soil and liberal mulching would prevent so much evaporation, with a corresponding benefit to the plants. Less water need be used, better results obtained, and fewer disappointments. Thus, instead of becoming disheartened and giving gardening up, it will be continued with more vigour and induce others to follow the example set.

I would desire to convey, through you, my thanks to Mr. McQueen for his kindness in showing me all that was to be seen in agricultural matters, thereby enabling me to obtain much valuable and useful information. My thanks are also due to Mr. Gleeson and Mr. Parr for their courtesy and attention while in their districts.

SHIPMENT OF LAMBS FOR ENGLAND.

An important step in the progress of land settlement and the development of the country was taken when an experimental shipment of 422 frozen lambs was exported to London on the R.M.S. " Britannia." The consignment has been despatched by the Producers' Union, Limited, and was made up of the following lots :—

Mr. J. C. Butcher (Beverley) ...	...	...	...	200
Messrs. Forrest, Emanuel, & Co.	...	...	...	80
Messrs. Wedge & Harper (Wagin)	...	...	...	60
Mr. V. Hamersley (Newcastle)	...	...	...	55
Messrs. McLean Bros. (Beverley)	...	...	...	27
Total	...	...	...	...	422

The shipment should mark a new era in the progress of sheep-raising in the State. The consignment is certainly a limited one, but every new industry must naturally start in a small way, and grow with the expansion of the country. It is now 12 years since South Australia sent her first experimental shipment of frozen mutton to London, and since then the exports have increased from a few hundred carcases in 1894 to over 200,000 in 1905, while it is anticipated that the figures will touch a quarter of a million for the current year. These results speak for themselves, and go to show that Western Australia, with her large area of lands suited in every way for sheep-raising, should in course of time become a large exporter of frozen carcases.

The lambs comprising the shipment will each bear the label of the Public Health Department. They were slaughtered under the supervision of Inspector Buckley, of the Public Health Department, and were then removed to the Fremantle Ice Works, and slowly frozen under the direction of the manager (Mr. Davey), who anticipates that they will reach London in excellent condition. The carcases were inspected at the Ice Works by a party organised by the Producers' Union, Limited, consisting of the Colonial Treasurer (Mr. Frank Wilson, M.L.A.), Mr. S. Wilson, of Sunderland (Eng.), Mr. Charles Harper, Mr. M. H. Jacoby, Mr. A. G. Layman, M.L.A., Mr. J. T. Smith; Mr. J. Savage, Mr. Mare (manager of the P. and O. Steam Navigation Compay), and Mr. A. M. Oliphant (manager of the Producers' Union, Limited). The gentlemen named evinced a lively interest in the project, and the question of the best class of lamb for the trade was freely discussed. The general and accepted opinion was that merinos ranging from 32lb. to 34lb. in weight would find the greatest favour in London. Many of the carcases included in the consignment are above that weight, but in the event of the experiment being successful farmers will have every encouragement to go in more extensively for sheep-raising, and will probably take steps to breed only the right class of lamb for the London Market. In larger shipments, which may be confidently expected to follow, more attention will assuredly have to be given to grading, for the Producers' Union, Limited, have been advised from London that this is essential to success. The advice stated that 28lb. carcases would bring the best price, and that 32lb. to 34lb. carcases would also find ready sale.

The farmers, it is stated, have more than overtaken the local demand for wheat, and have now to accept the export rates for the yearly increasing surplus, and this, it is considered, will be a very strong inducement to many settlers to give more attention to mixed farming, making a leading line of raising lambs for export. Experts agree that the quality of the lambs produced for export in Western Australia promises to be very good indeed, and all who know anything about the industry look forward with every confidence to a big export trade growing up.

The visitors were well satisfied with their inspection of the carcases, and are very sanguine as to the result of the experiment. Mr. Davey, of the Fremantle Ice Works, stated that the plant was capable of dealing with 500 lambs a day, or up to 1,000 a day if required, while they had storage accommodation for 30,000 frozen carcases. It is understood that the next experiment will be in the direction of exporting pork from Western Australia.—*West Australian.*

CONFERENCE OF AGRICULTURAL CHEMISTS.

The desirability has long been felt of holding a meeting of the agricultural chemists of the different States for the purpose of discussing and rendering uniform the work done by the official chemists and adopting uniform methods of analysis.

In February, 1904, the Council of Agriculture, Tasmania, despatched an official invitation to the Agricultural Departments of the other States for their chemists to attend such a conference to be held in Hobart in April, 1904. This date was subsequently altered to June, 1904, and was finally abandoned, as the representatives of Queensland, Victoria, South Australia, and Western Australia were unable to attend.

In November, 1904, a similar invitation was issued by the Victorian Department of Agriculture to a conference to be held in February, 1905, in Melbourne.

In January, 1905, the Victorian Department wrote stating that as the replies received did not indicate that the meeting would be sufficiently representative, it had been decided to postpone the conference.

In July of the present year an invitation was issued to the Agricultural Departments of the different States and New Zealand asking them to allow their chemists to attend a conference to be held in Sydney on 20th August.

Favourable replies having been received from all the States except South Australia and Tasmania, the conference was opened on the date mentioned, and was attended by the agricultural chemists of Queensland, Victoria, New Zealand, and New South Wales, the Western Australian representative being unable at the last minute to attend.

The meeting asked Mr. J. M. Hattrick, the local representative of the German Potash Syndicate, to act as honarary secretary, and held twelve meetings at the rooms of the Royal Society of New South Wales, which were kindly lent by the Society for the purpose.

The following is a short *résumé* of the work done by the Conference:—

Reports on Soils for Farmers.

> (a.) Details of form to be filled in by applicants for advice as to the treatment of soil.
>
> (b.) General directions for obtaining and forwarding samples of soil if an analysis is required.
>
> (c.) Form of report on the analysis of the soil.

Methods of analysis.

1. For soils :

   Mechanical analysis.—Meshes of sieves.   Apparatus for elutriation.   Preparation of air-dried fine sample.

   Chemical analysis.—Details of methods to be adopted for—

   > (a.) Hydrochloric acid method.
   >
   > (b.) Citric acid method.

2. Manures.—Bone-dust. Superphosphate. Basic slag. Nitrogen in different forms. Potash in fertilisers. Mixed manures.

3. Feeding stuffs.

4. Wheat and flour.

5. Dairy produce.

   > (a.) Milk and cream, including boric acid and formal dehyde.
   >
   > (b.) Butter.
   >
   > (c.) Cheese.

6. Water for irrigation, watering stock, and use in butter and cheese factories.

7. Other substances.
   Lime.
   Insecticides.
   Cattle dips.

Legislation regarding adulteration of fertilisers and other agricultural products.—In view of the importance of the subject, and the fact that all the States were not represented, the question of legislation and of fixing standards of purity was postponed until the next meeting.

Soil Surveys.—The great value of properly organised soil surveys of the different States was affirmed, but it was recognised that it was not feasible to carry out such a survey on the lines adopted by the United States Department, and a referee was appointed to investigate means for making short flying surveys and to test the rapid methods of analysis adopted by the American Bureau of Soils.

Field Experiments.— The Conference was unanimously of the opinion that all field experimental work should be carried out in conjunction with and under the supervision of the agricultural chemists, in so far as relates to design and conduct of the experiments themselves and the interpretation and publication of the results.

Further, that manure experiments in the States have in the past been carried out on a limited number of crops, and that it is desirable to conduct exact scientific experiments with a greater variety, special mention being made of fruit trees, vines, and potatoes.

The following was laid down as the objectives of field experimental work :—

1. To determine the effects of fertilising substances, separately and in conjunction.

2. The best and cheapest forms and quantities in which these ingredients should be applied, and the most effective means of applying the manures containing them.

3. Nitrification and the bacterial methods of soil treatment.

4. Action of amendments such as stable and organic manures, lime (as carbonate, ground quick-lime, and as slaked lime), ferreous sulphate, and magnesium salts.

5. Different methods of soil treatment, such as draining, subsoiling, ploughing to different depths, and green manuring.

6. Variety tests for the crops and varieties best adapted for given conditions of soil and climate.

7. Methods of treating special soils, such as salty and alkaline soils.

8. Eradication of noxious weeds by chemical or other means.

The above problems may be investigated in three ways :

(*a.*) By means of experiments conducted at State farms and agricultural colleges.

(*b.*) By experiments on the farms of private individuals.

(*c.*) By means of plots in school gardens.

Pot Experiments.—Field experiments are to be supplemented by pot experiments, by means of which certain problems can be best investigated.

Reciprocity.—The Conference affirmed the desirability of reciprocity between agricultural chemists, and passed the following resolution :—

That reciprocity between the chemists of the various States and New Zealand is highly desirable, and that this can be best brought about by the interchange of publications, and of such other matters as may be deemed of mutual interest.

and, secondly, by periodical meetings, which may be best secured by the formation of an Association.

Association of Official Agricultural Chemists.—The following constitution for the above Association was adopted :—

1. This Association shall be known as "The Association of Official Agricultural Chemists of Australasia." The objects of the Association shall be (1), to secure uniformity in the methods, results, and modes of statement of analyses of fertilisers, soils, feeding stuffs, agricultural products and other materials connected with this industry, and (2), to afford opportunity for the discussion of matters of interest to agricultural chemists.

2. The chief chemists for the Departments of Agriculture in the States and Colonies of Australasia shall be members *ex officio.* In the event of the unavoidable absence of one of the members from a meeting of the Association, he may nominate an official of his staff to act as his representative, and such representative shall have for the time being all the privileges of membership.

3. The officers of the Association shall consist of a president, vice-president, and a secretary, and these three officers, with one other member to be elected by the Association, shall constitute the Executive Committee.

4. The Executive Committee may appoint from time to time a recorder.

5. There may be appointed by the president at the regular meetings a referee for each of the subjects to be considered by the Association.

6. The special duties of the officers of the Association may be further defined when necessary by the Executive Committee.

7. The meetings of this Association shall be held at such places and at such times as shall be decided by the Executive Committee.

8. Any alterations or additions to this constitution shall only be made with the consent of a majority of the members of the Association.

The Association of Official Agricultural Chemists as above constituted was then formed, and the following office bearers were elected :—

President	...	...	...	F. B. Guthrie.
Vice-President		...	...	C. J. Erunnich.
Secretary	...	...	...	W. Percy Wilkinson.
Member of Executive Committee		...	B. C. Aston.

The proceedings of the present Conference were then formally adopted as the proceedings of the first meeting of the Association.

It was resolved that the second meeting should be held, if possible, in Sydney in March or April, 1907, as much important matter had been reserved for discussion with representatives of all the States.

It was resolved that the Governments of the various States and Colonies be advised of the formation of the Association, informed of its aims and objects, and asked to give it official recognition.

Other resolutions were passed as follow :—

1. Copies of analyses made by the official chemists should not be used for advertising purposes, and some steps should be taken to prevent such abuse.

2. Samples of soil for analyses should, when possible, be taken by an officer of the Department of Agriculture under the direction of the chemist.

3. The glassware used in dairies and butter factories ought to be of approved form and make, and all calibrated glassware should be submitted to the agricultural chemist for testing and verification, and if found correct should receive an official stamp. The limits of error tolerated to be decided at the next Conference.

4. Further investigation on Kjeldahl's method for the determination of nitrogen with and without the use of mercury is necessary. (Mr. Brunnich was appointed referee.)

5. It is desirable that in all cases of alleged poisoning of any animal in which a chemical analysis is required, a *post-mortem* examination by a veterinary surgeon should be made and the chemist advised of the result before he undertakes the analysis.

6. Mr. Aston was appointed referee in the matter of the determination of iron and alumina occurring in phosphate rock, to report to next Conference.

THE LABOUR BUREAU.

OCTOBER REPORT.

Mr. Jas. Longmore, the Superintendent of the Government Labour Bureau, reports as follows for the month of October :—

PERTH.

Registrations·—The total number of individual men who called during the month in search of work was 634. Of this number 282 were new registrations and 352 renewals, *i.e.*, men who called who had been registered during the year prior to the month of October. The trades or occupations of the 634 applicants were as follows: Labourers, 157; handy lads, 75; handy men, 59; bushmen, 54; farm hands, 46; carpenters, 17; cooks, 17; sawmill hands, 15; bricklayers, 12; painters, 11; horse-drivers, 10; miners, 10; grooms, 9; gardeners, 8; engine-drivers, 7; kitchenmen, 7; yardmen,

7; butchers, 5; fitters, 5; firemen, 5; shearers, 5; bakers, blacksmiths, gardeners (market), and hotel hands (4 of each); and 77 miscellaneous.

Engagements.—The engagements for the month numbered 227. The classification of work found was as follows:—Labourers, 34; bushmen, 28; farm hands, 27; sawmill hands, 25; handy men, 18; handy boys, 14; gardeners, 8; boys for farms, carpenters and shearers, 7 of each; cooks, 6; woodcutters, 6; painters, 5; yardmen, 5; bricklayers, carpenters (bridge), dairymen and horsedrivers, 3 of each; and 18 miscellaneous.

KALGOORLIE.

Registrations.—The applicants for work numbered 78. There were 47 new registrations and 31 renewals. The classification was as follows:— Labourers, 23; handy men, 23; miners, 7; handy youths, 4; blacksmiths, fitters, carpenters, and engine-drivers,' 3 of each; bricklayers, cooks, barmen, and firemen, 2 of each; and drivers, 1.

Engagements.—There were 11 engagements, classified as follows:— Labourers, 4; miners, 3; handy men, 2; carpenters and pressers, 1 of each.

The female servants who called numbered 36. There were 15 new registrations and 21 renewals. The classification was as follows:—Generals, waitresses, and cooks, 6 of each; charwomen, 5; barmaids, 4; shop assistants, housemaids, useful girls, and laundresses, 2 of each; and housekeepers, 1. There were 2 engagements, viz., shop assistants.

NORTHAM.

Registrations.—There were 54 applicants for work, classified as follows:—Farm labourers, 29; labourers, 10; handy men, 5; binder-drivers, shearers, and cooks, 2 of each; married couples, general servants, handy lads, and contractors, 1 of each.

Engagements.—The engagements for the month numbered 9, viz.;— Binder-drivers, clearers, and labourers, 2 of each; farm hands, handy men, and handy lads, 1 of each.

WOMEN'S BRANCH, PERTH.

Registrations.— The new registrations for the month were 55 and the renewals 94. The classification was as follows:—Generals, 29; laundress-charwomen, 29; housemaids, 28; cooks, 15: housekeepers, 13; light generals, 12; useful girls, 8; waitresses, 6; and 9 miscellaneous.

Engagements.—There were 71 engagements, classified as follows:— Generals, 25; laundress-charwomen, 18; light generals, 8; useful girls, 7; cook laundresses, 5; and 8 miscellaneous.

GENERAL REMARKS.

The number of individual men who called at the central office, Perth, during the month was 634. This is 94 short of the number for September, and 18 less than that for the month of October last year. The engagements were 227. There were 203 by private persons, this being 10 short of the number for September, and 36 in excess of that for the month of October last year; there were 24 engagements by Government departments. The railway fares refunded during the month totalled £32 6s. 5d., and the sum of £8 11s. 4d. was received from employers to send men, also £3 15s. 6d. to send women, the whole amounting to £44 13s. 3d.

During the month there was a fair demand for agricultural workers, the wages offered being from 20s. to 30s. a week and keep. The supply was about equal to the demand, although a few vacancies at 20s. were not filled. When the harvest is in full swing, it is doubtful whether the supply will be sufficient. Immigrants with a knowledge of agriculture are sought after and readily engaged.

At Kalgoorlie branch the callers numbered 114, viz.:—78 men and 36 women. There were 11 men and 2 women found situations. At Northam branch there were 54 applicants for work, and 9 engagements. At the Women's branch, Perth, there were 149 callers, and 71 engagements.

FRUIT-GROWERS' CONFERENCE.

The conference of fruit-growers from the various States of the Commonwealth, which was held on the 15th October in Sydney, was a gathering of some importance to Western Australia, and its representatives, Messrs. Newman, Piercy, and F. H. Piesse, M.L.A., were able to bring about a decision which will protect the State to a considerable extent from the introduction of further pests. In the course of an interview with a representative of the *West Australian*, Mr. Piesse was able to give an interesting account of what transpired at this gathering.

ANNUAL CONFERENCE.

" The conference is held annually," began Mr. Piesse, " to discuss questions affecting the interests of fruit-growers of the Commonwealth, and it has met three times. In the past, Western Australia, although requested to send delegates, has not been able to do so, but this year Messrs. Newman and Piercy travelled to Sydney as delegates, and I attended more by accident than intention, as I was at the time making a hurried health trip to the Eastern States. On reaching Adelaide I was communicated with, and requested to attend, and as some of the matters which had to be dealt with appeared to me to be important and affecting the interests of the fruit-growers of this State, I decided to accede to the request. The gathering took place in Sydney, and among the matters brought up, and which appeared to me to be of interest to this State, was the question of the inspection of fruit.

INSPECTION OF FRUIT AT THE PLACE OF IMPORT.

" It had been decided at a previous conference that the inspection should be made by officers appointed by the Agricultural Departments of the various States, only at the place of export and not at the place of import, as was the rule. Western Australia adopts the latter course, and there are strong objections from our standpoint to any variation from this rule. I found that while the decision arrived at at the previous conference was different from the practice in vogue in this State, a change of opinion among the members of the conference had taken place in the interim, and the view was that there should be a continuance of the existing methods. South

Australia appeared to be the strongest supporter of this, because the State is free from the dreaded fruit fly which has caused so much trouble in the orchards immediately surrounding Perth, and which is rampant in Queensland, and, to a lesser degree, has caused damage in New South Wales. Victoria, South Australia, and Tasmania are free from this scourge, and as they already have most of the other pests, and dreading this as the most serious if introduced, they were strong in the belief that the inspection should not be made under the conditions as had been previously proposed and decided upon. The presence of the West Australian delegates enabled the conference to carry a resolution in favour of the retention of the existing conditions, viz., that the inspection should be at the place of import, and not the place of export. It was opportune that Western Australia was represented, as it insured the continuance of an arrangement which is satisfactory to the State.

COOL STORAGE FOR EXPORT FRUIT.

"The other important matter was the question of space on steamships. Previously the practice has been to clear the space required by shippers at the latter end of October or the beginning of November, when it would be allotted by the companies carrying fruit in cold storage chambers. A difficulty has been experienced in consequence of this practice, for the reason that the fruit-grower has not been able to judge at so early a date what quantity of fruit he would have available for shipment. A resolution was passed at the conference requesting the companies to agree to an extension of the time limit, so as to enable the fruit-growers to obtain more reliable data as to the space they would require. At a subsequent meeting of the conference the representatives of the large shipping companies met the delegates, and agreed, after a discussion, to take into consideration the representations made by the conference, with a view of acceding to the wishes expressed. The object of obtaining this space is to enable the fruit-growers to make up shipments and despatch them to their own brokers in London without the aid of what are known as commission agents, who buy up and find the space on the ship. It was thought by the members of the conference, if inter-State action could be taken in the direction of securing space, that in the event of any one State not being in the position to fill the allotted space, another State which might be more favourably situated, because of its larger crops, should be permitted to make use of the space available. Very great attention is being given by the fruit-growers to the home market, preferring as they do to avail themselves of this rather than depend entirely, as appears to have been the case hitherto, upon the erratic conditions of the local markets.

UNIFORM FRUIT CASE.

"The other matters touched upon were questions of the uniform size of fruit cases, and it was decided that the cubical contents of the cases now used by Tasmania should be the standard for export. For local or inter-State uses it was decided that the same sizes should be adhered to, but the shape need not be uniform with that which, it is hoped, will be insisted upon for export purposes.

REPRESENTATION DESIRABLE.

"Speaking generally, I might say that this is the first opportunity I have had of being brought into contact with inter-State representatives. I found them most reasonable, the opinions expressed being those of practical men. The chairman (Mr. Wettenhall), who is a resident of Stawell, Victoria, is a thoroughly practical fruit-grower. It, therefore, means that from this gathering of men much good must result. It will be to the benefit of this State to be represented at similar conferences in the future. The next conference is to be held in Adelaide, and I hope delegates will again be sent from Western Australia to take part in the deliberations. The necessity for such an inter-State conference is more evident now than before Federation, as there is greater need for combined action in certain directions in order to obtain the best arrangements for export, and also to discuss the various State interests, so as to arrive at some uniform basis of protection, particularly with regard to pests and the general well-being of the industry throughout the Commonwealth."

THE DAIRYING INDUSTRY.

PROPOSED EXPERIMENTAL FARM.

A proposal for the establishment of a State experimental dairy farm was made to the Premier the other day by a deputation of representatives of the Brunswick Farmers' Association, accompanied by Messrs. Hayward and Ewing, Ms.L.A. It was urged by the deputation that the farm should be established on the Perrin Estate, which had been recently purchased by the Government.

Mr. Hayward said that the Association had passed a resolution to the effect that the Government be asked to resume 500 acres of average land on the Perrin Estate for the purpose of establishing an experimental dairy farm and butter factory. The climate and soil were admirably suited to dairy farming, and, if such a commencement were made as the deputation asked for, it would be found that many people in the South-Western part of the State would subsequently take up dairying. It was time that something was done by the State to check the drain upon the finances of the State owing to the large importations of dairy produce. The great difficulty in the past had, been the labour question, but with the introduction of improved machinery that trouble could be overcome. This industry had been the salvation of Victoria, and there was no reason why similar success should not follow its establishment in Western Australia.

The Premier, in reply, said that the Government recently purchased the Perrin Estate, and when instructions were issued for its subdivision provision was made for the reservation of a block of either 500 or 700 acres in extent for the purpose mentioned by the deputation. The estate was acquired by the Government at a fairly reasonable rate, and he thought that it would return a profit to the State. As far as the position for a dairy farm was concerned, it would be an ideal spot, more especially when the Collie to Narrogin line was completed. He was not at that stage prepared to say what the Government were going to do in regard to the establishment of an experimental dairy farm. The matter was under the consideration of Mr. Mitchell, the honorary Minister for Agriculture, who at the present time was visiting various parts of the State with the view of determining the locality where it would be best to start such a farm. It was the duty of the State to take active steps towards reducing the heavy imports of dairy produce, and so far as he was personally concerned he would promise to assist in that direction. In the Loan Bill which was being submitted to the House next week there would be found ample provision for the development of agriculture, and out of the sum that had been set aside the Government hoped to be able to allocate a portion not only for dairy farming, but also to give assistance towards the establishment of a frozen lamb trade, so that some day Western Australia would be able to take her place with other countries in this branch of production. The Government was determined to do all it could to encourage production in every form, and it was recognised that this could be brought about by giving State assistance. He promised that the particular request of the deputation should receive the best consideration.

THE SHEEP INDUSTRY.

A VISITING EXPERT'S OPINIONS.

PROMISING OUTOOK FOR BREEDERS.

INTERVIEW WITH MR. D. M. AITKEN.

Mr. D. M. Aitken, of Victoria, and a leading breeder of Shropshires in that State, came specially to Western Australia, at the invitation of the Royal Agricultural Society, to undertake the judging of the black-face classes at the Royal Show. Our visitor, in the course of an interview with a representative of the *West Australian*, expressed his high appreciation of all that he had seen.

" I must say that the Show has impressed me greatly. The grounds are superior to anything I have ever seen, and it is difficult to conceive of a more ideal site. It was impressive to see how the people gathered together, and how well the grounds held them. I wish also to express my appreciation of the splendid manner in which the Show was conducted. Everything moved smoothly, and all the events were up to time. Things worked so well that it was difficult to believe the Show had not been running for weeks. Of course there must have been some little friction at times, some untoward events happening which no amount of foresight can anticipate, but, whatever there was in this direction, few knew of it, and it did not in the least disturb the harmony of the Show."

You think we are up to date, then ?

" I was quite prepared to find things in the West abreast of the times, but my astonishment is to find you so well ahead of them. I may mention that I regularly receive the *Western Mail*, and am a close reader of it. From a perusal of the contents of this valuable publication I have for some time been struck with the fact that the agriculturists of the West were in touch with all modern developments. The few days that I have been here in the State convince me that things are more advanced with you than I thought."

Coming to the stock?

"They are of the best, and I am delighted with them. You have some sterling sheep and cattle men over here, who may be relied upon to push the stock industry to the front. It has occurred to me, however, that they might advance their mutual interests if they would work together on the lines that the breeders of the East adopt. The owner of a good sire in the East is always prepared to allow an opposition breeder to use him, always, of course, for only approved females. There is no spirit of exclusiveness. On payment of the prescribed fee, the custom is that the owner of any sire makes him available to suitable stock of even his keenest opponents."

And the system works well?

"It works excellently : indeed, it has much to do with the success of the stock industry of Victoria. Few men can afford to buy heavily-priced sires, but they can manage to send their ewes or their cows to a suitable ram or bull, and pay a fair price for the service. The consequence is that by the wider employment of high-grade sires which is made possible under this system, the average type of stock is being improved with advantage to everyone connected with the industry. Then the breeders of Victoria work together in other ways, and I speak from practical experience when I strongly urge the stockmen of Western Australia to work on similar lines. We have felt the benefit resulting from the existence of friendly relations amongst the breeding interests of the East, and I am confident that a like tale will be told here once the men engaged in the stock business work well together."

Have your own flocks benefited from the arrangement you suggest?

"Assuredly they have, and I have benefited too. For instance, we have in Tasmania Mr. A. E. Mansell, one of the greatest Shropshire breeders in the world. He had to leave the old country, where he made his reputation, from considerations of health. Naturally he brought some very superior black faces with him. Some few years ago, in a desire to improve my Shropshires, I sent three of my best ewes across to his ram 'Wildrose,' a sire of the first quality. I paid a stud fee of five guineas per head, while freight charges represented another three guineas each. In all it involved me in an expenditure of eight guineas a ewe to have them properly mated. Only a short time ago I sold one of their lambs for £50, while the other stock which are the result of the union are still in my possession."

You are a believer in breed?

"Yes; it tells every time. Not long ago I wished to improve my stud of Shropshires, which were considered very good, and the members of which had secured many show ring successes for me. I accordingly disposed of them all, and had fourteen ewes bought for me at Mr. Mansell's disposal sale on the occasion of his leaving the old country. I paid an extra fee to have these ewes served by the best Shropshire rams of the homeland. The ewes arrived in Australia, and bore in March 22 lambs, dropped according to English time. At the close of the year they again lambed, this time to an Australian sire and to Australian time, the number of their progeny being 20. It is interesting to know that 'Handroyd,' the sire used, had been the champion of England. Sent to Melbourne he also won champion honours there. Submitted to public auction he sold for 195 guineas, the record price paid in Australia for a Shropshire. Thus, in 12 months' time the increase was a considerable item, more particularly when consideration is given to the splendid quality of the parent sheep. But the point I want to make is that, except I could have had the services of these superior Shropshire sires, I could not have been successful as a breeder. And if the owners of the best stock in Western Australia will similarly place their best at the disposal of others, and even competing interests, the gain to the industry and the State will be considerable."

What about the export trade?

"In Victoria it is daily becoming a more important branch of the sheep-growing industry. Last year we sent away about a million carcases, and the trade is only in its infancy. Sheep men are beginning to see that it has enormous possibilities, and it is quite clear to my mind that we are on the eve of great changes in our Australian systems of stock husbandry. I was for 12 or 13 years engaged in the breeding of export sheep in New Zealand, so therefore I may be allowed to claim some special knowledge of the subject."

How does Australia compare with New Zealand as a sheep export country?

"Personally, I have no hesitation in saying that we can beat the island colony in the business. We have at least three factors—and very important factors as they are—in our favour. First, then, we have a much better foundation type in our merino. New Zealand is not a merino country, and, as this breed is the foundation of the best export classes, we at once start with a great advantage. Secondly, the Australian climate is much better for the raising of sheep than that of New Zealand, where there is an excess of bleak and wet weather. Finally land in Australia, paying full regard to its productive capacity, is one-third cheaper than it is in New Zealand."

Are you alone in these conclusions?

"No; strangely enough, I came across a New Zealand expert at a Victorian show the other day, who fully acquiesced in my views, and, indeed, added to them. He came over under agreement with a Victorian export firm, and is credited with being one of the best judges of 'freezers' in New Zealand. We were at the Shepparton Show together, and he told me that the sheep he was buying were the equal to anything he could get in New Zealand. There was this difference, however—that the pelt of a Victorian sheep is worth two or three shillings more than one of New Zealand, and we can make our first drafts for export in November, as against January in New Zealand. I remember when I first came across to Australia I was shown some pelts of ordinary wethers, and, judging them from a New Zealand standpoint, I could not believe anything but that they had come from rams."

Extending your observations, Mr. Aitken, what about Western Australia as a sheep export country?

"Of course, you can only expect me to answer that in a general way, as I have not seen your country outside of Perth. But I candidly confess that the developments of your sheep have fairly staggered me. When I examined them for judging purposes I, of course, had no clue to their age beyond what could be gathered from their teeth. To-day for the first time I obtained some particulars about the ages of the lambs, and I say without any reservation that I am amazed at their rapid maturity. Then, of course, as an exporting country you are a week or ten days nearer to London, which is a material advantage. From what I have seen of the sheep you can raise, I am decidedly inclined to take an optimistic view of the possibilities that lie ahead of Western Australia as a lamb and mutton exporting land. I am returning to Victoria almost immediately, very greatly impressed with your State, and full of the kindest recollections for the generous treatment that I have received in all directions. I shall indeed look forward with pleasure to making another trip in the not distant future."

POULTRY NOTES.

AMERICAN POULTRY FARMING.

By F. H. Robertson.

We all know the wonderful strides poultry breeding has made of late years in the United States of America, what an immense sum of money the annual crop of poultry products is worth, the large amount of capital laid out in plants to carry on breeding and fattening operations on an extensive scale, the great capacity of their artificial incubating and brooder appliances. From all accounts, they go into the thing in a very complete and systematic manner, and spare neither time nor money in planning out all details to evolve schemes which will produce the maximum results at a minimum expenditure of time or dollars. No doubt many of these big plants pay handsomely, and the most is made of that fact; on the other hand, there must be many large concerns which result in failure. The Yankee is nothing if not optimistic; it is part and parcel of his very existence, and well it is so; he is not in the habit of dwelling on the gloomy side of life, and if failure once befalls him, it is not for ever, but rather spurs him on to farther effort, and a fresh start is made under other conditions. It is a pity that there is not more of this go-ahead spirit among our West Australians. How often does one meet with the man who has, after mature consideration, gone in for poultry, and on finding it did not turn out as anticipated, thrown it up in disgust, firmly convinced that it does not pay, it cannot pay, and it is quite useless to waste any more time, thought, or capital over an industry which he is thoroughly convinced is absolutely worthless. He is too self-opinionated to ever dream that the fault could be with himself. He may have done one of the many wrong things which so many beginners indulge in; perhaps have started with the wrong class of birds, erected his houses and runs on an unsuitable locality, or, perhaps from want of knowledge, failed to rear chickens, and so on; and instead of ever afterwards becoming an enemy of poultry, he should try again, and, having gained experience by past failure, should profit by such and start afresh on other lines, taking the view that if other people can succeed, so can anyone else who applies himself to work and think out the correct manner of doing so in accordance with the existing natural conditions of soil, location, and climate. And now coming a to few American facts and figures:

The catering for the fresh egg trade forms a leading line with the Americans. and it has been found that, notwithstanding the enormous consumption, the supply of really first-class fresh eggs is not equal to the demand, and there is never likely to be over production. Great attention is paid to grading according to size, colour and quality, which is done by middle men in a large way of business, but many large egg farmers handle their own eggs, and frequently also those of their neighbours. Cold storage plays an important part in the egg business. The wholesale price averages about 10d. a dozen, the lowest quotations being 8½d. and the highest 1s. 9d. To give an idea of the large number of poultry kept, it is estimated that it takes nine million odd hens to supply the demand for Chicago alone.

The sticking to one variety of fowls is a striking feature of the American poultry farmer's mode of working things, and it is undoubtedly the best system, in a published interview of a breeder of White Plymouth Rocks who has stuck to the same breed for the past 16 years, sells from eight to ten thousand head of the one variety and two thousand sittings of eggs yearly; yet how few poultry breeders here who keep but one variety, or keep to it for any length of time. There is far too great an inclination on the part of the genuine poultryman to keep too many varieties; and when we come to the general all-round farmer he is, as a rule, a far greater offender, and mixes his breeds up without thought as to what the character of the progeny will be like from the haphazard mating.

KEEP ONLY ONE VARIETY.

The breeder of live stock, whether it be sheep, cattle, horses, or pigs, as a rule works on some system, and even the most careless sheep breeder would not, for instance, mix up all sorts of varieties of sheep in one flock, but keeps to one well-defined plan, otherwise he would be held up to ridicule, and be looked on as a fool by his neighbours; and yet how many who recognise the value of system in sheep and cattle fail to do so with their poultry? It stands to reason that what is correct in one instance must also be the right thing in another. If a first-class large egg supply is what is wanted, then for preference birds of the lighter varieties are kept, such as Leghorns, Andalusians, Minorcas; but as these do not go broody to any extent incubators become a necessity. But if table qualities are also desired, and no artificial incubation, then go in for a heavier class of fowls, such as Orpingtons, Wyandottes, Plymouth Rocks, or Leghorns. The same principal holds good with fowls as with other forms of live stock, viz., the impossibility of, for instance, combining in one horse the strongest and fleetest, or in cattle the best for beef and milk in the one animal. Therefore for the ordinary mixed farmer who grows the greater portion of his own poultry food it will be found most profitable to keep an all-round breed; his surplus stock, consisting chiefly of cockerels for the table, can be fattened on wheat which would otherwise have been lost. But the person who has to buy all his feed will find the profits small on table poultry, therefore it will pay much better to keep the lighter varieties and make egg production the chief source of profit.

EGG-LAYING COMPETITION.

NARROGIN MONTHLY RECORD.

	Breed.	Owner.	Total for Month.	Total to Date.
1.	White Leghorns ...	Mrs. A. Bristow	112	663
2.	Brown do. ...	E. E. Ranford	130	639
3.	Silver Wyandottes ...	A. M. Neitschke	138	616
4.	Buff Orpingtons ...	A. H. Hilton	106	590
5.	Silver Wyandottes ...	Miss Buttsworth	97	556
6.	White Leghorns ...	F. Piaggio	109	553
7.	Do. do. ...	C. W. Johnson	102	548
8.	Brown Leghorns ...	Mrs. R. A. Dusting...	124	545
9.	Silver Wyandottes ...	G. W. G. Lizars	98	502
10.	White Leghorns ...	A. F. Spencer	101	488
11.	Do. do. ...	Miss M. Parker	106	485
12.	White Wyandottes ...	Mrs. L. J. Hood	113	473
13.	Black Orpingtons ...	Sparks & Bonnington	98	472
14.	White Leghorns ...	Aveley Yard	125	464
15.	Do. do. ...	T. Handley	94	463
16.	Brown Leghorns ...	J. D. Wilson	120	453
17.	R.C. Brown Leghorns ...	Adelaide Yards	90	442
18.	Golden Wyandottes ...	W. G. Craig	85	437
19.	White Leghorns ...	F. G. Williams	102	431
20.	Black Orpingtons ...	Perth Yards...	107	428
21.	R.C. Brown Leghorns ...	E. Krachler	84	406
22.	White Leghorns ...	R. J. Flynn	105	405
23.	Do. do. ...	J. E. Tull	84	402
24.	Do. do. ...	J. Oneto	80	376
25.	Do. do. ...	O. C. Rath	111	352
		Totals	2,621	12,189

SUBIACO MONTHLY RECORD—OCTOBER.

FOWLS.

Six hens in each pen.

Owner and Breed.	Oct.	Total for four months.
1. Sunnyhurst (S.A.), *W. Leghorn	160	589
2. A. H. Padman (S.A.), *W. Leghorn	151	531
3. J. D. Smith, *W. Leghorn	123	511
4. S. Craig, *W. Leghorn	136	506
5. A. H. Padman (S.A.), *S. Wyandotte	129	489
6. A. F. Farrant, Partridge Wyandotte	110	489
7. E. Garbett, W. Leghorn	128	486
8. Ericville Egg Farm, *W. Leghorn	133	485
9. W. J. Clarke, Brown Leghorn	132	484
10. F. T. Rowe, *Black Orpington	125	479
11. F. Whitfield, Brown Leghorn	136	468
12. G. W. G. Lizars, *W. Leghorn	135	468
13. C. W. Johnson, *W. Leghorn	128	464
14. C. Attwell, *S. Wyandotte	101	462
15. E. Fitzgerald, W. Leghorn	134	461
16. Mrs. McGree, *W. Leghorn	125	460
17. Bungalow Farm, Brown Leghorn	126	457
18. Austin and Thomas, W. Leghorn	144	453
19. F. Piaggio, W. Leghorn	127	451

* Male birds in these pens.

FOWLS—*continued.*

Owner and Breed.	Oct.	Total for four months.
20. Ryan Bros., *W. Leghorn	127	448
21. B. Jones, *S. Wyandotte	94	437
22. J. R. Parkes, Brown Leghorn	134	436
23. G. M. Buttsworth, *W. Leghorn	121	434
24. Bungalow Farm, *W. Leghorn	123	434
25. F. Whitfield, *W. Leghorn	111	432
26. A. S. B. Craig, *W. Wyandotte	96	431
27. E. Palmerston, W. Leghorn	128	427
28. R. G. Flynn, W. Leghorn	107	426
29. Adelaide P. Yard, W. Leghorn	126	426
30. Bon Accord, W. Leghorn	139	423
31. Ericville Egg Farm, *Black Orpington	123	422
32. L. Meatchem, *G. Wyandotte	87	421
33. J. M. Buttsworth, *W. Leghorn	113	416
34. A. Snell, *Brown Leghorn	112	414
35. H. Jones, W. Leghorn	124	413
36. E. Hutchinson, *Minorcas	117	405
37. C. L. Braddock, S. Wyandotte	94	404
38. J. W. Buttsworth, S. Wyandotte	92	397
39. W. Snowden, Brown Leghorn	133	395
40. O. K. Poultry Farm, *Black Orpington	105	390
41. Perth P. Yard, W. Leghorn	110	381
42. Geo. Bolger, *Black Orpington	102	381
43. A. R. Keesing, Minorcas	97	380
44. W. Snowden, S. Wyandotte	87	375
45. Mrs. Hughes, *R. C. B. Leghorn	121	370
46. Honnor and Forbes, R. C., W. Leghorn	112	368
47. W. Wade, W. Leghorn	110	368
48. H. M. Kelly, *G. Wyandotte	108	366
49. C. R. Roberts, *W. Leghorn	106	365
50. A. Coombs, S. Wyandotte	94	359
51. Glen Donald Yard, G. Wyandotte	90	358
52. F. Mason, W. Leghorn	96	355
53. J. White, Brown Leghorn	132	354
54. R. G. Smith, W. Wyandotte	97	344
55. E. A. Newton, W. Leghorn	95	333
56. C. Crawley, B. Orpington	118	331
57. Mrs. McGree, W. Wyandotte	97	320
58. H. H. Wegg, G. Wyandotte	85	309
59. H. M. Kelly, *B. Orpington	103	306
60. W. Savage, Minorca	100	303
61. J. E. Redmond, S. Wyandotte	91	302
62. Jas. Kirk, G. Wyandotte	79	301
63. J. S. Miller, S. Wyandotte	87	287
64. J. B. Pettit, S. Wyandotte	87	272
Total for the month	7,291	11,687

DUCKS.

Four in each Pen.

Owner and Breed.	Oct.	Total for four months.
1. R. A. Dusting, *Indian Runner	104	404
2. E. A. Newton, *Indian Runner	117	389
3. Mrs. Mellen, *Indian Runner	109	372
4. Austin and Thomas, *Indian Runner	109	360
5. A. Snell, *Indian Runner	123	353
6. G. Stead, *Indian Runner	104	334

* Male birds n these pens.

Ducks—*continued.*

Owner and Breed.				Oct.	Total for four months.
7. Miss E. Parker, Indian Runner	...	...	...	121	326
8. F. T. Rowe, Indian Runner	...	...	...	119	324
9. W. Snowden, *Buff Orpington	...	...	...	107	323
10. C. E. Close, Indian Runner	...	...	...	116	321
11. Adelaide Poultry Yard, Indian Runner	...	...	123	315
12. Bon Accord, *Buff Orpington	...	...	...	109	313
13. Perth Poultry Yard, *Buff Orpington	...	...	119	312
14. Ericville Egg Farm, *Buff Orpington	...	...	110	306
15. S. Craig, Indian Runner	...	...	...	113	262
16. J. R. Parkes, Indian Runner	...	...	...	118	261
17. F. D. Vincent, *Indian Runner	...	...	...	121	247
18. Sargenfri (S.A.), *Buff Orpington	...	...	...	107	237
19. C. W. Johnson, *Indian Runner	...	...	...	116	230
20. Aveley Poultry Yard, Indian Runner	...	...	112	219
21. F. Piaggio, *Buff Orpington	...	...	...	111	187
22. J. B. Pettit, Indian Runner	...	...	...	101	169
Total eggs laid for month	...	...	...	2,489	6,566

* Male birds are in these pens, and eggs are obtainable for setting purposes, applications to be addressed to the Manager, Egg-laying Competition, Subiaco.

VALUE OF ANT-HILLS AS A FERTILISER.

—

The following interesting items on the value of ant hills as a fertiliser have been received from Mr. T. Church, of the National Bank ·—

Some months ago, when in search of special soils for the formation of beds for roses, Mr. William Paterson mentioned that experiments to determine the value of ant hills might lead to results not to be found in the use of ordinary soils.

Accordingly, being agreeable to give them a trial, he generously sent me a truck load. Half of the lot (a nine-ton truck) I pounded up, and the balance I burnt by the old English method of stifle burning or charring, on lines laid down by the eminent rose grower, Mr. William Paul, in his noted book on roses.

These parcels of earth I tried, using in some cases the pounded hills only, and in others burnt and unburnt mixed. I tried them with roses, cauliflowers, and (mixed with loam) potatoes. At the same time I handed samples to Mr. Despeissis, who as usual was pleased to try methods along new lines.

The result of Mr. Mann's analysis is annexed, and needs no comment from me.

But as to practical results, I planted a Bride rose in the unburnt earth, cauliflowers in a mixture of burnt and unburnt earth, and Carmen potatoes in holes partially filled with a mixture of burnt and unburnt hills. When pounded thoroughly the earth was almost as fine as flour, and this is reasonable to expect, seeing that it is believed it first passes through the body of the termite before being used for their hills.

It was also expected by me that the soil would consequently be rich in nitrogen. The results, however, all round were disappointing. The plants all made good growth at the outset, probably due to the fine nature of the earth particles furnishing a good root run for the tiny first roots. Later, however, when they commenced to demand nourishment—all being gross feeders —and same evidently not being forthcoming, they proceeded to grow with all the appearances of plants placed in uncongenial surroundings, and the ultimate results were no better than if the soil had been ordinary Perth sand.

A great defect in the soil, I found, was its impermeability to water. Unless carefully stirred it is as easy to pass water through it as through waterproof cloth.

Although the experiments in this case showed unsatisfactory results, I think the soil should not be accepted as useless, but believe that if obtained from the proper localities it has greater fertilising properties than the soil around it.

Experiments conducted at the Cape prove this, and Dr. Morrison drew my attention to the published results of a tour through Abyssinia by Dr. A. J. Hayes, who drew the conclusion that the great fertility of the delta of the Nile might be credited to the disintegration of these hills on the high lands and their subsequent washing down to the valleys.

Probably the case is one of environment. If the soil from which the hills are drawn is rich it is improved by treatment by the ants, but if poor, then there is little advance in its value.

The subject is one that is worthy of further tests, and results may prove that many areas of land at present covered with the hills might be greatly improved by the levelling down and distribution of the ant-hill earth over them.

TWO SAMPLES OF ANT HILLS FOR ANALYSIS.

—	1.	2.
Percentage of fine soil (passed by 2 m.m. sieve)	1 00·0	100·00
Percentage of roots and stones (retained by 2m.m. sieve) ...	*Nil*	*Nil*
Reaction of soil	Acid	Very strongly Acid

ANALYSIS OF FINE EARTH—AIR-DRIED.
PERCENTAGE OF FERTILISING CONSTITUENTS.

—	Total.	Available.	Total.	Available.	Required.
Phosphoric acid	·017	·0075	·032	·0046	·15
Potash	·066	·0179	·061	·0126	·2
Lime	·096	...	·071	...	·4
Nitrogen	·154	...	·182	...	...
Chlorine	·014	...	·009	...	...

" Total " represents percentage soluble in strong acid.
" Available " represents percentage soluble in 1 per cent. citric acid in seven days.

GARDEN NOTES FOR DECEMBER.

By PERCY G. WICKEN.

During the first days of November the annual show of the Royal Agricultural Society is the principal event of interest to agriculturalists, and that the show is appreciated by the public is evidenced by the number who attend during the principal days. The exhibits of farm and garden produce are shown in the Society's main pavilion, and although a very fair collection of garden produce was shown, the exhibits are not of the quality that we would expect to see, neither are the entries as numerous as they should be. Although farmers may exhibit vegetables at the country shows, it may perhaps not be profitable for them to go to the expense of exhibiting in Perth; but considering the number of market gardens about Perth, and the large quantity of vegetables grown about Jandakot and Wanneroo and other moist lands close to the city, it is a wonder that the competition for the prizes offered by the Society is not much keener. Nearly all classes of vegetables were represented, and some of them were very fine, but the average quality of the exhibits in this section were no better than may be seen in the windows of some of the best shops in the city. Some excellent samples of asparagus were shown, and if similar samples can be produced on a commercial basis there should be no occasion to import such quantities of the tinned article. The samples of bugle pumpkins were equal to anything that could be shown in a recognised pumpkin-growing district.

The principal work in the garden during this month will be to keep the ground well stirred, as this causes the surface soil to act as a mulch, the capillary action of the soil is destroyed and the ground retains the moisture for the use of the plants. As soon as plants have ceased bearing, they should be pulled up and either put on the compost heap or else dug into the ground, as after they have yielded their seeds they only become a harbour for insect pests.

Now is the time to commence to put in a system of subdrains to carry off the surplus water from any wet spots in the garden or orchard; during the winter these spots can be marked, and as soon as the water has run off trenches can be dug, drain pipes laid, and the surplus water carried out to the nearest water channel. By putting in a system of drains, the soil will be warmer in the winter and the plants will make much quicker growth in the spring and mature earlier, while during the summer months the drained soil will be much moister than the undrained soil, and vegetables can be grown which could not be raised on undrained land. Agricultural drain pipes of any diameter can now be purchased in Perth at a price that brings them within the means of most gardeners, and they will be found as cheap as any other system of drains that can be constructed, and more effective and durable.

Beans (French or Kidney) are now plentiful in the Perth markets. The pods should be picked before they become too old, as, if they are allowed to mature their seeds, the plants soon go out of bearing. A further supply of seed may be sown, but the soil must be kept well cultivated so as to conserve the moisture.

Beans (Lima).—Tie up to stakes or trellis all the climbing varieties. In moist localities a further supply of seed may be sown.

Beet (Silver).—Yields a supply of green leaves during the dry weather. They are useful for table and to supply the poultry with green leaves at a time when green feed is scarce. A little liquid manure, 1oz. nitrate of soda dissolved in one gallon of water, will help them along.

Cabbage.—Keep the plants already growing well cultivated. Except in moist localities it is not much use planting out more plants, but for garden purposes they may be planted if watered and shaded from the sun.

Celery.—Hill up the plants already growing so as to cause them to bleach.

Chokos.—The vines should now be running, and will require to be tied up to a trellis. A few more well-shot fruits may be planted out. The fruit somewhat resembles a squash, and is worth growing as a novelty for the table.

Cucumbers.—Early sown plants are now carrying ripe fruit. For garden purposes a little more seed may be sown. If grubs are troublesome they may be kept in check by laying a bait consisting of a little Paris green mixed with some pollard and treacle, as this will poison them.

Egg Plants.—Any strong seedlings may be planted out if shaded from the sun.

Maize (Sweet.)—Keep the ground between the rows well stirred, so as to conserve the moisture for the plants. A little more seed may be sown. The cobs should be used when they are young and full of milk, and not allowed to become hard.

Melons, Early.—Rock melons are now on the market, and water melons will soon be available. Keep the ground between the vines well cultivated until the plants take full possession of the ground. To obtain the best flavour a melon should always be picked first thing in the morning before the sun makes them warm, later in the day they become tougher and not so crisp.

Pumpkins and Squashes.—The early varieties of squashes are now plentiful, but the harder varieties are later. Keep the ground well worked between the vines.

Okras.—Put out any plants that are strong enough, and shade from the sun until they are established.

Sweet Potatoes.—Young vines should now be making strong growth, and all previous shoots planted should have taken root. They are best planted on ridges or hills, although in many instances they do well when cultivated on the level. The plants cannot be hilled up after planting, as the vines prevent the hilling machines from working. Sweet potatoes make an excellent vegetable, and as they are very easily grown they should be much more extensively cultivated than they are.

Tomatoes.—Tomatoes from the northern districts will now be on the market. In the cooler area seedlings can still be planted out. The smooth skinned varieties are the best for table use, and fetch the best price. Rough skinned tomatoes are hardly worth growing. As the plants make a growth, they should be tied up to stakes and kept off the ground.

Farm.—This is a busy month on the farm, haymaking and carting, stripping and harvesting, the grain will occupy all the farmer's time. Early in October the prospects of a bountiful harvest were very good, but the spell of dry warm weather which followed had a detrimental effect on the grain crops in the Eastern districts, and the average for these districts will be somewhat less than is estimated. As soon as a hay stack is completed, a fire-break should be ploughed round it, so as to minimise the danger from fire. Some varieties of wheat shed their grain when ripe much easier than others, and special attention should be given so as to harvest these varieties just before the grain becomes ripe enough to shell out. Farmers will probably have to accept a lower price for their wheat than they have done previously, but the price should not be less than the price in Adelaide, plus the freight from Adelaide to Fremantle. Should the yield prove so favourable that we have a surplus for export, the freight will not be any consideration, as we shall have to look for outside markets, and then shall have to accept the ruling rates of the corn markets of the world the same as the growers in the Eastern States, where there is a large surplus for export. Given proper methods of cultivation there is no doubt that wheat can be produced in this State as cheaply as it can elsewhere. As soon as the hay or grain is carted in, the sheep should be turned on to the stubble, as they will pick up all the fallen grain and soon fatten on it. Where there is sufficient moisture in the ground, a little sorghum, French millet, or cow-pea may be sown, but the cultivator must be kept going between the rows.

NOTES ON THE CLIMATE FOR THE MONTH OF OCTOBER, 1906.

The most noticeable feature of the weather during the month was the abnormal heat wave which broke up in coastal districts on the 20th, and on the Goldfields a day or two later.

During its prevalence the temperature at the Observatory and at many other places was higher than had ever previously been known in October. Great heat prevailed in the N.W. at times, the maximum temperature at Marble Bar averaging 104 degrees for the week ending 24th October, and reaching 113·0 degrees on the 26th, or 5·5 degrees higher than any previous October record, even in that very hot place ; otherwise conditions were fairly seasonable, fine and wet weather alternating in S.W. districts, and mostly fine elsewhere. On the whole the pressure was very slightly below the average for previous years, and temperature above.

The rainfall was somewhat below normal in the S.W. district, slightly above in the East Kimberley, and mostly nil or very light elsewhere. It is perhaps worthy of note that a few light showers were for the first time on record in October experienced on the N.W. coast.

W. E. COOKE,
Government Astronomer,
per E. A. W

The Observatory, Perth, 7th November, 1906.

The Climate of Western Australia during October, 1906.

Locality	Barometer — Mean of 9 a.m. and 3 p.m.	Barometer — Average for previous years	Barometer — Highest for Month	Barometer — Lowest for Month	Shade Temp. Oct. 1906 — Mean Max.	Mean Min.	Mean of Month	Highest Max.	Lowest Min.	Avg. previous Years — Mean Max.	Mean Min.	Highest ever recorded	Lowest ever recorded	Rainfall — Points (100 to inch) in Month	Wet Days	Total Points since Jan. 1
NORTH-WEST AND NORTH COAST:																
Wyndham	29·847	29·898	30·031	29·567	98·9	74·8	86·8	108·4	70·4	98·3	79·2	110·2	68·5	150	2	1466
Derby	29·852	29·916	30·062	29·95	97·7	41	85·9	110·9	66·0	96·9	70·8	112·2	58·6	2	1	1149
Broome	29·880	29·928	30·039	29·95	93·4	74·3	83·8	105·6	62·2	90·6	70·2	106·6	52·8	*Nil*		1016
Condon	29·890	29·96	30·041	29·770	98·7	64·0	78·8	107·6	50·8	90·3	61·6	108·2	49·2	2	1	678
Cossack	29·915	29·95	30·080	29·770	95·0	68·0	81·5	107·0	57·0	92·0	65·1	110·5	56·0	*Nil*		1013
Onslow	29·94	29·971	30·129	29·826	90·5	63·1	70·3	104·0	55·2	88·5	59·8	108·5	48·5	*Nil*		652
Winning Pool	29·940		33	29·77	9·2	55·9	75·0	103·8	50·6					25	3	928
Carnarvon	30·018	30·032	30·262	29·950	78·3	61·8	70·0	93·2	55·2	8·3	60·6	100·6	46·2	16	3	703
Hamelin Pool	29·997	30·018	30·207	29·821	82·9	59·3	71·1	94·8	46·6	81·7	54·9	101·6	44·6	13	2	559
Geraldton	30·044	30·064	30·293	29·826	74·9	55·8	65·4	8·6	9·3	31	54·9	90	41·0	44	6	2030
INLAND:																
Hall's Creek	29·871	29·928	30·087	29·69	99·1	72·2	85·6	109·0	0·8	99·7	67·8	108·0	48·4	91	3	678
Marble Bar	29·909	29·928	30·097	29·692	100·9	68·3	84·6	113·0	60·5	97·2	65·8	107·5	51·2	2	3	978
Nullagine	29·960	29·962	30·150	29·720	97·2	62·7	80·0	112·0	47·4	94·2	65	107·0	43·9	*Nil*		930
Peak Hill	29·935	29·940	30·145	29·603	87·3	59·9	73·6	100·6	49·0	81	58·3	97·6	41·3	40	2	981
Wiluna	29·992	29·999	30·208	29·821	84·3	56·2	70·6	101·6	45·0	82·2	53·7	98·2	9·1	22	3	719
Cue	30·003	30·006	30·212	29·765	82·0	56·2	70·2	99·0	44·9	82·2	54·7	99·0	41·5	51	3	925
Murgoo					80·4	6·1	69·0	98·0	46·0	90·5	52·4	98·6	38·9	20	1	734
Yalgoo						52·9	66·6	98·0	42·3					43	2	978
Nungarra																704
Darrs	29·952	29·977	30·178	29·618	83·8	56·6	67·1	108·4	45·4	81·2	55·0	99·9	41·2	*Nil*		752
Laverton	29·982	30·006	30·257	29·556	83·0	55·9	69·4	108·0	43·6	79·7	52·9	102·3	39·0	*Nil*		803
Menzies	29·992	29·987	30·265	29·652	81·1	53·7	67·4	9·0	42·0	78·7	52·9	99·0	39·2	*Nil*		887
Wna					9·1	51·3	65·4	9·0	39·8	75·0	48·8	98·6	38·3	*Nil*		794
Kalgoorlie	30·004	29·992	30·321	29·591	79·4	52·5	66·0	99·0	41·5	77·4	52·2	97·6	39·8	*Nil*		845
Coolgardie	29·982	29·996	30·321	29·588	79·5	69	64·8	99·6	90	78·9	50·7	99·8	39·7	*Nil*		857
urn Cross	30·009	29·990	30·306	29·658	79·7	49·2	64·4	98·2	39·0	77·3	48·6	107·0	36·0	7·	5	1013
K 1 Min					73·0	47·6	60	92·0	37·0	71·0	46·8	91·9	38·8	100	9	1907
Northam					74·9	47·5	61·2	94·5	37·8	73·0	46·9	93·0	34·7	56	7	1717
York	30·041	29·034	30·328		74·4	46·5	60·4	92·0	35·0	72·8	46·8	91·8	31·4	62	10	1382
Guildford				29·696	72·7	52·6	62·6	98·4	41·2	72·4	50·4	93·0	40·6	109	8	2985

* Average for the years only.

The Climate of Western Australia during October, 1906—continued.

Locality	Barometer Mean of 9 a.m. and 3 p.m.	Barometer Average for previous years	Barometer Highest for Month	Barometer Lowest for Month	Shade Temp. Oct. 1906 Mean Max.	Mean Min.	Mean of Month	Highest Max.	Lowest Min.	Avg. Mean Max.	Avg. Mean Min.	Highest ever recorded	Lowest ever recorded	Rainfall Points (100 to inch) in Month	W. Days	Total Points since Jan. 1
Perth Gardens	30·037	29·058	30·298	29·723	73·4	55·8	64·6	94·0	44·6	71·6	52·4	97·0	38·0	111	10	333
Perth Observatory	30·044	29·051	30·310	29·701	70·9	54·8	62·8	98·8	44·2	69·2	53·0	89·8	41·2	112	12	3211
…le	30·064	29·052	30·319	29·746	67·1	51	63·6	93·0	46·0	67·6	5·4	87·0	41·6	68	9	2450
…at	30·052	29·032	30·310	29·696	68·6	56·2	62·6	91·2	49·0	67·5	56·1	85·2	43·5	33	8	2069
…Mh	…	…	…	…	70·3	53·2	61·8	91·5	41·0	69·5	49·5	89·3	36·3	98	10	93
Marradong	…	…	…	…	69·8	44·0	56·9	89·0	33·0	68·2	40·6	85·0	30·1	29	8	2619
Wandering *	…	…	…	…	…	…	…	…	…	…	…	…	…	91	7	2385
Narrogin	…	…	…	…	69·3	45·8	57·6	92·0	34·0	6·1	43·8	88·6	31·2	241	14	3708
…lie	…	…	…	…	69·4	44·2	59·3	92·8	39·2	67·5	41	88·7	36·2	153	11	96
Donnybrook	30·020	29·047	30·385	29·635	67·1	53·0	61·6	88·0	41·4	68·2	50·6	89·2	37·4	122	10	3102
Bunbury	…	…	…	…	69·0	50·7	59·8	90·1	40·1	67·8	47·8	85·8	37·2	116	13	3320
Busselton	29·968	…	30·339	29·603	65·0	56·0	60·5	82·0	42·0	…	…	…	…	98	16	3066
…e Naturaliste	…	…	…	…	69·9	46·3	58·1	92·0	31·0	68·0	43·2	85·2	31·2	97	10	336
Bridgetown	…	29·036	…	29·460	67·0	50·0	58·5	91·0	38·0	65·7	49·7	85·2	36·8	246	15	37
Karridale	29·980	29·997	30·340	29·430	65·6	54·8	60·2	86·7	46·1	64·8	54·7	82·8	44·8	84	20	3264
Cape Leeuwin	30·020	30·007	30·310	29·600	70·3	45·5	57·9	90·0	35·0	68·2	45·6	87·0	31·0	96	7	135
Katanning	…	…	…	…	…	…	…	…	…	…	…	…	…	127	13	2370
Mt. Barker	29·990	30·005	30·370	29·520	61	46·8	8·4	91·2	41·0	65·0	49·3	83·0	36·2	40	16	681
Albany	29·984	29·999	30·371	29·449	62·7	49·7	57·4	85·8	43·5	61·6	51·8	78·0	39·0	285	17	30
Breaksea	29·986	30·006	30·324	29·558	70·0	52·0	59·9	88·0	39·0	69·0	50·8	101·4	8·2	93	11	2227
Esperance	30·010	30·028	30·386	29·559	76·4	49·8	61·6	99·3	34·5	74·2	47·4	98·0	35·7	6	2	640
Balladonia	29·990	30·028	30·346	29·552	71·7	46·9	60·0	100·3	39·2	71·5	50·8	99·5	30·0	13	3	852
Eyre						48·4										

(Left bracket label: SOUTH-WEST AND SOUTH COAST:)

INTERSTATE.

Locality	Bar. Mean	Bar. Avg prev	Bar. Highest	Bar. Lowest	Mean Max.	Mean Min.	Mean of Month	Highest Max.	Lowest Min.					Points	W. Days	Total Points
Perth	30·004	30·051	30·310	29·701	9·9	54·8	62·8	98·4	44·2					112	12	3211
Adelaide	30·001	30·021	30·362	29·445	71·2	50·6	60·9	96·0	42·0					166	12	2242
Melbourne	29·960	29·843	30·386		65·7	48·5	57·1	83·8	37·8					293	15	1918
Sydney	30·010	30·001	30·340	29·610	79·0	65·0	72·0	93·0	47·0					206	7	2816

* Averages for three years only.

The Observatory, Perth, 7th November, 1906.

W. E. COOKE, Government Astronomer.

RAINFALL for September, 1906 (completed as far as possible), and for October, 1906 (principally from Telegraphic Reports).

STATIONS.	SEPTEMBER.		OCTOBER.		STATIONS.	SEPTEMBER.		OCTOBER.	
	No. of points. 100 = 1in.	No. of wet days.	No. of points. 100 = 1in.	No. of wet days.		No. of points. 100 = 1in.	No. of wet days.	No. of points. 100 = 1in.	No. of wet days.
EAST KIMBERLEY:					N.W. COAST—contd.				
Wyndham	1	1	150	2	Balla Balla	...	...	...	...
6-Mile	...	...	...	...	Whim Creek	11	2	20	...
Carlton	140	1	...	...	Mallina	...	...	...	...
Ivanhoe	60	4	...	...	Croydon	8	1	...	...
Argyle Downs	308	5	...	...	Sherlock	...	...	...	...
Rosewood Downs	273	5	...	...	Woodbrooke	...	...	...	...
Lisadell	...	...	...	...	Cooyapooya	Nil	...	...	...
Turkey Creek	431	6	100	4	Roebourne	6	2	Nil	...
Ord River	...	...	...	...	Cossack	8	2	Nil	...
Alice Downs	714	6	...	...	Fortescue	3	1	...	...
Flora Valley	...	...	...	..	Mardie	11	4	...	...
Hall's Creek	195	4	91	3	Chinginarra	10	4	...	...
Nicholson Plains	...	...	...	...	Yarraloola	20	1	...	...
Ruby Plains	...	...	...	...	Peedamullah	41	3	...	...
Denison Downs	...	...	...	...	Onslow	44	5	Nil	...
					Point Cloates	...	...	...	...
WEST KIMBERLEY:									
Mt. Barnett	...	...	...	...	N.W. INLAND:				
Corvendine	...	...	...	...	Warrawagine	Nil	...	...	...
Leopold Downs	...	...	...	...	Eel Creek	...	...	...	...
Fitzroy Crossing (P.O.)	1	1	Nil	...	Muccan	...	...	...	...
					Ettrick	13	1	...	...
Cherrabun	...	...	...	...	Mulgie	Nil	...	...	...
Bohemia Downs	...	...	...	...	Strelly	...	...	...	...
Quanbun	...	...	...	...	Warralong	9	1	...	...
Nookanbah	...	...	...	...	Coongon	...	...	...	...
Upper Liveringa	...	...	...	...	Talga	...	...	...	...
Yeeda	...	...	...	...	Bamboo Creek	10	1	Nil	...
Derby	Nil	...	2	1	Moolyella	...	...	...	...
Pt. Torment	2	1	...	...	Marble Bar	7	1	23	...
Obagama	Nil	...	...	...	Warrawoona	10	1	Nil	...
Beagle Bay	...	...	...	...	Corunna Downs	11	1	...	...
Roebuck Downs	Nil	...	...	...	Mt. Edgar	...	...	...	...
Kimberley Downs	26	1	...	...	Nullagine	Nil	...	Nil	...
Broome	Nil	...	Nil	...	Middle Creek	25	1	...	...
Thangoo	...	...	...	...	Mosquito Creek	...	...	...	...
La Grange Bay	3	1	Nil	...	Roy Hill	...	...	...	...
					Bamboo Springs	...	...	...	...
					Kerdiadary	...	...	...	...
N.W. COAST:					Woodstock	25	1	...	...
Wallal	30	2	Nil	...	Yandyarra	...	...	...	...
Pardoo	18	1	...	...	Station Peak	Nil	...	...	...
Condon	12	1	2	1	Mulga Downs	...	...	...	...
DeGrey River	...	...	...	...	Mt. Florence	...	...	...	...
Port Hedland	5	1	21	1	Tambrey	...	...	...	...
Boodarie	9	1	...	...	Millstream	20	1	...	...

RAINFALL—*continued.*

STATIONS.	SEPTEMBER.		OCTOBER.		STATIONS.	SEPTEMBER.		OCTOBER.	
	No. of points. 100 = 1in.	No. of wet days.	No. of points. 100 = 1in.	No. of wet days.		No. of points. 100 = 1in.	No. of wet days.	No. of points. 100 = 1in.	No. of wet days.
N.W. INLAND—*contd.*					**YALGOO DISTRICT**— *contd.*				
Red Hill ...	39	1	...	...	Mullewa ...	62	10	24	5
Mt. Stewart ...	...	...	...	...	Kockatea ...	...	...	...	...
Peake Station ...	77	2	...	...	Barnong ...	24	1	...	...
Nanutarra ...	48	2	...	...	Gullewa ...	...	...	...	...
Yanrey ...	...	...	...	...	Gullewa House...	18	1	...	...
Wogoola ...	38	3	...	...	Gabyon ...	42	3	70	1
Towera ...	25	4	...	...	Mellenbye ...	27	7	...	...
					Wearagaminda...	31	2	17	2
GASCOYNE:					Yalgoo ...	47	2	43	2
Winning Pool ...	19	3	25	1	Wagga Wagga ...	20	3	...	...
Coordalia ...	...	...	...	...	Muralgarra ...	...	...	...	...
Wandagee ...	10	1	...	...	Burnerbinmah ...	26	2	...	...
Williambury ...	10	2	...	...	Nalbara ...	20	2	...	...
Yanyeareddy ...	...	...	...	...	Wydgee ...	36	2	Nil	...
Maroonah ...	...	...	...	...	Field's Find ...	9	4	...	...
Ullawarra ...	...	...	...	...	Thundelarra ...	47	4	...	...
Mt. Mortimer ...	...	...	...	...	Rothesay ...	59	6	...	...
Edmunds ...	...	...	...	...	Ninghan ...	34	3	...	...
Gifford Creek ...	...	...	...	...	Condingnow ...	...	..	...	...
Bangemall ...	...	...	...	...	163-Mile ...	24	2	...	...
Mt. Augustus ...	...	...	...	...	Palaga Rocks ...	35	2	...	...
Upper Clifton Downs	6	2	...	...	126-Mile ...	57	4	...	...
Clifton Downs ...	...	...	...	...	90-Mile ...	49	2	...	...
Dairy Creek ...	20	1	...	...	Mt. Jackson ...	38	6	Nil	...
Mearerbundie ...	...	...	...	...					
Byro ...	24	2	...	...	**MURCHISON:**				
Meedo ...	22	2	...	...	Wale ...	...	...	...	...
Mungarra ...	14	1	...	...	Yallalonga ...	27	3	...	...
Bintholya ...	...	...	...	...	Billabalong ...	...	...	...	...
Lyon's River ..	Nil	...	...	...	Twin Peaks ...	21	2	...	...
Mangaroon ...	25	2	...	...	Murgoo ...	12	2	20	1
Booloogooroo ...	...	...	...	...	Mt. Wittenoom ...	Nil	...	...	...
Doorawarrah ...	...	...	...	...	Meka ...	18	2	...	...
Brick House ..	29	3	...	...	Wooleane ...	11	1	...	...
Boolathana ...	24	3	...	...	Boolardy ...	...	...	...	...
Carnarvon ...	26	5	16	3	Woogorong ...	...	...	...	...
Dirk Hartog ...	117	1	...	...	Manfred ...	Nil	...	...	...
Sharks Bay ...	19	2	29	2	Yarra Yarra ...	13	1	...	...
Wooramel ...	49	4	33	3	Milly Milly ...	10	1	...	...
Hamelin Pool ...	11	3	13	2	Berringarra ...	9	1	...	...
Kararang ...	57	8	...	...	Miloura ...	33	1	...	...
Tamala ...	...	...	...	...	Mt. Gould ...	...	...	...	...
					Moorarie ...	Nil	...	...	...
YALGOO DISTRICT:					Wandary ...	...	...	...	...
Woolgorong ...	...	...	...	...	Peak Hill ...	15	3	40	2
New Forest ...	...	...	...	...	Mt. Fraser ...	...	...	...	...
Yuin ...	25	4	...	...	Minderoo ...	Nil	...	25	2
Pindathuna ...	7	1	Nil	...	Abbotts ...	7	1	...	...
Tallyrang ...	...	...	...	...	Belele ...	27	2	...	...

RAINFALL—*continued.*

STATIONS.	SEPTEMBER.		OCTOBER.		STATIONS.	SEPTEMBER.		OCTOBER.	
	No. of points. 100 = 1in.	No. of wet days.	No. of points. 100 = 1in.	No. of wet days.		No. of points. 100 = 1in.	No. of wet days.	No. of points. 100 = 1in.	No. of wet days.
MURCHISON—*contd.*					NORTH COOLGARDIE				
Meekatharra ...	...	...	...	...	GOLDFIELDS—*contd.*				
Gabanintha ...	28	1	21	4	Goongarrie ...	17	2	...	...
Quinns	...	...	...	...					
Bungalow ...	...	...	40	2	COOLGARDIE GOLD-				
Nannine	18	2	36	2	FIELDS:				
Annean	26	1	...	...	Waverley ...	...	...	Nil	...
Tuckanarra ...	25	1	25	1	Bardoc	3	1	Nil	...
Coodardy ...	Nil	...	...	...	Broad Arrow ...	5	2	Nil	...
Cue	21	3	51	3	Kanowna ...	2	1	Nil	...
Day Dawn ...	Nil	...	26	1	Kurnalpi ...	22	2	Nil	...
Lake Austin ...	23	...	...	...	Bulong	9	3	Nil	...
Lennonville ...	16	2	26	5	Kalgoorlie ...	2	1	Nil	...
Mt. Magnet ...	13	2	9	1	Coolgardie ...	16	3	Nil	...
Youeragabbie ...	7	1	...	...	Burbanks ...	26	2	Nil	...
Murrum	...	...	...	...	Bulla Bulling ...	27	3	...	...
Challa	35	2	...	...	Woolubar ...	...	...	...	...
Nunngarra ...	13	1	...	...	Waterdale ...	21	2	Nil	...
Berrigrin ...	21	1	...	...	Widgiemooltha...	99	9	18	4
					60-Mile	51	7	14	1
EAST MURCHISON:					Norseman ...	72	5	21	3
Gum Creek ...	Nil	...	...	...	Lake View ...	110	11	7	2
Dural	10	1	...	...	Frazer Range ...	69	6	...	...
Wiluna	12	1	22	3	Southern Hills ...	51	1	...	...
Mt. Sir Samuel ...	15	2	Nil	...					
Leinster G.M. ...	...	...	...	...	YILGARN GOLD-				
Lawlers	13	1	Nil	...	FIELDS:				
Wilson's Patch...	2	1	...	...	129-Mile... ...	153	8	...	...
Poison Creek ...	...	...	...	...	Emu Rocks ...	97	11	45	3
Lake Darlôt ...	Nil	...	...	...	56-Mile	88	2	...	...
Darda	11	2	...	...	Glenelg Rocks ...	101	14	...	...
Salt Soak ...	17	3	...	...	Burracoppin ...	71	6	55	4
Duketon ...	15	1	...	...	Bodallin ...	49	2	...	...
					Parker's Road ...	61	3	18	1
NORTH COOLGARDIE					Southern Cross ...	28	5	7	5
GOLDFIELDS:					Parker's Range...	65	9	21	5
Laverton ...	13	2	Nil	...	Yellowdine ...	41	2	Nil	...
Mt. Morgans ...	8	1	Nil	...	Karalee ...	40	2	10	2
Murrin Murrin...	10	2	Nil	...	Koorarawalyee..	90	6	2	1
Mt. Malcolm ...	5	1	Nil	...	Boorabbin ...	57	5	Nil	...
Mt. Leonora ...	5	1	Nil	...	Boondi	24	9	Nil	...
Tampa	Nil	...	Nil	...					
Kookynie ...	38	2	Nil	...	SOUTH - WEST				
Niagara	20	1	Nil	...	(NORTHERN DIVI-				
Yerilla	20	1	...	...	SION):				
Yundamindera ..	46	2	Nil	...	Murchison House	120	14	...	...
Mt. Celia ...	45	2	...	...	Mt. View ...	72	6	7	2
Edjudina ...	13	3	...	...	Mumby	163	12	...	...
Quandinnie ...	...	...	...	...	Northampton ...	200	10	49	4
Menzies	Nil	...	Nil	...	Chapman Experi-	146	10	...	...
Mulline	33	4	3	1	mental Farm				
Mulwarrie ...	41	5	...	...	Narra Tarra ...	251	11	...	...

RAINFALL—*continued.*

Stations.	No. of points 100=1in. (Sept.)	No. of wet days (Sept.)	No. of points 100=1in. (Oct.)	No. of wet days (Oct.)	Stations.	No. of points 100=1in. (Sept.)	No. of wet days (Sept.)	No. of points 100=1in. (Oct.)	No. of wet days (Oct.)
SOUTH-WEST (NORTHERN DIVISION)—*contd.*					**SOUTH-WEST (METROPOLITAN)**—*cont.*				
Oakabella	238	12	...	...	Fremantle	352	19	63	9
White Peak	215	10	...	...	Rottnest	308	16	...	...
Geraldton	246	17	44	6	Rockingham	439	18	26	4
Hinton Farm	138	7	...	...	Jandakot	417	15	85	5
Tibradden	243	12	83	6	Armadale	394	22	...	...
Myaree	247	15	79	8	Mundijong	330	19	127	11
Sand Springs	187	11	...	...	Jarrahdale	562	20	235	11
Nangetty	121	12	...	...	Jarrahdale (Norie)	505	18	...	...
Greenough	127	11	61	4	Serpentine	430	17	159	10
Bokara	239	17	64	4					
Dongara	245	14	27	3	**EXTREME SOUTH-WEST:**				
Strawberry	174	13	41	5	Mandurah	538	19	93	10
Yaragadee	...	...	...	...	Pinjarrah (Blythewood)	531	17	145	9
Urella	...	...	...	...	Pinjarrah	559	18	156	6
Opawa	88	11	33	6	Upper Murray	715	21	254	14
Manara	138	10	30	4	Yarloop	632	19	...	...
Mingenew	128	13	46	6	Harvey	515	21	...	...
Yandenooka	168	11	...	...	Brunswick	646	14	...	...
Arrino	218	14	21	4	Collie	514	17	241	14
Carnamah	161	13	57	5	Glen Mervyn	496	18	...	...
Jun Jun	180	15	25	2	Donnybrook	570	19	153	11
Watheroo	234	14	40	7	Boyanup	612	21	161	11
Nergaminon	...	...	...	...	Bunbury	516	20	122	10
Dandaragan	351	16	170	8	Elgin	616	19	189	14
Yatheroo	298	13	...	...	Busselton	423	24	116	13
Moora	316	14	87	8	Quindalup	476	17	216	14
Walebing	241	20	100	9	Cape Naturaliste	433	23	98	16
Round Hill	242	16	59	7	Glen Lossie	...	...	...	...
New Norcia	242	19	72	8	Karridale	532	24	246	15
Wongon Hills	162	16	...	...	Cape Leeuwin	437	26	184	20
Wannamel	373	17	181	9	Lower Blackwood	462	23	269	11
Gingin	397	12	183	8	Ferndale	462	12	...	...
					Greenbushes	422	14	131	8
SOUTH-WEST (METROPOLITAN):					Cooeearup	463	21	187	13
Wanneroo	262	13	79	4	Bridgetown	372	21	197	10
Belvoir	296	17	105	6	Hilton	411	8	...	...
Wandu	393	23	144	12	Greenfields	484	18	...	...
Mundaring	583	18	211	10	Dinninup	...	...	149	6
Canning Waterworks	485	16	136	11	Cundinup	317	10	68	4
Kalbyamba	413	16	107	10	Wilgarrup	404	21	249	14
Guildford	389	17	109	8	Balbarrup	500	16	204	16
Perth Gardens	343	18	111	10	Bidellia	457	12	325	7
Perth Observatory	393	19	112	12	Westbourne	387	13	...	...
Highgate Hill	323	18	118	10	Deeside	406	17	...	...
Subiaco	395	19	114	10	Riverside	411	20	...	...
Claremont	386	17	...	...	Mordalup	356	15	...	...
					Lake Muir	340	12	...	...

RAINFALL—*continued*.

STATIONS.	SEPTEMBER. No. of points. 100 = 1in.	SEPTEMBER. No. of wet days.	OCTOBER. No. of points. 100 = 1in.	OCTOBER. No of wet days.	STATIONS.	SEPTEMBER. No. of points. 100 = 1in.	SEPTEMBER. No. of wet days.	OCTOBER. No. of points. 100 = 1in.	OCTOBER. No of wet days.
EASTERN AGRICULTURAL DISTRICTS :					GREAT SOUTHERN RAILWAY LINE—*contd.*				
Emungin	224	17	...	...	Broomehill	291	13	77	6
Dowerin	146	11	...	...	Woodyarrup	312	11	66	4
Warramuggin	...	...	...	...	Pallinup	253	9	51	4
Oak Hill	...	...	...	...	Tambellup	...	...	66	4
Monglin	...	...	...	...	Toolbrunup	266	13	62	5
Hatherley	...	...	...	...	Cranbrook	291	17	80	11
Momberkine	210	10	...	...	Stirling View	362	20	128	11
Bolgart	212	12	93	8	Kendenup	384	22	148	10
Eumalga	209	15	...	...	Woogenellup	248	18	...	...
Newcastle	191	11	119	5	Wattle Hill	378	20	100	11
Craiglands	342	18	151	5	St. Werburgh's	322	22	160	12
Eadine	232	14	85	10	Mt. Barker	345	22	127	13
Northam	175	13	56	7					
Grass Valley	...	...	...	...					
Cobham	162	12	46	5					
York	144	17	62	10					
Burrayocking	130	13	41	6	WEST OF GREAT SOUTHERN RAILWAY LINE :				
Meckering	130	9	41	3	Talbot House	182	10	52	4
Cunderdin	134	8	33	3	Jelcobine	219	11	74	6
Doongin	106	9	...	...	Bannister	...	...	...	...
Whitehaven	...	...	...	...	Wandering	329	13	91	7
Mt. Caroline	128	9	31	4	Glen Ern	244	15	...	...
Cutenning	...	...	...	...	Marradong	414	10	29	3
Kellerberrin	78	8	34	4	Wonnaminta	286	15	...	...
Cardonia	96	11	32	5	Williams	305	11	102	5
Baandee	81	6	18	21	Rifle Downs	406	8	161	5
Nangeenan	144	7	21	2	Darkan	...	...	...	...
Merredin	82	9	37	3	Arthur River	300	11	69	7
Codg-Codgen	119	12	...	...	Gainsborough	216	11	47	6
Noongarin	106	8	26	3	Glenorchy	335	11	118	4
Mangowine	166	13	...	...	Kojonup	281	7	115	5
Yarragin	194	9	...	...	Blackwattle	...	...	...	...
Wattoning	...	...	...	...	Warriup	307	20	119	14
					Forest Hill	401	22	199	11
GREAT SOUTHERN RAILWAY LINE :									
Dalebridge	201	15	50	7					
Beverley	176	13	40	4	EAST OF GREAT SOUTHERN RAILWAY LINE :				
Brookton	183	12	32	2	Sunset Hills	178	10	...	...
Sunning Hill	208	18	...	...	Oakdale	150	11	...	...
Pingelly	194	9	67	5	Barrington	139	12	33	6
Yornaning	213	14	51	8	Bally Bally	143	8	30	9
Narrogin	268	11	81	7	Stock Hill	195	10	35	2
Narrogin Experimental Farm	324	12	...	...	Qualin	156	11	15	3
Wagin	290	8	68	5	Woodgreen	77	11	...	...
Katanning	350	15	86	9	Gillimanning	187	13	...	...
Sunnyside	281	17	86	9					

RAINFALL—*continued.*

STATIONS.	SEPTEMBER.		OCTOBER.		STATIONS.	SEPTEMBER.		OCTOBER.	
	No. of Points. 100 = 1in.	No. of wet days.	No. of points. 100 = 1in.	No. of wet days.		No. of points. 100 = 1in.	No. of wet days.	No. of Points. 100 = 1in.	No. of wet days.
EAST OF GREAT SOUTHERN RAILWAY LINE—*contd.*					SOUTH COAST—*contd.*				
					Peppermint Grove	431	15	98	12
Wickepin ...	230	14	50	4	Bremer Bay ...	341	13	91	7
Crooked Pool ...	258	14	55	5	Coconarup ...	229	15	36	8
Nalyring ...	317	13	82	6	Ravensthorpe ...	249	16	26	4
Bunking ...	252	10	52	2	Cowjanup ...	235	15	...	...
Bullock Hills ...	259	8	...	...	Hopetoun ...	235	15	...	...
Dyliabing ...	267	13	40	7	Fanny's Cove ...	271	16	64	4
Glencove ...	268	13	62	7	Park Farm ...	323	14	...	...
Cherillalup ...	303	16	...	...	Grass Patch ...	...	...	...	...
Mianelup ...	265	15	...	...	Swan Lagoon ...	176	12	...	...
Woolganup ...	261	11	54	4	30-Mile ...	204	12	...	...
Chillinup ...	251	4	...	...	Gibson's Soak ...	382	15	...	...
Jarramongup ...	...	...	...	...	Myrup	327	16	...	...
					Esperance ...	305	11	93	11
					Boyatup	246	10	...	...
					Lynburn ...	291	17	...	...
SOUTH COAST:					Middle Island ...	...	...	...	...
Wilson's Inlet ...	405	24	296	16	Point Malcolm ...	227	13	...	...
Grasmere ...	433	25	374	16	Israelite Bay ...	157	10	35	2
King River ...	430	18	228	11	Balbinia	183	11	...	...
Albany	451	24	430	16	Balladonia ...	63	8	6	2
Point King ...	520	17	321	12	Eyre	54	6	13	3
Breaksea ...	380	26	285	16	Mundrabella ...	...	...	...	...
Cape Riche ...	314	7	...	...	Eucla	15	3	50	3

The Observatory, Perth,
　　6th November, 1906.

W. E. COOKE,
Government Astronomer.

[Registered at the General Post Office for transmission by Post as a Newspaper.]

JOURNAL

OF THE

DEPARTMENT OF AGRICULTURE

OF

WESTERN AUSTRALIA.

By Direction of

The HON. THE MINISTER OF AGRICULTURE.

PUBLISHED MONTHLY.

Vol. XIV.—Part 6.

DECEMBER, 1906.

PERTH:
BY AUTHORITY: FRED WM. SIMPSON, GOVERNMENT PRINTER.

1906.

WESTERN AUSTRALIAN GOVERNMENT.

IMMIGRATION.

Nominated Passages.

Persons having friends and relatives in the United Kingdom who are desirous of emigrating to Western Australia may obtain passages at half the ordinary fares by nominating them to the Hon. Colonial Secretary in Perth.

Fares from £6 10s. to £14 10s.

Clerks, artizans, and mechanics will **not** be accepted.

Advanced Passages.

Working men and others resident in the State may obtain an advance of passage money, including railway fares from port of arrival to destination, to bring their wives and families from the Eastern States and New Zealand to this State.

Such advances to be repaid within six or twelve months, according to the amount advanced.

A responsible guarantor must be provided.

Special Concessions are provided for Settlers taking up Land.

Full particulars can be obtained upon application to the Under Secretary, Colonial Secretary's Department, Perth.

By order,

F. D. NORTH,
Under Secretary.

JOURNAL

OF THE

𝔇epartment of 𝔄griculture

OF

WESTERN AUSTRALIA.

Vol. XIV.   DECEMBER, 1906.   Part 6.

EDITOR'S NOTES.

NATIONAL SHOW FOR 1907.—It is announced that the National Show for 1907 will be held at Northam. The Statement was made by Mr. J. Mitchell, M.L.A., the Honorary Minister for Agriculture, at a meeting of the Northam Agricultural Society on the 8th inst.

THE CROPS.—The first truck of this season's wheat (says the *Northam Advertiser*) reached Northam on the 8th inst. It was stripped in the Goomalling district, and it is of excellent quality, the grain being large and clean; in fact, Messrs. Throssell, Son, & Stewart, the buyers, declare that it is superior to any they purchased last year. The same firm have also received a consignment of barley and oats (this year's), the quality of which was far beyond their expectations.

INSECTIVOROUS BIRDS.—The prevalence of insect pests of all kinds, cutworms and caterpillars especially, has been more pronounced this season than for many years past. The absence, at the same time, of insectivorous birds is also a cause of regret. It is as well to draw the attention of settlers and others to the wanton destruction of these useful birds by boys, who seem to take a delight in killing them. Boys should be taught the great good that insect-eating birds are to the country, and encouraged to protect them.

MANURING THE FARM.—The only successful and practical method of finding out what manures a farm requires is by properly arranged experiments. Every farmer should try the effect on his soil, and with different crops, of artificial fertilisers, taking as basis the three plant foods—ammonia, phosphate of lime, and potash—and make trials with them in combination, and then omitting one or the other. In this way, by carefully studying the the results, he can obtain most surely information as to the deficiencies of his soil, which he can then make good in an economical and satisfactory manner.

(2)

FRUIT FLY MAGGOTS.—The fruit fly maggots are once again in evidence, and their presence is reported in early apricots and peaches. Their number is, of course, still very restricted, and nothing but the watchfulness and care of the growers in continuously picking and destroying the wormy fruit help in keeping down the pest. The inspectors of the Department of Agriculture are already on the *qui vive*, and besides enforcing the regulations in gardens, they daily inspect auction rooms and fruit shops, and will seize and destroy any maggoty fruit offered for sale.

POULTRY JOURNAL.—We have received the first number of *The W.A. Poultry and Dog Gazette*, published by the Imperial Printing Company, of Perth. It is full of short pithy pars, and contains accounts of all the latest doings in the poultry world. One very good feature may be found in the reports of the egg-laying competitions now being carried on in this State, and that is, the records from the commencement of each contest is given, showing the leading pen for each month, the number of eggs laid being printed in bold black figures. The paper is a decided improvement on all previous ventures, and, providing the present standard is maintained, its success and usefulness should be assured.

PARASITES.—Mr. L. J. Newman, in a report to the Acting Director of Agriculture dealing with the distribution of parasites on insect pests, states :—"I am pleased to draw your attention to the fact that I have located the *Scutellista cyanea*, which is well established in black scales in several gardens, as well as on native bush. During the month I have sent out 12 colonies of this parasite to applicants, which I hope will soon become established in various parts of the State, the specimens I found being large and strong. I have also sent out 32 colonies of parasites on the black scale, 36 colonies of parasites on the brown scale, 5 colonies of parasites on the red scale, 4 colonies of parasites on aphis, and 2 colonies of parasites on the cabbage moth.

SOIL INOCULATION.—Two years ago (says the *Weekly Chronicle*) the American people were carried away by the " soil inoculation " fad. There is no doubt that soil can be inoculated with nitrogen-gathering bacteria, and that in good soil where such bacteria are lacking, inoculation will greatly promote the growth of legumes. The extensive distribution of the pure cultures and the resulting experiments were wise, for it is only by proving all things we can learn what is good to hold fast to. We never believed that in the present state of our knowledge soil inoculation would be found a workable addition to the art of practical husbandry, and said so. We think that is now the general conclusion of all the experiment stations.

SUBSOIL IRRIGATION.—At Narrabri, under the auspices of the local branch F.S.A., Mr. Fraser Hill delivered a lecture on a new system of subsoil irrigation, specially suited to districts with a limited water supply. The idea is to irrigate clayey hard land or black soil by means of drains to a depth of about two feet, at an approximate cost of 1d. per chain. The drains are to be cut by an inexpensive plough, necessitating a drawing power of, say, 16 horses or bullocks. The lecturer contended that one inch of rain put into the soil one foot below the surface had been demonstrated to be equal to three inches on the surface. The drains are cut perpendicularly, and form channels which, in hard land, become firm, and are not interfered with either by heavy rain or ploughing. Water put into the channels percolates under the soil, and sends the moisture towards the surface. The cost of supplying an inch of water to crops on our goldfields would be £2 4s. per acre, at the rate of 2s. per 1,000 gallons.

SILO.—There are exhibited at the Manufacturers' Exhibition now being held in Perth, two complete models of silos, which will repay any farmer to copy, those going in for dairy cattle particularly. They are both of the type known as "tub" silos; one is made of our hardwood (jarrah), and the other of hardwood framework, lined with pine matchboards, protected by B.P. paper, or with light-gauge smooth iron, painted with ruberoid paint. As dairying is now being established in this State, it behoves all interested in the industry to keep themselves posted in the latest inventions, methods of feeding, and labour-saving appliances. What with milking machines, separators, etc., dairying is rapidly developing a science of its own, and it is those who neglect to keep themselves well up with the times will find, too late, that they are left hopelessly behind, making, perhaps, a bare existence, while others following the more advanced methods will be reaping a rich reward for their study and application.

SALE OF STUD BULL.—The Government Auctioneer, Mr. Albert Clerk, has been commissioned by the Department of Agriculture to sell on Monday, the 7th of January next, the Shorthorn stud bull, "Pride of Argyle," for which the Department of Agriculture has no further use. The bull is in good nick, and has lately been subjected twice to the tuberculin test, and has not reacted. He was bred by Mr. McKenzie Grant, "Newmarracarra," near Geraldton, and was calved on 10th January, 1899. He comes from some of the best blood introduced into Australia, as shown by his pedigree. *Sire*—"Pride of the Lake," by Kirklevington, Count II., by Baron Graham (41,030); dam, Countess of Levington II., by Oxford Beau; grand-dam, Countess of Levington, by Lord of the Isles (34,631). *Dam*—"Campbell House Queen" bred by T. R. Bowman, Esq., of Campbell Park, S.A., and descended from the well-known "Canowie" herd, and noted M over 7 brand.

SPROUTING SEED POTATOES.—The system of sprouting early seed potatoes has been generally acknowledged to be a great factor in the success of good cropping, and adopted by most of our up-to-date farmers. The sprouting of seed for late or main crops, however, is not generally practised, yet it is quite as important as for the early planting. The advantage of sprouting seed is without doubt very considerable; for instance, the writer planted two lots of Beauty of Hebron at the beginning of last August, one-half the seed being sprouted, the other with dormant eyes. The weight of the tubers were uniform, being close on 2ozs. each. Those sprouted showed above the ground in seven days, while the others were three weeks. The plants were dug the first week in this month (December); the yield from the sprouted seed averaged 11½ tons to the acre, while that from the unsprouted seed was 4⅓ tons. The test, however, while showing the value of the system, must not be taken too literally, as such an enormous difference is too much to expect in every case. The general rule is an increase of from 25 to 50 per cent.

WATER FOR THE GOLDFIELDS.—It is officially announced that the price of water to residents of the Eastern Goldfields will be still further reduced as from the 1st of January next, as follows:—For domestic purposes a minimum charge of 6s. 8d. for rate, for first 5,000 gallons excess in the year 4s. per 1,000, for every thousand beyond this quantity 2s. 6d. per 1,000 gallons. In the case of market gardeners, fruit-growers, etc., a still further reduction will be made, when a charge of 2s. per 1,000 gallons only will be levied. This is the same price as that paid in Perth prior to 1st of January last. It speaks volumes for the administration, and must conduce, to a very considerable extent, to an increased demand. With water at 2s. and proper shade, vegetables should be grown at a profit right through the summer. In a future issue suggestions will be made by which gardening may be continued through the hot months with success, the main feature of which will be the complete shading by means of hessian or other light cheap material. The cost of the hessian, giving it a two seasons' life, will be repaid with profit if used with care, while the advantages obtained will be great and many.

GARDEN PESTS.—The following minute was recently addressed to the Minister controlling the Agricultural Department (Mr. J. Mitchell, M.L.A.) by Mr. A. Despeissis, the pomological expert :—" As a result of a methodical spring-time inspection of the nurseries established in this State, I regret having to report the introduction of two new pests, viz., the pear and cherry slug and the English snail. The snails were found at one nursery where pot plants and flowers are mostly kept. The pear and cherry slugs were seen at two nurseries and in four orchards in the vicinity of one of these nurseries. Steps have been taken by means of hand-picking and baiting to stamp out the snails, and by means of spraying with Paris green, pear, quince, and cherry trees, and also hawthorns, roses, etc., and dusting these plants with lime and sulphur, to prevent the escape of these leaf slugs, which ultimately develop into a saw fly. Any grower noticing on the above-mentioned trees leaves so eaten by an insect as to show either in patches or on the whole face the net work of the veins of these leaves should at once spray and dust their trees, and report to the Agricultural Department, when a complete examination will be conducted to locate the pest."

GREEN MANURING.—The practice of green manuring is increasing in this State, and the general consensus of opinion is that in nine cases out of ten the "Cow pea" is the best plant for use. In the United States an exchange states that the "Canada pea" is the best to use for green manuring. In naming this pea it really means only some hardy, smooth pea, which may or may not be one of the fifty or sixty varieties in common use in Canada for stock feed, and the seed which we get may or may not have been produced in Canada or any other district of short seasons and cold winters. In Canada where peas are grown very extensively, each one of these varieties has a name by which it is generally known, and they differ among themselves just as the varieties of other plants differ. It would appear that the subject is of sufficient importance to be taken up systematically by the experiment station with the view of ascertaining which of the varieties of hardy peas, whether grown in Canada or elsewhere, are best adapted to our purposes, and let us know the name of it and where seed can be procured. We are of the opinion that almost any of the varieties of smooth peas usually sold under the trade name of " Canada pea" will grow, if sown early, in an ordinary winter, but we ought to know which is best. While for spring sowing in this State the ordinary and well known "cow pea" is certainly the best.

SILK FROM SKIM MILK.—One of the latest patents in that wonderful country of inventions, the United States of America, is the production of silk from skim milk. An exchange, in referring to the matter, says:—" We have a sample of silk made from casein, prepared under a patent taken out by a German chemist that is a revelation of the possibilities of the cow. The sample consists of fine shredded threads as strong almost as silk, with a lustre that is as good or superior to the silk from the cocoon. We expect to have a sample of woven goods when suitable machinery has been made. In the early history of the dairy industry in the Elgin district, G. P. Lord made the statement that the by-products after the butter had been made were worth more than the butter. The present use of the sugar and casein has largely proved this. Now that the grand dames may soon be wearing gowns made from skim milk, further proves the chemistry of the cow in the production of milk is a wonder of nature. This new utilisation of the by-products will further increase the demand for a large supply of milk, and make the cow the most valuable animal on the farm. How good this fabric really is we do not know. How much it costs to produce nobody, probably knows. Nobody, therefore, can yet tell whether it will pay as a commercial proposition to engage in the production of dress goods from skim milk, but when we consider the prodigious amount of that product which is available for any use more profitable than feeding to swine we can see that the discovery is well worth looking into."

FROM TOWN TO COUNTRY.—While there is a constant drift of country-bred people to the cities from a desire to get rid of what they call the " drudgery " of the farm, there is a counter movement of less magnitude of city people to the country, usually for the accomplishment of certain ideals of happiness, usefulness, or " communion with nature." Unquestionably there will be more or less disappointment for both parties. It is certain that the drudgery of the farm is far less severe than the drudgery of the city. If anything were wanting to prove it, the fact that the country continually breeds the men to take the places of those who degenerate and die in the city is sufficient. Nevertheless, that there is hard work and long hours on the farm it would be foolish to deny. There were always hard work and long hours for those who have got on in the world, and there always will be. But there is another movement from city to country which should be noted. Wealthy men are acquiring a desire to found " estates " in the European meaning of the term. Until recently rich men have bought country places mainly for recreative purposes, and have usually preferred the picturesque—and therefore unprofitable—situation. Of late they are acquiring the notion of buying rich land as the best investment for their money. Such investments are made by men who have proved their sound judgment by getting wealthy. What these men think good investment ought to be accepted as such by the young men of the country. The best thing a young man can do for himself is to get ten acres, if he can get no more, of good land and improve it.

AFFILIATION OF SOCIETIES.—At a recent Agricultural Show, the Hon. the Minister for Agriculture made some very pointed remarks re the affiliation of Societies. Mr. Mitchell said :—" The matter of affiliation of societies he thought an excellent idea, but, as the secretary had pointed out, the question of control arose. He did not want to give the Society the same control as the W.A.T.C. exercised over horse racing, but he would give them consider-able control. He thought it would be a good idea if the Government could make grants upon the suggestion of a central body, and the Government would do all in its power to make affiliation possible. The idea had originated from the Northam Society, but since then nothing had been heard of it. The arrangement of dates was very important. About a fortnight ago three shows had been held on one day, all within a hundred miles of Perth. Then, again, there was the question of rules, concerning which is distinctly wrong, that when prizes were advertised for a certain class of stock they were awarded to animals not representative of that class. There ought to be some arrangement for appeal, to enable an owner to get redress. If judging at shows was bad, then the object lesson to be taught was also bad. People should be encouraged to appeal against wrong decisions. In his opinion there certainly ought to exist a controlling body, but he did not know exactly how it was to be constituted. Perhaps the Royal Agricultural Society would take the initiative in the matter ? If the Government were asked to make a grant for the improvement of show grounds, it was entitled to know how that money was spent, and it should be no hardship for the Government to ask that the grant should be subject to the approval of the controlling body."

———

FOUL BROOD, AND ITS REMEDY.—Foul brood is a disease commencing with a very minute germ called a spore, which comes in contact with a larva, or may be consumed by it. The spore has wonderful vitality, and once it finds suitable conditions, it germinates and develops into a bacillus. Having exhausted its feeding ground, spores are produced to again continue the disease, given suitable conditions. It should be noted that the disease attacks brood, and, without brood, cannot make any headway. When a larva has been attacked, it dies, and dries into a brown scale, which lies on the lower side of the cell. Should honey be stored in the cell, or an egg laid in it, the result is equally disastrous. The honey may be fed to other larvæ, and thus spread the disease, or the larvæ will hatch to die. Generally speaking, the beginner would notice a difference in the odour arising from the hive when the quilts were raised. The dead larvæ turn coffee-coloured, become a stringy mass, and, when in an advanced stage, smell like bad glue. The cappings over the diseased brood cells are broken and sunken. If a piece of stick be thrust into an infected cell, the sticky matter will adhere to it and stretch out an inch or more, then break and return like elastic to the cell. As a remedy, it must be carefully noted that should the disease be in an advanced stage, it will be well to destroy the quilts, hives, and bees, and make a fresh start. In the early stages the bees should be shaken from the frame into an empty skep, there to remain in confinement for 24 hours. Thoroughly cleanse the hive by washing with carbolic. The fittings are cheap, and should be destroyed by fire. Fit up the frames with starters. cage the queen, in three or four days remove the starters, melt into wax, and fit up with full sheets of foundation, keeping the queen caged for five or six days more. If the old combs are retained, they should be melted into wax by boiling, otherwise the wax will become a source of infection. The hive would stand on the old site. When the disease is discovered, act promptly but with discretion. Close all the entrances of the hives, so that one bee only may pass at a time, in order to prevent robbing; for this would only help to spread the disease. Generally speaking, it is useless to deal with a weak colony. The bees are not worth the trouble, nor is treatment likely to be successful. The best time of the year to eradicate the scourge is when the honey flow is in full swing.

SPRAYING.—The science of spraying for the prevention of disease and the destruction of insect pests is now very well understood by all intelligent fruit-growers, says a writer in the *San Francisco Chronicle*. The art has still to be learned by the majority. They know that spraying must be done at the right time and sufficiently often, but they cannot always tell when the right time is or how often spraying should be done. They know the work should be done thoroughly, but they do not know how to do it thoroughly. Winter spraying of deciduous trees is easy. All that is required is to give the trees a good coating with the least possible waste of material, and the eye will tell when that is being done. Summer spraying is a different thing. The work must be done thoroughly, but without injury to fruit or foliage. Injury is prevented by proper choice of spraying material and proper mixing. The production of dense, fine, even spray is a matter of mechanics. There is much failure in this. The even pressure which is necessary is maintained by keeping the pump in perfect order and all couplings perfectly tight. The greatest cause of failure is in the nozzle. As to this Professor M. B. Waite says:—"The most important part of the whole apparatus is the nozzle. Unfortunately, this feature has been much neglected by pump manufacturers, and many inferior nozzles have been sent out to farmers. There is a tendency to improvement in this direction, however. The actual results in the application of the spray mainly depend upon the efficiency of the nozzle. In general the best nozzle is the Vermorel, or a nozzle of that type. This consists of the 'cyclone' nozzle, as invented by Barnard, in which the spray enters a cylindrical eddy chamber through a tangential opening at the side. It circles violently in the eddy chamber and leaves the nozzle through a perforated cap, and, still whirling, flies in a minute, mist-like spray of the desired thinness. Vermorel added the plunger or degorger, which enables the operator to thrust the needle-shaped pin through the small opening to prevent clogging. With a good Vermorel nozzle, properly drilled on the inside, and having the correct style of eddy chamber, with a pressure of forty pounds to the square inch, a fine and satisfactory spray will be produced. Such nozzles are very rarely found in the market in recent years. Most of the nozzles require a pressure of 75 to 100lbs. to give a good spray. With this higher pressure almost any nozzle of this type gives good results. A good Vermorel nozzle is really an exact piece of work. The eddy chamber should be carefully drilled, and smooth on the inside, and the tangential inlet should also be correctly drilled and not simply cast in the brass. The cap itself is perhaps the most important. It should have its bearing on the outside, so as to avoid any interfering washers. The cap should be made of hard brass, and the size of the opening should vary from one-sixteenth to one-twenty-fourth of an inch, according to the pressure to be used. The greater the pressure the larger the opening and the greater the quantity of spray that can be thrown."

COOL STORAGE OF APPLES.

Report by A. Despeissis.

Among the exhibits which are being displayed in the agricultural court at the Manufacturers' Exhibition are some cases of apples from Mt. Barker. These apples, a specimen of which I now submit to you, have been in cool storage for a period of 22 weeks. A few bruised ones just show the spots where the flesh has been crushed, while the bulk, consisting of fruit which has been carefully picked, are absolutely without a blemish and look as fresh as if they had just been picked from the tree. These apples were worth 7s. to 8s. per case at the time of storing, at the end of May last. The cost of storage at 2d. per case is 3s. 8d., and they are now worth 30s. per case; as a matter of fact they are unprocurable at any price. The same exhibitor had some apples in the pavilion of the Department of Agriculture at the last Royal Agricultural Society's Show. They sold at the termination of the show week at 26s. to 28s. per case—cost of storing was 2s. 8d.—and the net profit resulting from storing, after making allowance for any bad fruit that had to be discarded, was about 15s. above market value at the time of storing. These examples unquestionably demonstrate the value of cool storage possessing keeping qualities, providing these fruits are carefully picked and handled.

The kinds which have come out best of the long-period tests carried out in the cool chamber, are:—Cleopatra, Dunn's Seedling, Stone Pippin, Ben Davis, Rokewood, Nick-a-Jack, Sturmer Pippin, Shockley, Yates, Granny Smith. Others, and amongst them some of the kinds best suited for the export trade, keep well for the first couple of months or so, namely, Jonathan, Rome Beauty, Esopus Spitzenberg—to only mention a few. So satisfied are Messrs. Sounness Bros. with their experiment that they intend next season to store not only a score or two of cases, but a thousand or two thousand cases. That others will do likewise, I have already satisfactory assurance, and Mr. Cairns, the manager of the Government Refrigerating Works, is prepared to handle and hold small or large consignments alike in the recently-overhauled chambers set apart for that purpose.

The following extract on the subject is taken from the daily Press:—

"An illustration (says the *Herald*) of the growing importance of cool storage as a means of keeping the market balanced and giving to producers a profitable return, whilst at the same time protecting the consumer against having to pay exorbitant prices for importations, is supplied by the above minute addressed to the Honorary Minister for Agriculture (Mr. Mitchell) by the Acting Director (Mr. Despeissis). The need for fruit-growers and producers generally utilising cool storage to a greater extent than at present has frequently been emphasised by Mr. Mitchell, and he is formulating a scheme for extending the operations of the Government refrigerators. At the same time, he has no desire to interfere with private enterprise, and, in urging the producer to adopt cool storage for the sake of themselves and the consumer, he points out that the different refrigerating firms are prepared to take produce into cool storage. There is, he affirms, ample cool storage accommodation for all fruit over and above that required for immediate consumption; and he advises farmers to make early application for space. There seems every prospect that, having regard to the fact that this State last year imported about £140,000 worth of fresh fruit, this means of keeping the local product on the market will be extensively adopted this year, and while, as the minute shows, this should be profitable to the producer, it should also tend to give the public their fruit supplies at a cheaper price than they are paying at the present time."

LAMB INDUSTRY AND COLD STORAGE NOTES.

BY A. D. CAIRNS.

The lamb industry, and its possibilities with regard to this State has been made a very prominent feature of late. It is one of those questions that must be studied entirely from the local conditions standpoint. What may have taken place in one State in slow or rapid development of this industry is only a guide to us so far as we avail ourselves of the experience gained and in the application of the knowledge to our own needs.

While South Australia may have taken years to attain the export of 2,678 tons of mutton for last year, Victoria, with practically the same number of stock (11 millions), rose to 9,761 tons, while New Zealand, with a total of less than both these States combined, viz., 20 millions, sent to London no less than 76,249 tons of the same commodity, while again Argentine with 120 millions (estimated) sheep sent 73,126 tons to London, and was practically unheard of as a frozen mutton producer before the year 1902. In that year Argentine sent to London about 112,000 lambs; this year she will probably exceed 80,000 tons of fresh mutton, to the British capital.

Australia, according to the Agent General's, report exceeded all previous efforts last year by an increase of over 900,000 carcases. This means practically nine-tenths of the total increase for Australasia. New Zealand, with a flock of twenty millions, supplied 1,751,229 sheep, and 1,953,337 lambs, which 'seems to be nearing the limit of production, and stands in strong contrast to the comparatively insignificant total of 461,902 sheep and 906,536 lambs for the whole of Australia, from a flock of eighty millions.

While Western Australia has made a small beginning in lamb export, it behoves us to look into any practical contributory causes that makes the industry of New Zealand the despair and envy of the pastoral world.

One thing stands out boldly which we might imitate, and that is, there are about 7,000 farmers with flocks under 200 head each, while flocks from 200 to 500 are owned by a further 5,000 growers. These 12,000 farmers probably with cream, bacon, and grain added to the above form, in the writer's opinion, the best possible example for our farmers to follow. In a year or two's time, this class of farmer will have graduated from the 200 to the 500 class into probably the 500 to the 1,000 class. Thus increasing his own prosperity and incidently that of his district. A thousand small holders are better for us than 10 large holders, as the larger number of small owners can give closer attention to the details of market requirements whether for local or oversea requirements, than can be obtained by isolated individuals on large stations.

Of the 150,000 live or local sheep and lambs consumed between Fremantle and the goldfields last year, still too many frozen came round the Leeuwin for our good. Small holdings in the Southern part of our State would go a long way to stop this.

For lamb raising, good milk-producing feed must be provided for the ewes during the few months of the lambing season. The fat lambs then are sold, and a quick annual return is made without further risk, and the chaffed silage in the silo can be held in reserve till herbage is scarce.

Some change in the local meat supply is bound to take place soon. The sufferings and beef losses of live stock from the North-West cannot go on much longer in the present light of cold storage advancement. A depôt to receive chilled meat at Fremantle can also accommodate the killing of mutton both for export and local requirements.

The necessary cold storage to accommodate this can also handle our fruit for the same destination.

Lambs will precede fruit from say November till March. If the chambers are then cleared the many thousands of cases of fruit can be stored for a rise for the grower, and it might be within the scope of most of the banks to advance a 50 or 60 per cent. value on such produce on the day of storing, thereby keeping our fruit or mutton growers going while the market is stiffening.

With an increase of 267,000 in our sheep total this year, it will provide us with one sheep per head of population, and, roughly, 10,000 over for reserve. This number per head of population is slightly over coastal towns requirements and slightly under goldfields average. With a similar or proportionate increase next year, not only should Eastern mutton be shut out, but preparation should be considered for dealing with the export possibilities in a most thorough manner.

Surplus chaff and such herbage must be turned into mutton. Small holdings increased in number will widen the distribution of flocks and give a larger area to collect from when a shipment is being prepared.

Another great advantage of small flocks in New Zealand is that many weed pests are kept in check. The method is adopted of panelling off a section of a field infested by the ox-eye daisy (as they would panel off root feed sections) or other weed pest, and turning in a few hundred nibblers for a day or two before seeding time. This plan should commend itself to our settlers as being extremely practical. Other seeding pests of the grass family, which injure the sight of lambs or destroy the pelts by perforation, and render the mutton unsightly, besides lowering its grade below export standard, can thus be controlled by a mob of sheep to the benefit of themselves and their owners by dealing with the herbage at the proper time. It is more efficacious than any hand labour, and makes the weed pest a source of profit.

It is a noticeable feature among the small farmers of New Zealand that co-operation is firmly believed in and practised. By this means not only are they able to buy machinery cheaper, distribute seeds and implements, but they are so close in touch with each other and the centres of information that the markets are never glutted.

No time should be lost in starting a small flock of some good strain of crossbred or comeback breed. The study of a good sheep book which has been boiled down and shorn of its dreary detail, containing only facts of practical value for this special industry, sifted and simplified for the student of lamb raising, would do much as an educational factor. The mixed farmer, having several lines going at the same time, and with crops, dairying, pork, and perhaps a little fruit, he has to be a fairly all-round, well-informed man, so that books containing concrete reading will be found to be of the most value.

The following interesting article on this question of lamb raising is taken from the *West Australian* of a recent date:—

" Mr. James Mitchell, Honorary Minister for Agriculture, recently conveyed his observations of the local frozen lamb trade. During the course of a conversation with a representative of the *West Australian* the Minister gave some interesting particulars about the future before sheep husbandry in Western Australia. He said: ' The frozen meat industry is bound to become one of the first importance in this State. We have the sheep, we have the lands, and all that is wanting is the right method. It goes without saying that ample refrigeration conveniences are the key to the whole position. The refrigerator lifted New Zealand from the verge of bankruptcy to the present pinnacle of prosperity which she enjoys. It has sent the meat trade forward by leaps and bounds in Victoria and South Australia. And what it has done for these countries, it will do for Western Australia. Indeed, I am bold enough to say it will do more. We have in this State large areas of land eminently suitable for sheep and lamb-raising, on which to-day there is scarcely a hoof. Once the proper conveniences are provided these waste lands will jump into favour, and be made wealth-producing. To that extent, therefore, refrigeration will do for us more than it has done for the Eastern States, which are already pretty well stocked up. We have our own markets to catch up, and we can never adequately supply local requirements until a proper system of refrigeration is in vogue. Our imports of mutton, beef, etc., during 1905 exceeded in value £200,000, and obviously the first work is to catch up this shortage. Nothing can be done, however, until a proper system of cold storage is available. For two or three months in the year we have a surplus of lamb and mutton, afterwards there is a shortage. If we could store the surplus of the spring months of the year in cool chambers there should be no need to import a single carcase. This is what other meat-producing lands are doing, and it is what we will have to do in the very near future. It is a simple matter to keep meat in good condition in a refrigerator for six months, if need be. In Victoria, for instance, they are now maintaining in cool storage lambs that were killed six months ago, and what is being done there is, of course, equally possible here. The erection of an adequate number of cool chambers is the first essential. If there were proper refrigerator conveniences available, the sheep-owners of the State could send to them next year a quarter of a million lambs. But until the refrigerator is actually in existence it would be folly for them to arrange for such an extensive output, which is far beyond the immediate requirements of the consumers of the State. The

whole future of the sheep industry of our South-West land division is
dominated by the cool storage problem. Provide adequate refrigerating
facilities, and Western Australia will see her sheep industry expand by
leaps and bounds. Leave matters as they are, and sheep-raising
will always have a very limited scope in the State. Personally,
I believe in cool storage works being conducted by private enterprise,
although at the same time I think there should be some measure of
State control to prevent monopolies being formed prejudicial to both consuming and producing interests. It seems to me that this work of catering
for the local mutton and lamb trade is eminently one for private enterprise
to undertake, and I have hopes that the opportunity now offering will be
grasped by private persons. But as I have already said, the position is
sufficiently serious to call for immediate attention. If private enterprise
fails to rise to the occasion, it will become necessary to work out other means
of providing the cool storage facilities, without which the mutton and
lamb industry of Western Australia will remain only a fraction of what it
ought to become. The export trade will follow immediately we have overtaken local requirements. Indeed, the one will lead to the other. I look
forward to the day when the value of our meat export will be equal to the
value of our gold export. New Zealand to-day sends away six million
pounds' worth of frozen meat, and there is no reason why in time we should
not reach similar figures in this State. We have just as great possibilities
of raising prime lamb as New Zealand, and with our large areas of safe
rainfall country, and our good climate, there is nothing extravagant
in the contention that mutton and lamb raising should be as important
an industry in Western Australia as it is in Maoriland. And in my
opinion there can be no doubt of the economic importance of
building up a large meat-exporting industry. There can be no comparison set up as between the gold and the meat industry. No
one values more highly than I do the great worth of our gold mining industry, but I say emphatically that in days to come the permanent prosperity
of the State must rest upon its agricultural lands. There is no way in
which they can be turned to better account than by utilising them for
intense grazing methods. Roughly speaking, we have 40 million acres of
land in the south-west land division of the State—the division specially
adapted for agricultural pursuits—and I see no reason why five million sheep
should not be maintained on them. There can be no question that the direct
and indirect benefits of the industry, when fully developed, will far transcend
the benefits that the people of the State derive from the gold-mining industry.
In days to come the sheep, and not the gold mine, will be the symbol of our
progress, though, of course, we all hope and believe that the mining industry
will continue to prosper for many years to come. To my mind the future
of the lamb and mutton industry will belong to the small men. In New
Zealand the farmer who has a few hundred 'freezers' to sell is the back-
bone of the industry. We want a similar state of affairs to prevail in Western
Australia. What can be done in this direction is suggested by the experience
of Mr. Thomas Wilding, of Mokine, near Northam, who from 800 ewes realised
£800. Our meat export trade is to be built up by the men who have four
and five hundred sheep to sell during the year, and who so till their lands that
they can maintain this number on a relatively speaking small area of land.
There is a great field before all the southern districts in the domain of meat
production. I am sure that the settlers are waking up to the fact. They
will naturally alter their methods as the opportunities of making a ready
sale of the stock they raise are expanded. During a recent trip from

Donnybrook to Kojonup and Katanning, I was greatly impressed with the sheep-carrying capacity of the country.   At Mr. Wilfred Steere's station I saw magnificent grasses on land that had been ringbarked, and on which the blackboys had been topped.   Throughout the journey the possibilities which the district offers to the up-to-date sheep farmer were very suggestive. I believe that in these favoured latitudes the sheep man will use the plough to produce fodder for his stock, and thus follow the lines of approved stock husbandry as practised in New Zealand and England.   Rape, peas, and turnips will grow readily all over the South-West, and for fattening purposes we could not produce a better fodder.   Once the trade is properly organised fat lambs will be the same as gold.   There will always—for the market is practically unlimited—be a ready demand for "freezers." The man with a thousand lambs of the proper type will be able to turn them into cash at a moment's notice, where the owner of a thousand ordinary sheep may experience some little delay in finding a buyer. With the appreciation in value of the right sort of lamb that follows the establishment of proper cool storage facilities, it goes without saying that our farmers will endeavour to increase the carrying capacity of their lands.   It is only a matter of time when they will maintain their sheep largely by the product of the plough.   That is to say, they will not be content with the natural grasses, but will raise for the sustenance of their stock approved fodders of the kinds I have already named.   You will perceive, therefore, that the solution of the cool storage problem means a great many good things for the State.   My idea, then, is to encourage the small conditional-purchase men to become breeders of lambs suitable for export. These are the men from whom we must look for results.   And that it will be distinctly to their advantage to energetically pursue this form of stock husbandry cannot be gainsaid.   A well-organised lamb export trade means this for them.   Their lambs will bring a fixed cash price at the nearest railway station, and, so far as one is able to judge, there will be. no material fluctuation in prices.   The small farmer will be able to gauge his income to a nicety from the number of lambs that he has to sell.   The overseas market is practically unlimited, and we have the satisfaction of knowing that Western Australia, in addition to being a remarkably healthy stock country, is from a week to ten days' nearer to the markets of the old world than other portions of Australia.   Once the industry is properly organised it will produce a fixed source of regular revenue that can be depended upon with more confidence than the monthly gold yield.   Unlike the mining industry, which is permanently depreciated in value by every ounce of gold taken from the earth, it will show an upward tendency as each additional acre is brought under pasture year by year. We know what the industry can do, and we know what our lands can do. There is no guesswork about it at all.   Our seasons are thoroughly safe.   In the most arid portions of the South-West division, with proper precautions, there should be no trouble experienced during even the most unfavourable seasons; while in the more coastal districts the possibilities before the industry have yet to be generally realised.   Competent sheep men, who know something of the conditions of the frozen meat business, are quite satisfied that Western Australia has an assured future in exploiting it.   The time is ripe for action, and I am anxious to see what private enterprise will do in meeting the position that has already risen in the local lamb trade.   It is satisfactory to recognise that there are not wanting indications of the value of such an industry being thoroughly well recognised by those who are conversant both with the trade itself and also with the potentialities of the Western State."

HAMEL EXPERIMENTAL STATION.

ANNUAL REPORT 1905-6.

G. F. BERTHOUD.

The report in full of Mr. G. F. Berthoud, the manager of the Experimental Station at Hamel, is now given, as exigencies of space compelled its being printed in a condensed form in the Annual Report of the Department:—

SEASON.

The rainfall during the winter and spring months was very heavy, about 50 inches. The brook overflowed its banks many times, covering all low lying lands, doing serious damage to the cereal plots. Owing to this cause, the yields of grain are light. The summer was a mild one, very favourable to the growth of maize, cotton, potatoes, and other summer crops.

WORK.

The general objects of the work carried out here are purely experimental: chiefly for testing new varieties of grasses, cereals, fruits, and tubers. I think that seed potatoes should be grown in larger quantities, to permit of choice seed from selected kinds being sold to planters.

PRISON LABOUR.

The fences—boundary and divisional—are all well built of substantial posts, wire, and netting. The jarrah posts were split, the fencing and gates erected by the prisoners. The outbuilding, pig and poultry yards, etc. were built, the drains opened, and part of the heavy clearing on this farm was done by prison labour.

VISITORS.

The farm adjoins Hamel Siding on the South-Western Railway, about 70 miles south of Perth and 40 miles north of Bunbury. The plots are usually at their best from October to Christmas and March and April. During the past season many agriculturists and others have called to inspect the various plants. Visitors are always welcome.

BULLETINS.

One or more bulletins should be issued in cheap form annually, illustrated with photo-blocks, showing plants of the most useful grasses, fruits, tubers, etc., grown here. The work would thus be made more interesting and useful to all who may desire reliable information on such matters.

EXCHANGE OF SEEDS.

Several parcels containing seeds of native plants and grasses have been sent out to South Africa, Argentina, the United States of America, and other places. Small lots of new and useful seeds were received in return. Thus, by means of friendly intercourses, with those interested in the progress of agriculture outside of Australia, seeds of many useful grasses may be obtained.

INFORMATION SUPPLIED.

Many queries relating to crops, seeds, mode of culture, etc., have been replied to by post. This work, and also that of showing visitors round the plots—which, owing to the various blocks being scattered over different parts of Hamel Estate—takes up a considerable share of time.

FLOWERS.

Applications are frequently received for cut flowers, seeds, bulbs, and ornamental shrubs. Such are not cultivated on the farm, and cannot be supplied.

YIELDS.

Owing to the large number of varieties of cereals, etc., which are annually tested here, the area of each plot is limited; therefore the yields of each are computed by carefully weighing the matured crop, gathered on a measured average portion of each plot, thus gauging the approximate results obtainable per acre.

MANURING.

Many persons who have no practical knowledge of this locality may naturally think that the soil is very rich, and should not require much fertiliser. Such a notion is incorrect and misleading. This soil when first broken up is very sour, and unless it is thoroughly well cultivated and manured the results are *nil*. The costs of the complete fertiliser used here for potato and other crops is at the rate of about 9s. per cwt.

WHEAT.

Fifty varieties, including a few new crossbreds, and several new kinds imported from Europe. Taken as a whole, the crop was very poor, and the worst harvested on the farm, due chiefly to excessive rainfall. The best and most prolific—early varieties, Alpha and Cumberland; late, Tardent's Blue, Lucky Talavera, Bobs, Galland's Hybrid.

Yield—Highest, 22 bushels; lowest, 8 bushels; average, 11 bushels.

MANURE TEST PLOTS.

Wheat, "Alpha,"

Sown in drills, 28th June, 1905, on new land fallowed during the summer. Owing to these plots being twice flooded during the winter, the complete soluble fertilisers were washed out. The best returns are from fine ground bonedust, and blood and bone mixed. Yields, light and below fair average in all cases.

Yield—Highest, 17 bushels; lowest, 1¼ bushels; average, 8¼ bushels per acre.

OATS.

Eighteen varieties grown. Of these, several were new, and tested here for the first time. Seed introduced from America and elsewhere. All the varieties were badly damaged by the prolonged wet season, and also floods over the low-lying land. Yields poor, and grain light. The best are, Burt's Early, Early Ripe, Giant Dakota, and Falman's White.

Yield--Highest, 30 bushels; lowest, 10 bushels; average, 21 bushels per acre.

BARLEY.

Twelve varieties. A few of these were new. Seed introduced from Europe and America. The results were poor, owing to the unfavourable season. The soil on this farm does not appear to be suitable for the successful culture of this cereal. The best were Champion Beardless, Hofbran, and Russian Black.

Yields—Highest, 23 bushels; lowest, 8½ bushels; average, 16 bushels per acre.

RYE.

Five varieties, including new ones introduced from Germany. This hardy cereal withstood unfavourable conditions of soil and climate very well, and is worthy of more general attention on the part of farmers for culture on poor land. The best are Markisoher and Summer Saxon.

Yields—Highest, 18 bushels; lowest, 8 bushels; average, 13 bushels per acre.

CEREALS, 1906.

This season's experimental plots comprise 52 varieties of wheat (including 10 new), 12 oats, 5 barley, 2 rye. Sown end of May and first week in June, on new land, Block No. 10. So far the season is not too wet, the plots are all looking well.

HAY.

Sixteen acres sown 4th May, on new land, ploughed in narrow lands, and fertilised broadcast at the rate of 2 cwts. per acre, as follows:—

Block 12: Six acres, Algerian Oats, now looking fairly well.
Block 13: Five acres, Rye and Field Peas, mixed, coming on well.
Block 14: Five acres, Cape Barley, not doing well.

FIELD PEAS.

Two varieties cultivated here. The common (Grey) and white Chilian. Both are strong growers. Sown in May the vines attained to 8 feet in length. First-class cover crop for sowing on old weedy land. They clean off sorrel and improve the land greatly for succeeding crops. The grain supplies superior feed for pigs.

Yield: 27 bushels per acre.

MAIZE.

Twenty-four varieties, including some recently introduced from America. Sown during November, 4 feet by 3 feet apart, allowing two plants in each hill. All plots hoed and hilled twice, all weeds kept down. All suckers broken off for stock feeding. By doing so the cobs are larger, and fill out better.

Soil deeply worked lowland, rather light, and peaty. Complete manure rate of 6 cwts. per acre, applied and mixed with soil below the seed. The season was a very favourable one for the proper growth and ripening of this crop, the soil retaining fair moisture during the summer months. Returns from all sorts payable and good. Grain of nice colour and well matured. Dent varieties are most prolific, the grain large, floury, of excellent nutritive quality for stock. Being tall vigorous growers they require a richer and stronger soil than the more hardy Yellow Flint, also a longer season, as they mature late. In this State maize may be profitably grown only on good low or swampy lands which remain moist during the hot season.

Dent sorts, the best are, early—" Pride of the North "; late—" Kansas 4568 "; Reid's " Yellow "; Funk's " Yellow "; " Old Gold "; Flint's " Ninety Day."

Yields—Highest, 81 bushels per acre; lowest, 17 bushels per acre; average, 52 bushels per acre.

POTATOES.

No. 1 Plot.

Planted from 18th to 25th August, 1905, 30 by 18 inches apart. Soil, good loam, clean and deeply worked. Complete fertiliser rate of 8cwt. per acre, applied along the drills, and well mixed with soil below the sets; depth of covering, 5 inches. All tubers were cut, and any showing signs of disease rejected. The selected sets were dipped in a dry mixture of lime, sulphur, and bluestone. Heavy rains followed shortly after planting; the overflow from the brook soaked through part of the land, thereby rotting a large number of sets; otherwise the crop turned out well. Foliage fairly clean, and the tubers of good size and quality. Varieties in this lot comprised six imported and 180 new seedlings; of these many failed to germinate, and a large number have been rejected; a few only are promising, the stock of which is now being increased.

Yields—Highest, 12 tons per acre; lowest, 4 tons per acre; average, 7 tons per acre.

No. 2 Plot.

Planted first week in November, 1905; sets whole, 30 by 24 inches apart; soil, low land, light and peaty, a class of land that dries out quickly in summer; fertiliser same as No. 1 Plot. Varieties, 28 seedlings and 16 imported; of these 21 seedlings and six imported have been rejected owing to bad qualities. The growth was healthy. Crop dug first week of March, 1906, with good results, the " Factor " giving the record yield rate of 25 tons per acre. The best in this lot are—Early, " Noroton Beauty "; main crop, " Factor," " Pink Blossom," " Radium," and " Duchess of Norfolk."

Yields—Highest, 25 tons per acre; lowest, 1 ton per acre; average, 8 tons per acre.

No. 3 Plot.

Eight varieties planted 4th December, 1905. Sets whole; 36 by 24 inches apart. Seed local; being first growth from imported stock. Soil, moist low land of excellent quality. Fertiliser same as No. 1 plot. Growth strong and clean; dug first week in April, 1906, with good results. The best in this trial were early " Noroton Beauty," main crop " Pink Blossom," " Radium," " Snowball." The " Factor " was not planted in this lot.

Yields—Highest, 19 tons per acre; lowest, 9 tons per acre; average, 14 tons per acre.

No. 4 Plot.

Five varieties planted 3rd January, 1906. Sets whole; 36 by 24 inches. All American imported seed, which arrived in fair condition. Soil and fertiliser same as No. 3. The plants made nice healthy growth; were dug 4th April, and gave fair returns. The best are:—Early—" Red River Triumph "; second early—" Clinton" and " Early Rose."

Yields—Highest, 19 tons per acre; lowest, 8 tons per acre; average, 12 tons per acre.

No. 5 Plot.

Fourteen varieties planted 25th January. Sets whole ; 34˙ by 24 inches. Soil and fertiliser same as No. 3. The 12 seedlings included in this trial lot are those grown and selected on No. 1 Plot. Growth very vigorous and healthy. Dug first week in May. Results good, tubers of nice even market size and clean. The best are—Seedling Second Early No. 150; main crop Nos. 151, 140.

Yields—Highest, 14 tons per acre ; lowest, 6 tons per acre ; average, 9 tons per acre.

No. 6 Plot.

Six varieties. Planted 10th February, 1906. Sets whole, 36 by 24 inches. Soil and fertiliser same as No. 3. All American seed, which reached here in excellent order and germinated freely, producing strong healthy plants. Dug 7th May. All gave satisfactory returns, but the two noted below were most prolific. Second early " Rose of Erin," " Red Jacket."

Yields—Highest, 8¾ tons per acre ; lowest, 6 tons per acre ; average, 7 tons per acre.

No. 7 Plot.

Twenty-four varieties. Planted 12th to 25th May. Cut sets, 30 by 24 inches apart. Soil, sandy loam, high and well drained. Previous crop field peas. Complete fertiliser at the rate of 6 cwts. per acre, same as No. 1 plot. The above comprise 11 of the newest sorts from England and France, including " Violet," the new hybrid of *Solanum Commersoni* ; balance are seedlings. They are all making fair growth so far. The most promising are " Midlothian Early," " Southern Queen," and " Table Talk."

NOTE.

The potato is subject to the ravages of numerous injurious pests. Among these the moth, whose grubs cause serious annual loss by eating their way into the tubers, thereby rendering many useless for seed or table use. Here, keeping sound seed is now very difficult. To facilitate this work a specially-built brick house is urgently needed. Such a place of moderate size would not be costly. The floor should be cemented, walls and ceiling plastered, doors and ventilators to be provided with two close-fitting frames, the inner covered with fine wire gauze. This would prevent the ingress of moths, and permit free circulation of air, the outer one to be air-tight and closed when desired for fumigation, thus killing any germs or insects which may have entered. Inside of room to consist of strong upright frames, fitted to carry shallow trays made of light wood to allow of the seed tubers being packed in layers two deep to admit of contents being easily inspected, and allow a free current of air for keeping the seed dry and in good condition. Such a room would be very useful for storage of maize and other seeds liable to the depredations of mice and weevils.

I respectfully desire to suggest that the work of raising good seed potatoes should be extended on this farm, which is really too small, ever to be very successful or payable as a dairy, but by growing and supplying sound seed of good varieties only to farmers at a fair price—the place would bring in a revenue to the Department, and meet a long felt want among agriculturists in this State. Good reliable seed is hard to get at any price, except by direct importation from Europe, which is a very expensive way, beyond the means of ordinary cultivators.

By extending this work here on commercial lines, private enterprise would not be interfered with, and farmers would gain the advantage of being able to procure reliable seed.

DISEASE.

Bacterial and fungoid pests are yearly getting worse on the potato throughout Australia. The sale and use of infected tubers for seed, is no doubt a fruitful source for spreading the evil. The task of divising effective means of prevention is one beset with many difficulties. One plan by which useful results may be attaineth would be for all the Australian Agricultural Departments to combine and carry out a series of carefully conducted experiments on identical lines as regards treatment of seed, mode of planting, and varieties. Also noting the influence of fertilizers, and benefit or otherwise to be gained by chemical treatment of the sets and soil, and which are the most hardy and disease resistant kinds. I have raised a large number of seedlings—these, as a rule, are more vigorous growers than the old sorts. From experience gained here, the germs of disease appear to be in the soil. For instance, seed was grown in boxes of clean soil in the green house, the young plants set out in other boxes of clean soil, and finally out on new land, a considerable distance away from any other potato plots. A large number of the plants were attacked by disease, especially the late sorts. For second planting only the best and cleanest cut seed was used; all treated with bluestone, lime, and sulphur; planted on clean land, manured with chemical fertilizers only. The resulting crop was also diseased, although not badly. From this experiment it would appear that the germs of disease are in the soil.

SWEET POTATO.

(Tpomœa Batatas.)

Four varieties introduced by tubers from Queensland sprouted in shallow boxes of sandy soil, under glass. The rooted slips were planted out in November on prepared land 4ft. x 3ft. apart.

Soil light ·peaty lowland, manured with complete fertiliser, rate of 6cwts. per acre, well mixed with the soil, below the sets.

The vines made fine healthy growth. Taken up 12th June. Tubers of fair size, sound, and very satisfactory. This valuable and easily grown plant will thrive well in many parts of this State, and should be more extensively cultivated. The tubers are excellent for table use, also relished by stock, and are more nutritious than the ordinary potato. The vines make a superior green feed for milch cows.

The best varieties are " Spanish " and " White Maltese."

Yields—Highest: 17 tons per acre.
       Lowest: 7 ,, ,,
       Average: 12 ,, ,,

COTTON.

(Gossypium herbaceum.)

Seven varieties were sown on prepared land, 16th November, 4ft. x 3ft. apart, one or two plants per hill. Soil light low land of fair quality. Complete manure, used at rate of 6cwts. per acre. The plants made slow, but fair healthy growth, attaining the height of 4 feet. Owing to the Autumn being dry and warm, a good proportion of the bolls ripened nicely before the wet season set in, yielding a fair return of lint, excellent in colour and quality. Much the best lot yet raised here. This crop to mature properly needs fine warm weather until late in Autumn. Here, the early rains usually discolour the lint. Although perennials here, the plants are best treated as annuals, and resown each season. Along the more congenial coastal districts North of Geraldton better and payable results will be easily obtained. The only kinds which mature here are the early American sorts. Highest yield harvested here is at the rate of about 350lbs. clean lint per acre. Best varieties "Shine's Early Prolific," and "Louisiana Prolific." The yield from the first named variety, being at rate per acre of clean lint 350lb.

Seed ½ ton, equal to 16 gallons of oil, and 300lbs. of oil-cake.

Hops (*Humulus lupulus*).

One variety, "Oregon," planted two years ago; strong, hardy grower, clean and healthy; bears a fair crop of large catkins; ripens well; some were discoloured and damaged by the high east wind; crop gathered early in March and sun-dried in shallow trays covered with hessian. This system of curing is cheap, and produces a superior sample of hop, with good aroma and strength, our fine warm climate being very favourable for this work.

Yield, good, rate of 2,250lbs. (green) per acre. Cured 600lbs., worth 1s. 4d. per lb.

The hop plant will do well in the South-West, providing that it is planted on good low land which remains moist during the summer months. However, the high cost of labour for picking will be a drawback for a while.

NOTE.—Two other kinds will be planted here this spring.

Beans.

Six varieties; sown 5th December, thinly in drills three feet apart; the vines were healthy and yielded well.

La Vallee.—An excellent new sort from France; pods long, fleshy, and of delicate flavour.

Zulu.—A very distinct dwarf free-growing kind from Africa, which produces its fruits underground like pea-nuts.

Rice (*Oryza sativa*).

Block No. 24. Sown in November; two varieties; Bertone (Italian), Yamani (Egyptian); drills 18 inches apart; ripe in April; results fair.

New Zealand Hemp (*Phormium tenax.*)

Block No. 7. Rooted plants were set along the division fence in June, 1905. They have made but slow growth; thrives best along the edge of brooks.

Tomatoes.

Nine varieties, being the leading new sorts introduced from England and America. Plants set out in November 6 x 4 feet apart, all fruited well. The choicest and most prolific are "King Edward VII." and "Magnificent;" fruits, bright red, large and smooth. "Tenderloin," fruit very large, heavy and fleshy; colour pink.

POMPKINS.

Six varieties. Sown 5th December, hills 8 x 10 feet apart. All made vigorous growth, yielding heavy crops of sound fruit. For stock feeding the most productive is "King of the Mammoths." For home use and market, "Table Crown" and "Bugle" are good sorts.

WATER MELONS.

Sown 7th December in hills 8 x 8 feet apart. Ten varieties, including new ones from America; all made fine growth, which produced a heavy crop. Specimen fruits weighing 40lbs. For quality the best are "Halbert Honey," "Seminole," and "Kleckley Sweet." For market "Rattlesnake" and "Sugarstick" are good carriers.

ROCK MELONS.

Six varieties; sown 1st December in hills 6 x 6 feet apart. Vines made nice healthy growth, producing a fair crop of good fruit. The best are "Trondegouit," "Tip-top" and "Lewis' Perfection."

CUCUMBERS.

Three varieties; sown 1st October, hills 6 x 4 feet. Growth fine and healthy. "Satisfaction" and "Early White" are prolific. Fruit of medium size and superior quality.

NOTE.—Seeds of pumpkins, melons, cucumbers and tomatoes have been saved from the finest selected fruits.

BANANAS.

Suckers of four varieties were introduced from Ceylon five years ago. One died. Two, "Atikikel" and "Kollkulla," have made fine growth, and set fruit, which has not matured owing to cold climate. The third, a dwarf sort, has made nice healthy growth, but not yet fruiting.

ORCHARD.

Area, four acres; block 7. Planted August, 1904. Four hundeed trees (197 varieties), about 20ft. x 20ft. apart. Trees are all healthy; and making fair progress.

Almonds (six sorts).—Annual growth very strong up to six feet on "Nonpareil." "Lewelling" and "Burbank" are also free branching and fine.

Apples (56).—These are the leading family here. Season's growth on "Statesman" five feet. "Lady Hopetoun," "Sharp's late Red," "Reinette du Canada," "General Carrington," "Cleopatra," "Dunn's Seedling," and "White Winter Pearmain" are also vigorous growers.

Apricots (11).—Healthy and doing well. "Newcastle Early" and "Gooley" are strong, quick growers.

Cherries (4).—All doing fairly well. The strongest are "Lewelling" and "Chapman." "Suda" produced some fruit.

Chestnuts (5).—Doing well, "Downton" being the most rapid grower.

Figs (9).—All doing exceedingly well, soil and climate being very suitable for the growth of this useful fruit. Strongest growers are "Adam," "Brunswick," and "Adriatic White."

Guava (1).—Purple ; dwarf, but healthy growth.   Produces fruit freely of good size and quality.

Lemons (3).—All doing well and making better headway than the oranges ; "Thornless" being the most robust grower.

Loquat (4).—All doing well.   Soil and climate very suitable for this useful fruit, which should be more extensively cultivated.   It ripens its fruit in October, when all others are scarce.   "Victory" and "Advance" are the most vigorous.

Medlar (2).—Doing nicely.   Produced a few fruits.

Mulberry (3).—Making fair growth, Downing's "Everbearing" being the most vigorous.

Nectarines (6).—All healthy and robust ; "Goldmine," "Zealandia," and "New Boy" are very fine.   "Goldmine" produced a few nice fruits.

Oranges (12).—Are doing fairly well.   The Indian variety, "Santalah," makes fine branching growth ; "Mediterranean Sweet" bore two nice fruit ; "Siletta," "Charley Baker," and "Jaffa" are also fine growers.

Peaches (15).—All healthy and branching out freely.   "Stump the World," "Kalamwhoo," and "Beauty of Taupaki" are the strongest.

Pears (24).—All making fine headway.   This family is likely to be successful here.   "Broompark's" season's wood six feet long.   "Keiffer's Hybrid," "Koonce," "Mount Vernon," and "River's Fertility" are also very fine.

Persimmons (8).—These have done exceedingly well ; growth sturdy and branching.   They appear to be well adapted for culture here. "Yemon," "Dai-Dai-Maru," and "Gibio Shin" are the best growers.

Pomegranate (1).—Growth dwarf and bushy.   Fair.

Plums and Prunes (7).—Although not as vigorous as the Japanese sorts they are doing well, "King of the Damsons" making 6 feet of new wood. *Prunes*—"Splendour," "Golden," and "Prolific" are also very fine.

Japanese Plums (10).—All looking very well.   "Early Yellow" made shoots 10 feet long and nearly one inch thick. "Hay's Seedling," "Nikko," "Sultan," and "October Purple" are also vigorous growers.

Walnuts and Peccan Nut (3).—Making slow but fair progress.

Quinces (7).—All making good headway.   "Bourgeat" made seven feet of new wood. "Meeche's Prolific," "Van Deiman," and "Champion" are also very fine.

Note.—The above experimental orchard was established chiefly with the view of testing the value of new varieties of fruits to ascertain which are really suitable for general culture.

Growers, later on will need to export to distant over-sea markets, therefore it is most important that intending planters may obtain correct and disinterested information as to which are the most reliable and best sorts to plant.   With this object in view the plot should be enlarged, and two trees of all new varieties—in apples and pears chiefly—be introduced annually. When in bearing, fruit to be submitted to severe tests to ascertain those which possess real merit.   By doing so, this branch of work will at no distant date prove to be an interesting and instructive feature of the farm.

FIG PLANTATION.

Planted June, 1905. Area. six acres, viz., one on block 7 and five on block 8. Varieties, 6, comprising the drying figs "Smyrna" or Calimyrna and "Kassaba," with a suitable proportion of wild figs—Capri No. 1 and No. 2 for fertilising purposes, imported direct from California. Nearly one half failed to grow owing to being heated on the long sea voyage. The others have made free growth, which will give a fair lot of cuttings for propagation. The "Smyrna" fig should prove to be a valuable acquisition to the State, where the fine warm climate will be an ideal place, for maturing superior fruits of this class. The other two kinds are "Adam" and "Brown Turkey," which have made fine vigorous growth.

FUMIGATED PEACH TREES.

Twelve young trees of the Alexander Peach were received on 4th August, 1905, from Inspector Beatty, of Fremantle. The object of this test being to show if fumigation has an injurious effect on the trees. Planted in the orchard, block No. 7, these trees appeared to be rather dry and shrivelled.

No. 1.—Not fumigated. In leaf 5th September; buds and shoots weak.

No. 2.—Fumigated at the ordinary strength. Came out in leaf a few days earlier than the last, with stronger shoots.

No. 3.—Fumigated at 50 per cent. stronger than the ordinary. Out in leaf 25th August; buds and shoots fairly strong.

No. 4.—Fumigated double ordinary strength. Out in leaf 25th August; buds and shoots stronger than No. 3. One tree in this lot came in leaf later, viz., 5th September.

There is hardly any difference in the vigour of Nos. 3 and 4, and they are better than No. 1, which started growth later.

From above trial it appears that fumigation does not injure deciduous trees. However, the gas may have an injurious effect on the foliage of evergreen trees and shrubs.

DATE PALMS (*Phœnix dactylifera*).

Fifteen strong suckers of these valuable plants were imported from Algeria, North Africa, and planted last winter on homestead blocks Nos. 23 and 24. Six are dead, the others are alive, but a few only have made new leaves, which are weak and sickly. But they will recover and improve next spring when the weather becomes warmer.

MISCELLANEOUS PLANTS.

Several new introductions are now being grown here, including: The "Guango" or Rain-tree, a valuable shade and fodder tree, suitable only for naturalisation and extensive planting in the Northern portion of this State, where the climate is warm and moist.

Pine-apple, "*Cayenne*."—Rooted plants of this useful smooth leaved variety have been sent out for trial to residents in suitable localities. The supply of young plants is now exhausted.

"*Buck Yams*" and "*Tanniers*."—Two varieties of these plants, which produce edible tubers like sweet potatoes were received by parcel post from the Botanical Gardens, Georgetown, British Guiana.

Young plants have been propagated, and are now making fair progress in the greenhouse. These will be available for field trial during next summer.

Being tropical plants they are not likely to do well in the temperate part of this State, except during the hot season. The "Buck Yams" stand the winter best. The "Tanniers" are very delicate, and several have died off under glass this winter.

SOIL INOCULATION.

In the early part of the season six plots were treated with some of Dr. Moore's nitrogen bacteria cultures, which were obtained from the Agricultural Department, as follows:—Three plots each of red clover and garden peas. On one of each the seed was carefully inoculated, as per instructions supplied, and on one of each the soil was inoculated. On the last two plots the seed was sown without any treatment. No difference could be seen between any of the plots. Perhaps the cause of failure may be owing to the cultures losing their vitality on the long sea voyage.

INSECT AND OTHER PESTS.

During the past year several of these have been troublesome among cultivated plants, the potato moth being one of the worst. The grubs find their way among the seed tubers when stored, and cause a great deal of damage. The common black spot fungus of the potato leaves, and the grey mildew on melon vines, damage these plants.

SHADE TREES.

Useful and ornamental; planted last season near the homestead around the pig and poultry runs, have made fair progress, and will, later on, provide nice shade in summer. Several small groves will be planted on the pasture land on blocks 10 and 11 to provide shelter for the live stock.

SEEDS AND GRASS PLANTS.

Numerous applications have been received from residents in various parts of the State for trial lots. When possible these have been supplied, with directions for planting. ·

VINE CUTTINGS.

A part of block 23 has been set aside for use as a quarantine station for striking imported vine cuttings. One lot only was received and grown here during the past season.

FODDER PLANTS.

Several summer kinds of these were cultivated on blocks 21 and 24 with successful results, as under:—

Cow Peas—Four varieties. Seed sown in drills 3 feet apart early in December. All made nice leafy growth to the height of 3 feet, shading and covering the soil nicely. This crop is useful for improving the soil, and makes good green feed for stock. Seed should be sown only after the soil is warm, say, here from middle October to December, and apply a liberal dressing of superphosphates say from two to four cwts. per acre. The most reliable and robust sorts grown here are the "Black" and "Iron" cow pea.

TEOSINTE (*Euchluena luxurians*).

Block 21, sown 5th December, 4 x 4 feet apart, on good moist low land; complete manure applied and mixed with soil below seed, rate of 6cwts. per acre. By the end of autumn the plants had stooled out remarkably well, and attained the height of 10 feet. Makes excellent green feed for cattle, but can be grown to perfection only on very rich soil, moisture, and warm climate. Under these conditions it will yield wonderful returns. Does not mature seed here. Estimated yield per acre from plants weighed here in June: Tons, 26.

MAZAGUA (*Sorghum cernum*).

This is a strong-growing variety of African millet or Dhoura. Seed sown 22nd November thinly in drills three feet apart; complete manure, 4cwts. per acre in the drills; stools out freely, and makes remarkable vigorous growth; height in June 12 feet, level and even, stands up fairly well, but failed to mature seed owing perhaps to late sowing; cut and carefully weighed; end of June estimated yield of green fodder per acre: Tons, 22.

PEARL MILLET.

Sown 24th November, 1905, drills three feet apart; growth, good; height, six to eight feet; fair green feed if cut while young; will yield several cuttings.

Sorghum saccharatum and amber cane.—Sown 7th December, 1905, drills three feet apart; growth, very good; height to 10 feet; useful fodder if cut when sweet; late in autumn.

GIANT MILLET.

Sown 23rd December, 1905, drills 18 inches apart; growth, tall and even, five feet; good for green feed; ripe early in April; large drooping heads; seeds useful for poultry.

HUNGARIAN MILLET.

Sown in drills 18 inches apart 23rd November, 1905; growth rapid, very even; height, four feet; ripe early in April; heads well filled, good.

NOTE.—Four other varieties of millets were grown, but these did not prove of any special value.

RESULTS OF TRIALS OF POTATOES GROWN AT PERTH EAST.

By T. Church.

The following notes may be of interest, as showing in some degree the merits of some of the newer introductions of seed potatoes and also of some of the well-known varieties extensively grown in the Eastern States. It may be mentioned that in this State little regard in the majority of cases seems to be given to the virtue of any potato except Early Rose, Beauty of Hebron, and Vermont. The comparatively poor eating qualities of these three and their uncertain yields seem to furnish ample reasons for exhaustive experiments with the view of getting a better flavoured, heavier cropping, and hardier potato. If some enthusiastic grower will strike out in this direction I have no doubt his labours will be well rewarded and will tend to lift potato-growing on to the proper lines. At the present time the majority of growers seem to be satisfied to grow their Early Roses without much regard to quality or size of seed and to accept potato culture as a hazardous and uncertain occupation. If they will try a few experimental plots with new varieties and spend a few pounds on obtaining guaranteed seed, instead of the leavings of their previous crop, I am certain they will find it far more profitable than present methods.

Mr. Berthoud is working in this direction and, having proved the qualities of "Factor" and other varieties, deserves commendation.

He kindly sent me, in May last, 2½lbs. each of the following varieties:— Factor, Radium, Duchess of Norfolk, Vermont, Gold Coin, and Pink Blossom. Of these, Factor and Radium were sprouting and therefore I planted them at once, 12th May, 1906.

They were planted in a prepared bed of brown soil from the Armadale brook. The chief virtue of this soil I found was its colour, but I manured it well with cow manure and wood ashes and a sprinkle of sulphate of potash and superphospate. Planted in holes partially filled with the manure, five inches deep, 18 inches apart in the rows, and 24 inches between the rows. Seed planted on top of the manure. These two were planted in the worst season of the year, having the whole of the winter to contend with, consequently they were not grown under favourable climatic conditions.

Factor.—13 tubers; planted whole; lifted at end of 16 weeks; average 1¼lb. to the root. Tubers even in size, healthy, and of good flavour. Skin smooth and white eyes, shallow and few. Yield per acre, 9½ tons.

Radium.—15 tubers, some cut, making in all 21 sets; yield, 12lbs.; matures before Factor—a week or two; skin rough and light brown colour, quality good; might be grown as a second early; yield disappointing, but worth another trial. Yield per acre, 3½ tons.

The balance of the lots were planted in similar soil with same manures on 29th July, 1906.

Duchess of Norfolk.—22 tubers, seed rather small; lifted after 16 weeks; yield, average 1lb. per root; even size, good quality; skin white, shape long and tapering, eyes shallow, and infrequent; promising, with larger seed. Yield per acre, 6½ tons.·

Vermont Gold Coin.—14 tubers, good size, grown 16 weeks; yield, 11¼lbs., disappointing; good shape, netted yellowish skin; quality excellent. Yield per acre, 5¼ tons.

Pink Blossom.—13 tubers; matured, with others, about 16 weeks; quality good, but potatoes small; yield, 9¼lbs., poor; these grow better at Hamel. Yield per acre as mentioned. I think the soil used unsuitable, being too light, and coming from the brook was "washed out"; they should do far better in a stronger soil; 5¼ tons.

Subsequently I made a layer bed with red clayey loam from the hillside at Bellevue, near Lacey's brickyard, and mixed it with road scrapings, pounded out hill sand. In this on 8th August I planted the following:— Carmen, Early Vermont, Up to Date, Sutton's Flourball, Manhattan, Hebron, and Early Rose; seed planted whole, 5in. deep; manure, cowdung and kainit, the latter spread a month before planting; seed planted in holes partially filled with dung except alternate rows planted without; rows 2 feet apart, seed planted 18 inches in the rows. The freely-manured rows made fine growth, many of the Up to Date, Flourball, and Vermont haulms being 30 inches high. The rows without the dung were fully 50 per cent. behind those fully manured.

Manhattan.—Matured just 14 weeks; 16 sets, weight 7lbs.; some of the roots weighed 3½ to 4 lbs., and individual tubers up to 1lb. each; yield, 36¼lb.; tubers rather oblong, colour blue, blotched; tubers baked good flavour, large ones inclined to be coarse. Yield per acre, 14½ tons.

Up to Date.—14lbs., 54 seed, took 16 weeks to mature; crop even, many of large size, ¾lb.; yield, 84lbs.; some roots yielded 3 to 3¾ lbs. each; quality good. I think this should do well along the red soil streaks of the Darling Ranges as a main crop; there were very few small tubers. Yield per acre, 9½ tons.

Early Vermont.—7lbs., 28 sets; well grown; eating quality not of the best; matured in fourteen weeks; some of the roots weighed 3 to 3½lbs.; a good many small tubers. Yield, 44lbs.; yield per acre, 9½ tons.

Sutton's Flourball.—7lbs., 28 sets; a long season potato; would have done with 18 weeks; lifted at 16 weeks; coloured reddish with purple eyes; not many (average about six) to a root. Yield, 29lbs.. Would do well where it can have a long growing season. Yield per acre, 6¼ tons. Flavour good.

Carmen.—7lbs., 28 sets; 15 weeks; yield disappointing; did not make good growth. This is the second trial with Carmen and both did not do well with me. Yield, 28lbs.; tubers are of good quality, white, and a good cooking potato. Yield per acre, 6½ tons.

The "yields per acre" mentioned in the foregoing, based on a very small area, must only be taken as an approximate estimate. Samples of each of these potatoes may be seen at the agricultural stalls in the W.A. Manufacturers' Exhibition now open, where their points may be considered better than I can here describe them. A fair sample of each is being exhibited. From my trials to date I think growers should try Factor, Manhattan, and Up to Date. As the yield and quality differ according to locality I think those interested sufficiently to spend a few shillings in seed to try them all for themselves, and I am sure that good results will be the outcome. If a smaller area were cultivated and cultivated well instead of adopting the rough and ready methods now used, I think potato growing would become a profitable business, and the present complaint of housewives, that it is impossible to get good potatoes, stopped. It may be mentioned that the five varieties last described were sprayed twice with Strawson's mixture, which I understand is really "bluestone," available for direct use by dissolving in water, 1 pound to 5 pints. One pound sufficed for the two sprayings of the whole plot, and the results warranted the time and cost. There was no trace of disease in any of the tubers.

I have not given the results of the Roses and Hebrons for the reason that they are not yet all dry, but the results from those lifted do not compare favourably with any of those described.

PIGGERIES.

By A. DESPEISSIS.

Both private and State enterprise have of late years been the means of stocking Western Australia with some of the best strains of pigs that ready money, commanded by sound judgment, could procure. While no effort was spared to obtain from the most renowned breeders in England and in Australia pigs of aristocratic pedigree, the housing accommodation provided for these pigs and their valuable progeny has not in many cases been a matter to boast about. Yet it is only by studying the comfort, the cleanliness, and the economic working of the home of the pig that the maximum amount of profit can be expected by feeding wholesome and easily digested food to pigs of the right class. Because of the lack of suitable conveniences and method in housing pigs, the work of looking after that class of farm stock is often regarded as a drudgery. The pigs are in consequence too often left in the winter to wallow knee-deep in sour-smelling slush, and in the summer to burrow in dusty pens overrun with lice and vermin.

Renewed attention has of late been given to pig-raising by the opening in this State of an extensive Bacon and Ham Factory, by the firm of J. & C. Hutton.

The same firm have also shown their readiness to assist farmers in rearing the right class of pigs. For that purpose they have commissioned one of their representatives, Mr. A. Dundas, to travel the country, and by means of advice and friendly criticism convey that information born of practice which they have acquired after a long and successful career.

It is in the course of conversation on the methods of pig fattening that the opportunity offered of obtaining, on the subject of the erection of piggeries, Mr. A. Dundas's views.

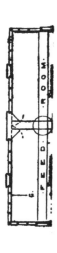

The plan published in this issue is the outcome of the ideas on the subject expressed by that experienced pig breeder. The piggery, a plan of which was drawn to scale in the architectural branch of the Public Works Department, is capable of development to suit any size pig farm.

This is done by providing sets of two or more pens as required.

It is all under one roof, compact, well aerated, but not draughty, clean, and in every respect convenient for sorting and handling and feeding pigs without any effort and without hustling them about in any way.

The material used in the construction of the structure can vary according to circumstances.

The piggery consists of a Receiving Yard, into which the pigs are quietly driven. An inclined gangway leading from the floor of the dray to the ground is here found a great convenience for both loading and unloading.

From this a funnel shaped race, narrowing down to 2 feet 6 inches, and commanded at its extremity by a swinging drafting gate, leaving the way open to either Drafting Yard, allows of the automatic grading and sorting of the pigs.

Strong pig-proof netting is a suitable material for fencing if fastened to a stout board resting edgways on the surface of the ground to prevent the pigs rooting their way out underneath. As a temporary fence double posts and saplings, although rough and ready, may serve for a few years.

From the Drafting Yards narrow lanes 3 feet 6 inches wide extend on each side of the shed.

On these lanes open Fattening Pens, 8 feet x 12 feet, which are large enough to comfortably hold six young pigs. The number of these pens depend on the scale it is intended to operate. Thus ten pens will be sufficient to fatten 60 pigs at a time, and every two pens in excess of that number will accommodate another dozen pigs.

At the end of the piggery opposite that of the Drafting Yards is the Feed Room, where corn, pollard, meal are stored, and where the boiler is located.

A small truck on wheels running on light iron or wooden rails carries the prepared food from the Feed Room along the Central Feeding Lane.

On each side of that Feeding Lane, and extending the whole width of the pen, are the feeding and drinking troughs, separated by means of iron tie rods into six feeding places, one for each pig.

A swinging flap hanging over the centre of each trough permits of shutting off the pigs when the troughs are being cleaned or before the the feed is served out from the Central Feeding Lane.

The pens should be enclosed by walls 3 feet 6 inches high, which is enough for young pigs. For boars and big sows the walls should be a foot higher. They should be open above, but closed all round to keep out draughts.

The doors which open on the gangways are of the same width as these lanes.

An important feature of this sty is the floor, and no false economy should be made in having a concrete one which can be swept and flushed clean and at times disinfected, without fear of germs of maladies impregnating the floor.

A concrete floor three inches thick would be strong enough. Such floors consist of three parts :—First, the porous foundation for drainage also minimises the swelling or contracting of the earth, which often cause cracks; the body which furnishes strength and supports the surface which receives the wear. For the formation, coarse sand or cinders, free from ashes, do very well. This should be wetted and rammed to a solid bed. On the foundation set guides of 2 x 3in. on edge, into these compartments pour Portland cement concrete made of sand, cement and broken stones in the proportion of 1 : 2 : 4 respectively. For mixing these constituents of the concrete, spread on a platform or on clean floor, the sand about six inches deep and deposit the cement evenly on top. With a shovel mix these dry; add sufficient water to make a rather thin mortar; upon this mortar deposit the measured stone or clean gravel, which should preferably have been moistened previously, and mix again. The right amount of water has been added when by spreading the concrete in place and tamping lightly the water flushes to the surface. Remove the guides after a day or so and fill in the spaces with strips of tarred paper or felt and fill the spaces with liquid mortar.

The surface of the floor is composed of mortar alone, containing the same proportion of cement and sand as used in the concrete, but with a little less water; it is well smoothed with a wooden float. The surface will thus be less slippery than if finished with the trowel, which imparts a polish to it.

The floor is protected by means of spread bagging against the direct rays of the sun, to reduce evaporation, and for a few days before using, it should be kept moist by sprinkling with water.

The diagram shows the roof to be high enough to allow plenty of head room and ventilation. The roof can be of iron, painted white to reduce the heat, or covered with sheets of bark, or, better still, with a neat thatch made of rye straw or of rushes or bracken fern, sprayed over with a strong solution of silicate of soda to make it less inflammable.

If water be laid on over the building and supplied by a high tank, it will be found very convenient for flushing the floor, which should be laid with a slope from the centre to the outside towards a concrete pit, where it all runs. In the morning the doors are all open. Most of the pigs after awhile avail themselves of the opportunity offered of making their mess outside, and during the time the doors are thus left open a certain amount of sun and light penetrates the pens. With a stiff broom and shovel the dung and dirty litter is swept out into the cement concrete pits on each side of the building, when as often as occasion requires a chain and disc pump lifts the liquid manure into a tank on wheels and it is carted away to the fields. In that way all the manure, both solid and liquid, is secured and utilised; the pig-sty is kept clean and sweet, and every chance is offered to the pigs to settle down comfortably to the business of converting foodstuff into the more valuable meat. In one corner of the pen a little dry litter is provided for the pigs to lie on. A good plan to keep them from sleeping on the cold cement floor is to have a movable board floor with an inch of space underneath. This floor can be canted up when the sty is being cleaned and hosed.

For breeding pigs more room is required, as exercise is necessary to the brood sow. For that purpose breeding pens of about one acre each, provided with a pen similarly designed in one corner are recommended wherever possible.

The doorway should be against the fence, so that the pigs may be easily penned by quietly driving into the corner whenever required.   A secure sty is very useful for catching young pigs for marking, castrating, or sending to market.

Those who have handled pigs know that it is advisable in doing so to separate the sow from the young pigs.   Some sows when their temper is aroused are very free with their snouts, especially when suckling their young

A large breeding pen while affording plenty of room for exercise, can also be separated by a temporary fence in the winter, and sown with some kind of crop which is left to the sow herself to harvest.   The ground is then sweetened, manured, and turned to a profitable account.

The inducement offered by our local market in pig rearing is one which is capable of considerable development.

A reference to the list of agricultural produce imported into Western Australia shows that only four groups of comestible articles imported reach in value six figures.

Dairy produce heads the list, with somewhat less than half a million pounds' worth.   Fruit and vegetables come next, with £185,500 worth.   This item is now on a rapid decline.

Next comes meats—salt, fresh, and preserved—with £140,000, and bacon, hams, and lard, with £124,000 worth.

Porkers weighing 60 to 80lbs. dead weight are, as shown by the produce price list, commanding 5d. to 6d. per lb.

Baconers weighing 100lbs. to 150lbs., sell for 4½d. per lb.

These prices are much better than those obtained by Eastern farmers, who get from 3½d. to 4d. per lb. for baconers up to as much as 5d. per lb. for prime porkers.

The bedrock price for pork of fair average quality, however, is indicated by London price list which is 4½d. per lb.   The charge for killing, freezing, freights, and commission amount to 1⅓d. per lb., leaving a net price to producer of 3d. to 3½d. per lb.

With these prices as a guide, the farmer can gauge whether it is more advantageous for him to sell his corn at low market value or whether it is more profitable to convert it into pork; in other words is it more advantageous to sell wheat at 3s. a bushel or to turn it into pork and receive the equivalent of 6s. for it, after deducting the cost of raising, feeding, and marketing the pigs.

Apart from marketable corn, however, there is always, on the farm, a proportion of small shrivelled or cracked corn which commands a very low value, and much of this, as well as other foodstuff produced on the farm, can, with profit, be converted into pork.

The following concise advice is offered by Mr. Dundas in the leaflet " Profit in Pigs " issued by the firm of J. and C. Hutton :—

" When near pigging, each sow should be kept by herself for the protection of the young pigs, and all should be fed three times a day with boiled mangolds, potatoes, pollard, crushed wheat, barley, or peas, in a mashed condition. This should be continued till the sow decides to wean her young, when mother and her progeny should be separated, and the same feeding continued until the youngsters are three months old, when a little more meal should be added for a couple of months. They should then be shut up and fed on a ration of crushed peas, wheat, barley, or oats, soaked thirty hours before using, and as much given as they can eat. Use a little sulphur in the food occasionally, also charcoal, and a handful of any green food now and then to keep them in health. Let the sty be dry-bedded, clean, and well ventilated, but not draughty.

" By the foregoing method of treatment breeders should be able to turn out a first-class bacon pig of 130lbs. weight at six months old."

Where breeders have milk to assist, it is not uncommon to surpass that weight at six months, and get pigs of the Berkshire and Middle Yorkshire breeds, and their cross, scaling 150 to 160lbs. dead weight.

Good healthy pigs, eating to their full appetite, and comfortably housed, give for every 6lbs. of raw grain—a good daily ration—an increase of 1lb. per diem. In other words, a bushel of wheat, weighing 60lbs., and worth 3s., yields, when fed to good pigs, a return of 10lbs. of pork, worth 3s. 4d. to 5s., plus the manure produced by the animal.

POULTRY NOTES

By F. H. ROBERTSON.

Poultry breeders are now in the off season so far as regards shows, hatching, and selling birds for stock or show purposes. One is not, however, to think that there remains but little to do. On the contrary, there is much requiring attention, in fact all the year round, and all the time the poultry farmer can always notice something to do. The incubators and brooders are practically all now out of use, so look them over; clean out all drawers and drying chambers; carefully pack away the thermometers, and see that levers, rods, and all the light metal parts are out of harm's way. If any repairs are required now is the time to get them done; far better than leaving everything until hatching season comes round again. Run off the water from tank machines and drain dry if possible. Should the tank be an iron one, turn the machine upside down as a precaution against rusting the bottom of the tank. Clean all lamps and take out oil and wicks and pack away in a box with lid to keep out dirt and dust, also thoroughly overhaul the brooders and put in good clean order for immediate use when again required.

Next season's results now depend on the care given to the young stock. The early hatched cockerels require attention; those intended for sale for stock purposes, or for showing should be kept in a run by themselves, and all unsuitable for either should be eaten or sent to the market. The cockerel run should not be too small; for say 40 birds, not less than $\frac{1}{4}$ of an acre, and then it should not be a run which has been in use as a breeding pen, but on ground which has had a good spell. The more tree shade it has the better, as it cannot be expected that birds can have good coloured plumage if they are constantly exposed to the sun. If the run has not already growing foliage, bough sheds must be erected; they are cooler than iron or wood; are inexpensive, and easily made. First put in four posts of of any old timber, sink them deep enough to be quite firm, and if the soil is of a sandy nature, the easiest mode of making the post holes is by means of a garden trowel. On to the uprights firmly nail the cross pieces, and over those place the boughs. They should be made secure by tying with fine wire. These sheds need not be high, about three feet will be found quite sufficient, and if any surplus water is thrown under them it will be much appreciated by the fowls, as it is always noticeable how much they enjoy dusting themselves in damp, cool ground on a hot day.

The early hatched birds are now roosting at night time, but the later chickens still assemble in mobs under coops or boxes. Care must be taken to see that they are not too hot and over-crowded at night time; the accommodation which was quite snug two months ago, is now too stuffy, therefore either remove the birds to more airy quarters or put down a larger coop in the place of the old one, or a simple plan is to place a brick or block of wood under the coop and raise the front a few inches; but care must be exercised in doing this or too strong a draught may be created.

The hot weather has come suddenly upon us in real earnest; the heavy layers are looking seedy, and the young stock pout under every available shady nook. Be sure that there is always a supply of clean water, and a little tonic in it is now very serviceable; an occasional dose of Epsom Salts is advisable, or a pinch of sulphur in the mash will help to keep the blood cool and tone up the system. Give as much greenstuff as obtainable; if but little available, buy lucerne chaff, steam it well and mix with the mash. This is always made of bran and pollard in Australia, but the quantities of each vary greatly as the qualities vary so much, when the pollard is very fine and flowry it is necessary to use two parts by measure of bran to one of pollard.

It is early yet to think of mating up or buying stock birds for next year's breeding pens; still the time soon comes round, and when it does, the tardy poultryman often finds he is too late to buy what he wanted, therefore it is not a bad plan to buy early hatched chickens and develop them under one's own supervision. Not many breeders will sell such, but when the opportunity does occur it is wise to take advantage of it. Good pure bred chickens are sometimes on offer at 4s. or 5s. apiece, and I have often seen fine strapping young cockerels sold at the auction rooms at that price per pair. One, on seeing such, will say: "I'ts too early to buy; I do not want a cockerel for five or six months yet, and then there is the risk of tick." My advice is: buy when the opportunity offers, and as for the risk of tick that danger is easily surmounted by placing the birds in quarantine for 10 days, if they have any young tick on them they will have dropped off in that time, and will be found secreted in the woodwork of the box they were kept in; therefore burn it, or if the birds are old enough to take to the roost, tie strips of flannel round the perch and if the bought birds came with tick on them the rest will now be found secreted in the folds of the flannel, and are thus easily destroyed.

(3)

THE NARROGIN POULTRY FARM.

The poultry at Narrogin farm are making satisfactory progress, and about 600 head of the following varieties have been hatched during the past season, the numbers being approximately in the following order, viz.:— White Leghorns, Brown Leghorns, Silver Wyandottes, Plymouth Rocks, Minorcas, Black Orpingtons, Bronze Turkeys, Indian Runner Ducks, Pekin ducks, and Toulouse geese.

The White Leghorns are bred from two pens, viz., No. 1 the original hens which are a combination of Wicker, Mason, and Cuddihy's stock, these were mated to a Leven's laying strain cockerel, with the object of breeding large bodied birds of good laying qualities. No. 2 pen consisted of about 30 well-grown pullets, the progeny of the old hens of No. 1 pen, mated to two cockerels obtained from Mrs. Bristow, whose birds have done so well in the Narrogin competition. The Brown Leghorn pen consists of pullets bought from Dusting mated to a cockerel from Wilson, of Crawley. A nice lot of early birds were bred from this pen, the cockerels of which are well grown birds now fit for use, and are for sale. The pullets from this pen have been laying well for the past five or six weeks. The Wilson cockerel was sold, and a fresh cockerel obtained, and a nice lot of later chickens have been bred from this mating.

The Plymouth Rocks bred are all from a selected lot of hens which are proved good layers. Some nice young cockerels are now for sale.

Only a few Minorcas have been bred, as the pen was bought rather late in the season.

About 50 Pekin and Indian Runner ducks have been hatched, and are doing remarkably well, no losses having occurred with the ducklings. The old Pekin ducks were on the farm on my arrival here, and these were mated to typical young drakes from Gladstone Heath, but fertility has not been good with the Pekins. The Indian Runners, on the other hand, have been remarkably fertile. Two quite unrelated pens have been bred from, viz., one from Johnson, the other was purchased by the department some time ago from Woodward. Later on unrelated breeding pens will be for sale from these two pens. One Runner duck stole a nest, sat, and hatched every egg.

Two Silver Wyandotte hens were bred from both matings, being with the object of producing stock of good laying qualities.

The breeding of a good useful class of poultry for supplying farmers is the chief object held in view, particular attention being paid to laying qualities. The raising of birds for show purposes does not receive consideration, and no pampering of the stock is indulged in, and but little attention paid to the doctoring of sick birds. Should any illness be noticeable, the bird is either killed at once or cooped up and given a tonic in the drinking water. If it does not quickly recover, no further remedies are applied. The locality is so far very free of pests, such as hawks and cats, but quite recently an iguana played sad havoc in one of the chicken pens, having accounted for no less than ten well-grown pure-bred chickens in a single morning. The brute was fortunately killed, and on opening him up he was found to have swallowed three chickens, the legs of the last of them almost protruding from his jaws; the other seven were found dead or dying, having been badly bitten on head or body. The pest was 39 inches in length, and of rather attractive-looking markings of a partridge colour, could run very fast, and was favoured with formidable looking fangs which gave him a rather ferocious aspect.

With the view to keeping up the egg-laying qualities of the fowls, sittings of eggs of the best laying strains were procured from the Subiaco Competition, and a nice lot of chickens have been hatched from the best birds there, viz., 14 White Leghorns, 8 Silver Wyandottes, 6 Black Orpingsons, and 10 Minorcas. It is hoped to rear these for mating with the flocks now on the farm, and by this means have birds of the best laying qualities procurable.

CLIPPINGS FROM "THE FEATHERED WORLD."

FEATHERS AS MANURE.

Excellent results are obtained in some hop gardens by using about 20 to 25cwt. of feathers, and the limited supply (amounting probably to only a few hundred tons a year) is rather keenly sought after. Large feathers are slow in action, the shafts especially taking a long time to decay; a sample containing many of them is not as valuable as one composed mainly of small, more easily decomposable feathers. The ammonia obtained is usually a little over 10 per cent., a not uncommon price being £5 per ton delivered, giving a unit price of 10s. In spite of the generally good mechanical condition, this price is, perhaps, too high. The price naturally fluctuates; farmers have been known to pay £5 15s., while samples have also recently been offered at 70s. to 80s. At these lower prices, where the unit value is 7s. to 8s., feathers must be considered cheap. Copies of any of the above, and many other similar pamphlets, can be had free on application to above address, and letters of application need not be stamped.

SEX OF EGGS.

As a rule the earliest hatches of eggs produce the most cockerels, and the later hatches pullets, but beyond this we cannot go. I do not infer that all the first hatches will be cockerels or all the later ones pullets, as the rule only infers the majority in each case.

SALES AT THE DAIRY SHOW.

The highest price realised at the Dairy Show sales was that of £25 for Mr. J. L. Galway's second-prize buff Orpington pullet, while Mr. Norris's second-prize black Orpington cockerel fetched £21. Mr. Stuart Heaton's fourth-prize bird in the same class was sold for £15, for which sum Mr. W. Slater's v.h.c. barred Rock cockerel changed hands. The following are the other highest prices realised:—Mr. E. Cowing's first Goose, £10 10s.; Mr. W. Harrison's v.h.c. breeding pen of silver-pencilled Wyandottes, £10; Mr. R. H. Lingwood's second partridge Cochin cockerel, £6 6s.; Mr. W. H. Bell's first Orpington pullet in the A.O.V. selling, £6; Mr. H. L. Wade's first selling Brahma cockerel, £5 5s.; Mr. W. G. Goldsmith's first selling gold Wyandotte cockerel, £5 5s.; Mr. W. G. Watson's reserve Goose in 1906 class, £5 5s.; and Mrs. Wainwright's third Buff Orpington pullet, £5.

MAKING A CAPSULE.

You are not the only plumber that has an ambition to make a capsule, and you are not the only one that has tried and failed. They are most difficult to make, as the spirit boils at about 94 to 96deg., consequently the solder is scattered all over the shop as soon as you put the hot iron on it. The little capsule, you will note is made of exceedingly fine brass. I believe it is known as 33 gauge, but am not quite sure. You might take the old one to pieces, and so obtain a sample. The bottom of the capsule is thicker brass than the top. Very often a thickness of blotting paper is placed between the two strips of brass, and all is soldered up but a small opening through which the necessary spirit is poured. It is in closing this aperture that the difficulty arises. I do not think anyone knows the exact composition of the contents of the Hearson capsule. The principal fluids in use for capsules are sulphuric ether and alcohol, two parts of the former and one of the latter being a favourite prescription ; others only use a few drops of ether. I have seen good, sensitive capsules made from methylated ether alone.

— — —

THE EGG-LAYING COMPETITIONS.

These are progressing in a satisfactory manner, the yield at Subiaco being especially good, and is so far of a higher average right through than at Narrogin, but it must be remembered that the Metropolitan Competition is worked under much more favourable conditions than the one in the country. In the first place the Narrogin event was sprung as a surprise on Poultry Breeders, and they were not prepared for it, which, of course, placed them at a great disadvantage ; then again Narrogin pens only number 25, against the 64 of the other, and unfortunately the frequent absence of the writer from Narrogin broke the continuity of supervision, particularly as regards the feeding of the fowls. This occurred at least once every month, and the absence lasted several times for a week to ten days, the care of the birds being on these occasions left entirely in inexperienced hands.

At the Subiaco Competition the conditions are entirely different. Poultry owners had good notice of the event, and had ample time to make up pens of the best laying strains of hens procurable. This was fully availed of, as several pens were imported from the Eastern States especially for the purpose. In addition, the three pens which were sent by South Australian Competitors have done remarkably well, as at time of writing they occupy foremost positions, viz., 1st, 2nd, and 5th. The care of the birds at Subiaco has been in the experienced hands of one man all the time, viz., Mr. G. Allmon, so that altogether it is not a fair comparison, neither should it be expected under such conditions to look for an equal return from the two competitions.

The following are the Records for November :—

EGG-LAYING COMPETITION.

SUBIACO MONTHLY RECORD—NOVEMBER.

[Commenced on July 1. To close on June 30, 1907.]

Prizes as follows :—For fowls and ducks respectively :—For the greatest number of eggs in the twelve months :   1st prize, £7 ; 2nd prize, £4 ; 3rd prize, £3 ; 4th prize, £2 ; 5th prize, £1 ; 6th prize, 10s.

For the first three months (Winter test)—Greatest number of eggs : 1st prize, £3 ; 2nd prize, £2 ; 3rd prize, £1.

For the greatest market value of eggs : 1st prize, £3 ; 2nd prize, £2 ; 3rd prize, £1.

For the greatest number of eggs during the last three months of the competition: 1st prize, £3; 2nd prize, £2; 3rd prize, £1.

For the greatest number of eggs each month during the competition: £1 each month.

The following prizes have been awarded to date:—*Fowls.*—Monthly prize of £1: 1st month, Sunnyhurst, White Leghorns, 139 eggs; 2nd month, A. F. Farrant, Partridge Wyandottes, 159 eggs; 3rd month, Sunnyhurst, White Leghorns, 150 eggs; 4th month, Sunnyhurst, 160 eggs; 5th month, Sunnyhurst, W.L., 140 eggs. *Ducks.*—Monthly prize of £1: 1st month, R. A. Dusting, Indian Runners, 64 each; 2nd month, E. A. Newton and R. A. Dusting, equal, Indian Runners, 116 each; 3rd month, R. A. Dusting, C. E. Close, and S. Craig, equal, 120 each; 4th month, A. Snell and Adelaide Poultry Yard, 103 each; 5th month, Miss Parker and F. D. Vincent, 106 each.

Prizes for first three months (Winter test).—*Fowls.*—1st prize, £3, Sunnyhurst (S.A.), White Leghorns, 429 eggs; 2nd prize, £2, J. D. Smith, White Leghorns, 388 eggs; 3rd prize, £1, A. H. Padman (S.A.), White Leghorns, 380 eggs. *Ducks.*—1st prize, £3, R. A. Dusting, Indian Runners, 300 eggs; 2nd prize, £2, E. A. Newton, Indian Runners, 272 eggs; 3rd prize, £1, Mrs. L. Mellen, Indian Runners, 263 eggs.

FOWLS.

Six hens in each pen.

Owner and Breed.				Nov.	Total for five months.
1. Sunnyhurst (S.A.), *W. Leghorn	...	...	...	140	729
2. A. H. Padman (S.A.), *W. Leghorn ...		...	...	139	670
3. S. Craig, *W. Leghorn ...	...	...	...	129	635
4. J. D. Smith, *W. Leghorn	...	...	...	112	623
5. A. H. Padman (S.A.), *S. Wyandotte		...	...	125	614
6. Ericville Egg Farm, *W. Leghorn	...	...	...	119	604
7. E. Garbett, W. Leghorn	...	...	...	116	602
8. W. J. Clarke, Brown Leghorn		...	...	111	595
9. G. W. G. Lizars, *W. Leghorn		...	...	127	595
10. A. F. Farrant, Partridge Wyandotte		...	...	104	593
11. F. Whitfield, Brown Leghorn ...		...	...	118	586
12. Austin and Thomas, W. Leghorn		...	...	129	582
13. Bungalow Farm, Brown Leghorn		...	...	122	579
14. E. Fitzgerald, W. Leghorn	...	...	...	117	578
15. F. Piaggio, W. Leghorn	...	...	...	125	576
16. C. W. Johnson, *W. Leghorn ...		...	...	105	569
17. Mrs. McGree, *W. Leghorn	...	...	...	103	563
18. F. T. Rowe, *Buff Orpington ...		...	...	83	562
19. J. R. Parkes, Brown Leghorn ...		...	...	124	560
20. Ryan Bros., *W. Leghorn	...	...	...	111	554
21. E. Palmerston, W. Leghorn ...		...	...	123	550
22. G. M. Buttsworth, *W. Leghorn		...	...	111	545
23. Bon Accord, W. Leghorn	...	...	...	121	544
24. Bungalow Farm, *W. Leghorn		...	...	109	543
25. C. Attwell, *S. Wyandotte	...	...	...	80	542
26. Adelaide Yard, W. Leghorn ...		...	...	112	538
27. F. Whitfield, *W. Leghorn	...	...	...	104	536
28. J. W. Buttsworth, *W. Leghorn		...	...	110	526
29. A. Snell, *Brown Leghorn	...	...	...	110	524
30. H. Jones, W. Leghorn	...	...	...	108	521
31. A. S. B. Craig, *W. Wyandotte		...	...	89	520
32. B. Jones, *S. Wyandotte	...	...	...	82	519
33. R. G. Flynn, W. Leghorn	...	...	...	86	512

* Male birds were placed in these pens on August 1.

FOWLS—continued.

Owner and Breed.	Nov.	Total for five months.
34. E. Hutchinson, *Minorcas	106	511
35. W. Snowden, Brown Leghorn	113	508
36. L. Meatchem, *G. Wyandotte	86	507
37. Ericville Egg Farm, *Black Orpington	75	497
38. A. R. Keesing, Minorcas	113	493
39. Mrs. Hughes, *R. C. B. Leghorn	108	478
40. W. Wade, W. Leghorn	107	475
41. O. K., *Black Orpington	85	475
42. C. L. Braddock, S. Wyandotte	70	474
43. C. R. Roberts, *W. Leghorn	109	474
44. J. W. Buttsworth, S. Wyandotte	74	471
45. Geo. Bolger, *Black Orpington	87	468
46. J. White, Brown Leghorn	112	466
47. Perth Yard, W. Leghorn	84	465
48. H. M. Kelly, *G. Wyandotte	86	452
49. Honnor and Forbes, R. C., W. Leghorn	82	450
50. Glen Donald Yard, G. Wyandotte	86	444
51. F. Mason, W. Leghorn	89	444
52. W. Snowden, S. Wyandotte	67	442
53. A. Coombs, S. Wyandotte	83	442
54. R. G. Smith, W. Wyandotte	85	429
55. E. A. Newton, W. Leghorn	92	425
56. C. Crawley, B. Orpington	91	422
57. Mrs. McGree, W. Wyandotte	70	390
58. A. Savage, Minorca	85	388
59. H. M. Kelly, *B. Orpington	80	386
60. J. E. Redman, S. Wyandotte	76	378
61. H. H. Wegg, G. Wyandotte	69	378
62. Jas. Kirk, G. Wyandotte	73	374
63. J. S. Miller, S. Wyandotte	85	372
64. J. B. Pettit, S. Wyandotte	68	340
Totals for the month	6,400	32,597

DUCKS.

Four in each Pen.

	Nov.	Total for five months.
1. R. A. Dusting, *Indian Runner	98	502
2. E. A. Newton, Indian Runner	81	470
3. Austin and Thomas, *Indian Runner	95	455
4. Mrs. Mellen, *Indian Runner	70	442
5. A. Snell, *Indian Runner	84	437
6. Miss E. Parker, Indian Runner	106	432
7. F. T. Rowe, Indian Runner	104	428
8. G. Stead, *Indian Runner	85	419
9. C. E. Close, Indian Runner	98	419
10. Adelaide Poultry Yard, Indian Runner	106	419
11. Bon Accord, *Buff Orpington	95	408
12. Ericville Egg Farm, *Buff Orpington	94	402
13. Perth Poultry Yard, *Buff Orpington	89	401
14. W. Snowden. *Buff Orpington	73	396
15. S. Craig, Indian Runner	91	353
16. F. D. Vincent, *Indian Runner	106	353
17. J. R. Parkes, Indian Runner	90	351
18. C. W. Johnson, *Indian Runner	104	334
19. Aveley Poultry Yard, Indian Runner	104	323
20. Sargenfri (S.A.), *Buff Orpington	80	317
21. F. Piaggio, Buff Orpington	100	287
22. J. B. Pettit, Indian Runner	103	272
Total eggs laid for month	2,054	8,620

* Male birds were placed in these pens on August 1.

NARROGIN MONTHLY RECORD.

[Commenced on May 1. To close on April 30, 1907.]

Prizes awarded as follows:—Greatest number of eggs in twelve months: 1st prize, £10; 2nd prize, £5; 3rd prize, £2.

For the first three months (Winter Test)—Greatest number of eggs: 1st prize, £3; 2nd prize, £2; 3rd prize, £1.

For the greatest market value of eggs: 1st prize, £3; 2nd prize, £2; 3rd prize, £1.

For the greatest number of eggs during the last three months of competition: 1st prize, £3; 2nd prize, £2; 3rd prize, £1.

The following prizes have been awarded to date:—First three months (winter test): 1st prize, £3—Mrs. A. Bristow, Armadale, White Leghorns; 2nd prize, £2—Mr. E. E. Ranford, 100 Carr Street, West Perth, Brown Leghorns; 3rd prize, £1—Mr. E. W. Johnson, Osborne Park, Leederville, White Leghorns.

	Breed.	Owner.	Total for Month.	Total to Date.
1.	Brown Leghorns ...	E. E. Ranford	127	766
2.	White do. ...	Mrs. A. Bristow	102	765
3.	Silver Wyandottes ...	A. M. Neitschke	127·	743
4.	Buff Orpingtons ...	A. H. Hilton	95	685
5.	White Leghorns ...	F. Piaggio	101	654
6.	Do. do. ...	C. W. Johnson	108	651
7.	Brown Leghorns ...	Mrs. R. Dusting	88	633
8.	Silver Wyandottes ...	Miss Buttsworth	68	624
9.	White Leghorns ...	A. F. Spencer	100	588·
10.	Do. do. ...	Miss M. Parker	108	588
11.	Silver Wyandottes ...	G. W. G. Lizars	69	571
12.	Black Orpingtons ...	Sparks & Binnington	97	569·
13.	White Leghorns ...	Aveley Yard	101	565·
14.	Brown Leghorns ...	J. D. Wilson	109	562·
15.	White do. ...	T. Handley	98	561
16.	White Wyandottes ...	Mrs. S. J. Hood	79	552
17.	R.C. Brown Leghorns ...	Adelaide Yards	89	531
18.	White Leghorns ...	F. J. Williams	99	530
19.	Golden Wyandottes ...	W. J. Craig	75	512
20.	Black Orpingtons ...	Perth Yards...	77	505
21.	White Leghorns ...	R. G. Flynn	90	495
22.	R.C. Brown Leghorns ...	E. Krachler	70	476
23.	White Leghorn ...	J. E. Tull	64	466
24.	Do. do. ...	G. Oneto	71	447
25.	Do. do. ...	O. C. Rath	90	442
		Totals	2,335	14,524

NATIONAL SHOW FOR 1907.

TO BE HELD AT NORTHAM.

Great enthusiasm was displayed at the annual meeting of the Northam Agricultural Society on Saturday afternoon, the 8th inst., when members were informed that the National Show for 1907 was to be held in Northam, under the auspices of the society.

The President (Mr. T. H. Wilding) referred to the matter in submitting the annual report, and at a later stage

The Minister for Agriculture said he desired to make an announcement which he hoped would give satisfaction to the Society. They were aware that the Government had spent a considerable sum of money in show subsidies—£3,000 in ordinary subsidies and £500 for the National Show. It was entirely the duty of the Government to see that it got good value for its money. He believed they had obtained value in the past, but there was no reason why they should not get still better value, and so long as he was in control of the Agricultural Department, he would see that that was done. At present Western Australia imported yearly something like £1,500,000 worth of food stuffs from the Eastern States. From this State very little was sent away, excepting gold, and it was not right that they should send gold to keep people at work growing food for them in the Eastern States when they had equally good land here. A very great deal might be done by the Society in the encouragement of stock-breeding. He would like to put dairying first, but he knew that it was an arduous occupation, which might not be taken up so readily as stock-raising. New Zealand every year exported lambs and wool to the value of six millions sterling, and there was no reason why Western Australia should not steadily build up a similar trade. It was absurd that they should go on sending out of the State £1,000 per day for dairy produce, and £500 per day for fruit, all of which might be produced in the State. Horse-breeding was another industry that should be encouraged, and all these things could be helped by the intelligent distribution of show subsidies. Under the Federal Constitution the Government were prohibited from giving bonuses, but the subsidies distributed by the agricultural societies might be made to serve the same end. At present things were not too bright with the wheat producer. Prices were low, and a firm basis would not be reached until they were able to export on a large scale. In the meantime it would be a great thing to increase the output of lambs. The Government had determined to ask the Northam Agricultural Society to undertake the duty of carrying out the National Show for 1907. (Applause.) The special subsidy of £500 that the society would receive would not be given unconditionally. He was going to make conditions in regard to these subsidies in future, and he welcomed the opportunity of making them apply in the first instance to his own district. (Hear, hear.) He was sure that they would have a show that would be a credit to the State. The Society would not be permitted to spend one penny of the £500 in buildings. Every copper must be legitimately spent on the prize schedule, and in such a way as to stimulate production of the right sort. In the following year he intended to recommend that the show should go to Busselton, which he regarded as a centre of very great possibilities. He hoped that the Northam Society, in drawing up its schedule, would give attention to the encouragement of horse and sheep breeding and in a minor degree to dairying. He wished to emphasise the condition that the grant of £500 and the usual subsidy must be spent. They would have to provide for a large number of visitors, and produce a schedule that would attract exhibitors from all parts of the State. He was giving them ten months' notice, because he believed that it would take ten months to do the work properly. They would have to get to work on the schedule without delay, and he believed they would make the show the best ever held in the State. He wanted it to be an object lesson to every one who visited it, and a vindication of the policy of the Government in granting the subsidies. By means of special trains from the goldfields and the city they would be able to attract thousands of visitors. He hoped that before the date of the show an affiliation would be arrived at between the different societies, so that they might all work together for the good of the producer. He had much pleasure in asking them to undertake the National Show for 1907. An official communication to the same effect would be forwarded to the Society in a few days, and he hoped no time would be lost in getting to work. He hoped they would take into consideration the advisableness of offering some special prizes, not necessarily for permanent pastures, which might be difficult to maintain in the district, but for the man who could utilise the plough for the production of feed for sheep, such as rape, turnips, etc. The time was very opportune for such a work. Until they were in a position to export largely the producer of wheat was going to experience some trouble. One way to get over it was to produce lambs. He looked with every confidence to the Northam Agricultural Society to assist him in making the National Show of 1907 a great success. (Loud cheers.)

Mr. Wilding said that it would give the society very much pleasure to accept the trust. With ten months in which to make preparations, they could arrange a show that people would find worth coming to see. He was sure that every farmer in the district would do his best. Already their show was an easy second to the Royal, and better than any of the national shows held at other centres, and now that they were to have the National Show they would prove that the district was worthy of the distinction. He wished to emphasise what Mr. Mitchell had said in regard to the breeding of lambs. If some of the farmers took to breeding and fattening lambs on hay and crushed wheat, they would find that they would get far more for their crops than at present prices. He thanked Mr. Mitchell for having secured for them the National Show for next year, and for having given them ample notice. He felt certain that it would prove a great success.

Mr. H. W. Hancock, Vice-president, said it would be the duty of every one connected with the society to try to make the National Show a success. The Northam district had the land, the stock, and the men, and if they all worked together they could make a better show than had yet been seen in Western Australia.

Mr. G. L. Throssell, Vice-president, spoke in similar terms, and emphasised the necessity of continuing the monthly meetings that had proved so successful last year and would be the means of keeping their members together. During the next few months fruits, etc., should be placed in cool storage for the show, and he had no doubt the Government would assist them in that way.

Mr. Mitchell said he would arrange storage for fruits for exhibition and also for use at the show luncheon. The Government would help the society in every way to make the show a success.—*Northam Advertiser.*

NARROGIN STATE FARM.

REPORT FOR THE MONTH OF NOVEMBER.

By R. C. BAIRD.

Hay cutting was commenced during the month, and is now almost completed. The crop cut for hay is principally wheat, about 90 acres of which will be used for this purpose. Some portions of the crop are very good, while other portions, owing to excessive wet in winter, together with late sowing, are very light. The average yield will be about one ton per acre. The quality of the hay is excellent.

Owing to the continued absence of rain the summer crops are not making such rapid growth as I would like.

The Ninety Day maize is suffering from want of moisture, and in some patches beginning to dry off.

The sorghums are healthy and of good colour, and only require a few showers to insure a vigorous growth.

The millets and cow peas have not done well.

An exhibit of grain, fodder plants, grasses, etc., was sent to the National Show held at Narrogin, also some live stock consisting of horses and cattle. These animals were not competing, but on exhibition only.

Thirty one students are now in residence, most of whom have lately arrived from England. The work of the farm is largely carried out by students, the majority of whom evince a great desire to become acquainted with all farming operations.

CHAPMAN EXPERIMENTAL FARM.

REPORT FOR THE MONTH OF NOVEMBER.

By J. KEAYS.

Hay carting was commenced and finished during the month. We have about 50 tons in stack, sufficient to carry us through the coming summer and winter. The yield was not so high as formerly owing to the lighter rainfall and poorer class of soil under crop. Threshing will not be commenced in a general way until the middle of December, when all the cereal crops will be harvested. The weather during the month was favourable to the filling out and ripening of grain and the quality of grain will compare favourably with past seasons; but not so as regards yield, which can be accounted for, viz., 4in. less rainfall and a larger area of sand plain under cultivation; however, we have threshed a small paddock of Jade wheat sown 5th June for a yield of 21 bushels per acre. The largest portion of this area was apparently poor white sand that in its natural condition only grew a low stunted scrub, but with ordinary cultivation and 1cwt. superphosphates per acre gave the above return, and there is no doubt that with similar cultivation and sown in April the yield would be considerably higher.

The variety wheat test plots and manurial tests are not threshed, but as soon as they are detailed results will be forwarded on.

The potato crop gave a return of 28cwt. per acre. This crop is rather precarious to grow here owing to having to plant late to escape the frosts, then the dry weather sets in which has a detrimental effect on the growth; of course on swamp land in this district the potato crop gives good results.

The onion crop promises a fair return; they apparently adapt themselves more readily to our soil and climate than the potato. All stock on the farm are in excellent condition and we have a liberal supply of grass and herbage in paddocks to last over the summer months.

No rain for November; the rainfall from January 1st to November 30th is 15 inches.

A SCRUB-CUTTING ROLLER.

Such a roller can be constructed by any country blacksmith. A heavy log of wandoo, jarrah, or salmon gum, say six feet long by two in diameter, made true with the adze, girt by means of strong iron rings at intervals of one foot along the length, and armed longitudinarily with half a dozen strong iron flanges, would constitute a very serviceable roller.

A substantially built square frame made of four pieces of wood 8 by 3, armed with angle irons and through the two side pieces of which the axle of the roller pass through, complete the appliance.

Much of our scrub country in Western Australia which is too thickly covered with brush, could by means of such a roller be economically rolled previously to burning and subsequent to ploughing, as referred to in the explanatory notes accompanying these illustrations, which are taken from the *Pastoralists' Review.*

This roller is used on Mr. Victor Foy's Toologooa Estate, N.S.W., designed by Mr. H. Hollibone, and built to his order by the Meadowbank Manufacturing Company for cutting ti-tree. It is drawn by 16 bullocks walking on the fallen scrub, and is worked with side draft to allow bullocks to keep out of green bush. The roller cuts from 5 to 6 feet wide, goes round and round the block, and rolls from 5 to 8 acres per day, according to thickness of scrub and size of block. The scrub is all chopped twice over, consequently burns splendidly after lying about three weeks, and after burning-off the land is ready for the plough, effecting a saving of at least 25s. per acre against hand-cutting. Tenders were called for scrubbing this land by hand labour, the lowest being 26s., the men not making near wages. Mr. Hollibone also uses a six-furrow plough, which is another great saving against the single-furrow set plough, the saving being 10s. per acre. Without the roller and the big plough the ti-tree would be left untouched.

FRUITGROWERS' FEDERAL CONFERENCE.

RESOLUTIONS, 1906.

The following resolutions were carried at the Fruitgrowers' Conference held in Sydney recently :—

1. "That this conference urges the necessity of deferring the date at which cool chamber space for the carriage of fruit to oversea markets is to be definitely declared from November to December 31, and that interchange of allotted space between States be permitted.

2. "That the size of the case for the oversea trade in apples should be 18in. x 8⅞in. x 14in.

Scrub-cutting Roller (*see* letterpress).

Scrub-cutting Roller at work.

3. " That the standard fruit case throughout the Commonwealth for oranges and other fruits, except pineapples and such soft fruits as are sold in trays, crates, or punnets, may be of any shape, but shall be of one Imperial bushel capacity, or $\frac{1}{4}$, $\frac{1}{2}$, or double of such.

4. " That the inter-State trade in fruits be encouraged, each State retaining its rights of inspection at the port of discharge, without any more drastic measures than have been adopted in the past.

5. " That the Commonwealth should include fruit products in the Bonus Act by providing for a bounty on fruit exported to countries outside Australia and New Zealand.

6. " That in view of the fact that the Federal Government is arranging preferential trade terms with South Africa, the Prime Minister be urged to insert a clause in his list of proposals that will secure the free entry of clean fruit, fruit trees, and plants through the different South African ports.

7. " That it is advisable that immediately upon inspection of fruit for export a certificate shall be forwarded to the port of destination, containing a full list of the fruit so inspected, and that the Secretaries be instructed to write to the authorities responsible for the same, asking them to give it their attention.

8. " That the shipping companies be asked to provide fumigating chambers on the wharves, the fumigating to be done under Government inspection.

9. " That sub-section 3 of the Commerce Act Regulations be amended, to provide that fruit infected with any disease to the extent of not more than 5 per cent. shall be considered sound.

    That the Minister for Customs be asked to eliminate the word " Australia," and be asked to sustitute the letters " AUS " in the Commerce Act.

    " That the clause requiring that registered trades marks shall be registered under the Trades Mark Act be amended, to provide that registration of brands shall mean registration with the Minister for Customs.

    " That Part 3, Section 12, be amended, so as to include India in the list of the countries exempted.

    " Owing to the difficulty of shippers in the country making declarations as to the soundness of fruit before a J.P. or Customs officer, that the section imposing this procedure be eliminated from the regulations.

    " That it be a recommendation that for the purposes of this Act, New Zealand, Fiji, and adjacent islands be included in the regulations as States of the Commonwealth.

10. " That the New Zealand Government be approached with the view of getting the embargo on grapes removed.

11. "That the resolution passed at the 1905 conference *re* sugar duties be re-affirmed."

> The resolution in question was to the effect that the Minister for Customs should be asked to allow a rebate of the Customs or excise duty on sugar in respect of all manufactures having fruit as their base.

12. "That, in the opinion of this conference, it is highly desirous that an expert entomologist be sent to California to investigate the matter of parasites for the destruction of fruit pests.

13. "That, in the case of fruits, such as pine-apples and cherries, in which there is no known disease, steps be taken to have the fee for inspection abolished.

14. "That an executive be formed in connection with the conference, to be composed of the delegates of the one year from the State in which the ensuing conference is to be held."

NEXT CONFERENCE.

It was decided that the next Conference be held at Adelaide, South Australia, about the middle of October, 1907, and that Mr. G. F. Mepean Smith be President. Each State or Colony to be represented by three delegates.

Mr. H. H. Davey to be secretary, and the hon. sec. of the South Australian Fruitgrowers' Association assistant secretary.

HERBERT J. RUMSEY, } Joint Secs.
W. BEAN SMITH,

BOTS IN HORSES.

A correspondent writes to the department saying that a mare he had had passed some small grubs.

In reply, Mr. Despeissis states that the specimen submitted for identification is that of the chrysalis of the Bot Fly. These grubs are cast off by horses in the spring or early summer and burrow into the ground, from whence they emerge as a fly, commencing straight away to lay its eggs under the jaws, on the flanks, and on the fetlocks of the horse. On hatching, these newly transformed grubs create irritation, with the result that the horse nibbles the part effected and swallows a number of the pests, which fasten themselves to the walls of the horse's stomach. It is essential that horses turned out in the field should be looked over every few days this time of the year, and, as a good precaution, the horse's jaws, chest, and nose should be rubbed with a mixture of kerosene and tar, which would kill the eggs adhering to the hair and also act as a deterrent for the fly.

Should the animal be run down on account of hard work and the strain created by the presence of these grubs the Chief Inspector of Stock—Mr. Weir—suggests giving the following powder:—

Sulphate Iron	...	...	...	...	1oz.
Sulphate Copper	...	...	...	...	1oz.
Tarter Emetic	...	...	...	...	1½oz.
Arsenic	...	...	...	...	1 drachm.

Divide this into twelve (12) powders: one to be given daily to the animal in its food.

AGRICULTURAL SOCIETIES.

The following article was published in the *Southern Argus* of the 17th ultimo, and is deserving of more than passing interest :—

" The agricultural show season of 1906 is quickly drawing to a close, and it is pretty safe to assume that the various committees responsible for the holding of these functions will recede into a state of semi-somnolency for several months to come. This would make it appear to the casual observer that the only duty of an agricultural society is to hold an annual exhibition. However, to emphatically state that such is the case is but to seriously reflect on the common sense of the agriculturist endowed with an ordinary amount of intelligence. Agricultural societies should be made a medium for educating the members comprising them in both primitive and scientific metholds of farming in all its phases, as embodying cereal and fruit-growing, vegetable cultivation, stock-raising, etc. To accomplish anything in this direction, periodical meetings—monthly for a start—should be held, at which various agricultural matters could be discussed, and papers contributed by those who had made special studies or experiments in some particular branch of farmers' work. One man may have made such experiments in the cultivation of fodder grasses as has enabled him to launch out as a successful grazier ; whilst another might have evolved from special experiments a system of rotation of crops, that enables him to utilise his land for many years in succession without the use of artificial fertilisers. Papers on these or any other successful experiments would be of incalculable benefit to other members, and some item in them may supply authors of unsuccessful experiments with the missing link (so to speak) which would have made their trials a success. Also, all must concede, that an interchange of ideas between the various members should be productive of a considerable amount of good. There are also many matters which are inseparable from the welfare of the man on the land that could, with advantage, be discussed, but for the consideration of which no time is available at the ordinary business committee meetings of the various societies. For instance, the all-important question of the land tax was one that could well have been discussed by agricultural societies in various centres, and a concerted course of action adopted to protest against what was considered the iniquitous features of the same becoming law. Such discussions would really ultimately have a more beneficial effect than results from the public meetings as at present organised. At the present time these public meetings are usually addressed by certain persons who are not landholders, and very often those having nothing at all at stake, but who, for the sake of gaining a little cheap notoriety, are only too anxious to make themselves heard on matters of which their knowledge is both superficial and limited. By the time two or three of these individuals air their knowledge—or rather lack of it—the men really concerned (the farmers) are more bewildered on the question than they were at the outset. On the other hand, leave a body of farmers of the ordinary class together to discuss matters that affect their avocation, and they usually arrive at an intelligent decision concerning the matter at issue. They address one another in their ordinary everyday language which they understand, and avoid the emulation of the man who has picked up a few grandiloquent phrases which he trots out on every possible occasion to the bewilderment of the tillers of the soil, whose misfortune it is to be compelled to listen to him. As said before, leave a body of ordinary farmers together and they are capable of intelligently discussing matters affecting their welfare. They may discuss the question at issue in a round about fashion, but they eventually get there just the same. If the agricultural societies in the Great Southern districts were to devise a scheme of meetings as suggested, a strong combination in watching the interests of their members could ultimately be evolved. Take for example the question of the present excessive railway freights. This iniquity could first be discussed by the societies separately. The motions carried at each place could be discussed and amended by the other societies, until the outcome would be the adoption of a decisive line of action that must eventually succeed in combatting the action of the Railway Commissioner in penal s ng the producer by the imposition of such excessive freights. The adage, " Union is Strength," is just as applicable to those engaged in agricultural pursuits, as to those whose duties lead them in other walks of life. This brings us back to the suggestion contained in the beginning of this article, viz., monthly meetings to discuss matters concerning the profession of the farmer, and also anything which threatens to jeopardise his chance of reaping a maximum of profit for his arduous labours."

DISTRICT NOTES.

THE NARROGIN DISTRICT.

By Inspector G. M. May.

The increase of settlement in this district has been steady and very satisfactory ; numbers who selected in the rush of two and three years ago have taken possession of their holdings, many being accompanied by their wives and families, and though it may appear to the traveller by train or along the chief roads, east and west, that there is not over-much new settlement going on, it is only necessary to go a short distance along the by-roads and new tracks leading off the main highways to come across numberless new selectors making determined efforts to clear the timber off the land, and intent on forming comfortable homes for themselves and their families. There is a hard time ahead of them doubtless, but I feel certain most will succeed, and in a few years become prosperous and contented farmers, though a few, through no fault of their own, perhaps, are fated to fail not being by nature born cut out " for the land." This satisfactory state is taking place in all directions, and will be very noticeable in two or three years' time, when all these new-comers have had time to clear and ringbark an appreciable portion of their holdings.

The general development of the district has been progressing quietly, though steadily, and each year must see a marked increase in the area of land cleared.

So far, the settlers about here have not, with few exceptions, gone in very extensively for fruit trees ; the best known orchards are those at Messrs. Clayton and Rentoul, seven acres, Jesse Martin, W. Weisse, W. Graham, and W. H. Ingram, each about four or five acres, and others. These are in the bearing stage, and promise to give good returns to their owners. At the last-named there are some well-grown cherry trees, which are now nearly in full bearing, and yield a good crop annually. Travelling round the district it is noticeable that nearly every new settler, when starting, is putting a small area under assorted fruit trees, generally about one acre to 100 trees. These where cared for, and in suitable localities, are in most cases doing well, and it looks as if the time is fast approaching when a shortage of seasonable fruit and exhorbitant prices will be at an end.

Settlement is too new around here for much attention to have been paid to root crops, the time of the settler being all taken up in clearing and preparing more land for the growth of cereals. In many gardens—in fact, most—however, a few mangels and swedes, etc., are to be found, and the fine size they attain is sufficient proof that later on, when time permits, more attention will be paid to these valuable products. The growth of summer grasses, though still in its experimental stage. is fast coming to the front.

Messrs. Wilkie Bros. planted a quantity of various grasses on their poison leases when grubbing out the plants, and when I saw them the cocksfoot, clover, and Chewings fescue were growing strongly in many places, with every appearance of being firmly established. Personally, I planted a few small plots, about 6ft. by 30ft. each, of Turkestan lucerne, Hungarian forage grass, Johnston grass, wallaby grass, and paspalum dilitatum. The first-named is growing, but does not look too well, the early starting of summer and hard state of the ground being against it. The Hungarian forage grass is still growing, and keeping quite green, and is worthy, I consider, of being given a good trial. Some of the paspalum is also growing, and will, I think, be ready for transplanting next spring. The others, although growing well in the spring, do not look too good now.

With the advent of dairying, which should come about in the near future, the farmers must, if they are to be successful, pay attention to a growth of root crops and summer grasses for their stock during the long, dry summer, and experiments which are now being made at the State farm will doubtless be watched with keen interest. At present, as before stated, the new selector has not the time to devote to this, but there are many holdings with paddocks ringbarked and growing good grass, and free from poison, which would yield a handsome return to the owner if provision were only made to tide the stock over the end of summer and early winter in good condition.

As seen by the exhibits at the shows, the class of stock in the district is quickly improving, and it is also pleasing to note the desire of nearly all the settlers to have a small flock of sheep, which yield such a handsome return, and also obviate the necessity of so much tinned meat. Of course, the presence of poison on many of the holdings renders this at present impossible, but I think a year or two will see this righted and mixed farming more general.

Most of the good country in the district as far east as the first rabbit-proof fence has been applied for, and a considerable part of it has already been taken possession of. A railway eastward from here is eagerly discussed and looked forward to. This would serve a large area of splendid wheat-growing lands, which now give large returns where cultivated, but the holders have to spend so much of their time on the road, carting their produce and stores, that they cannot increase their cultivation areas to any great extent. It should also cause a large portion of the morrel and salmon-gum forest country east of the lakes to be placed under crop, for which it is eminently suited, instead of being used almost exclusively for stock as the present holders mostly intend, the distance from a railway and bad roads rendering the growth of cereals almost impracticable. This railway would also be a further section of the Collie Coalfields line, and for that reason alone will doubtless receive attention in the near future.

GERALDTON DISTRICT.

BY INSPECTOR W. W. THOMPSON.

This district has always been considered one of the best in the South-Western division of the State, and has always upheld its reputation for sheep-raising, and the thousands of bales of wool that leave Geraldton by boat for London annually is a sure sign of the progress of the industry.

Although the percentage for lambs was high, since I arrived in the district, 30,000 sheep have been imported into it from the Nor'-West, and yet it is not-overstocked, and although a stranger might wonder where the sheep get their feed on the large sandplains that are seen from the railway carriage windows, these sandplains are more valuable than the best grass paddocks in the summer on account of the succulent herbs and scrubs growing on them. There are now 20 different species which the sheep are fond of, and were these plants growing in some other country they would be imported and classed with lucerne, paspalum, and other fodder plants.

It is the fact of the herbage growing on the land that makes some " sand-plains " more valuable than others for grazing purposes, and a classifier must have a thorough knowledge of these plants before he is competent to value land under grazing and poison leases.

In regard to the number of sheep in the Victoria district, it would be a difficult matter to obtain the correct number, but, making a rough estimate, I should say there were fully half a million sheep in this district, and yet it would be a difficult matter to purchase 20,000 young breeding ewes, as the surplus stock is snapped up to stock new country farther east. In my annual report for 1904 I drew attention to the fact of the seasons changing along the Great Southern Railway, and I am of opinion, from what I can gather, the same thing is happening here, and wetter winters and cooler summers are experienced than formerly, for land is being selected as pastoral leases that would not be thought of years ago on account of the danger from drought. It is to these lands that the surplus stock mentioned above are being taken.

CATTLE.

Although the country immediately along the coast of the Indian Ocean, and to within 50 miles, is better adapted for sheep than cattle, still a fair number of the latter are kept, and it is pleasing to note that it is rare to see a beast that has no breeding about it, for, as a rule, they are a fine healthy lot, and keep in good condition all the year round. I have seen as fine a herd of fat bullocks within 20 miles of Mullewa as could be seen anywhere in the Kimberleys to draw the meat supplies from, the Victoria district would be raising cattle instead of sheep.

HORSES.

The fact of this district being eminently adapted for horse breeding is shown by the splendid stamp of horses that come off the stations of the following men, whose names are a sufficient guarantee of a horse, in regard to breed-ing, wherever it is sold :—Messrs. Grant, Burgess, M'Pherson, " The Mission,"

Roberts, Brockman, and others too numerous to mention here. I have myself used a number of these horses during the ten years that I have been constantly travelling about inspecting, and have found them better for the hard work and rough feed than any imported horse.

It is a great pity that more attention is not paid to the question of horse-breeding for the Indian market, for I contend that a better class of horse for that market can be bred on the pastures of Western Australia than on the grasses that grow on the soft, wet flats of the Murray and Mitta Mitta rivers in Vicotria, and yet thousands of pounds are paid annually for horses for India from these two rivers alone.

PIGS.

Farmers in this district are beginning to turn their attention more fully to pig-raising; that is on account of the Messrs. Hutton establishing a bacon-curing establishment at Fremantle. The drawback will be, unless the farmer has a swamp, or at least a good water supply, the trouble attached to growing root crops or green stuffs, without which the pigs will not thrive during the summer months. No doubt the latter can be grown, for a number of crops of rape have been sown this season, and all I have seen are looking well. Some have made wonderful growth after a shower we had a few weeks ago.

There is practically no dairying carried on, and possibly the farmer may, when starting pig-raising, find out that it will pay him to combine the two industries.

The Chapman River has for years been noted for its orangeries and other citrus fruits; some of the finest oranges I have ever seen have been grown there. A good many settlers have started planting in earnest on Mount Erin and elsewhere.

Very few fruit trees, other than citrus fruits, have been tried. Mr. Patrick, M.L.C., has a fine young orchard coming on in the Northampton district, and in my travels for years in the Blackwood district I never saw anything to beat his. He deserves great credit for attempting an orchard, for he was advised by all old settlers not to attempt it, for they said the trees would not grow. However, they have done so, and his advisers, I notice, have started planting for themselves.

Should this orchard be a success, and there is not the slightest doubt, so far. that it will be, Northampton will, in the future, be as noted for its fruit as is Bridgetown to-day, for there are thousands of acres of as good land as Mr. Patrick's in and round Northampton, and the situation for orchards could not be beaten.

YORK AND BEVERLEY.

BY INSPECTOR H. ST. BARBE MORE.

The York and Beverley district inspector of lands writes to the department in his annual report:—

"There is an increasing amount of enterprise in the direction of experimental pasture plots, but it is to be regretted that operations are being almost

-entirely confined to paddocks where water exists at shallow depths. Paspalum is fairly astonishing those who are trying it. It is now seeding. The roots are stooling in a most promising manner, and this grass looks as if it will take more even than pigs to prevent its forming a permanent sole. I write at the end of summer, and the plants are all green. Mr. McDonald, of East Beverley, has some cow peas in. These are as healthy-looking as the paspalum, and one cannot help thinking that we shall see this fodder plant and soil renovator grown seriously for milk-production beloie very long. The cow-pea thrives best in the hot weather, and the white vaiiety has been known under adverse conditions of soil, temperature, and moisture to cut $9\frac{1}{2}$ tons of green stuff per acre. Lucerne is also to be seen here and there about t e district. I have not, however, observed any noteworthy results from it.

"In my report to the Government Statistician, in December last, I estimated the probable wheat yields for the York and Beverley police districts of the York magisterial district at $14\frac{1}{2}$ bushels per acre. I am pretty confident that this average will be maintained, if not exceeded. With the exception of a few localities which got a bad drenching in the winter, the hay and grain harvests have been gratifying to practically all. The inequality of the crops was rather conspicuous, however, and was evident where physical conditions were similar, nearly as much as where they were dissimilar. Inexperience was chiefly at the bottom of this. Instructions given on the fallow at convenient central places, before the approaching sowing-time, would accordingly be greatly appreciated by the novices, and doubtless not come amiss to the more enlightened husbandmen too, and would lead to increased yields: an object lesson is intelligible; literature is obscure, say to a miner who has turned farmer. Evening lectures may be good as a finish, but without the preliminary demonstration on the land, a large number of settlers whom I know would derive very little benefit from them.

" One who has to travel the district over like I have to, to say nothing of the isolated farmer, would like to see all road-gangs kept off made roads and put on those which are merely formed or cleared for the last five years, taking the gangs at their present strength. The latter highways spoken of are being more and more used every year, and are therefore becoming worse and worse every year. I would particularly call attention, in the interests of the outlying settlers, to the very bad state of the roads, who have remoteness from railway facilities to handicap them as well.

"Of the 34 homestead farms inspected, 21 were unimproved and abandoned and three slightly improved but apparently abandoned. The conditional purchases, with few exceptions, showed that the obligations under the Act were being more than complied with. The 64 inspections I made for the Agricultural Bank all proved the applicants to be farmers with little or no capital. The districts generally present a succession of ever-spreading clearings as each road and track is traversed. One frequently comes on new settlers taking possession of their embryonic homes. The land guides, who seem to be going constantly, are now piloting selectors out beyond Quajabin, Cubbine, and Dangin, where there are still vast stretches of good land awaiting them. West of the Great Southern line there are vacant spaces within a few miles of York and Beverley, but this white-gum country is not a popular hunting ground. It certainly looks hungry and dry, but let a trip through it be timed when the strippers are at work on its wheat-fields, or when valuable flocks are depasturing in the spring, where it has been ringbarked, and there will be no doubts left as to its capabilities. As for water, springs break out after the timber is killed. The secret is to burn the stumps down well, and use a single-furrow plough so that preparations by tillage may be thorough. Here is where you will see some of the old local agriculturists, and they should know.

" A little dairying is being carried on, notably by Mr. Hamersley, of Babbyalla, Beverley. The feeling is growing tha tthis great industry should at any rate be given a systematic trial in the district. It has always appeared to me that the smaller holder, having a long way to cart, would find cheese-making profitable. He would only need to bring in his produce three or four times a year, and it would be in such a compact form and so light that it would be nothing compared with wheat. Besides, the spring-cart has to go in for stores occasionally in any case. The lack of green summer feed is, of course, made somewhat of as against the idea, but do not the pastures in recognised dairying parts fail the dairyman in the winter months and necessitate his growing auxiliary crops? There is a full bite here most of the year on our strong forest land; in fact, tons upon tons of fattening, succulent herbage are now utilised. Neither ensilage nor legumes have been exploited. I had an interesting talk on the subject of cheese-making lately with a new arrival in the State—Mr. Thomas Richards—who is now settled on some fine forest country about 30 miles east of Beverley. Mr. Richards was paying £215 per annum rent for 150 acres in Shropshire, England; yet, against these, one would think, crushing odds, he declares he did really well by making Cheshire cheeses by the quick-ripening process, the article thus manufactured being ready for market in three weeks and freely saleable. I believe that, if one or two skilled dairymen in the district were set up with small cheese-making outfits by the Government, the cost to be repayable over, say 20 years, and then left to their own resources, it would be the best method to solve this important question once and for all. They would have to make their livelihood at the business or go down. And there is nobody like a farmer to convince a farmer."

ALBANY DISTRICT.

By Inspector C. A. Vaughan.

" I am pleased to be able to report that fruit-growing is making great strides in these parts, especially at Mount Barker—I might almost, to specialise, say apple-growing, as this is the chief fruit grown. Twenty thousand cases of fruit were sent away from Mount Barker last year, and as several orchards are only just coming into bearing, I see no reason why forty thousand should not be sent away this year, and, if planting ceases altogether, enough has been planted to give over an annual output of 100,000 cases from this station alone.

" Mr. Sounness, of Merryup orchard, Mount Barker, one of the largest apple-growers in the State, who has over one hundred acres planted with this fruit, recently went East for a trip, visiting all the Eastern States including Tasmania, where he naturally collected all the information he could with reference to apple-growing, comes back perfectly satisfied that these parts can hold their own in the production of apples, not only in quantity, but quality, and can see no reason why these parts should not equal Tasmania in the production of apples, especially as in Tasmania land is expensive, while here we have thousands of acres suited for fruit-growing, available under the most liberal land laws of the Commonwealth. What we want to do now is to stimulate the industry by working up an export trade. Pioneer growers have proved the land equal to any in Australia for apple growing, and if we can guarantee a fair maket there is no reason why thousands of cases of apples should not be exported from this district only.

" It is not out of place to say that this State has additional advantages of being free from most of the worst pests that trouble the fruit-growers, such as the Codlin Moth, and several of the worst scale insects, thanks to the wise administration of the Insect Pest Act, under the Department of Agriculture. While I am on the subject of fruit, I would also mention that the cherry trees at the Mount Barker Estate, owned by Mr. Teesdale Smith, have borne very well this year, and this fruit promises to do well in this district. We know thousands of cases of this fruit are imported annually to this State from South Australia, so that we have a good market to overcome.

" It is interesting to note that the majority of trees planted in these parts are apples, export varieties, the favourites being Jonathan, Cleopatra, Munroe's Favorite, Rome Beauty. One of the most profitable apples has been the Rookman, an apple too late for export, but a fine keeper for the late local market.

" Three growers in the Mount Barker district have over 100 acres of orchard, and several from fifty downwards, so you see from this the industry will soon assume big proportions, as growers are still extending ; 40,000 trees were imported through this port this year, which is sufficient to plant 500 acres. If growers continue to plant at this rate we shall certainly have a big surplus to dispose of outside the requirements of the State."

HAMEL AND NANGEENAN DISTRICTS.

The Under Secretary for Lands, in his annual report, refers to the Hamel and Nangeenan settlements as follows :—

" Within the past year the contractors on the Hamel settlement completed their clearing work, and in accordance with the terms of the agreements were entitled to take up the land included in such contracts either under leasehold conditions for 99 years or conditional purchase extending over a term of years, the selling price of the land being calculated on the original value of the land, plus amount expended on clearing and advances made to the contractors by way of seed and manures, ploughing and sowing, fares and freights, etc. The whole of the contractors preferred to take the land under ordinary conditional purchase, and in order to further assist them the Government promised support from the Agricultural Bank to the extent of £150 to each settler. These contractors now come under the provisions of the Land Act, 1898, as landholders under Section 56, with the result that Hamel has now in fact ceased to exist as a special settlement, though it will, doubtless. still be known as such.

" Nangeenan, being situated about 95 miles east of Northam, practically beyond the confines of what has in the past been considered the cultivable belt of country east of the Avon Valley, makes it of more than ordinary interest as an experiment and object-lesson, and judging by last year's crops, and the appearance of those of the present year, the department has no reason to be dissatisfied with the experiment : in fact, bearing in mind that the rainfall for the year has been rather light, the results are distinctly encouraging. Thirty-five blocks are now being worked, and from the manager's remarks it would appear that the contractors are well satisfied with their prospects.

ANIMAL PHYSIOLOGY.

THE INFLUENCE OF EXERCISE ON THE DIGESTION AND ASSIMILATION OF HORSES.

Dr. A. Scheunart, Berlin, has made experiments on twenty-three aged horses, all of the same age and all in perfect health, which were, for a certain time, fed entirely on oats. This preparatory period facilitated the study of the manner in which each animal took his food, the mastication, the salivation, the rapidity of consumption, etc. Those horses which exhibited no anomaly at this stage were stabled at the Veterinary Institute at Dresden, and were fed for several days on the usual rations, but immediately before the close of the experiment they only received pure hay. This diet, which had for its object the getting rid of all residue of oats in the intestines, was followed by a period of 36 hours during which the animals only received water, and could obtain no other nutriment, solid or liquid. After this, they were given a ration of 1,500 gr. ($3\frac{3}{10}$lb.) of oats. Then the test horses were kept in the stable, whilst the others were exercised, either by lunging or with the saddle. Great care was taken to avoid fatiguing them. When they had been exercised for an hour, they were rested for intervals varying from 10 to 25 minutes.

After periods of repose or of exercise lasting exactly 1, 2, 3, 4, and 5 hours, the horses were killed by means of an apparatus charged with powder, and were at once bled. The stomach and intestines being always subject during the death throes to very pronounced movements which might have drawn into the small part of the stomachic content passes into the intestine of a horse, by the eviscerated immediately after they were slaughtered, in order to apply ligatures to the pylorus (the lower orifice of the stomach) and the intestines, the small intestine was ligatured in sections of from 1 to 2 metres ($3\frac{1}{4}$ to $6\frac{1}{2}$ feet), so as to prevent all displacement of its contents.

Of the 23 horses utilised in the experiment 14 were rested after feeding, whilst 9 were exercised; 7 were killed after the lapse of 1 hour, 7 after 2 hours, 4 after 3 hours, 2 after 4 hours, and 2 after 5 hours. The conclusions arrived at by Scheunart may be summarised as follows:—

1. That exercise during digestion retards the passage of food in the intestine, and consequently the emptying of the stomach. This is proved even by the gait. During the first hours following a moderate feed, only a very small part of the stomachic content passes into the intestine of a horse, if the animal is kept moving. After the first hours this retarding action diminishes in intensity, but is still very marked.

2. The stomach of animals in motion always contains more fluid than that of animals in repose (70 to 80 per cent., as against 60 to 70 per cent.).

3. This abundance of fluid is attributable to the more active secretion of the mucous membrane of the stomach.

4. But, notwithstanding this abundance of fluid content, the gait or pace, when trotting or even galloping, does not affect the mashing up of the contents of the stomach. The physical and chemical differences between the ingesta near the cardia, those close to the pylorus, and those which occupy the centre of the organ remain distinct. This fact has been proved by Ellenberger, Hofmeister, and Goldschmit in the case of horses, pigs, and dogs. The making up of the alimentary materials is, therefore, not produced in the stomach, which is quite contrary to the teachings of the greater number of physiologists.

5. The stomachic digestion of the carbo-hydrates, always a matter of importance, is notably increased by exercise. The carbo-hydrates of oats present in the stomachs of horses at rest were not digested by 30 to 40 per cent. until about three hours after feeding, whilst the same proportion of digested matter was observed in two hours in the case of horses which had been exercised. Thus motion had notably accelerated digestion.

It was likewise proved that animals which had been set to work after feeding had rendered in one hour more starch soluble than the resting horses had succeeded in doing in two hours. This seems to be due to the fact that acidity can only be produced slowly, the stomach being filled with an alkaline saliva rich in ptyalin.

6. The nitrogenous matters, on the other hand, were digested in less proportion during the first hours by exercised horses, which appears to be due to the quantity of fluid contained in the stomach, where the acidity can only slowly attain the concentration necessary to proteolysis. After some hours, on the contrary, proteolysis becomes stronger.

7. Exercise increases the stomachic secretions, notably of the enzymes, the hydrochloric acid, and the water. The acceleration of amylolysis and of proteolysis is only explicable by this fact.

8. Motion not only accelerates digestion, but also the absorption of alimentary matter.

9. Five hours after feeding, it may be admitted that half the carbo-hydrates and nitrogenous matter remaining in the stomach are absorbed, both in the case of horses at rest and horses at work. Therefore, the stomach possesses a very high power of absorption.

10. The passing of food from the stomach to the intestine is performed very regularly; consequently, there is no rapid transmission of food easy of digestion, nor slow passage of less digestible food.

11. The digestion and absorption carried on in the stomach are more important than has hitherto been believed to be the case, notably in view of the results obtained by the evacuation of this organ. The greater portion of the food remains in the stomach for at least six hours.

12. The passage of the contents of the stomach into the intestine begins early, probably actually during the act of feeding, but the quantities which thus pass are very small until the fourth or fifth hour, as has been proved by Ellenberger.

13. The digestion and resorption of chyme in the intestine are scarcely influenced by exercise. Still it can be shown that, in this case, there is a greater abundance of fluid and a certain increase in solubility and absorption of carbo-hydrates.

14. Digestion of food is, to sum up, markedly favoured by exercise. After two or three hours, the digestion of the starch is in the proportion of 35 to 50 per cent., according to whether the horses rest or work; 33 to 35 per cent. of nitrogenous materials are then digested.

15. The total absorption itself is accelerated by corporal exercise. After two or three hours, from 20 to 30 per cent. of hydro-carbons and 20 to 25 per cent. of nitrogenous matter are absorbed. The second figures of these proportions refer to animals which have been kept moving. After five hours, the absorption reaches 50 to 60 per cent.

16. The horses which had been exercised before feeding, and which afterwards had rested during and after feeding, showed neither acceleration nor diminution of the activity of the stomach.—*Revue générale Agronomique.*

THE FRUIT INDUSTRY IN AUSTRALIA.

When one comes to think of the hundreds of tons of raisins, currants, and sultanas that are annually imported into the United Kingdom from foreign countries, it is astonishing that few people know how these fruits are grown and prepared, and what a healthy, pleasant, and profitable occupation their culture affords. There are thousands of acres waiting to be turned into fruit gardens, at a comparatively small outlay, on British soil in sunny Australia.

Everybody who wishes to become a colonial farmer seems to rush off to Canada to grow wheat, while this almost equally useful industry seems left in the background. As an ex-fruit grower who has turned out tons of dried fruit for the market, and having had experience as a wine grower, I may claim to know pretty thoroughly what I am writing about. Wheat growing, to be profitable nowadays, has to be taken up on a very large scale, requiring expensive machinery, and it cannot safely be undertaken by a man with small capital, who wishes to become his own master. On the other hand, let a man start in Australia with a comparatively small capital, and he can be sure of a pleasant out-door life and a good living if he chooses to take up a carefully selected plot of ground for fruit farming. An enormous sum of money goes from English firms annually to foreign countries for dried fruit, and I venture to assert that such fruit is inferior as to size, flavour, colour, and cleanliness than Australia can and does produce, and I have seen fruit in Mildura and Renmark, the Irrigation Settlements, which would bear favourable comparison with even the famous Californian products.

One of the objections raised against Australian fruit culture is the question of cost, it being argued that southern European and Californian labour is cheap and plentiful. But one must consider that the only time when the small Australian fruit farmer needs to call in extra help is during the harvest; also, considering the superior quality of the fruit produced there, the Australian is able to command a much higher price, and there is always a ready market for a superior and really good article. It is by no means necessary to start in an irrigation settlement. There are districts in either of the five colonies where there is sufficient regular rainfall, and the respective Governments practically give the land away to new settlers. The principal and only drawback is the delay in seeing a return for the capital invested. Three years must be allowed in raisin culture before one can expect any return. But in the Australian colonies, if a man is blessed with energy and common-sense, he can always find something to serve as a pot boiler while waiting for his crops, and I maintain that a bachelor can manage well on 10s. a week.

The raisins are the product of the Gordo Blanco vine (the muscatel), which thrives best on a rather light sandy loam. At any of the big nurseries in the cities plants ready rooted or cuttings are to be obtained at a cheap rate. Having taken up a piece of ground, the settler clears it of trees and bushes, fences it in with rabbit-proof wire netting, and it is then ploughed and ready for pegging.

The planting is done most carefully, so as to keep all the rows of vines perfectly straight. This is by no means the easy task it would seem, and much depends on the care taken over this branch of the work. The land is divided off into 10ft. lengths, which are marked by pegs stuck into the earth, and at each of these points a hole has to be dug. This is carried out in such a way that a regular square is formed of rows going each way at distances of 10ft., like the squares on a draught board. When planting the vine, a shaped board is used to keep the young vine in position until the earth is filled in, thus insuring every vine a straight, regular start. The Gordo Blanco (muscatel) vine is not grown on trellis, but is pruned into a bush not above 2ft. from the ground. Great care is taken to prune and shape the young vines, not allowing them to possess more than six or seven branches. Thus, formed into the shape of a plate, every part of the plant gets its full share of sunshine.

When the grapes are thoroughly ripe they are picked and conveyed in baskets or buckets to the dipper. A copper of water is kept boiling containing a solution of caustic soda, and into this the grapes are dipped for not more than two or three seconds, when they are taken out and thinly spread on wooden trays made of unplaned pine boards. The dipping breaks the skin slightly, and makes them get dried more quickly. These trays, when filled, are laid out in rows between the vines to dry in the sun, and the fruit has to be turned carefully when sufficiently dried on the top side. Great care has to be exercised to avoid their exposure to rain, as moisture would destroy their colour and cause mildew. The raisins are put into open boxes and left for five or six weeks to sweat. After this they are stemmed, graded, sorted, and packed in neat little boxes for the market,yand marked according to quality, colour, and size. It may be interesting to mention here that it takes on an average about 3 tons of grapes to produce 1 ton of dried fruit, and in my own experience I found that by the third year my vines were producing at the rate of £40 per acre, increasing yearly from that time, while the working cost per acre was about £4 per annum.

The sultana vine is grown on trellises, and is far more delicate than the Gordo Blanco. The processes of drying sultanas and currants are the same as raisins, with the exception that the currants are not dipped. Altogether, the question of fruit culture in Australia is not, in my humble opinion, taking the prominent position it deserves as a means of finding profitable employment for hundreds of men who, with perhaps a little capital, would scarcely venture to risk it by following up industries already as overcrowded in the colonies as at home.—EMILE DONNIER, in the *Field.* ;

THE CONSERVATION OF OUR FORESTS.

PINE PLANTATIONS.

Anyone who reads agricultural notes or the other items of news from the country districts must be familiar with paragraphs intimating that, on certain dates, so many thousand acres, comprising numerous blocks, will be made available for selection under certain conditions. The average reader is pleased to know that the country is fast filling up, and that the stability of Australia as a nation is assured by the ever-increasing number of successful farms brought under cultivation throughout the land. The splendid oversea market for butter has made the small farm a success, and for the production of butter, scrub land, cleared and in grass, provides the finest pasture. It follows that the opening up of scrub lands, divided into small areas, results in the rapid disappearance of the scrub itself; and the demand for such land is so strong that the preservation of large areas as timber reserves is a policy that any Government must have a difficulty in maintaining.

There are still magnificent assets in the shape of timber lands in the Commonwealth, but the pressure of the farmer, anxious for the possession of the best dairying land, is already severe, and such pressure is sure to increase as railways open up facilities for transport. The individual farmer cannot be expected to conserve timber for the use of future generations under the present regulations, and it is open to question if the locking-up of scrub lands suitable for dairying for the purpose of preserving the timber growing on such land is a satisfactory solution of the problem.

For the growth of the pine-tree, scrub land is necessary. Nature, however, does not plant her wild scrubs with pine-trees as an orchardist plants his acres with fruit-trees. Many acres may have few pine-trees, and a few acres may have many. In all timber reserves the really valuable trees are scattered, and, if brought together, would occupy a comparatively small area. Pine-trees improve, for commercial purposes, when they grow in close proximity. The sizes, when the trees have matured, are most suitable for mill requirements. Trees that have too much space are frequently too large to handle, and much of their growth has to be wasted before they can be removed from the land to the mill. The pine-trees are well adapted for artificial planting, and the occupation of scrub lands by farmers might be a means of increasing, instead of decreasing, the supply of this valuable timber, under new regulations.

With this object in view, the State should make it a condition of selection that a certain number of pine-trees should be planted for every acre selected. Instead of being scattered far and wide, the trees would be in plantations. By mutual arrangement the farmers might easily bring their plantations together at boundary-lines, and, at the end of the lease, when the purchasing terms were fulfilled, the plantations would prove their value to every farmer, and their preservation would be certain.

In many ways such plantations would be to the advantage of a neighbourhood, and a farmer who produces butter should take an interest and pride in producing the timber in which his butter must be packed to reach the market. Such plantations could be easily protected from fires, and should a fire destroy one plantation it would be confined to a limited area. Every State in the Commonwealth is deeply interested in the future supplies of good pine; and the throwing open of scrub lands, combined with proper regulations for the permanent production of this valuable timber, is surely a solution of the difficulty, more reasonable in every way than the closing of lands that may not average more than one or two good trees to the acre.—*Sydney Morning Herald.*

GOVERNMENT LABOUR BUREAU.

REPORT FOR NOVEMBER.

Mr. James Longmore, the Superintendent of the Government Labour Bureau, reports as follows for the month of November:—

PERTH.

Registrations.—The total number of individual men who called during the month in search of work was 663. Of this number 325 were new registrations and 338 renewals, *i.e.*, men who called who had been registered during the year prior to the month of November. The trades or occupations of the 663 applicants were as follows:—Labourers, 211; handy lads, 85; handy men, 52; farm hands. 45; bushmen, 29; cooks, 23; carpenters. 18; painters, 18; drivers, 14; yardmen, 14; gardeners, 11; grooms, 9; miners, 9; kitchenmen, 6; shearers. 6; bakers, butchers, blacksmiths, engine-drivers, firemen, fitters, and platelayers, 5 of each; bricklayers, brickmakers, and plumbers, 4 of each; clerks, carpenters (rough), electricians, hotel hands, ironmongers, joiners, orderlies, and strikers, 3 of each; and 42 miscellaneous.

Engagements.—The engagements for the month numbered 264. The classification of work found was as follows:—Labourers, 124; farm hands, 44; handy boys, 17; bushmen, 14; handy men, 14; painters, 8; carpenters, 5; cooks, 4; boys for farms, 3; kitchenmen, 3; gardeners, horsedrivers, ironmoulders. orderlies, plumbers, shepherds, woodcutters, and yardmen, 2 of each; and 12 miscellaneous.

KALGOORLIE.

Registrations.—The applicants for work numbered 60. There were 23 new registrations and 37 renewals. The classification was as follows:— Labourers, 19; handy men, 14; fitters, 5; cooks, 4; miners, 4; handy youths, 3; engine-drivers, carpenters, ironmoulders, and firemen, 2 of each; bakers, blacksmiths, and printers, 1 of each.

Engagements.—The engagements were 3, viz,:—2 labourers and 1 handy man.

The female servants who called numbered 32. The classification was as follows:—Charwomen, 5; cooks, 4; housemaids, waitresses, generals, housekeepers, and useful girls, 3 of each; barmaids, 2; and laundresses, 1. There were two engagements, viz:—1 general and 1 laundress.

NORTHAM.

Registrations.—There were 58 applicants for work, classified as follows:—Farm hands, 26; labourers, 14; stack builders, 3; handy men, 3; contractors, 5; bushmen 2; handy lads, 2; kitchenmen, engine-drivers, and carpenters, 1 of each.

Engagements.—The engagements for the month numbered 18, viz.:— Chaff-cutters, 7; farm hands, 5; contractors, 2; bushmen, kitchenmen, stack builder, and engine-driver, 1 of each.

WOMEN'S BRANCH, PERTH.

Registrations.—The new registrations for the month were 61, and the renewals 77. The classification was as follows:—Laundress-charwoman, 29; generals, 21; housemaids, 18; cooks, 16, housekeepers 15; useful girls, 12; light generals, 11; waitresses, 5; lady helps, 3; and 8 miscellaneous.

Engagements.—There were 86 engagements, classified as follows:— Laundress-charwomen, 29; generals, 21; useful girls, 11; light generals, 6; cooks, 5; housemaids, 4; cook-laundresses, 3; wardsmaids, 2; kitchenmaids, 2; and 3 miscellaneous.

GENERAL REMARKS.

The number of individual men who called at the Central Office, Perth, during the month was 663. This total is 29 in excess of the number for October, and also 4 for that of the month of November of last year. The engagements totalled 264, this being the third highest monthly total for the year, being 37 in excess of the previous month, and also 58 for that of the month of November of last year. The railway fares refunded during the month amounted to £31 17s. 6d., and the sum of £13 15s. 1d. was received from employers to send men, also £4 17s. 5d. to send women; the whole amounting to £50 10s.

At Kalgoorlie branch the callers numbered 92, viz.:—60 men and 32 women. There were 3 men and 2 women found situations. At Northam branch there were 58 applicants for work, and 18 engagements. At the women's branch, Perth, there were 138 callers, and 86 engagements.

AGRICULTURE IN TRANSVAAL.

The last file of newspapers from Johannesburg relate the healthy development of the recently established Experimental Farms. The farm at Potchefstrom is a particularly bright example of it.

Already the sphere of its usefulness is being felt in the Colony, but its work has barely commenced, though its equipment is rapidly nearing completion.

Early in November a representative gathering, headed by the Governor General, Lord Selborne, accompanied by Dr. A. Jameson, the Commissioner of Lands, attended the second sale of the progeny of the pure-bred stock recently imported into the country.

In his speech at the luncheon which preceded the sale, Lord Selborne, referring to the initatory work done on the farm as only the beginning of far greater work—the beginning of an agricultural college where the sons of farmers, intending themselves to be farmers, can go and learn all that can be learnt from experiment and from science to supplement their native knowledge. Because more and more the farmer must realise that science is necessary in the promotion of agriculture. You have a wonderful example of it here in the Transvaal. What but science carried out by assiduous labour over a continuous period of time has resulted in the immunisation of mules from horse-sickness? And what will you say when horses are immunised too? Just think of the immense assistance to the farmer, which he never could have done for himself, but which could only be done by continuous and sustained work in a Government institution by trained scientists.

In the afternoon a number of bulls, sheep, and pigs were offered for sale under the hammer and were distributed at highly satisfactory prices. The purchasers hailed from all parts of the Colony, and the stock will in consequence be well distributed.

In connection with this sale and after the auctioneer's conditions had been announced, Mr. Holm, the farm manager, announced those of the Department of Agriculture, chief amongst which was that farmers and stockbreeders only owning or occupying land in the Transvaal Colony, may purchase any of the animals at the sale, and by such purchase they shall be deemed to have undertaken not to export any of the said animals from the Colony within two years after the date of purchase.

To us in Western Australia it is pleasant to chronicle this successful sale, as since the present Minister for Agriculture, Mr. James Mitchell, has assumed the control of the agricultural interest of this State, it has been his policy to hold such annual stock sales in connection with the disposal of the pure-bred stock reared on the State farms.

CONSTRUCTING SILOS.

ESSENTIAL QUALITIES WHICH THEY MUST HAVE.

It does not matter what material the silo is made of; it must be air-tight on sides and at bottom. Any crack or knothole or poor joint at the door will admit air, and the silage will rot just in proportion to the amount of air that enters. The receptacle must be strong enough to withstand the lateral pressure of the silage when it settles. This lateral pressure at 10 feet from the top is 110 pounds per square foot, at 20 feet 220 pounds, and at 30 feet 330 pounds, and at 40 feet 440 pounds. It is very difficult to make deep rectangular silos whose walls will not spring enough to allow air to circulate up and down the sides and cause losses.

DEPTH OF THE SILO.

This should be made as great as practical, because, first, in this way the largest amount of food per cubic foot of space may be stored; and, second, the silage keeps better because packed so solid; and third, there is less relative loss at the surface. The top of the silage always spoils to a depth of two to eight inches. No silo should be less than twenty-five feet deep. A silo 20 x 40 will hold twice as much as one 20 x 25, and one 36 feet deep will hold five times as much as one 12 feet deep.

Summer silos should be deeper in proportion than those intended for winter use, because the silage spoils faster in summer and must be fed down at the rate of about three inches a day to have always fresh silage.

FOUNDATION.

This must stand on level, firm earth, and should extend about two feet above the surface of the ground. If the foundation is started deep, the hole should be dug large enough to give ample room outside of the wall to thoroughly tamp the earth up close to the foundation. There is a tremendous outward pressure against the wall, especially in deep silos, and if it is not made strong it will crack and admit air. It is also well to build into this wall, about eighteen inches above the surface of the ground, several heavy wires to keep the wall from cracking. It should be made of stone or brick, laid in cement mortar, or of concrete, and from twelve to eighteen inches thick, depending on the height the silo is to extend above it.

PLACED PARTLY IN GROUND.

It is a good plan to dig down four or five feet in order to secure good firm earth on which to start the foundation, and also in order to get the greatest capacity in the silo without going too high into the air. Deeper than five feet would not be either convenient or safe.

Care must be taken in wet places not to dig down much, or else the soil must be drained. In many places even a good wall of stone, laid in cement and well plastered inside with cement, will not keep the water out. In some parts of the South the houses can have no cellars on this account.

PAINTING OF WOOD SILOS.

A coat of paint or tar on the inside of a wooden silo does not prevent the silage juice getting into the wood, but does retard it drying out when the

(4)

silo is empty and thus hastens decay. The outside may be painted and the inside washed with a wood preservative—something that will not hold the water and will destroy the mold plant in the wood.

PLOUGHING BY STEAM.

Mr. G. Buchanan, late of this Department, has handed us a most interesting letter on the use of steam engines for ploughing, from which we clip the following :—

" I had a very interesting time (at Geelong), and saw many up-to-date methods of getting a lot of work done in a little time, and a good deal of the latest machinery in the agricultural line. With regard to steam traction, I think it is the coming power on large farms wherever the country is fairly solid and not too hilly. Of course the initial outlay is somewhat large ; but a good engine, with reasonable care, will last a lifetime, and it will plough land in a condition that no man would care to tackle with horses. No matter how hard and dry it is, if you can get a plough to go into it, you can plough it. I saw three steam ploughs on the Lara Plains (a continuation of the Werribee Plains), and the particular one that I went to see was an object lesson to any man. The engine is an eight-horsepower compound, built by Burvill & Sons, England, and she was pulling three seven-furrow ploughs. When I was told of this I did not believe it, for I thought 21 furrows beyond any eight-horsepower engine ; but when I saw it 1 had to admit that it was a fact. The ploughs were discs, built for the purpose, by T. Robinson & Co., whose agent went out with me.

" The young fellows who are running this plant bought it on spec., and it has turned out a good one. The engine cost £800, and the ploughs cost about £40 each, and they have broken up about 6,000 acres of that country with it. They are contractors, and average about 15 acres a day in all weathers. Their price is 8s. an acre.

" This engine is the same make as ours, and is the same H.P., though of a slightly different type. She weighs 15 tons, and works up to 150 lbs. pressure, and she was not all out even with that load on. You can calculate how many horses and how much hard swearing it would take to do the same work.

" Another plant was an 8 h.p. Fowler pulling 8 furrows (Mouldboards), and was also doing good work, these ploughs of course pulling heavier than the discs, but making a nicer job.

Another plant, an 8 h.p. Ransome and Sims engine, with three five-furrow disc ploughs, was waiting for fine weather for a start. One thing worthy of note was that on account of heavy rain these two engines were laid up, while the Burvill, the heaviest engine by two tons, was working comfortably, which proves that it is a question of manufacture and not of weight. The idea in this part of the world is that English engines are too heavy, and that the country will only carry them in the summer ; but it is a mistaken idea, for the Burvill 15-ton engine will work where a wagon with a 4-ton load will bog. One engine has driving wheels 7 feet in diameter and

20 inches wide, and will go anywhere as long as the ground is not greasy. By using grips that difficulty can be overcome.

" N. and I are busy ploughing now. We are not pulling 21 furrows— we content ourselves with two three-furrows, and stick another on on fine days. We get along very well, and are doing about seven acres a day and have about 70 done; but this is awful country to break up, and in its present condition eight horses would not pull a three-furrow constantly. This may sound rash, but it is a fact. All the same I struck it out with four horses in a double, and they were all out though they were big powerful horses. I get along very well with the engine for a new chum, and we make as good a job as possible because the farmers for miles round are visiting us. We work the job ourselves with a lad carting wood and water. We only use 600 gallons daily, and about a ton of wood, so that the working expenses are small. By and by, when we get into our gait, I will find out about the cost per acre and let you know. I have kept a careful record of all the expenses of cropping this year, so that when we get our returns for the coming harvest, I will be able to give you a pretty accurate account of the cost of obtaining a crop. The cost per acre for labour is surprisingly small, but we got our crops in very quickly this year."

THE FUTURE OF THE HORSE.

The horse is declared by some people to be doomed on account of the extending use of tramcars, motors, and motor 'buses. The impression is fostered by the noisiness of the innovation, and the compulsory idleness of many horse vehicles. " Cab, sir," is frequently uttered to inattentive ears, as the newly-arrived passengers in many towns make their way to the trams. Horses of a certain class are cheap, but, on the other hand, hunters and agricultural horses are dear. It therefore seems as though electricity and petrol have affected the value of some classes of horses, but not others; and the question as between horses and mechanical power is by no means settled. The public is not unanimous in opinion as to the relative merits of the two systems. A great number of people look upon trams, motors, and motor 'buses with intense antipathy. They consider them dangerous, noisy, ugly, and nerve-shaking; that they injure the roads and depreciate the value of property near the highways; and that they are injurious to hay and other crops, and destroy the beauty of hedgerows and trees. The letters which appear every day in the daily papers are often couched in the strongest possible language, and yet the " nuisance " grows, and probably will continue to grow. There will be improvements, and in a few years many of the objections may possibly be met. Still, at the present time they undoubtedly exist, and the idea that our old friend and companion the horse is being gradually thrust out of existence is sometimes expressed. Hunters and polo ponies are safe, although the novelty of motoring has proved in some cases attractive.

The principal fact against the view of the extinction, or even the considerable diminution, of the horse is that there are more horses in the country now than there were six years ago, and, probably, more than at any previous period. Whether there are more in the towns it is impossible to say, in the absence of a horse census, but the agricultural statistics are against the idea of extinction. So is the price of oats, which are essentially horse-corn, for no cereal has kept up in value better, in spite of foreign competition. Hay is not likely to be cheap this winter, so that neither of the principal horse foods afford indications of diminished demand. That hay has been cheap must be attributed to superabundance, owing to successive good crops, and to foreign competition, largely due to the high prices of three or four years since. Many farmers at that time went in exclusively for hay-growing and selling, and spoiled their own market; but hay is now likely to be dear again. It would be a great misfortune to agriculture if horses were generally supplanted by motor-power, but there are many reasons why this fear is not likely to be consummated. The present craze for speed and dust is inconsistent with true pleasure, and we may soon see a re-action. The horse has many advantages which it may be well to mention. He is a unit of power which can be much more conveniently applied than motor-power. We can drive one horse in a light trap, or two horses in a four-wheeler, or three or four in a brake; whereas the many-horse-power motor must be used for one individual at a very considerable waste of energy. Again, horses are less liable to breakdowns and accidents, and do not require repairs, but only rest. Neither are they subject to the same depreciation in value as a machine, and may increase in value, while motors must depreciate, and that very rapidly.

So far as agricultural horses are concerned, there are no complaints, for good horses of this class are at a premium. The convenience of horse-power on farms is even more marked than in the case of carriage horses. One may be used to draw a wagon or cart, and the power is easily doubled, trebled, or quadrupled without waste. The horses are not puzzled by soft ground, which entails two or three instead of one, and they are easily cleaned, and kept in good order. They have stood their ground wonderfully against steam, and may be relied upon to stand against motor-power. Besides, they are cheaper than mechanical power. They may be managed so as to be profitable, as a £40 3-year-old may become a £60 4-year-old, and an £80 5-year-old; but a 5-year-old motor would be difficult to dispose of at any price. Horses are adaptable to any sort of farm-work. They can cut the corn and carry it, plough the land, and drill the seed, and haul out dung over muddy roads without clogging or breaking. They make manure, and thus return a large proportion of their food to the land. They live well upon fodder which is not of the most saleable sort, and eat up the lighter oats which would only fetch a low price on the market. They graze rough ground at little expense, and, in fact, this cost cannot be estimated on the basis of ordinary market values. There are, therefore, many advantages to the credit of horses beyond a hard-and-fast calculation based on the market prices of hay and corn. The depreciation owing to age is very light, not amounting to more than £2 or £3 a year on an average, and the risks from accident, disease, or death are not heavy. On the other hand, the deprecia-tion, supercession, and risks of motor-power are simply incalculable, as an improvement in mechanism may quickly reduce the value of a machine to that of old iron. We may therefore say with confidence, "Long live the horse!" May he continue to reap our harvests and plough our land, to carry us, and trot before us on the road. There is room for him as well as for motors, and there is no reason why both should not exist together, each in the sphere most appropriate to its peculiar advantages.—*English Live Stock Journal.*

GARDEN NOTES FOR JANUARY.

By Percy G. Wicken.

This is not the best time of the year for the vegetable garden. Where a supply of water is not available for irrigation, most of the more delicate plants will be feeling the effects of the dry weather. As soon as any plant ceases to be profitable or productive, it should he pulled up and placed on the manure heap or destroyed. Old peas, cabbages, beet, etc., which have started to run to seed, are of no further use in the garden, and should be destroyed unless it is intended to save a few plants for seed. All weeds should be cut down before the seed become ripe, and by this means they can be kept in check. The number of seeds shed from one plant is enormous, and as many as 1,000 to 1,500 young plants, as the result of allowing a dock-weed to shed its seed, are not uncommon. Many weed plants will ripen their seed after being cut down, if allowed to remain on the ground, and for this reason it is better to burn all weeds, or to place them on a compost heap, where the seeds will be destroyed. As soon as the ground becomes idle it should be dug up deeply and allowed to lie fallow until time for autumn planting takes place. The ground will then become well aerated, and will be in better condition for growing vegetables than if allowed to remain in a hard-baked condition during the summer.

Cut-worms are particularly troublesome at the present time; they eat the leaves and stems of plants and often cause the stem to break off and the plant dies. They are generally to be found in the ground close round the stem of the plant, and if the ground is disturbed may be easily found. They are a brownish colour, somewhat the same as the soil. Constant stirring of the soil helps somewhat to keep them in check, as also does liming the soil with caustic lime; but the most effective way to destroy them is to spray the plants with a mixture of Paris green and water at the rate of 1oz. of Paris green to 10 gallons of water. First mix the Paris green to a paste and then add the water, spray the plants on both sides of the leaves and keep the mixture well stirred while using.

If the black rot appears among the tomatoes, the plants should be tied up to stakes to keep the fruit off the ground and all diseased fruit should be picked and burned.

The early tomatoes are now coming into market. If sprayed earlier in the season with Bordeaux mixture to which a little Paris green has been added they will not be so likely to be attacked by disease. If the ground is kept well stirred, in addition to helping to conserve the moisture, the attacks of insect pests are kept in check, as the turning up to the sun of many insects in their immature state destroys them.

Beans. —Any kind of the summer-growing beans may be sown where the ground is sufficiently moist to germinate the seed. Beans should not be sown on the same ground as they were grown in the previous year, but this ground should be reserved for root crops, or some other tribe that will make use of the nitrogen collected from the air by these leguminous plants.

Madagascar beans are prolific bearers, and grow well in the hottest weather. They are somewhat strong in flavour, but are relished by many people.

Lima beans are one of the most delicious of the bean tribe, but have been very little cultivated in this State. The Black Pole Lima will stand a great amount of heat and drought. The white seeded varieties are the best for table and bear well.

BEET (Silver).—This is one of our most valuable summer plants; in many gardens it is the only thing that continues to give a supply of green leaves when all else is dried up   It is valuable both for table and for providing green food for poultry and other farm stock.   It is late for sowing now, except in exceptionally favourable localities, but large quantities should be sown earlier in the season.   If the outer leaves are cut off as required it will continue to send out leaves from the centre for some months.

CABBAGE.—Keep those already up well cultivated and give them a little liquid manure if available.   A little seed may be planted in a shady place where they can be watered to keep up a supply of plants.

CELERY.—Earth up any plants that are well forward, but care must be taken not to let any earth get into the hearts.

CHOKOS.—Those planted early in the season should now have climbed over the trellis and be bearing young fruits.   The best way to cook chokos is to boil for a short time until soft and then bake with the meat.

CUCUMBERS are now plentiful and cheap.   In moist situations a further supply of seed may be sown, but the holes should be deeply worked and the young plants shaded by a few bushes as soon as they break the ground.

EGG PLANT.—If enough plants are not out a few more may be transplanted but they will require to be well shaded, and are not likely to yield so well as the early sown ones.

MAIZE.—The cultivator should be kept going between the rows of maize already up and the earth should be hilled up towards the plants.   A few more rows may be sown in moist situations.   The cobs should be picked before they become hard, if required for table use.

MELONS should be fit for market.   Pick out a few of the best of each kind, true to name and mark them with a knife for seed; the marks will soon show and they can then be reserved.

OKRAS.— If required for pickles the pods should be picked while green if seeds are required allow the pods to become dry before picking.

ONIONS.—A little seed may be sown for garden purposes if water is available and any young plants put out.   The main crop should now be fit for market.

PUMPKINS AND SQUASHES.—All the early varieties should be ripe by now, and supplies will be plentiful; keep the cultivator going between the rows until the vines cover the ground.   A few more of the quick-growing bush varieties of squashes may be sown in moist localities to provide for a late supply.

SWEET POTATOES.—Early planted shoots should now be making a good growth.   As soon as the runners have become strong, the plants, unless planted on hills, should be hilled up and the centres between the hills kept well cultivated; this can be done by a special attachment to the cultivator, which lifts the vines.

TOMATOES.—The market is fairly well supplied with tomatoes, but the quality is inferior. Good prices can be obtained for first-class smooth-skinned fruit, free from disease, and growers should select only good varieties when sowing and obtain their seed from a reliable source. Tomatoes should not be planted on the same ground two seasons running, and should not follow after the potato crop, as they belong to the same species. All plants should be staked as soon as high enough, so as to keep them off the ground. A few more young plants can be put out if well shaded and watered.

FARM.—Harvesting in the field, except in a few late localities, will be over before these Notes appear. There will remain, however, plenty of work in thrashing, winnowing, chaff-cutting, etc., before the crop is ready for market. These operations, although not so urgent as the getting the crop in from the field, require to be carried out as soon as possible. Those who intend to keep their hay until later in the season should get their stacks thatched as soon as possible, so as to protect it from any chance storms that may occur and also to plough a fire-break round the stack so as to protect it from bush fires. As the harvesting machinery is finished with it should be thoroughly cleaned and given a good coat of oil before being put away; more machinery is ruined by exposure and neglect than is worn out harvesting the crop. Before the wheat is sent off the farm it will pay to run it through a grader, as a better sample can be secured and a higher price obtained, especially if the best sample can be sold for seed. Any surplus straw should be stacked and saved for the winter, when it will form a valuable addition to the feed for the store stock when grass is scarce. Potatoes have given fairly good returns, but the proportion lost by disease still continues to form a large percentage of the crop. This is due in some respect to the seed obtainable being so weakened by excessive propagation that it is very susceptible to disease, and also in a great measure to the lack of precautions to prevent attacks of insect pests. If the tops were sprayed with Bordeaux mixture before any signs of disease occur it would help to keep diseases in check. Most people wait until the attack is so bad that the crop is almost lost before they take any steps to spray the plants. The increased vigour of the plant can only be secured by the raising of new varieties from seed and not from tubers, and this is a business of itself. Onions are a most profitable crop, and why they are not more extensively grown is a question hard to answer. They certainly require care and attention, but the returns are sufficient to pay for the labour. At Northam this season the average return from one garden has been eight tons per acre, and there were several acres under this crop; the price has been from £15 to £20 per ton, and at times higher, consequently this ought to make the crop a profitable one to grow.

Bot-flies become troublesome at this time of the year. Once the larvæ of the fly gets into the intestines of the horse very little can be done to dislodge them, consequently the only thing to do is to prevent the larvæ from obtaining entrance. The bot-fly lays its eggs on the jaw and shoulder of the horse, the animal licks them off, and the eggs hatch out in the stomach of the animal. If the jaw and shoulder of the horse are well washed every night and rubbed with carbolised oil it will prevent the fly from laying its eggs, as the smell is objectionable to it. When the eggs are swallowed the grub hatches out and attaches itself to the intestines of the animal and feeds in the juices in the stomach, often causing the loss of the animal.

NOTES ON THE CLIMATE FOR THE MONTH OF NOVEMBER, 1906.

The weather on the whole has been of a normal character. Several "lows" have passed across from the N.W. coast towards the Bight, causing slight weather disturbances, principally inland.

On the 16th the disturbance was somewhat marked in extreme eastern settlements, the temperature reaching 100° at Laverton, with a fresh N.W. gale. This "low" passed across to South Australia, and caused very heavy rain in that State. Towards the end of the month very heavy rain was recorded at Port Darwin, in South Australia, and a little later at Wyndham. where 355 points fell during the 24 hours ending 8 a.m. on the 30th, This was connected with a "low" which travelled down the Indian Ocean, keeping, roughly, parallel to the coast all the way from Wyndham (and probably even from Port Darwin), round to the Leeuwin, which it passed on 4th December, being preceded by considerable heat (100° at the Perth Observatory), and followed by a cool change, with a little coastal rain. On the whole, pressure was below the average for previous years in the tropics, but elsewhere about normal. Temperature was mostly about normal, except on the Murchison and Coolgardie Goldfields, especially the latter. At Coolgardie the mean maximum was only 79·7°, or 7·2° below the average for previous years, and considerably lower than in any other November since records commenced in 1897. The hottest place in the State was, as usual, Marble Bar, where the mean of the daily maxima was 106·3°, and the absolute maximum for the month was 114·0° The mean monthly temperature there was 89·0°, and even this was exceeded at Wyndham (89·9°) owing to the very hot nights which prevail there. As a contrast to these unpleasant temperatures we notice that the mean maximum at Cape Naturaliste was only 68·6°, at Cape Leeuwin 69·5°, and at Breaksea Island, in the extreme South, 63·2°.

Owing to the disturbance at the end of the month the rainfall was above the average in the extreme N.E. It was also moderately heavy at scattered places on the goldfields and in the S.E. owing to occasional thunderstorms, but otherwise it was very light.

W. E. COOKE,
Government Astronomer.

The Observatory, Perth, 11th December, 1906.

The Climate of Western Australia during November, 1906.

Locality	Barometer (corrected and reduced to sea-level).				Shade Temperature.									Rainfall.		
	Mean of 9 a.m. and 3 p.m.	Average for previous years.	Highest for Month.	Lowest for Month.	November, 1906.					Average for previous Years.				Points (100 to inch) in Month.	Wet Days.	Total Points since Jan 1.
					Mean Max.	Mean Min.	Mean of Month.	Highest Max.	Lowest Min.	Mean Max.	Mean Min.	Highest ever recorded.	Lowest ever recorded.			
NORTH-WEST AND NORTH COAST:																
Wyndham	29·764	29·856	29·975	29·487	98·1	81·7	89·9	105·0	74·0	98·5	80·9	111·6	69·2	367	4	1833
Derby	29·832	29·865	29·998	29·614	100·9	77·2	89·0	106·8	70·0	98·4	76·7	112·5	66·8	12	1	1161
Broome	29·794	29·875	29·947	29·609	95·7	76·9	86·3	103·5	69·8	92·9	76·0	111·0	67·4	Nil		1016
Condon	29·811	29·876	29·966	29·611	96·3	69·3	82·8	110·0	60·4	94·4	68·5	112·8	49·2	Nil		678
Cossack	29·835	29·880	29·950	29·580	96·0	70·0	83·0	110·0	60·0	97·7	71·1	111·7	57·6	Nil		1013
Onslow	29·858	29·902	29·953	29·666	92·9	65·6	79·2	108·0	60·8	93·8	65·3	111·0	50·0	Nil		652
Winning Pool														7	1	960
Carnarvon	29·932	29·978	30·106	29·805	80·0	65·9	73·0	92·0	56·4	81·6	64·9	109·1	50·4	Nil		744
Hamelin Pool	29·912	29·954	30·109	29·753	86·6	61·1	73·8	99·0	53·8	89·4	59·8	109·0	46·6	8	1	503
Geraldton	29·978	30·020	30·151	29·706	76·5	58·1	67·3	98·3	47·0	76·7	57·7	103·8	45·0	11	1	2041
Hall's Creek	29·785	29·876	30·021	29·609	100·8	73·7	87·2	109·0	57·0	100·8	74·6	109·4	56·4	6	2	684
Marble Bar					106·3	71·8	89·0	114·0	67·5	106·3	72·7	116·4	59·8	7	1	985
Nullagine	29·785	29·842	30·047	29·563	103·4	69·8	86·6	112·6	55·3	101·9	69·5	114·0	52·0	Nil	2	980
Peak Hill	29·840	29·866	30·061	29·603	98·2	65·6	79·4	108·0	55·2	94·2	67·1	108·5	45·4	8	1	939
Wia	29·829	29·848	30·183	29·530	90·2	62·6	76·4	103·0	52·0	93·2	68·5	107·2	38·5	4	1	720
Ge	29·870	29·910	30·142	29·617	91·4	60·9	76·2	104·7	50·3	93·2	62·9	108·2	45·0		1	929
Murgoo		29·930			88·6	61·5	75·0	101·0	52·0					38	1	772
Yalgoo	29·916		30·168	29·600	86·0	57·1	71·6	102·2	48·0	91·1	59·2	107·7	42·8	46	2	1024
INLAND:																
Nungarra	29·897	29·906	30·236	29·550	87·5	61·0	74·2	102·0	51·0	91·1	63·6	105·4	41·1			718
Lawlers	29·895	29·935	30·276	29·563	85·4	59·8	72·6	100·2	47·3	90·8	62·9	105·6	42·7	14	1	768
Barton	29·936	29·926	30·279	29·574	83·7	57·1	70·4	100·8	44·0	89·0	61·0	105·9	39·3	16	3	808
Menzies					80·5	54·2	67·4	90·2	43·0	83·3	57·4	106·1	40·3	Nil		976
Kanowna	29·946	29·954	30·319	29·586	81·2	54·3	67·8	99·6	44·4	87·3	58·6	107·8	40·6	89	4	874
Kalgoorlie	29·949	29·953	30·324	29·512	79·7	53·1	66·4	98·0	42·9	86·9	57·1	107·1	39·3	84	4	944
Coolgardie	29·960	29·946	30·310	29·520	83·0	55·0	69·0	99·0	42·0	87·7	55·3	109·5	37·8	99	6	912
Southern Cross														55	3	1063
Kellerberrin					81·4	53·3	67·4	98·2	44·2	80·7	51·9	108·8	36·4	50	3	2040
Walebing					83·4	53·4	68·4	97·5	42·9	88·4	53·5	109·1	38·3	73	5	1745
Northam					82·6	52·8	67·7	98·0	42·0	82·9	52·5	110·2	39·2	28	2	1435
York	29·977	30·007	30·306	29·541	79·3	54·9	67·1	98·0	47·0	79·4	55·0	106·2	40·7	53	2	1436
Guildford														18	4	3008

The Climate of Western Australia during November, 1906—continued.

Locality	Barometer (corrected and reduced to sea-level).				Shade Temperatures. November, 1906.					Average for previous Years.				Rainfall.		
	Mean of 9 a.m. and 3 p.m.	Average for previous years.	Highest for Month.	Lowest for Month.	Mean Max.	Mean Min.	Mean of Month.	Highest Max.	Lowest Min.	Mean Max.	Mean Min.	Highest ever recorded.	Lowest ever recorded.	Points (100 to inch) in Month.	Wet Days.	Total Points since Jan. 1.
SOUTH-WEST AND SOUTH COAST:																
Perth Gardens ...	30·000	30·027	30·324	29·650	77·6	57·1	67·4	92·0	50·8	78·6	57·1	102·1	44·0	18	3	3551
Perth Observatory	30·010	30·036	30·279	29·638	75·1	56·8	65·8	89·0	49·9	74·8	56·4	100·9	42·0	22	4	3233
Fremantle ...	30·016	30·044	30·305	29·667	72·9	57·7	65·3	89·0	51·0	72·0	58·1	98·6	42·5	20	3	2470
Rottnest ...	30·026	30·024	30·282	29·681	70·5	58·2	64·4	87·0	52·8	71·0	59·1	96·3	48·6	5	3	2096
Mandurah ...	...	...	...	...	75·8	54·6	65·2	89·3	46·0	76·9	53·9	98·4	36·9	112	8	1965
Marradong ...	...	...	...	...	...	...	...	...	...	...	...	...	...	6	4	2625
Wandering ...	...	...	...	...	77·9	47·9	62·9	99·8	37·0	78·6	46·7	16·0	35·8	1	1	2386
Narrogin ...	...	...	...	...	...	...	...	...	...	...	...	...	...	...	...	...
Collie ...	...	...	...	...	76·1	48·0	62·0	87·8	38·5	75·7	48·1	99·8	35·9	13	3	3721
Donnybrook ...	30·087	30·049	30·46	...	76·6	51·9	64·2	88·9	41·3	75·0	49·9	97·8	36·8	11	3	1607
Bunbury ...	...	...	...	...	74·8	52·8	63·8	86·9	43·5	73·2	53·1	97·2	39·3	4	2	3106
Busselton ...	...	...	...	...	74·0	51·2	62·6	86·2	41·2	73·6	50·6	93·8	39·2	10	3	3330
Cape Naturaliste	30·056	...	30·334	29·693	68·6	53·3	61·0	80·8	45·5	...	...	...	...	17	7	3115
Bridgetown ...	...	...	...	...	75·1	47·1	61·1	89·1	35·0	75·1	47·0	98·0	35·5	45	6	3361
Karridale ...	30·050	30·054	30·340	29·854	70·0	52·0	61·0	86·0	43·0	76·1	52·1	95·0	38·0	43	7	3844
Cape Leeuwin ...	30·036	30·024	30·322	29·689	69·5	57·8	63·6	78·5	51·5	68·2	57·6	88·4	44·0	52	15	3316
Katanning ...	30·18	30·010	30·365	29·733	75·8	48·5	62·2	91·0	38·0	77·8	49·5	106·0	37·0	108	4	1803
Mt. Barker ...	...	...	...	...	74·1	48·7	61·1	86·8	41·9	...	...	...	...	165	20	2535
Albany ...	30·060	30·032	30·382	29·975	68·0	53·5	60·8	83·0	47·0	68·7	52·4	98·5	40·6	60	14	3691
Breaksea ...	30·052	30·038	30·385	29·801	63·2	54·5	58·8	77·8	48·2	65·2	54·9	88·0	43·2	51	17	3191
Esperance ...	30·18	30·029	30·320	29·780	68·5	53·3	60·9	85·0	48·8	78·4	54·4	105·0	39·2	180	9	2407
Balladonia ...	29·96	30·025	30·317	29·783	74·3	49·2	61·6	89·9	39·0	81·5	51·1	106·4	40·0	161	10	801
Eyre ...	29·78	30·035	30·311	29·889	69·7	51·6	60·6	91·8	35·4	74·0	54·3	108·1	34·5	148	12	601
INTERSTATE.																
Perth ...	30·010	30·036	30·279	29·888	75·1	56·6	65·8	89·0	49·9	74·8	56·4	100·9	42·0	22	4	3233
Adelaide ...	29·912	30·008	30·281	29·843	73·2	52·7	63·0	90·4	44·3	79·0	55·4	113·5	40·9	245	11	2487
Melbourne ...	29·871	29·875	30·231	29·811	67·0	49·5	58·2	87·3	40·6	71·3	50·9	105·7	38·5	247	12	2165
Sydney ...	29·920	29·961	30·260	29·860	74·0	58·0	66·0	92·0	48·0	74·3	59·6	102·7	46·2	412	12	3028

The Observatory, Perth, 7th December, 1906.

W. E. COOKE, Government Astronomer.

RAINFALL for October, 1906 (completed as far as possible), and for November, 1906 (principally from Telegraphic Reports).

Stations.	October. No. of points 100 = 1in.	October. No. of wet days.	November. No. of points 100 = 1in.	November. No. of wet days.
EAST KIMBERLEY:				
Wyndham ...	150	2	367	4
6-Mile ...	...	...	...	...
Carlton ...	229	3	...	...
Ivanhoe ...	275	4	...	...
Argyle Downs ...	...	...	...	...
Rosewood Downs	518	8	...	...
Lisadell ...	...	...	...	...
Turkey Creek ...	100	4	203	5
Ord River ...	...	...	...	...
Alice Downs ...	...	...	...	...
Flora Valley ...	...	...	...	...
Hall's Creek ...	91	3	6	1
Nicholson Plains	...	...	...	...
Ruby Plains ...	...	...	...	...
Denison Downs	...	...	...	...
WEST KIMBERLEY:				
Mt. Barnett ...	...	...	...	...
Corvendine ...	...	...	...	...
Leopold Downs...	44	3	...	...
Fitzroy Crossing (P.O.)	Nil	...	20	2
Fitzroy Station...	...	...	...	...
Brooking ...	17	1	...	...
Cherrabun ...	21	2	...	...
Bohemia Downs	...	...	...	...
Quanbun ...	Nil	...	...	...
Nookanbah ...	...	...	...	...
Upper Liveringa	...	...	...	...
Yeeda ...	...	...	...	...
Derby ...	2	1	12	1
Pt. Torment ...	...	...	...	...
Obagama ...	19	2	...	...
Beagle Bay ...	...	...	...	...
Roebuck Downs	...	...	...	...
Kimberley Downs	Nil	...	...	...
Broome ...	Nil	...	Nil	...
Thangoo ...	...	...	...	...
La Grange Bay...	Nil	...	Nil	...
N.W. COAST:				
Wallal ...	Nil	...	Nil	...
Pardoo ...	3	1	...	...
Condon ...	2	1	Nil	...
DeGrey River ...	2	1	...	...
Port Hedland ...	21	1	Nil	...
Boodarie ...	6	1	...	...

Stations.	October. No. of points 100 = 1in.	October. No. of wet days.	November. No. of points 100 = 1in.	November. No. of wet days.
N.W. COAST—contd.				
Balla Balla ...	...	...	...	...
Whim Creek ...	20	1	Nil	...
Mallina ...	...	...	...	...
Croydon...	71	1	...	...
Sherlock...	...	...	...	...
Woodbrooke ...	Nil	...	...	...
Cooyapooya ...	Nil	...	...	...
Roebourne ...	Nil	...	...	...
Cossack ...	Nil	...	...	...
Fortescue ...	4	1	...	...
Mardie ...	Nil	...	...	...
Chinginarra ...	Nil	...	...	...
Yarraloola ...	Nil	...	...	...
Peedamullah ...	Nil	...	...	...
Onslow ...	Nil	...	Nil	...
Point Cloates ...	...	...	...	...
N.W. INLAND:				
Warrawagine ...	Nil	...	...	...
Eel Creek ...	Nil	...	...	...
Muccan ...	Nil	...	...	...
Ettrick ...	Nil	...	...	...
Strelly ...	14	1	...	...
Mulgie ...	Nil	...	...	...
Warralong ...	Nil	...	...	...
Coongon ...	Nil	...	...	...
Talga ...	Nil	...	...	...
Bamboo Creek ...	Nil	...	3	1
Moolyella ...	...	...	...	...
Marble Bar ...	2	2	7	2
Warrawoona ...	Nil	...	Nil	...
Corunna Downs ...	2	1	...	...
Mt. Edgar ...	...	...	...	...
Nullagine ...	Nil	...	Nil	...
Middle Creek ...	Nil	...	...	...
Mosquito Creek ...	...	...	...	...
Roy Hill ...	...	...	...	...
Bamboo Springs	Nil	...	...	...
Kerdiadary ...	6	1	...	...
Woodstock ...	Nil	...	...	...
Yandyarra ...	...	...	...	...
Station Peak ...	8	1	...	...
Mulga Downs ...	21	1	...	...
Mt. Florence ...	57	2	...	...
Tambrey ...	29	1	...	...
Millstream ...	39	1	...	...

RAINFALL—continued.

STATIONS.	October. No. of points 100=1in.	October. No. of wet days.	November. No. of points 100=1in.	November. No. of wet days.	STATIONS.	October. No. of points 100=1in.	October. No. of wet days.	November. No. of points 100=1in.	November. No. of wet days.
N.W. INLAND—*contd.*					**YALGOO DISTRICT**—*contd.*				
Red Hill	Nil	...	...	...	Tallyrang	...	...	...	...
Mt. Stewart	...	...	...	...	Mullewa	24	5	Nil	...
Peake Station	28	2	...	...	Kockatea	22	5	...	...
Nanutarra	Nil	...	...	...	Barnong	23	1	...	...
Yanrey	Nil	...	...	...	Gullewa	...	...	37	1
Wogoola	...	...	...	...	Gullewa House	25	1	...	...
Towera	18	2	...	...	Gabyon	70	1	...	...
					Mellenbye	10	2	...	...
GASCOYNE:					Wearagaminda	17	2	40	1
Winning Pool	25	1	7	1	Yalgoo	43	2	42	2
Coordalia	...	...	...	...	Wagga Wagga	6	1	29	2
Wandagee	...	...	...	...	Muralgarra	Nil	...	...	...
Williambury	182	3	...	...	Burnerbinmah	Nil	...	...	...
Yanyeareddy	...	...	...	...	Nalbara	9	3	...	...
Maroonah	...	...	...	...	Wydgee	Nil	...	...	...
Ullawarra	129	2	...	...	Field's Find	7	1	30	2
Mt. Mortimer	...	...	...	...	Thundelarra	19	4	42	2
Edmunds	106	2	...	...	Rothesay	...	...	...	...
Gifford Creek	...	...	...	...	Ninghan	5	1	...	...
Bangemall	21	1	...	...	Condingnow	Nil	...	...	...
Mt. Augustus	...	...	...	...	163-Mile	Nil	...	95	1
Upper Clifton Downs	...	...	...	...	Palaga Rocks	3	1	...	...
Clifton Downs	Nil	...	...	...	126-Mile	Nil	...	60	1
Dairy Creek	...	...	...	...	90-Mile	...	...	54	2
Mearerbundie	31	1	...	...	Mt. Jackson	Nil	...	...	...
Byro	45	4	...	...					
Meedo	29	3	...	...					
Mungarra	57	3	...	...	**MURCHISON:**				
Bintholya	...	...	...	...	Wale	19	2	...	...
Lyon's River	15	2	...	...	Yallalonga	...	...	...	...
Booloogooroo	...	...	...	...	Billabalong	...	...	...	...
Doorawarrah	7	2	Nil	...	Twin Peaks	10	1	...	...
Brick House	...	...	...	...	Murgoo	20	1	38	1
Boolathana	...	...	...	...	Mt. Wittenoom	...	...	...	...
Carnarvon	23	4	92	13	Meka	18	1	...	...
Point Charles	11	1	...	...	Wooleane	10	1	44	1
Dirk Hartog	...	...	...	...	Boolardy	...	...	...	...
Sharks Bay	29	2	14	1	Woogorong	32	1	...	...
Wooramel	33	3	13	2	Manfred	61	2	27	1
Hamelin Pool	13	2	8	1	Yarra Yarra	64	5	...	...
Kararang	...	...	...	...	Milly Milly	32	1	32	1
Tamala	...	...	...	...	Berringarra	41	1	16	1
					Miloura	25	1	...	...
YALGOO DISTRICT:					Mt. Gould	...	...	...	...
Woolgorong	Nil	...	45	1	Moorarie	49	2	...	...
New Forest	25	1	...	...	Wandary	...	...	...	...
Yuin	...	...	...	...	Peak Hill	40	2	8	1
Pindathuna	Nil	...	...	...	Abbotts	40	2	Nil	...
					Belele	...	...	...	...

RAINFALL—continued.

STATIONS.	October. No. of points 100=1in.	October. No. of wet days.	November. No. of points 100=1in.	November. No. of wet days.	STATIONS.	October. No. of points 100=1in.	October. No. of wet days.	November. No. of points 100=1in.	November. No. of wet days.
MURCHISON—contd.					**NORTH COOLGARDIE GOLDFIELDS—contd.**				
Minderoo	25	2	...	...	Mulwarrie	Nil	...	24	3
Gabanintha	21	4	Nil	...	Goongarrie	...	...	55	4
Quinn's	...	...	...	...	**COOLGARDIE GOLDFIELDS:**				
Bungalow	40	2	Nil	...	Waverley	...	...	...	...
Nannine	36	2	7	3	Bardoc	Nil	...	35	2
Annean	40	2	...	...	Broad Arrow	Nil	...	65	4
Tuckanarra	25	1	...	...	Kanowna	Nil	...	89	4
Coodardy	Nil	...	...	...	Kurnalpi	Nil	...	75	4
Cue	51	3	4	1	Bulong	Nil	...	80	4
Day Dawn	26	1	Nil	...	Kalgoorlie	Nil	...	84	4
Lake Austin	51	3	36	1	Coolgardie	Nil	...	99	5
Lennonville	26	5	34	3	Burbanks	Nil	...	74	4
Mt. Magnet	9	1	24	2	Bulla Bulling	Nil	...	...	...
Youeragabbie	22	2	...	...	Woolubar	Nil	...	...	...
Murrum	Nil	...	...	...	Waterdale	Nil	...	76	3
Challa	6	1	...	...	Widgiemooltha	18	4	109	9
Nunngarra	Nil	...	...	...	50-Mile	14	1	177	6
Berrigrin	...	...	...	...	Norseman	21	3	190	9
					Lake View	7	2	172	7
EAST MURCHISON:					Frazer Range	Nil	...	...	...
Gum Creek	70	1	Nil	...	Southern Hills	12	1	...	...
Dural	...	...	...	...	**YILGARN GOLDFIELDS:**				
Wiluna	22	3	1	1	129-Mile	41	2	...	...
Mt. Sir Samuel	Nil	...	24	2	Emu Rocks	45	3	11	1
Lawlers	Nil	...	14	1	56-Mile	...	...	61	2
Granite Station	Nil	...	17	2	Glenelg Rocks	22	3	33	2
Wilson's Patch	Nil	...	...	...	Burracoppin	33	4	60	1
Poison Creek	...	...	...	...	Bodallin	9	1	59	2
Lake Darlôt	Nil	...	17	3	Parker's Road	18	1	...	...
Darda	Nil	...	Nil	...	Southern Cross	7	5	55	3
Salt Soak	Nil	...	...	...	Parker's Range	21	5	97	7
Duketon	16	2	...	...	Yellowdine	Nil	...	125	3
					Karalee	10	1	140	3
NORTH COOLGARDIE GOLDFIELDS:					Koorarawalyee	2	1	150	4
Laverton	Nil	...	16	3	Boorabbin	Nil	...	113	4
Mt. Morgans	Nil	...	14	3	Boondi	Nil	...	184	4
Murrin Murrin	Nil	...	27	3	**SOUTH-WEST (NORTHERN DIVISION):**				
Mt. Malcolm	Nil	...	23	1	Murchison House	55	4	6	1
Mt. Leonora	Nil	...	38	3	Mt. View	7	2	Nil	...
Tampa	Nil	...	26	1	Mumby	99	5	7	1
Kookynie	Nil	...	30	1	Northampton	49	4	12	2
Niagara	Nil	...	55	3	Chapman Experimental Farm	24	1	Nil	...
Yerilla	Nil	...	...	...	Narra Tarra	...	...	...	...
Yundamindera	Nil	...	36	4					
Mt. Celia	Nil	...	12	1					
Edjudina	Nil	...	52	4					
Quandinnie	Nil	...	...	...					
Menzies	Nil	...	52	2					
Mulline	3	1	36	5					

RAINFALL—*continued*.

Stations.	October. No. of points 100=1in.	October. No. of wet days.	November. No. of points 100=1in.	November. No. of wet days.	Stations.	October. No. of points 100=1in.	October. No. of wet days.	November. No. of points 100=1in.	November. No. of wet days.
SOUTH-WEST (NORTHERN DIVISION)—*contd.*					SOUTH-WEST (METROPOLITAN)—*cont.*				
Oakabella ...	...	...	...	...	Fremantle ...	63	9	20	3
White Peak ...	70				Rottnest ...	35	9	5	3
Geraldton ...	44		11	2	Rockingham ...	26	4	32	2
Hinton Farm ...	...	.2	...	...	Jandakot ...	85	5	7	1
Tibradden ...	83	6	2	1	Armadale ...	...	...	...	...
Myaree ...	74	8	6	2	Mundijong ...	127	11	50	5
Sand Springs ...	...	...	...	...	Jarrahdale ...	235	11	80	4
Nangetty ...	...	...	...	...	Jarrahdale (Norie)	203	11	95	5
Greenough ...	61	4	14	3	Serpentine ...	159	10	40	3
Bokara ...	64	4	...	...					
Dongara ...	27	3	20	2	EXTREME SOUTH-WEST:				
Strawberry ...	41	5	14	3	Mandurah ...	93	10	112	4
Yaragadee ...	...	...	...	...	Pinjarra (Blythewood)	145	9	51	4
Urella ...	...	...	...	...	Pinjarra ...	156	6	27	2
Opawa ...	33	6	25	4	Upper Murray ...	254	14	32	4
Manara ...	30	4	11	1	Yarloop ...	170	13	11	3
Mingenew ...	46	6	30	4	Harvey ...	229	13	16	4
Yandenooka ...	...	...	...	...	Brunswick ...	158	6	...	...
Arrino ...	21	4	...	...	Collie ...	241	14	13	3
Carnamah ...	51	5	84	3	Glen Mervyn ...	218	8	54	6
Jun Jun ...	25	2	22	2	Donnybrook ...	153	11	11	3
Watheroo ...	49	7	184	3	Boyanup ...	161	11	5	8
Nergaminon ...	...	...	...	...	Bunbury ...	122	10	4	2
Dandaragan ...	170	8	115	4	Elgin ...	189	14	24	4
Yatheroo ...	101	7	...	...	Busselton ...	116	13	10	3
Moora ...	85	9	114	3	Quindalup ...	216	14	33	4
Walebing ...	100	9	73	5	Cape Naturaliste	98	16	17	7
Round Hill ...	59	7	135	2	Glen Lossie ...	...	...	...	...
New Norcia ...	72	8	120	4	Karridale ...	270	17	52	7
Wongon Hills ...	58	9	64	2	Cape Leeuwin ...	184	20	52	15
Wannamel ...	181	9	53	3	Lower Blackwood	269	11	112	8
Gingin ...	183	8	122	2	Ferndale ...	...	...	...	...
					Greenbushes ...	131	8	26	2
SOUTH-WEST (METROPOLITAN):					Cooeearup ...	187	13	...	...
Wanneroo ...	79	4	37	3	Bridgetown ...	197	10	45	6
Belvoir ...	105	6	23	3	Hilton ...	137	6	...	...
Wandu ...	144	12	9	4	Greenfields ...	154	8	...	...
Mundaring ...	211	10	*Nil*	...	Duminup ...	149	6	52	3
Canning Waterworks	136	11	4	2	Cundinup ...	68	4	...	...
Kalbyamba ...	107	10	26	3	Wilgarrup ...	249	14	64	10
Guildford ...	109	8	18	4	Balbarrup ...	204	16	...	...
Perth Gardens ...	111	10	18	3	Bidellia ...	325	7	...	...
Perth Observatory	112	12	22	4	Westbourne ...	81	5	118	5
Highgate Hill ...	118	10	18	2	Deeside ...	237	10	89	6
Subiaco ...	114	10	15	3	Riverside ...	287	12	101	7
Claremont ...	65	4	...	...	Mordalup ...	192	8	...	...
					Lake Muir ...	239	11	120	9

RAINFALL—continued.

STATIONS.	OCTOBER. No. of points. 100 = 1in.	OCTOBER. No. of wet days.	NOVEMBER. No. of points. 100 = 1in.	NOVEMBER. No. of wet days.	STATIONS.	OCTOBER. No. of points. 100 = 1in.	OCTOBER. No. of wet days.	NOVEMBER. No. of points. 100 = 1in.	NOVEMBER. No. of wet days.
EASTERN AGRICULTURAL DISTRICTS:					**GREAT SOUTHERN RAILWAY LINE—contd.**				
Emungin	50	10	72	3	Woodyarrup	66	4	...	...
Dowerin	39	2	147	2	Pallinup	51	4	77	5
Warramuggin	...	...	..	...	Tambellup	66	4	49	4
Oak Hill	...	...	...	...	Toolbrunup	62	5	...	...
Monglin	...	...	...	...	Cranbrook	80	11	75	10
Hatherley	31	4	...	...	Stirling View	128	11	98	10
Momberkine	...	...	...	...	Kendenup	148	10	78	8
Bolgart	93	8	...	...	Woogenellup	108	10	...	...
Eumalga	108	8	...	...	Wattle Hill	100	11	...	...
Newcastle	119	5	21	1	St. Werburgh's	160	12	...	...
Craiglands	151	5	5	1	Mt. Barker	127	13	165	20
Eadine	85	10	...	...					
Northam	56	7	28	2					
Grass Valley	...	...	...	...					
Cobham	46	5	84	3	**WEST OF GREAT SOUTHERN RAILWAY LINE:**				
York	62	10	53	2	Talbot House	52	4	96	2
Burrayocking	41	6	210	3	Jelcobine	74	6	6	1
Meckering	41	3	103	3	Bannister	126	5	18	2
Cunderdin	33	3	...	...	Wandering	91	7	84	2
Doongin	36	4	...	...	Glen Ern	50	6	...	...
Whitehaven	10	1	...	...	Marradong	29	3	6	2
Mt. Caroline	31	4	71	2	Wonnaminta	70	10	30	4
Cutenning	...	...	...	...	Williams	102	5	23	1
Kellerberrin	34	4	50	2	Rifle Downs	161	5	...	...
Cardonia	32	5	88	2	Darkan	...	...	...	...
Baandee	18	2	Nil	...	Arthur River	69	7	82	3
Nangeenan	21	2	46	2	Gainsborough	47	6	69	4
Merredin	37	3	45	1	Glenorchy	118	4	10	1
Codg-Codgen	...	...	...	...	Kojonup	115	5	22	2
Noongarin	26	3	...	...	Blackwattle	97	2	...	...
Mangowine	...	...	...	...	Warriup	199	14	137	13
Yarragin	22	3	...	...	Forest Hill	199	11	166	13
Wattoning	...	...	...	...					
GREAT SOUTHERN RAILWAY LINE:					**EAST OF GREAT SOUTHERN RAILWAY LINE:**				
Dalebridge	50	7	82	2	Sunset Hills	30	3	...	...
Beverley	40	4	84	2	Oakdale	...	...	160	10
Brookton	32	2	69	2	Barrington	33	6	235	3
Sunning Hill	68	11	93	2	Bally Bally	30	9	...	...
Pingelly	67	5	128	2	Stock Hill	35	2	28	1
Yornaning	51	8	90	4	Qualin	15	3	104	2
Narrogin	81	7	36	4	Woodgreen	13	6	...	...
Wagin	68	5	39	4	Gillimanning	44	4	93	3
Katanning	91	8	103	...					
Sunnyside	86	9	92	7					
Broomehill	77	6	62	4					

RAINFALL—*continued.*

STATIONS.	October. No. of Points 100 = 1in.	October. No. of wet days.	November. No. of points. 100 = 1in.	November. No. of wet days.	STATIONS.	October. No. of points. 100 = 1in.	October. No. of wet days.	November. No. of Points. 100 = 1in.	November. No. of wet days.
EAST OF GREAT SOUTHERN RAILWAY LINE—contd.					SOUTH COAST—contd.				
Wickepin ...	50	4	...	...	Peppermint Grove	98	12	164	14
Crooked Pool ...	55	5	...	...	Bremer Bay ...	91	7	177	12
Nalyring ...	82	6	55	5	Coconarup ...	36	8	113	9
Bunking ...	52	2	62	2	Ravensthorpe ...	26	4	150	10
Bullock Hills ...	34	2	163	4	Cowjanup ...	48	9	...	...
Dyliabing ...	46	7	...	...	Hopetoun ...	64	4	198	9
Glencove ...	62	7	83	3	Fanny's Cove ...	83	7	153	5
Cherillalup ...	...	...	...	...	Park Farm ...	62	10	201	8
Mianelup ...	54	4	74	7	Grass Patch ...	Nil	...	...	...
Woolganup ...	54	4	46	4	Swan Lagoon ...	16	2	204	7
Chillinup ...	...	...	...	...	30-Mile ...	40	3	199	8
Jarramongup ...	...	...	...	...	Gibson's Soak ...	48	3	217	10
					Myrup ...	77	8	175	9
SOUTH COAST:					Esperance ...	93	11	180	9
Wilson's Inlet ...	296	16	153	12	Boyatup ...	67	4	246	10
Grasmere ...	374	16	106	16	Lynburn ...	64	7	257	10
King River ...	228	11	92	8	Point Malcolm ...	45	3	...	...
Albany	430	16	60	14	Israelite Bay ...	35	2	223	11
Point King ...	321	12	40	5	Balbinia ...	19	3	...	...
Breaksea ...	285	17	61	19	Balladonia ...	6	2	161	10
Cape Riche ...	...	...	...	...	Eyre	13	3	148	12
					Mundrabella ...	50	1	...	...
					Eucla	50	3	200	2

The Observatory, Perth,
    11th December, 1906.

W. E. COOKE,
Government Astronomer.

By Authority FRED. WM. SIMPSON, Government Printer, Perth.

INDEX.

VOL. XIV.

July to December, 1906, inclusive.

INDEX.

INDEX—*continued.*

B.

C.

INDEX—*continued.*

D.

INDEX —*continued.*

E.

F.

INDEX—*continued.*

G.

H.

INDEX —*continued.*

INDEX—*continued.*

N.

O.

P.

INDEX—*continued.*

INDEX—*continued.*

INDEX—*continued.*

By Authority: Fred. Wm. Simpson, Government Printer, Perth.

Lightning Source UK Ltd.
Milton Keynes UK
UKHW020605120219
337137UK00005B/757/P